Springer Series in Cognitive Development

Series Editor
Charles J. Brainerd

Jeffrey Bisanz, Charles J. Brainerd, and Robert Kail
Editors

Formal Methods in Developmental Psychology

Progress in Cognitive Development Research

With 52 Illustrations

Springer-Verlag
New York Berlin Heidelberg
London Paris Tokyo

Jeffrey Bisanz
Department of Psychology
University of Alberta
Edmonton, Alberta T6G 2E9
Canada

Charles J. Brainerd
Program in Educational Psychology
University of Arizona
Tucson, AZ 85715
U.S.A.

Robert Kail
Department of Psychological Sciences
Purdue University
West Lafayette, IN 47907
U.S.A.

Library of Congress Cataloging in Publication Data
Formal methods in developmental psychology.
(Springer series in cognitive development)
Includes bibliographies and index.
1. Developmental psychology—Statistical methods.
2. Developmental psychology—Mathematical models.
3. Developmental psychology—Data processing.
I. Bisanz, Jeffrey. II. Brainerd, Charles J.
III. Kail, Robert V. IV. Series.
BF713.F67 1987 155 86-26202

Typeset by TCSystems, Shippensburg, Pennsylvania.
Printed and bound by R.R. Donnelley & Sons, Harrisonburg, Virginia.
Printed in the United States of America.

9 8 7 6 5 4 3 2 1

ISBN 0-387-96441-X Springer-Verlag New York Berlin Heidelberg
ISBN 3-540-96441-X Springer-Verlag Berlin Heidelberg New York

Series Preface

For some time now, the study of cognitive development has been far and away the most active discipline within developmental psychology. Although there would be much disagreement as to the exact proportion of papers published in developmental journals that could be considered cognitive, 50% seems like a conservative estimate. Hence, a series of scholarly books devoted to work in cognitive development is especially appropriate at this time.

The *Springer Series in Cognitive Development* contains two basic types of books, namely, edited collections of original chapters by several authors, and original volumes written by one author or a small group of authors. The flagship for the Springer Series is a serial publication of the "advances" types, carrying the subtitle *Progress in Cognitive Development Research*. Each volume in the *Progress* sequence is strongly thematic, in that it is limited to some well-defined domain of cognitive-developmental research (e.g., logical and mathematical development, development of learning). All *Progress* volumes will be edited collections. Editors of such collections, upon consultation with the Series Editor, may elect to have their books published either as contributions to the *Progress* sequence or as separate volumes. All books written by one author or a small group of authors are being published as separate volumes within the series.

A fairly broad definition of cognitive development is being used in the selection of books for this series. The classic topics of concept development, children's thinking and reasoning, the development of learning, language development, and memory development will, of course, be included. So, however, will newer areas such as social-cognitive development, educational applications, formal modeling, and philosophical implications of cognitive-developmental theory. Although it is anticipated that most books in the series will be empirical in orientation, theoretical and philosophical works are also welcome. With books of the latter sort, heterogeneity of theoretical perspective is encouraged, and no attempt will be made to foster some specific theoretical perspective at the expense of others (e.g., Piagetian versus behavioral or behavioral versus information processing).

C. J. Brainerd

Preface

The focus of this volume in the *Springer Series in Cognitive Development* is methodology, especially as it concerns the development and testing of formal theories. The choice of this topic reflects an increasing concern for the development of sophisticated methodological tools that yield more perceptive insights into children's behavior, a theme that was evident in an earlier volume in this series (*Learning in Children*) and that, in our judgment, required more specific attention.

The need for more powerful methods of developing and testing theories is not new, of course. Experimental research on cognitive development has proliferated over the past 30 years, partly because of an infusion of concepts and paradigms from learning theories in the 1950s, from Piaget's work in the 1960s, and from the perspective of information processing in the 1970s. Theories and methods of research have become more sophisticated with each step in this progression. One problem that consistently emerges, however, is the tendency to formulate theories in terms that preclude unambiguous predictions about performance. Similarly, methods of analysis often have been insufficient for providing the kinds of precise, quantitative, and theoretically meaningful measurements necessary for identifying process variables on diverse tasks. Difficulties in making clear-cut predictions and sensitive measurements have resulted in extended, and often unproductive, controversies. One outcome of these continuing controversies is the growing realization that the complexity and relative inaccessibility of cognitive processes require greater precision in the formulation and testing of theories. As a consequence, there has been a notable increase in the use of *formal models* in cognitive developmental research over the past several years. Computer simulations, mathematical models, and advanced statistical methods are now being used to investigate a wide range of developmental phenomena.

Research involving formal models is far from the modal approach in cognitive developmental research, however. One reason for the common failure to use more sophisticated methods and theories is that many approaches to formal modeling are closely linked in the literature to specific issues or processes. Authors typically do not have the opportunity to discuss issues and details that are pertinent to applying the methods more broadly. Thus most developmental researchers do not realize how generally appropriate these approaches are for diverse phenomena. A second reason is that many of these newer techniques are quite complex, and rarely are the details necessary for implementation available in journal articles.

Our goal in publishing this volume is to communicate the insights and methodological details researchers need to adopt or develop techniques that may be useful for advancing their own investigations. The chapters in this volume are based on presentations at a conference on the use of formal methods in developmental psychology that was held at the University of Alberta in May, 1985. The conference served as a forum for proponents of different methodological approaches. Participants took the opportunity to explain the assumptions and procedures associated with their particular methods, to illustrate the use of the methods, to highlight particular strengths and shortcomings, and to exchange information about recent developments. In the resulting chapters, most authors chose to describe their methods in the context of specific investigations, and in each case careful attention is given to the reasons for selecting a particular method and for implementing or adapting it in useful ways. This approach allows readers to gain an appreciation of the complex and sensitive manner in which relations between theoretical concepts and empirical outcomes must be explored in the course of developing and testing a theory.

Taken as a whole, the volume represents a sampling of current methods and, perhaps more importantly, the issues that must be addressed in developing more sophisticated methods for theory construction and validation. Readers interested in a particular method, such as the use of computer simulation, are encouraged to peruse the pertinent chapters to gain a broad perspective on the issues, constraints, and procedures associated with that method. Brief descriptions are provided below to assist readers in the selection of chapters.

The volume is divided into two sections. Included in the first section is a wide range of mathematical and statistical approaches. Charles Brainerd uses several examples to illustrate the generality and pervasiveness of measurement problems in developmental research, and he illustrates how some of these problems can be addressed in certain types of investigation. The broad issues that are raised provide a context for the contributions of the other authors in the volume. Johannes Kingma describes the use of mathematical models in general, and he also provides a very detailed illustration of how Markov models can be used to understand differences in memory processes among groups of children that vary in age and learning ability. Alex Cherry Wilkinson and Beth Haines use a variety of mathematical techniques, including Markov modeling, to study three different types of transitions in knowledge acquisition: changes that result from repeated testing; changes that occur as components of a skill are acquired; and changes that reflect the process of assembling familiar components into a workable strategy. The chapter is very useful for illustrating how various methods can be combined and how precision in measurement often requires greater specialization of method.

Several chapters represent relatively novel applications of statistical methods. Colleen Surber illustrates the use of functional measurement techniques in the study of reversible operations. In the process, she shows how certain methods of developing and testing theories, many of which arise from the literature on judgment and decision making, enable her to examine an expanded concept of reversibility and to identify several possible sources of developmental change in children's thinking. Robert Sternberg shows how a variety of multivariate methods can be used systematically to examine implicit theories and belief systems, a new topic of research that is gaining considerable attention. Hoben Thomas provides an elegant illustration of how exploratory data analyses and careful analyses of probabilities can yield revealing insights about possible sources of individual differences in achievement. In the final chapter of this section, Kevin Miller provides a thoughtful discussion of issues associated with geometric methods of analyzing and representing data. He also illustrates how nonmetric multidimensional scaling and nonhierarchical clustering can be used productively in developmental research.

The chapters in the second section all pertain to the use of computer simulation. Michael Rabinowitz, Malcolm Grant, and Louis Dingley provide a broad overview of the concepts and issues that are associated with the use of computer simulation in the development of psychological theories, and they also review a number of studies in which simulations have been used to understand children's performance. Mark Ashcraft describes a specific simulation of mental arithmetic and, more generally, how simulation became a useful tool for him in his effort to integrate concepts and test ideas about the organization and development of cognitive processes. Martin Banks argues that computational theories, implemented in computer simulations, provide a more promising way of understanding perceptual development than existing approaches. Finally, Donald Heth and Edward Cornell show how Monte Carlo simulations can be used to test hypotheses about spatial search behavior in children, and they provide a set of simulation tools that can be used in a variety of contexts by researchers.

The conference and subsequent preparation of this volume were made possible by support from the Natural Sciences and Engineering Research

Council of Canada and by the Department of Psychology, the Centre for Research in Child Development, the Conference Fund Committee, and the Office of the Vice-President of Research at the University of Alberta. We are grateful for the stimulating comments provided by the conference discussants (Terry Caelli and Frederick Morrison) and by the many individuals who attended the conference and contributed significantly to the discourse. We are also thankful for the expert assistance of Cindy Scott, Lorri Broda, Frances Russell, and Cecile Cochrane in preparing the conference and this volume.

Jeffrey Bisanz
Charles J. Brainerd
Robert Kail

Contents

Contributors

Mark H. Ashcraft Department of Psychology, Cleveland State University, Cleveland, Ohio 44115, U.S.A.

Martin S. Banks School of Optometry, University of California, Berkeley, California 94720, U.S.A.

Charles J. Brainerd Program in Educational Psychology, University of Arizona, Tucson, AZ 85715, U.S.A.

Edward H. Cornell Department of Psychology, University of Alberta, Edmonton, Alberta T6G 2E9, Canada

H. Louis Dingley Department of Psychology, Memorial University of Newfoundland, St. John's, Newfoundland A1B 3X9, Canada

Malcolm J. Grant Department of Psychology, Memorial University of Newfoundland, St. John's, Newfoundland A1B 3X9, Canada

Beth A. Haines Department of Psychology, University of Wisconsin, Madison, Wisconsin 53706, U.S.A.

C. Donald Heth Department of Psychology, University of Alberta, Edmonton, Alberta T6G 2E9, Canada

Johannes Kingma Department of Psychology, University of Alberta, Edmonton, Alberta T6G 2E9, Canada

Kevin F. Miller Department of Psychology, University of Texas at Austin, Texas 78712, U.S.A.

F. Michael Rabinowitz Department of Psychology, Memorial University of Newfoundland, St. John's, Newfoundland A1B 3X9, Canada

Robert J. Sternberg Department of Psychology, Yale University, New Haven, Connecticut 06520-7447, U.S.A.

Colleen F. Surber Department of Psychology, University of Wisconsin, Madison, Wisconsin 53706, U.S.A.

Hoben Thomas Department of Psychology, Pennsylvania State University, University Park, Pennsylvania 16802, U.S.A.

Alex Cherry Wilkinson AT&T Bell Laboratories, Holmdel, New Jersey 07733, U.S.A.

1. Structural Measurement Theory and Cognitive Development

Charles J. Brainerd

The overriding function of scientific theories is to reduce uncertainty about the world we live in by explaining how things work. A basic dilemma in psychological theories, probably the most basic dilemma of all, is that we do not possess what is sometimes called *fundamental measurement control* over the constructs that we use to explain behavior. On one hand, we regularly resort to notions such as short-term memory capacity, retrieval from long-term memory, attitudes, hypotheses, rule knowledge, preference, attention, motivation, intelligence, and the like when formulating explanations. On the other hand, these notions are not amenable to physical measurement operations such as weighing and counting. They lie somewhere in the uncharted region between true physical reality and metaphysical speculation. Consequently, we are not certain of how to go about quantifying them through experimentation. Here, a familiar catechism is that the most that can defensibly be assumed is that data are related to psychological constructs by unknown but order-preserving transformations. This is the familiar monotonicity constraint on the measurement of psychological constructs. To take a hoary instance, while we can presumably say that a person with a Stanford-Binet IQ of 150 is at least as intelligent as a person with a Stanford-Binet IQ of 100, we cannot say much more than this. And we certainly cannot say that the first person is half again as intelligent as the second.

The monotonicity constraint would be less a cause for concern if we were content with qualitative theories, that is, if we did not seek to quantify such variables and were content instead with nominal-scale measurements. However, theories in all areas of psychology, especially the most refined theories, routinely make quantitative statements about their explanatory constructs. To test these theories, it is necessary to evaluate such statements, but the means of doing so under monotonicity restrictions are usually obscure.

The problem is conveniently encapsulated by an illustration that Krantz and Tversky (1971) gave some years ago. Hull once proposed that an organism's reaction potential (or response strength) was a multiplicative function of three variables, namely, drive, habit strength, and incentive. That is,

$$R = DHK, \tag{1}$$

where R, D, H, and K are numerical scales denoting reaction potential, drive, habit strength, and incentive, respectively. Shortly thereafter, Spence argued that reaction potential was a multiplicative function of the sum of habit strength and incentive, on the one hand, and drive, on the other. That is,

$$R = D(H + K). \tag{2}$$

Both models assume that response strength is a simple algebraic function of three psychological variables. But how do we secure a differential test of the two models? Under the monotonicity constraint, we can presumably obtain ordinal-scale measurements of the pertinent variables by using, for example, running speed to a goal box for response strength, amount of prior deprivation for drive, amount of prior training for habit strength, and amount of reward in the goal box for incentive. But because only the subjects' ordering along each of the four dimensions is invariant under such measurements, how do these data help us to choose between a model in which drive is distributed over the sum of habit strength and incentive and a model in which response strength is a simple product of drive, habit strength, and incentive? If we had ratio-scale measurements of all the variables, then naturally it would be a trivial matter to decide whether the value calculated from the right side of Equation 1 or the value calculated from the right side of Equation 2 was nearer to the observed value of response strength. We do not have such measurements, however. (See Chapter 4, this volume, by Surber for a discussion of related problems in research on human judgment.)

One reason that measurement theories have evolved in psychology is to show us how to decide between different quantitative statements about psychological variables. Some say, not without justification, that measurement theories are merely quasitheological devices that allow us to avoid the bitter fact that we ought not to be using metaphysical ideas in our theories. I shall let this possibility pass, however.

In this chapter, there are two features of most measurement theories that I wish to focus on. First, the monotonicity constraint is taken as a given—that is, most measurement theories operate with ordinal-scale measurements and do not usually deliver ratio-scale information about constructs. Second, they are local theories. They do not attempt to solve the monotonicity problem in general terms for all areas of psychological theory. Instead, they solve particular manifestations of the problem in well-defined areas of experimentation. Broadly speaking, then, measurement theories have sought to discover how much mileage can be gotten from particular classes of theories having only ordinal information about subjects' status on psychological constructs.

These points can be illustrated by two familiar, contemporary measurement frameworks, conjoint-measurement theory (Krantz, Luce, Suppes, & Tversky, 1971; Krantz & Tversky, 1971) and functional-measurement theory (e.g., Anderson, 1970, 1974; Anderson & Cuneo, 1978). (See Chapter 4 by Surber and Chapter 3 by Wilkinson and Haines, this volume, for additional discussions of functional-measurement theory.) The Hull-Spence example is an instance of a large class of theories in which some psychological variable is expressed as a simple algebraic function of a small number of additional psychological variables, which conjoint-measurement theorists have termed *polynomial composition rules*. Another particularly rich source of examples is provided by classical theories of attitude change, where subjects' current attitudinal status is expressed as some polynomial function of constructs such as balance, congruence, valence, and so forth. In both conjoint-measurement theory and functional-measurement theory, it is often possible to decide between different polynomial formulations of the relationship between variables with data that deliver at most ordinal information. A central feature of both frameworks turns out to be the interpretation of interaction terms in the analysis of variance. One framework, Anderson's functional-measurement theory, has been far more productive of experimentation than the other, owing primarily to the fact that its statistical machinery has been more completely developed and, in particular, its connections to analysis of variance have been carefully spelled out. With functional-measurement techniques, certain contrasting polynomial composition rules can be distinguished by merely conducting factorial experiments and examining plots of various interactions. (See Chapter 4, this volume, by Surber for illustrations.)

In the study of cognitive development, the realization that measurement theory is critical to research has come very late. Even today, this point is neither widely understood nor commonly acknowledged in the literature. The most likely, though by no means complete, explanation is that the field has historically been dominated by theoretical traditions that were purely qualitative, with the Piagetian tradition being the prototype. Piaget coupled a lack of serious quantitative theorizing with an active antipathy to such work. He believed that theories that incorporated precise numerical statements about the relationship between children's understanding of various concepts and developmental changes in certain process variables (e.g., attention to relevant dimensions, knowledge of pertinent rules, capacity of working memory) were somehow inconsistent with the proposition that cognitive development is a stagelike process. This is not to say that Piaget's writings abjured formal modeling of any sort. They did not. However, his use of modeling technologies such as group theory and propositional logic (e.g., Piaget, 1949) was normally metaphorical and invariably opaque.

Because cognitive development theory has traditionally been qualitative, the need for measurement frameworks has been less clear than in other areas of psychology. Lately, however, two trends have made this need more apparent. First, there is a growing awareness that some classical questions about cognitive development, questions originally brought to prominence by qualitative theories, are implicitly quantitative in the sense that different answers turn on assumptions about quantitative relationships between psychological variables. Three well-known examples (the stage-learning hypothesis, sequences in concept development, and the relative contributions of age changes in storage and retrieval to memory development) are discussed below. Second, there is, for the first time, a vigorous literature concerned with quantitative theories of cognitive development, particularly in concept and memory development. Illustrations of such theories are also discussed below.

The general purposes of this chapter are to argue for the importance of measurement-theoretical considerations in the study of cognitive development and for an evolving perspective on measurement that relies on the theory of maximum likelihood. The chapter consists of three main sections. In the first section, I review some important research questions that, although ostensibly qualitative, seem to require careful attention to measurement issues. Next, I discuss four goals for measurement theories of cognitive development that follow from the material in the first section. In the final section, some illustrations of quantitative theories of concept and memory development are presented. It is suggested some progress has been made toward a general measurement system for cognitive development and, more explicitly, that the objectives set forth in the second section have sometimes been met. Curiously, this progress has occurred more or less without any realization that a general measurement framework, one that is adapted to the specialized demands of cognitive development theory, is being created.

Three Examples

In the literature on concept and memory development, some long-standing questions are rooted in failures to give due consideration to measurement issues, specifically to response scaling issues that arise from the monotonicity constraint on measurement. In the standard scenario, several studies concerned with a predicted (qualitative) relationship among certain variables are reported, but upon reflection it turns out that the predictions being tested are informative only if it can be assumed that the response scales (output transformations) that map different theoretical variables with their empirical measures are identical. Since monotonicity is normally the strongest assumption that can be made about response scales, the question then arises, What do the data actually tell us about the predicted relationships? I give three instances of this situation, examples that have been chosen with a view toward their familiarity rather than their profundity.

Example 1: The Stage-Learning Hypothesis

Experiments on the relationship between children's concept learning and their levels of cognitive development provide a textbook illustration of the response scaling problem. Piagetian theory anticipates that children's ability to learn concepts such as conservation, perspective taking, classification, and the like will "vary very significantly as a function of the initial cognitive levels of the children" (Piaget, 1970, p. 715). Most studies concerned with this prediction have used level of posttraining performance to measure the theoretical variable "concept learning" and have used level of pretraining performance on tests of the to-be-trained concept to measure the theoretical variable "level of cognitive development," all of which seems natural enough at first glance. The featured results in these studies have been dependencies between the two types of measures; the conditional probability of being at a higher posttest level given that the child occupied a higher pretest level is greater than the unconditional probability of occupying a higher posttest level. Clearly, however, such dependencies bear upon the predicted relationship only in the unlikely (and unproven) event that the response scales for the two measures are identical.

In the usual design of an experiment of this sort, first children are given a battery of pretests for some Piagetian concept such as conservation. This is followed by a training session in which the target concept is taught, with the most common types of instruction being observational learning, rule instruction, attentional training, and simple corrective feedback. Training is followed immediately and/or a few days later and/or a few weeks later by another battery of tests for the trained concept and sometimes for other related concepts. With such designs, there are four psychological variables of interest for which ordinal-scale information is available. First, there are the children's pretraining levels of cognitive development (variable D). Second, there is the power of the training procedure to produce concept learning (variable P). Third, there is the amount of learning produced by a given amount of training (variable L). Fourth, there is the children's posttraining knowledge of the target concept (variable K). Variables D, K, L, and P are all distinct theoretical concepts that cannot necessarily be defined in terms of each other; hence, it is important to include them all in the formulation for completeness. For example, one cannot simply define L as $K - D$ because learning might be something very different from the difference between children's pretraining stage and their posttraining knowledge of the target concept. Similarly, the power of the training manipulation must be considered because the relationship between learning and pretraining stage may depend critically on the effectiveness of training.

To begin, learning is related to the effectiveness or power of the training method. That is, more effective procedures should tend to produce more learning. For example, a small number of trials with a given method ought to produce less learning than a larger number of trials. In short, we assume that

$$L = f_1 (P) \tag{3}$$

holds, where f_1 is any monotonic function that maps scale values of P with scale values of L. Essentially, the familiar Piagetian claim that children's concept learning depends on their stage of cognitive development implies that this expression is an incomplete representation of the relationship between learning and the power of the training method. Specifically, the learning function f_1 should accelerate or decelerate, depending on developmental status, which is to say that L depends on D as well as on P.

Therefore, learning must be expressed as some joint function

$$L = f_2 (D, P) \tag{4}$$

of development and power, where f_2 is another monotonic function that maps scale values of L with scale values of D and P. This latter function would usually be called a *composition rule* in conjoint-measurement theory or an *integration rule* in functional-measurement theory. Bear in mind that, except for the monotonicity assumption, nothing whatsoever is known about f_2.

Now, consider some numerical examples from a mythical conservation training experiment. The experiment is a 3×3 design in which three levels of development (D) have been factorially crossed with three levels of training power (P). The examples appear in Table 1.1, and each is based on a different assumption about f_2 *that satisfies Equation 4*. The composition rule is additive in one case ($L = D + P$), multiplicative in the second case ($L = DP$), and a power function in the third case ($L = P^D$). To generate these examples, the scale values for D were set at 2, 3, and 4, and the scale values for P were set at 5, 7, and 9.

The crucial question that Table 1.1 answers is whether the claim that concept learning depends on developmental stage leads to some unique result for $D \times P$ factorial designs that must be true for all monotonic composition rules. To begin, note that scale values of L vary both down the rows and across the columns when the composition rule is additive. But if learning depends only on the effectiveness of training and not on development (i.e., Equation 3, not Equation 4, is correct), then L should only vary across rows. When scale values of L are inspected for the other two composition rules, the same pattern is observed. This suggests a basic research strategy for discriminating Equations 3 and 4: Conduct $D \times P$ factorial experiments and test for D main effects, concluding that Equation 4 is or is not correct accordingly as such effects are or are not observed.

A difficulty arises, however, in implementing this strategy, namely, the question of how to measure learning. Learning—like developmental level, training power, and posttraining knowledge—is a theoretical con-

TABLE 1.1. Some numerical examples from a hypothetical conservation learning experiment.

	Rule and developmental level	Power of training method		
		$P_1 = 5$	$P_2 = 7$	$P_3 = 9$
f_2:	$L = D + P$			
	$D_1 = 2$	$L = 7$	$L = 9$	$L = 11$
	$D_2 = 3$	$L = 8$	$L = 10$	$L = 12$
	$D_3 = 4$	$L = 9$	$L = 11$	$L = 13$
f_2:	$L = DP$			
	$D_1 = 2$	$L = 10$	$L = 14$	$L = 18$
	$D_2 = 3$	$L = 15$	$L = 21$	$L = 27$
	$D_3 = 4$	$L = 20$	$L = 28$	$L = 36$
f_2:	$L = P^D$			
	$D_1 = 2$	$L = 25$	$L = 49$	$L = 81$
	$D_2 = 3$	$L = 125$	$L = 343$	$L = 729$
	$D_3 = 4$	$L = 625$	$L = 2401$	$L = 6561$

struct that is subject to the monotonicity restriction. Experiments of this type provide two measures of learning. First, there are pretest to posttest improvements in concept-test scores. In other words, pretest scores on the concept tests are subtracted from posttest scores, and the residual is regarded as being monotonically related to amount of learning. Different scores, however, are subject to well-known reliability problems. The other, more attractive candidate for the learning measure is the rate at which concept-test performancc improves during training.

With the aid of these distinctions and examples, it is now easy to see why the prediction usually tested in concept-learning studies with children does not actually bear upon the issue of whether developmental stage constrains learning. The essence of this prediction is that learning depends jointly on the power of the training method and on the developmental stage, not merely on the former. A simple factorial design evidently is required to test this possibility. But the prediction that has actually been evaluated in research is that posttraining performance depends on pretraining performance, which merely says that scale values of K are some monotonic function of scale values of D. Note (1) that L does not enter into this prediction in any direct way, although K is presumably some joint function of L and D, (2) that the prediction does not provide any clear basis for discriminating Equations 3 and 4, and (3) that, indeed, as long as the concept tests are reliable, the prediction would be consistent with either expression.

Example 2: Concept Sequence Research

Sequentiality, the study of the order in which things develop, has always been a prominent concern in developmental sciences, but its appearance in the concept development literature dates to the revival of Piagetian theory two decades ago. The theory leads to two familiar predictions about sequences in concept development. First, children should invariably acquire some concepts, those that belong to earlier stages, before they acquire certain other concepts, those that belong to later stages. Second, concepts that belong to the same stage should not be acquired in any particular order. Predictions of this ilk are also centerpieces of most other theories that are closely connected to Piaget's work, with Kohlberg's theory of moral development being a well-known instance.

Although Piaget's stages provided the initial impetus, a second, instructional motivation for sequence research soon emerged. Curriculum sequencing, the order in which new concepts and skills are introduced in the classroom, is a key issue in the design of any curriculum, but especially in preschool and elementary school curricula. Here, a common assumption has been that if two (or more) concepts develop in some fixed order, then teachers should introduce them in that same order in the classroom. Since many of the concepts associated with Piagetian stages are also taught as part of elementary school curricula (e.g., number, classification, seriation, proportionality), some of the earliest studies in the literature focused on such concepts. At the time, it was widely believed that this research simultaneously afforded tests of theoretical hypotheses and generated data that were useful in instruction.

The bulk of the early literature was concerned with concrete and formal operational concepts, and the subjects were usually elementary schoolers. The designs of these studies were simple. Typically, a single test of each target concept was administered to a sample of children drawn from an age range during which, according to theory or extant data, the concepts developed. An overall performance measure based on the average probability of a correct response was then used to score the data of each test. As a rule, performance on given tests either was scored pass-fail or was stratified into a small number of levels deemed analogous to stages. The empirical evidence of sequentiality consisted of statistically reliable differences in the pass-fail rates for different tests (if the tests were scored pass-fail) or statistically reliable differences in stage classifications. In other words, concept A was said to develop before concept B if the pass rates or the stage classifications were higher for test A.

Most of these studies produced what, in the minds of investigators of that era, appeared to be quite striking evidence of sequentiality. Some early reviewers went so far as to conclude that sequentiality was far more pronounced than even stage theories would expect. However, an ambiguity materialized with respect to specific sequences that, for one reason or another, were sufficiently interesting to prompt multiple studies. Minor procedural variations (e.g., introducing visual illusions, requiring children to explain their answers) were found to perturb the order of test difficulty rather badly. Hooper and his associates seem to have been the first reviewers to focus attention on this fact in connection with the frequently studied ordering of quantity, weight, and volume conservation (Hooper, Goldman, Storck, & Burke, 1971). They pointed out that while some data on this sequence were in precise agreement with theoretical predictions, other studies, using the same basic tests with slight modifications, had produced quite different patterns of test difficulty.

Some illustrations of theoretically important sequences that produced literatures with inconsistent patterns of test difficulty are compensation versus conservation, class inclusion versus conservation, identity versus equivalence, ordinal number versus cardinal number, and transitivity versus conservation. Perhaps the longest tradition of inconsistent findings is for the developmental ordering of transitivity and conservation. Smedslund (1959, 1963) originally reported that children conserve before they make transitive inferences, a result that agreed with theoretical predictions (Piaget & Szeminska, 1941) and that was subsequently replicated by others (e.g., McManis, 1969). At the same time, however, Lovell and Ogilvie (1961) reported that children conserve and make transitive inferences at about the same age. Several other investigators have found that children make transitive inferences before they conserve (e.g., Brainerd, 1973, 1974; Hooper, Toniolo, & Sipple, 1978). There is even one experiment by Keller and Hunter (1973) in which some comparisons showed that conservation is understood before transitivity, other comparisons showed that transitivity is understood before conservation, and still other comparisons showed that conservation and transitivity are simultaneous achievements.

Conflicting data of this sort eventually led to a realization that children's performance on a concept test is not merely a measure of their grasp of the target concept. There is now general agreement that three types of variables need to be taken into account: (1) children's knowledge of the concept being measured; (2) the possibility that both children who have the concept and children who do not have the concept often make correct responses by relying on nonconceptual factors (called *false-positive errors* in the literature); and (3) the possibility that both children who have the concept and children who do not have the concept often make errors by relying on nonconceptual factors (called *false-negative errors*). The distinction between these variables merely acknowledges the intuitively obvious fact that there are always three paths to a correct response on a concept-test item: A child may possess the target concept and manage to avoid various sources of false-positive and false-negative error, the child may possess the target concept but make a correct response by relying on some source of false-positive error, and the child may not possess the target concept but may make a correct response by relying on some source of false-positive error. It is the proportion of responses in the first category that most investigators would regard as the true measure of conceptual knowledge.

The literature contains numerous illustrations of potential types of false-positive and false-negative errors proposed for class inclusion, conservation, transitive inference, probability judgment, and other familiar concepts. However, the dimensions of the underlying problem are clear enough without a recitation of further examples. On the one hand, several procedural manipulations (some of which apply to several tasks and others of which are specific to given tasks) are known to inflate or deflate performance on concept tests. Moreover, the presence or absence of these manipulations dramatically affects the developmental ordering of tests of different concepts. On the other hand, the fact that there are three paths to any correct response means that we do not know whether the effects of such manipulations are on the false-positive error rate, the false-negative error rate, or both. That is, a manipulation that inflates performance may do so by expanding the pool of false-positive error sources or by shrinking the pool of false-negative error sources or by doing both. Conversely, a manipulation that deflates performance may do so by producing the opposite effects.

Owing to these ambiguities, inferences about the developmental ordering of concepts that are based on the relative difficulty of tests are profoundly suspect. To make such inferences, correct responses must be factored into those that are based on the concept and those that derive from possible sources of false-positive error. As in Example 1, these requirements are beyond our current capabilities because we lack appropriate measurement frameworks. The problem here is more difficult than in Example 1 because the relevant theoretical variables are harder to disentangle. We saw with concept learning that there were four such variables (developmental stage, training efficiency, amount of learning, and posttraining conceptual knowledge) and that four empirical measures were available that could reasonably be supposed to be monotonic functions of the respective variables. But in concept sequence studies, the picture is more muddied. Only two statements can be made with some confidence about measurement of the relevant variables. First, the probability of a correct response on a concept test is some monotonic function of conceptual knowledge, the false-positive error rate, and the false-negative error rate. Second, when two versions of a concept test that produce different levels of performance are administered, the conceptual knowledge variable is presumably not affected because the subjects are the same in both cases. But it is not clear whether the false-positive variable, the false-negative variable, or both are affected. Unlike Example 1, therefore, measurements that are uniquely related to all the theoretical variables do not seem to be available, which makes the task of a measurement theory more difficult.

Example 3: Contributions of Storage and Retrieval Factors to Memory Development

In the study of memory development, an interesting set of questions turns on whether the developmental improvements observed on most memory tasks are due to age changes in the ability to get information into memory and/or age changes in the ability to get information out again. The general issue of whether the development of storage processes or the development of retrieval processes is more important to age changes in particular paradigms has often been raised (e.g., Emmerich & Ackerman, 1978). The question is also implicit in theoretical controversies associated with certain paradigms. For example, the current disagreement over capacity versus efficiency explanations of age changes in short-term memory span (e.g., Dempster, 1985) can be interpreted as a disagreement about the relative importance of storage development (capacity) versus retrieval development (efficiency). Similarly, the controversy over automatic versus strategic theories of the development of organization in semantic memory (e.g., Bjorklund, 1985) can be interpreted as a dispute over the relative importance of storage development (automatic organizational processes) and retrieval development (strategic organizational processes). One need not, of course, agree with these interpretations of either controversy. They are merely illustrations.

This same issue crops up in the study of age × treatment interactions on memory tasks. Normally, a task-difficulty manipulation that enhances or inhibits performance in some standard paradigm (e.g., free recall, paired-associate learning) has the same qualitative effect at all age levels—that is, crossover age × treatment interactions are rather uncommon in memory development. However, a given manipulation's effects are often greater or less in adults than in children, which is to say that divergent and convergent age × treatment interactions are common. Prominent instances of manipulations that show either divergent or convergent developmental interactions include serial position in serial learning (divergent), list organization in recall (divergent), cuing in categorized recall (convergent), imposed elaboration in paired-associate learning (convergent), and concreteness in recall (divergent). One goal of any theory of memory development is to explain such interactions, and existing explanations vary in the emphasis placed on the development of mechanisms for reproducing traces on test trials.

In the literature, the standard device for weighing the relative influence of storage and retrieval factors in memory development has been to conduct experiments that incorporate manipulations designed to reduce the effects of one class of factors on certain aspects of the data. But because these manipulations are not informed by measurement-theoretic considerations, particularly the monotonicity problem, they actually confound the issue more than clarify it. I illustrate this claim with a brief discussion of two familiar procedures for separating storage and retrieval development, the study-test technique and the recognition-recall technique.

The assumption that underlies the study-test technique seems sensible enough: On most list-learning tasks, subjects are administered a series of trials in which study cycles alternate with test cycles. By *study cycles* or *study trials,* I mean opportunities that subjects are given to study the individual list items. By *test cycles* or *test trials,* I mean opportunities that subjects are given to remember items after having studied them. Since subjects see the material only on study trials, it is assumed that storage difficulty is more important on study trials than on test trials. Or, conversely, because subjects must reproduce the material on test trials but do not see it, it is assumed that retrieval difficulty is more important on test trials than on study trials. Now, suppose some manipulation is known to interact with age and that it can be *independently* varied on study and test trials in what is basically an A (type of trial: study vs. test) $\times$ B (treatment) $\times$ C (age) factorial design. Picture cues versus word cues in paired-associate learning are a simple example: The effect of this manipulation is known to increase with age, and the type of cue can be independently varied on the study and test trials of each cycle.

The logic of the procedure says that because storage difficulty and retrieval difficulty are of differential significance on study and test trials, certain patterns of results can be interpreted as showing, first, that a manipulation's effects are primarily localized within storage or within retrieval and, second, that the age × treatment interaction is therefore a consequence of either storage development or retrieval development. For instance, suppose that the picture-word manipulation produced a main effect and the usual diverging age × treatment interaction. But suppose that there was also an age × treatment × type of test interaction such that age divergence in the picture-word effect is greater for study trials than test trials. This would probably be interpreted as a demonstration that the interaction of age with picture-word cuing is localized mainly within storage development. As another example, suppose that the results were the same, except that the age × treatment × type of test interaction did not occur. This would probably lead to the conclusion that the age × cuing interaction is localized within both storage and retrieval development.

Another procedure for separating storage development and retrieval development in list learning is the recognition-recall technique. This method relies on the (presumably) differential contributions of storage and retrieval difficulty to different tests of the same material. The underlying logic is that if age × treatment interactions vary across testing procedures to which storage difficulty and retrieval difficulty differ in importance, this is informative with respect to the contributions of storage and retrieval development to such interactions. This method could, in principle, be used with many testing procedures. However, it has almost always been used with recognition versus recall. This variation has been chosen because memory theorists normally regard recognition as being more under the control of storage factors than recall is (e.g., Estes & DaPolito, 1967). Some theorists (e.g., Greeno, James, DaPolito, & Polson, 1978) have viewed recognition as a pure storage paradigm, although others maintain that such a strong assumption is inconsistent with findings such as recognition failure (e.g., Flexer & Tulving, 1978). In any event, there seems to be widespread consensus that storage difficulty contributes more to recognition performance than to recall performance.

As with the first procedure, the logic of this method is that factorial experiments of the form A (recognition vs. recall) $\times$ B (treatment) $\times$ C (age) provide evidence about the relative contributions of storage development and retrieval development. If we continue the picture-word illustration, the type of cue could be manipulated over recognition tests versus recall tests rather than over study trials versus test trials. As before, certain patterns of main effects and interactions would be interpreted as localizing the usual interaction between age and cuing within either storage or retrieval development. For example, suppose that the usual main effects for A, B, and C were observed, plus an $A \times B \times C$ interaction such that the effects of the picture-word manipulation were always greater for older children, but this discrepancy was more pronounced with recognition tests than recall tests. The interpretation here would be that the cuing effect is storage based and the usual age $\times$ treatment interaction is primarily a consequence of storage development. In contrast, suppose that the pattern of results were the same, except the picture-word manipulation always had larger effects for recall than for recognition, and this difference was greater with older children than with younger children. Now the interpretation would be that the cuing effect is retrieval-based and that the age $\times$ treatment interaction is due to retrieval factors.

In the earlier example of research on the stage-learning hypothesis, I used numerical illustrations to highlight interpretative difficulties. Here, I resort to similar illustrations to demonstrate why, under monotonicity restrictions, paradigms such as the study-test technique and the recognition-recall technique do not provide unambiguous information about the comparative roles of storage and retrieval processes in memory development. First, a minimum of three theoretical variables must be considered, namely, memory strength, storage difficulty, and retrieval difficulty. Let M, S, and R be the scales that denote these respective variables.

On memory tasks, global memory strength is some joint function of global storage difficulty and global retrieval difficulty. The exact manner in which scale values of the last two variables combine to produce scale values of the first variable specifies a composition rule. As usual, this composition rule is unknown. Also about all we can claim is that it is monotonic—that is, larger values of S correspond to equal or larger values of M when R is invariant, and larger values of R correspond to equal or larger values of M when S is invariant.

Let P be the probability of a correct response on some memory task. Under the monotonicity assumption, P is some order-preserving function of internal memory strength, which is to say

$$P = f_r(M), \tag{5}$$

where f_r is the function in question. However, we also know that memory strength is some monotonic function of storage and retrieval difficulty. This allows us to eliminate the concept of memory strength and express performance directly in terms of the storage and retrieval scales. The general form is

$$P = f_r[f_c(S, R)], \tag{6}$$

where f_c is the composition rule that maps values on the memory-strength scale with values on the storage and retrieval scales and f_r is still the output transformation for memory strength. Under the monotonicity assumption, f_c and f_r may be any order-preserving transformations whatsoever.

To localize the effects of a manipulation within storage or retrieval, the methods that we have considered assume that storage difficulty and retrieval difficulty vary in their contributions to different aspects of the data (study trials vs. test trials or recognition tests vs. recall tests) and that this somehow implies that comparisons of these different aspects of the data provide differential evidence on storage and retrieval. However, the numerical examples show that even if the theoretical assumptions of both methods are sound, this implication does not follow under monotonicity constraints. We have already considered a prototype $A \times B \times C$ experiment for each method. Recall that the first factor in the design is always the methodological variable (study trials vs. test trials or recognition tests vs. recall tests), the second factor is always a substantive treatment known to interact with age (e.g., picture cues vs. word cues), and the third factor is always age. It is clear from the illustrations that each method's ability to deliver storage-retrieval explanations of age × treatment interactions depends on the validity of using results for the first two factors in the design to make inferences about the respective contributions of storage difficulty and retrieval difficulty. To simplify the numerical examples, therefore, I confine attention to the first two factors.

The initial series of examples is for the study-test procedure. Recall that the key assumption is that storage difficulty contributes more to study trials than to test trials or, equivalently, that retrieval difficulty contributes more to test trials than to study trials. We now reconsider the earlier experiments in which picture cues versus word cues are manipulated factorially over study and test trials. The first step is to insert some scale values for the S and R variables in this experiment (see Table 1.2). For the

TABLE 1.2 Some numerical examples from a hypothetical study—test experiment.

	Condition and scale values			
	A_1B_1: $S = 4$ and $R = 4$	A_2B_1: $S = 16$ and $R = 6$	A_1B_2: $S = 6$ and $R = 8$	A_2B_2: $S = 16$ and $R = 10$
f_c: $M = S + R$ and f_r: $P = M$	8	22	14	26
f_c: $M = S + R$ and f_r: $P = \ln M$	2.08	3.09	2.64	3.26
f_c: $M = \ln S + R$ and f_r: $P = M$	5.39	8.77	9.79	12.77
f_c: $M = \ln S + R$ and f_r: $P = \ln M$	1.69	2.17	2.28	2.55

Note: A_1B_1 = word/word, A_2B_1 = picture/word, A_1B_2 = word/picture, and A_2B_2 = picture/picture.

four cells of the $A \times B$ matrix, suppose that the scale values are $S = 4$ and $R = 4$ for A_1B_1 (word cues on study and test trials), $S = 16$ and $R = 6$ for A_2B_1 (picture cues on study trials and word cues on test trials), $S = 6$ and $R = 8$ for A_1B_2 (word cues on study trials and picture cues on test trials), and $S = 16$ and $R = 10$ for A_2B_2 (picture cues on both study and test trials). These four sets of values satisfy the method's assumption that storage difficulty is more important on study trials than on test trials. When the cuing variable is manipulated over study trials, the increase in S values is greater than the increase in R values, with the average scale differences between conditions having different study cues but the same test cues being 11 for S and 2 for R. When the cuing variable is manipulated over test trials, the increase in R values is greater than the increase in S values, with the average scale differences between conditions having different study cues but the same test cues being 11 for S and 2 for R. When the cuing variable is manipulated on test trials, the increase in R values is greater than the increase in S values, with the average scale differences between conditions having different test cues but the same study cues being 4 for R and 1 for S. Also, according to the four pairs of scale values, the cuing effect is more a consequence of storage than of retrieval: The average difference in scale values between conditions is 7.67 for S and 3.33 for R. Under the logic of the study-test method, we should find that the cuing variable has larger effects on study trials than on test trials because study trials depend more on storage difficulty than on retrieval difficulty and so does cuing.

Table 1.2 shows, however, that the results of an actual factorial experiment will depend more on the nature of the composition rule than on the validity of the assumptions about storage and retrieval. As we have already seen, a very large class of functions is consistent with the constraint that the function mapping values of memory strength with values of storage and retrieval difficulty must be order-preserving. Two such functions have been used in the examples that appear in Table 1.2, namely, an additive rule ($M = S + R$) and a log-additive rule ($M = \ln S + R$). These two functions have been combined, for purposes of illustration, with an additive output transformation ($P = M$) and a logarithmic output transformation ($P = \ln M$).

In Table 1.2, the composition rules and output transformations have been crossed with four pairs of scale values. In general, we see that the patterns of between-conditions results for the performance measure P mirror the relationships in the underlying scale values for storage and retrieval *only* when the compositive rule is additive. In the first two rows of Table 1.1, where the composition rule is always additive and the output transformation is either additive or logarithmic, the data are in the same direction as the scale values. In the first row, the average difference in P values is greater for comparisons where the cues are different on study trials but the same on test trials ($\Delta P = 13$) than for comparisons where the cues are the same on study trials but different on test trials ($\Delta P = 5$). In the second row, the difference in P values is in the same direction, with $\Delta P = .82$ for the former comparisons and $\Delta P = .73$ for the latter comparisons. In short, cuing affects study and test trials, and there is an interaction such that the study-trial effect is larger. Given that storage difficulty is more important on study trials than on test trials (an assumption that is confirmed by the scale values), the conclusion would be that the cuing effect is more a matter of storage difficulty than of retrieval difficulty, which also happens to be the correct inference in this case. But if we now consider the last two rows in Table 1.2, the between-conditions pattern is reversed. In row 3, the average difference in P values is *smaller* for comparisons where the cues are different on study trials but the same on test trials ($\Delta P = 3.18$) than for comparisons where the cues are the same on study trials but different on test trials ($\Delta P = 4.20$). In the fourth row, the P difference is .38 for the first type of comparison and .49 for the second type of comparison. Thus, there are again two main effects and an interaction, but this time the cuing effect for study trials is smaller than that for test trials. This result would presumably be interpreted as showing that retrieval difficulty is more responsible for the effect than storage difficulty is, an inference that is wrong.

The second series of examples is for the recognition-recall procedure. With this method, the key assumption is that storage difficulty contributes more to recognition performance than to recall performance. We return to the hypothetical experiment in which picture cues versus word cues are factorially combined with recognition tests and recall tests. Suppose that the scale values for storage and retrieval for the four cells of the experiment are $S = 4$ and $R = 8$ for A_1B_1 (word cues on both tests), $S = 16$ and $R = 14$ for A_2B_1 (picture cues on recognition tests and word cues on recall tests), $S = 12$ and $R = 14$ for A_1B_2 (word cues on recognition tests and picture cues on recall tests), and $S = 28$ and $R = 18$ for A_2B_2 (picture cues on both tests). These scale values are consistent with the assumption that storage difficulty is more important on recognition tests than on recall tests. The average R scale value is greater on recall tests than on recognition tests. The scale values, like those for the study-test illustration, are also consistent with the conclusion that storage difficulty contributes more to the cuing effect than retrieval difficulty does: The manipulation produces larger average differences in S scale values than in R scale values.

The numbers in Table 1.3 illustrate that relationships between scale values for different conditions may or may not be reflected in results for a factorial experiment. We saw in Table 1.2 that variations in the composition rule produce variations in apparent support for theoretical conclusions, even though scale values are invariant. In Table 1.3, both the composition rule and the output transformation can have this effect. The two composition rules and output functions are the same as before. Only the scale values are different.

The first row of Table 1.3, where both functions are linear, produces data consistent with the underlying state of affairs. There is a main effect for type of test (such that recognition is easier than recall), there is a main effect for cue (such that pictures are easier than words), and there is an interaction such that the cuing effect is greater on recognition tests than on recall tests. This pattern would, naturally, be interpreted as establishing that cuing depends more on storage factors than on retrieval factors. But each of the remaining three rows produces the opposite interaction (i.e., cuing effects are greater on recall trials than on recognition trials), even though the scale values are consistent with theoretical hypotheses. Relative to row 1, the composition rule is invariant and the output function changes in row 2, the composition rule changes and the output function is invariant in row 3, and both functions change in row 4.

To conclude, both methods discussed in this section make some otherwise sensible assumptions about the relative influences of storage difficulty and retrieval difficulty on different aspects of list-learning data.

TABLE 1.3. Some numerical examples from a hypothetical recognition—recall experiment.

	Condition and scale values			
	A_1B_1: $S = 4$ and $R = 8$	A_2B_1: $S = 16$ and $R = 14$	A_1B_2: $S = 12$ and $R = 14$	A_2B_2: $S = 28$ and $R = 18$
f_c: $M = S + R$ and f_r: $P = M$	12	30	26	46
f_c: $M = S + R$ and f_r: $P = \ln M$	2.49	3.40	3.26	3.83
f_c: $M = \ln S + R$ and f_r: $P = M$	9.39	16.77	16.49	21.33
f_c: $M = \ln S + R$ and f_r: $P = \ln M$	2.24	2.82	2.80	3.06

Note: A_1B_1 = word cues on both tests, A_2B_1 = picture cues on recognition tests and word cues on recall tests, A_1B_2 = word cues on recognition tests and picture cues on recall tests, and A_2B_2 = picture cues on both tests.

However, elementary measurement considerations, especially the empirical consequences of monotonicity restrictions, indicate that these assumptions do not lead to unambiguous conclusions about the memory loci of either treatment effects or developmental interactions.

Some Objectives

The principal aim of these examples was to illustrate that our historical tendency to ignore even the most basic measurement distinctions in cognitive development research is perilous. In addition, however, these examples adumbrate some goals or motivations that we should bear in mind when attempting to develop measurement systems for cognitive development research. In this section, I discuss four objectives that can be drawn from the examples, namely, the need to factor relevant theoretical variables, the need to obtain ratio-scale measurements of these variables, the need to validate particular formulations of theoretical variables, and the need to test psychological interpretations of theoretical variables.

It is worth mentioning, before we proceed, that these objectives have not been casually or arbitrarily chosen from recondite questions of concern only to measurement theorists. On the contrary, the issues of how to disentangle theoretical variables from each other, how to obtain ratio-scale measurements of such variables, how to assess the validity of different formulations of such variables, and how to pit different conceptualizations of theoretical variables against each other are, by consensus, fundamental to theory construction in psychology. In treatises on measurement, these questions often serve as textbook instances of foundational crises in psychology (e.g., Krantz & Tversky, 1971). Frankly, one motivation for the preceding examples is that they implicate these questions.

Factoring Variables

In Example 1 (concept learning), there were four theoretical processes of interest: stage, power of the training regimen, amount of learning, and posttraining conceptual knowledge. For each process, an empirical measure was available in the design of traditional concept-learning experiments that could be assumed to be uniquely and monotonically related to that process. That is, there was a manipulable variable for each process such that changes in its observed values could be assumed to be a consequence of changes in the target process, and *not* of changes in the other three. This general situation, where experimental variables exist that presumably are unique monotonic funtions of process variables, is the standard one that frameworks such as conjoint-measurement theory and functional-measurement theory are designed to handle. Unfortunately, this is not a very common circumstance in cognitive development research. Instead, a persistent difficulty is that our experimental variables are complex functions of multiple process variables.

The endemic nature of this problem is apparent from Examples 2 and 3. In Example 2 (concept sequence research), there were three theoretical processes of interest: children's concept knowledge, the false-positive error rate of a concept test, and the false-negative error rate of a concept test. There are two classes of experimental variables in the relevant studies. First, there are the concept tests, performance on which is assumed to be monotonically related to all three processes. Second, there are various task-difficulty treatments such as requiring children to give extemporaneous explanations, presenting test items nonverbally, imposing visual illusions, and so forth. As long as all levels of such a treatment are administered to the same subjects, its effects are assumed to be monotonically related to the two error rates but not to concept knowledge. Reviewers of this literature have concluded that no conceivable task-difficulty manipulation can, in principle, be said to be uniquely controlled by one of the two error rates (Brainerd, 1977). As we saw, therefore, the changes in a child's concept-test performance observed as a consequence of imposing a given manipulation may occur because it changes the false-positive error rate or changes the false-negative error rate or changes both. This would be a less serious problem if such manipulations normally left the order of difficulty of tests of different concepts invariant. We know, however, that they perturb these orderings. The result is a vast literature on developmental ordering that, it now seems, is a sea of ambiguity.

In Example 3, the two theoretical variables of interest were storage difficulty and retrieval difficulty. Here, the picture was analogous to that for concept sequence research. On one hand, there are different types of memory variables and performance measures, such as study trials versus test trials and recognition tests versus recall tests. In the present state of our theoretical knowledge, storage and retrieval ostensibly contribute at different rates to these variables and tests. On the other hand, storage and retrieval both appear to be involved in all variables and tests.

Two overriding goals of memory development research have been to decide whether the effects of particular treatments are more a consequence of storage processes or of retrieval processes and to use this information to tease apart developmental interactions in these effects. As with concept sequence studies, we do not seem to possess memory measures that can legitimately be assumed to be unique monotonic functions of either category of processes. The situation is nominally better than with concept sequences because there is reason to suppose that certain measures are more directly controlled by storage than by retrieval and that certain other measures are more directly controlled by retrieval than by storage. Under monotonicity constraints, however, this advantage is not sufficient to avoid contradictory conclusions from experimentation. Therefore, the consequences—namely, an ambiguous literature on the relative contributions of storage development and retrieval development to age × treatment interactions—are the same as in concept sequence research.

Evidently, procedures are required for obtaining measurements that are uniquely controlled by cognitive development processes. Because there seem to be important areas of research where this cannot be done merely by introducing empirical variables into experimental designs, attempts to factor processes mathematically appear to be the most promising strategy. In other words, frameworks that allow one to obtain independent measurements of theoretical processes from data in which these processes are partly or completely confounded would be especially useful in cognitive development work.

Ratio-Scale Measurement

Assuming that appropriate factoring technologies can be devised, it would be desirable if the independent measurements of theoretical processes were something more than monotonically related to these processes. Although systems such as conjoint-measurement theory and information integration theory have revealed a surprising amount of inferential power in monotonic information, they have also shown that there are clear limitations. One can, it is true, draw precise conclusions about the algebraic relationships between process variables with such information, but it is not usually possible to make statements about the relative magnitudes of different process variables' effects on performance.

As a rule, inferences of the latter sort have been of greatest concern to students of cognitive development. In the concept-learning example, for instance, the stage-learning hypothesis does not specify what amount of learning is determined exclusively by developmental stage, nor does it propose a particular algebraic relationship between the power of the training method and developmental stage. Instead, effectiveness of training is presumed to depend on stage; or, more simply, stage is said to make a larger contribution to learning than training does. Likewise, in the concept sequence example, we need to know the relative magnitudes of the contributions of conceptual knowledge, false-positive error, and false-negative error across many versions of a concept test before we can conclude that there is a robust sequence in knowledge of different concepts. Again, information about how different versions are ordered with respect to the three variables would not be adequate for our purposes. Finally, in the storage-retrieval example, assigning memory loci to treatment effects and the subsequent use of such interpretations to explain developmental interactions also require information about relative magnitude. In fact, with both the study-test procedure and the recognition-recall procedure, it is possible to have information about the ordering of storage difficulty and retrieval difficulty in distinct features of the data and still be unable to make unambiguous statements about the loci of treatment effects. Something more powerful than monotonic information is again necessary.

In short, another very useful feature of measurement systems for cognitive development would be to deliver estimates of theoretical processes that permit statements about relative magnitude. If such measurements were on at least a common interval scale, such statements would ultimately be possible. But in specific applications to data, it would be necessary to confront the bothersome technical problem of finding the zero point for all the relevant scales. Applications would, therefore, be much smoother if independent measures of processes could be made on a common ratio scale (see also Chechile & Richman, 1982).

Validity

If it is possible to obtain independent estimates of theoretical processes on common ratio scales, the next question is whether our characterization of these processes as controlling performance on particular tasks is actually correct. In the three examples, the process descriptions simply were assumed correct. Explicitly, it was assumed that the four variables of stage, training power, learning, and posttraining conceptual knowledge provided an accurate characterization of concept-learning experiments. Three processes (conceptual knowledge, false-positive error, and false-negative error) were assumed to account for concept-test performance, and performance on memory tests was said to be adequately represented by two classes of processes, storage factors and retrieval factors.

But how do we know that these characterizations are even remotely accurate? More particularly, two questions, one about parsimony and one about completeness, can normally be posed: How do we know that all the processes specified are actually involved? In the concept-learning illustration, for example, perhaps developmental stages do not exist and concept-test performance on both pretests and posttests merely reflects different levels of the same knowledge scale (cf. Brainerd, 1978). If so, we can reduce the set of process variables that must be measured to training power, learning, and conceptual knowledge. Similarly, perhaps separate storage and retrieval processes do not exist and, instead, what we usually call storage factors and retrieval factors are indistinguishable components of a common memory-strength variable. Concerning completeness, how do we know that processes other than those specified are not also involved? In the storage-retrieval illustration, for example, perhaps encoding and decoding processes operate independently of whatever processes fix traces in storage and whatever processes find them on test trials. If so, the number of processes for which independent measurements must be sought is 4 rather than 2.

In general, then, we would like to know whether our sets of theoretical variables are either too rich or too impoverished for the data spaces. Conceptually, this is a question about goodness of fit, and consequently it suggests that goodness-of-fit machinery would be a useful component of measurement theories for cognitive development.

Interpretation of Theoretical Variables

Assuming that the first three objectives can be met, we are still left with the problem of making psychological interpretations of theoretical constructs such as developmental stage, concept learning, false-positive error, storage, and retrieval. Saying that certain processes are critical to certain types of data and confirming such statements with goodness-of-fit tests do not necessarily tell us anything about the nature of these processes. Normally, there are a number of competing psychological interpretations of any process. This is perhaps most apparent in Example 3. The current memory literature contains many physical metaphors for retrieval that stand as competing interpretations of how traces are located on performance tests. The metaphors include such things as conveyer belts, decision trees, junk boxes, and tuning forks. Similarly, concept learning in Example 1 can be interpreted as discrete shifts in the use of selected rules (e.g., Brainerd, 1979) or as the gradual accretion of skills such as attention (e.g., Gelman, 1969). In the same example, between-subject differences in conceptual knowledge can be viewed as all-or-none differences in rule state or quantitative differences in component skills. (See Chapter 3, this volume, by Wilkinson and Haines for a related discussion.)

Clearly it is important to gain leverage on contrasting interpretations of process variables. Differences between such interpretations can often be embodied in experimental manipulations of some sort. For example, if concept learning is more a matter of changes in rule usage than a matter of attentional shifts, rule instruction should affect concept learning more than attentional instruction, other things being equal. In other words, these manipulations should affect the power of the training procedure in predictable ways, though not necessarily some of the other processes. So we would like to be able to compare the relative effects of training methods that are inspired by different theories of concept learning on the training power variable. More generally, we would like to be able to compare the relative effects of manipulations that embody different interpretations of a given process variable on that particular variable independently of the other variables being measured.

Three Models

I now summarize a concept-learning model, a concept sequence model, and a storage-retrieval model from the recent literature. In each case, the synopsis shows how it is possible both to address the specific problems raised in the first section of this chapter and to satisfy some of the general objectives discussed in the preceding section with a single model.

Two-Stage Model of Concept Learning

Experiments of the type discussed in Example 1 have been principally concerned with the learning of Piagetian concepts such as conservation, class inclusion, proportionality, perspective taking, subjective morality, and so forth, especially conservation. A feature of overriding significance is that children's performance on tests of these concepts appears to be strongly rule-governed: Children's responses tend to be highly consistent rather than haphazard, a fact that serves as the basis for nonverbal rule assessment methodologies (e.g., Siegler & Vago, 1978). When asked to justify their responses, moreover, children normally state simple rules that are strongly correlated with these responses. In short, the evidence seems overwhelming that children retrieve simple rules on concept tests, although the specific rules and the manner of their application may be in doubt. (On this point, see also Chapter 3, this volume, by Wilkinson and Haines.)

Although we may not know the precise rules guiding a child's performance on any given occasion, it is possible to make an exhaustive, abstract characterization of such rules in terms of the probabilities with which correct responses occur. We can say that any rule that a child might conceivably use on any concept test must fall into one and only one of the following sets:

W = set of *wrong* rules, each of which produces errors on items of target test with probability 1
V = set of *valid* rules, each of which produces correct responses on items of target test with probability 1
P = set of *partially valid* rules, each of which produces correct responses on items of target test with some average probability $0 < p < 1$

Because every conceivable rule must be a member of exactly one of the sets, this classification system can be used with any concept test whatsoever without regard to the nature of the rules that are actually retrieved.

I have noted elsewhere that the normative data on many Piagetian tests follow a pattern that can be explained by a simple rule-sampling interpretation of children's concept learning (Brainerd, 1979, 1982). This theory can, in turn, be implemented as a Markov model. The normative pattern to which I refer is one in which performance on tests of concepts such as conservation, class inclusion, and the like seems to show a stereotyped, three-step sequence. During an early age range, which usually corresponds to the preschool and early elementary school years with Piagetian concepts, children make errors more or less across the board. During an intermediate age range, which usually corresponds to the early-middle elementary school years, children sometimes make correct responses. During a final age range, which usually corresponds to the late elementary school and adolescent years, errors rarely occur. The rule-sampling theory being considered makes two primary assumptions: (1) Children in the early, intermediate, and final age ranges use predominately W, P, and V rules, respectively, and (2) the improvements in test performance that occur as a function of training consist of surrendering current rules and sampling new rules with a view toward securing rules that always produce correct responses. At the start of a learning experiment, a child may be in state W (using a wrong rule), state P (using a partially correct rule), or state V (using a valid rule) with respect to the items on the test. Children in such experiments normally are administered an extensive pretest battery, and only children who make at least some errors are retained for training. In terms of rule-state classification, the children in a concept-learning experiment are always in either state W or state P. For children who start in state W, test performance can be improved by sampling either rules from P or rules from V. For children who start in state P, however, performance can improve only if V rules are sampled.

The notions that children occupy discrete rule states and that concept learning consists of moving from more error-prone states to less error-prone states imply a particular three-state Markov model. The mathematical aspects of the model have been described elsewhere (Brainerd, 1979, 1982; Wilkinson and Haines, Chapter 3, this volume) and need not concern us here. The main feature of interest is that the model provides different parameters which measure the difficulty of learning in the sense of abandoning wrong rules and the difficulty of learning in the sense of abandoning partially valid rules. The specific learning parameters of interest are

a = on any trial, the probability that children who occupy state W escape that state by sampling either a P rule or a V rule
b = on any trial, where a child escapes state W, the probability that a V rule is sampled
d = on any trial where a child occupies state P and makes an error on a test item, the probability that the child escapes state P by sampling a V rule

It is now possible to conduct simple tests of the stage-learning hypothesis by noting that children who currently occupy more error-prone states (W in the model) should be at lower stages of cognitive development, on the average, than children who occupy less error-prone states (P in the model). Consequently, one would expect that children who occupy state W should have more difficulty learning than children who occupy state P, a prediction that can be tested by comparing observed values of a to observed values of d. Procedures are available for estimating these parameters via the method of maximum likelihood (Brainerd, 1979, 1982;

Kingma, Chapter 2, this volume; Wilkinson and Haines, Chapter 3, this volume). Contrary to the stage-learning hypothesis, the difficulty of learning for children who occupy state *W* is not generally greater than for children who occupy state *P*. In a series of experiments on conservation and classification (Brainerd, 1982), either the estimated values of *a* and *d* did not differ, or *a* was larger than *d*. Another surprising result from the standpoint of the stage-learning hypothesis is that the majority of children who start in state *W* learn by moving directly from *W* to *V* without ever entering *P;* the estimates of the parameter *b* ranged consistently from 0.6 to 0.7. (Wilkinson and Haines report some similar data in Chapter 3.)

In addition to delivering direct tests of the stage-learning hypothesis, the parameters of the rule-sampling model satisfy the four objectives mentioned in the preceding section. First, they manage to factor the pertinent process variables by providing separate estimates of the difficulty of concept learning for children who occupy less advanced and more advanced states at the start of an experiment. To test the stage-learning hypothesis, about all that is necessary is to conduct a learning experiment, estimate the parameters *a* and *d,* and determine whether they differ reliably. Second, concerning ratio-scale measurement, because the three-state Markov model gives a complete expression of concept-test performance in terms of its parameters, the process variables that serve as interpretations of these parameters are measured on a common ratio scale (cf. Brainerd, 1982). In other words, variables such as the difficulty of learning a *P* rule and the difficulty of learning a *V* rule are measured on a common ratio scale. When the parameters have been estimated, therefore, statements such as "learning in state *W* was twice as difficult as in state *P*" and the like can be made.

Third, the validity of the rule-sampling theory's interpretation of concept learning can be tested. An extensive battery of goodness-of-fit tests is available that allows one to assess whether three-state Markov processes give statistically tolerable accounts of learning data (Brainerd, Howe, & Desrochers, 1982; Brainerd, Howe, & Kingma, 1982). If the theory is correct in describing learning as progress through three, discrete states, then the correspondence between the model and fine-grain statistics of learning data should be virtually exact, a result that has usually been obtained (Brainerd, 1979, 1982). Fourth, the model also permits advances in our theoretical understanding of children's concept learning. As we have seen, parameters are in hand that measure the difficulty of learning in different rule states, and learning has been tentatively interpreted as a rule-sampling process. However, other interpretations are possible, some of which were mentioned earlier. It is quite feasible to pit such interpretations against each other by manipulating treatments that embody these ideas in experiments and determining how the learning parameters of different states react. An illustrative research program has been reported by Wilkinson (1982b; Chapter 3, this volume). In his experiments, Wilkinson has contrasted the simple rule-sampling view described here with another interpretation in which concept learning involves both sampling rules and assembling them into more complex solution procedures.

A Model of Measurement Error in Mental Arithmetic

In Example 2, the underlying dilemma of concept sequence research is that it is not possible to distinguish conceptual knowledge from false-positive and false-negative reasoning errors. When children perform better on tests of one concept than on tests of another concept, therefore, it is not possible to tell whether this is due to a developmental sequence in knowledge of the concepts or to differences in the intrinsic error rates for the two types of tests. Apparently a model is needed that provides separate estimates of the probability that children have the target concept, that they will make false-positive errors, and that they will make false-negative errors. As yet, a satisfactory framework that encompasses the full range of traditional concept sequence studies has not been developed. However, progress has been made lately in connection with sequences in basic number concepts (Brainerd 1983b; Wilkinson, 1982a, 1982b; Wilkinson & Haines, Chapter 3, this volume). Here, I describe a procedure that permits the detection of sequences in two such concepts (addition and subtraction) independently of the inherent error rates of the relevant tests.

When children are administered arithmetic word problems, a common finding is that addition problems are solved before subtraction problems of equivalent logical complexity. For example, items of the form "$5 + 3 = ?$" and "$7 + 2 = ?$" are normally solved before the logically equivalent items "$5 - 3 = ?$" and "$7 - 2 = ?$". Cognitively, performance on such simple problems might break down in two general ways, namely, processing failure and short-term memory failure. Concerning processing, children might not have addition and/or subtraction operations available in their long-term knowledge stores. Concerning short-term memory, children might not be able to encode some of the relevant information in a word problem, or they might not be able to store the information long enough to execute the necessary processing operations. If children are constrained to give a response on every item, they presumably guess or select a numeral on the basis of irrelevant contextual factors whenever processing or short-term memory fails.

In this situation, we wish to determine whether the usual sequence in addition and subtraction performance is due to a sequence in the processing operations or to noise factors, such as guessing and short-term memory. An elementary model is available that is defined over a modified mental arithmethic paradigm in which addition and subtraction items are occasionally followed by short-term memory probes for the problem information. Consider an addition item of the form "$m + n = ?$" that is followed by a recall probe requiring the child to restate the problem. Let $p(AM)$, $p(\bar{A}M)$, $p(A\bar{M})$, and $p(\bar{A}\bar{M})$ be, respectively, the probability that both the addition and probe responses are correct, the probability that the addition response is wrong and the probe response is correct, the probability that the addition response is correct and the probe response is wrong, and the probability that both responses are wrong. Also, let P_A be the probability that the child possesses the necessary addition operations, S_A the probability that the child correctly encodes that problem information into short-term memory and retains it until processing is completed, and g the probability that the child guesses the correct number on addition items when processing or short-term memory fails and on probe items when short-term memory fails. The first four probabilities, all of which correspond to observable data events, can now be expressed in terms of the latter three probabilities, all of which are theoretical constructions.

First, correct responses might occur on both the addition and probe items in three general ways: (1) Short-term memory and processing might both function correctly (with probability $P_A\ S_A$); (2) short-term memory might function correctly (with probability S_A), which produces a correct response on the probes, but processing might fail on the addition item and be accompanied by a correct guess [with probability $(1 - P_A)g_A$]; and (3) short-term memory might fail, and the subject might guess correctly on both items [with probability $(1 - S_A)g_A^2$]. Hence, $p(AM)$ can be expressed as

$$p(AM) = P_A S_A + (1 - P_A)S_A g_A + (1 - S_A)g_A^2. \tag{7}$$

Second, an error might occur on the addition item and be accompanied by a correct probe response in the following ways: (1) Short-term memory might function correctly (with probability S_A), which produces a correct probe response, but processing might fail and be accompanied by an incorrect guess on the addition item [with probability $(1 - P_A)(1 - g_A)$]; and (2) short-term memory might fail and be accompanied by correct and incorrect guesses on the probe and addition items, respectively [with probability $(1 - S_A)g_A(1 - g_A)$]. The expression for $p(\bar{A}M)$, then, is

$$p(\bar{A}M) = (1 - P_A)S_A\ (1 - g_A) + (1 - S_A)g_A\ (1 - g_A). \tag{8}$$

Third, a correct addition response might be followed by an incorrect probe response in just one way, namely, short-term memory fails (with probability $(1 - S_A)$ and the child guesses correctly on the addition item and incorrectly on the probe [with probability $(1 - g_A)g_A$]. This gives the following expression for $p(A\bar{M})$:

$$p(A\bar{M}) = (1 - S_A)g_A\ (1 - g_a). \tag{9}$$

Last, an error might occur on both items in just one way, namely, short-term memory fails (with probability $1 - S_A$) and the child guesses incorrectly on both items [with probability $(1 - g_A)^2$]. The expression for $p(\bar{A}\bar{M})$, then, is

$$p(\bar{A}\bar{M}) = (1 - S_a)(1 - g_A)^2. \tag{10}$$

Turning to subtraction, let $p(SM)$, $p(\bar{S}M)$, $p(S\bar{M})$, and $p(\bar{S}\bar{M})$ be, respectively, the probability of a correct subtraction response followed by a correct probe response, the probability of an incorrect subtraction response followed by a correct probe response, the probability of a correct subtraction response followed by an incorrect probe response, and the probability of errors on both the subtraction and probe items. Obviously, these probabilities, like those for addition problems, can be expressed in terms of the theoretical events of processing failure, short-term memory failure, and guessing. Let P_S, S_S, and g_s be the probabilities of these respective events for subtraction items followed by a probe for the problem information. The parallel equations for subtraction are

$$p(SM) = P_S S_S + (1 - P_S) S_S g_S + (1 - S_S) g_S^2, \tag{11}$$

$$p(\bar{S}M) = (1 - P_S) S_S (1 - g_S) + (1 - S_S) g_S (1 - g_S), \tag{12}$$

$$p(S\bar{M}) = (1 - S_S) g_S (1 - g_S), \tag{13}$$

$$p(\bar{S}\bar{M}) = (1 - S_S)(1 - g_S)^2. \tag{14}$$

The method of maximum likelihood can be used to estimate the three parameters for addition in experiments where addition problems are followed by short-term memory probes (Brainerd, 1983b, appendix). The same procedures can be used to estimate the three parameters for subtraction in experiments where subtraction problems are followed by short-term memory probes. To decide whether there is a developmental sequence in children's knowledge of addition and subtraction, it is only necessary to conduct studies in which both types of probed arithmetic problems are administered, estimate the three parameters separately for addition and subtraction, and then determine whether performance differences are due to differences in the processing parameter P or to differences in the two noise parameters S and g. I have previously reported four experiments of this sort (Brainerd, 1983b). In the first two experiments, probed addition items (experiment 1) or probed subtraction items (experiment 2) were administered to mixed samples of preschool and kindergarten children. In experiment 1, the average values of the three parameters were $P_A = .68$, $S_A = .40$, and $g_A = .14$. In experiment 2, the average values of the three parameters were $P_S = .46$, $S_S = .40$ and $g_S = .13$. It appeared, therefore, that sequence in addition versus subtraction knowledge was independent of noise factors. Similar findings were obtained in two follow-up studies. In experiment 3, probed addition items were administered to both preschool and kindergarten children and first-grade children. In experiment 4, probed subtraction items were administered to children from the same grades. The average values of the three parameters in the addition experiment were $P_A = .67$ (younger children) and $P_A = .72$ (older children), $S_A = .40$ (younger children) and $S_A = .60$ (older children), and $g_A = .18$ (younger children) and $g_A = .30$ (older children). The corresponding values in the subtraction experiment were $P_S = .44$ (younger children) and $P_S = .56$ (older children), $S_S = .41$ (younger children) and $S_S = .64$ (older children), and $g_S = .08$ (younger children) and $g_S = .26$ (older children). In these latter experiments, the processing parameter differed reliably at both age levels, although the difference for the younger children (.23) was somewhat greater than the difference for the older children (.16).

These data illustrate that by using fairly simple stochastic models one can measure children's underlying knowledge of target concepts independently of potential sources of measurement error. Further illustrations can be found in Wilkinson's (1982a, 1982b, Chapter 3 in this volume) models of partial knowledge. All these models are confined to elementary numerical reasoning paradigms, where the major sources of false-positive and false-negative errors are rather obvious. Nevertheless, concept sequence data from these models represent a considerable advance over the types of studies discussed in Example 2. Moreover, there is reason to suppose that the basic strategy of segregating performance into parameters that measure conceptual knowledge and parameters that measure error sources can be extended to more complex tasks where these error sources are not self-evident.

Models such as these also provide leverage on the four measurement objectives. First, in Equations 7 to 10 and in Equations 11 to 14, the present model slices up performance on mental arithmetic items in such a way that conceptual knowledge and measurement error can be assessed independently of each other. Second, because performance on probed arithmetic items is completely expressed in terms of the probabilities of events such as processing failure, short-term memory failure, and guessing, the latter events are being measured on a single ratio scale. This, in turn, allows for relative-magnitude statements about the respective probabilities of these events. Third, because the parameters are estimated via the method of maximum likelihood, familiar likelihood ratio tests of goodness of fit can be used to assess the model's validity. Mathematically, the expressions in Equations 7 to 10 (as well as those in Equations 11 to 14) constrain the four observable probabilities in specific ways. One constraint is easy to see by manipulating Equations 8 and 9. $p(\bar{A}M)$ must always be larger than $p(A\bar{M})$. If these constraints are violated, the model is invalid.

Fourth, the theoretical interpretations of the three parameters—namely, that P measures processing accuracy, S measures short-term memory accuracy, and g measures guessing accuracy—can all be tested by studying the effects of manipulations that should, under the stated interpretations, selectively affect certain parameters. For example, suppose that identical probed arithmetic items involving the same numbers were administered, except that some were addition items (for example, 5 + 3 = ?) and some were subtraction items (for example, 5 − 3 = ?). Because the problems are identical except for the processing operation required, one would expect, if the interpretations of the parameters are sound, that only *P* should be affected by such a manipulation. Clearly, from the data reported above, such a result has already been obtained. In contrast, suppose that identical probed addition (or subtraction) items are administered except that some problems are stated in more difficult language than others. (For example, stating a problem in ordinal terminology is usually easier for children to comprehend than stating it in cardinal terminology.) Since the language in which a problem is posed is a pure encoding manipulation, one would anticipate, under the model's interpretations, that the processing parameter would not be affected but the short-term memory parameter would be. Data consistent with this expectation have been reported (Brainerd, 1983b).

Two-Stage Model of Storage-Retrieval Development

We saw in Example 3 that a number of theoretical questions about memory development turn out to be questions about changes in the ability to get information into memory versus changes in the ability to get information out again. In some instances, these questions are focused on a specific memory paradigm (e.g., free recall). In other cases, the questions are in the nature of general theoretical controversies, such as current disagreements over capacity versus efficiency explanations of short-term memory development and automatic versus strategic explanations of organizational development. As in concept sequence research, the fact that independent measurements of storage and retrieval development are not made has contributed to confusing and inconsistent literatures on such questions.

During the past few years, an especially rich and varied array of models has been implemented to deal with this problem. These models make it possible to study the comparative rates of storage and retrieval development, plus the development of other theoretical variables, quite independently of each other. Different models are defined over different families of memory tasks, which allows for truly convergent research on storage-retrieval development. For example, Chechile and his associates (Chechile & Meyer, 1976; Chechile & Richman, 1982; Chechile, Richman, Topinka, & Ehrensbeck, 1981) have proposed a model whose parameters provide independent estimates of storage and retrieval development in short-term memory. The model is defined over a modified version of the familiar Brown-Peterson distractor task in which recognition tests are intermingled with the normal recall tests (see Chechile & Meyer, 1976). However, Wilkinson and his associates (Wilkinson, DeMarinis, & Riley,

1983; Wilkinson & Koestler, 1983, 1984) have developed a model whose parameters provide independent estimates of storage and retrieval development in long-term memory. This model, naturally, is defined over different tasks than Chechile's model, namely, Buschke-type repeated recall procedures. A separate review of these models, together with other techniques for measuring storage-retrieval development, is available (Brainerd, 1985).

Of extant techniques, three-state Markov models of storage-retrieval development have been by far the most commonly employed procedures. They have been used to study the respective contributions of storage and retrieval development in such varied contexts as memory deficits in the aged (Howe & Hunter, in press), age changes in semantic organization (Howe, Brainerd, & Kingma, 1985) age changes in the effects of response knowledge on associative memory (Bisanz, Voss, & Vesonder, 1978), memory deficits in learning-disabled children (Brainerd, Howe, & Kingma, in press, a; Howe, Brainerd, & Kingma, in press), age changes in the effects of concreteness on associative memory (Brainerd & Howe, 1982), age changes in the rate of forgetting from long-term memory (Brainerd, Kingma, & Howe, in press b), and age changes in recall (Brainerd, Howe, Kingma, & Brainerd, 1974). These models, which are extensively discussed in Chapter 2, this volume, by Kingma, have the advantage, relative to other models, of being applicable to a broad range of memory paradigms. In particular, they can be used with *any* of the standard list learning paradigms as long as the response measure is some sort of recall (e.g., cued recall, free recall, paired-associate learning, serial learning). A pedagogically instructive point is that the underlying mathematical model is the same as the three-state model of concept learning considered earlier in this chapter and in Chapter 3, this volume, by Wilkinson and Haines.

The logic behind the model is fairly straightforward. When children memorize a supraspan list under standard recall conditions, the protocols of individual items show a stereotyped pattern of errors and successes: An initial series of one or more trials on which only errors occur is followed by a series of trials on which recall is sometimes successful and sometimes unsuccessful, and this is followed by a final series of trials (criterion run) on which recall is always successful. (The complete pattern is observed only when performance is driven to a stringent criterion.) Conceptually, this pattern is interpreted as follows. Because the guessing probability is effectively zero on recall tasks, it is assumed that a correct recall is not possible until a permanent trace of an item has been deposited in long-term memory. Because permanent storage does not mean that retrieval will be infallible on test trials, some further learning may be necessary before a retrieval algorithm is acquired. The states of the model are then defined as follows. First, there is an *unstored* state U in which only errors are observed because a trace has not yet been fixed in long-term memory. Second, there is a *stored* state S in which a trace has been deposited but a retrieval algorithm is not yet available. During state S, the probability of successful recall is some value $0 < p < 1$. Third, there is a *retrievable* state R in which a retrieval algorithm is available for the trace.

As I mentioned, these assumptions imply the same three-state model as the one discussed in connection with concept learning. Not surprisingly, the same parameters are used to measure storage and retrieval development on recall tasks. In particular, parameters a, b, and d are redefined as follows:

a = on any trial, the probability that an item escapes initial state U by having a trace stored in long-term memory

b = on any trial where a trace is stored, the probability that a retrieval algorithm is already available for the trace, so the item can proceed immediately to state R without entering state S

d = on any trial where an item is already in state S (i.e., a trace was stored on some earlier trial but a retrieval algorithm was not yet available) and an *unsuccessful* recall occurs, the probability that a retrieval algorithm is learned and the item enters state R

Another parameter concerned with retrieval is added to these models:

c = on any trial where an item is already in state S and a *successful* recall occurs, the probability that a retrieval algorithm is learned and the item enters state R

In specific research applications, then, one merely estimates parameters such as these from recall protocols and evaluates the respective contributions of storage and retrieval development to the data. Such experiments evidently satisfy the first objective of measurement theories of cognitive development because they factor the effects of the pertinent theoretical processes on the target data: If storage development contributes more to a certain age effect than retrieval development does, the a parameter ought to show more age change than the other parameters do; but the reverse should be true if retrieval development contributes more to the effect. The most vigorous applications of this factoring strategy have been to age × treatment interactions—that is, to manipulations whose effects on list learning tend to increase or decrease with age (e.g., category cuing, concreteness, degree of list organization, elaboration). In most instances, such interactions appear to be either mainly storage effects or mainly retrieval effects. For example, Howe and I found that the divergent age × treatment interaction in the effects of concreteness was primarily the result of storage development during the early childhood years but primarily the result of retrieval development later on (Brainerd & Howe, 1982). Other investigators have reported age × treatment interactions in the effects of factors such as learning disability (Brainerd, Howe, and Kingma, in press, b) and cuing that are consistently due to retrieval development (Howe et al., in press). Finally, age × treatment interactions in certain variables can be chiefly storage-based with some tasks and chiefly retrieval-based with other tasks. The familiar divergent interaction for degree of list organization, for instance, has been found to be due to retrieval development on free-recall tasks (Howe, et al., 1985) and to storage development on paired-associate tasks (Brainerd et al., in press, b).

Three-state models of storage-retrieval development also meet the second measurement objective by providing ratio-scale measurements of storage and retrieval development. The reason is the same as for the concept-learning and concept sequence models, namely, the model gives a complete specification of performance on the target task (recall paradigms) in terms of its parameters. Hence, conclusions about the relative impact of storage and retrieval development on age changes in memory performance have become routine features of experiments in which these models, and other storage-retrieval models, have been used (for a review, see Brainerd, 1985).

Concerning the third measurement objective, well-developed procedures exist for estimating the model's parameters via the method of maximum likelihood by using either data from criterion experiments or data from fixed-trials experiments (Brainerd, in press). As for the concept-learning and concept sequence models, therefore, a likelihood ratio technology is also available for assessing the model's fit to data, which is to say that the validity of its assumptions about list-learning data are subject to precise tests. In most developmental studies conducted so far, the model's predictions about fine-grain features of data have agreed closely with observation (for a review, see Brainerd, 1983a).

The final measurement objective, that of interpreting theoretical variables, is especially well met by this model. If escape from the initial, pure error state is synonymous with depositing a permanent trace, then manipulations that affect the difficulty of getting information into memory should affect parameters such as a without affecting parameters such as b, c, and d. If escape from the intermediate, mixed error-success state is synonymous with learning how to retrieve a trace, then manipulations that affect the difficulty of getting information out of memory should affect parameters such as b, c, and d without affecting parameters such as a. There is a reasonably extensive literature with both adults and children that tends to agree with the predictions. Insofar as storage is concerned, visual discriminability of list items appears to be a pure storage-difficulty treatment: Items that are harder to differentiate visually but are otherwise (e.g., orally or conceptually) quite distinctive should make it more difficult to encode a unique trace of each item but should not make it more difficult to find traces once they are stored. In line with this prediction, Humphreys and Greeno (1970) found that visually confusable consonant trigrams decreased the value of parameter a but left the values of parameters *b, c,* and *d* invariant. Turning to retrieval, we see that category cuing would seem to be a pure retrieval-difficulty manipulation: Since cuing the category to which a word belongs cannot help one retrieve a trace that has not yet been stored, this manipulation should affect retrieval difficulty without affecting storage difficulty. Howe et al. (1985) have reported supportive results.

Concluding Remarks

We have traditionally paid very little attention to measurement issues, in particular the monotonicity problem, in research on memory and cognitive development. An inevitable consequence has been the accumulation of a large research literature in which there are fundamental disagreements about the reality of certain findings and their theoretical interpretability. The bodies of literature concerned with stage-learning effects in children's concept learning, the sequence of acquisition of various concepts, and the relative contributions of storage and retrieval processes to memory development are all prominent illustrations.

Recent research, however, provides some grounds for believing that this situation may be changing. Mathematical models developed by a number of investigators allow researchers to deal with some important measurement issues. Examples include models that factor the relative contributions of different theoretical variables to performance data, models whose parameters deliver ratio-scale measurements of interesting theoretical processes, models that permit validity tests of their assumptions, and models that allow one to pit different theoretical interpretations of psychological processes against each other in experimentation. Models that accomplish some of or all these objectives are now available for concept learning, concept sequentiality, and storage-retrieval development. The data base on the latter model is particularly extensive.

In short, we have progressed in a few short years from a state in which fundamental measurement distinctions were almost entirely ignored to a state in which some fairly powerful techniques for implementing some of these distinctions in specific research contexts have been reported. Logically, the next step is to formulate general measurement frameworks that focus on uniquely developmental measurement problems. It remains to be seen, of course, whether this step will be taken.

References

Anderson, N. H. (1970). Functional measurement and psychophysics. *Psychological Review 77,* 153–170.

Anderson, N. H. (1974). Information integration theory: A brief survey. In D. H. Krantz, R. C. Atkinson, R. D. Luce, & P. Suppes (Eds.), *Contemporary developments in mathematical psychology* (Vol. 2). San Francisco: Freeman.

Anderson, N. H., & Cuneo, D. O. (1978). The height + width rule in children's judgments of quantity. *Journal of Experimental Psychology: General, 107,* 335–378.

Bisanz, G. L., Voss, J. F., & Vesonder, G. T. (1978). Knowledge of one's own responding and the relation of such knowledge to learning. *Journal of Experimental Child Psychology 25,* 116–128.

Bjorklund, D. F. (1985). The role of conceptual knowledge in the development of organization in children's memory. In C. J. Brainerd & M. Pressley (Eds.), *Basic processes in memory development: Progress in cognitive development research* (pp. 103–142). New York: Springer-Verlag.

Brainerd, C. J. (1973). Order of acquisition of transitivity, conservation, and class inclusion of length and weight. *Developmental Psychology, 8,* 105–116.

Brainerd, C. J. (1974). Training and transfer of transitivity, conservation, and class inclusion. *Child Development, 45,* 324–344.

Brainerd, C. J. (1977). Cognitive development and concept learning: An interpretative review. *Psychological Bulletin, 84,* 919–939.

Brainerd, C. J. (1978). The stage question in cognitive-developmental theory. *The Behavioral and Brain Sciences, 1,* 173–213.

Brainerd, C. J. (1979). Markovian interpretations of conservation learning. *Psychological Review, 86,* 181–213.

Brainerd, C. J. (1982). Children's concept learning as rule-sampling systems with Markovian properties. In C. J. Brainerd (Ed.), *Children's logical and mathematical cognition: Progress in cognitive development research* (pp. 177–212). New York: Springer-Verlag.

Brainerd, C. J. (1983a). Structural invariance in the developmental analysis of learning. In J. Bisanz, G. Bisanz, & R. V. Kail (Eds.), *Learning in children: Progress in cognitive development research.* New York: Springer-Verlag.

Brainerd, C. J. (1983b). Young children's mental arithmetic errors: A working-memory analysis. *Child Development 54,* 812–830.

Brainerd, C. J. (1985). Model-based approaches to storage and retrieval development. In C. J. Brainerd & M. Pressley (Eds.), *Basic processes in memory development: Progress in cognitive development research* (pp. 143–207). New York: Springer-Verlag.

Brainerd, C. J. (in press). Three-state models of memory development: A review of advances in statistical methodology. *Journal of Experimental Child Psychology.*

Brainerd, C. J., & Howe, M. L. (1982). Stages-of-learning analysis of developmental interactions in memory, with illustrations from developmental interactions in picture-word effects. *Developmental Review, 2,* 251–273.

Brainerd, C. J., Howe, M. L., & Desrochers, A. (1982). The general theory of two-stage learning: A mathematical review with illustrations from memory development. *Psychological Bulletin, 91,* 634–665.

Brainerd, C. J., Howe, M. L., & Kingma, J. (1982). An identifiable model of two-stage learning. *Journal of Mathematical Psychology, 26,* 263–293.

Brainerd, C. J., Howe, M. L., & Kingma, J. (in press, a). Long-term memory development and learning disability: Storage and retrieval loci of disabled/nondisabled differences. In S. J. Ceci (Ed.), *Handbook of cognitive, social, and neuropsychological aspects of learning disabilities.* Hillsdale, N J: Erlbaum.

Brainerd, C. J., Howe, M. L., & Kingma, J. (in press, b). On the development of forgetting. *Child Development.*

Brainerd, C. J., Howe, M. L., Kingma, J., & Brainerd, S. H. (1984). On the measurement of storage and retrieval contributions to memory development. *Journal of Experimental Child Psychology, 37,* 478–499.

Chechile, R. A., & Meyer, D. L. (1976). A Bayesian procedure for separately estimating storage and retrieval processes. *Journal of Mathematical Psychology, 13,* 269–295.

Chechile, R. A., & Richman, C. L. (1982). The interaction of semantic memory with storage and retrieval processes. *Developmental Review, 2,* 237–250.

Chechile, R. A., Richman, C. L., Topinka, C., & Ehrensbeck, K. (1981). A developmental study of the storage and retrieval of information. *Child Development, 52,* 251–259.

Dempster, F. N. (1985). Short-term memory development in childhood and adolescence. In C. J. Brainerd & M. Pressley (Eds.), *Basic processes in memory development: Progress in cognitive development research* (pp. 209–248). New York: Springer-Verlag.

Emmerich, H. J., & Ackerman, B. P. (1978). Developmental differences in recall: Encoding or retrieval? *Journal of Experimental Child Psychology, 25,* 514–525.

Estes, W. K., & DaPolito, F. (1967). Independent variation of information storage and retrieval processes in paired-associate learning. *Journal of Experimental Psychology, 75,* 18–26.

Flexer, A. J., & Tulving, E. (1978). Retrieval independence and recall. *Psychological Review, 85,* 153–171.

Gelman, R. (1969). Conservation acquisition: A problem of learning to attend to relevant attributes. *Journal of Experimental Child Psychology, 7,* 167–187.

Greeno, J. G., James, C. T., DaPolito, F. J., & Polson, P. G. (1978). *Associative learning: A cognitive analysis.* Englewood Cliffs, NJ: Prentice-Hall.

Hooper, F. H., Goldman, J. A., Storck, P. A., & Burke, A. M. (1971). Stage sequence and correspondence in Piagetian theory: A review of the middle-childhood period. *Research relating to children* (Bulletin 28). Washington: Government Printing Office.

Hooper, F. H., Toniolo, T. A., & Sipple, T. S. (1978). A longitudinal analysis of logical reasoning relationships: Conservation and transitive inference. *Developmental Psychology, 14,* 674–682.

Howe, M. L., Brainerd, C. J., & Kingma, J. (1985). Development of organization in recall: A stages-of-learning analysis. *Journal of Experimental Child Psychology, 39,* 230–251.

Howe, M. L., Brainerd, C. J., & Kingma, J. (in press). Storage-retrieval processes of normal and learning-disabled children: A stages-of-learning analysis of picture-word effects. *Child Development.*

Howe, M. L., & Hunter, M. A. (in press). Adult age differences in storage-retrieval processes: A stages-of-learning analysis of developmental interactions in concreteness effects. *Canadian Journal of Psychology.*

Humphreys, M. S., & Greeno, J. G. (1970). Interpretation of the two-stage analysis of paired-associate memorizing. *Journal of Mathematical Psychology, 7,* 275–292.

Keller, H. R., & Hunter, M. L. (1973). Task differences on conservation and transitivity problems. *Journal of Experimental Child Psychology, 15, 287–301.*

Krantz, D. H., Luce, R. D., Suppes, P., & Tversky, A. (1971). *Foundations of measurement* (Vol. 1). New York: Academic.

Krantz, D. H., & Tversky, A. (1971). Conjoint-measurement analysis of composition rules in psychology. *Psychological Review, 78,* 151–169.

Lovell, K., & Ogilvie, E. (1961). A study of conservation of weight in the junior school child. *British Journal of Educational Psychology, 31,* 138–144.

McManis, D. L. (1969). Conservation and transitivity of weight and length by normals and retardates. *Developmental Psychology, 1,* 373–382.

Piaget, J. (1949). *Traite de logique.* Paris: Colin.

Piaget, J. (1970). Piaget's theory. In P. H. Mussen (Ed.), *Carmichael's manual of child psychology.* New York: Wiley.

Piaget, J., & Szeminska, A. (1941). *La genese du nombre chez l'enfant.* Neuchatel, Switzerland: Delachaux & Niestle.

Siegler, R. S., & Vago, S. (1978). The development of the proportionality concept: Judging relative fullness. *Journal of Experimental Child Psychology, 25,* 371–395.

Smedslund, J. (1959). Apprentissage des notions de la conservation et de la transitivité du poids. *Etudes d'epistemolgie genetique, 9,* 3–13.

Smedslund, J. (1963). Development of concrete transitivity of length in children. *Child Development, 34,* 389–405.

Wilkinson, A. C. (1982a). Partial knowledge and self-correction: Developmental studies of a quantitative concept. *Developmental Psychology, 18,* 874–891.

Wilkinson, A. C. (1982b). Theoretical and methodological analysis of partial knowledge. *Developmental Review, 2,* 274–304.

Wilkinson, A. C., DeMarinis, M., & Riley, S. J. (1983). Developmental and individual differences in rapid remembering. *Child Development, 54,* 898–911.

Wilkinson, A. C., & Koestler, R. (1983). Repeated recall: A new model and tests of its generality from childhood to old age. *Journal of Experimental Psychology: General, 112,* 423–451.

Wilkinson, A. C., & Koestler, R. (1984). Generality of a strength model for three conditions of repeated recall. *Journal of Mathematical Psychology, 28,* 43–72.

2. The New Two-Stage Model of Learning: A Tool for Analyzing the Loci of Memory Differences in Intellectually Impaired Children

Johannes Kingma

In modern cognitive theories, memorizing has been conceptualized as a process of storing information and remembering as a process of retrieving information. These memory processes have commonly been studied in standard list-learning paradigm tasks such as free recall, paired-associate learning, cued recall, serial learning, and recognition memory. When several seconds of distracting activity are inserted between consecutive study and test trials, these tasks can be considered to be long-term memory tasks (Brainerd, in press). Since the early 1950s, the simple mathematical concept of finite Markov chains has been used to account for the data of adults in these long-term memory tasks (Estes, 1962; Feller, 1950; Kemeny & Snell, 1960). Many fruitful hypotheses about the mechanisms of memory in adults have been generated by using these finite Markov chains (Greeno, 1970, 1974; Greeno, James, DaPolito, & Polson, 1978; Levine & Burke, 1972; Norman, 1972).

Before the early 1980s, however, developmental psychologists were rather disinterested in mathematical modeling techniques (Brainerd, 1982b). In contrast, mathematical psychologists provided some classic studies with children (e.g., Atkinson & Crothers, 1964; Spiker, 1970; Suppes & Ginsburg, 1962), but these studies were mostly ignored by developmental psychologists. It seems that the zeitgeist is changing, because serious mathematical modeling is becoming more important in developmental psychology (Bisanz, Vesonder, & Voss, 1978; Brainerd, 1979, 1982a; Heth & Cornell, 1983; Wilkinson & Koestler, 1983, 1984).

Finite Markov models are so fruitful for analysis of list-learning data in developmental studies because age-level effects can be tested and explained in a refined way. For example, complex learning can be represented as a collection of elementary processes (storage, retrieval, etc.), and the roles of these processes in a learning task can be distinguished (see Greeno, 1974).

Markov models are also very useful for analyzing the loci of memory differences in normal achieving children and learning-disabled children. For example, some aspects of retrieval learning have been found to be responsible for the poorer performance of learning-disabled children on these tasks (Brainerd, Kingma, & Howe, in press, b; Howe, Brainerd, & Kingma, in press, b). However, as far as we know, information about the loci of memory differences between atypical subjects (e.g., learning-disabled and educable mentally retarded children) is scarce in the literature.

My principal goal is to illustrate how Markov models can be used to study the development of memory processes in atypical children. In the following section I describe the use of mathematical models in general, and Markov models in particular, in the analysis of data from list-learning tasks. Then I review some existing research on memory processes in intellectually impaired children and describe an experiment in which Markov models are used to clarify the loci of memory difficulties in learning-disabled children and mentally retarded children. Assumptions and analytic procedures are described in some detail to illustrate the process by which mathematical models can be used, applied, and evaluated.

Mathematical Models

General Characteristics

According to Torgeson (1958), "The principle objective of science, other than the description of empirical phenomena, is to establish, through laws and theories, general principles by means of which the empirical phenomena can be explained, or accounted for." Mathematical models serve as mediators between theory and empirical data. A mathematical model is a translation of some theoretical (verbal) constructs into mathematical expressions, and it is connected to the data by means of measurement. *Measurement* is usually defined as the assignment of numbers to the quantities of properties of objects in accordance with certain rules (Bohrnstedt, 1982; Torgeson, 1958). Such quantification is necessary for determining whether a mathematical model hence the translated theoretical constructs fit the data (Stevens, 1951). In contrast to verbal models, mathematical models have the advantage that relations between the elements in their expressions are well defined. A discussion about the relationship between mathematical model and theory lies outside the scope of this chapter (for a discussion, see Blalock, 1982; Bohrnstedt, 1982; Kaplan, 1973; Nagel, 1961). In the next section, I describe some issues and procedures that pertain to the use of mathematical models generally, including how a model is "tied" to the data and how it is tested.

Tying the Model to the Data

Suppose a model builder wants to explain a person's behavior in a list-learning task. According to a particular verbal theory, learning can be explained in terms of two long-term memory processes, storage and retrieval. A specific model must be described in which some elements (storage and retrieval) are related, manifesting the *structure* of the model. In mathematical models, these relations are described in mathematical expressions. If a model describes changes in the state of the subject, it is often profitable to express this in the language of probability theory. The mathematical expressions of the model contain different parameters for estimating the probability of the occurrence of some process in the learning task. They specify the process underlying the joint distribution of a set of observable variables.

The process of building and testing models is illustrated in Figure 2.1. The first step is to formulate the relation into mathematical expressions. When one is starting to build a new model, it is sometimes convenient to make simple and complex versions, or exemplars (see Brainerd, Howe, and Kingma, 1982). This approach has the advantage that the two models may be tested against each other to determine which is more satisfactory. Of course, a model is sometimes presented only in the less complex form. In such a case, Figure 2.1 may be read as a path for one model in which the necessity test (see below) is deleted.

As an example, Brainerd, Howe, and Kingma (1982a) used two models for explaining the processes of storage and retrieval in a list-learning task. The simple version was a one-stage Markov model, and the complex version was a two-stage Markov model. The mathematical expressions of these models contain 6 and 11 parameters, respectively, for estimating the probability of some process (storage and retrieval) in a list-learning task.

The first two steps in model building are formulating the relationships between the theoretical psychological processes and putting these relationships into mathematical expressions (see Figure 2.1). Next, a proof is performed to analyze whether the mathematical model is identifiable. The logic-of-identifiability proof runs as follows. A model contains a number of parameters that measure theoretical processes. The outcome space contains a number of observable variables as measured in the experiment. In the identifiability proof, the theoretical parameters (unknowns) are algebraically expressed in terms of the observable variables (knowns). The model is called *identifiable* when it is shown that each of the theoretical parameters can be independently expressed in observable variables. If the model is identifiable, then we are able to estimate the parameters because the system of expressions with knowns and unknowns is solvable. If a model is nonidentifiable, then we are unable to estimate the parameters because the system cannot be solved. Unless some alterations are made, a nonidentifiable model is not suitable for estimating the parameters from the data of a particular experiment for which it was designed.

FIGURE 2.1. A schematic representation of the way in which a model may be tied to the data. ▷

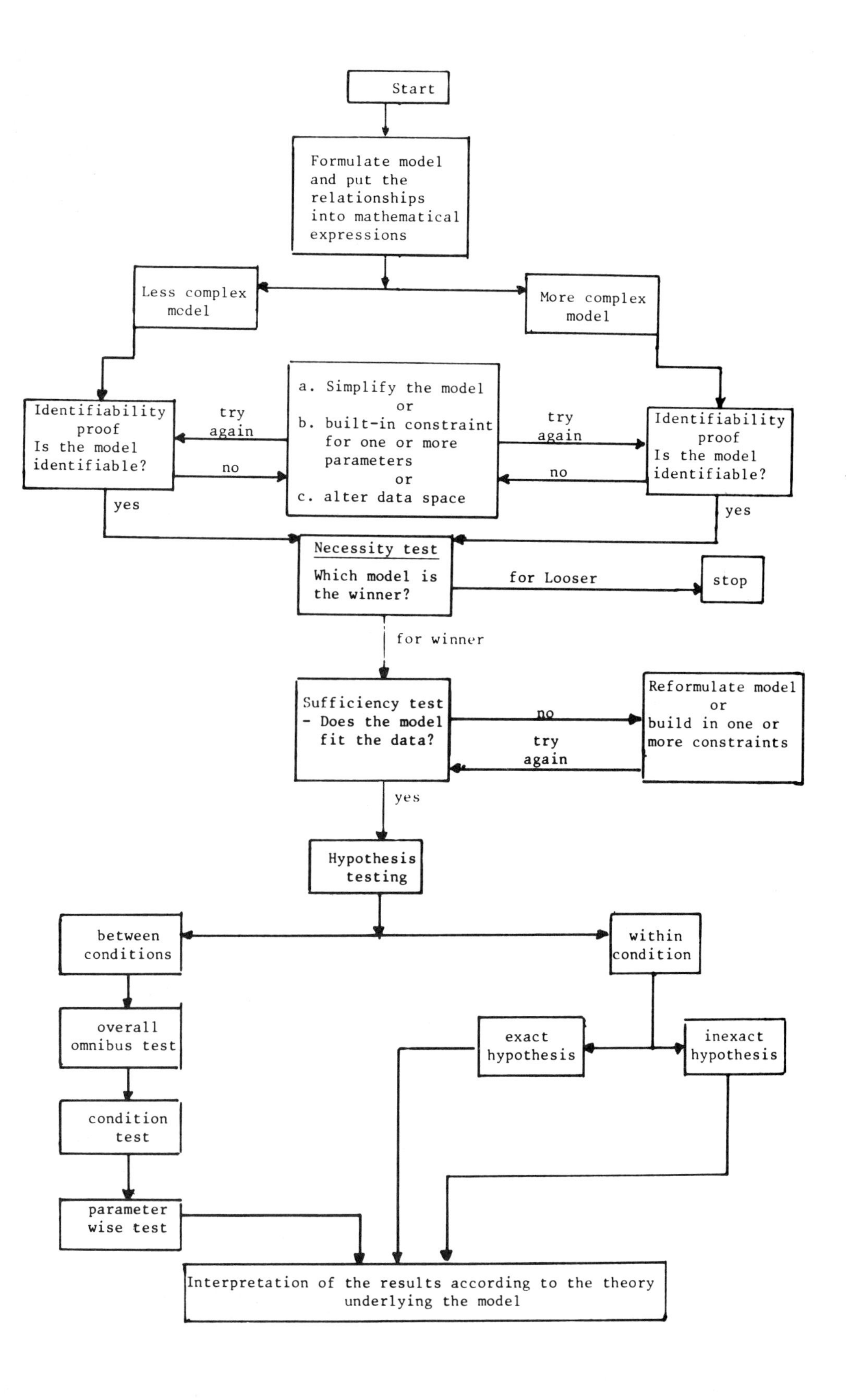
Start
Formulate model and put the relationships into mathematical expressions
Less complex model
More complex model
Identifiability proof
Is the model identifiable?
try again
no
a. Simplify the model
or
b. built-in constraint for one or more parameters
or
c. alter data space
try again
no
Identifiability proof
Is the model identifiable?
yes
yes
Necessity test
Which model is the winner?
for Looser
stop
for winner
Sufficiency test - Does the model fit the data?
no
try again
Reformulate model
or
build in one or more constraints
yes
Hypothesis testing
between conditions
within condition
overall omnibus test
condition test
parameter wise test
exact hypothesis
inexact hypothesis
Interpretation of the results according to the theory underlying the model

To check whether a model is identifiable, a general counting rule is easy to apply (Duncan, 1975). Count the number of theoretical parameters T. Then count the number of observable variables O. A *necessary* condition for identification is that $O \geq T$. This counting rule is, of course, only a rule of thumb. Necessary and sufficient conditions for identifiability are obtained when identification proof, such as the one proposed by Greeno (1967, 1968; Greeno & Steiner, 1964), shows that *unique* estimators can be delivered for each of the parameters. A variety of techniques are available for testing identifiability, including ordinary algebra proofs (Brainerd, Howe, & Desrochers, 1982), proofs using matrix algorithms (Greeno, Millward, and Merryman, 1971) and computer search programs (Polson & Huizinga, 1974).

When the number of observable variables in the data is smaller than the number of theoretical parameters, that is, $O < T$, the model is *nonidentifiable* (Brainerd, Howe, & Desrochers 1982; Restle & Greeno, 1970; Wilkinson, 1982) and the model is improper for the proposed experiment. Conceptually, such a model requires more degrees of freedom than exist in the data. There are basically three methods of dealing with a nonidentifiable model (Brainerd, Howe, & Kingma, 1982). One procedure is to simplify the model. However, such a strategy is often not desirable, especially when the model contains a very small number (for example, 2 or 3) of theoretically important parameters (see Brainerd, 1985). Simplifying such a model may reduce the explanatory power of the model. When the model contains a larger number (for example, 10) of theoretical parameters, the simplification rule may be a reasonable way to make the model identifiable.

A second approach to making a nonidentifiable model identifiable is to introduce testable restrictions on some parameters. A nonidentifiable parameter may be given a certain value between 0 and 1, or some parameters may be equated. In general, a testable identifying restriction is a constraint on the freedom of the parameters to vary. The model becomes identifiable when the introduction of one or more constraints delivers a unique expression for each theoretical parameter in terms of identifiable parameters (Brainerd, Howe, & Kingma, 1982). Suppose a model contains 10 parameters: a', b', a, b, c, d, e, g, h, and r. Suppose further that nine parameters can be shown to be identifiable. One may equate, for example, $g = h$, or $c = 0$ to make the model identifiable. These testable restrictions should make sense theoretically. Several of these restrictions can be evaluated statistically by using likelihood-ratio tests developed by Greeno (1968). One also may try to investigate different sets of constraints empirically. The advantage of using testable restrictions is that the model becomes identifiable. A disadvantage is that the model may become too specific because one constraint may not be acceptable for all the conditions of a given experiment, especially if the experiment contains a large number of conditions with treatments that have powerful effects on the parameters of the given model (Brainerd, Howe, & Kingma, 1982). In addition, comparisons cannot be made between experiments with the same conditions but using different identifying restrictions. Different patterns of parameter values observed in the experiment could be attributed simply to these restrictions rather than to actual discrepancies in the findings. (For some examples, see Brainerd, Howe, & Kingma, 1982.)

A third way of changing a nonidentifiable model to an identifiable one is by increasing the complexity of the data so that all parameters can be estimated (for examples, see Brainerd, Howe, & Kingma, 1982; Chechile & Meyer, 1976; Chechile & Richman, 1982). That is, the design of the experiment may be altered by increasing the number of observable variables to obtain enough degrees of freedom for the model's parameters. For example, the structure of the standard list-learning tasks to which Markov models apply is normally $S_1T_1S_2T_2S_3T_3$ . . . , where S_i denotes the ith study trial and T_i denotes the ith test trial. Study and test trials alternate until either some performance criterion is met or some fixed number of study-test cycles is administered. Greeno (1968, 1974) used a nine-parameter Markov model for list-learning tasks. Only seven parameters were identifiable for experiments with the standard $S_1T_1S_2T_2$ structure. Some restrictions had to be made to obtain an identifiable model. However, a small change in the structure of the experiment will deliver sufficient degrees of freedom in the new data space. For example, Brainerd, Howe, and Kingma (1982) showed that an 11-parameter Markov model was identifiable for the new data space. When the structure of the proposed experiment and consequently, the data space, can be altered so that the model becomes identifiable, then this method is preferred to that of using identifiable constraints. With the former method, the parameters from different conditions of an experiment may be compared, whereas such comparisons may become impossible when different constraints have been used for those conditions.

Following the identifiability proof, the researcher may now actually perform the experiment and tie the model to the obtained data. The mathematical expressions of the model contain different parameters for estimating the probability of the occurrence of some process in the learning task. However, it is not enough for the mathematical model to describe a psychological process. It must do so with sufficient completeness to tie it to the data (Wickens, 1982). Goodness-of-fit tests are used to assess whether the model fits the data, that is, whether good agreement is obtained between theoretical distributions using the estimated parameters and some data distributions (e.g., the learning curve, errors before first success). Such tests of learning models have usually involved two phases (Brainerd, Howe, Kingma, 1982a; Greeno, 1968): Necessity tests are followed by sufficiency tests (see Figure 2.1).

Necessity tests are concerned with whether simpler models give a statistically acceptable account for the data. Much of the usefulness of a model lies in the fact that it is as simple as possible and as complex as necessary (Blalock, 1969, 1982). The necessity test provides information about which model is favorable from the principle of parsimony. The logic behind the necessity test runs as follows. The likelihood function (containing the mathematical expressions with the theoretical parameters) is computed for each model. Then the likelihood ratio is computed, which has a χ^2 distribution with the number of degrees of freedom equal to the difference between the number of parameters of the two models (Greeno, 1968, 1970). If we let L_1 denote the likelihood of some set of data under one model and L_2 denote the likelihood of the same set of data under the more complex model, then the following likelihood ratio is used for the necessity test:

$$\chi^2\ (n) = -2 \log \frac{\hat{L}_1}{\hat{L}_2} \tag{1}$$

where $\hat{L}_1$ and $\hat{L}_2$ are the estimates for L_1 and L_2, respectively, and n indicates the degrees of freedom. When χ^2 exceeds the critical value at a certain alpha level, the more complex model is more satisfactory. If the value is below the critical value, the simpler model is chosen. For example, Brainerd, Howe, and Kingma (1982) showed that an identifiable two-stage Markov model with 11 parameters provided a more satisfactory account for free-recall data than an identifiable one-stage model with 6 parameters.

Subsequently, sufficiency tests are performed for the model that passes the necessity test (see Figure 2.1). Sufficiency tests are used to determine whether the model fits the data. First, because mathematical expressions of the model represent the probabilities of various aspects of the data as functions of the parameters of the model, parameters can be estimated from the data. These estimates provide measurements of some aspects of learning (e.g., the probability that on the first trial an item has been stored in long-term memory). After the numerical estimates are obtained, the second step is to perform tests of the differences between observed data distributions and distributions predicted by the estimated parameters. Examples of the observed data distributions include such variables as errors before first success, the learning curve, total errors, and trial number of the last error. Predicted distributions are obtained from formulas containing the parameters (see Brainerd, Howe, & Kingma, 1982, equations 47*a*–52*b*). Both necessity and sufficiency tests must be performed for all the conditions of the experiment. A nonparametric test, such as the Kolmogorov-Smirnov test, may be used for testing the differences between the two distributions for each condition of the experiment.

When the sufficiency tests fail for a condition [i.e., the difference between the two distributions (observed and predicted) is significant], we conclude that the model does not tie to the data of that particular condition. The fault may lie in the theory or in the parameter values (Restle, 1971). The solution may be either to reformulate the model or to build new identifiable constraints. In the latter case, the different conditions cannot be compared when different constraints are used. Fortunately, Markov models of free-recall list learning generally fit the data (Greeno et al., 1978; Howe, 1982).

The evidence from both necessity tests and sufficiency tests has been quite consistent (Brainerd, 1985). In necessity tests, the two-stage Markov model is almost always more satisfactory than the one-stage model in applications to recall data, regardless of whether the subjects are children or university undergraduates. Brainerd (1985) mentioned only two exceptions in which a one-stage Markov model was adequate to account for recall data: relearning of paired-associate lists that had been memorized to a stringent acquisition criterion one week earlier (Brainerd, Desrochers, & Howe, 1981), and memorization by undergraduates of short paired-associate lists comprised of very easy words (Humphreys & Yuille, 1973). The results of sufficiency tests have been similarly positive. In most experiments, the predicted distributions of two-stage Markov models closely approximate the observed data distributions (Brainerd, 1985). Despite these very positive results, the necessity and sufficiency tests must always be performed to ensure that the model ties with the data of the experiment. Parameter estimation and the goodness of fit are technical prerequisites for interpretation of the data.

Hypothesis testing (see Figure 2.1) is performed for all conditions of the experiment that pass the sufficiency tests. Between- and within-condition comparisons are both of interest. The general aim of the between-condition tests is to localize treatment effects within particular parameters (see Brainerd, Howe, & Kingma, 1982; Greeno et al., 1971; Humphreys & Greeno, 1970), whereas within-condition tests are used to determine whether obtained parameter values differ (Brainerd, Howe, & Desrochers, 1980; Brainerd et al., 1981). Both types of tests concern likelihood ratio tests for which χ^2 distributions are known (see Brainerd, Howe, & Kingma, 1982).

Between-condition tests are performed in three steps: experimentwise tests, conditionwise tests, and parameterwise tests. The first question that must be answered is whether there are global statistical grounds for supposing that the parameter values differ between conditions. A likelihood ratio statistic has been developed (Brainerd, 1982a, equation 53) for the experimentwise test that resembles the omnibus F test in the analysis of variance. When there are some overall differences (i.e., the null hypothesis fails), a conditionwise test is used, which is conceptually similar to the well-known t statistic. If L_a denotes the likelihood of the set of data of condition a and L_b denotes the likelihood of condition b, then the following likelihood ratio statistic is used for the conditionwise test (see Brainerd et al., 1982, equation 54):

$$\chi^2_{(n)} = -2 \log \frac{\hat{L}_{ab}}{\hat{L}_a \hat{L}_b}, \tag{2}$$

where $\hat{L}_a$ and $\hat{L}_b$ are the estimated likelihoods of the data for, respectively, conditions a and b, $\hat{L}_{ab}$ is the estimated likelihood of the data when the protocols for conditions a and b are pooled, and n is the degrees of freedom. This procedure is repeated for all possible combinations of the conditions of the experiment. Repeated testing of this sort may inflate alpha levels. To reduce this problem, a small numerical alpha value may be used.

When some pair of conditions differs significantly, the parameterwise test is performed to identify the parameters to which these differences may be attributed. A likelihood ratio statistic has also been developed for the parameterwise test (see Brainerd, Howe, & Kingma, 1982, equation 55).

The majority of hypothesis testing concerns testing between conditions. However, within-condition tests are often of interest. Two types are distinguished: *exact* numerical hypotheses and *inexact* hypotheses. The former refer to any prediction which specifies that one of the parameters shall take a particular value, whereas inexact numerical hypotheses concern predictions that specify that a particular algebraic relationship will be obtained between two or more parameters. Likelihood ratio statistics have been developed for evaluating these two types of hypotheses (see Brainerd, Howe, & Kingma, 1982, equation 56). Following these tests, the results are interpreted in terms of the theory underlying the model.

To summarize, after a model has been shown to be identifiable, necessity and sufficiency tests are used to determine whether the model ties to the data. If the model fits the data, between- and within-condition tests are performed. Next, the difference between statistical inference and model testing is described.

Model Testing and Conventional Statistical Testing

Mathematical models enable the researcher to separate different process variables, such as storage and retrieval. One may argue, however, that mathematical models are not needed because such research questions can be investigated with an adequate experimental design and conventional statistical tests. That is, separating different process variables is seen as a problem in experimental design rather than a problem in measurement theory (see Brainerd, 1985).

Although the methodology of an experiment may appear to be correct, interpretation of the results may be wrong when conventional statistical testing, e.g., analysis of variance, is used (Brainerd, 1985). For example, in a free-recall experiment, performance on the test trials is the dependent variable (the total number of errors and trial of last error).

However, this performance is the result of both storage and retrieval; that is, storage and retrieval are interwoven in only *one* dependent variable in free-recall experiments. Owing to limitations of the structural linear model, which is the basis of the analysis of variance, the effects of experimental manipulations on either storage or retrieval cannot be computed separately, because a compound dependent variable has been used (Krantz & Tversky, 1971; Brainerd, 1985). This problem cannot be solved with multivariate techniques, because it seems impossible to create two different types of dependent variables that only measure either storage or retrieval. The difficulty with the conventional approach is that statistical models describe what the data look like, but not how they came about (Wickens, 1982). In contrast, mathematical models can be used to separate the process variables by incorporating fine grained assumptions about underlying measurement (Brainerd, 1985).

Of course, the goodness-of-fit tests of mathematical models also are pure statistical tests. They are derived from the fact that the algebraic assumptions that comprise a model normally constrain the data of performance in certain respects; the data must have specific statistical properties if the assumptions are correct. A goodness-of-fit test is simply a mechanical procedure. When the data do not pass such tests, a model-based theory is rejected. However, testing the parameters with the between- and within-condition tests provides information about each of the processes. Thus, the quantities on which the mathematical model is dependent reflect characteristics of the behavior under study. The process-oriented nature of these mathematical models make them useful both for data analyses and for testing the processes themselves.

Markov Models

Learning as Discrete Events

Learning has been viewed historically either as a gradual change or as a discrete change. Gradual change was assumed in early versions of association theory (Boring, 1950), in which strength of associative connection between ideas was assumed to increase each time the concepts were experienced together. Pavlov (1927) assumed gradual learning in conditioning of reflexes. Gradualist ideas were popular for a variety of conceptual and philosophical reasons (Greeno, 1974). Although some psychologists viewed learning as a discrete change in the 1920s (Kohler, 1927; Lashley, 1928), not until the 1950s did the mathematical tools exist for studying learning as a discrete process. For example, Feller (1950) introduced the probability theory for discrete sample spaces, while Kemeny and Snell (1960) and Kemeny, Snell, and Thompson (1957) introduced finite mathematics for social scientists (see Estes, 1962). From the early 1950s, Markov models were used by psychologists to study learning as discrete events (Greeno et al., 1978).

Models of learning may be deterministic or stochastic. A deterministic model predicts the effect of any change in the model with certainty. In practice, however, there is usually an element of uncertainty in any prediction of human behavior. This uncertainty can be accommodated because the equations of a model may include random variables. Such a model is stochastic, i.e., its mathematical entities are known as stochastic processes. A stochastic process is one that develops in time according to probabilistic laws (Bartholomew, 1973). Therefore, its future behavior cannot be predicted with certainty; the most that can be done is to attach probabilities to the various possible future states of this process. The mathematical two-stage learning model is such a stochastic Markov model (see Brainerd, Howe, & Kingma, 1982). Learning can be considered a "construct," an indication that a new state has been reached. In an all-or-none learning model, two states are distinguished, namely, a learned and an unlearned state. In a two-stage model a partially learned state is placed between these two. The number of states can be increased so that long-term memory processes involved in the learning process may be described in terms of state changes.

In the study of memory, a Markov chain is a model of changes in the subject's *cognitive* states of knowledge and the way in which these knowledge states change. However, these postulated cognitive states cannot be observed directly in, for example, a list-learning task. The only thing that can be observed is the subject's response pattern for each item from the list. The Markov process is considered a model of the subject's internal states, and the responses are the functions of these states. In other words, there is a mapping function between the space of unobservable cognitive states and the observable response space.

Characteristics of Markov Models

Markov models, as presented in this chapter, have three main characteristics: The states are countable, no backward transitions are allowed, and the future of the process depends only on the current state. The denumerable, or finite-state, Markov process is characterized by a set of countable states. The state of the process is specified by one of a discrete set of alternatives, that is, by a member of a set of states. The set of states in the model is called its *state space*. Changes, such as learning, are represented by the transitions from one state to another. Defining an appropriate state space is crucial for building a suitable model, and it involves a balance between complexity and simplicity. That is, the state space has to be sufficiently large to allow interesting properties to appear, but not so complex that it becomes unworkable (see Wickens, 1982).

The second characteristic mostly appeared in list-learning task studies; that is, the transitions between the different states are usually defined in a way that no backward transitions occur. When, for example, an item has been learned or "escaped," no backward transition to the unlearned state is possible, that is, it cannot become unlearned again.

The third feature of the Markov model concerns the Markov property (Breiman, 1969) about the relationship between the process in the current and future states. Specifically, the state of the processes at trial $n + 1$ depends only on the state at trial n. States of the process on trials prior to trial n are not relevant to the probability of entering a state on trial $n + 1$; that is, all information about the past is embodied in the current state on trial n. How the process enters a particular state is not important. In other words, the past may determine where the subject is now, but the subject's current state determines future activity (Wickens, 1982).

In the simplest case, learning involves a single transition between two states. In such an all-or-none model, the subject's state of knowledge about an item to be learned is either that it is unknown or it has been learned. These two states are represented in Figure 2.2. In free-recall experiments, the words from a list are presented for study and followed by a distractor task (e.g., counting backward) to prevent rehearsal. Subsequently, the subject is asked to remember the learned words on the test trial. This sequence of study trial, distractor task, and test trial can be repeated until the subject has reached a criterion such as all items recalled correctly on two consecutive trials. The items are usually unknown at the beginning of the experiment. At this point each item is in state U. According to the all-or-none hypothesis there is a fixed probability c that an item is learned at each presentation. If an item is learned, it has "escaped" state U. If the item "remains" in U, no learning occurs. When an items "enters" (is learned) state L, the probability of a correct response always is 1.0.

These one-stage (one type of transition) Markov models are rarely adequate for representing free-recall data (Brainerd et al., 1981; Humphreys

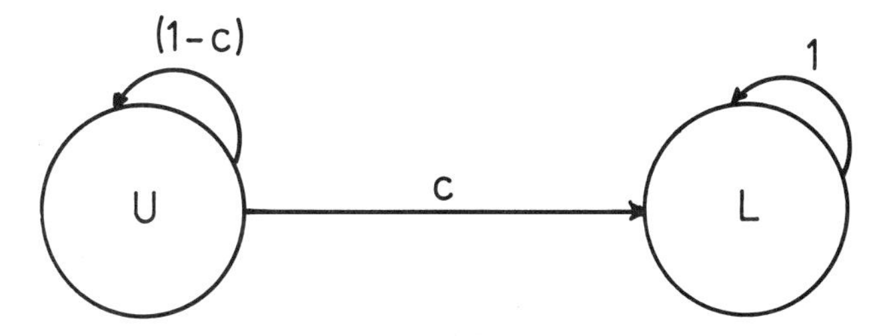

FIGURE 2.2. One-stage model.

& Yuille, 1973), but may be satisfactory for recognition data (Brainerd, 1983; Greeno et al., 1978; Kintsch & Morris, 1965). The two-stage model is more successful for free-recall data.

Representation of the Markov Chain

A denumerable, or finite-state, Markov process is typically represented as a branching tree or as a transition matrix (see Kemeny & Snell, 1960; Levine & Burke, 1972; Wickens, 1982). For instance, a tree diagram for the transition probabilities in an all-or-none model of the previous section is depicted in Figure 2.3. It can be seen from Figure 2.3 that any one branch (continuous route) of this tree represents the sequence of joint events necessary to reach a particular state on a particular trial by a particular route. On the first trial, the probability of escaping the unlearned state U_1 and entering state L_2 is c, whereas the probability of staying in the unlearned state is $1 - c$ at U_1. On the second trial the

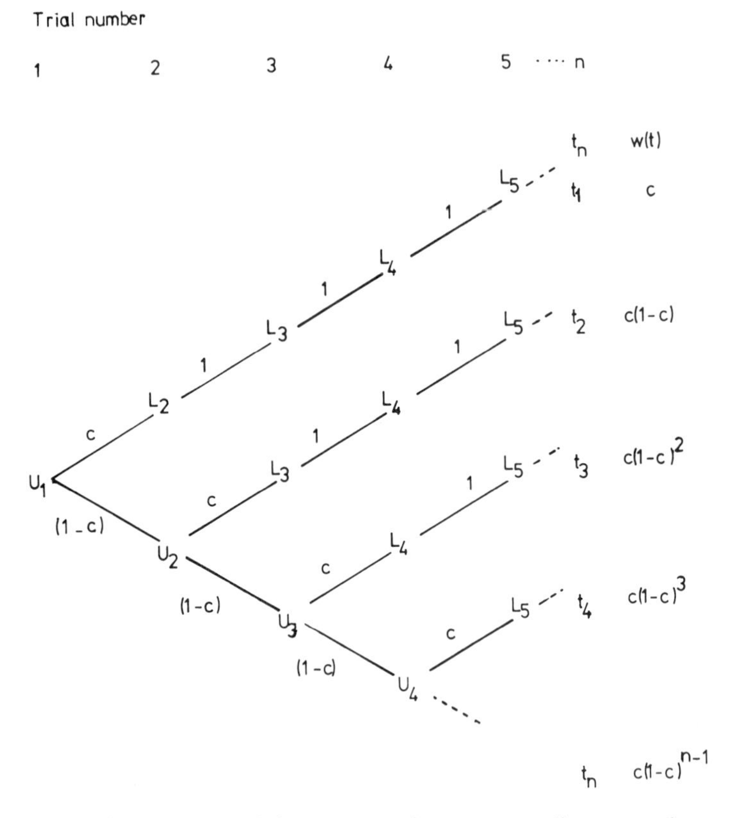

FIGURE 2.3. One-stage model represented as a tree diagram, where t_1, t_2, t_3, . . . , t_n represent the trial numbers, L_n is the learned state at trial t_n, and U_n is the unlearned state at trial t_n.

probability of staying in state L_2 is 1 since L_2 is an absorbing state, whereas the probability of escape from U_1 on the second trial is c for entering the learned state L_3 and that for staying in the unlearned state U_2 is $1 - c$.

The above procedure, depicted in Figure 2.3, can be carried out for any experiment that takes place in phases or trials. The only requirements are a finite number of possible outcomes and probabilities for any particular outcome at the jth phase given the knowledge of the outcome for the first $j - 1$ stage must be known (Kemeny & Snell, 1960).

The probability of a particular route in Figure 2.3 is simply the product of the transition probabilities joining the states in that branch, whereas the probability of being in a particular state on a particular trial is the sum of all the different branch probabilities that lead to that state on that trial. For example, in Figure 2.3 there are four paths, each representing a different way of reaching a learned state L_5 on or before the fourth trial t_4. The probability of reaching L_5 on the fourth trial t_4 is $P(L_5)$, and that of reaching L_5 on the fourth trial t_4 is $P(L_5)$

$$\begin{aligned} P(L_5) &= t_1 + t_2 + t_3 + t_4 \\ &= c + c(1 - c) + c(1 - c)^2 + c(1 - c)^3 \\ &= c^4 + 4c^3 - 6c^2 + 4c \\ &= 1 - (1 - c)^4, \end{aligned}$$

where t_n is the probability of reaching the learned state L_{n+1} on trial n. More generally, the probability of reaching the learned state on some trial n is

$$P(L_{n+1}) = 1 - (1 - c)^n,$$

whereas the probability of staying in the unlearned state on some trial n is

$$P(U_{n+1}) = (1 - c)^n.$$

Although the probabilities of reaching a particular state at a particular trial can be determined from Figure 2.3, they can also be expressed as conditional probabilities. Since the probabilities are independent of the steps prior to the immediately preceding one (the Markov property), the probability of reaching the learned state at, for example, the third trial is

$$\begin{aligned} P(L_4) &= P(L_4|L_3)P(L_3|L_2)P(L_2|U_1) + P(L_4|L_3)P(L_3|U_2)P(U_2|U_1) \\ &\quad + P(L_4|U_3)P(U_3|U_2)P(U_2|U_1) \\ &= (1 \cdot 1 \cdot c) + [1 \cdot c \cdot (1 - c)] + [c \cdot (1 - c)^2] \\ &= 1 - (1 - c)^3. \end{aligned}$$

With the help of such a tree it is easy to derive the probabilities of reaching some state on a certain trial. However, when the number of trials is very large, such a tree becomes rather complex. Therefore, the transitions are usually collapsed into matrix form. Because there is only one-trial dependency in the Markov process, the most general form of such a matrix is the representation of the transition probabilities on a single trial n to trial $n + 1$. For instance, the transition matrix for the all-or-none model represented in Figure 2.3 is

$$\begin{array}{c} \\ L_n \\ U_n \end{array} \begin{array}{c} L_{n+1} \quad U_{n+1} \\ \left[\begin{array}{cc} 1 & 0 \\ c & 1-c \end{array}\right] \end{array} .$$

In this matrix, the probability of a transition from U_n to L_{n+1} is c, and the probability that the process remains in the unlearned state on trial $n+1$ is $1 - c$, and so on.

It is important to keep in mind that with this transition matrix only the transition probabilities are depicted which are conditional on some trial n. The probabilities of being in each of the states on trial n must still be computed. Suppose the row vector $[P(L_{n+1}), P(U_{n+1})]$, represents the probabilities of either being in the learned state on trial $n+1$ or staying at the unlearned state. Those probabilities are computed by multiplying the row vector for trial n and the transition matrix as follows:

$$[P(L_{n+1}), P(U_{n+1})] = [P(L_n), P(U_n)] \times \left[\begin{array}{cc} 1 & 0 \\ c & 1-c \end{array}\right]$$

$$= [\{P(L_n) + P(U_n)c\}, \{P(U_n)\,(1 - c)\}].$$

Thus, the probability of being in a particular state on a particular trial can be computed easily with the transition matrix. By substituting a certain number for n it can be shown that, with the help of a transition matrix, the same results are obtained as with the branching tree.

Although the probabilities of the transitions can be represented for the individual items of a free-recall list, most theorists use probabilities for the list as a whole for all subjects in a condition. This simplification is often needed to reduce complexity.

Researchers are often interested in the probability of some transition on the first trial; for example, a high probability of entering the learned state on trial 1 would indicate early learning or ease of storage, depending on the definition of the parameters of the model. The probabilities of the transitions on the first trial are represented in the *starting* vector, or initial vector. After the first study trial, learning of an item is assumed to be governed by the matrix of transition probabilities (Greeno et al., 1978). A response vector is used to represent states on which correct responses occur. The starting vector and the corresponding transition matrix for the all-or-none model and the response vector are

$$W_1 = P[L_1, U_1] = [c', (1 - c')],$$

$$M_1 = \begin{array}{c} \\ L_n \\ U_n \end{array} \begin{array}{c} L_{n+1} \quad U_{n+1} \\ \begin{bmatrix} 1 & 0 \\ c & 1 - c \end{bmatrix} \end{array}, \qquad C_1 = \begin{bmatrix} 1 \\ 0 \end{bmatrix}.$$

By using a starting vector, a new parameter c' has been introduced for estimating difficulty of learning on the first trial. Response vector C_1 represents only the state on which correct responses occur. This vector has not been used for computing the probabilities of being in a certain state.

In sum, the transition matrix represents the probabilities of a change from a particular state to another one on a particular trial. It is used for computing the probability of being in a certain state, which can also be represented by a branching tree. However, when the model is complex, the transition matrix is used for computing the probabilities. Introducing a starting vector provides information about learning on the first trial, which is often used when the overall probabilities of all the items of a list as a whole are the focus of interest.

The New Two-Stage Model

In the preceding section the all-or-none one-stage model was used to illustrate the terminology of the Markov models. However, acquisition data from list-learning tasks are normally in close agreement with the prediction of a two-stage Markov process (see Brainerd, in press; Greeno, 1974). These models assume that learning consists of an initial state U in which only errors are possible, an intermediate state P in which errors occur with some average probability $0 < q < 1$, and a fully learned (final absorbing) state L in which only successes are possible. Such models have given a good account in animal studies of avoidance conditioning (Theios, 1963) and escape conditioning (Theios, 1965). Analogous findings with human adults have been reported for free recall (Kintsch & Morris, 1965), cued recall (Humphreys & Greeno, 1970), eyelid conditioning (Bower & Theios, 1964), and discrimination reversal (Bower & Theios, 1964). Recent applications of the two-stage model in children include, for example, cued recall (Bisanz, Vesonder, & Voss, 1978), free recall (Brainerd, 1983), children's learning of logical concepts (Brainerd, 1982b), infants' learning of spatial concepts (Heth & Cornell, 1983), free recall in disabled children (Brainerd, Kingma, and Howe, in press, c; Howe et al., in press, b).

Since the initial appearance of these two-stage models in the psychological literature (Theios, 1961), their statistical machinery has undergone gradual development. In the course of this development most of the technical obstacles that one encounters in applying any model to data have been overcome. For instance, the sampling distributions of several learning statistics have been derived, a maximum likelihood procedure now exists for estimating the parameters of these models, and tests have been developed for within- and between-parameter values (see Brainerd, Howe, & Kingma, 1982).

However, a key problem remains, namely, that these models are not identifiable. For example, Greeno (1968; Greeno et al., 1971) demonstrated that a 9-parameter two-stage Markov model had only 7 identifiable parameters. Brainerd, Howe, and Desrochers (1982) showed that an unrestricted 10-parameter model has only 8 identifiable parameters. In other words, these models involve more degrees of freedom than the data space onto which they are mapped. To solve these problems, identifiable restrictions were introduced.

As discussed previously, using these identifiable restrictions may lead to difficulties for comparing the results of different conditions in one experiment, as well as for making comparisons between different types of experiments. In the new two-stage model, this obstacle has been removed by altering the data space. Brainerd, Howe, and Kingma (1982) proved that a completely identifiable version of the two-stage model can be devised for list-learning experiments in which children are required to meet a stringent acquisition criterion (e.g., two or three consecutive errorless test cycles). The major change was a slight adjustment of the outcome space over which the model is defined. The normal outcome space of criterion list-learning experiments is $S_1T_1S_2T_2 \ldots$, whereas the modified outcome space is $S_1T_1T_2S_2T_3\,S_3T_4 \ldots$ etc. The only alteration is the insertion of an extra test trial between the first and second study trial; in the remaining part of this chain, study and test trials alternate in the usual way.

The new model assumes that list learning consists of three discrete states: an initial state U (unlearned state) before a trace has been stored in which only errors can occur; an intermediate "partially learned" state P in which both errors (substate P_E) and success (substate P_C) can occur; and a terminal "well-learned" or absorbing state L in which only successes can occur (see Figure 2.4).

In this two-stage model, as in the one-stage model, no backward transitions are allowed. This model contains 11 parameters that reflect a theory of paired-associate memorizing which is based on an account developed originally by Greeno and his associates (e.g., Greeno, 1970, 1974; Greeno et al., 1971; Humphreys & Greeno, 1970). Because the terminal state L can be reached from U directly or via the partial state (either P_E or P_C), two stages of learning can be distinguished. When a distracting activity is

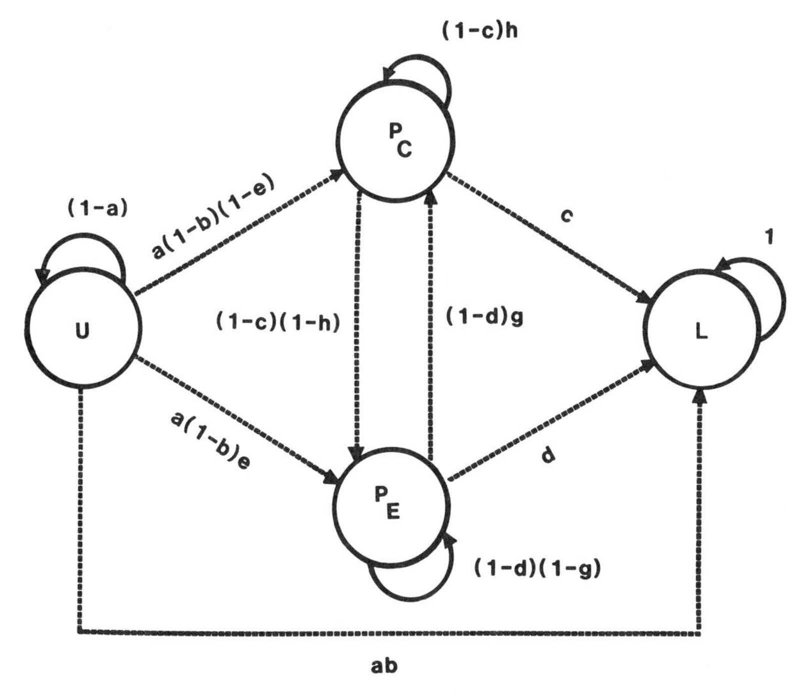

FIGURE 2.4. The new two-stage model with the transition probabilities between the four different states after the second study trial.

performed between each study trial and the following test trial, performance on the test trial cannot be based on retrieval from short-term memory; instead, an item can be successfully recalled only after a trace of that item has been established in long-term memory. Therefore, the difficulty of the first stage of learning (escape from the unlearned state *U*) has been identified with the difficulty of storing a trace in long-term memory. However, because storing a trace does not guarantee that the subject will be able to retrieve it reliably on test trials, the difficulty of the second stage of learning (escape from an intermediate partial-success state, either P_C or P_E) has been identified with the difficulty of learning how to retrieve.

When the hypotheses about storage and retrieval are combined with the states depicted in Figure 2.4, the parameters associated with each of these states become measures of theoretically important processes: parameters a' and a measure the difficulty of storing a permanent trace; parameters b', b, c, and d are measures of the difficulty of learning a retrieval algorithm; parameters e, g, h, and r measure the difficulty of retrieving a trace between the time of storage and the acquisition of a retrieval algorithm; parameter f is a measure for forgetting a previous stored trace between test trials T_1 and T_2. Definitions for each of the individual parameters are shown in Table 2.1.

TABLE 2.1. Theoretical interpretations of the 11 parameters in the two-stage model.

Parameter	Interpretation
Storage	
a'	Probability of storing a trace on the first study trial.
a	Probability of storing a trace on any study trial after the first trial.
$1 - f$	Probability of retaining a previously stored trace between the first and second test trials.
Retrieval learning	
b'	Probability of acquiring a retrieval algorithm for an item on the first study trial, given that the item was also stored on the same trial. No further retrieval learning is needed.
b	Probability of acquiring a retrieval algorithm for an item on any study trial after the first study trial, given that the item was also stored on the same trial. No further retrieval learning is needed.
c	Probability of learning a retrieval algorithm after a success in state P.
d	Probability of learning a retrieval algorithm after an error in state P.
Retrieval performance:	
$1 - r$	Probability of a success or heuristic retrieval for items entering state P on the first study trial.
$1 - e$	Probability of a success or heuristic retrieval for items entering state P after the first study trial.
g	Probability that, for any two consecutive trials in state P, unsuccessful heuristic retrieval (error) is followed by a successful heuristic retrieval (success).
h	For two consecutive trials in state P the probability that a success is followed by a success (or successful heuristic retrieval is followed by successful heuristic retrieval).

The transitions can now be described in terms of the parameters that may occur on the first test trial in free-recall learning in the altered data space $S_1T_1T_2S_2T_3S_3T_4$. . . . Before the first study trial, all items are in the initial unlearned state U. As a consequence of learning on the first study trial S_1, some items are learned; that is, they "escape" the unlearned state on study trial T_1 with a probability a'. Others from the list are still unlearned with a probability $1 - a'$. For items that are learned, a distinction can be made between those that are directly "fully" learned, state L, with a probability b', and those that are partially learned, state P_C or P_E, with a probability $1 - b'$. Furthermore, when an item is partially learned, either an incorrect response can be given (state P_E) with a probability r or a correct response occurs (state P_C) with a probability $1 - r$. On the first test trial, items can be in four distinct states: state U (with probability $1 - a'$), state L (with a probability $a'b'$), state P_E [with a probability $a'(1 - b')r$], and state P_C [with probability $a(1 - b')(1 - r)$].

Between the first and second test trials T_1 and T_2, no learning would have occurred. If an item is either unlearned (state U) or fully learned (state L), it remains there. An item in either state P_C or P_E can remain there with probability $(1 - f)h$ or $(1 - f)(1 - g)$, respectively. However, on this second test trial, the subject's partial knowledge of an item may diminish and fall back to the unlearned state for that item. That is, an item may drop from either state P_C and P_E to state U (the only possible backward transition in this model is on T_2) with a probability f. The possibility also exists that the subject gives a correct response on an item on test trial 2, whereas on the first test trial that item was in state P_E, with a probability $(1 - f)g$. The reverse can also be found; that is, on the first trial the item is in the state P_C (subject recalled it correctly), and on the second test trial the subject cannot recall that item (state P_E) with a probability $(1 - f)(1 - h)$. The transitions and their associated probabilities are summarized in Table 2.2.

On the second study trial, if an item is unlearned, state U, it may be learned with a probability a, or it may still be unlearned and staying in state U with a probability $1 - a$. These newly learned items may be either fully learned (state L) or partially learned (state P_C or P_E) with probabilities, respectively, $(1 - b)(1 - e)$ and $(1 - b)e$. If an item is in state P_C, the subject may recall that item correctly, and it will still be in state P_C with a probability $(1 - c)h$; and an incorrect recall (state P_E) may occur with a probability $(1 - c)(1 - h)$, or such an item may be fully learned (state L) with a probability c. If an item is in state P_E, the subject may be still unable to recall it (this item remains in state P_E) with a probability $(1 - d)(1 - g)$, or the subject will recall it correctly (but still not fully learned, i.e., the item goes in state P_C) with a probability $(1 - d)g$, or the item will be fully learned (state L) with a probability d. The transitions and their associated probabilities are summarized in Table 2.3.

The probabilities that appear in Table 2.3 are in fact the probabilities that occupy the transition matrix of a new two-stage model of learning.

TABLE 2.2. Probabilities of transitions between the first study trial and the first test trial and between the first and second test trials.

Transition	Probability
Study trial 1 → test trial 1	
$U \rightarrow U$	$1 - a'$
$U \rightarrow P_C$	$a'(1 - b')(1 - r)$
$U \rightarrow P_E$	$a'(1 - b')r$
$U \rightarrow L$	$a'b'$
Test trial 1 → test trial 2	
$P_C \rightarrow P_C$	$(1 - f)h$
$P_E \rightarrow P_E$	$(1 - f)(1 - g)$
$P_C \rightarrow U$	f
$P_E \rightarrow U$	f
$P_C \rightarrow P_E$	$(1 - f)(1 - h)$
$P_E \rightarrow P_C$	$(1 - f)g$

TABLE 2.3. Transition probabilities on the second study trial.

Transition	Probability
Study trial 2 → test trial 3	
$U \to U$	$1 - a$
$U \to P_E$	$a(1 - b)e$
$U \to P_C$	$a(1 - b)(1 - e)$
$U \to L$	ab
$P_E \to P_E$	$(1 - d)(1 - g)$
$P_E \to P_C$	$(1 - d)g$
$P_E \to L$	d
$P_C \to P_E$	$(1 - c)(1 - h)$
$P_C \to P_C$	$(1 - c)h$
$P_C \to L$	c

After the first study trial, an item may be in any of the four states. On the third and following study trials, the interstate transition probabilities as described for study trial S_2 are assumed to apply. Although the probability that an item has not yet entered the learned state L becomes increasingly small as the number of study trials increases, the transition probability of that item from a certain state to the learned state L on some study trial is always identical to that described in Table 2.3.

With the transition probabilities from Tables 2.2 and 2.3, the identifiable two-stage model can be derived from the revised outcome space (see Brainerd, 1984; Brainerd, Howe, & Kingma, 1982):

$$\begin{aligned} W_1 = [&L(1)L(2) = a'b',\ L(1)P_E(2) = 0,\ L(1)P_C(2) = 0,\ L(1)U(2) \\ &= 0,\ P_E(1)L(2) = 0,\ P_E(1)P_E(2) = a'(1 - b')r(1 - f)(1 - g), \\ &P_E(1)P_C(2) = a'(1 - b')r(1 - f)g,\ P_E(1)U(2) = \\ &a'(1 - b)rf,\ P_C(1)L(2) = 0,\ P_C(1)P_E(2) \\ &= a'(1 - b')(1 - r)(1 - f)(1 - h),\ P_C(1)P_C(2) = \\ &a'(1 - b')(1 - r)(1 - f)h,\ P_C(1)U(2) \\ &= a'(1 - b')(1 - r)f,\ U(1)L(2) = 0,\ U(1)P_E(2) = 0,\ U(1)P_C(2) \\ &= 0,\ U(1)U(2) = 1 - a']; \end{aligned}$$

$$M_1 = \begin{array}{c} \\ L(n) \\ P_E(n) \\ P_C(n) \\ U(n) \end{array} \begin{array}{c} \begin{array}{cccc} L(n+1) & P_E(n+1) & P_C(n+1) & U(n+1) \end{array} \\ \left[\begin{array}{cccc} 1 & 0 & 0 & 0 \\ d & (1-d)(1-g) & (1-d)g & 0 \\ c & (1-c)(1-h) & (1-c)h & 0 \\ ab & a(1-b)e & a(1-b)(1-e) & 1-a \end{array}\right] \end{array} ; \quad C_1 = \left[\begin{array}{c} 1 \\ 0 \\ 1 \\ 0 \end{array}\right]. \tag{3}$$

When we consider the first term of the starting vector $L(1)L(2)$, the probability of reaching the learned state on T_1 is $a'b'$. On the second test trial the probability is 1 for staying in L (since no backward transition is allowed from state L); the product of both probabilities is therefore $a'b'$ for staying in the learned state on both test trials T_1 and T_2. The only backward transition allowed is from the partial state to the unlearned state U on the test trial T_2 [e.g., the probability $P_E(1)U(2) = a'(1 - b)rf$ represents the backward transition from the partial state on test trial T_1 to the unlearned state on the second test trial T_2]. In fact, the transition probabilities that occur in the starting vector are the products of the probabilities in Table 2.2 for test trials T_1 and T_2. Thus, the starting vector gives the probabilities of being in various pairs of states on the first two test trials.

The zero probabilities in this starting vector correspond to transitions that cannot occur according to the assumptions of the model. And $P_E(1)L(2)$ has a zero probability, because between test trial T_1 and T_2 no learning event has taken place; consequently, the protocol cannot escape between these two test trials.

The matrix M_1 gives the probabilities of the various possible intertrial transitions after test trial T_2 on the following study trials. The zero probabilities refer once again to impossible transitions according to the assumptions of the model. The probability of a transition from $U(n)$ to $L(n + 1)$ is ab. The probability that the process remains in the unlearned state $U(n + 1)$ is $1 - a$. The probabilities in the transition matrix are the same between trial $n + 1$ and trial $n + 2$, and so on. Therefore, the descriptions of the probabilities on study trial 2 (S_2) (see Table 2.3) already deliver the probabilities of this transition matrix.

The model described in Equation 3 contains the theoretical parameters. Brainerd, Howe, and Kingma, (1982) have proved that this model is identifiable in its outcome space. Because there is a set of functions that maps each parameter onto the parameter space of Equation 3, the observable process has 11 identifiable parameters. Also the set of functions delivers unique estimators of the parameters of Equation 3.

The parameter estimation procedure for the two-stage model involves, first, the construction of an observable-state Markov model. Only the outcome space is presented here (see Brainerd, Howe, & Kingma, 1982a, for the identifiability proof), because it provides the link to observable features of the data from free-recall experiments. The observable model for the new two-stage learning model has the following states for experiments with the structure $S_1T_1T_2S_2T_3S_3T_4$. . . :

Q = state on all T_i after the last error in protocols with one or more errors and the state on all T_i in protocols with no errors
R = state on all T_i where the response is an error and at least one success has occurred on some earlier T_i
S = state on all T_i where the response is correct and at least one error occurs on some later T_i
E_1 = event of an error on T_1
E_2 = event of an error on T_2 if an error also occurred on trial T_1
E_3 = event of an error on T_3 if an error occurred on both T_1 and T_2
.
.
.
E_i = event of an error on trial T_i if errors also occurred on trials T_1 to T_{i-1}

The starting vector, the transition matrix, and the response vector for the observable model are

$$W_2 = [Q(1)Q(2),\ Q(1)R(2),\ Q(1)S(2),\ Q(1)E_1,\ Q(1)E_2,\ \cdots,\ Q(1)E_i(2),\ R(1)Q(2),\ R(1)R(2),\ R(1)S(2),\ R(1)E_1(2),\ R(1)E_2(2),\ \cdots,\ R(1)E_i(2),\ S(1)Q(2),\ S(1)R(1),\ S(1)S(2),\ S(1)E_1(2),\ S(1)E_2(2),\ \cdots,\ S(1)E_i(2),\ E_1(1)Q(2),\ E_1(1)R(2),\ E_1(1)S(2),\ E_1(1)E_1(2),\ \cdots,\ E_i(1)E_i(2)]$$

$$= [\pi_1, 0, 0, 0, 0, \cdots, 0, 0, 0, 0, 0, 0, \cdots, 0, 0, \pi_2, \pi_3, 0, 0, \cdots, 0, \pi_4, 0, \pi_5, 1 - \pi_1 - \pi_2 - \pi_3 - \pi_4 - \pi_5, \cdots, 0],$$

$$M_2 = \begin{array}{c} \\ Q(n) \\ R(n) \\ S(n) \\ E_2(n) \\ \vdots \\ E_i(n) \end{array} \begin{array}{cccccc} Q(n+1) & R(n+1) & S(n+1) & E_3(n+1) & \cdots & E_{i+1}(n+1) \\ \hline 1 & 0 & 0 & 0 & \cdots & 0 \\ u & (1-u)v & (1-u)(1-v) & 0 & \cdots & 0 \\ 0 & z & 1-z & 0 & \cdots & 0 \\ \alpha_1 & 0 & \beta_1 & 1-\alpha_1-\beta_1 & \cdots & 0 \\ \cdots & \cdots & \cdots & \cdots & \cdots & \cdots \\ \alpha_i & 0 & \beta_i = 1-\alpha_i & 0 & \cdots & 0 \end{array}, \quad C_2 = \begin{bmatrix} 1 \\ 0 \\ 1 \\ 0 \\ \cdot \\ \cdot \\ \cdot \\ 0 \end{bmatrix}. \tag{4}$$

The index variable i is defined as the length of the longest initial error run. For instance, if the latest occurrence of the first correct response in the protocols is T_9, then $i = 9$; but if the latest occurrence of the first correct response is T_{25}, then $i = 25$.

The starting vector W_2 represents the observed probabilities of the various state pairings for test trials T_1 and T_2. The zero probabilities refer to transitions that are logically impossible on the basis of the definitions of the observable states. The transition matrix gives the observed probabilities of all inter- and intrastate transitions for $n = 2, 3, 4, \ldots$. As with the starting vector, the zero entries in M_2 refer to impossible state combinations.

The second step of the parameter estimation procedure involves the construction of a likelihood function. The observable model contains five identifiable parameters in the starting vector $[\pi_1, \pi_2, \pi_3, \pi_4, \pi_5]$ and six parameters in the transition matrix $[u, v, z, \alpha_i, \beta_i]$. After the identifiability proof (see Brainerd, Howe, & Kingma, 1982) the likelihood function for the observable process can be derived from the maximum likelihood of all parameters (see, e.g., Hays & Winkler, 1970)

$$\begin{aligned} L = {} & (\pi_1)^{N(Q_1Q_2)} \times (\pi_2)^{N(S_1R_2)} \times (\pi_3)^{N(S_1S_2)} \times (\pi_4)^{N(E_1Q_2)} \times (\pi_5)^{N(E_1S_2)} \\ & \times (1 - \pi_1 - \pi_2 - \pi_3 - \pi_4 - \pi_5)^{N(E_1E_2)} \\ & \times (u)^{N(R_nQ_{n+1})} (1 - u)^{N(R_nR_{n+1}) + N(R_nS_{n+1})} \\ & \times (v)^{N(R_nR_{n+1})} (1 - v)^{N(R_nS_{n+1})} (z)^{N(S_nR_{n+1})} (1 - z)^{N(S_nS_{n+1})} \\ & \times \prod_{i=2}^{j} [(\alpha_i)^{N(E_nQ_{n+1})} (\beta_i)^{N(E_nS_{n+1})} (1 - \alpha_i - \beta_i)^{N(E_nE_{n+1})}] . \end{aligned} \tag{5}$$

The variables inside the parentheses are the parameters of the observable model. The exponents are empirical numbers obtained from the protocols of some experiment. For example, $N(S_n, R_{n+1})$ is simply the total number of times that protocols were observed to be in observable state S on trial n and in observable state R on trial $n + 1$. As mentioned earlier, the overall frequency of each type of transition is computed across all items of a list for the whole condition in order to compute the parameters for an experimental condition as a whole. The subscript i = n is an integer which is always greater than or equal to 2, because between the second and third test trials T_3 and T_4 the first transitions as described in the transition matrix can be observed. The letter j is the maximum length of the initial error run.

The third step in the parameter estimation procedure involves the expression of the probabilities of observable features of the data in terms of theoretical parameters of the new two-stage model (see Tables 2.2 and 2.3). When these expressions are substituted in the likelihood function of the observable model equation 5, the parameters of the theoretical two-stage model can be estimated. The definitions that are substituted are shown in Appendix 2A. The substitution delivers the following likelihood function:

$$
\begin{aligned}
L = {} & [a'b' + (a'(1-b')(1-r)(1-f)hc)/(1-(1-c)h)]^{N[Q(1)Q(2)]} \\
& \times [a'(1-b)(1-r)(f+(1-f)(1-h))]^{N[S(1)R(2)]} \\
& \times [(a'(1-b')(1-r)(1-f)h(1-c)(1-h))/(1-(1-c)h)]^{N[S(1)S(2)]} \\
& \times [(a'(1-b')r(1-f)gc)/(1-(1-c)h]^{N[E(1)Q(2)]} \\
& \times [(a'(1-b')r(1-f)g(1-c)(1-h))/(1-(1-c)h)]^{N[E(1)S(2)]} \\
& \times [1-a'+a'(1-b')r(f+(1-f)(1-g))]^{N[E(1)E(2)]} \\
& \times [d+((1-d)cg)/(1-(1-c)h)]^{N[R_nQ_{n+1}]} \\
& \times [((1-g)(1-(1-c)h))/((1-g)(1-(1-c)h) \\
& + (1-c)(1-h)g)]^{N[R_nR_{n+1}]} \\
& \times [1-((1-g)(1-(1-c)h))/((1-g)(1-(1-c)h) \\
& + (1-c)(1-h)g)]^{N[R_nS_{n+1}]} \\
& \times [1-d-((1-d)cg)/(1-(1-c)h]^{N[(R_nR_{n+1})] + N[(R_nS_{n+1})]} \\
& \times [1-(1-c)h]^{N[S_nR_{n+1}]} \\
& \times [(1-c)h]^{N[S_nS_{n+1}]} \prod_{i=n=2}^{j} \{[\alpha_i]^{N[E_nQ_{n+1}]} \\
& \times [\beta_i]^{N[E_nS_{n+1}]} \times [1-\alpha_i-\beta_i]^{N[E_nE_{n+1}]}
\end{aligned} \tag{6}
$$

where α_i and β_i are described in Appendix 2A.

This maximum likelihood function has 11 unknown theoretical parameters, and the exponents are the known total numbers of the transitions in the protocols of an experimental condition. To maximize the likelihood function for these 11 parameters, the logarithm of this function has been used. Because the logarithm of a positive argument is a monotonically increasing function of that argument, maximizing the likelihood function is equivalent to maximizing the logarithm of the likelihood function. To maximize the function with respect to each of the individual parameters, the technique of partial differentiation is often employed (see, e.g., Hays & Winkler, 1970). However, the maximum likelihood function of the two-stage model is too complex to find a miximum for each individual parameter by means of partial differentiation. Because no analytic solutions for the first partial derivatives can be obtained for the 11 parameters, numerical methods must be used in parameter estimation. The logic is as follows. The logarithm of the likelihood function in Equation 6 has to be programmed, and data counts of the total number of each type of transition of a condition are read as the input for this programmed function. The minimum of the likelihood equation 6 is found via computer search by using some standard optimization algorithm. (Because the function concerns probabilities, the minimum and the maximum of the likelihood function are equal.) Another important aspect of the minimization is that the minimum of the likelihood function is found for some values of the 11 theoretical parameters. These values are in fact the maximum likelihood *estimates* for those data. The calculated value of the function itself, $\hat{L}$, serves as the basis for the necessity and sufficiency tests (see Brainerd, Howe, & Kingma, 1982).

Various types of numerical methods have been described and evaluated (Avriel, 1976; Brainerd, Howe, & Desrochers, 1982; Foulds, 1981; Powell, 1970). Two methods, the simplex algorithm and the quasi-Newton algorithm, are widely available in optimization programs. The simplex algorithm tends to be slow, especially when the number of parameters is greater than 8 (Avriel, 1976).

To summarize, a way of building the new two-stage model has been presented. One starts by defining the theoretical parameters (see Figure 2.5) and then constructing a theoretical model. Subsequently, the observable model is built. After this, the identifiability proof is performed. Because this model is identifiable, the likelihood function of the observable model is formulated. Next, the theoretical parameters are substituted for the parameters of the observable model in this likelihood function, and the logarithm of this function is programmed. Finally, this function is minimized for the transition counts of experiments, which provides both the minimum of the function and the maximum likelihood estimates of the parameters. Because this model is identifiable, one can take the logarithm of the likelihood function of Equation 6. However, before parameters obtained after the minimization of the function can be interpreted, the necessity test must be performed. A less complex, one-stage model is described in the next section that can be used for this test.

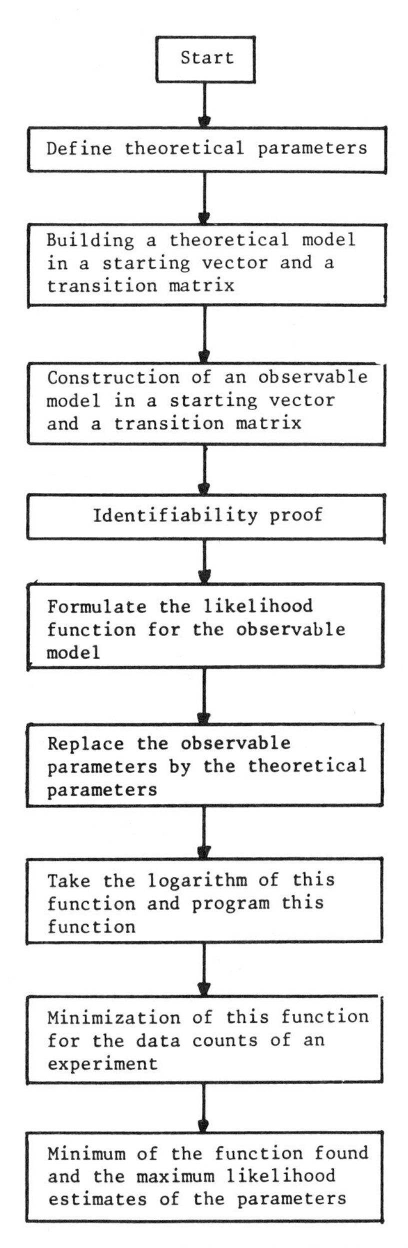

FIGURE 2.5. Steps for minimizing the likelihood function.

Necessity and Sufficiency Tests

Because the two-stage model assumes that learning involves exactly two stages, the necessity test determines whether a model with only one stage will do as good a job of accounting for the data as one with two stages. If so, then the two-stage model would fail on grounds of parsimony.

The one-stage model described here is quite similar to the general one-stage model (e.g., Greeno, 1968), except that the outcome space has been altered. This model assumes that learning consists of an initial unlearned state U in which both errors (substate U_E) and successes (substate U_C) occur, followed by a terminal learned state L in which only successes occur. When the likelihood function of Equation 6 is called $\hat{L}_2$, the likelihood function for the one-stage model is called $\hat{L}_1$. The steps for deriving the likelihood function are identical to those depicted in Figure 2.5. Because this model is also identifiable in the altered outcome space, only the likelihood function of the observable model is presented here. For the derivation see Brainerd, Howe, and Kingma (1982). The likelihood function for the one-stage model (in which the theoretical parameters are substituted) is

$$
\begin{aligned}
L = {} & [m + (1 - m)(1 - n)pc'/(1 - (1 - c')p]^{N[Q(1)Q(2)]} \\
& \times [(1 - m)ns(c'(1 - (1 - c')p))]^{N[R(1)Q(2)]} \\
& \times [(1 - m)n(1 - s)]^{N[R(1)R(2)]} \\
& \times [(1 - m)ns(1 - c')(1 - p)/(1 - (1 - c')p]^{N[R(1)S(2)]} \\
& \times [(1 - m)(1 - n)(1 - p)]^{N[S(1)R(2)]} \\
& \times [(1 - m)(1 - n)p(1 - c')(1 - p)/(1 - (1 - c')p]^{N[S(1)S(2)]} \\
& \times [d' + (1 - d')sc'/(1 - (1 - c')p)]^{N[R_nQ_{n+1}]} \\
& \times [1 - d' - (1 - d')sc'/(1 - (1 - c')p)[^{N[R_nR_{n+1}] + N[R_nS_{n+1}]} \\
& \times [(1 - s)(1 - (1 - c')p)/((1 - s)(1 - (1 - c')p) \\
& + (1 - c')(1 - p)s)]^{N[R_nR_{n+1}]} \\
& \times [1 - (1 - s)(1 - (1 - c')p)/((1 - s)(1 - (1 - c')p) \\
& + (1 - c')(1 - p)s)]^{N[R_nS_{n+1}]} \\
& \times [1 - (1 - c')p]^{N[S_nR_{n+1}]} [(1 - c')p]^{N[S_nS_{n+1}]}]
\end{aligned}
\tag{7}
$$

where $n \geq 2$ and the exponents of six task terms are summed across all values of n. The variables inside the parenthese are the six theoretical parameters of the one-stage model (c', d', m, n, p, s). The exponents, as in Equation 6, are observed states in the data.

Three observable states can be distinguished in this one-stage model, namely, Q, R, and S. The Q and S states have the same definitions as in the two-stage model. However, R has been defined as the state on any error trial; in other words, the E and R states of the two-stage model are combined in state R of the one-stage model. Each exponent in Equation 7 refers to the total numbers of times that the process was observed to be in the indicated states on the consecutive trials for the experimental condition as a whole. Differentiating the logarithm of Equation 7 does not produce simple algebraic expressions for the minima of the partial derivatives of the six parameters. Therefore the logarithm of Equation 7 has to be programmed, and the counts of the transitions of some experimental condition serve as the input.

Subsequently, both the minimum value of L_2 and the parameters are estimated for that condition by numerical methods, as with the likelihood function for the two-stage model. Following this, the necessity test is performed. The statistic from Equation 1 is

$$\chi^2(5) = -2 \ln \hat{L}_1/\hat{L}_2,$$

where $\hat{L}_1$ is the calculated likelihood of the data under the one-stage model and $\hat{L}_2$ is the calculated likelihood of the data under the two-stage model. The null hypothesis tested by this statistic is that the two likelihoods are not reliably different versus the alternative hypothesis that $\hat{L}_2$ is larger. The two-stage model passes the necessity test in those instances where this null hypothesis is rejected for some critical value of (5), $\chi^2(5)$, such as $p = .05$.

If the null hypothesis is rejected, the sufficiency tests are performed. It is common practice in two-stage analysis to study three types of statistics, namely, those concerned with the first stage of learning, those concerned with the second stage of learning, and those concerned with the learning process as a whole. The motivation for this procedure is that the model should predict the results for the individual stages as well as for the overall course of learning. Several goodness-of-fit measures have been developed for the identifiable model, including (1) sampling distributions for one first-stage statistic (errors before first success; see Brainerd, Howe, & Kingma, 1982, equations 47a and 47b), (2) two second-stage statistics (length of R runs and length of S runs, see Brainerd et al., 1982a, equations 48 and 49), and (3) three overall statistics (the learning curve, total errors, and trial number of the last error; see Brainerd, Howe, & Kingma, 1982, equations 50a, 50b, 51a, 51b, 52a, and 52b). When it is shown that the model fits the data, tests of hypotheses can be performed.

In sum, the likelihood functions of both the two-stage model and the one-stage model, as presented here, Equations 6 and 7, respectively, must be programmed. Such a program reads the input as data transition counts of some experimental condition. To find the minimum of the logarithm of these likelihood functions, an optimization program is used that is available in the majority of the mathematical libraries on most mainframe computers. When parameter values and the minimum function values are obtained for these likelihood functions, the necessity test is performed. If a model passes the necessity test, then sufficiency tests can be performed very easily by substituting the parameter values in the equations of the sufficiency tests provided in Brainerd et al. (1982a).

The likelihood function of the two-stage model is also the basis for hypothesis testing. For example, the appropriate statistic for the experimentwise testing is

$$\chi^2[k(11)-11] = -2 \ln [\hat{L}_2'/\hat{L}_{21} \times \cdots \times \hat{L}_{2k}] \,. \tag{8}$$

In the denominator, each term is the likelihood of the data for one of the k treatment combinations, as already estimated by the likelihood function of Equation 6. In the numerator, the value $\hat{L}_2'$ is found by pooling the protocols (transition counts) for all k conditions and then estimating the likelihood of the pooled data used in Equation 6. Also for the other hypothesis testing, the likelihood function of Equation 6 is used.

This new two-stage model can be used immediately. The investment in time will be small because only two functions have to be programmed and the identifiability proofs have already been performed (see Brainerd, Howe, & Kingma, 1982). In the next section, these models are illustrated in a free-recall experiment with intellectually impaired children.

Storage and Retrieval Processes in Intellectually Impaired Children

In this study the performance of free-recall tasks is investigated in learning-disabled children and educable mentally retarded children. An exact definition of learning disability is still being debated (Bryan & Bryan, 1980; Mercer, Forgogne, & Wolking, 1976). However, it is generally accepted that these children show a marked discrepancy between intellectual ability and scholastic performance (e.g., Hallahan & Kauffman, 1976). Learning-disabled children have IQs in the normal range, but perform below their intellectual ability in one or more academic subjects, mostly reading or arithmetic.

Most research on children with specific learning disabilities has centered on tasks that are rather closely related to the disability, such as grapheme encoding in reading-disabled children or syntactical anomalies in language-impaired children (Brainerd et al., in press, a). However, there has been a growing interest in the loci of memory differences in learning-disabled children and normal achieving children. Learning-disabled children with normal IQs perform more poorly on long-term memory tasks (Ceci, Ringstrom, & Lea, 1981; Ceci, Lea, & Ringstrom, 1980; Howe et al., in press, b; Wong, Wong, & Foth, 1977), but the basis of this performance in terms of the storage and retrieval concepts is still unclear.

A number of theories concern long-term memory deficits in learning-disabled children. Most of these theories employ a deficit hypothesis (for an overview, see Manis & Morrison, 1985). The most prominent cases in point are the structural deficit hypothesis, the strategy deficit hypothesis, the perceptual deficit hypothesis, and the short-term memory deficit hypothesis. According to the structural deficit hypothesis, neurological defects account for the poor performance on list-learning tasks in learning-disabled children (Beaumont & Rugg, 1978; Newell & Rugel, 1981; Swanson & Mullen, 1983; Witelson, 1977). However, a key weakness of the structural deficit position is its imprecision with respect to the specific long-term memory processes in learning-disabled children (Brainerd et al., in press, a). For instance, it is unclear whether this position would anticipate that learning-disabled children will primarily have problems with encoding, storage, retaining previously stored traces, or retrieving previously stored traces. Therefore, the implications of the structural deficit hypothesis for standard process variables of memory theories are rather ambiguous.

According to the strategy deficit hypothesis, learning-disabled children use inefficient mnemonic strategies on long-term memory tasks, especially organizational strategies (Dallago & Moely, 1980; Freston & Drew, 1974; Parker, Freston, & Drew, 1975; Wong et al., 1977). However, the weakness of the strategy deficity hypothesis position is that performance on long-term memory tasks is assumed to depend on the spontaneous use of mnemonic strategies. Although the evidence favors this assumption with adults, the evidence with children does not. Apparently, children often do not use strategies on these list-learning tasks spontaneously (Pressley, Heisel, McCormick, & Nakamura, 1982). Furthermore, neither the amount of subjective organization nor the amount of category clustering correlates with accuracy of recall before adolescence (Moely, 1977).

According to the perceptual deficit hypothesis position, perceptual disorders lie at the root of learning impairment (for a review see Bender, 1957; Cruickshank, 1972; Morrison & Manis, 1982; Vellutino, 1979). Topics that have been investigated under this umbrella include perceptual capacity, duration of initial information registration, and perceptual processing speed. Concerning the former two aspects, recent research failed to uncover deficits in learning-disabled children in either the capacity or the duration of initial information registration (Arnett & DiLollo, 1979; McIntyre, Murray Cronin, & Blackwell, 1978; Morrison, Giordani, & Nagy, 1977). However, Morrison et at. (1977) found that reading disability involves some problems in the processing of information in stages following initial perception. Research has also failed to find major differences in speed of perceptual processing between learning-disabled and normal achieving children (Arnett & DiLollo, 1979; Katz & Wicklund, 1972; Stanley, 1975). In addition, visual memory in learning-disabled children is not necessarily deficient (Vellutino, Smith, Steger, & Kaman, 1975; Vellutino, Steger, & Kandel, 1972). The perceptual deficit hypothesis, although on the surface appealing, is unsatisfactory because systematic research has failed repeatedly to find differences between normal achieving and learning-disabled children in basic perceptual processes (Morrison & Manis, 1982).

More recently, it has been suggested that short-term deficits in learning-disabled children underlie many of their difficulties on general cognitive and long-term memory tasks. For example, it has been hypothesized that the lower recency effect in immediate free recall is due to some short-term memory deficit (Morrison & Manis, 1982). Unfortunately, this suggestion has little empirical support because differences in the effect between learning-disabled and normal achieving children are not reliable (Bauer, 1979). In contrast, differences in primacy effects tend to be stable and well replicated (Bauer, 1977, 1979).

Despite a failure to find consistent evidence for the different types of deficit hypotheses, there is considerable evidence that learning-disabled children have difficulty in the basic process of storing and retrieving information (e.g., Vellutino, 1979). Unfortunately, this research on long-term memory deficits has relied on purely qualitative considerations in separating storage processes from retrieval processes. The conjoint measurement of these two processes makes it impossible to break up the two basic processes by the conventional statistical methods used in these experiments.

In contrast, Brainerd et al. (in press, a) and Howe et al. (in press, b) employed the new two-stage model for analyzing the loci of memory differences in normal achieving and learning-disabled children. The most important finding was that while differences between learning-disabled and normal achieving children remained age-invariant in free recall at storage, differences in retrieval increased with age. Thus, the new two-stage model may be a valuable instrument for analyzing the loci of memory differences in normal achieving and learning-disabled children.

Educable mentally retarded children have IQs between 50 and 80 (Ellis, 1979) and generally perform worse on list-learning tasks than either learning-disabled or normal achieving children of the same chronological age (Evans & Bilsky, 1979). Some researchers argue that this poor performance on list-learning tasks may be attributed to a deficiency in the use of rehearsal strategies rather than to a long-term memory deficit per se. In fact, inducing the use of such rehearsal strategies experimentally has typically resulted in marked facilitation of recall performance in retarded persons (Ashcraft & Kellas, 1974; Belmont & Butterfield, 1971; Kellas, Ashcraft, & Johnson, 1973; Moely, Olson, Halwes, & Flavell, 1969). However, even this finding alone need not imply that poorer recall performance of educable mentally retarded children in standard free-recall tasks might be due to rehearsal strategy per se (Ashcraft & Kellas, 1974; Flavell, 1970).

There is some evidence that the learning impairment for educable mentally retarded children may be attributed to long-term memory processes.

Educable mentally retarded and normally achieving children do not differ significantly on any portion of the serial position curve in a free-recall task; only normal achieving children produced a significant primacy effect (Spitz, Winters, Johnson, & Carroll, 1975). Although educable mentally retarded children have lower performance on free-recall tasks than either normal achieving or learning-disabled children, the loci of these memory differences is not well understood. Using the stages-of-learning analysis, Brainerd, Howe, and Kingma (in press, a) and Howe et al. (in press) showed that the memory differences between normal achieving and learning-disabled children could be localized in retrieval processes. However, these intellectually impaired groups have rarely been compared. The purpose of the present research was both to pinpoint the loci of memory differences between learning-disabled and educable mentally retarded children and to assess with the new stages-of-learning model whether these differences varied across two age levels.

An important stimulus variable in free recall is the picture-word manipulation. Such a manipulation permits comparisons of recall involving the same semantic concepts presented in different visual formats (printed words versus line drawings). Such comparisons may be of value in assessing whether certain storage-retrieval deficits are a function of printed words. In some studies with learning-disabled children, material has been presented in a pictorial format (e.g., Dallago & Moely, 1980) and in a word format (e.g., McFarland & Rhodes, 1976). However, few long-term memory studies exist in which pictures and words were directly compared. Evidence from these and other studies indirectly suggests that the learning-disabled child's memory deficit may be the result of a failure to interconnect verbal and visual codes when storing and retrieving visually presented information (e.g., Ceci, 1982; Ceci et at., 1980; Perfetti, Finger, & Hogaboom, 1978; Swanson, 1984; Vellutino, Steger, Desoto, & Philips, 1955). In addition, Howe et al. (in press, b) found that although learning-disabled and normal achieving children benefited from the presentation in pictorial format, normal achieving children were consistently better than the learning-disabled children at storing and learning to retrieve both pictures and words.

The performance of mentally retarded subjects has also been shown to improve on list-learning tasks in which pictures are used. Evans (1970) found that combined visual and auditory conditions led to better recall than did either modality alone. However, recall did not differ for the visual and auditory conditions. Similarly, Geruoy and Winters (1970) found that bimodal presentation, in which each picture was labeled by the experimenter, resulted in a better recall than did auditory presentation. However, in these studies, learning-disabled and mentally retarded children were not compared. The new two-stage model was used to analyze the loci of memory differences between learning-disabled and educable mentally retarded children in terms of storage and retrieval effects by using picture-word manipulation in a free-recall task.

Method

Subjects

The sample consisted of two age levels, 8- and 11-year-olds. The 8-year-olds were 60 (45 males and 15 females) learning-disabled children (mean age = 8 years, 4 months; SD = 6 months) and 60 (40 males and 20 females) educable mentally retarded children (mean age = 8 years, 6 months, SD = 6 months). The 11-year-olds were 60 (46 males and 14 females) learning-disabled children (mean age = 11 years, 5 months, SD = 4 months) and 60 (41 males and 19 females) educable mentally retarded children (mean age = 11 years, 4 months, SD = 5 months).

All learning-disabled children had measured IQs from 97 to 106, and the educable mentally retarded children had IQs from 60 to 75. Learning-disabled children had been classified by their schools as being at least one year behind their classmates in either reading or arithmetic, but not both.

Materials and Procedure

Lists were composed of either concrete nouns or line drawings of the objects denoted by these nouns. All items were drawn from the Paivio, Yuille, and Madigan (1968) norms and were highly familiar (A or AA on the Thorndike-Lorge count). Each list was composed of 16 items.

Half of the children in each age and ability level were randomly assigned to the picture list, and the remaining half were assigned to the word list. Lists were learned by using an alternating sequence of study-distractor-test cycles. In each study phase, items were presented individually in random order at a 5-s rate. To avoid any potential differences owing to naming or reading ability, the experimenter pronounced the name of each

TABLE 2.4. Necessity tests for the learning-disabled and educable mentally retarded children data.

Experiment and condition	Statistic		
	$-2 \ln L_1$	$-2 \ln L_2$	$\chi^2(5)$
Learning-disabled children			
8-year-olds			
Pictures	4521.27	4197.72	323.55
Words	5240.53	4784.41	456.12
11-year-olds			
Pictures	2992.02	2839.41	152.61
Words	3725.82	3515.01	210.81
Educable mentally retarded children			
8-year-olds			
Pictures	4895.66	4526.54	369.12
Words	6100.01	5698.55	432.46
11-year-olds			
Pictures	4104.46	3930.34	174.12
Words	4903.84	4618.61	285.23

item at the time of visual presentation. After all items had been presented, the child circled pairs of letters for 30 s to eliminate short-term memory effects. Following this, the child was instructed to recall aloud as many of the items as he or she could remember. A test trial ended when 30 s had elapsed without an item being recalled. This sequence of study phase followed by distractor task followed by test phase continued until the child reached an acquisition criterion of two consecutive errorless recall trials. The one exception to this routine occurred on the initial sequence. Here, in accordance with a methodological requirement of the two-stage model, instead of following the first study-distractor-test sequence with another study opportunity, the subject was immediately presented with the distractor task followed by a test trial.

Results and Discussion

Preliminary Analysis

First, the minima of maximum likelihood functions were computed for both one- and two-stage models for all conditions. Estimates of L_1 (one-stage model) and L_2 (two-stage model) and the test statistic of Equation 1 appear by treatment condition in Table 2.4. For all treatment conditions, the two-stage model passes the necessity test. (Because logarithms are used, estimates of L_2 are subtracted from the estimates of L_1.)

Next, sufficiency tests were performed for the two-stage model for all treatment conditions in order to analyze whether the model fitted all these data sets. The observed-predicted comparisons for four learning statistics (errors before first success, length of S runs, length of R runs, and the learning curve) for the 8-year-old learning-disabled children are presented in Table 2.5. (The sufficiency data for the other treatments were quite

TABLE 2.5. Illustrative sufficiency tests for the learning-disabled 8-year-old children data.

Age level and statistic	k													
	0	1	2	3	4	5	6	7	8	9	10	11	12	13
E														
Observed	.30	.24	.19	.12	.07	.03	.02	.01	.01	.01				
Predicted	.29	.25	.20	.14	.09	.04	.01	.00	.00	.00				
LR														
Observed		.53	.10	.04	.02	.01								
Predicted		.47	.18	.09	.03	.00								
LS														
Observed		.33	.18	.08	.06	.03								
Predicted		.29	.25	.08	.06	.01								
$P(X_{k=0})$														
Observed		.24	.50	.60	.71	.75	.80	.84	.86	.91	.95	.96	.97	.99
Predicted		.20	.48	.62	.71	.74	.80	.85	.87	.91	.95	.96	.98	.99

Note: The number of errors before first success is E, LR is the length of error runs after first success, LS is the length of success runs before last error, and X_k is the learning curve.

TABLE 2.6. Estimates of the parameters by age and ability level.

Ability, age level, and list condition	Trace storage and retention			Retrieval learning: Prestorage		Retrieval learning: Poststorage		Poststorage retrieval performance: Early		Poststorage retrieval performance: Late	
	a'	a	$1-f$	b'	b	c	d	$1-e$	$1-r$	g	h
Learning-disabled children											
8-year-olds											
Pictures	.51	.47	1.00	.28	.00	.28	.31	.77	.82	.48	.73
Words	.38	.44	1.00	.17	.01	.17	.36	.68	.89	.50	.67
11-year-olds											
Pictures	.50	.67	1.00	.33	.31	.36	.37	.67	.85	.59	.69
Words	.40	.48	1.00	.17	.21	.24	.33	.43	.91	.54	.78
Educable mentally retarded children											
8-year-olds											
Pictures	.36	.45	1.00	.34	.00	.15	.35	.74	.90	.47	.40
Words	.26	.44	1.00	.31	.00	.00	.34	.60	.86	.46	.32
11-year-olds											
Pictures	.44	.55	1.00	.16	.17	.26	.37	.49	.86	.64	.71
Words	.34	.44	1.00	.20	.11	.17	.36	.54	.81	.49	.66

comparable.) No significant differences were observed between the observed and the predicted values by using the Kolmogorov-Smirnoff test. Therefore, the two-stage model was used for analyzing all the treatment conditions.

Subsequently, the *experimentwise* test was conducted to determine whether parameter values differed between conditions for the experiment as a whole (see Equation 8). At $\chi^2(77) = 874.21$, $p < .001$ was found for the test, indicating significant differences. The remaining steps in this sequence involved *conditionwise* tests to determine which pairs of conditions differed as well as *parameterwise* tests to determine which of the parameters differed between conditions. Three mains sets of comparisons were made, each of which involved four conditionwise pairings: 8- versus 11-year-olds, pictures versus words, and learning-disabled versus educable mentally retarded children. (See Table 2.6.)

Picture-Word Effects

The four conditionwise tests revealed significant picture-word differences for all four groups of children. *Parameterwise* tests were performed to determine the locus of parameter differences for those pairs of conditions which differed statistically (see Brainerd, Howe, & Kingma, 1982, equation 55). Each of these tests is distributed as $\chi^2(1)$. As noted previously, four types of memory processes are measured with the new two-stage model, namely, storage difficulty (parameters a' and a), retention difficulty (parameter f), retrieval learning difficulty (parameters b',b, c, and d), and accuracy of retrieval (parameters e, g, h, and r). Statistically reliable differences are reported separately for learning-disabled and educable mentally retarded children.

Learning-Disabled Children

Parameterwise tests revealed that a' and a taken together were reliably larger for pictures than for words for both 8- and 11-year-olds. The magnitude of the average numerical difference at storage was statistically greater for the older children (.15) than for the younger children (.07). In other words, pictures were easier to store than words, and the magnitude of this effect increased with age. However, despite the greater ease with which pictures were stored, pictures and words were retained equally once they had been stored (see parameter $1 - f$).

With respect to retrieval learning, the prestorage retrieval parameter b' was reliably larger for pictures than for words at both ages. However, prestorage retrieval learning (parameter b) occurred only for 11-year-olds and was larger for pictures than for words. Poststorage retrieval learning following a success (parameter c) was also found easier for pictures than for words for the younger and older children. Finally, poststorage retrieval performance was found for the 8-year-olds to be larger for the pictures (parameters $1 - e$ and h), but these children had a better performance on words on the first study trial (parameter $1 - r$). The 11-year-olds also found pictures easier than words (parameter $1 - e$), but they showed a better performance on words on two other parameters ($1 - r$ and h).

Educable Mentally Retarded Children

Picture-word differences at storage resembled those found for the learning-disabled children. Both 8- and 11-year-old children found pictures easier to store than words (as measured by a' and a). Here also, the picture superiority effect at storage increased with age. As before, the retention parameter $1 - f$ did not vary between pictures and words.

Unlike with the 8-year-old learning-disabled children, the picture advantage was not maintained in the prestorage retrieval learning in the young educable mentally retarded children. For the 11-year-olds the prestorage retrieval learning was more reliable for pictures than words on the study trials following the first one (as measured by parameter b), whereas the learning-disabled children at this age level also showed a picture superiority on both prestorage parameters b' and b. Concerning the poststorage retrieval learning, following a success, the picture superiority was shown for parameter c for both age levels, which resembles the pattern found with the learning-disabled children. Although pictures had an effect on more retrieval parameters in the 11-year-old children (parameters b' and b) than in the 8-year-old children, the effect on the retrieval parameters in the older educable mentally retarded children was less (only one parameter b was affected) than in the learning-disabled children at the same age level.

With respect to the poststorage retrieval performance, 8-year-old educable mentally retarded children found pictures easier than words (as measured by $1 - e$, $1 - r$, and h). However, the 11-year-old children showed a better retrieval performance on three of the four parameters ($1 - r$, g, and h).

To summarize, pictures facilitated both storage and retrieval at both ability levels. The probability of a heuristic retrieval (after the first study) was greater for pictures than for words. The picture effect showed an increase in the 11-year-olds of both ability levels on the storage side on the first study trial (parameter a') as well as on the following study trial (parameter a). Striking differences in picture-word effects were observed on the retrieval side for prestorage retrieval on both the first and following trials. Thus, the use of pictures involves a greater effect than words in the older children than in the younger children of both ability levels. Overall, the pictures were superior on the poststorage retrieval learning for both ability groups and age levels. The probability of heuristic retrieval was only greater for pictures than for words in the 11-year-old educable mentally retarded children. However, a word superiority effect (in terms of algorithm retrieval was observed for the 11-year-old learning-disabled children. Overall, then, differences in ability were primarily reflected in older children's heuristic and algorithmic retrieval skills.

Age Effects

The 8- and 11-year-olds differed significantly on the conditionwise test for each of the ability levels, $\chi^2(11)$ values were greater than 35.64, $p < .001$. The results of the parameterwise test are discussed separately for the learning-disabled and the educable mentally retarded children.

Learning-Disabled Children. Pronounced age differences were found at storage; specifically pictures (as measured by a) were easier for older children. No differences in trace retention were found ($1 - f$).

Age-level differences for retrieval learning were rather variable. The 11-year-olds had a reliably larger prestorage retrieval performance for both pictures and words (as measured by b) than the 8-year-old learning-disabled children. Older children were also better than the younger children at poststorage retrieval of pictures (as measured by c). For retrieval performance, age differences tended to interact with materials. Older children were better than younger children at the retrieval performance for words (as measured by $1 - e$, $1 - r$, and h). In contrast, younger children were better than older children at the retrieval performance for pictures on the first state P test trial (as measured by $1 - e$) and subsequent state P test trials that preceded a success (as measured by h). However, older children performed better than younger children for pictures on those later state P trials that were preceded by an error (as measured by g).

Educable Mentally Retarded Children. In contrast to the situation with learning-disabled children, for the educable mentally retarded there were more age differences during storage. Both pictures and words (as measured by a' and a, respectively) were easier for older children than younger children at storage. Trace retention still did not vary between age levels. Age differences at retrieval were also observed for the educable mentally retarded children, but these effects were larger and more variable than those reported for the learning-disabled children. Younger children were better than older children in retrieval at the first test trial (as measured by b'), whereas the reverse was observed for the second and following test trials (as measured by b). In addition, older children were better than younger children at poststorage retrieval learning for both pictures and words (as measured by c). Age differences on the poststorage retrieval performance were rather mixed. Younger children were better than the older children at early heuristic retrieval for pictures (as measured by $1 - e$). In contrast, the poststorage retrieval parameters g and h were more reliable for older children than for younger children when pictures were used.

Overall, major developmental advances were most predominant for the learning-disabled children at storage after the first study trial, prestorage retrieval learning, and early poststorage retrieval performance. Developmental differences in memorization skills for the educable mentally retarded children were more pronounced for both storage parameters and the prestorage retrieval parameters. The development of heuristic retrieval was rather mixed, whereas pronounced developmental effects were found for algorithmic retrieval for both pictures and words.

Ability Effects

Four conditionwise tests revealed differences between learning-disabled and educable mentally retarded childen. The following numerical results were obtained: All $\chi^2(11)$ values were greater than 37.64, $p, < .001$. Because ability effects varied with age, reliable parameter differences are reported separately for 8- and 11-year-old children.

Eight-Year-Old Children. Concerning the trace storage, learning-disabled children were better than educable mentally retarded children at storing both pictures and words (as measured by a') with average storage differences being significantly greater for words than for pictures. Although storage differed as a function of ability level, no differences were found for trace retention $(1 - f)$.

On the retrieval learning side, only minor differences were found. Educable mentally retarded children were better than learning-disabled children at retrieving words (as measured by b'), and learning-disabled children were better than educable mentally retarded children at poststorage retrieval for words (as measured by c). Note that no reliable ability differences were observed for pictures. Ability differences at retrieval were also reflected in the retrieval performance parameters. The difference was located on one parameter h: The learning-disabled children were better than the educable mentally retarded children for both pictures and words on the second and following test trials in state P which were preceded by a success.

Eleven-Year-Old Children. Ability differences found for the younger children at the trace storage side were almost diminished in the older children. The only reliable difference was observed for pictures on parameter a: The learning-disabled children were better than the educable mentally retarded children at storing a trace on the second and following study trials. In contrast, major ability differences were found on the retrieval side. Specifically, learning-disabled children were better than educable mentally retarded children at learning to retrieve both pictures (as measured by b', b, and c) and words (as measured by b). These differences were also reflected in the early poststorage retrieval performance. Learning-disabled children were reliably better at retrieval performance in the first test trial in state P (as measured by $1 - e$) for pictures, whereas learning-disabled children were better on subsequent state P trials (as measured by h for words).

Turning to the parameter invariance, two types are distinguished, *quantitative* and *qualitative*. *Quantitative invariances* refer to situations in which the numerical values of the parameters remain stable across conditions, whereas *qualitative invariances* are those in which *relationships* between parameter values remain stable across conditions. Concerning quantitative invariance, it has already been noted that the numerical value of the parameter $1 - f$ did not vary reliably across conditions. Thus, despite differences in trace storage as a function of material and ability (in the younger children) no differences were observed to retain a trace once it was stored in long-term memory.

Concerning qualitative invariance, Table 2.6 shows that $g < h$ (except for the 8-year-old educable mentally retarded children). This outcome implies that for all learning-disabled children and the older educable mentally retarded children, retrieval performance was superior if the preceding recall attempt was successful. This result has been interpreted as a priming effect in heuristic retrieval (see, e.g., Brainerd et al., 1981).

Summary and Conclusions

In this chapter, some features of mathematical modeling have been discussed. The issue of tying a model to the data was illustrated with the new two-stage Markov model. A sequence of proofs and a battery of tests are needed before the parameter estimates may be interpreted. First, it must be proved that the model is identifiable in its data space. When the model passes the identifiability proof, the necessity test is performed to determine whether a simpler model will do a better job. A number of sufficiency tests have to be performed for models that pass the necessity test. The sufficiency tests tells us whether the model fits the data. When the sufficiency tests show that the predictions of the model are in very close agreement with the data, the between-condition and conditionwise tests are used to locate the conditions with reliable parameter differences. Parameterwise tests are used for analyzing whether differences between parameters are reliable.

Although these modeling procedures resemble conventional statistical testing, a mathematical model can do a better job than the conventional statistical methods, because conventional methods fail to separate the relative contributions of storage and retrieval processes as reflected in the performance on a free-recall task. In contrast, mathematical models enable us to separate these two processes.

Subsequently, characteristics of Markov models were discussed. It was emphasized that a Markov chain is a model of changes in the subject's cognitive state of knowledge, that elements of the state space correspond to the subject's state of knowledge about a task, and that the transition mechanism shows how these knowledge states change. For a simple Markov model, a branching tree can be used to represent the transitions, whereas in a more complex model a transition matrix of the transitions between the states on trials n and $n + 1$ is more suitable.

I then described the new two-stage learning model and an alternative one-stage learning model. The way of linking the theoretical model to the data was illustrated with a free-recall experiment in which stimulus presentation (picture versus words) was manipulated in learning-disabled and educable mentally retarded children. Pictures facilitated learning for both types of children. Ability effects on the parameter estimates were evident. For younger learning-disabled and educable mentally retarded children (8-year-olds), pictures were more easily stored than words. Differences were found for retrieval as well as for retrieval performance. Pictorial superiority at the storage side diminished in the older (11-year-old) educable mentally retarded children, but memory differences were found in retrieval.

The two-stage Markov models can be used successfully for analyzing the loci of memory differences in intellectually impaired children. However, it can be argued that this model has some limitations for atypical subjects because of the underlying assumption that the child has to reach a criterion of two consecutive correct test trials. When a list consists of more difficult words, intellectually impaired children may be unable to meet this criterion. As a consequence, the two-stage model as presented in this chapter cannot be used. However, Brainerd (1985) has shown that for fixed trial experiments, two-stage Markov models can be constructed that are nested in the present model (that is, the same parameters are employed). Thus, a family of different two-stage models exists that are applicable for different experimental situations.

Two-stage Markov models, although quite successfully applied in list-learning tasks, are rarely used for analyzing the development of concepts (Brainerd, 1982a). Because the acquisition of concepts resembles learning in free-recall and paired-associate tasks, it may be worthwhile to employ these models for conceptual development.

Acknowledgments

This research was supported by a Killam Memorial Award of the University of Alberta.

References

Arnett, J. L., & DiLollo, V. (1979). Visual information processing in relation to age and to reading ability. *Journal of Experimental Child Psychology, 27,* 143–152.

Ashcraft, M. H., & Kellas, G. (1974). Organization in normal and retarded children: Temporal aspects of storage and retrieval. *Journal of Experimental Psychology, 103,* 502–508.

Atkinson, R. C, & Crothers, E. J. (1964). A comparison of paired-associate models having different learning and retention axioms. *Journal of Mathematical Psychology, 1,* 285–315.

Avriel, M. (1976). *Nonlinear programming: Analysis and methods.* Englewood Cliffs, NJ: Prentice-Hall.

Bartholomew, D. J. (1973). *Stochastic models for social processes.* New York: Wiley.

Bauer, R. H. (1977). Memory processes in children with learning disabilities: Evidence for deficient rehearsal. *Journal of Experimental Child Psychology, 24,* 415–430.

Bauer, R. H. (1979). Memory, acquisition, and category clustering in learning-disabled children. *Journal of Experimental Child Psychology, 27,* 365–383.

Beaumont, J., & Rugg, M. (1978). Neurophychological laterality of function in dyslexia: A new hypothesis. *Dyslexia Review, 1,* 18–21.

Belmont, J. M., & Butterfield, E. C. (1971). Learning strategies as determinants of memory deficiencies. *Cognitive Psychology, 2,* 411–420.

Bender, L. (1957). Specific reading disability as a natural lag. *Bulletin of the Orton Society, 7,* 9–18.

Bisanz, G. L., Vesonder, G. T., & Voss, J. F. (1978). Knowledge of one's own responding and the relation of such knowledge to learning: A developmental study. *Journal of Experimental Child Psychology, 25,* 116–128.

Blalock. H. M. (1969). *Theory construction: From verbal to mathematical formulations.* Englewood Cliffs, NJ: Prentice-Hall.

Blalock, H. M. (1982). *Conceptualization and measurement in the social sciences*. Beverly Hills, CA: Sage.
Bohrnstedt, G. W. (1982). Measurement. In P. H. Rossi, J. D. Wright, & A. B. Anderson (Eds.), *Handbook of survey research*. New York: Academic.
Boring, E. G. (1950). *A history of experimental psychology*. New York: Appleton Century Crofts.
Bower, G. H. & Theios, J. (1964). A learning model for discrete performance levels. In R. C. Atkinson (Ed.), *Studies in mathematical psychology*. Stanford, CA: Stanford University Press.
Brainerd, C. J. (1979). Markovian interpretation of conservation learning. *Psychological Review, 86,* 181–213.
Brainerd, C. J. (1982a). Children's concept learning as rule-sampling systems with Markovian properties. In C. J. Brainerd (Ed.), *Children's logical and mathematical cognition: Progress in cognitive development research*. New York: Springer-Verlag.
Brainerd, C. J. (1982b). Editorial. *Developmental Review, 2,* 209–212.
Brainerd, C. J. (1983). Structural invariance in the developmental analysis of learning. In J. Bisanz, G. Bisanz, & R. V. Kail (Eds.), *Learning in children: Progress in cognitive development research*. New York: Springer-Verlag.
Brainerd, C. J. (1984). *The general theory of two-stage learning: An update on statistical methodology* (Research Rep.). University of Alberta, Department of Psychology.
Brainerd, C. J. (1985). Model approaches to storage and retrieval development. In C. J. Brainerd and M. Pressley (Eds.), *Basic processes in memory development: Progress in cognitive development research*. New York: Springer Verlag.
Brainerd, C. J. (in press). Developmental constancy in memory: Structural invariance and parameter stability. *Psychological Bulletin*.
Brainerd, C. J., Desrochers, A., & Howe, M. L. (1981). Stages-of-learning of developmental interactions in memory. *Journal of Experimental Psychology: Human Learning and Memory, 7,* 1–14.
Brainerd, C. J., Howe, M. L., & Desrochers, A. (1980). Interpreting associative-learning stages. *Journal of Experimental Psychology: Human Learning and Memory, 6,* 754–765.
Brainerd, C. J., Howe, M. L., & Desrochers, A. (1982). The general theory of two stage learning: A mathematical review with illustrations from memory development. *Psychological Bulletin, 91,* 634–665.
Brainerd, C. J., Howe, M. L., & Kingma, J. (1982). An identifiable model of two-stage learning. *Journal of Mathematical Psychology, 26,* 263–293.
Brainerd, C. J., Howe, M. L. & Desrochers, A. (1982). The general theory of two-stage learning: A mathematical reviw with illustrations from memory development. *Psychological Bulletin, 91,* 634–665.
Brainerd, C. J., Kingma, J., & Howe, M. L. (in press,a). Long-term development and learning disability: Storage and retrieval loci of disabled/nondisabled differences. In S. Ceci (Ed.), *Handbook of cognitive, social, and neuropsychological aspects of learning disabilities*. Hillsdale, NJ: Erlbaum.
Brainerd, C. J., Kingma, J., & Howe, M. L. (in press, b). Processing of item-level and catagory-level features in children's recall. *Journal of Experimental Child Psychology*.

Breiman, L. (1969). *Probability and stochastic processes*. Boston: Houghton Mifflin.

Bryan, T. H., & Bryan, J. H. (1980). Learning disorders. In H. E. Rie & E. D. Rie (Eds.), *Handbook of minimal brain dysfunctions*. New York: Wiley.

Ceci, S. J. (1982). Extracting meaning from stimuli: Automatic and purposive processing of the language-based learning disabled. *Topics in Learning and Learning Disabilities, 2,* 46–53.

Ceci, S. J, Lea, S. E. G., & Ringstrom, M. D. (1980). Coding processes in normal and learning-disabled children: Evidence for modality specific pathways to the cognitive system. *Journal of Expermimental Psychology: Human Learning and Memory, 6,* 785–797.

Ceci, S. J., Ringstrom, M., & Lea, E. G. (1981). Do language-learning disabled children (L/LDs) have impaired memories? In search for underlying processes. *Journal of Learning Disabilities, 14,* 159–162, 173.

Chechile, R. A., & Meyer, D. L. (1976). A Bayesian procedure for separately estimating storage and retrieval components of forgetting. *Journal of Mathematical Psychology, 13,* 269-295.

Chechile, R. A., & Richman, C. L. (1982). The interaction of semantic memory with storage and retrieval processes. *Developmental Review, 2,* 237–250.

Cruickshank, W. M. (1972). Some issues facing the field of learning disability. *Journal of Learning Disabilities, 5,* 380–383.

Dallago, M. L. L., & Moely, B. E. (1980). Free recall in boys or normal and poor reading levels as a function of task manipulations. *Journal of Experimental Child Psychology, 30,* 62-78.

Duncan, O. D. (1975). *Introduction to structural equation models*. New York: Academic.

Ellis, N. R. (1979). *Handbook of mental deficiency, psychological theory and research*. Hillsdale, NJ: Erlbaum.

Estes, W. K. (1962). Learning theory. In P. R. Earnsworth, O. McNemar, and W. McNemar (Eds.), *Annual review of psychology* (Vol. 13). Palo Alto, CA: Annual Review, Inc.

Evans, R. A. (1970). Use of associative clustering technique in the study of reading disability: Effects of presentation mode. *American Journal of Mental Deficiency, 74,* 765–770.

Evans, R. A., & Bilsky, L. H. (1979). Clustering and categorical list retention in the mentally retarded. In N. R. Ellis (Ed.), *Handbook of mental deficiency, psychological theory and research*. Hillsdale, NJ: Erlbaum.

Feller, W. (1950). *An introduction to probability theory and its applications* (Vol. 1). New York: Wiley.

Flavell, J. H. (1970). Developmental studies of mediated memory. In H. W. Reese & L. P. Lipsett (Eds.), *Advances in child development and behavior* (Vol. 5). New York: Academic.

Foulds, L. R. (1981). *Optimization techniques*. New York: Springer-Verlag.

Freston, C. W., & Drew, C. J. (1974). Verbal performance of learning disabled children as a function of input organization. *Journal of Learning Disabilities,* 7, 424–428.

Geruoy, I. R., & Winters, J. J. (1970K). Subjective organization by retardates in free recall bimodal presentation. *American Journal of Mental Deficiency, 74,* 509–516.

Greeno, J. G. (1967). Paired associate learning with short-term retention: Mathematical analysis and data regarding identification of parameters. *Journal of Mathematical Psychology, 4,* 430–472.
Greeno, J. G., (1968). Identifiability and statistical properties of two-stage learning with no successes in the initial stage. *Psychometrika, 33,* 173–215.
Greeno, J. G. (1970). How associations are memorized. In D. A. Norman (Ed.), *Models of human memory*. New York: Academic.
Greeno, J. G. (1974). Representation of learning as discrete transition in a finite space. In D. H. Krantz, R. C. Atkinson, R. D. Luce, and P. Suppes (Eds.), *Contemporary developments in mathematical psychology* (Vol. 1). San Francisco: Freeman.
Greeno, J. G., James, C. T., DaPolito, F., & Polson, P. G. (1978). *Associative learning: A cognitive analysis*. Englewood Cliffs, NJ: Prentice-Hall.
Greeno, J. G., Millward, R. B., & Merryman, C. T. (1971). Matrix identifiability of some finite Markov chains. *Psychometrika, 36,* 389–408.
Greeno, J. G., & Steiner, T. E. (1964). Markovian processes with identifiable states: General considerations and application to all-or-none learning. *Psychometrika, 29,* 309–333.
Hallahan, D. P., & Kaufman, J. M. (1976). *Introduction to learning disabilities: A psychobehavioral approach*. Englewood Cliffs, NJ: Prentice-Hall.
Hays, W. L., & Winkler, R. L. (1970). *Statistics: Probability, inference and decision*. New York: Holt, Rinehart & Winston.
Heth, C. D. & Cornell, E. H. (1983). A learning analysis of spatial concept development in infancy. In J. Bisanz, G. Bisanz, & R. V. Kail (Eds.), *Learning in children: Progress in cognitive development research*. New York: Springer-Verlag.
Howe, M. L. (1982). *The structure of associative traces: A mathematical analysis of learning associative clusters*. Unpublished doctoral dissertation, University of Western Ontario.
Howe, M. L. Brainerd, C. J., & Kingma, J. (in press,). Storage-retrieval processes or normal and learning-disabled children: A stages -of-learning analysis of picture-word effects. *Child Development*.
Humphreys, M. A., & Yuille, J. C. (1973). Errors as a function of noun concreteness. *Canadian Journal of Psychology, 27,* 83–94.
Humphreys, M. S., & Greeno, J. G. (1970). Interpretation of the two-stage analysis of paired-associate memorizing. *Journal of Mathematical Psychology, 7,* 275–292.
Kaplan, A. (1973). *The conduct of inquiry*. San Francisco: Chandler.
Katz, L., & Wicklund, D. (1972). Letter scanning rate for good and poor readers in grades two and six. *Journal of Educational Psychology, 63,* 363–367.
Kellas, G., Ashcraft, M. H., & Johnson, N. S. (1973). Rehearsal processes term memory performance of mildly retarded adolescents. *American Journal Of Mental Deficiency, 77,* 670–679.
Kemeny, J. G., & Snell, J. L. (1960). *Finite Markov chains*. Princeton, NJ: Van Nostrand.
Kemeny, J. G., Snell, J. L., & Thompson, G. L. (1957). *Introduction to finite mathematics*. Englewood Cliffs, NJ: Prentice-Hall.
Kintsch, W., & Morris, C. J. (1965). Application of a Markov model to free recall and recognition. *Journal of Experimental Psychology, 69,* 200–206.

Kohler, W. (1927). *The mentality of apes.* New York: Harcourt, Brace.
Krantz, D. H., and Tversky, A. (1971). Conjoint-measurement analysis of composition rules in psychology. *Psychological Review, 78,* 151–169.
Lashley, K. S. (1928). *Brain mechanisms and behavior.* Chicago: Chicago University Press.
Levine, G., & Burke, C. J. (1972). *Mathematical model techniques for learning theories.* New York: Academic.
Manis, F. R., & Morrison, F. J. (1985). Reading disability: A deficit in rule learning? In L. S. Siegel & F. J. Morrison (Eds.), *Cognitive development in atypical children: Progress in cognitive development research.* New York: Springer-Verlag.
McFarland, C. E., & Rhodes, D. D. (1978). Memory for meaning is skilled and unskilled readers. *Journal of Experimental Child Psychology, 25,* 199–207.
McIntyre, C. W., Murray, M. E., Cronin, C. M., & Blackwell, S. (1978). Span of apprehension in learning disabled boys. *Journal of Learning Disabilities, 11,* 13–30.
Mercer, C. D., Forgogne, C., and Wolking, W. D. (1976). Definitions of learning disabilities used in the United States, *Journal of Learning Disabilities, 9,* 376–386.
Moely, B. E. (1977). Organizational factors in the development of memory. In R. V. Kail, Jr., and J. W. Hagen (Eds.), *Perspectives on the development of memory.* Hillsdale, NJ: Erlbaum.
Moely, B., Olson, F., Halwes, T., & Flavell, J. (1969). Production deficiency in childrens recall. *Developmental Psychology, 1,* 26–34.
Morrison, F. J., Giordani, B., & Nagy, G. (1977). Reading disability: An information processing analysis. *Science, 196,* 77–79.
Morrison, F. J., & Manis, F. R. (1982). Cognitive processes and reading ability: A critique and proposal. In C. J. Brainerd & M. Pressley (Eds.), *Verbal processes in children: Progress in cognitive development and research.* New York: Springer-Verlag.
Nagel, E. (1961). *The structure of science: problems in the logic of scientific explanation.* New York: Harcourt, Brace & World.
Newell, D., & Rugel, R. (1981). Hemispheric specialization on normal and disabled readers. *Journal of Learning Disabilities, 14,* 296–297.
Norman, M. F. (1972). *Markov processes and learning models.* New York: Academic.
Paivio, A., Yuille, J. G., & Madigan, S. A. (1968). Concreteness, imagery, and meaningfulness values for 925 nouns. *Journal of Experimental Psychology Monograph, 76 (1, pt. 2).*
Parker, T. B., Freston, C. W., & Drew, C. J. (1975). Comparison of verbal performance of normal and learning disabled as a function of input organization. *Journal of Learning Disabilities, 8,* 386–393.
Pavlov, I. P. (1927). *Conditioned reflexes* (G. V. Anrep, trans.). New York: Oxford University Press.
Perfetti, C., Finger, T., & Hogaboom, T. (1978). Sources of vocalization latency differences between skilled and less skilled young readers. *Journal of Educational Psychology, 70,* 730–739.
Polson, P. G., & Huizinga, D. (1974). Statistical methods for absorbing Markov-chain models for learning: Estimation and evaluation. *Psychometrika, 39,* 3–22.

Powell, M. J. (1970). A survey of numerical methods for unconstrained optimization. *SIAM Review, 12,* 79–97.

Pressley, M., Heisel, B. E., McCormick, C. B., & Nakamura, G. V. (1982). Memory strategy instruction with children. In C. J. Brainerd & M. Pressley (Eds.), *Verbal processes in children: Progress in cognitive development research.* New York: Springer-Verlag.

Restle, F. A. (1971). *Mathematical models in psychology.* Baltimore: Penquin.

Restle, F., & Greeno, J. G. (1970). *Introduction to mathematical psychology.* Reading, MA: Addison-Wesley.

Spiker, C. B. (1970). An extension of Hall-Spence discrimination theory. *Psychological Review, 77,* 496–515.

Spitz, H. H., Winters, J. J., Johnson, S. J., & Carroll, J. G. (1975). The effects of spatial, temporal, and control variables on the free-recall serial position curve of retardates and equal-MA normals. *Memory and Cognition, 3,* 107–112.

Stanley, G. (1975). Visual processes in dyslexia. In D. Deutsch & J. A. Deutsch (Eds.), *Short-term memory.* New York: Academic.

Stevens, S. S. (1951). Mathematics, measurement, psychophysics. In S. S. Stevens (Ed.), *Handbook of experimental psychology.* New York: Wiley.

Suppes, P., & Ginsburg, R. (1962). Application of a stimulus sampling model to children's concept formation with and without overt correct responses. *Journal of Experimental Psychology, 63,* 330–336.

Swanson, H. L. (1984). Semantic and visual codes in learning disabled readers. *Journal of Experimental Child Psychology, 37,* 124–140.

Swanson, H. L., & Mullen, R. C. (1983). Hemispheric specialization in learning disabled reader's recall as a function of age and level of processing. *Journal of Experimental Child Psychology, 35,* 457–477.

Theios, J. (1961). *A three-state Markov model for learning.* (Tech. Rep. No. 40). Stanford, CA: Stanford University, Institute for Mathematical Studies in the Social Sciences.

Theios, J. (1963). Simple conditioning as two-stage all-or- none learning. *Psychological Review, 70,* 403–417.

Theios, J. (1965). The mathematical structure of reversal learning in a shock-escape T maze: Overtraining and successive reversals. *Journal of Mathematical Psychology, 2,* 36–52.

Torgeson, W. S. (1958). *Theory and methods of scaling.* New York: Wiley.

Vellutino, F. R. (1979). *Dyslexia: Theory and research.* Cambridge, MA: M.I.T.

Vellutino, F. R., Smith, H., Steger, J. A., & Kaman, M. (1975). Reading disability and the perceptual deficit hypothesis. *Child Development, 46,* 487–493.

Vellutino, F., Steger, J., Desoto, L., & Philips, F. (1975). Immediate and delayed recognition of visual stimuli in poor and normal readers. *Journal of Experimental Child Psychology, 19,* 223–232.

Vellutino, F. R., Steger, J. A., & Kandel, G. (1972). Reading disability: An investigation of the perceptual deficit hypothesis. *Cortex, 8,* 106–118.

Wickens, T. D. (1982). *Models for behavior stochastic processes in psychology.* San Francisco: Freeman.

Wilkinson, A. C., DeMarines, M., & Riley, S. J. (1983). Developmental and individual differences in rapid remembering. *Child Development, 54,* 898–911.

Wilkinson, A. C., & Koestler, R. (1983). Repeated recall: A new model and tests

if its generality from childhood to old age. *Journal of Experimental Psychology, General, 112,* 423–451.
Wilkinson, A. C., & Koestler, R. (1984). Generality of a strength model for three conditions of repeated recall. *Journal of Mathematical Psychology, 28,* 43–72.
Witelson, S. (1977). Developmental dyslexia: Two right hemispheres and none left. *Science, 195,* 309–311.
Wong, B., Wong, R., & Foth, D. (1977). Recall and clustering of verbal material among normal and poor readers. *Bulletin of the Psychonomic Society, 10,* 375–388.

Appendix 2A

The definitions that are substituted for the observable parameters in Equation 5 (for the derivation see Brainerd et al., 1982a) are

$$\pi_1 = a'b' + a'[1 - b'(1 - r)(1 - f)ch]/[1 - (1 - c)h] \, , \tag{9}$$

$$\pi_2 = a'(1 - b')(1 - r)[f + (1 - f)(1 - h)] \, , \tag{10}$$

$$\pi_3 = [a'(1 - b')(1 - r)(1 - f)(1 - c)(1 - h)h]/[1 - (1 - c)h] \, , \tag{11}$$

$$\pi_4 = [a'(1 - b')r(1 - f)cg]/[1 - (1 - c)h] \, , \tag{12}$$

$$\pi_5 = [a'(1 - b')r(1 - f)(1 - c)(1 - h)g]/[1 - (1 - c)h] \, , \tag{13}$$

$$u = d + (1 - d)gc/[1 - (1 - c)h] \, , \tag{14}$$

$$v = (1 - g)[1 - (1 - c)h]/\{(1 - g)[1 - (1 - c)h] + (1 - c)(1 - h)g\} \, , \tag{15}$$

$$z = 1 - (1 - c)h \, , \tag{16}$$

$$\alpha_i = \{(1 - a)^{i-1} [1 - a' + a'(1 - b')rf] \{ab + a(1 - b)(1 - e)c/[1 - (1 - c)h]\} + (a(1 - b)e[1 - a' + a'(1 - b')rf] \{ \sum_{k=0}^{i-2} (1 - a)^k[(1 - d)(1 - g)]^{i-2-k} + a'(1 - b')r(1 - f)(1 - g)[(1 - d)(1 - g)]^{i-1}\} \{d + (1 - d)cg/[1 - (1 - c)h]\} \div \{(1 - a)^{i-1} [1 - a' + a'(1 - b')rf] + a(1 - b)e[1 - a' + a'(1 - b)rf] \times \sum_{k=0}^{i-2} (1 - a)^k[(1 - d)(1 - g)]^{i-3-k} + a'(1 - b')r(1 - f(1 - g)[(1 - d)(1 - g)]^{i-1})\} \tag{17}$$

and

$$
\begin{aligned}
\beta_i = {} & \{(1-a)^{i-1}\,[1-a'+a'(1-b')rf]\,\{a(1-b)(1-e)(1-c) \\
& \times (1-h)/[1-(1-c)h] + \{a(1-b)e[1-a'(1-b')rf] \\
& \times \sum_{k=0}^{i-2} (1-a)^k[(1-d)(1-g)^{i-2-k}] \\
& + a'(1-b')r(1-f)(1-g)[(1-d)(1-g)]^{i-1}\}\,\{(1-d)(1-c) \\
& \times (1-h)g/[1-(1-c)h]\}\} \div \{(1-a)^{i-1}(1-a'+a'(1-b')rf \\
& + (a(1-b)e[1-a'+a'(1-b')fr] \\
& \times (\sum_{k=0}^{i-2} (1-a)^k[(1-d)(1-g)]^{i-2-k}) + a'(1-b')r(1-f)(1-g) \\
& \times [(1-d)(1-g)]^{i-1})\}\,. \qquad (18)
\end{aligned}
$$

3. Learning a Cognitive Skill and Its Components

Alex Cherry Wilkinson and Beth A. Haines

Learning a Cognitive Skill and Its Components

In this chapter, we analyze transitions during cognitive growth. Our approach contrasts with traditional methods of studying children's cognition, which typically identify stages or sequences of development but are vague or altogether silent about processes of transition. We present detailed analyses of three kinds of transitions that occur as children acquire a cognitive skill. For each of the three kinds of transition, we propose a mathematical model.

Views of Children's Cognition

We begin with a brief summary of some classical and contemporary views of cognitive development and with a sketch of our own perspective.

States and Transitions in Cognitive Development

In research on cognitive development, biological growth is a venerable, popular, and powerful metaphor (Carmichael, 1970; Piaget, 1970, 1971). It uses a sequence of stages to describe the child's progress in reasoning, thinking, or remembering. Thus, the major way to analyze development according to a biological view is to break it down into discrete steps.

Another view, which is more recent but increasingly popular, comes from artificial intelligence. This view derives from expert systems that contrast the mature knowledge of an expert and the tenuous knowledge of a novice (Chase & Simon, 1973; Chi, Glaser, & Rees, 1982). Here, in a sense, there are two stages. The goal is to understand development by specifying clearly where it starts and where it ends.

Still another view, which is also recent and is becoming more visible in the field of cognitive development, derives from mathematical models of judgment. It is the perspective of information integration theory. (For reviews, see Anderson, 1980; Surber, 1984 and Chapter 4, this volume.)

As applied to children's cognition, it contrasts two or more mathematical equations that formalize alternative processes by which a child might use information to reach a decision or make a judgment. A typical finding from studies using this view is that different equations fit children's decisions or judgments at different ages (e.g., Wilkening, 1981). Thus, information integration, like the other two views, aims to understand development by identifying discrete states of cognition that characterize children of different ages.

Finally, a fourth view of cognitive development comes from the componential theory of intelligence (Sternberg, 1977; Sternberg & Powell, 1983). Like information integration theory, the componential theory of intelligence provides different equations that characterize different mental processes. The focus here, however, is not on judgments or decisions but on reasoning and problem solving. A typical finding from mathematical models of componential intelligence, like models of information integration, is that different equations characterize children of different ages (e.g., Ashcraft, 1982; Sternberg & Nigro, 1980).

To be sure, biological metaphors, expert systems, information integration theory, and componential theories of intelligence differ in many important ways. We have neglected their differences to cast a spotlight on a feature they all share. The common feature is that they all analyze children's cognition by isolating fixed points in development. Only indirectly or by inference do they study the actual process of development. To their credit, these views tell us much that is valuable about points on the path of a child's developmental journey. In short, they tell us much about where the child travels. They tell us less, however, about the method of travel.

In this chapter, we describe models of studying cognitive development that take the opposite approach. We limit any discussion of stages, states, or points that might demarcate the course of development. Instead, we concentrate our efforts on mathematical models that analyze processes of developmental transition.

Cognitive Skills and Their Components

Our models analyze several properties of developmental transition. Before we explain these properties, however, we must define the domain to which our models apply. Briefly, the domain of our models is children's procedural knowledge (knowing how), not their factual or semantic knowledge (knowing that). Within this domain, we study developmental transitions that occur as children explore strategies for assembling the components of a multifaceted cognitive skill. We define our key concepts as follows.

Cognitive skills are complex mental capabilities that one can learn to proficiency. Reaching proficiency will require long, repetitive experience to make the complex skill highly reliable. Knowing how to play chess well is an example of a cognitive skill. Other examples are knowing how to count with dexterity or how to search intelligently for elusive memories.

Components are constituent elements of a cognitive skill. A given component need not be limited to a single skill. For example, one handy component is knowing how to match manual gestures one to one with vocal recitation of the items in a memorized list. This component is part of the cognitive skill of counting, in which one points at objects individually while reciting numbers from memory. The same component could also help a child to learn how to read letters, because the child could use it to point at printed, alphabetized letters while reciting the alphabet song.

Strategies are ways of assembling components to accomplish an immediate purpose. If it is used many times and found to be effective, a strategy may become a routine that changes little and succeeds often. When it becomes routine, a strategy joins with other routines that use similar components, and together the routinized strategies form a cognitive skill. Before becoming a skill, these strategies may change often, and their success is erratic.

Our goal is to analyze how children learn a cognitive skill, including its individual components and strategies for assembling them to solve problems. We make no attempt to identify a universal sequence of stages in the development of the skill, or even a typical or modal sequence. Instead, we observe the transitional period between children's initial awkwardness in exercising the skill and their eventual proficiency. While observing this transitional period, we analyze the children's efforts in three ways.

1. *Stability of knowledge*. To begin, we analyze the stability of a child's knowledge of a task over repeated occasions of testing. Quantifying the stability of knowledge casts light, we shall argue, on the psychological architecture of a developing skill.
2. *Learning individual components*. Next, we examine ways in which a child's knowledge changes while the child is practicing and learning a cognitive skill. Here we concentrate on alternative ways of describing how children acquire the individual components of the skill.
3. *Strategies for assembling components*. Finally, we analyze children's strategies for assembling components into workable methods of solving problems. This analysis looks at how children take isolated components they already know and seek ways to make them work together effectively.

Thus, we have models that analyze, first, whether children's knowledge of a cognitive skill is stable, second, how children learn to use individual components that make up the skill, and, third, how children assemble the components into strategies. In each of these three cases, our models quantify transitions that occur during development.

Method

The source of data for testing all our models was a single study in which preschool children tried to solve problems of constructing towers with wooden blocks. The study had the standard design of a training study, with a pretest, a training period, and a posttest. Haines (1983) thoroughly analyzed the results of the training. In this report, we concentrate on other findings, minimizing any discussion of training methods or their effectiveness.

Apparatus

We used a metal rod 40 cm tall that stood on a wooden base. Wooden blocks, each with a hole drilled heightwise through it, could be placed on the rod. The blocks were identical in width (10 cm), depth (5 cm), and color (unfinished oak); they varied, however, in height. The heights and their code letters were 12.5 cm, *A;* 10 cm, *B;* 7.5 cm, *C;* 5 cm, *D;* and 2.5 cm, *E*. Sizes *B* and *D* were used in testing; sizes *A, C,* and *E* appeared only in training and control activities.

Procedure

The children were shown the materials and told how to place blocks on the rod. The experimenter explained that the child would earn one poker chip for each block placed on the rod and that the child could later use the chips to buy a toy. The experimenter dumped the blocks from a box, letting them fall haphazardly on the floor. Then the experimenter asked the child to build a tower by stacking blocks on the rod, using as many blocks as possible.

The child had a pretest, training or a control activity, and a posttest, all in a single session lasting about 20 min. The pretest and posttest were identical in every respect. They contained three problems. The *mostly short* problem had 16 short (*D*) blocks and 8 tall (*B*) ones, the *mostly tall* problem had 16 tall (*B*) blocks and 8 short (*B*) ones, and the *equally balanced* problem had 12 each of short (*D*) and tall (*B*) blocks. The order of problems was counterbalanced. Between the pretest and posttest, a child had one of the following activities.

Short-Size Training

In this activity, the children were told that they would play a game and that it would help them earn many chips. The experimenter showed the child a pair of blocks and asked which block the child should use to get many blocks on the rod. The pairs of blocks were *AB, BC, CD,* and *DE.* The experimenter showed the pairs in random order. After making a choice, the child got feedback either affirming that the shorter size was right or saying that the child should have picked the shorter size. Notice that in the training pairs we used, the testing sizes *B* and *D* were correct as often as they were wrong (Bryant & Trabasso, 1971). Training continued until the child made eight consecutive correct choices.

Same-Size Training

For this activity, the children were told that they would play a game and that it would help them earn many chips. The experimenter put one or two *C* blocks on the rod, telling the children that this was the good size and that they wanted blocks matching this size. Notice that this size is exactly halfway between the *B* and *D* sizes used in testing. The child then drew a block from a covered box that contained one *A*, one *E*, and two *C* blocks. After getting a block, the child was to give it to the experimenter if it was the good size and put it aside if it was different. Verbal feedback emphasized that "we want that one, it's the same" or that "we don't want that one, it's different." Training continued until the child made eight consecutive correct choices.

Control Condition

In this activity, a child chose whether to play with puppets or with cars. After choosing, the child engaged in free play, interacting with the experimenter and using *A*, *C*, and *E* blocks and the chosen puppets or cars. The free play lasted 4 to 5 min, which was the typical duration of the training conditions.

Subjects

Ninety-nine children, aged 37 to 78 months, participated in the study. Six of them were randomly eliminated to form three groups that were perfectly matched on pretest performance. The three groups each had 31 children, of whom 12 children got no problem correct on the pretest, 8 got one correct, 6 got two correct, and 5 got three correct. The criterion of correct performance was at least six short blocks on the rod. The three groups were differentiated only by the activity they got between pretest and posttest, with each group getting one of the activities described above.

Stability of Knowledge

Our first analysis measured the stability of the children's knowledge of the block-stacking task. The analysis derived from Wilkinson's (1982b, 1984) theory of partial knowledge and used a mathematical model of double assessment. Previous data applying the theory and model to the block-stacking task appeared in Wilkinson (1982a). With ample detail given in these earlier papers, we limit the discussion here to the most essential information.

Theory of Partial Knowledge

The theory of partial knowledge applies to children (or older persons) who are neither novices nor experts. Given a set of problems that test some cognitive skill, children with partial knowledge would perform some of the problems correctly and others erroneously. For a preview and summary of the theory, see Table 3.1.

The theory makes a critical distinction between *restricted knowledge* and *variable knowledge*. With restricted partial knowledge, a child would perform certain problems erroneously on every occasion and other problems correctly on every occasion. In this respect, restricted knowledge is stable across different occasions of its use. With variable partial knowledge, a child would get a reasonably constant percentage of the problems correct across occasions, but the problems done correctly one time might be done erroneously another time. Thus, variable knowledge is unstable.

The theory assumes that restricted and variable knowledge differ in stability because they have different cognitive structures. Restricted knowledge derives from a *unitary algorithm*. This type of cognitive structure is an invariant procedure or method that one uses in the same way with the same result on different occasions. Variable knowledge, in contrast, derives from cognitive structures that have a fragmented quality.

More precisely, variable knowledge may have two kinds of cognitive structure. One kind of structure is a collection of methods from which one samples a single method, taking a different method on different occasions. This cognitive structure is a set of *unitary substitutes*. The elements of this set are substitutes because they are interchangeable; they are unitary because each of them is algorithmic. Alternatively, the cognitive structure for variable knowledge may be separate *modular components* that the child must assemble into a workable method. This cognitive structure produces variable knowledge because the process of assembly is successful on some occasions but not on others.

To see the difference between the two kinds of cognitive structure for variable knowledge, consider what a child might know about counting. According to Siegler and Robinson (1982), children learn to count by

TABLE 3.1. Summary of the theory of partial knowledge.

Type of knowledge	Cognitive structure	Process of learning
Restricted	Unitary algorithm	Amendment
Variable	Unitary substitutes	Sampling
Variable	Modular components	Self-correction

progressing through a sequence of increasingly sophisticated algorithms for generating numbers in the proper order. Suppose that at a transitional point, a child vacillates between using two algorithms, one that can generate numbers in the teens and another that cannot. This child has two interchangeable algorithms that form a set of unitary substitutes. Alternatively, according to Gelman and Gallistel (1978), the child may know several principles of counting, such as the principles that each item counted must get exactly one numerical tag and that the tags must have an invariant order. Suppose that a child sometimes applies both these principles and at other times applies only one or the other. Then the principles are modular components that the child may or may not assemble properly. (See Wilkinson, 1984, for a study that compared these two views of children's cognitive structure for counting.)

The theory of partial knowledge pairs each type of cognitive structure with a unique process of learning. For the unitary algorithms of restricted knowledge, the process of learning is *amendment*. This process revises or replaces a faulty algorithm. For unitary substitutes, the process of learning is *sampling,* a process of trying different methods, getting feedback, discarding faulty methods, and possibly adding new ones, until only effective methods remain. Finally, for modular components, the process of learning is *self-correction*. Here, children know the right components and in this sense know what to do. The children find it difficult, however, to assemble the components smoothly and make them work together reliably. Through self-correction, children monitor and adaptively improve their own attempts to assemble the components.

Studies using the block-stacking task (Haines, 1983; Wilkinson, 1982a) have shown that young children aged 3 to 6 years have partial knowledge of the cognitive skill that the task requires. The extant data suggest strongly that the children's partial knowledge is variable rather than restricted. Finally, the data also suggest that the underlying cognitive structure is a set of two modular components and that children use self-correction while they try to assemble the components into a reliable skill. We have much more to say later about the two components and about self-correction. Before doing so, however, we turn to measuring the stability of children's knowledge of the block-stacking task.

Model of Double Assessment

We studied the children's stability with a model of double assessment that analyzed transitions between the pretest and posttest. Here, a transition is one of the sequences *CC, CE, EC,* or *EE,* where, for example, the notation *CC* means correct performance on a particular problem of block stacking in both the pretest and the posttest. We applied a series of models to the observed frequencies of these transitions, adopting in the end a single, parsimonious model.

TABLE 3.2. Descriptions of parameters in the model of double assessment.

Parameter	Description
$\alpha(i)$	Level of initial ability for children in group i.
β_{CE}	Regression from C to E. Estimate of measurement error or forgetting or both.
β_{EC}	Regression from E to C. Estimate of measurement error or learning or both.
ω	Degree to which data conform to predictions of restricted knowledge ($\omega = 0$) or variable knowledge ($\omega = 1$).

Note: All parameters are probabilities.

Wilkinson (1982b, 1984) explains the series of models and the procedure for selecting a parsimonious one. Other recommended sources of advice on statistical and computational methods are Mood, Graybill, and Boes (1974) on estimation by maximum likelihood; Bishop, Fienberg, and Holland (1975) on models for contingency data; and Bazaraa and Shetty (1979) on algorithms for parameter estimation. These are important methodological topics that, unfortunately, we cannot cover in the space available here.

Conceptually, the value of the model of double assessment is best explained by describing its parameters. Table 3.2 gives these descriptions. The model estimates level of ability for separate groups of children with parameters $\alpha(i)$. In addition, it uses parameters β_{CE} and β_{EC} to fit a linear regression function. This function accounts for changes in correctness between pretest and posttest that stem from learning, foregetting, or measurement errors. The last and most important parameter in the model, ω, measures the extent to which the data exhibit the stability typical of restricted knowledge (ω near 0) or the instability typical of variable knowledge (ω near 1).

Empirically, the values of these parameters may differ across problems or across groups of children. However, a parsimonious model would constrain the parameters to be constant across problems and children. The goal of our analysis was to find a parsimonious model by constraining parameters to be constant without sacrificing goodness of fit.

Data

Data for the analysis came from classifying a child's response as correct (C) or erroneous (E) on a particular problem of blockstacking. Our criterion for crediting a response as correct was a stack containing six or more short blocks. We expressed transitions from the pretest to the posttest as the response patterns *CC, CE, EC,* or *EE*. Separately, we classified children according to the number of C's they produced in the first session. This classification yielded four levels of initial ability corresponding to values of 0 to 3 for the number of initial C's. At this point, we had a contingency table with two dimensions: response pattern and level of ability.

To extend the table, we added a third dimension. In fact, we added it in two different ways. First, following Wilkinson (1982b, 1984), we classified data according to problem type, producing separate tallies for the mostly short, mostly tall, and equally balanced sets of blocks. Second, we classified data according to training condition, separating the tallies for short-size training, same-size training, and the control condition. Thus, we analyzed the data twice, as two contingency tables, each with three dimensions. (Of course, we could have generated a four-dimensional table, but the density of data in this very large table was too meager to justify analyzing the table statistically. Bishop et al., 1975, pp. 401–433, give recommendations for analyzing large, sparse contingency tables.)

Results

In the analysis with problem type as the third dimension, one parameter exhibited a significant interaction. The parameter for level of initial ability (α) varied over problem types, $\chi^2(2) = 14.75$, $p < .01$, indicating that the children showed more ability on the mostly short problem than on the mostly tall and equally balanced problems. Thus, the mostly short problem, in which correct blocks were abundant, was easier. See Table 3.3 for the numerical values of these parameters.

The other parameters had the following values, which were constant across problem type and level of ability: $\beta_{CE} = .12$, $\beta_{EC} = .33$, and $\omega = .92$. The values of β_{CE} and β_{EC} differed significantly, $\chi^2(1) = 31.76$, $p < .001$, indicating that some learning occurred between sessions because the children were more likely to switch from error to correct than the reverse. Finally, the high value of ω replicated Wilkinson's (1982a) finding that children's performance of block-stacking problems is highly unstable. This finding implies that the underlying partial knowledge is predominantly variable, not restricted.

In the analysis with training condition as the third dimension, the values

TABLE 3.3. Interaction between ability and problem.

	Ability parameter			
Problem	$\alpha(0)$	$\alpha(1)$	$\alpha(2)$	$\alpha(3)$
Mostly short	.00	.41	.75	1.00
Equally balanced	.00	.17	.47	1.00
Mostly tall	.00	.12	.38	1.00

Note: $\alpha(0)$ must always be 0, and $\alpha(3)$ must always be 1. Only $\alpha(1)$ and $\alpha(2)$ were free to vary.

TABLE 3.4. Interaction between parameters and condition.

Condition	Parameter		
	β_{CE}	β_{EC}	ω
Short-size training	.09	.56	1.00
Same-size training	.19	.24	.70
Control—no training	.08	.21	.83

of α were constant across conditions. They were 0, .24, .48, and 1 for children who got 0 to 3 C's, respectively, in the initial session. Training interacted, however, with the values of β_{CE}, β_{EC}, and ω, $\chi^2(6) = 19.76$, $p <$ .01, as shown in Table 3.4. The main finding here is that the difference between β_{CE} and β_{EC} was the greatest in the condition of short-size training, indicating that the children learned best in this condition. The value of ω varied somewhat over conditions. Interestingly, it increased as the difference between β_{CE} and β_{EC} increased, perhaps because ω was, in part, correlated with learning.

Although ω was not constant, it was high in all the training conditions. The high values are evidence that the children's partial knowledge was mainly variable. This finding of mainly variable knowledge is the most important one. The other findings, which concerned problem difficulty and the effects of training, were results that we could have shown by other, simpler methods. The unique value of the double assessment model is its measurement of ω, which shows the relative amounts of variable and restricted knowledge. As a diagnostic tool, the model enabled us to tell which of the two hypothesized kinds of partial knowledge was closer to the reality of the data.

Learning to Use Individual Components

Once we showed that the children's partial knowledge was mainly variable, our next goal was to identify the underlying cognitive structure. Recall from our earlier discussion of cognitive structures that the theory of partial knowledge offers two possibilities. One possibility is that the child samples from a collection of unitary substitutes; the other is that the child assembles modular components. In this section, we explicate these possibilities and test them with two Markov models. Importantly, the models are both special cases of a single general Markov model of learning. We show that a learning model for modular components was better than a learning model for unitary substitutes. The data for these analyses were sequences of correct and erroneous blocks that a child selected within a single problem.

Theory of Cognitive Structure

One type of cognitive structure for variable knowledge is a collection of unitary substitutes, each of the substitutable elements in the collection being a fixed algorithm. Given this cognitive structure, a child would sample from the collection, get feedback, discard algorithms found faulty, and perhaps add new algorithms that the child believes to be better than the discarded ones. We borrowed a Markov model from Brainerd (1979, 1982) to formalize this possibility.

An important assumption of the learning model for unitary substitutes is that the child knows several algorithms, rules, or methods for solving a block-stacking problem. Some of these methods always produce an erroneous result, others always produce a correct one, and the rest are inconsistent. An inconsistent method is correct on some problems and erroneous on others. For example, in our block-stacking problems, preferring to select the most numerous blocks would be an inconsistent method. It would be correct (fortuitously) on the mostly short problem, indeterminate on the equally balanced problem, and wrong on the mostly tall problem.

Another important assumption of the learning model for unitary substitutes is that learning is progressive. After abandoning a method found to be erroneous or inconsistent, a child never reverts to using it later. In essence, a child may learn to solve block-stacking problems in any of the following ways.

1. *Always correct.* The child starts by sampling a correct method from the collection and uses it exclusively.
2. *From inconsistent to correct.* The child starts by sampling an inconsistent method from the collection. After producing an error, the child discards the inconsistent method with some probability, samples a new inconsistent or correct method, and never revives the discarded method. After sampling a correct method, the child uses it exclusively.
3. *From erroneous to inconsistent to correct.* The child starts by sampling an erroneous method from the collection. With some probability, the child discards the erroneous method, samples an erroneous or inconsistent method, and never revives the discarded method. After sampling an inconsistent method, the child never reverts to an erroneous method and with some probability discards the inconsistent method in favor of a correct one. After sampling a correct method, the child uses it exclusively.
4. *From erroneous to correct.* The child starts by sampling an erroneous method from the collection. With some probability, the child discards the method, samples a new erroneous or correct method, and never revives the discarded method. After sampling a correct method, the child uses it exclusively.

Our second type of cognitive structure for variable knowledge is a set of modular components that the child must assemble into a workable strategy for solving a block-stacking problem. Wilkinson (1982a) gave evidence that favored this type of cognitive structure. He argued for two components. One component, called INDICATE, sets a criterion for selecting blocks. If used correctly, INDICATE would set a criterion of shortness; if used in error, it would set a criterion such as tallness, nearness, or perhaps summed smallness of height, width, and depth. The other component, called REPEAT, is a loop for performing several iterations of a single action. In block-stacking, REPEAT governs iterative selection of blocks matching the criterion that the INDICATE component has set.

To test this cognitive structure, we generated a learning model for modular components. The model assumed that a child may learn to solve block-stacking problems in any of the following ways.

1. *Correct strategy*. The child starts with a strategy that uses both components properly. Having started a problem with this strategy, the child retains it throughout the problem.
2. *Switching strategy*. The child starts with a strategy that invokes INDICATE anew for every block, using a mixture of correct and erroneous criteria. With some probability, the child discovers the correct criterion, begins using the REPEAT component, and thereby moves to the correct strategy. Having adopted the correct strategy, the child retains it until the end of the current problem.
3. *Repeat-errors strategy*. The child starts with a strategy that sets an erroneous criterion with INDICATE and uses REPEAT to make consistent but erroneous selections. With some probability, the child notices that the criterion is wrong, self-correctively invokes INDICATE anew to set the right criterion, and thereby moves to the correct strategy. Having adopted the correct strategy, the child retains it until the end of the current problem.

These descriptions of the two kinds of cognitive structure emphasize that there are alternative paths of learning. We assume no fixed sequence of states or stages through which every child must go. Instead, both models assume that children may take any of several paths. We turn next to expressing the models mathematically and testing them with out data.

Markov Models of Learning

We formulated a general model and from it derived two constrained models that we tested against our data. One constrained model was for unitary substitutes; the other, for modular components. The following explication of the model covers the general model first and then the two constrained models.

Despite differences in notation and terminology, the general model was equivalent to the classical, two-state Markov model of learning (for reviews, see Brainerd, Howe, & Desrochers, 1982; Greeno, 1974; and Kingma, Chapter 2, this volume). The model assumed that on a given problem of block stacking, the child is in one of these states: (1) U, an unlearned state in which the child uses an erroneous method and therefore selects tall blocks consistently; (2) S, a partially learned state in which the child uses an inconsistent method and happens to select a short block; (3) T, a partially learned state in which the child uses an inconsistent method and happens to select a tall block; or (4) L, a fully learned state in which the child uses a correct method and therefore selects short blocks consistently.

The child can move among these states, but must do so progressively. Having left the unlearned state U, the child could go to the partially learned state S or T or to the fully learned state L. Having left either of the partially learned states S or T, the child could go to the other partially learned state or to the fully learned state L, but could not retreat to the unlearned state U during the current block-stacking problem. Finally, having reached the fully learned state L, the child must stay there for the remainder of the current problem.

The model has a starting vector that gives the probabilities of a child starting in each of the states. It also has a response vector that gives the probability of a child selecting a correct block when the child is in a given state. Finally, it has a transition matrix that gives the probability of the child moving from one state to another. The starting vector, transition matrix, and response vector of the general model are:

$$\Pr[L(1), S(1), T(1), U(1)] = [p, (1-p)(1-q)k, (1-p)(1-q)(1-k), (1-p)q]$$

$$\begin{array}{c} \\ L(i) \\ S(i) \\ T(i) \\ U(i) \end{array} \begin{array}{c} \begin{array}{cccc} L(i+1) & S(i+1) & T(i+1) & U(i+1) \end{array} \\ \left[\begin{array}{cccc} 1 & 0 & 0 & 0 \\ a & (1-a)g & (1-a)(1-g) & 0 \\ b & (1-b)(1-h) & (1-b)h & 0 \\ c & (1-c)(1-d)m & (1-c)(1-d)(1-m) & (1-c)d \end{array}\right] \end{array} \begin{array}{c} \Pr(\text{correct}) \\ \left[\begin{array}{c} 1 \\ 1 \\ 0 \\ 0 \end{array}\right] \end{array}$$

The model has 10 parameters, as summarized in Table 3.5. (For additional explanation of this model, see Chapter 2, this volume, by Kingma.)

To derive a learning model for unitary substitutes, we applied the constraints $k = m$ and $a = 0$. Under these constraints, the model has eight free parameters and is identical to Brainerd's (1979, 1982) model of the process by which children learn rules for Piagetian concepts. We applied these constraints to make the model more parsimonious and to allow direct comparison between our data and Brainerd's.

TABLE 3.5. Descriptions of parameters in the general Markov model of learning.

Parameter	Description
p	Probability of starting in L
q	Probability of starting in U, conditional on not having started in L
k	Probability of starting in S, conditional on not having started in U or L
a	Probability of moving to L from S
b	Probability of moving to L from T
c	Probability of moving to L from U
g	Probability of staying in S
h	Probability of staying in T
d	Probability of staying in U, conditional on not moving from U to L
m	Probability of moving to S from U, conditional on not staying in U and not moving to L

The constraint $k = m$ concerns the probabilities of entering the partially learned states S and T, either from the unlearned state U or at the outset of a problem. The other constraint, $a = 0$, is more important theoretically. It specifies that when children use an inconsistent method, they may go directly to the learned state L from state T but may not do so from state S. In effect, the constrained model specifies that children learn correct methods only after making errors. The formal expression of the learning model for unitary substitutes is

$$\Pr[L(1), S(1), T(1), U(1)] = [p, (1-p)(1-q)k, (1-p)(1-q)(1-k), (1-p)q]$$

$$\begin{array}{c} \\ L(i) \\ S(i) \\ T(i) \\ U(i) \end{array} \begin{array}{c} \begin{array}{cccc} L(i+1) & S(i+1) & T(i+1) & U(i+1) \end{array} \\ \left[\begin{array}{cccc} 1 & 0 & 0 & 0 \\ 0 & g & (1-g) & 0 \\ b & (1-b)(1-h) & (1-b)h & 0 \\ c & (1-c)(1-d)k & (1-c)(1-d)(1-k) & (1-c)d \end{array}\right] \end{array} \begin{array}{c} \Pr(\text{correct}) \\ \left[\begin{array}{c} 1 \\ 1 \\ 0 \\ 0 \end{array}\right] \end{array}$$

With this model, we can restate the child's possible paths of learning, expressing them formally as the following sequences of states.

1. *Always correct.* The child starts in state L with probability p and stays there.
2. *From inconsistent to correct.* The child starts in state S or T with probabilities governed by parameters p, q, and k. The child moves back and forth between S and T for one or more selections, with probabilities governed by parameters b, g, and h. The child advances to L only from T, with probability b. Once in L, the child stays there.

3. *From erroneous to inconsistent to correct.* The child starts in state U with probability $(1 - p)\,q$. For one or more selections, the child stays there. The child advances to S or T, with probabilities governed by parameters c, d, and k. Otherwise, the child moves back and forth between S and T for one or more selections, with probabilities governed by parameters b, g, and h. Only from T can the child advance to L, with probability b. Once in L, the child stays there.
4. *From erroneous to correct.* The child starts in state U with probability $(1 - p)q$. For one or more selections, the child stays there. The child advances to L with probability c and stays there.

To derive a learning model for modular components, we applied the constraints $d = m = 1$. These constraints reduced the number of free parameters to eight and produced the following Markov model:

$$\Pr[L(1), S(1), T(1), U(1)] = [p, (1-p)(1-q)k, (1-p)(1-q)(1-k), (1-p)q]$$

$$\begin{array}{c} \\ L(i) \\ S(i) \\ T(i) \\ U(i) \end{array} \begin{array}{c} \begin{array}{cccc} L(i+1) & S(i+1) & T(i+1) & U(i+1) \end{array} \\ \left[\begin{array}{cccc} 1 & 0 & 0 & 0 \\ a & (1-a)g & (1-a)(1-g) & 0 \\ b & (1-b)(1-h) & (1-b)h & 0 \\ c & 0 & 0 & 1-c \end{array}\right] \end{array} \begin{array}{c} \Pr(\text{correct}) \\ \left[\begin{array}{c} 1 \\ 1 \\ 0 \\ 0 \end{array}\right] \end{array}.$$

The constraints in this model specify that children never go from the unlearned state U to the partially learned states S and T. Although this restriction may seem puzzling, it made good sense when we interpreted the states as strategies and used the model to specify formally the paths of learning that children might take. We defined the following correspondence between states and strategies: The learned state L is the correct strategy, the partially learned states S and T are the switching strategy, and the unlearned state U is the repeat-errors strategy. Given this correspondence, the model specifies that children's use of strategies could take them along the following paths on a given problem of block stacking.

1. *Always correct.* With probability p, the child uses the correct strategy throughout the problem. Here the child starts with and retains both of the essential components, INDICATE and REPEAT.
2. *From switching to correct.* With probability $(1-p)(1-q)$, the child starts with the switching strategy, initially selecting a short block with probability k and a tall block with probability $1 - k$. After the initial selection, probabilities a and b govern moves from the switching strategy to the correct strategy, while probabilities g and h govern changes in size of block within the switching strategy. The path of learning is

that the child begins with occasionally correct use of INDICATE, depending on the value of k. Then the child may improve in using INDICATE, depending on the values of g and h, and may learn to use REPEAT, depending on the values of a and b.

3. *From repeat errors to correct.* With probability $(1 - p)q$, the child starts with the repeat-errors strategy. The child selects tall blocks when using this strategy. After each selection, the child retains the repeat-errors strategy with probability $1 - c$ and moves to the correct strategy with probability c. Here the child's path is to start with REPEAT and then, depending on the value of c, learn to use INDICATE.

Data

To test the models of learning, we analyzed children's selections of individual blocks. Within a single block-stacking problem, we classified each block placed on the rod as correct (c) or erroneous (e). (Notice that we used lowercase c and e for performance on individual blocks, whereas we previously used uppercase C and E for performance on a whole problem.) Next we classified each problem according to the sequence of the first four blocks the child selected. Examples are the sequences *cccc, ccce,* and the like. We used sequences of this length because four blocks of any size would always fit on the rod. With four selections, there are 16 possible sequences.

In a preliminary analysis, we tallied frequencies in a one-dimensional table of the 16 sequences, collapsing over children, problems, testing sessions, and training conditions. This analysis was tractable because the table of data was small, but it might have masked effects of the collapsed factors. Therefore, in a follow-up analysis, we collapsed only over children and problems, tallying frequencies in a table with three dimensions (16 sequences $\times$ 2 testing sessions $\times$ 3 training conditions). The frequencies in these two tables were the data to which we fitted our Markov models.

Results

We concentrate on the results for the smaller, one-dimensional table. The learning model for unitary substitutes fit this table well, $\chi^2(7) = 6.24$, and so did the learning model for modular components, $\chi^2(7) = 6.47$. Having found equally good fits with the two eight-parameter models, we then tested more constrained versions of each model.

We simplified the learning model for unitary substitutes to six free parameters by applying the constraints $k = g = 1-h$. These constraints specify that when children used an inconsistent method, their probability of selecting a short block was the same under all the following conditions: on the first selection, after selecting a short block, and after selecting a tall block. Brainerd (1979) used equivalent constraints in a successful effort to model children's learning of the concept of conservation. Our data, however, rejected this six-parameter model, $\chi^2(9) = 30.36$, $p < .01$. Admittedly, it is possible that if we had used some other constraints, we might have been able to fit the data. We did not, therefore, reject all simplified versions of the learning model for unitary substitutes; we only concluded that our data rejected Brainerd's (1979) simplification,

In contrast, we were able to fit the data well with a simplified version of the learning model for modular components that had only five free parameters, $\chi^2(10) = 7.10$. The constraints we applied to simplify this model were $a = b = 0$ and $k = .5$. The meaning of the double constraint $a = b = 0$ is that the children did not move from the switching strategy to the correct strategy. The meaning of the constraint $k = .5$ is that when children used the switching strategy, their first selection was equally likely to be a short or tall block.

We also found two interesting results for the unconstrained parameters in the simplified version of the learning model for modular components. First, our estimate of c was .08, and we rejected the hypothesis $c = 0$, $\chi^2(1) = 7.68$, $p < .01$. This result shows that the children occasionally moved from the repeat-errors strategy to the correct strategy while selecting blocks. Such moves are evidence of self-correction. Second, estimated values were $g = .44$ and $h = .30$, and we rejected the hypothesis $g = h$, $\chi^2(1) = 12.63$, $p < .01$. Notice, however, that neither g nor h was greater than .5, the value for random switching. This result means that when using the switching strategy, the children tended *not* to stay with the size of their previous selection. They were more likely to stay with the short size, however, than with the tall size. The children's restraint in switching away from short blocks is mild evidence of self-corrective learning.

In a follow-up analysis that looked for other possible effects, we used the larger three-dimensional table of data (16 sequences × 2 testing sessions × 3 training conditions) and fit the simplified version of the learning model for modular components. The model gave a good fit to these data, with two new findings. First, parameters p and q from the starting vector interacted with testing session and training condition. Thus, the probability of starting a problem with a particular strategy in the first session differed from the probability of starting a problem with that same strategy in the second session. The main difference was that the probability of starting a problem with the correct strategy increased more after short-size training than after same-size training or the control condition. Second, parameters c, g, and h from the transition matrix were constant across all the data. Thus, the probabilities for self-corrective learning within a problem remained the same over testing sessions and training conditions.

To summarize the major findings, our investigation of the learning models showed that the one for modular components gave a more parsimonious fit to the data than did the one for unitary substitutes. Furthermore, the estimated parameters in the learning model for modular components gave evidence of self-correction, a finding consistent with the theory of partial knowledge.

Strategies for Assembling Components

The evidence from our learning models implied that children's cognitive structure for the block-stacking task is a set of modular components. An important limitation of this evidence, however, is that it looked at children's strategies for selecting blocks within one block-stacking problem. It did not investigate whether children tended to keep the same strategy from one problem to the next. In this section, we develop a new model to diagnose whether and how children changed strategies across problems. The new model gave us insight into the processes by which children explored ways of assembling the components into strategies. It also provided a new diagnostic tool that has some advantages over methods used in other studies of children's strategies.

Theory of Using Strategies

We have already described three strategies for solving block-stacking problems, the correct, switching, and repeat-errors strategies. Table 3.6 summarizes how these strategies use the components INDICATE and REPEAT. The correct strategy uses both components properly. The switching strategy uses the INDICATE component anew for each block, sometimes properly and sometimes not. Last, the repeat-errors strategy uses REPEAT properly but with an erroneous criterion resulting from improper use of INDICATE. However, while using the repeat-errors strategy, the child may self-correctively discover that the criterion is wrong and invoke INDICATE anew, this time using it properly.

From the theory of partial knowledge, we derived an account of the ways in which children use these strategies. The main idea is that children know the components but exhibit variable partial knowledge because they fail to assemble the components properly and reliably. Success in assembling the components on one occasion is no guarantee of successful as-

TABLE 3.6. How strategies make use of components.

Strategy	Use of components
Correct	INDICATE used correctly. REPEAT use correctly.
Switching	INDICATE used often, sometimes correctly, sometimes not. REPEAT not used.
Repeat errors	INDICATE used in error, but self-correction may occur. REPEAT used correctly.

sembly on the next occasion. Consequently, a strategy that a child uses on one problem need not be the same as the child's strategy on the next problem. Assembling the components in different ways is the underlying cause of strategic inconsistency. To test this account of children's strategies, we developed a model that analyzed transitions among strategies from one problem to the next.

Diagnostic Model of Strategies

Overview

To test this theory, we used a model that gave us a new and powerful tool for diagnosing children's strategies. Because of its novelty, the model requires some explanation. The essence of the model is that it generated predictions for our data in three steps.

First, the diagnostic model of strategies took advantage of our earlier results from the learning model for modular components. The learning model allowed us to look at a child's sequence of selections on a given block-stacking problem and, from this datum alone, identify the child's probable strategies. For example, given the sequence *eecc,* there are two possibilities, according to the final, simplified version of our learning model. Either the child started with the repeat-errors strategy and moved to the correct strategy after two errors, or the child used the switching strategy. The diagnostic model of strategies gave us mathematical expressions for all such possibilities. Thus, the first step in applying the diagnostic model was to generate mathematical probabilities that a child was using any of the three strategies, given only a sequence of four blocks that the child had selected. In short, it took observable data and generated probabilities for unobservable strategies.

Second, the diagnostic model estimated the probabilities of keeping or changing strategies between block-stacking problems. To take this step, the model applied a transition matrix that gave the probability of starting a problem with any strategy, given the strategy with which the child had ended the previous problem.

Third, the diagnostic model took advantage, once again, of results from the learning model. Using the learning model, we generated the probability that a child would produce any sequence of four blocks, given the strategy with which the child started to work on the problem. Thus, the final step was to take the probability of an unobservable strategy and predict the probability of an observable sequence.

In summary, the diagnostic model took as input the empirical probabilities of observable sequences on a problem and computed the probabilities of observable sequences on the next problem. Mediating the computation were unobservable strategies and equally unobservable changes in strategy. The main advantage of the diagnostic model was that it precisely estimated the probabilities of changes in strategy. It enabled us to study children's use of strategies without requiring us to know with certainty the strategy that any individual child was using on a particular problem.

This method of diagnosing strategies has some advantages, we think, over other methods currently in use in developmental psychology. One such method is Siegler's (1976, 1981) procedure of rule assessment. Siegler's method assumes that a child uses a single strategy (he calls it a *rule*) consistently over a series of problems. Based on the pattern of a child's behavior over the series, the method classifies the child as having used one of several predefined strategies (or rules). The main disadvantage of the method, in our view, is that it assumes no change in strategy but offers no test of the assumption. Another method is Brainerd's (1979, 1982) Markov model of rule sampling, which is formally equivalent to our earlier learning model for unitary substitutes. Brainerd's method estimates the probabilities of changes in types of rules or classes of strategies that groups of children use. A disadvantage of the method is that it applies only to broad classes of strategies and, consequently, does not identify any specific strategy.

Our diagnostic method avoided the disadvantages of these other methods. We measured changes in strategy, rather than assuming consistency by default, as Siegler did. We also identified three particular strategies that the children used, thus gaining specificity over Brainerd's method.

Model

To develop the mathematics of our diagnostic model of strategies, consider the sequence *eecc,* for example. The simplified version of our learning model for modular components states that this sequence occurs with probability

$$\Pr(eecc) = (1 - p)qc(1 - c) + .5(1 - p)(1 - q)gh(1 - h).$$

On the right side of this expression, the term $(1-p)qc(1-c)$ is for sequences that come from beginning with the repeat-errors strategy and moving to the correct strategy after two errors. The term $.5(1-p)(1-q)gh(1-h)$ is for sequences that come from the switching strategy. After simplifying algebraically, it follows that with probability

$$qc(1 - c) \,/\, [qc(1 - c) + .5(1 - q)gh(1 - h)]$$

an observed case of the sequence *eecc* represents a child who has moved to the correct strategy, and with probability

$$.5(1 - q)gh(1 - h) \,/\, [qc(1 - c) + .5(1 - q)gh(1 - h)]$$

it represents a child who has been using the switching strategy.

We generated similar expressions for each of the 16 sequences. The result was a 16×3 matrix **X** that mapped observable sequences to unobservable strategies. Essentially, the **X** matrix served the same function in our diagnostic model as a starting vector would serve in a classical Markov model. It gave the probabilities that a child was using the correct, repeat-errors, or switching strategy, given the sequence of the first four blocks the child had produced on the problem. Note that matrix **X** identified the probable strategy a child was using after having selected four blocks. To keep the diagnostic model mathematically tractable, we assumed that the child's probable strategy after selecting four blocks would be a good indicator of the child's probable strategy at the completion of a block-stacking problem.

To save space in displaying **X**, we use the following notational abbreviations:

$$\begin{array}{ll}
A = p & B = .5(1-p)(1-q)g^3 \\
C = (1-p)qc & D = .5(1-p)(1-q)g^2(1-h) \\
E = (1-p)q(1-c)c & F = .5(1-p)(1-q)gh(1-h) \\
G = (1-p)q(1-c)^2c & H = .5(1-p)(1-q)h^2(1-h) \\
I = .5(1-p)(1-q)h^3 & J = (1-p)q(1-c)^3.
\end{array}$$

With these abbreviations, the formal definition of **X** is

$$\begin{array}{c} \\ cccc \\ ccce \\ ccec \\ ccee \\ cecc \\ cece \\ ceec \\ ceee \\ eccc \\ ecce \\ ecec \\ ecee \\ eecc \\ eece \\ eeec \\ eeee \end{array}
\begin{array}{c}
\begin{array}{ccc} \text{Correct} & \text{Switching} & \text{Repeat errors} \end{array} \\
\left[\begin{array}{ccc}
A/(A+B) & B/(A+B) & 0 \\
0 & 1 & 0 \\
0 & 1 & 0 \\
0 & 1 & 0 \\
0 & 1 & 0 \\
0 & 1 & 0 \\
0 & 1 & 0 \\
0 & 1 & 0 \\
C/(C+D) & D/(C+D) & 0 \\
0 & 1 & 0 \\
0 & 1 & 0 \\
0 & 1 & 0 \\
E/(E+F) & F/(E+F) & 0 \\
0 & 1 & 0 \\
G/(G+H) & H/(G+H) & 0 \\
0 & I/(I+J) & J/(I+J).
\end{array}\right]
\end{array}$$

With matrix **X** as our clue to the child's strategy at the end of a problem, we needed another matrix to specify the probabilities of the child keeping that strategy or adopting a new one for the next problem. For this purpose, we used a 3×3 matrix **Y** that gave the probabilities of keeping or changing strategies. Matrix **Y** is a transition matrix in the terminology of Markov models. Here is its formal definition:

	Strategy $i + 1$		
Strategy i	Correct	Switching	Repeat errors
Correct	u	$(1 - u)r$	$(1 - u)(1 - r)$
Switching	$(1 - v)s$	v	$(1 - v)(1 - s)$
Repeat errors	$(1 - w)t$	$(1 - w)(1 - t)$	w

See Table 3.7 for definitions of the transition parameters in **Y**.

Using **X** and **Y** as starting and transition matrices, we completed the diagnostic model with a 3×16 matrix **Z** that is analogous to a response vector in a classical Markov model. Matrix **Z** mapped the child's unobservable strategy at the outset of a problem onto the probabilities of the 16 observable sequences. These probabilities followed from our learning model for modular components.

For example, consider the sequences a child could produce, given that the child started a problem with the repeat-errors strategy. The only possible sequences and their respective probabilities are

$$\Pr(eccc) = c, \qquad \Pr(eeec) = c(1 - c)^2,$$
$$\Pr(eecc) = c(1 - c), \qquad \Pr(eeee) = (1 - c)^3.$$

TABLE 3.7. Descriptions of transition parameters for diagnostic model of strategies.

Parameter	Description
r	Probability of moving to the switching strategy, conditional on not staying with the correct strategy
s	Probability of moving to the correct strategy, conditional on not staying with the switching strategy
t	Probability of moving to the correct strategy, conditional on not staying with the repeat-errors strategy
u	Probability of staying with the correct strategy
v	Probability of staying with the switching strategy
w	Probability of staying with the repeat-errors strategy

Notice that these are conditional probabilities and that they sum to 1. The formal expression of all such probabilities defined matrix **Z** (which we show transposed to fit the page):

$$
\begin{array}{l}
 \\
cccc \\ ccce \\ ccec \\ ccee \\ cecc \\ cece \\ ceec \\ ceee \\ eccc \\ ecce \\ ecec \\ ecee \\ eecc \\ eece \\ eeec \\ eeee
\end{array}
\begin{array}{ccc}
\text{Correct} & \text{Switching} & \text{Repeat errors} \\
\end{array}
$$

$$
\begin{array}{l}
cccc \\ ccce \\ ccec \\ ccee \\ cecc \\ cece \\ ceec \\ ceee \\ eccc \\ ecce \\ ecec \\ ecee \\ eecc \\ eece \\ eeec \\ eeee
\end{array}
\left[\begin{array}{clc}
1 & .5g^3 & 0 \\
0 & .5g^2(1-g) & 0 \\
0 & .5g(1-g)(1-h) & 0 \\
0 & .5g(1-g)h & 0 \\
0 & .5g(1-g)(1-h) & 0 \\
0 & .5(1-g)^2(1-h) & 0 \\
0 & .5(1-g)h(1-h) & 0 \\
0 & .5(1-g)h^2 & 0 \\
0 & .5g^2(1-h) & c \\
0 & .5g(1-g)(1-h) & 0 \\
0 & .5(1-g)(1-h)^2 & 0 \\
0 & .5(1-g)h(1-h) & 0 \\
0 & .5gh(1-h) & c(1-c) \\
0 & .5(1-g)h(1-h) & 0 \\
0 & .5h^2(1-h) & c(1-c)^2 \\
0 & .5h^3 & (1-c)^3
\end{array}\right].
$$

The matrix product **XYZ** generated a 16 × 16 matrix of predicted transitions from an observed sequence on one problem to the observed sequence on the next problem. To fit these predictions to our data, we used standard methods of maximum likelihood. These methods gave us estimates of the parameters in matrices **X, Y,** and **Z** that yielded the best-fitting predictions for our empirical 16 × 16 matrix. In addition, we imposed constraints on the parameters to test various hypotheses.

Data

To test the diagnostic model of strategies, we formed a 16 × 16 table. The rows in the table were the 16 possible sequences of four blocks; the columns were the same 16 sequences. In the body of the table, we tallied the frequencies with which children moved from the row sequence on one problem to the column sequence on the next problem. For example, the entry corresponding to row *eecc* and column *cccc* contained the frequency with which children produced *eecc* on one problem and *cccc* on the next. To keep the table from being too sparse, we collapsed over children, problems, pre- and posttest, and training conditions. However, to minimize training effects, we omitted data for the move from the last problem in the pretest to the initial problem in the posttest. This move was the one most likely to be affected by the training condition.

Results

A summary of the results appears in Table 3.8. Embedded in these results are several tests of hypotheses. Mathematically, all the hypotheses concerned values of parameters in matrix **Y** which defined transitions among unobservable strategies. Conceptually, each of the hypotheses assumed that the transitions were, in some respect, random. Our purpose in testing these hypotheses was to determine whether changes in the children's strategies were systematic or random.

First, we tested the hypothesis $r = s = t = .5$. Acceptance of this hypothesis would imply that when children abandoned a strategy, they were equally likely to move to either of the two remaining strategies. We could not reject this hypothesis, $\chi^2(3) = 5.53$.

Next, we tested the hypothesis $u = v = w$. Acceptance of this hypothesis would imply that the children were equally likely to keep any of the three strategies. We rejected this hypothesis, $\chi^2(2) = 13.65$, $p < .01$. Following up on this result, we could not reject the hypothesis $u = w$, $\chi^2(1) = .45$, or the hypothesis $v = .33$, $\chi^2(1) = 1.94$. We did, however, reject the hypothesis $u = w = .33$, $\chi^2(2) = 128.32$, $p < .001$. From these results we drew three conclusions about the children's use of strategies.

First, the children often changed strategies between problems. Even the correct strategy was sometimes discarded. One interpretation of this finding is that whatever children knew or learned within a problem, they sometimes abandoned or forgot between problems.

Second, the children favored strategies containing the REPEAT component. The value .33 for v shows that the children had no better than a random tendency to retain the switching strategy, which lacks the REPEAT component. In contrast, the value .71 for u and w shows that the children tended to stay with the correct and repeat-errors strategies, both of which contain the REPEAT component.

TABLE 3.8. Fitted values of transition parameters.

	Strategy $i + 1$		
Strategy i	Correct	Switching	Repeat errors
	Initial unconstrained fit		
Correct	.69	.17	.14
Switching	.36	.44	.20
Repeat errors	.17	.09	.74
	Final constrained fit		
Correct	.71	.14	.14
Switching	.33	.33	.33
Repeat errors	.14	.14	.71

Finally, except for retention of the correct and repeat-errors strategies, the children's use of strategies was effectively random. Following the switching strategy, the children were equally likely to use any of the three strategies. Furthermore, if the children abandoned the correct or repeat-errors strategy, they were equally likely to adopt either of the two remaining strategies.

The reasons for this randomness may be partly methodological. The sparseness of data in our large contingency table reduced the power of our analysis to detect significant effects. In addition, our diagnostic model assumed that the child's strategy after selecting the fourth block on a problem was the same as the child's strategy at the end of the problem. Although the first four blocks are a good diagnostic of the child's strategy, they are surely imperfect. We might have done better, had we used a matrix that mapped transitions from the last four blocks on one problem to the first four blocks on the next problem. Then, however, the **X** matrix for our diagnostic model would have been very complex. Thus, some randomness in the data may have been a price we paid for keeping the model tractable.

The data were not entirely random, however, and there were theoretical reasons to expect a mixture of systematic effects and randomness. According to the theory of partial knowledge, the children knew the components needed to solve block-stacking problems, but had trouble assembling the components into a correct and consistent strategy. Correct knowledge of the components, coupled with imperfect assembly, would cause the children's strategies to be right on occasion but inconsistent.

To see why such behavior fits the results from our diagnostic model, consider the example of a child who used the correct strategy on a given problem. The child must have used both components, INDICATE and REPEAT, correctly. However, on the next problem, according to the results from the diagnostic model, the child could use any of the three strategies. (1) With probability .71, the child would again adopt the correct strategy and use both components correctly. (2) With probability .14, the child would apply the switching strategy, which uses INDICATE alone, sometimes correctly and sometimes not. (3) With probability .14, the child would apply the repeat-errors strategy, which always uses REPEAT correctly and occasionally corrects an initial misuse of INDICATE.

As this example shows, the estimated probabilities in the diagnostic model supported our assertion that the children knew the individual components for block stacking, but needed to learn how to assemble them into an effective strategy. The children's inconsistency in assembling components was the reason for their sporadic correctness and the basis of their shifts in strategy.

Conclusions: States and Transitions Reconsidered

At the outset, we asserted that our research concentrated on analyzing transitions during development, not on identifying states or stages in a developmental sequence. A good way to summarize and evaluate our research is to review this assertion in light of our findings.

There were three kinds of transitions in our analyses, each with its own mathematical model. First, the model of double assessment used transitions between pretest and posttest to study the stability of children's knowledge. Second, the Markov models of learning used transitions from block to block within a single problem to study how children learn components. Finally, our diagnostic model of strategies used transitions between problems to study how children assemble components into strategies. Concentrating on these three kinds of transitions enabled us to analyze in unusual detail how the children's behavior changed over time.

In effect, by studying transitions we observed the fine points of cognitive development as it unfolded. None of our models, however, specified a traditional developmental sequence, in which children pass through an ordered series of fixed states or stages. The closest we came to specifying a developmental sequence was in the Markov model of learning. The states in the general Markov model might be viewed as developmental states. Nonetheless, the model failed, on two counts, to qualify as a traditional developmental sequence. First, the model explicitly assumed that a child could pass through the states in any of several possible orders. Second, we eventually interpreted the states to be labile strategies. Thus, even in the model that best fit the traditional mold, the sequence of states was more variable than in a fixed developmental sequence, and the states themselves were fluid.

One might argue that, because we did not identify stages of growth and because we observed children's progress in a 30-minute study, our research was about learning, not about development. Indeed, we got one of our models, the Markov model of learning, from mathematical learning theory. The issues we examined with our models of transition, however, were issues central to developmental theory.

There are three such issues. First, the model of transitions between pretest and posttest used ω to measure the stability of children's emerging knowledge. In this way, we quantified the assumption made by Piaget (1970, 1971) and others that children's knowledge is unstable during developmental transitions. Second, by fitting models to transitions within individual problems, we found evidence that the children detected and corrected their own errors as they worked on block-stacking problems. This self-corrective behavior, which we quantified with parameters c, g, and h in the componential model of learning, was solid evidence of self-regulation. Brown, DeLoache, and their colleagues (Brown & DeLoache,

1978; Brown, Bransford, Ferrara, & Campione, 1983; DeLoache & Brown, 1984; DeLoache, Brown, & Sugarman, 1985) have argued that self-regulation is important in children's cognitive growth. Finally, the model of transitions between problems provided a new way to quantify how children investigate alternative strategies. Arguing both sides of the question, other developmentalists have claimed that children are consistent (e.g., Siegler, 1976, 1981) or flexible (e.g., Flavell, 1980; Klahr, 1985; Shatz, 1976, 1983) in using strategies. Rarely have developmentalists been able to substantiate their claims by measuring children's probability of keeping or switching strategies; Brainerd (1979, 1982) is the exception.

Thus, the major contribution of the methods discussed in this chapter is to quantify concepts that many psychologists have proposed qualitatively in analyses of cognitive development. Quantifying the concepts makes them testable.

While arguing that our methods are a substantive advance, we recognize that they have limitations. One restriction is that they work only for certain tasks. The Markov models of learning and the diagnostic model of strategies require a task in which the child produces a sequence of discrete actions, such as selecting individual blocks. Furthermore, the actions must be scorable as individually correct or erroneous. The model of double assessment requires a task in which a child's performance on a whole problem can be scored as correct or erroneous, and the problem must allow repeated testing. Important areas of development, such as children's acquisition of language, may lack tasks that fit these requirements. Another limitation of our methods is that they look at fine details of children's behavior, and in doing so they risk missing the forest for the trees. Advances in mathematical models, here and elsewhere, are a two-edged sword. Better models offer more detailed analyses of increasingly specific phenomena. But the benefit of precision comes at the cost of specialization.

References

Anderson, N. H. (1980). Information integration theory in developmental psychology. In F. Wilkening, J. Becker, & T. Trabasso (Eds.), *Information integration by children* (pp. 1–45). Hillsdale, NJ: Erlbaum.

Ashcraft, M. H. (1982). The development of mental arithmetic: A chronometric approach. *Developmental Review, 2,* 213–236.

Bazaraa, M. S., & Shetty, C. M. (1979). *Nonlinear programming: Theory and algorithms.* New York: Wiley.

Bishop, Y. M. M., Fienberg, S. E., & Holland, P. W. (1975). *Discrete multivariate analysis: Theory and practice.* Cambridge, MA: M.I.T.

Brainerd, C. J. (1979). Markovian interpretations of conservation learning. *Psychological Review, 86,* 181–213.

Brainerd, C. J. (1982). Children's concept learning as rule-sampling systems with Markovian properties. In C. J. Brainerd (Ed.), *Children's logical and mathematical cognition: Progress in cognitive development research* (pp. 177–212). New York: Springer-Verlag.

Brainerd, C. J., Howe, M. L., & Desrochers, A. (1982). The general theory of two-stage learning: A mathematical review with illustrations from memory development. *Psychological Bulletin, 91,* 634–665.

Brown, A. L., Bransford, J. D., Ferrara, R. A., & Campione, J. C. (1983). Learning, remembering, and understanding. In J. H. Flavell & E. M. Markman (Eds.), *Cognitive development* [P. H. Mussen (Ed.), *Handbook of child psychology* (Vol. 3, pp. 75–166]. New York: Wiley.

Brown, A. L., & DeLoache, J. S. (1978). Skills, plans, and self-regulation. In R. S. Siegler (Ed.), *Children's thinking: What develops?* (pp. 3–35). Hillsdale, NJ: Erlbaum.

Bryant, P. E., & Trabasso, T. R. (1971). Transitive inferences and memory in young children. *Nature, 232,* 456–458.

Carmichael, L. (1970). Onset and early development of behavior. In P. H. Mussen (Ed.), *Carmichael's manual of child psychology* (3d ed., Vol. 1, pp. 447–564). New York: Wiley.

Chase, W. G., & Simon, H. A. (1973). Perception in chess. *Cognitive Psychology, 4,* 55–81.

Chi, M. T. H., Glaser, R., & Rees, E. (1982). Expertise in problem-solving. In R. J. Sternberg (Ed.), *Advances in the psychology of human intelligence* (Vol. 1, pp. 7–75). Hillsdale, NJ: Erlbaum.

DeLoache, J. S., & Brown, A. L. (1984). Intelligent searching by very young children. *Developmental Psychology, 20,* 37–44.

DeLoache, J. S., Brown, A. L., & Sugarman, S. (1985). The development of error correction strategies in young children's manipulative play. *Child Development, 56,* 928–939.

Flavell, J. H. (1980). On cognitive development. *Child Development, 53,* 1–10.

Gelman, R., & Gallistel, C. R. (1978). *The child's understanding of number.* Cambridge, MA: Harvard.

Greeno, J. G. (1974). Representation of learning as discrete transition in a finite state space. In D. H. Krantz, R. C. Atkinson, R. D. Luce, & P. Suppes (Eds.), *Contemporary developments in mathematical psychology* (Vol. 1, pp. 1–43). San Francisco: Freeman.

Haines, B. A. (1983). *Children's partial knowledge: Training the components of a quantitative concept.* Unpublished master's thesis, University of Wisconsin, Madison.

Klahr, D. (1985). Solving problems with ambiguous subgoal ordering: Preschoolers' performance. *Child Development, 56,* 940–952.

Mood, A. M., Graybill, F. A., & Boes, D. C. (1974). *Introduction to the theory of statistics* (3d ed.). New York: McGraw-Hill.

Piaget, J. (1970). Piaget's theory. In P. H. Mussen (Ed.), *Carmichael's manual of child psychology* (3d ed., Vol. 1, pp. 703–732). New York: Wiley.

Piaget, J. (1971). *Biology and knowledge.* Chicago: University of Chicago Press.

Shatz, M. (1976). The relationship between cognitive processes and the development of communication skills. In C. B. Keasey (Ed.), *Nebraska symposium on motivation.* Lincoln: University of Nebraska Press.

Shatz, M. (1983). Communication. In J. H. Flavell & E. M. Markman (Eds.), *Cognitive development* [P. H. Mussen (Ed.), *Handbook of child psychology,* Vol. 3, pp. 841–889]. New York: Wiley.

Siegler, R. S. (1976). Three aspects of cognitive development. *Cognitive Psychology, 8,* 481–520.

Siegler, R. S. (1981). Developmental sequences within and between concepts. *Monographs of the Society for Research in Child Development, 46* (2, Serial No. 189).

Siegler, R. S., & Robinson, M. (1982). The development of numerical understandings. In H. W. Reese & L. P. Lipsitt (Eds.), *Advances in child development and behavior* (Vol. 16, pp. 242–312). New York: Academic.

Sternberg, R. J. (1977). *Intelligence, information processing, and analogical reasoning: The componential analysis of human abilities.* Hillsdale, NJ: Erlbaum.

Sternberg, R. J., & Nigro, G. (1980). Developmental patterns in the solution of verbal analogies. *Child Development, 51,* 27–38.

Sternberg, R. J., & Powell, J. S. (1983). The development of intelligence. In J. H. Flavell & E. M. Markman (Eds.), *Cognitive development* [P. H. Mussen (Ed.), *Handbook of child psychology* (Vol. 3, pp. 341–419)]. New York: Wiley.

Surber, C. F. (1984). Issues in using quantitative rating scales in developmental research. *Psychological Bulletin, 95,* 226–246.

Wilkening, F. (1981). Integrating velocity, time, and distance information: A developmental study. *Cognitive Psychology, 13,* 231–247.

Wilkinson, A. C. (1982a). Partial knowledge and self-correction: Developmental studies of a quantitative concept. *Developmental Psychology, 18,* 874–891.

Wilkinson, A. C. (1982b). Theoretical and methodological analysis of partial knowledge. *Developmental Review, 2,* 274–304.

Wilkinson, A. C. (1984). Children's partial knowledge of the cognitive skill of counting. *Cognitive Psychology, 16,* 28–64.

4. Formal Representation of Qualitative and Quantitative Reversible Operations

Colleen F. Surber

In this chapter I present an approach using contemporary mathematical models of human judgment to explore the issue of whether the relations among a set of variables are conceptualized reversibly. Specifically, are the judgments of each of a set of variables based on a single, fully reversible set of mental operations?[1] This topic is important to psychologists for three reasons. Piaget (1947/1960) proposed that reversible mental operations distinguish true intelligence from intuition and perception. If the transition to reversible thought is an important developmental event, then there is a need for precise representations of knowledge that is reversible. It is equally important to describe states of irreversible and partially reversible knowledge in order to describe the transition from irreversible to reversible thought.

Second, the study of reversibility is important because of the proposal that reversible mental operations or structures are the basis of social inferences and that predictions of an event and attributions of its causes should be based on the same cognitive operations or structure (Kelley, 1972, 1973). Kelley's idea is very similar to Piaget's proposal that reversible thought underlies true intelligence. Third, collecting judgments of one variable given other related variables is a commonly used way of assessing a person's concept of the relations among the variables (Birnbaum, 1976; Brehmer, 1974; Brehmer & Slovic, 1980; Slovic & Lichtenstein, 1971). If judgment methods are to be useful for this purpose, it is important to know the extent to which the results depend on what variable of a set is judged. Examining reversibility by having the subject judge two or more variables gives a more complete picture of the underlying concept in that it uses the principle of converging operations to assess the concept.

An obvious way to determine whether a person possesses a reversible structure for a set of variables *A, B,* and *C* is to ask the person to make three types of judgments: (1) judge variable *A* given information about variables *B* and *C,* (2) judge variable *B* given information about variables *A* and *C,* and (3) judge variable *C* given information about variables *A* and *B*. If the person conceptualizes variables *A, B,* and *C* as part of the same reversible structure, then judgments of the three variables ought to show some sort of correspondence. Although we can all probably agree with this assertion, when we ask exactly what type of correspondence is necessary to conclude that a person has a reversible structure, the issue becomes less clear.

In the exposition below, first, I present the general approach and a theoretical perspective on human judgment. Second, I summarize previous research on whether social judgments are based on reversible mental operations or structures, as hypothesized by Kelley. By using judgments of ability, effort, and performance, my research (as well as that of others) provides evidence that although there is development in the reversible operation that Piaget termed *compensation,* even the judgments of college-age subjects cannot be characterized as based on a fully reversible structure. Third, I present findings from judgments of nonsocial variables that are similar to the results for social judgments. Finally, I consider the implications of the results for the appropriate theoretical representation of the mental operations and cognitive states of judgment. Specifically, what is the nature of the mental operations of judgment that are represented by mathematical models? How can we construct a theory that predicts when judgments will show reversibility and when they will not?

A Theoretical Perspective on Human Judgment

Figure 4.1 presents the functional-measurement approach to the judgment process (Anderson, 1979; Birnbaum, 1982; Birnbaum, Parducci, & Gifford, 1971). The objective stimuli presented to the subject are represented at the left of the diagram. These stimuli are evaluated subjectively, resulting in implicit values or scale values, denoted S_i. The psychophysical function H relates the objective stimuli to their subjective, psychological values.

The subjective values of the stimuli are then combined according to some set of assumptions to form an integrated impression, denoted ψ_{ij}. The manner in which the subjective values are combined is called the *information integration function* and is represented by the symbol I in Figure 4.1. The information integration process is usually represented by an equation in terms of the scale values and other parameters such as weights. The final step in the judgment process is to translate the impression ψ_{ij} to a response R_{ij} on the judgment scale. This final transformation is called the *judgment function* by Birnbaum et al. (1971) or the *psychomotor law* by Anderson (1980) and is denoted by J in the figure. And J is assumed to be at least a strictly monotonic function of the values of ψ_{ij}, although some researchers explicitly or implicitly assume it to be linear. The observable response R_{ij} is thus the result of the composition of the functions H, I, and J.

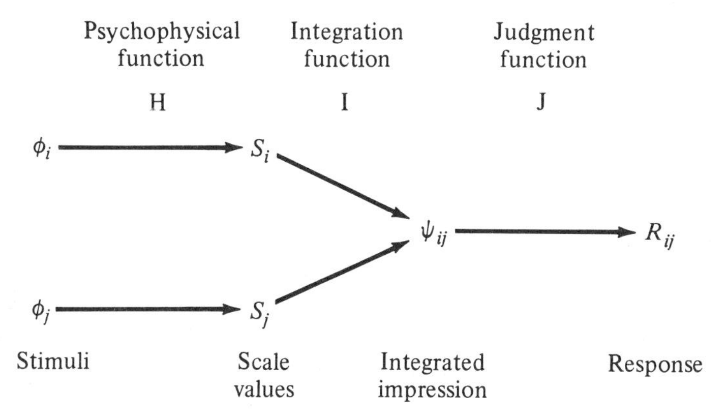

FIGURE 4.1. Outline of judgment (after Birnbaum, 1974b). Subscripts i and j at left represent the stimuli that are presented, S_i and S_j represent the subjective values of the stimuli, ψ_{ij} represents the integrated impression based on the stimuli, and R_{ij} represents the subject's response on the rating scale.

Several aspects of the functional-measurement approach make it particularly useful for developmental research. First, it provides a powerful tool for formally expressing and testing theories of how people combine information. This is an advantage because many developmental experiments are concerned with changes in information integration (see Surber, 1985a, for a review of applications of the functional-measurement approach to a variety of social concepts). Second, the approach allows description of both gradual, quantitative developmental changes (as change in parameter values in the equations representing information integration) and qualitative developmental changes (as changes in the form of the equation representing the information integration process). Third, as I have discussed in detail elsewhere (Surber, 1984c), individual strategies for combining information can be assessed, although a relatively large number of observations are needed on each subject. Fourth, the three global processing stages outlined in Figure 4.1 force the researcher to consider the possible loci of developmental change: the psychophysical function, the integration function, or the judgment function. As is shown below, age differences in rating scale responses do not necessarily imply age differences in information integration, although many researchers attempt to draw such conclusions.

Given the analysis of judgment processes in Figure 4.1, what constitutes evidence of a reversible mental structure or operations? Theoretically, the judgment function J in Figure 4.1 does not represent the person's underlying concept of the relations among a set of variables. Rather, J represents how the person translates the underlying impression or concept into a response and is influenced by variables such as the distribution of stimuli (Birnbaum, 1974a; Mellers & Birnbaum, 1983) and instructions (Birnbaum & Viet, 1974). According to this view, evidence of a reversible mental structure for a set of variables should be found in the integrated impressions but not necessarily in the final responses. Therefore, the integration functions I for judgments of a set of variables are what should be reversible.

Algebraic versus Statistical Reversibility

The integration functions for a set of variables can constitute a reversible structure in two different ways. Suppose that judgments of variable A can be represented as an additive function of the scale values of variables B and C, $R_A = J_A(B + C)$, where R_A is the observed judgment of A, J_A is a monotonic function representing the judgment function, and B and C represent the scale values of variables B and C. A fully reversible mental structure for variables A, B, and C could require that judgments of variable B be a monotonic transformation of the difference between A and C, $R_B = J_B(A - C)$, and analogously for variable C. In other words, the integration functions for judgments of a set of variables should be based on a single equation solved for the variable to be judged. Henceforth, I call this *algebraic reversibility*.

A second possible criterion for reversibility states that the integration functions for judgments of a set of variables should be based on the same set of subjective statistical relationships among the variables. This approach assumes that humans are "intuitive statisticians" (Peterson & Beach, 1967). In this view of reversibility the integration functions for the judged variables are all subjective multiple regression equations derived from a single set of subjective correlations. The weight of each variable is then the standardized regression weight (Birnbaum, 1976). For example, if judgments of A could be represented by the equation

$$R_A = J_A \left[\frac{(r_{AB} - r_{AC}r_{BC})S_B}{1 - r_{BC}^2} + \frac{(r_{AC} - r_{AB}r_{BC})S_C}{1 - r_{BC}^2} \right],$$

then judgments of B should agree with the equation

$$R_B = J_B \left[\frac{(r_{AB} - r_{AC}r_{BC})S_A}{1 - r_{AC}^2} + \frac{(r_{BC} - r_{AB}r_{AC})S_C}{1 - r_{AC}^2} \right],$$

where the r's represent the subjective correlations between the subscripted variables and the S's are the scale values of the subscripted variables. This criterion is termed *statistical reversibility*.

Inverse Compensation

These two criteria for reversibility, algebraic and statistical, lead to different predictions about the results of an experiment in which a person is asked to judge each of a set of interrelated variables. Assume that when a person is asked to judge variable A, given B and C, the person judges A to increase as either B or C increases. The algebraic criterion of reversibility predicts that judgments of B should increase as A increases but decrease as C increases. For example, if $A = B + C$, then $B = A - C$, and if $A = B \cdot C$, then $B = A/C$. Thus, the result that is termed *compensation* or *inverse compensation* in the developmental literature is predicted by using the criterion of algebraic reversibility. The higher variable C, the lower variable B, with A constant. Mathematically sophisticated readers will recognize compensation as the partial derivative of B with respect to C or vice versa (cf. Norman & Schemmer, 1977). In the social attribution literature, this same effect is called the *discounting principle* (Kelley, 1972, 1973).

In contrast, the statistical model for reversibility allows, but does not clearly predict, inverse compensation. Whether inverse compensation occurs will depend on the subjective correlations between the variables. For our example above, the statistical model can predict either that (1) variable B will be judged to be directly related to variable C, holding A constant, or (2) variable B will be judged to be inversely related to variable C, holding A constant. If all the subjective correlations are assumed to be positive, the former result is obtained if $r_{BC} > r_{AB}r_{AC}$, whereas the latter occurs if $r_{BC} < r_{AB}r_{AC}$

Piaget (1947/1960) was clearly considering algebraic reversibility, not statistical reversibility, when he wrote about reversible operations. Algebraic reversibility embodies the basic principles that we think of as involved in functional relations in science, such as the ideal gas law (pressure times volume equals number of moles times temperature times constant), Newton's laws, and simple geometric equations (area of a rectangle equals height times width and volume of a cylinder equals cross-sectional area times height). Piaget used such deterministic functional systems to explore the development of the reversible operation of compensation. The major focus of this chapter is algebraic reversibility, not statistical reversibility. However, statistical reversibility may occur in social judgments (Surber, 1984b) or in situations in which relations among variables are probabilistic. Statistical reversibility may also represent a part of the developmental transition to algebraic reversibility. Thus, the reader should keep the statistical model in mind as an alternative.

Correspondence of Interaction Patterns

A second type of reversibility predicted by the algebraic criterion is termed *correspondence of interaction patterns* (Surber & Gzesh, 1982).[2] As an example, assume that a person's integration rule for judging A is a multiplicative function of variables B and C. For the moment we ignore any potential distortions introduced by the judgment function J. The person's judgments of A should show a significant B by C interaction that should be concentrated in the linear $\times$ linear, or bilinear, component.

When judgments of A are graphed with the marginal means of one given variable (B or C) on the abscissa and a separate curve for each level of the other given variable, the curves should form a linear fan, which, if extrapolated, would intersect in a common point (Anderson, 1974). If the judgments of B (given A and C) are based on the same reversible structure or operations, then judgments of B should also show an $A \times C$ interaction concentrated in the bilinear component and should plot as a linear fan. A set of ideal responses based on the multiplying model for judgments of ability, effort, and performance is shown in Figure 4.2. For an additive integration function, correspondence of interaction patterns predicts that all three types of judgments should show no interaction in analysis of variance and should graph as a set of parallel lines. Correspondence of interactions obviously requires more precise quantitative knowledge of the relations among the variables than does inverse compensation.

An important feature of using judgments to test for reversible operations is that reversibility can be assessed regardless of whether the individual makes judgments that are "correct" or accurate according to some external criterion. According to Acredolo (1981), Piaget's view of the reversible operation of compensation does not entail quantitative accuracy in making judgments. Proportional concepts, described by Piaget (1941/1965, pp. 17–24) as involved in the development of conservation, also do not entail quantitative accuracy in making judgments. In using functional measurement, proportional concepts are revealed by the way variables are combined (represented by the integration function) rather than by whether the judgments are accurate or agree with some external criterion. For example, use of proportional concepts would be shown if judgments of variable A could be represented as a multiplicative combination of the subjective values of variables B and C, and judgments of B could be represented as a ratio of the subjective values of variable C to variable A. The judgments of A and B could be numerically inaccurate. This characteristic of the functional-measurement approach allows us to explore reversibility for social concepts and other tasks where there is no standard for correctness.

The Judgment Function and Reversibility

If reversible structures are represented by the integration function, then testing the hypothesis that a person conceptualizes a set of variables reversibly requires methods of separating the integration function from the judgment function. Failure to include the possibility that the judgment function can change with the variable being judged is equivalent to requiring the judgments to be in exact numerical agreement. For example, imagine that judgments of variable A, given information about variables B

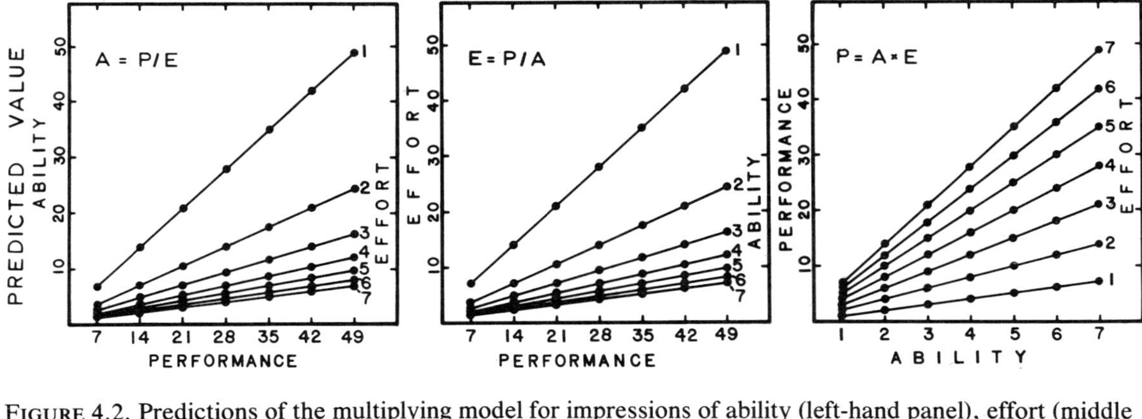

FIGURE 4.2. Predictions of the multiplying model for impressions of ability (left-hand panel), effort (middle panel), and performance (right-hand panel).

and C, were plotted in a three-dimensional space with B on the x axis, C on the y axis, and judged A on the z axis. Then imagine judged B, given that A and C were plotted in the same three-dimensional space. The view that the judgment function cannot vary requires that all the points fall on the same surface in the three-dimensional space. This view of a reversible structure would be contradicted if the data for the three types of judgments fit separate but similarly shaped surfaces in the space. It seems implausible that we would want to say that such a data set is based on irreversible mental operations because the results are merely off by a constant. Thus, allowance must be made for at least linear transformations introduced by the judgment function and possibly other sorts of distortions.

Inverse compensation is a prediction of algebraic reversibility that can be tested without concern for the form of the judgment function J, because J is assumed to preserve rank order (monotonicity) and lack of inverse compensation drastically alters the rank orders of the responses. If two individuals or age groups differ in their use of inverse compensation, the differences can be attributed confidently to differences in either the integration function or the psychophysical function (or in both), rather than to the judgment function. This fact allows the development of inverse compensation to be studied without concern for age shifts or individual differences in the judgment function. To assess correspondence of interaction patterns, however, it is necessary either to make assumptions about the judgment function and use those assumptions to make inferences about the integration function or to use some methods of separating the integration function from the judgment function.

Judgment Function Assumed Linear

A common strategy has been to assume that the judgment function is linear (see Surber, 1984c, for a review). Under this assumption, the integration function can be directly inferred from the pattern of the judgments. For example, a parallel set of curves and a nonsignificant interaction implies an additive integration function (Butzin & Anderson, 1973), a diverging linear fan and a significant bilinear interaction (with a nonsignificant residual component) implies a multiplicative integration function (Kun, Parsons, & Ruble, 1974), and a plot showing a "slanted barrel" shape with a significant (but not bilinear) interaction implies a relative ratio integration function, for example, $A = B/(B + C)$ (Anderson & Butzin, 1978). The assumption that the judgment function is linear allows a test of the correspondence of interactions by examining the judgments of two or more variables. For example, if judgments of A, given B and C, show a bilinear pattern interpretable as a multiplicative integration function, do judgments of B, given A and C, show a bilinear interaction pattern consistent with a ratio integration function?

Judgment Function Not Necessarily Linear

Interpreting the results of any experiment involving judgments becomes considerably more complex if the judgment function J is not assumed to be linear, but only monotonic (Anderson, 1977; Birnbaum, 1974a; Bogartz, 1976; Bogartz & Wackwitz, 1970; see also Brainerd, Chapter 1, this volume). Presented in Figure 4.3 are three hypothetical data patterns, all derived from the additive integration function shown in the center panel. A negatively accelerated judgment function (in this case, a logarithmic transformation) was applied to produce the results in the left-hand panel and a positively accelerated judgment function (exponential in the example) was applied in order to produce the results in the right-hand panel. The rank orders in the three panels are identical, and the lines connecting the panels show the transformations of the ordinate that map one data set onto another.

Comparison of Figure 4.2 with Figure 4.3 should clarify some of the implications of the preceding example for testing correspondence of interactions. Suppose that the panels of Figure 4.3 were the results of an experiment in which the subjects judged three different interrelated variables. Under the assumption that the judgment function is linear, the investigator would conclude that the judgments do *not* show correspondence of interactions and would reject the hypothesis that the judgments derive from a fully reversible cognitive structure or set of operations. However, if the investigator were more cautious and assumed the judgment function to be only monotonic, then the hypothesis that the judgments are based on a fully reversible cognitive structure would be retained. Thus, we see that the conclusions about correspondence of interactions drawn from a set of data depend on the assumption made about the judgment function.

Methods for Separating the Judgment and Integration Functions

Fortunately, there are methods for separating the judgment function from the integration function, although these methods are difficult to apply in developmental research and consequently have been used infrequently. There are two approaches: two-operation experiments and the scale convergence criterion. Both approaches are based on the idea that by obtaining a richer network of data the number of interpretations that are com-
that are compatible with the complete pattern will be reduced.

Two-Operation Experiments

There are two types of two-operation experiments, those in which subjects are instructed to judge the aggregation (or total) of two stimuli, each composed of components, and those in which subjects are instructed to

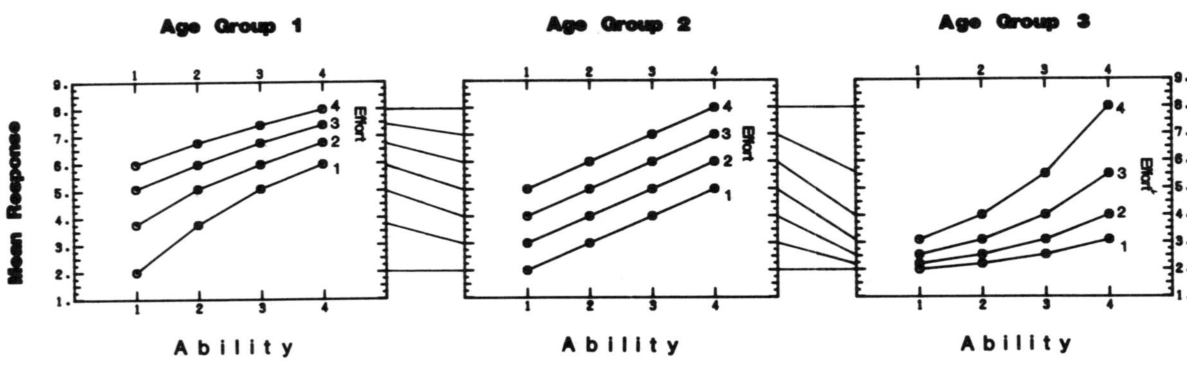

FIGURE 4.3. Hypothetical results illustrating that differences in response patterns do not necessarily imply differences in information integration. The three panels represent predictions of performance based on an additive integration function (performance = effort + ability), subjected to a log transformation (left-hand panel), no transformation (middle panel), and an exponential transformation (right-hand panel). The rank orders of the data are identical in all three panels. Lines connecting the panels show the transformations.

make a judgment based on a comparison of two stimuli, each composed of components. Although both methods provide some additional evidence, collection of comparative judgments has much greater leverage for separating the integration and judgment functions.

Aggregation Approach

An example of an aggregation experiment is found in Anderson and Cuneo (1978, experiment 6). In this experiment, children were asked to judge the combined area of two rectangles at a time (e.g., "How much is there to eat in both rectangles?"). Children were shown combinations of rectangles generated by a 4(7 × 7, 7 × 11, 11 × 7, and 11 × 11 cm) × 2(6 × 5 and 10 × 8 cm) factorial design. Anderson and Cuneo hypothesized that combined area should be judged according to an additive combination rule $R_{12} = J(\psi_1 + \psi_2)$, where R_{12} is the response to the two rectangles, J is any monotonic function, and ψ_1 and ψ_2 represent the impressions of the area of each rectangle. Anderson and Cuneo's goal was to decompose ψ_1 and ψ_2 to discover how width and height are combined in forming an impression of the area of a single rectangle.

One approach to decomposing the total area judgments is to test the fit of the additive model for judgments of total area by using the significance test of the interaction in an analysis of variance. If the rectangle 1 × rectangle 2 interaction is nonsignificant (given reasonable statistical power), then the additive model can be retained, and the judgment function for total area is assumed to be approximately linear. Note that this just moves the assumption that the judgment function is linear from the task of judging single rectangles to the task of judging pairs of rectangles.

Aggregation judgments can also be decomposed by assuming that J is only monotonic. In this case the judgments are monotonically transformed to fit the additive model by using a procedure such as MONANOVA (Kruskal & Carmone, 1969). MONANOVA is a computer program that removes interactions and generates scale values for the stimuli from which the rank-order characteristics of the data can be reproduced. The scale values from MONANOVA can be used to test between additive and nonadditive integration processes for the components in an aggregation experiment. This approach does not require the assumption that the judgment function is linear, but it assumes the validity of the additive model for the aggregation judgments. A discussion of problems in monotonic transformations of response scales is found in Busemeyer (1980).

An important drawback of aggregation models is that the rank-order characteristics of the aggregation ratings cannot discriminate between additive and multiplicative integration of the components because aggregation ratings will be ordinally consistent with the additive model in both cases. Table 4.1 shows a hypothetical set of results for an aggregation experiment involving rectangles. The upper panel shows the predicted

TABLE 4.1. Judged total area for pairs of rectangles.

		Multiplicative combination			
		First rectangle			
		7 × 7	7 × 11	11 × 7	11 × 11
Second rectangle	7 × 7	1	2	2	5
	7 × 11	2	3	3	6
	11 × 7	2	3	3	6
	11 × 11	5	6	6	9
		Additive combination			
		First rectangle			
		7 × 7	7 × 11	11 × 7	11 × 11
Second rectangle	7 × 7	1	3	3	5
	7 × 11	3	5	5	7
	11 × 7	3	5	5	7
	11 × 11	5	7	7	9

Note: The scale values assigned to 7 and 11 were 1 and 3, respectively. The scale values for each rectangle were combined either multiplicatively (top) or additively (bottom) followed by summing the values to produce the predicted aggregated impression. The aggregation values were then linearly transformed to fit a 1-to-9-scale. (The linear transformation is analogous to the judgment function J in that it transforms implicit impressions to fit the designated range of rating scale responses.)

results when the dimensions of each rectangle are combined multiplicatively, whereas the bottom panel shows the predicted results when the dimensions are combined additively. Although the rank orderings in the table differ slightly, both tables meet the tests for additivity of the underlying dimensions (Krantz & Tversky, 1971).

COMPARISON OR "SCALE-FREE" APPROACH

In spite of the fact that developmental researchers frequently ask children to make choices between stimuli (Piaget, 1947/1960; Siegler, 1976, 1981), there has been very little use of comparison designs in developmental research as a method for separating integration and judgment functions. In Birnbaum's (1974a, 1978, 1982) scale-free method, the subject is asked to judge the difference between two stimuli, each of which is composed of two attributes. The judged difference is hypothesized to follow the subtractive model $R_{12} = J(\psi_1 - \psi_2)$, where R_{12} is the judged difference between stimulus compound 1 and 2, J is a monotonic function, and ψ_1 and ψ_2 are the impressions of the two stimulus compounds. For example, in judgments of area children could be presented with pairs of rectangles and asked, "Who would have more to eat, the person with cookie 1 or the person with cookie 2?" Following an initial decision, the child can then be asked to make a quantitative rating of how much more. The difference ratings can be used to test the integration process for height and width for each rectangle.

If the integration function is additive, then when the difference between stimuli that differ on only one dimension is judged, the judgment should depend only on the varying dimension. For example, for judgments of the area of rectangles

$$R = J[(h_i + w_j) - (h_i + w_k)]$$
$$= J(w_j - w_k).$$

In contrast, for the multiplicative integration function, the judgment of the difference between stimuli should depend on both dimensions:

$$R = J[(h_i w_j) - (h_i w_k)]$$
$$= J[h_i(w_j - w_k)].$$

These predictions are shown in Table 4.2, which is analogous to Table 4.1, and presents a hypothetical set of results for an experiment using Birnbaum's scale-free test. The difference data based on the multiplicative combination show ordinal violations of the joint independence axiom required for additivity (Krantz & Tversky, 1971), whereas the data in Table 4.1 based on the additive model do not. If the height and width of rectangles are combined additively, then the difference judgment data should satisfy joint independence for all pairs of factors. Since the difference task is a $2 \times 2 \times 2 \times 2$ design (height of rectangle $1 \times$ width of rectangle $1 \times$ height of rectangle $2 \times$ width of rectangle 2), we can denote each data point as a quadruple (h_1, w_1, h_2, w_2). Joint independence of H_1 and H_2 from W_1 and W_2 requires that if

$$(7, 7, 7, 11) \geq (11, 7, 11, 11),$$
then
$$(7, 11, 7, 7) \geq (11, 11, 11, 7).$$

TABLE 4.2. Judged differences in area for pairs of rectangles.

		Multiplicative combination			
		First rectangle			
		7 × 7	7 × 11	11 × 7	11 × 11
Second rectangle	7 × 7	5	6_b	6	9
	7 × 11	4_a	5	5	8
	11 × 7	4	5	5	8_b
	11 × 11	1	2	2_a	5
		Additive combination			
		First rectangle			
		7 × 7	7 × 11	11 × 7	11 × 11
Second rectangle	7 × 7	5	7_b	7	9
	7 × 11	3_a	5	5	7
	11 × 7	3	5	5	7_b
	11 × 11	1	3	3_a	5

Note: The scale values assigned to 7 and 11 were 1 and 3, respectively. The scale values for each rectangle were combined either multiplicatively (top) or additively (bottom) followed by subtracting the value for rectangle 2 from the value for rectangle 1. The difference values were then linearly transformed to fit a 1-to-9 scale, with 1 indicating rectangle 2 larger than rectangle 1. Subscripted values provide a test of joint independence.

These comparisons are marked with the subscripts *a* and *b*, respectively, in Table 4.2. When height and width are combined multiplicatively (top portion of Table 4.2), joint independence is violated (4 is greater than 2, but 6 is not greater than 8). Thus, the scale-free method provides an ordinal test of the additive model without assuming a linear judgment function. The ordinal violation of additivity makes the scale-free method quite powerful.

Assumptions in Two-Operation Experiments

One assumption that has already been mentioned is that the aggregation or comparison follows a particular hypothesized model (for the examples above, either an additive or a subtractive model). This assumption can be tested ordinally, however, so that a linear judgment function need not be assumed. A second assumption is that the information integration process of primary interest (for example, the combination of height and width to estimate area, or the combination of ability and effort to estimate performance) is not disturbed by embedding it in the aggregation or comparison task. This assumption is obviously open to question in developmental research. When presented with complex cognitive tasks, children may ignore some of the information (Anderson & Butzin, 1978) or may change to a strategy that is more completely mastered (Shatz, 1978). Thus, the results of a two-operation experiment may contradict those of a one-operation information integration experiment and not provide an answer to the original research question.

When subjects do change strategies in making judgments in a two-operation task, it seems likely that they would either center on one dimension of both stimuli across all trials or cancel a stimulus dimension that has equal value across the two stimuli of a trial. For example, subjects might judge the total area of two rectangles by attending only to height (centration). If this were the case, the additive model would fit the total area judgments, but the derived ψ values would show an effect of only height. Thus centration should be obvious in the data.

The strategy of canceling a dimension that has equal value for a stimulus pair seems most likely to occur in comparison judgments. For example, given a 7×11 and a 7×7 cm stimulus, the subject may judge the difference in area by canceling the equal-valued dimension and relying only on the dimension for which the values differ. Which dimension differs will vary between stimulus pairs. For the difference judgment task, this strategy will produce data that agree with the subtractive model. The ψ values derived will show an additive pattern, however. Under these conditions, the investigator could be led to the erroneous conclusion that an additive integration function holds. If the judgments in a one-operation task show significant interactions but the impression values derived from difference judgments support the additive model, then the investigator should be cautious about concluding that the two dimensions are combined additively. Thus, difference judgments provide the most leverage when they support a nonadditive integration process also found in a one-operation experiment.

Scale Convergence Criterion

Integration and judgment functions sometimes can be separated by using more than one type of judgment task and assuming that the scale values for the stimuli are independent of the judgment task. The rationale behind the scale convergence criterion is that measured psychological values should have at least some generality across tasks if they are to have predictive power and theoretical utility (Birnbaum, 1982). In contrast, Marks (1982) prefers to assume that psychological values vary with the experimental procedure, for example, magnitude estimation versus category rating.

The scale convergence criterion is illustrated by an experiment by Birnbaum and Viet (1974), in which adults judged both the differences and ratios of weights lifted simultaneously in the left and right hands. The authors initially hypothesized that the two types of judgments would be based on subtractive and ratio integration processes, respectively, with linear judgment functions. Analyses of variance showed the expected results: Instructions to judge differences resulted in a parallel set of curves; instructions to judge ratios resulted in a bilinear fan of curves.

In practice, the scale convergence criterion requires that scale values derived from the fit of the integration functions to the two sets of judgments be linearly related, allowing the scale values to be unique to a linear transformation. In Birnbaum and Viet's experiment, however, scale values from the subtractive and ratio models showed a nonlinear relationship. Scale values were linearly related when the data from the ratio judgment task were monotonically transformed to fit the subtractive model. Theoretically, the monotonic transformation of the ratio judgments corrects for a nonlinear judgment function. Birnbaum and Viet concluded that rather than using two different integration operations when instructed to judge ratios and differences, subjects used the same integration process and scale values but different judgment functions. Thus, the assumption of scale convergence provides a criterion for distinguishing between the information integration process and the judgment function.

Scale convergence is tested by plotting the scale values for a set of stimuli derived from one judgment task against the scale values derived from a second judgment task. One way to obtain estimates of the scale values is by fitting a hypothesized integration function to the data, by using any of a variety of iterative "brute force" algorithms, such as STEPIT (Chandler, 1969). For the additive and multiplying integration models, it is a convenient fact that the marginal means are a linear function of the scale values if the judgment function is assumed to be linear. For a ratio model, the inverses of the marginal means of the denominator variable can be used. In principle, the scale convergence criterion seems important for assessing reversible operations. Algebraic reversibility requires not only that the integration functions should derive from the same equation, but also that the scale values should correspond across judgment tasks.

Are Social Judgments Reversible?

Correspondence of Interaction Patterns

Functional-measurement methods were first used with judgments of social concepts to test for reversibility in judging a set of interrelated variables (Anderson & Butzin, 1974; Graesser & Anderson, 1974). These studies were conducted with college students and led to the conclusion that "cognitive algebra is not a simple mirror of mathematical algebra" (Anderson & Butzin, 1974, p. 598). Anderson and Butzin (1974) tested three hypotheses: (1) Judged performance equals the product of motivation and ability, (2) judged motivation equals the ratio of performance and ability, and (3) judged ability equals the ratio of performance and motivation (Heider, 1958). Judgments of performance for two different tasks (athletic and academic performance) showed a significant bilinear interaction as predicted by the multiplying model, but judgments of ability for one type of performance showed no significant interaction. For the other type of performance there was a small but not bilinear interaction. The results for judgments of motivation were similar. Under the assumption that the judgment function is linear, Anderson and Butzin's data allow us to reject the hypothesis that the three types of judgments are based on integration functions derived from a single equation. Anderson and Butzin's data showed inverse compensation, however, in that motivation and ability were judged to be inversely related. As we will see, inverse compensation is not a universal finding.

A second experiment testing reversibility was conducted by Graesser and Anderson (1974) who hypothesized that gift size would be judged to be the product of a donor's generosity and income and analogously that generosity would be judged by using the subjective ratio of gift size and income and income would be judged by the subjective ratio of gift size and generosity. The results were quite similar to those of Anderson and Butzin (1974). Judgments of gift size showed a large bilinear interaction of income and generosity, but judgments of generosity and income showed departures from bilinearity. If the judgment function is assumed to be linear, Graesser and Anderson's (1974) data also contradict the hypothesis that a fully reversible structure or reversible operations underlie social predictions and inferences. As in the Anderson and Butzin (1974) study, Graesser and Anderson's data also showed inverse compensation. Generosity and income were judged to be inversely related at constant levels of gift size. If the assumption of response scale linearity is questioned, however, the hypothesis that judgments reflect a fully reversible system cannot be rejected. The data of both studies are ordinally consistent with additive and subtractive models, and so some method of separating the integration and judgment functions should be employed.

I conducted two studies with college students to separate the integration and judgment functions and provide a better test of the hypothesis that judgments of performance, ability, and effort were based on a reversible operational system (Surber, 1978). In the first experiment I used seven values for each variable, thereby providing a better assessment of scale convergence. In the second experiment, subjects judged the differences in performance, ability, and effort between pairs of hypothetical individuals, so that the scale-free test could be applied. The results were disappointing but also informative. In the first experiment I found inverse compensation for judgments of ability and effort, but my data did not replicate Anderson and Butzin's finding of a bilinear interaction of ability and effort in judgments of performance. Since then I have replicated my own findings (Surber, 1981a, 1981b, 1985c), and data collected in India appear quite similar to mine (Singh, Gupta, & Dalal, 1979). For judgments of ability and effort the data also showed unexpected interactions, but they did not agree with the performance judgment pattern. Assessments of scale convergence for the three variables both before and after rescaling to additivity were again inconclusive. Seven scale values may be adequate, but where the interactions are not dramatic there is little effect of rescaling to additivity on scale convergence. In Birnbaum and Viet's (1974) study, the judgments of ratios of lifted weights were dramatically nonparallel, so that rescaling to additivity noticeably changed the scale values. My data were also ordinally consistent with additive and subtractive models, and because the scale convergence test did not provide the leverage to separate the integration and judgment functions, the experiment did not allow rejection of the reversibility hypothesis.

My second experiment was designed around Birnbaum's scale-free test and also failed to separate the integration and judgment functions. In the scale-free test judgments of the differences between pairs of stimuli (e.g., how much better will person 1 perform than person 2?) are assumed to follow a subtractive integration function. Metric properties of my data were inconsistent with the subtractive model (there were large interactions for judgments of differences in performance, ability, and effort). Rescaling the means to additivity by using MONANOVA showed that there were some ordinal violations of the subtractive model, invalidating the scale-free test.

The real problems with my scale-free experiment were not immediately evident, however. It appeared that a fair proportion of the subjects were using a cancellation strategy when stimuli had one component in common. A second problem was that a number of the subjects seemed to be confusing the ends of the response scale in judging the differences in ability and effort. For example, when asked to judge who has higher ability, someone with an examination score of 150 who studied 20 h or someone with an exam score of 150 who studied 5 h, a fair proportion of subjects rated the one who studied 20 h as *higher* in ability. I assumed that these responses were a confusion of the ends of the response scale owing to inattentiveness. I discarded subjects who made a large number of these "errors" for failing to follow instructions. For those with only a few of these errors, I reversed their responses. Based on more recent findings (Surber, 1984b), I now believe these subjects were failing to show inverse compensation. Thus, the difference judgment task, in this case, may have induced a fundamentally different strategy for combining the information for a number of subjects. This makes use of the difference judgments to separate the integration and judgment function impossible in this case.

I again tested the hypothesis that judgments of ability, effort, and performance are based on a single reversible operational system, but for a physical task (lifting weights) and with a wide age range of subjects (6-year-olds to college students) (Surber, 1980). In addition, to apply the scale-free test, I included six trials of difference judgments. A disadvantage of this study was that each subject judged only one variable. The college students' judgments of performance showed the bilinear pattern predicted by the multiplying integration model, replicating Anderson and Butzin (1974). The scale-free test in this experiment supported the interpretation of the bilinear interaction in performance judgments as due to the integration function. The interactions in the judgments of ability and effort did not show the bilinear form, so once again social judgments failed to show a fully reversible pattern.

In another study (Surber, 1981b), I manipulated the difficulty of the task on which performance was to be judged, and I collected judgments of performance, ability, and effort from college students. The performance judgments showed three different patterns. For the task described as difficult, judged performance showed an approximately bilinear and diverging interaction of ability and effort, as predicted by a multiplying model. For the easy task, judged performance showed a converging interaction of ability and effort, and for the moderate-difficulty task the pattern was approximately parallel. The key question is whether the patterns of judgment of ability and effort agreed with the pattern of performance judgments for each type of task. They did not. For all three tasks, judgments of ability and effort showed a pattern similar to that predicted by the ratio model (ability = performance/effort, and effort = performance/ability). As in previous work with college students (Anderson & Butzin,

1974; Kun, 1977; Surber, 1978, 1980), these judgments showed inverse compensation.

An important issue is whether task difficulty influenced the information integration process or the judgment function for judgments of performance. If change in the judgment function cannot be excluded, then it is possible to assume that judgments of ability, effort, and performance are based on fully reversible operations. Because this experiment used only four stimulus values for each variable, I did not assess scale convergence, nor did I attempt the scale-free method. Instead I administered a questionnaire assessing subjects' beliefs about how ability and effort are related to performance for each of the three tasks: easy, moderate, and difficult. The questions asked the subjects to report the degree to which a given level of performance was determined by *either* one of the two factors (e.g., to get a low score on the difficult examination, either a low IQ or low study effort is alone sufficient) or by both variables in combination (e.g., to get a high score on the difficult examination, both a high IQ and a high study effort are necessary). Questionnaire ratings varied with task difficulty in the expected way. For the difficult task, subjects believed that high performance required both high ability and high effort, but that low performance would occur in the presence of either low ability or low effort. For the easy task, high performance was seen as possible based on either high ability or high effort, whereas low performance required both low ability and low effort.

These results constrain the possible interpretations of the different patterns of judgment of performance. One might assume that the belief responses are based on the subject's reflection on his or her pattern of judgments, not on a reflection on how one combines the information. This viewpoint questions the concept of a reversible cognitive structure as a set of assumptions about the relations among the variables that can be used to make judgments of any of the variables, as proposed by Kelley (1972, 1973). Reported assumptions, in this interpretation, are unrelated to the way subjects actually combine information, and so there would be no reason to predict coherence across judged dimensions. An alternative is to view the belief questionaire as a different way of assessing some aspects of the integration function. In this case, the belief questionnaire could then be taken as evidence that the information integration process (and not just the judgment function) for judgments of performance varies with the difficulty of the task on which performance is judged. To answer the reversibility question, however, we are still left with the issue of whether variation in the judgment function could have disguised the integration function for the judgments of ability and effort. Thus the hypothesis that judgments of ability, effort, and performance are based on an algebraically reversible structure can maintain its viability if it is assumed that there are different nonlinear judgment functions for the three task difficulty levels for judgments of ability and effort.

Summary

I have reviewed five studies testing the hypothesis that social judgments are based on a fully reversible cognitive structure or set of operations. None produced solid evidence supporting the hypothesis. However, the hypothesis that the judgments are not a linear function of the subjective impressions produced by combinations of information prevents a firm rejection of the reversibility hypothesis.

Inverse Compensation

In the studies described so far, college students typically showed inverse compensation in judging social variables. One exception was in my dissertation study (Surber, 1978) in which college students judged the differences in ability and effort between pairs of hypothetical individuals. Based on the developmental literature on the development of compensation (Brainerd, 1976; Larsen & Flavell, 1970), we would expect to see rather dramatic developmental change in inverse compensation in social judgments. Since I have recently reviewed these findings in detail (Surber, 1984a), I recapitulate them here only briefly.

Kun (1977, study 1) gave children in first, third, and fifth grades combinations of information about the performance (1, 4, or 7 puzzles done) and effort (barely tried at all, tried a little, tried very hard) of hypothetical individuals solving puzzles. Subjects were asked to judge how "good at puzzles" each story character was. Kun found no significant main effect of effort and no interaction of age group and effort. I replicated these results in a study in which children in kindergarten, third and fifth grades, and college students judged the strength of hypothetical weight lifters, given the size of weight lifted (very very light, kind of light, kind of heavy, or very very heavy) and the effort expended (did not try at all, tried a little bit, tried pretty hard, and tried very very hard). There was no main effect of effort and no age by effort interaction when the college sample was excluded. Examination of the data showed that some children judged ability to be directly related to effort (a pattern Kun called the *halo schema*) and others judged ability to be inversely related to effort.

Formal criteria were developed to separate the children into groups based on the slope of their judgments of ability as a function of effort. For each of the elementary school age groups, some of the children showed inverse compensation whereas others judged ability to increase as effort increased. Analyses of judgments of the differences in ability showed the same two response strategies. Thus, the lack of a main effect of effort on the children's ability judgments was not due to neglect of the effort information. Almost all the children made use of the effort information, but they used it in two different ways. A second finding was that age was not related to the proportion of children showing inverse compensation. Reanalyses of the data of Kun's (1977) study 1 showed the same type of individual differences in inverse compensation, with little age change. Based on these two studies it appears that there is only a small age trend in use of inverse compensation to judge ability during the elementary school years, but there are individual differences. This conclusion is also supported by Karabenick and Heller (1976).

There are between-study differences in use of inverse compensation, however. Approximately 60 percent of the elementary school children in Karabenick and Heller's study used inverse compensation, whereas 49 percent did in my study and 38 percent did in Kun's study. Note that Karabenick and Heller's procedure made the lowest memory demands of any of the studies, because they held performance constant over the whole experiment (all characters succeeded). Kun's study and my study were similar with the exception that I presented line drawings representing the values of the component stimuli as memory aids on each trial. Kun also presented line drawings, but the drawings did not represent the values of the stimulus components. This post hoc ordering of the three studies in terms of their memory demands suggests that the information-processing demands of the task may interfere with use of the "mature" strategy of inverse compensation, as suggested by Shatz (1978) and Anderson (1980).

Further evidence that information-processing load influences use of inverse compensation is provided by an experiment with college students (Surber, 1984a). In this experiment, subjects judged the ability of hypothetical students described in terms of study effort and performance information that varied in reliability. Effort was described as based on one of three different-size samples of the student's studying (1 day, 1 week, or 1 month), and performance was described as based on one of three different tests (a 10-item quiz, a midterm, or a comprehensive final examination). Suprisingly, there was no main effect of effort in the total sample, but approximately half the sample judged ability to increase as the given level of effort increased, whereas the other half of the sample judged ability to be inversely related to effort. The addition of reliability information can be assumed to have raised the overall processing load of the task, because each trial now required integration of four pieces of information rather than just two. The increase in processing load may have decreased use of inverse compensation.

Similar conclusions about inverse compensation emerge from the literature on judgments of effort except that subjects at all ages are more likely to use inverse compensation in judging effort than in judging ability. In summary, there is little evidence of age change in use of inverse compensation during the elementary school years, and more complex judgment tasks yield a lower proportion of use of inverse compensation.

Are Nonsocial Judgments Reversible?

I began by studying reversible operations in social judgments to determine whether concepts of the physical and social worlds develop synchronously (Surber, 1985b). However, there are a number of problems inherent in studying social judgments, some of which are avoided by studying nonsocial concepts. First, in the course of everyday experience individuals may have acquired different ways of judging concepts such as performance, ability, and effort. That is, something about the social ecology may lead to inconsistent judgments across the variables. It is less likely that an individual will have had inconsistent experiences with physical variables than with social variables.

Second, stimuli presented may induce the subject to modify her or his mental representation of the relations among a set of variables, especially if stimuli were presented that seemed impossible (Kun & Weiner, 1973). For example, for a person of high ability to attain a very low grade on an easy test might seem impossible at any level of effort and might lead the subject to modify his or her assumptions about relations among the variables. With nonsocial concepts it should be easier to determine what stimuli are consistent with a set of assumed relations among variables. Third, if hypothetical events are used, the experimenter can control the amount and type of experience the subject receives about the variables. For social events, the experimenter has no control of the subject's experience. For these reasons we turn to an examination of judgment tasks involving nonsocial variables.

Correspondence of Interaction Patterns

Wilkening (1981) collected judgments of time, velocity, and distance traveled in an experiment with 5-year-olds, 10-year-olds, and college students. Wilkening concluded that judgments of distance were a multiplicative combination of time and velocity for all three age groups, that time was judged as a subjective ratio of distance and velocity by the 10-year-olds and college subjects, but that the 10-year-olds' and college students' judgments of velocity were based on a subtractive combination, velocity = distance − time. Thus, for 10-year-olds and college students, Wilkening's data showed correspondence of interaction patterns across two judged variables, distance and time, but not across all three. Wilkening's conclusions depend on the assumption that the judgment function is linear.

In another study, judgments of weight and distance from the fulcrum on a two-arm balance scale were examined (Surber & Gzesh, 1984). Subjects from five age groups (5-year-old preschoolers, second graders, fifth graders, eighth graders, and college students) made three types of judgments about balancing the scale: (1) Judge the distance of a constant weight on the left arm, given the number of weights on the right and their distance from the fulcrum; (2) judge the distance of a variable number of weights on the right, given the distance of the constant weight on the left and the number of weights on the right; and (3) judge the number of weights to be placed on the right, given their distance from the fulcrum and the distance of the constant weight on the left. The correct models for solving all three versions of the task can be derived from the equation $cD_L = W_R D_R$, where c is the constant weight on the left, D_L is the distance of the constant weight from the fulcrum, W_R is the weight on the right, and D_R is the distance from the fulcrum on the right. The results for the college-age subjects were consistent with the multiplying model for judged distance on the left, were consistent with the ratio model for judgments of distance on the right, but were not consistent with the ratio model for judgments of weight on the right. Thus, the results are analogous to those of Wilkening (1981). College-age subjects showed correspondence of interaction patterns across two of three variables. The conclusions of this study also depend on assuming a linear judgment function. (The children did not show inverse compensation, and so correspondence of interactions cannot be considered for their data.)

The previous studies of nonsocial reversibility all involved multiplicative and ratio combination of information (torque = weight × distance, and distance = velocity × time). Anderson and Butzin (1974) hypothesized that a subjective ratio operation was difficult, if not impossible, and that the difficulty of subjective ratios accounted for the lack of complete reversibility in their data. Given Anderson and Butzin's hypothesis, it is important to study relations among variables that are not multiplicative. For these reasons, I have also conducted a series of studies with college-age subjects of reversibility for judgments of hypothetical events. Using hypothetical events allows the investigator to determine the nature of the relations among the hypothetical variables involved, so that different ways of combining the variables can be trained, followed by testing for reversibility.

In my first study using hypothetical events (Surber, 1982), I taught subjects either a diverging pattern for predicting the amount of a hypothetical chemical Z produced from combinations of hypothetical chemicals A and B or a converging bilinear pattern. The trained patterns correspond to an approximate conjunctive rule for combining A and B and an approximate disjunctive rule, respectively (Oden, 1977). The amounts of A and B were described verbally, and the subjects predicted the amount of Z by marking a line with endpoints labeled *extremely high* and *extremely low*. After a series of training trials in which Z was predicted with feedback, subjects then predicted Z without feedback, given different verbal levels of A and B, and inferred the amount of A needed to produce a given amount of Z when combined with a specified amount of B. The predictions of Z are presented in Figure 4.4. The solid lines show the untrained

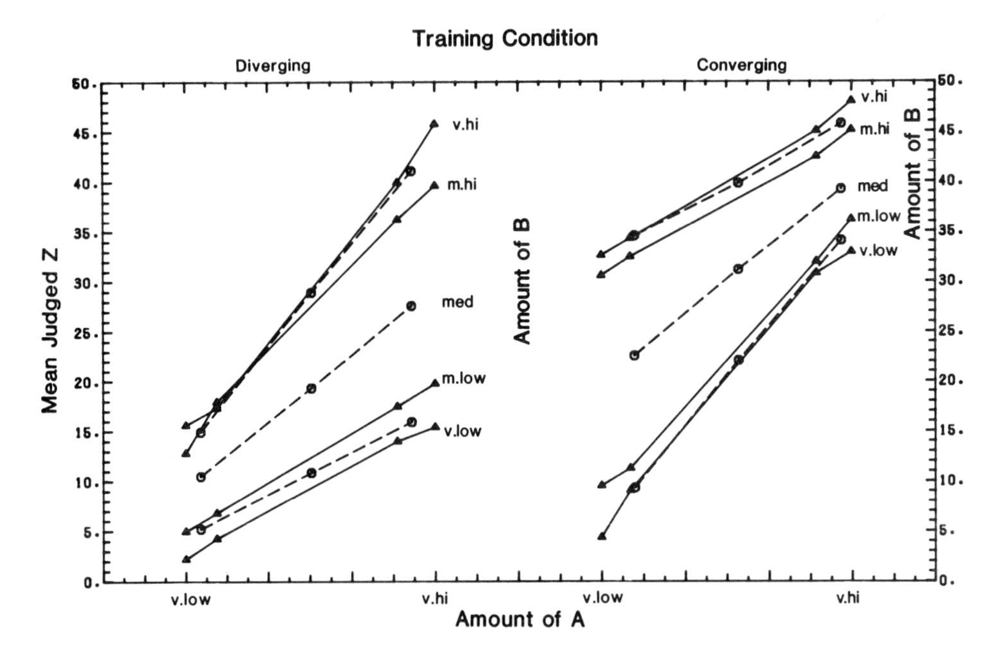

FIGURE 4.4. Mean judgments of the generalization trials of experiment 1 (points connected by solid lines). The left-hand panel shows the mean judged amount of Z for groups trained in the diverging bilinear condition, and the right-hand panel shows the mean judged Z for groups trained in the converging bilinear pattern. The abscissa is spaced according to the marginal mean A values. Points connected by dashed lines are the no-feedback means.

values of A and B, and the dashed lines show the trained values. As can be seen, the training successfully produced two different judgment patterns.

The judgments of A are shown in Figure 4.5, with the diverging condition in the top two panels and the converging condition in the bottom two panels. There were two separate designs for judgments of A. In one condition, shown in the left-hand panels of Figure 4.5, Z values of medium or less were combined with B values of medium or greater. In the right-hand panels of Figure 4.5, Z values of medium or greater were combined with B values of medium or less. As can be seen in Figure 4.5, the pattern of A predictions depended *not* on the training condition, but on the distribution of trials presented for judgments of A. When the Z values were less than the B values, a diverging bilinear pattern was obtained (left-hand panels), but where the Z values were greater than the B values (right-hand panels), a converging pattern was obtained.

These data were somewhat puzzling to me. One hypothesis is that the distribution of stimuli altered the judgment function in ways that might be expected based on range-frequency theory (Birnbaum, 1974a; Mellers, 1982; Mellers & Birnbaum, 1982,1983; Parducci, 1974). According to

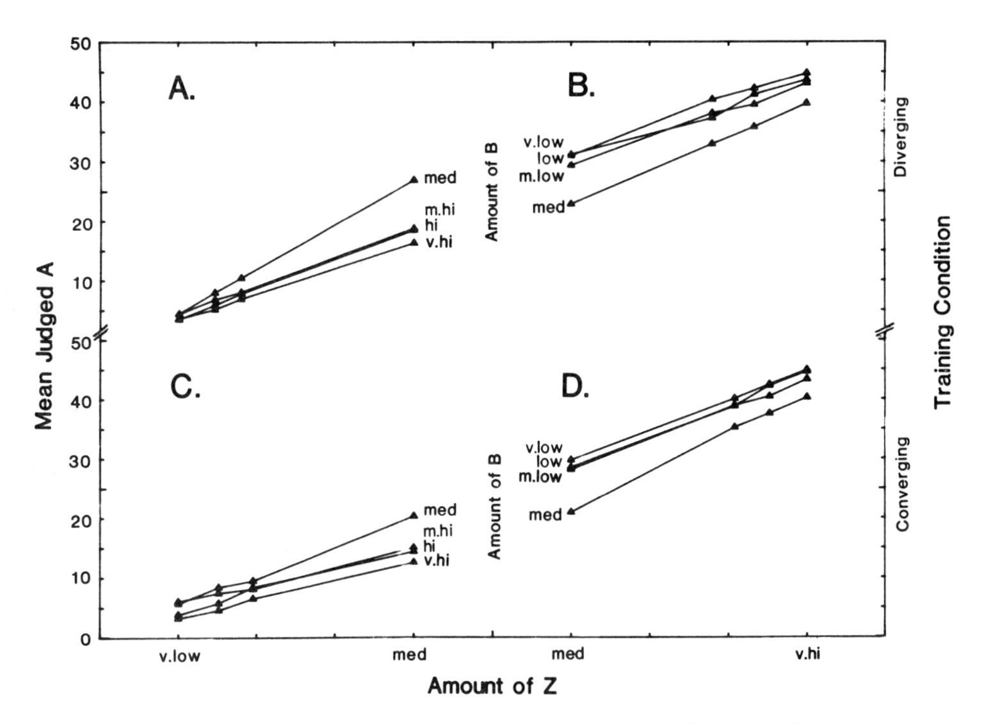

FIGURE 4.5. Mean judgments of the amount of A in experiment 1. The top two panels (A and B) are the diverging bilinear training groups, and the bottom panels (C and D) are the converging bilinear training groups. The left-hand panels (A and C) are the groups that answered trials in which $Z \leq B$, and the right-hand panels (B and D) are the groups that answered trials in which $Z \geq B$. The abscissa is spaced according to the marginal mean Z value, and each curve in a panel is a different level of B.

range-frequency theory, the judgment function is positively accelerated when the distribution of impressions is positively skewed and negatively accelerated when the distribution is negatively skewed. For an additive combination of cues, a positively accelerated judgment function produces a diverging interaction when it is plotted as in Figure 4.5, whereas a negatively accelerated judgment function produces a converging interaction. Thus, one explanation of the data is to propose that (1) training influenced the judgment function, but not the information integration function for predicting Z, and the integration function is additive for both groups; (2) the information integration function for inferences of A is subtractive ($A = Z - B$) for both training conditions, but the skewed distribution of A impressions altered the judgment function so that the responses were not parallel in either stimulus condition. This explanation saves the hypothesis that the judgments of Z and A are based on reversible operations.

To test this explanation, I conducted a second experiment, using the same two training conditions, a diverging bilinear and a converging bilinear pattern. The design for the judgments of *A* was not skewed this time; instead it was a 7 × 7 factorial of *Z* and *B* values. If the skewed designs of the first experiment produced the interactions of *B* and *Z*, they should be eliminated (or at least altered) by the uniform factorial design. In addition, I administered a questionnaire, analogous to that used in my 1981 study of judgments of performance, asking subjects to report their beliefs about how *A* and *B* combine to produce *Z*.

The results for the judgments of *Z* replicated those shown in Figure 4.4. The results for the judgments of *A* are shown in Figures 4.6 and 4.7. The two training conditions showed patterns of judgments of *A* that were quite similar, as shown statistically by the nonsignificance of the training condition × *Z* × *B* interaction in spite of high power. In addition, if the data from the first experiment in Figure 4.5 are superimposed on the data of Figures 4.6 and 4.7, the results can be seen to be very close. The skewed stimulus designs in the first experiment do not appear to be the source of the interactions that do not agree with the trained patterns.

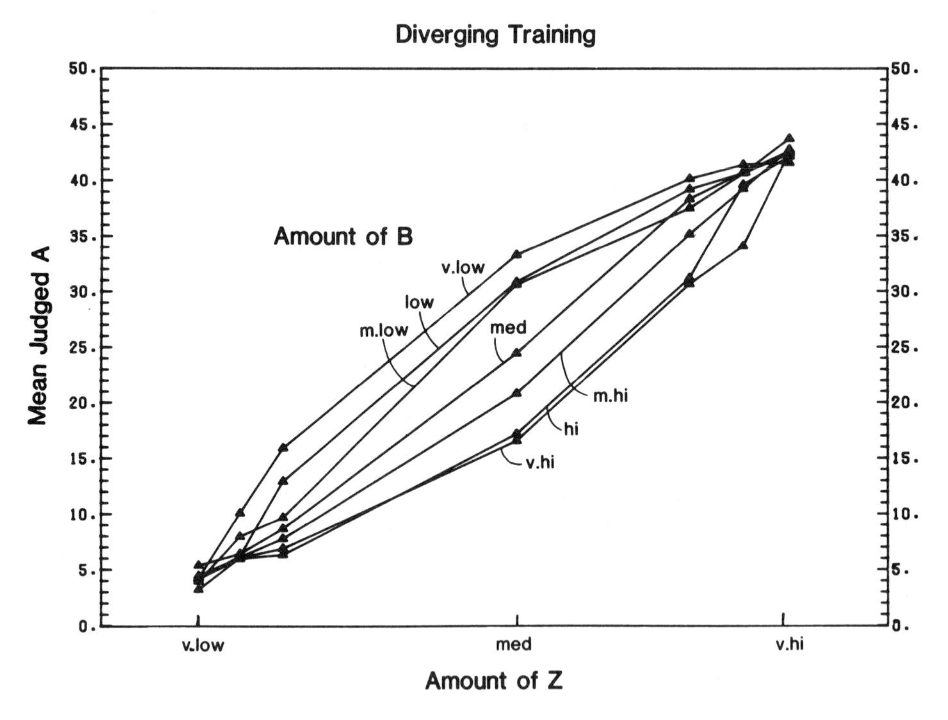

FIGURE 4.6. Mean judgments of the amount of *A* in experiment 2 for the diverging bilinear training group. The abscissa is spaced according to the marginal mean *Z* value, and each curve represents a different level of *B*.

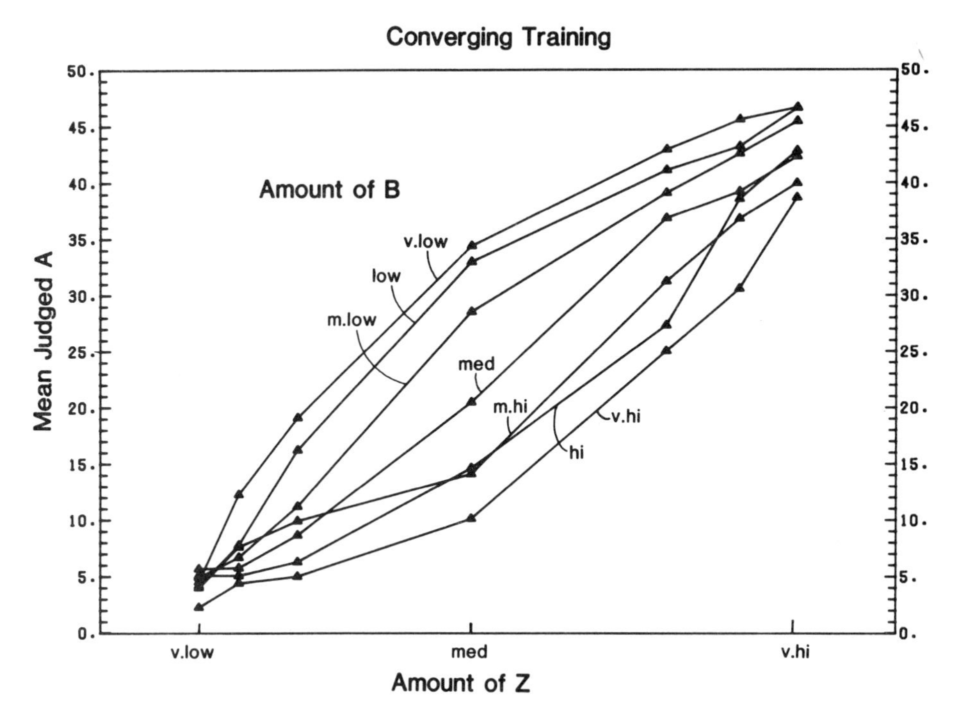

FIGURE 4.7. Mean judgments of the amount of A in experiment 2 for the converging bilinear training group. The abscissa is spaced according to the marginal mean Z value, and each curve represents a different level of B.

The questionnaire ratings, however, supported the hypothesis that the training influenced the way subjects believed A and B combined to produce Z. Subjects in the converging training condition reported high belief in the statement that low Z required both low A and low B, whereas subjects in the diverging condition expressed high belief in the statement that high Z required both high A and high B. Thus, to explain the data as resulting from a reversible structure with the response patterns distorted by the judgment function, one has to discount both the questionnaire results and the failure of the change in the stimulus distribution to influence the response pattern. The hypothesis that humans base judgments on a fully reversible mental structure begins to lose credibility.

A remaining explanation of the hypothetical chemical experiments that preserves the reversibility hypothesis is that some of the stimulus combinations for judgments of A may have seemed impossible to the subjects, inducing them to change their representations of the way A and B combine to produce Z. In a recent experiment, I included a condition in which the subjects learned an additive or parallel response pattern for predicting Z, given A and B. For the bilinear patterns there are a priori rationales for expecting the subjects to view some combinations of Z and B as impossible. But for an additive combination of A and B there is really no a priori reason to hypothesize that the subjects would view any combinations of Z and B values as impossible. The judgments of A in this experiment showed a pattern almost identical to that in Figures 4.6 and 4.7.

The overall conclusion from my hypothetical chemical experiments is that judgments are not based on a fully reversible set of operations or structure. Once again, the judgment function for judgments of either variable Z or variable A may be nonlinear. However, to save the reversibility hypothesis, it is necessary to assume that (1) the training influenced the judgment function but not the integration function, (2) the integration function for predictions of Z was additive for all three training conditions, (3) the subjects based their answers to the questionnaire on their judgments and not on how they combined the information, (4) the integration function for inferences of A was subtractive regardless of training condition, and (5) the judgment function for inferences of A is nonlinear and independent of training condition and stimulus distribution. Accepting this set of postulates saves the reversibility hypothesis, but at the cost of concluding that complete reversibility may occur only for additive combinations of information.

An exception to the conclusion that judgments are not based on a completely reversible structure can be found in a study of judgments in the balance scale task (Surber & Gzesh, 1984). We found that a few of the college students reported explicitly using the correct multiplying and ratio equations to find their answers. The judgments of those subjects who used calculations were, not surprisingly, fully reversible. In a second experiment (Haines, Surber, Walden, & Gzesh, 1985), we confirmed that fully reversible response patterns are produced by subjects who are capable of the appropriate calculations and who are urged to calculate. However, when the task was presented such that calculation was impossible, results similar to those reported by Surber and Gzesh (1984) were obtained: The college students' judgments showed the diverging bilinear pattern for only two of the three types of judgments.

Inverse Compensation

Three of the experiments on nonsocial concepts above provide information on developmental change in inverse compensation. Wilkening (1981) found that even 5-year-olds judged time to be inversely related to velocity, but that 5-year-olds did not judge velocity to be inversely related to time. Ten-year-olds and adults showed inverse compensation in judging both variables. Surber and Gzesh (1984) found an increase with age in use of inverse compensation in the balance scale task, with college students showing almost 100 percent inverse compensation. Surprisingly, only about half of the eighth-graders showed inverse compensation, and they did so inconsistently across the two types of judgments for which it was required. Inconsistency in use of inverse compensation across judged dimensions is similar to the inconsistency in using inverse compensation found in judgments of ability and effort.

Haines et al. (1985) found that, after training subjects to make judgments that show the bilinear pattern of the multiplying model, there was considerably higher use of inverse compensation for both eighth-graders and fifth-graders than in the study by Surber and Gzesh (1984). The training in the Haines et al. study did not directly involve inverse compensation. It is possible that the subjects abstracted the inverse relationship between weight and distance on one arm of the balance when the position of the constant weight on the other arm was fixed. For example, in training the subject would discover that the constant weight should be placed a certain distance from the fulcrum for two different stimulus combinations: a weight larger than the constant weight placed closer to the fulcrum, or a weight smaller than the constant weight placed farther from the fulcrum. From such trials, the subject can abstract the inverse relation between weight and distance on one arm of the balance.

Data on developmental change in inverse compensation for nonsocial judgments are found also in the extensive literature on "anticipation of levels" tasks used by researchers exploring the development of conservation. The general conclusion in this literature is that inverse compensation is poorly developed in children 4 years or younger but is relatively well developed in children about 7 years or older (Larsen & Flavell, 1970).

Representations of the Mental Operations of Judgment

At this point the reader may feel that studying the reversible operation of correspondence of interaction patterns is not only fruitless (because of the problems introduced by the judgment function) but also somewhat purposeless. Developmental research has been predominantly concerned with the reversible operation of inverse compensation, which can be studied without regard for possible nonlinearity on the judgment function. However, I think correspondence of interactions is an important type of reversibility for several reasons. First, testing correspondence of interactions allows us to test the central hypothesis in attribution theory, that how one assumes causes combine to produce an event will determine how one will make inferences of the causes (Kelley, 1972, 1973). To distinguish the effects on inferences of different causal schemata, the interaction pattern must be considered. If the interaction pattern is not considered, the schemata are indistinguishable.

Second, Piaget proposed that the development of proportionality concepts begins with logical multiplication (or factorial combination of two variables) and additive compensation (or compensation "in the sense of an additive difference,'' Inhelder & Piaget, 1958, p. 218). Development then proceeds through an understanding of qualitative proportionality in which it is understood that ''an increase in one variable gives the same result as a decrease in the other'' (p. 219), to an understanding of metric proportions and multiplicative compensation. This description of the development of proportionality concepts implies that correspondence of interaction patterns would occur for an additive combination of variables but not for a multiplicative combination, because multiplicative combination requires extensive quantification and *metric* proportions. It seems clear that a test of the proposed developmental sequence requires a method for distinguishing what Inhelder and Piaget (1958) call additive and multiplicative compensation. These two types of compensation might be taken to correspond to subtractive and ratio information integration functions, respectively. As has been shown here, distinguishing these two models of information integration is not simple, but is a central part of testing for correspondence of interaction patterns or quantitative reversibility.

Third, I think testing correspondence of interaction patterns has forced me to seriously consider just what underlying representations or operations are involved in human judgment. The findings of the experiments reviewed above require a theory to predict the different aspects of reversibility and lack of reversibility found in inconsistent use of inverse compensation across dimensions and use of inverse compensation but failure of the interaction patterns to correspond. In addition, it is necessary that the theory distinguish between mental operations that are explicit mathematical calculations and the mental operations of subjective judgment, which do not involve explicit calculation. Models of judgment have been called *paramorphic models* because many types of mental operations could produce results agreeing with a given model (Hoffman, 1960). Several possible representations are considered below: a list of triadic (for systems of three variables) associations among the variables, a spatial representation, a set of conditional functions, and a production system in J. Anderson's (1982, 1983) Act* model.

Associative Model

According to the associative representation, a person's knowledge about the relations among a set of variables is encoded as a list. For three variables *A*, *B*, and *C*, the person would have in long-term memory a list of triadic associations of *A*, *B*, and *C*. For example, the person might have stored A = low, B = low, C = low; A = medium, B = high, C = low; and A = medium, B = low, C = high; and so on. The process of making a judgment would then consist of using the values of the given variables to retrieve the associated value of the variable to be judged. The psychophysical function (*H* in Figure 4.1) then represents the transformation of the given stimulus values to match the form in which the values of the variables are stored. The integration function (*I* in Figure 4.1) is instantiated in the list of associations; it is not really a function at all. The judgment function (*J* in Figure 4.1) represents the way the person transforms the retrieved value of a variable to something that corresponds to the response scale.

What does the associative model predict about reversibility? If it is assumed that the list of associations can be accessed with equal facility from any pair of variable values (*A* and *B*, *A* and *C*, or *B* and *C*), then the associative model predicts algebraic reversibility, both inverse compensation and correspondence of interaction patterns. Under the associative model, lack of reversibility would be expected if the person had stored separate lists of associations among the variables for each variable to be judged, or if the person were unable to retrieve a value for a variable when given the values of the other variables. In the associative model there are also difficulties if the person is given more stimulus values than she or he has stored. For example, suppose the person has stored information about how low, medium, and high values of *B* and *C* are associated with *A*, but is asked to judge *A* given values of *B* and *C* such as very very low, very low, low, medium, high, very high, and very very high. The associative model by itself has no mechanism for extrapolating and interpolating beyond the stored values. Thus, if the person encounters stimulus values that do not fit those in memory, some other method of generating a judgment must be used, and there would be no a priori reason to expect reversibility.

Spatial Representation

A second possibility is that a person organizes knowledge about the relations among the variables as a surface in *n*-space (where *n* is the number or variables). If the person acquired the knowledge as a list of associations, then a surface would be fit to the points and filled in by interpolation. When asked to make a judgment about a variable, the person locates the positions of the given variables on their axes and projects the resulting point onto the surface. The value of the variable to be judged is then obtained by projecting the point on the surface onto the judged variable's axis. In this model, the psychophysical function corresponds to the process of finding the value on the axis of a given variable that corresponds to the given stimulus value. The integration function corresponds to the surface itself and essentially represents the person's assumptions, based on limited knowledge, about how the variables in the set are related. The judgment function corresponds to the process of transforming the value from the axis of that variable into a response.

The spatial model predicts algebraic reversibility, as long as the stimulus values can be transformed to the axes in a region where the surface exists. It is possible, however, that a person could have regions over which the surface if undefined. That is, the surface may have "holes" in it or may be undefined above or below extreme values of the variables. For stimulus values that fall above or below the defined region of a surface, it seems natural for the person to extrapolate the same shape in that direction, however, and algebraic reversibility would then be expected. A surface would be expected to have holes in it only if the knowledge on which the surface was based were very incomplete.

A variation on this representation allows the surface to have a thickness that varies with the subjective uncertainty about the relations among the variables; the more uncertainty, the thicker the surface. Within the bounds of the thickness, one might also imagine the surface as varying in density (analogous to a probability density function) such that variable values in the denser regions are viewed as more likely than those in less dense regions.

A Set of Conditional Functions

Another possibility is that when initially acquiring knowledge about the relations among the variables, a person structures this knowledge in the form of conditional functions that represent the relation between two of the variables by holding one of the variables constant at a particular value.[3] For example, a person might have a set of 10 functions giving the relation between variable B and variable A, each associated with a different value of variable C. For a more concrete example, imagine that a person's judgments of variable A agree with the additive model $A = B + C$. This could be mentally represented as a set of linear functions conditional on the value of C. When called on to judge variable A, the person retrieves the function that is stored under the given value of C and, using the given value of B, finds the appropriate A value. For the additive case, the variable C changes the intercept of the function that is retrieved. A different function is retrieved for each C value. The functions themselves might be represented spatially as lines in a 2-space, or they might be represented with imagery.

In the conditional-function model, the psychophysical function for variable B represents the process of finding a value of B to use in a retrieved function that corresponds to the given B stimulus value. For Variable C, the psychophysical function represents the transformation of the stimulus value to match the form in which the values of variable C are stored. The integration function consists of the stored set of conditional functions, and the judgment function represents the process of translating the value of A into a response.

The conditional-function model does not make clear predictions about reversibility. For example, suppose a person judges A by using a set of linear functions in terms of B, conditional on C. When the person is asked to judge *C*, there is no given value of *C* to use as a cue to retrieve a function. Alternatively, when the person is asked to judge *B*, the given *C* value will allow retrieval of a function, but the retrieved function must be solved for variable *B*. If the functions are represented spatially or with imagery, however, they could be used to find the value of either of the two variables with equal facility. Algebraic reversibility would then be shown for judgments of two of the variables but not the third (in the example, judgments of variables *A* and *B* would show algebraic reversibility, but not judgments of variable *C*). Algebraic reversibility for three variables would be predicted if a person had stored two sets of conditional functions that embody the same relations—for example, a set of functions for *A* in terms of *B* conditional on *C* and a set of functions for *B* in terms of *C* conditional on *A*. Thus, the conditional-function model predicts that reversibility depends on the manner in which the information is stored. More experience with a set of variables would be likely to establish alternative storage forms for the conditional functions and would therefore increase the probability of reversibility.

Act*

Another possible approach to representing mental operations of judgment is to use the production systems of J. Anderson's (1982, 1983) Active Control of Thought, or ACT*, theory.[4] The Act* model is intended to be a general theory of cognition and is based on a number of principles. First, the mind consists of three memories: working memory (containing information immediately available for use or currently activated), declarative memory (long-term memory, represented as a tangled hierarchy of cognitive units), and production memory (containing condition-action or if-then pairs for operating on the information in working memory). Second, thought is goal-directed, with goals held in working memory. The production that is applied in a given cognitive act depends in part on the degree of match between the condition and the goal in working memory.

Third, all knowledge is initially encoded declaratively and is used by general interpretive procedures. With practice, people show a gradual improvement in skill performance. Anderson postulates that skill acquisition goes through three stages: declarative, knowledge compilation, and tuning. Fourth, ACT* includes several mechanisms for learning that take the learner through the three stages: (1) Productions are strengthened by successful use and become more likely to be selected in the future, (2) productions are modified and new productions are acquired through principles of generalization and discrimination, and (3) new task-specific productions are acquired through practice via the processes of proceduralization (acquisition of a specific production to replace use of a general production) and composition (the process of combining two or more productions into a single production).

Smith (1984) applied the Act* model to phenomena in social inference and included some discussion of reversibility in social judgments. Smith primarily considered inference tasks involving only two variables and did not speculate on the type of reversibility we have called *correspondence of interaction patterns*. For two variables, Smith posits that inference rules are bidirectional only if they are encoded declaratively rather than procedurally. This assertion is based on the hypothesis in Act* that a declaratively encoded concept can be retrieved from either the premise or the conclusion through spreading activation. Procedures, however, are applied only if the condition segment of the condition-action pair is sufficiently well matched by the contents of working memory. The action segment cannot be used to retrieve a procedure. Thus, social inferences should be bidirectional when judgments are made in the interpretive stage but not necessarily once the judgments are proceduralized. Smith pointed out that use of an inference rule in one direction more than in the reverse direction will result in the development of a procedure for making the judgment in one direction but not the other.

Smith also attempted to explain how an information integration function could be represented in Act*. He proposed that a declarative inference rule of the following form might represent information integration: "(object) has properties $(P_1)(P_2)$, . . . and $(P_1)(P_2)$, . . . are relevant to (characteristic) of (object) = = (object) has (characteristic) with level average (P_1, P_2, . . .)" (Smith, 1984, p. 408). The parentheses denote variables that can be instantiated with values depending on the particular task content, and = = separates the premise and conclusion of a biconditional, declaratively encoded inference rule. Smith points out that if the information integration rules of social judgment are represented as above, they would not be usable bidirectionally because it is not possible to retrieve the properties (P_1, P_2, etc.) from the level of the characteristic that is the conclusion.

Smith's attempt to assimilate the information integration approach to Act* is laudable and important, but it is incomplete. For example, he has not specified how the characteristics (P_1, P_2, etc.) are translated to values that can be averaged (i.e., the psychophysical function is unspecified) or how the characteristics are weighted. Also, as Smith acknowledges, there are other possible ways of applying Act* to the problem of how people make judgments. An alternative is to express the possible information integration functions as productions, with information about the context of the task used to choose which production (information integration function) to apply and the combination of information in a given trial used to fill the local variables in the selected production. There might be a general-purpose production for determining scale values from characteristics by positioning the characteristic on a continuum between the possible extremes of the characteristic indicated by the instructions or past experience, and there might be a general-purpose production for positioning the integrated psychological impressions (ψ_{ij}) on the response scale, perhaps embodying principles such as those of range-frequency theory.

In principle, Act* is an interesting model for representing the acquisition of reversible operations. For example, it should be possible to specify productions for the four different aspects of the development of proportionality hypothesized by Inhelder and Piaget (1958): additive compensation, qualitative proportionality, multiplicative compensation, and quantitative proportionality. Furthermore, the learning mechanisms in Act* should allow specification of how these aspects of reversibility develop and what types of experiences will promote or inhibit the development of reversibility. For example, the compensatory relation between two variables should be abstracted in Act* by the generalization process that finds similarities between productions and creates a new production. The process of knowledge compilation (via proceduralization and composition) could result in the higher-level organization of operations postulated by Piaget to constitute the INRC group.

Conclusions

In this chapter I have reviewed the literature applying the functional-measurement approach to the study of the development of reversible operations. In addition to the general advantages of the functional-measurement approach in developmental research mentioned at the outset, two particular contributions of the approach are evident. First, use of the functional-measurement approach has made it possible to reach beyond the kind of reversibility that Piaget called *compensation* to the type of reversibility called *correspondence of interactions,* or what Piaget termed *multiplicative compensation* or *qualitative proportionality*. This makes it possible to test Piaget's proposed developmental sequence for proportional reasoning. Second, it is clear that testing correspondence of interaction patterns requires methods for separating the integration function and judgment function. Most developmental research using rating scale responses has ignored the possibility of developmental change in the way rating scales are used, the process represented by the judgment function. Although the experimental attempts to separate the integration and judgment function were not completely successful, they demonstrate methods that could be used in other developmental research addressing the general issue of developmental change in information integration. Appropriate use of the functional-measurement approach (or, indeed, any type of rating scale responses) in developmental research requires consideration of the possibility that there is developmental change in any of the three global processing steps in Figure 4.1. Making clear these three possible loci of developmental change is a contribution of the approach in itself. The functional-measurement approach, because it addresses the question of how information from several sources is combined, is well tailored for many developmental research topics, from moral judgment to cue use in conservation, and could be used profitably in many other settings.

Acknowledgments

Portions of the research by the author reported in this chapter were supported by a grant from the Spencer Foundation to the School of Education, University of Wisconsin-Madison, by a grant from the Graduate School, University of Wisconsin-Madison and by grant 79-12414 from the National Science Foundation.

References

Acredolo, C. (1981). Acquisition of conservation: A clarification of Piagetian terminology, some recent findings, and an alternative formulation. *Human Development, 24,* 120–137.

Anderson, J. R. (1982). Acquisition of cognitive skill. *Psychological Review, 89,* 369–406.

Anderson, J. R. (1983). *The architecture of cognition.* Cambridge, MA: Harvard.

Anderson, N. H. (1974). Cognitive algebra. In L. Berkowitz (Ed.), *Advances in experimental social psychology* (Vol. 7, pp. 1–101). New York: Academic.

Anderson, N. H. (1977). Note on functional measurement and data analysis. *Perception and Psychophysics, 21,* 201–215.

Anderson, N. H. (1979). Algebraic rules in psychological measurement. *American Scientist, 67,* 555–563.

Anderson, N. H. (1980). Information integration theory in developmental psychology. In F. Wilkening, J. Becker, & T. Trabasso (Eds.), *Information integration by children* (pp. 1–45). Hillsdale, NJ: Erlbaum.

Anderson, N. H., & Butzin, C. A. (1974). Performance = motivation × ability: An integration-theoretical analysis. *Journal of Personality and Social Psychology, 30,* 598–604.

Anderson, N. H., & Butzin, C. A. (1978). Integration theory applied to children's judgments of equity. *Developmental Psychology, 14,* 593–606.

Anderson, N. H., & Cuneo, D. O. (1978). The height + width rule in children's judgments of quantity. *Journal of Experimental Psychology: General, 107,* 335–378.

Birnbaum, M. H. (1974a). The nonadditivity of personality impressions. *Journal of Experimental Psychology, 102,* 543–561.

Birnbaum, M. H. (1974b). Using contextual effects to derive psychophysical scales. *Perception and Psychophysics, 15,* 89–96.

Birnbaum, M. H. (1976). Intuitive numerical prediction. *American Journal of Psychology, 89,* 417–429.

Birnbaum, M. H. (1978). Differences and ratios in psychological measurement. In N. J. Castellan & F. Restle (Eds.), *Cognitive theory* (Vol. 3, pp. 33–74). Hillsdale, NJ: Erlbaum.

Birnbaum, M. H. (1982). Controversies in psychological measurement. In B. Wegener (Ed.), *Social attitudes and psychophysical measurement* (pp. 401–485). Hillsdale, NJ: Erlbaum.

Birnbaum, M. H., Parducci, A., & Gifford, R. K. (1971). Contextual effects in information integration. *Journal of Experimental Psychology, 88,* 155–170.

Birnbaum, M. H., & Viet, C. (1974). Scale convergence as a criterion for rescaling: Information integration with difference, ratio, and averaging tasks. *Perception and Psychophysics, 15,* 7–15.

Bogartz, R. S. (1976). On the meaning of statistical interactions. *Journal of Experimental Child Psychology, 22,* 178–183.

Bogartz, R. S., & Wackwitz, J. H. (1970). Transforming response measures to remove interactions or other sources of variance. *Psychonomic Science, 19,* 87–89.

Brainerd, C. J. (1976). Does prior knowledge of the compensation rule increase susceptibility to conservation training? *Developmental Psychology, 12,* 1–5.

Brehmer, B. (1974). Hypotheses about relations between scaled variables in the learning of probabilistic inference tasks. *Organizational Behavior and Human Performance, 11,* 1–27.

Brehmer, B., & Slovic, P. (1980). Information integration in multiple cue judgments. *Journal of Experimental Psychology: Human Perception and Performance, 6,* 302–308.

Busemeyer, J. R. (1980). Importance of measurement theory, error theory, and experimental design for testing the significance of interactions. *Psychological Bulletin, 88,* 237–244.

Butzin, C. A., & Anderson, N. H. (1973). Functional measurement of children's judgments. *Child Development, 44,* 529–537.

Chandler, J. D. (1969). Subroutine STEP IT—Finds local minima of a smooth function of several parameters. *Behavioral Science, 14,* 81–82.

Graesser, C. A., & Anderson, N. H. (1974). Cognitive algebra of the equation Gift size = generosity × income. *Journal of Experimental Psychology, 103,* 692–699.

Haines, B. A., Surber, C. F., Walden, J., & Gzesh, S. M. (1985, April). *Reversibility of intuitive versus analytic mental operations.* Paper presented at the biennial meeting of the Society for Research in Child Development, Toronto, Canada.

Heider, F. (1958). *The psychology of interpersonal relations.* New York: Wiley.

Hoffman, P. J. (1960). The paramorphic representation of clinical judgment. *Psychological Bulletin, 57,* 116–131.

Inhelder, B., & Piaget, J. (1958). *The growth of logical thinking from childhood to adolescence.* New York: Basic Books.

Karabenick, J. D., & Heller, K. A. (1976). A developmental study of effort and ability attributions. *Developmental Psychology, 12,* 559–560.

Kelley, H. H. (1972). *Causal schemata and the attribution process.* New York: General Learning Press.

Kelley, H. H. (1973). The processes of causal attribution. *American Psychologist, 28,* 107–128.

Krantz, D. H., & Tversky, A. (1971). Conjoint-measurement analysis of composition rules in psychology. *Psychological Review, 78,* 151–169.

Kruskal, J., & Carmone, F. (1969). MONANOVA: A FORTRAN-IV program for monotone analysis of variance. *Behavioral Science, 14,* 165–166.
Kun, A. (1977). Development of the magnitude-covariation and compensation schemata in ability and effort attributions of performance. *Child Development, 48,* 862–873.
Kun, A., Parsons, J., & Ruble, D. (1974). Development of integration processes using ability and effort information to predict outcome. *Developmental Psychology, 10,* 721–732.
Kun, A., & Weiner, B. (1973). Necessary versus sufficient causal schemata for success and failure. *Journal of Research in Personality, 7,* 197–207.
Larsen, G. Y., & Flavell, J. H. (1970). Verbal factors in compensation performance and the relation between conservation and compensation. *Child Development, 41,* 965–977.
Marks, L. E. (1982). Psychophysical measurement: Procedures, tasks, scales. In B. Wegener (Ed.), *Social attitudes and psychophysical measurement* (pp. 43–71). Hillsdale, NJ: Erlbaum.
Mellers, B. (1982). Equity judgment: A revision of Aristotelian views. *Journal of Experimental Psychology: General, 111,* 242–270.
Mellers, B., & Birnbaum, M. H. (1982). Loci of contextual effects in judgment. *Journal of Experimental Psychology: Human Perception and Performance, 8,* 582–601.
Mellers, B., & Birnbaum, M. H. (1983). Context effects in social judgment. *Journal of Experimental Social Psychology, 19,* 157–171.
Norman, K. L., & Schemmer, F. M. (1977). Functional processing in information integration tasks (Tech. Rep. No. 14). University of Maryland, Center for Language and Cognition.
Oden, G. C. (1977). Integration of fuzzy logical information. *Journal of Experimental Psychology: Human Perception and Performance, 3,* 565–575.
Parducci, A. (1974). Context effects: A range-frequency analysis. In E. C. Carterette and M. P. Friedman (Eds.), *Handbook of perception: Vol. 2. Psychophysical judgment and measurement* (pp. 127–141). New York: Academic.
Peterson, C. R., & Beach, L. R. (1967). Man as an intuitive statistician. *Psychological Bulletin, 68,* 29–46.
Piaget, J. (1941/1965). *The child's conception of number.* New York: Norton.
Piaget, J. (1947/1960). *The psychology of intelligence.* Totowa, NJ: Littlefield, Adams & Co.
Shatz, M. (1978). The relationship between cognitive processes and the development of communication skills. In C. B. Keasey (Ed.), *Nebraska symposium on motivation 1977* (Vol. 25, pp. 1–42). Lincoln: University of Nebraska Press.
Siegler, R. S. (1976). Three aspects of cognitive development. *Cognitive Psychology, 8,* 481–520.
Siegler, R. S. (1981). Developmental sequences within and between concepts. *Monographs of the Society for Research in Child Development* 46 (2, Serial No. 189).
Singh, R., Gupta, M., & Dalal, A. K. (1979). Cultural difference in attribution of performance: An integration-theoretical analysis. *Journal of Personality and Social Psychology, 37,* 1342–1351.
Slovic, P., & Lichtenstein, S. C. (1971). Comparison of Bayesian and regression

approaches to the study of information processing in judgment. *Organizational Behavior and Human Performance, 6,* 649–744.

Smith, E. R. (1984). Model of social inference processes. *Psychological Review, 91,* 392–413.

Surber, C. F. (1978). *Organization in social inference: Is there a schema for judgments of ability, effort, and task performance?* Unpublished doctoral dissertation, University of Illinois at Urbana-Champaign.

Surber, C. F. (1980). The development of reversible operations in judgments of ability, effort and performance. *Child Development, 51,* 1018–1029.

Surber, C. F. (1981a). Effects of information reliability in predicting task performance using ability and effort. *Journal of Personality and Social Psychology, 40,* 977–989.

Surber, C. F. (1981b). Necessary versus sufficient causal schemata: Attributions for achievement in difficult and easy tasks. *Journal of Experimental Social Psychology, 17,* 569–586.

Surber, C. F. (1982, November). *Relationships between predictions and inferences.* Paper presented at the meeting of the Psychonomic Society, 1982, Minneapolis, MN.

Surber, C. F. (1984a). The development of achievement-related judgment processes. In J. Nicholls (Ed.), *The development of achievement motivation.* Greenwich, CT: JAI Press.

Surber, C. F. (1984b). Inferences of ability and effort: Evidence for two different processes. *Journal of Personality and Social Psychology, 46,* 249–268.

Surber, C. F. (1984c). Issues in using quantitative rating scales in developmental research. *Psychological Bulletin, 95,* 226–246.

Surber, C. F. (1985a). Applications of information integration to children's social cognitions. In J. B. Pryor & J. D. Day (Eds.), *The development of social cognition* (pp. 59–94). New York: Springer-Verlag.

Surber, C. F. (1985b). Developmental changes in inverse compensation in social and nonsocial attributions. In S. Yussen (Ed.), *The growth of reflection in children* (pp. 149–166). New York: Academic.

Surber, C. F. (1985c). Measuring the importance of information in judgment: Individual differences in weighting ability and effort. *Organizational Behavior and Human Decision Processes, 35,* 156–178.

Surber, C. F., Gzesh, S. M. (1984). Reversible operations in the balance scale task. *Journal of Experimental Child Psychology, 38,* 254–274.

Wilkening, F. (1981). Integrating velocity, time and distance information: A developmental study. *Cognitive Psychology, 13,* 231–247.

Notes

1. Mental structure and mental operations are not distinguished in most of this paper. It is possible that the same behavior (judgments of a set of variables that are reversible in ways defined below) could result from either retrieval of values (a mental representation) or operations on the subjective values of stimuli.
2. The statistical model of reversibility can be expanded to include inter-

action terms. However, its equations become quite complex, and I have not yet worked out the details of the model's predictions for the interactions across judged variables.

3. This possibility was suggested to me by Jerome Busemeyer.
4. Application of the Act* model was suggested to me by John R. Surber.

5. Implicit Theories: An Alternative to Modeling Cognition and Its Development

Robert J. Sternberg

Theories of cognition can be classified as being of two kinds: explicit and implicit. Explicit theories of cognition are constructions of psychologists or other scientists that are based, or at least tested, on data collected from people performing tasks presumed to measure cognitive functioning. For example, a battery of cognitive tests might be administered to a large group of people and the data from these tests analyzed to isolate the proposed sources of cognitive functioning in test performance. *Implicit theories* of cognition are constructions of people (psychologists or laypersons) that reside in the minds of these individuals. Such theories need to be discovered rather than invented because they already exist, in some form, in people's heads. The goal in research on implicit theories is to find out the form and content of people's informal theories of cognition. Thus, one attempts to reconstruct already existing theories rather than to construct new theories. The data of interest are people's communications regarding their notions about the nature of cognition or its aspects. For example, a survey of questions regarding the nature of cognition might be administered to a large group of people and the data from this survey analyzed in order to reconstruct people's belief systems.

Most modeling of cognitive structure and processing is based on explicit theories of cognition. In most domains and research situations, such modeling via explicit theoretical analysis makes perfect sense: One tests an explicit theory of cognitive functioning on data collected from people performing various cognitive tests. Sometimes, however, modeling based upon implicit theoretical analysis may be called for. Because of the unfamiliarity of many investigators with implicit theoretical techniques, students of cognition may miss the opportunity to collect valuable data in cases where explicit theoretical analysis is inappropriate, impossible, or in need of supplementation by implicit theoretical analysis.

The goal of this chapter is to acquaint readers with the nature of implicit theoretical modeling of human cognition and its development. The chapter is divided into four major parts. In the first, I discuss the nature and uses of implicit theoretical modeling in the study of human cognition. In the second, I discuss methodologies for performing implicit theoretical analysis. In the third part, I provide illustrations of the use of implicit theoretical analysis, primarily from my own research but also from the research of others. In the fourth part, I draw some conclusions about the use of implicit theoretical analysis in the study of human cognition.

The Nature of and Need for Implicit Theoretical Modeling of Human Cognition and Its Development

Implicit theoretical analysis is a method for understanding people's conceptions of their cognitive structures and processes. Under what kinds of circumstances might one seek such understanding?

Understanding Behavior Motivated by Implicit Theories

Implicit theories of cognition drive the way in which people perceive and evaluate both their own cognition and that of others. To understand better the judgments people make about their own and others' cognition, it is useful to learn about their implicit theories. For example, parents' implicit theories of their childrens' language development will determine at what ages they will be willing to make various corrections in their children's speech. More generally, parents' implicit theories of children's cognitive development will determine at what ages they believe their children are ready to perform various cognitive tasks. In sum, knowledge about implicit theories is important because it is so heavily used by people in making judgments in their everyday lives.

Defining the Scope of an as yet Poorly Understood Phenomenon

Certain kinds of methodology can be particularly useful at different stages of research into various phenomena. For example, rigorous mathematical modeling of stimulus variance requires that one have an a priori model of task performance and hence tends to be useful in the middle or later stages of research. In contrast, exploratory factor analysis and protocol analysis can be useful for gleaning an idea of just how individuals approach a task that is poorly understood. Because of its exploratory nature, implicit theoretical analysis probably has some of its greatest uses during the early stages of research into a given phenomenon.

Because implicit theories of scientific investigators ultimately give rise to their explicit theories, it is useful to find out what these implicit theories are, perhaps even before the explicit theories have been proposed. Implicit theories essentially provide a framework, or a lay of the land, that can be useful in defining the general scope of a new phenomenon to be investigated. Sometimes, the phenomenon is not itself newly discovered, but there is a need for a new approach to an old phenomenon. Again, understanding implicit theories can suggest what aspects of the phenomenon have been more or less attended to in previous investigations. Finally, studying implicit theories can be useful when an investigator suspects that existing explicit theories are wrong or misleading. If an investigation of implicit theories reveals little correspondence with the explicit theories, the implicit theories may be wrong. The possibility also has to be taken into account, however, that the explicit theories are wrong and in need of correction or supplementation. For example, it will be argued later that implicit theories of intelligence suggest the need for expansion of some of our explicit theories of the construct.

Understanding Developmental and Cross-Cultural Differences

Many, if not most, psychological investigators have a tendency to extrapolate the validity of their results beyond the population from which their sample(s) can reasonably be construed as having been drawn. Consider, for example, the field of intelligence. Investigators were drawing universal conclusions about the nature of intelligence before they had ever systematically investigated the intelligence of people in other cultures. They continue to do so to this day, using tasks on single or multiple homogeneous populations and drawing conclusions about others as well (see, e.g., chapters in Eysenck, 1982).

Similarly, investigators make unwarranted extrapolations about developmental phenomena. For many years, the standard operating procedure in the study of intelligence across the adult life span was to administer various kinds of standard psychometric tests and to draw conclusions about the growth versus decline of levels of intelligence with age. More recently, investigators have come to realize the importance of defining exactly what intelligence is at various ages. For example, we do not measure the intelligence of infants or even young children in the early school years in the same way that we measure the intelligence of adults. Analogously, it may be necessary to measure the intelligence of older adults in ways that are different from those we use to measure the intelligence of younger adults. For example, tests such as the Scholastic Aptitude Test and the Graduate Record Examination require fairly extensive knowledge of algebraic and geometric concepts in their mathematical sections. Such knowledge may or may not be fairly common among high school and college students, but it is not likely to be common knowledge among older adults, many of whom will not have used algebraic formulas and geometric principles for as much as half a century or more.

The point, quite simply, is that we cannot blindly assume that intelligence or any other aspect of mental functioning is necessarily the same across populations, especially if the construct is, at least in part, a social construction. Analysis of implicit theories can provide a useful means for suggesting similarities and differences in psychological constructs across populations. Berry (1984), for example, has provided a masterful review of implicit theories of intelligence across various cultural groups. The review shows the sometimes astonishing range of conceptions harbored by people in various cultures with regard to the nature of intelligence. Parents in some cultures may literally bring their children up in ways that are opposed to the ways of parents of other cultures, with both sets of parents being convinced that they are bringing up their children to be intelligent. The work of Heath (1983) demonstrates that this phenomenon is not limited to different cultures around the world, but applies as well to different subcultures within the United States.

The idea that intelligence may vary across cultural or subcultural groups is not nearly as exotic as it sounds. Consider, for example, the respective roles of memory and reasoning in intelligence. In today's middle-class world, children are brought up to be reasoning individuals, and mere memorization of facts is scoffed at. Few middle-class parents wish to bring up their children to be "automatons" who merely recite facts. Yet, throughout most of our history and throughout most of the world, a good memory has been, and is still considered to be, a major part of intelligence (Laboratory of Comparative Human Cognition, 1982). Many schools, even today, place far more emphasis on the products of memory skills than on the products of reasoning skills. Often the child with a good memory is identified as being intelligent and thus will be at an advantage throughout his or her scholastic career.

Fry (1984) has done a fascinating study of conceptions of children's intelligence held by teachers at different levels of schooling. She found that teachers of primary school children tend to emphasize social skills in their definitions of intelligence, teachers of secondary school students tend to emphasize verbal skills, and teachers of college students tend to emphasize abstract reasoning and symbol-manipulation skills. These different notions about the nature of intelligence are bound to have an effect on the kinds of children that the teachers label as intelligent (Heath, 1983). As a result, children with varying patterns of abilities are likely to be at a relative advantage or disadvantage at different points in schooling.

There are at least three ways in which to approach data such as Berry's and Fry's. One is to conclude that intelligence truly is universal and that many people throughout the world have misconceptions about intelligence. From this point of view, it is the layperson who needs an education. A second approach is to conclude that intelligence is particularistic with respect to populations differing in attributes such as age or culture. From this point of view, it is the majority of psychologists who need education. The psychologists are making assumptions of uniformity that simply do not apply across populations. A third possible conclusion is that intelligence has both universal and particularistic attributes and that each of these attributes must be understood both separately and in interaction. In other words, there may be a common core to intelligence across cultures and across the life span.

Berg and Sternberg (1985a) have taken this latter position. They assert that the ability to cope with novelty in the environment is a source of continuity in the nature of intelligence throughout the life span, whether or not it is adequately measured by existing tests. Conceivably, this ability may be common across cultures as well, because members of any culture need to cope with novelty to develop cognitively and even to survive. One could make an evolutionary argument that species are selected for reproduction in part because of their ability to cope with novelty and that this ability is thus essential to the intelligence of survival of a species (Jerison, 1982). Berg and Sternberg have found that implicit theories of intelligence differ across the life span: Intelligence is not viewed as being exactly the same thing at every possible age level. These two lines of research need not be viewed as mutually contradictory if one views intelligence as having both universal and particularistic aspects. Berg and Sternberg take such a point of view, adopting Sternberg's (1985a) triarchic theory of human intelligence as a basis. In this theory, intelligence is viewed as having both a universal (componential) and a particularistic (contextual) aspect.

To conclude, investigation of mental constructs such as intelligence can provide a useful supplement to explicit theoretical investigation. It would be foolish to suggest, of course, that implicit theoretical investigations should replace explicit theoretical ones. Implicit theoretical investigations cannot substitute for explicit theoretical ones. Rather, they provide complementary information that can provide a useful perspective on the results of explicit theoretical investigations. The nature of this complementation is illustrated throughout this chapter.

Methodology of Implicit Theoretical Analysis

Before some examples are given of how implicit theoretical analysis can be useful in studying various aspects of cognition and its development, it is helpful to provide some basic guidelines as to the forms that implicit theoretically motivated research can take. Although the exact methodology needs to be tailored to the specific constructs and population under investigation, there are some commonalities in the ways such investigations proceed. Those commonalities are outlined in this section.

Defining the Domain of Inquiry: Behavioral Listings

The first step in implicit theoretical analysis is almost always the collection of listings of behaviors or traits that characterize people's conceptions of the domain of inquiry. For example, if one wishes to investigate implicit theories of wisdom, one would start by asking people in a specified population to list behaviors or traits that characterize wise individuals. If one wishes to study implicit theories of creativity, similarly, one would begin by asking people to list behaviors or traits characteristic of creative individuals. It is important to specify in advance exactly what population or populations are the targets for obtaining such listings and hence the population or populations to which findings will be generalized.

Typically, individuals provide listings that have some degree of overlap, but not full overlap. Some of the listed traits or behaviors are idiosyncratic to particular individuals; others are common to practically all the individuals. Hence, it is necessary to analyze the content of the behavioral listings, quantifying the number of individuals who list each behavior or trait. Such quantification will require merging behaviors or traits that are the same but are worded differently by different individuals. For example, *thinks rapidly* and *thinks quickly* presumably refer to the same characteristic, even though the words are slightly different. In some cases, the conceptual equivalence of different semantic units is less obvious. For example, *acts impulsively* and *acts too quickly* probably refer to the same basic concepts, even though the words are somewhat different. In merging lists across individuals, errors in the direction of keeping listed attributes separate are better than bringing the attributes together if it is uncertain whether two attributes do indeed correspond. Later the attributes can be merged after further statistical analysis, if such a merger is warranted.

The end product of these listings is a long list of behaviors accompanied by a frequency of response for each. At this point, we typically eliminate from the master list of traits or behaviors any attributes that have not been listed by at least two individuals, thereby weeding out totally idiosyncratic attributes. Almost inevitably, a substantial proportion of behavior listings will be idiosyncratic.

Determining the Structure of People's Implicit Theories: Latent-Structure Analysis

Behavioral listings are useful for limiting the scope of cognitive phenomena, but they are not useful for revealing the organization of these phenomena. Further data collection and analysis are needed to determine the implicit theories of the organization of cognitive phenomena.

In the next phase of research, new subjects are presented with the edited list of behaviors from the first phase of research. They are asked to rate or sort these behaviors or traits in a way that is appropriate for the investigator's goals. One possibility is to have individuals sort the behaviors into as many or as few piles as they wish, putting together attributes that seem psychologically related. Another procedure, which may be used instead of or in conjunction with the first, is to have individuals rate the listed behaviors. Typically, we asked subjects to rate how *characteristic* each behavior or trait is in the repertoire of an exceptionally _____ person, where the blank is filled in with the appropriate term, such as *intelligent, wise,* or *creative*. Alternatively, we might ask subjects to rate how *important* each behavior or trait is in defining the construct under investigation. It is important to determine the reliabilities of these and all other measures, in order to adequately assess the meaning of various data sets and statistics derived from them.

Ratings of degree of characteristic and ratings of importance yield overlapping but distinct information. An attribute can be highly characteristic of a certain kind of individual, but not necessarily important in defining the psychological construct under investigation. For example, intelligent people characteristically eat food, but eating is probably not very important to defining the psychological construct of intelligence. Similarly, attributes can be important for defining given classes of people, but not very characteristic. For example, some people might view the ability to solve complex logical problems as important to defining the concept of intelligence, but even very intelligent people do not characteristically solve such problems on a routine basis in their everyday lives.

Characteristic and importance ratings also have different scale properties. Consider, for example, the behavior *continually solves problems incorrectly*. Such a behavior would probably be rated as extremely *uncharacteristic* of a highly intelligent person, but it would not be meaningful to refer to this behavior as *unimportant* in defining the concept of intelligence. In general, a negative pole for characteristic ratings is conceptualized easily: People who are notably unintelligent or unwise, or whatever the characteristic, do not exhibit certain traits or behaviors, and hence the traits or behaviors are referred to as *uncharacteristic* of the individuals. But such traits and behaviors do not fit well into a scheme for importance ratings. Importance ratings do not carry with them the polarities that characteristicness ratings have. Including behaviors or traits that correspond to the pole opposite to that of interest (such as *unintelligent* or *unwise*) works for characteristicness ratings but not for importance ratings. Unintelligent behaviors are uncharacteristic of intelligent people, but they may be important for defining the concept of intelligence.

Sometimes, one will wish to investigate the characteristicness or importance of traits or behaviors not for the positive end of a continuum (for example, *intelligence*), but for the negative end of the continuum (for example, *unintelligence* or *stupidity*). Ratings for marked forms of the construct under investigation can be solicited in the same way as ratings for the unmarked form. Similarly, one may wish to examine an "average prototype" rather than an ideal one. In other words, one might be interested in the traits or behaviors of the typically intelligent or the typically wise person, rather than the extremely intelligent or wise one. Again, ratings can be collected in the same way. Indeed, if one wishes to examine what distinguishes the highly intelligent person from the typically intelligent one, one may wish to collect ratings for both ideal and average prototypes and then use difference scores as a basis for further analysis. In using such difference scores, it is the difference between the exceptional and average person, rather than the absolute characteristics of the exceptional or average person, that becomes the object of analysis.

Ratings of characteristicness and importance differ in one critical respect from sortings of behaviors. In ratings, one must tell the subjects what to rate the attributes for, say, intelligence or wisdom. In sorting tasks, one typically does not tell the individual on what basis to sort. Thus, the sorting task is less structured than the ratings task. Which is appropriate will depend on the particular purposes of the investigator. For example, if one wished to discover the latent dimensions in people's conceptions of intelligence, it would be quite appropriate to have subjects rate various behaviors or traits with regard to their characteristicness or importance for intelligence. But if one wished to determine whether people distinguished between traits or behaviors that characterize intelligent versus wise individuals, one might simply ask subjects to sort behaviors and then determine whether the latent structure (see below) of the sortings distinguishes between the two constructs. An alternative to the sorting procedure would be to have subjects rate the behaviors for their characteristicness or importance for intelligent individuals and for wise individuals and then to use the difference scores as a basis for further data analysis.

After the ratings or sortings are collected, the data are subjected to a variety of techniques for latent-structure analysis, such as principal-component analysis, common-factor analysis, metric or nonmetric multidimensional scaling, or hierarchical or nonhierarchical clustering. The choice of technique depends on the type of data collected, the investigator's hunches about the structure of the data, and the constraints built into the data themselves. For example, principal-component analysis will probably be preferred to common-factor analysis if the correlation matrix to be analyzed is singular, and metric multidimensional scaling will probably be preferred to nonmetric multidimensional scaling if the data are not highly constrained. Sometimes, more than one of these techniques is used to analyze the data in several ways.

It is not possible to give here a detailed accounting of how each method may be applied to rating or sorting data. (See Chapter 7, this volume, by Miller.) For information on component and factor analysis, the reader is referred to Gorsuch (1983). For information on multidimensional scaling, see Kruskal and Wish (1978). For information on cluster analysis, the reader is referred to Hartigan (1975).

The outcomes of these methods are series of either dimensions (in the case of factor analysis and scaling analysis) or clusters (in the case of cluster analysis). The structures are named by the investigator on the basis of the variables having salient loadings on them. Of course, the names are only as good as the analyst's intuitions in selecting them. For example, factors showing salient loadings for traits or behaviors measuring verbal skills might be labeled *verbal ability*. Usually, the strengths as well as the interpretations of the factors, dimensions, or clusters are of interest. For example, in principal-component solutions, factors are extracted in order of strength, and priority of extraction indicates a component that is likely to more salient in people's implicit theories.

Prototypical Analysis

For People's Evaluations of Themselves

A motivating idea in many implicit theoretical analyses is that underlying people's implicit theories are one or more prototypes representing their normative standards, whether for the ideal or the typical. These normative standards can be used as a basis for scoring people's ratings about themselves.

Implicit theories, like explicit theories, can serve as bases for the construction of scales to measure various kinds of ability patterns. When implicit theories are used, a first set of subjects rates the ideal individual on a given dimension, for example, intelligence. A second set of individuals rate themselves for each of the traits or behaviors relevant to measuring this dimension. Thus, two sets of ratings are obtained, one for the ideal and the other for the actual subjects in the study, which can then be compared.

There are at least two standard ways of making this comparison. The first involves calculating a correlation coefficient between the real and ideal response patterns. In this case, resemblance to the prototype is a function of similarity of a given individuals' response pattern to the prototypical response pattern, without regard to possible differences in the use of the two scales. The correlation coefficient, of course, is insensitive to absolute magnitudes of scale values. The advantage of this insensitivity is that if the scale was used differently for the two sets of subjects (real and ideal), this difference will not be reflected in the correlation. The disadvantage of the correlation coefficient is that one may actually wish to take scale differences into account. For example, one might argue that even if two response patterns are identical, one would not wish to give a perfect score to an individual who shows the same response pattern as the "ideal" subject but whose responses are low on the scale in absolute magnitudes.

The second method of scoring involves computation of a measure of badness of fit between the real and ideal response patterns. For example, one can compute the root-mean-square deviation (RMSD) between the real and ideal response patterns. This index is computed by taking the square root of the mean of the squared deviations between real and ideal response patterns. This measure, unlike the correlation measure, is on the same scale as the original data, and it is sensitive to the values of numbers on the scale. For example, even if two response patterns are identical, the RMSD will be high if there are large absolute discrepancies between the two sets of values.

It is also possible, of course, simply to compute sums of ratings of the trait or behavioral checklists while taking into account the direction in which each item should be scored. For example, in measuring intelligence, one would add scale values for "intelligent behaviors" but subtract scale values for "unintelligent behaviors." This method of scoring yields a simple sum, much as in traditional test scoring. Nevertheless, this method of scoring may be less satisfactory for tests based on implicit theories than for those based upon explicit theories or for an atheoretical test. First, the summing of item values fails to make use of the theoretical notion of resemblance to the prototype underlying the data (Neisser, 1979). Second, the method is more susceptible to "faking good", wherein the perfect score will be identical to the most socially desirable one. Thus, a subject who rates herself or himself highest on the positive traits and behaviors and lowest on the negative traits and behaviors will receive the best possible score. This will not necessarily be the case in the prototype method of scoring, however, because the ideal is not necessarily at the top of the scale on all positive traits or behaviors or at the bottom of the scale on all negative traits or behaviors. If this direct method of scoring is used, it is perhaps best used in conjunction with one or both types of prototype scoring.

Prototypical analysis of individuals' questionnaire scores is probably best used in conjunction with scores from standard psychometric or cognitive measures. The standard measures differ in several key respects from the implicit theoretical ones and provide an important complement to the implicit theoretical measures, just as the implicit theoretical measures provide an important complement to the more standard measures. First, standard measures are typically maximum-performance ones, whereas the new kinds of measures are usually typical-performance ones. Second, the standard measures require one to perform certain tasks that directly measure cognitive skills, whereas the new measures require one to describe one's performance on such tasks. Third, the new measures are obviously more susceptible to various kinds of faking than the old measures, which is an especially important reason for using the old measures in conjunction with the new ones. Fourth, the new measures are less susceptible to test anxiety and other forms of blocking in the taking of the examinations and can be more responsive to cultural and age differences. Indeed, it is possible to form different prototypes for subjects of different ages and cultural groups and to score a given protocol for just one of these prototypes. On this notion, the response pattern of, say, a highly intelligent individual from an African country need not ideally look the same as the response pattern of an intelligent individual from North America. This accounting for prototypes is much more difficult to do with standard kinds of test batteries.

It is useful, if both implicit and explicit kinds of tests are used, to correlate scores between the two kinds of measures as well as within multiple measures of the same kind. In this way, it is possible to discern the extent to which scores for the two types of measures reflect various constructs as opposed to methods of measurement. For example, one would probably have more confidence in a result if implicit and explicit measures of a given construct showed higher correlations than implicit measures of different constructs or explicit measures of different constructs.

For People's Evaluations of Others

Prototypical analysis can be used not only to understand people's evaluations of themselves, but also to understand people's evaluations of others. Typically, we have constructed profiles of hypothetical individuals who are described to exhibit certain traits or behaviors that were previously listed as more or less characteristic of ideally intelligent individuals. (Attributes other than intelligence can be, and have been, used.) The hypothetical individuals are described in ways that result in considerable variance in their intelligence or other characteristics, as would be predicted from the characteristicness ratings obtained in earlier phases of research. For example, one individual might be described in a way that would render her quite intelligent according to the characteristicness ratings from the implicit theories, whereas another individual might be described in a way that would render him quite unintelligent. We then have subjects rate each of the hypothetical individuals on the attribute under consideration, for example, intelligence.

There are at least two questions of primary interest in this procedure. The first concerns the correlation between the observed ratings for each of the hypothetical individuals and the predicted ratings, based on the characteristicness ratings obtained in the earlier phases of research. To obtain predicted ratings for the attribute, one takes these characteristicness ratings from the earlier phases of research and then finds a mean for the behavior of each hypothetical individual (or, alternatively, a sum, if one prefers a summative to an averaging model). The correlations between the predicted and the observed ratings gives one a sense of the extent to which people use their implicit theories in evaluating others.

A second datum of interest concerns the beta weights (standardized regression coefficients) for predicting observed ratings from factor or scale scores obtained from the earlier phases of research. Suppose, for example, one performed a factor analysis for the ideal-subject rating. One can then obtain approximate factor coefficients by weighing each salient trait or behavior 1 and each nonsalient trait or behavior 0. One can compute factor scores for each hypothetical individual on each of the obtained factors by taking the mean value for each hypothetical individual on these coefficients (see Gorsuch, 1983). Thus, one uses the approximation coefficients to obtain a score for each given individual on constructs such as verbal ability, problem-solving ability, and so on, by relating the behaviors describing the individuals to the behaviors factor analyzed earlier. One can then predict the overall observed rating from the factor scores for the hypothetical individuals and determine the extent to which subjects weigh each factor in evaluating each hypothetical individual on the construct under investigation.

All these procedures may become more clear through illustration by concrete examples. In the next section, such concrete examples are provided from three sets of studies we have done that use implicit theoretical analysis.

Review of Studies Implying Implicit Theoretical Analysis

My collaborators and I have performed three sets of studies that make fairly heavy use of implicit theoretical analysis. The first was on implicit theories of intelligence, academic intelligence, and everyday intelligence in laypersons (novices) and experts (Sternberg, Conway, Ketron, & Bernstein, 1981). The second set of studies was done on implicit theories of intelligence across the adult life span (Berg & Sternberg, 1985b). The third set of studies was on implicit theories of intelligence, wisdom, and creativity in adults who were either laypersons or experts in various fields of endeavor (Sternberg, 1985b). Each set of studies is described in turn. The studies are numbered consecutively throughout the chapter for ease of reference.

Implicit Theories of Intelligence, Academic Intelligence, and Everyday Intelligence

Study 1

We sought to compile a master list of intelligent and unintelligent behaviors and to ascertain various characteristics of these behaviors and their relations to the people who supplied them.

The experiment involved 180 subjects, including 61 people studying in a college library, 63 waiting for trains in a railroad station during morning and afternoon rush hours, and 62 people entering a local supermarket. Students predominated among the library sample, commuters among the railroad sample, and homemakers among the supermarket sample. People were approached by one of four experimenters in each locale and were asked to give 5 minutes of their time to the experiment. Those who agreed received a blank page on which to list behaviors characteristic of intelligence, academic intelligence, everyday intelligence, or unintelligence.

People were also asked to rate themselves on intelligence, academic intelligence, and everyday intelligence. Each individual listed behaviors characteristic of just one of the four investigated attributes.

The behaviors listed by the subjects were compiled into a master list of 250 behaviors, of which 170 were for the various kinds of intelligence and 80 were for unintelligence. We simply listed frequencies for the various behaviors and correlated these frequencies for each group. Intelligence and academic intelligence were significantly correlated for the library group, but not for either the railroad group or the supermarket group. In contrast, intelligence and everyday intelligence were significantly correlated for the railroad and the supermarket groups, but not for the library group. In other words, subjects in the library viewed intelligence as closer to academic intelligence, whereas the other subjects saw intelligence as closer to everyday intelligence. This analysis permits examination of the relations among intelligence, academic intelligence, and everyday intelligence for stimulus variance. The self-ratings enable one to perform the same examination for subject variance within each group. In the library group, the correlation between self-rated intelligence and academic intelligence was .80, compared to the correlation of .42 between intelligence and everyday intelligence. Thus, intelligence was perceived as much closer to academic than to everyday intelligence. In contrast, the comparable correlations for the railroad group were .73 and .74, respectively. In other words, the commuters viewed their academic intelligence and their everyday intelligence as equally related to their intelligence. The supermarket group came out in between: Their comparable correlations were .83 and .65, respectively. The correlations between academic and everyday intelligence reflected the same pattern: .28 for the library group, .60 for the railroad group, and .41 for the supermarket group. Thus, the library group saw these two entities as most distinct, and the railroad group saw them as least distinct.

Study 2

Two principal groups of subjects were tested. The first group comprised 120 persons who responded to newspaper advertisements. Because the results of the first study suggested that students' conceptions of intelligence can differ substantially from nonstudents' conceptions, and because our primary interest was in the general population, students were excluded from participation. The second group comprised 140 experts in the field of intelligence who responded to our questionnaire. All experts were psychologists with doctoral degrees doing research on intelligence in major university and research centers around the country. They answered a questionnaire sent by mail. The return rate on the questionnaire was 48 percent. Materials consisted of a list of 250 behaviors compiled from Study 1. A page on which laypersons could rate themselves by using a percentile scale on intelligence, academic intelligence, and everyday intelligence was also included. Laypersons received the Henmon-Nelson Test of Mental Abilities.

Four different questionnaires were prepared. All four questionnaires were distributed to laypersons; only the first two questionnaires were distributed to experts. No individual received more than one questionnaire. All items required ratings on a scale of 1 (low) to 9 (high).

One group of subjects provided ratings of how *important* each of the 170 behaviors associated with intelligence (as opposed to unintelligence) was in defining their conception of an ideally (1) intelligent person, (2) academically intelligent person, and (3) everyday intelligent person. The ideal was described as the best possible in a given dimension, but no further information was given. Subjects in a second group were asked to rate how *characteristic* each of 250 behaviors was of an ideally (1) intelligent person, (2) academically intelligent person, and (3) everyday intelligent person. Subjects in a third group were asked to rate how *characteristic* each of 250 behaviors was of their ideal concept of (1) intelligence, (2) academic intelligence, and (3) everyday intelligence. Note that in subjects in the second group rated an ideal person, whereas subjects in the third group rated an ideal conception. In group 4, subjects rated how *characteristic* each of 250 behaviors was of (1) themselves and (2) the adult whom they knew best. The order in which ratings for intelligence, academic intelligence, and everyday intelligence were made was counterbalanced across subjects.

Several major points of interest emerged from the data. First, experts view intelligence as very closely related behaviorally to both academic and everyday intelligence. The correlations between patterns of ratings were .90 between intelligence and academic intelligence and .90 between intelligence and everyday intelligence for the experts' importance ratings. The comparable correlations for their characteristicness ratings (group 2) were .83 and .84, respectively. Laypersons view academic and everyday intelligence as less closely related to intelligence, especially in terms of the importance of the behaviors to defining ideal persons. The correlations between their importance ratings for intelligence, on one hand, and academic and everyday intelligence, on the other, were .81 and .76. The comparable correlations for the characteristicness ratings (group 2) were .75 and .86, respectively. Experts see academic and everyday intelligence as less closely related than they see intelligence as related to each of academic and everyday intelligence, but again the laypersons see an even weaker relationship. The correlations between ratings for academic and everyday intelligence were .67 (importance) and .46 (characteristicness) for the experts and .36 (importance) and .45 (characteristicness) for the laypersons. Clearly, both experts and laypersons distinguish between behaviors associated with academic intelligence and behaviors associated with everyday intelligence.

Second, ratings of importance (group 1) and of characteristicness (group 2) showed generally similar trends and were, in fact, highly correlated. These correlations were typically in the .90s for the experts and in the .70s to .80s for the laypersons.

Third, ratings of experts and laypersons for comparable kinds of intelligence are quite highly correlated, with all but one of the six correlations ranging in the .80s. In each case (importance and characteristicness ratings), the correlation is highest for academic intelligence and lowest for everyday intelligence. In view of the small range in the correlations, one can probably conclude that experts and laypersons have similar, but not identical, perceptions of the nature of intelligence.

The data from the second group were subjected to principal-component analysis, followed by varimax rotation of the factorial axes. Because of the unwieldiness of the original set of 170 intelligent behaviors as input to the final analysis, preliminary factor analyses were done to reduce the original set to a more tractable set of 98 behaviors.

Three interpretable factors emerged from the analysis of ratings of the ideally intelligent person as supplied by the laypersons. The factors were labeled *practical problem-solving ability, verbal ability,* and *social competence,* and they accounted for 29, 10, and 7 percent of the variance in the data, respectively. The first factor includes behaviors such as *reasons logically and well, identifies connections among ideas,* and *sees all aspects of a problem.* The second factor includes behaviors such as *speaks clearly and articulately, is verbally fluent,* and *converses well.* The third factor includes behaviors such as *accepts others for what they are, admits mistakes,* and *displays interest in the world at large.*

Factor analyses were also conducted on the ratings of academic intelligence and everyday intelligence. For academic intelligence, three interpretable factors emerged, *verbal ability, problem-solving ability,* and *social competence,* accounting for 20, 8, and 7 percent of the variance in the data, respectively. For everyday intelligence, four interpretable factors emerged, *practical problem-solving ability, social competence, character,* and *interest in learning and culture,* accounting for 26, 10, 8, and 6 percent of the variance in the data, respectively.

Several points are worth noting. First, the factors for the three kinds of intelligence are highly overlapping. Second, problem-solving ability and social competence cross-cut all three kinds of intelligence. Third, the cognitive factors that constitute people's belief system for intelligence seem closely to resemble the two principal factors in Cattell and Horn's theory of fluid and crystallized intelligence (Cattell, 1971; Horn, 1968). Fluid intelligence emphasizes reasoning and problem-solving skills, whereas crystalized intelligence emphasizes verbal-comprehension skills.

Comparable factor analyses were conducted for the experts. Three interpretable factors emerged in the experts' ratings of characteristicness of behaviors, *verbal intelligence, problem-solving ability,* and *practical intelligence*. These factors accounted for 23, 19, and 9 percent of the variance in the data, respectively. The first factor included behaviors such as *displays a good vocabulary, reads with high comprehension,* and *displays curiosity*. The second factor included behaviors such as *able to apply knowledge to problems at hand, makes good decisions,* and *poses problems in an optimal way*. The third factor included behaviors such as *sizes up situations well, determines how to achieve goals,* and *displays awareness to world around him or her*. Comparable factor analyses were conducted for academic and everyday intelligence. For academic intelligence, three factors accounting for 26, 12, and 9 percent of the variance in the data, respectively, were labeled *problem-solving ability, verbal ability,* and *motivation*. For everyday intelligence, three factors accounting for 26, 13, and 6 percent of the variance in the data, respectively, were labeled *practical problem-solving ability, practical adaptive behavior,* and *social competence*.

Four main points emerged from these analyses. First, as was the case for laypersons, problem-solving ability is perceived as playing a major role in all three kinds of intelligence. Second, practical intelligence sometimes emerged in the factors for intelligence and everyday intelligence. Third, a motivation factor emerged in the analysis of data for ratings regarding academic intelligence. Finally, the first two cognitive factors in the experts' conceptions of intelligence, like those in the laypersons' conceptions, seemed to correspond closely to fluid and crystallized abilities, whereas the third factor again seemed to represent some kind of practical or social adaptation.

Laypersons' mean self-ratings on the percentile scale were 74 for intelligence, 71 for academic intelligence, and 74 for everyday intelligence. The mean ratings of others on the percentile scale were 76, 74, and 74 for intelligence, academic intelligence, and everyday intelligence, respectively. For the self, the intercorrelations of the three ratings were .60 for intelligence and academic intelligence, .62 for intelligence and everyday intelligence, and .54 for academic and everyday intelligence. Correlations for the ratings of the other were lower: .25, .48, and .39, respectively. Correlations of these self-ratings with Henmon-Nelson IQ were .23 for intelligence, .36 for academic intelligence, and .30 for everyday intelligence.

We also computed a prototypicality measure by correlating each layperson's pattern of self-ratings with the pattern of ideal-subject ratings of characteristicness of behaviors from the data set described earlier. The mean prototypicality index (i.e., mean correlation between self-described actual and ideal behaviors) was .40 for intelligence, .31 for academic intelligence, and .41 for everyday intelligence. Correlations of the prototypicality measure with IQ were .52 for the intelligence measure, .56 for the academic intelligence measure, and .45 for the everyday intelligence measure. Thus, the prototypicality measure actually serves as a relatively good predictor of IQ, especially for academic intelligence.

Study 3

In this study, we sought to ascertain the extent to which people actually use behaviors associated with intelligence and unintelligence in their evaluations of other people's intelligence, particularly when they are presented with written behavioral descriptions of the others.

A questionnaire was sent to 168 persons selected at random from a local telephone book. Of these persons, 65 responded in time for their data to be used in the study.

The principal experimental material was a 90-item questionnaire. Each item consisted of a verbal description of behaviors characterizing some particular person. People were told that they would "find a brief description of different people, listing various characteristics they had. Assume that the list for each person is made of characteristics that teachers have supplied to describe that person as accurately as possible." The subject's task was to "read the characteristics for each person and then to rate each person on how intelligent" the subject considered the person to be. Ratings were made on a scale from 1 to 9, where 1 was labeled *not at all intelligent,* 5 was labeled *average intelligent,* and 9 was labeled *extremely intelligent.* Half of the items on the questionnaire presented unquantified behavioral descriptions (e.g., "She converses well"), and half presented a mixture of quantified (e.g., "She often converses well") and unquantified descriptions. Moreover, half of the descriptions were paired with male names and half with female names: A given description was paired half the time with a name of each sex.

An example of a problem from this study was:

Susan:
She keeps an open mind.
She is knowledgeable about a particular field of knowledge.
She converses well.
She shows a lack of independence.
She is on time for appointments.

All subjects received the same questionnaire items, except that half of the subjects received quantified items presented before unquantified ones, and the other half received the reverse ordering, and different names were paired with different descriptions so that those that were male for half the subjects were female for the other half, and vice versa.

The mean rating of intelligence over the 45 unquantified descriptions was 5.09; the mean rating over the 45 quantified descriptions was 4.49. The difference between ratings was significant, indicating the quantification generally lowered ratings of intelligence. The correlation between the unquantified statements and their paired quantified versions was .87, indicating that although quantification lowered ratings, it changed their pattern only slightly. It made no difference in means whether a given description was paired with a male or a female name. The means for the male and female names were practically indistinguishable (within .01 on the rating scale), and the correlation between identical descriptions paired for male versus female names was .99 in the unquantified condition and .98 in the quantified condition.

Two basic kinds of modeling were done for the unquantified descriptions. In the first, we took means and sums of characteristicness ratings from experts from Study 2 and computed means on the basis of those behaviors listed in each description given in the present experiment. The correlation between ratings of intelligence and the mean characteristicness rating for each fictitious person was .96; the correlation between ratings of intelligence and the summed characteristicness ratings for each fictitious person was .97. Comparable correlations were obtained if laypersons' rather than experts' prototypes were used. Hence, the prototype ratings from the earlier experiment provided excellent predictions of the ratings in the present experiment.

In the second kind of modeling, multiple regression was used to predict the overall rating of the intelligence of the fictitious person from counts of numbers of behaviors in each of the factors of intelligence (and the behaviors characterizing unintelligence) found in each description. The multiple correlation between the ratings of the intelligence of the fictitious person, on one hand, and the aspects of perceived intelligence and unintelligence, on the other, was .97. Regression weights were .32 for practical problem-solving ability, .33 for verbal ability, .19 for social competence, and −.48 for unintelligence. All weights were significant and in the predicted directions. The same kinds of analysis were performed on the data for quantified descriptions, with very similar results. Thus, we can conclude that people use their implicit theories of intelligence in evaluating the intelligence of others as well as themselves. As in the self-ratings, people seem to weigh cognitive factors more heavily than noncognitive ones and to take into account negative as well as positive information.

Implicit Theories of Intelligence across the Adult Life Span

The studies described above concerned different conceptions of intelligence held by experts and nonexperts. In a second set of studies, Berg and Sternberg (1985b) investigated the development of implicit theories of intelligence over the life span.

Study 4

The main purpose of Study 4 was to compile a master list of behaviors associated with intelligence. In this study, 152 subjects ranging in age from 20 to 83 years were asked to list as many behaviors as they could that characterize an exceptionally intelligent individual and an exceptionally unintelligent individual of 30, 50, or 70 years of age. The subjects themselves were divided into three age groups: a young group (mean age = 29.8, range of 20 to 39), a middle-aged group (mean age = 49.4, range of 40 to 59), and an older group (mean age = 68, range of 60 to 83). Subjects received a questionnaire by mail or else were contacted by telephone.

The master list consisted of 130 intelligent and 120 unintelligent behaviors. Correlations were computed between the frequencies of each of the 130 intelligent behaviors for each age prototype. The correlations between the frequencies of listed behaviors for the different aged prototypes range from .35 to .56. The correlations suggested that the frequency with which the items were listed was most similar between the exceptionally intelligent 50-year-old prototype and the exceptionally intelligent 70-year-old prototype and was least similar between the exceptionally intelligent 30-year-old prototype and the exceptionally intelligent 70-year-old prototype. Thus, the closer the ages of the prototypes, the more similar the frequencies of listed behaviors.

Study 5

In this study, we sought to reduce the number of behaviors to a more manageable set and to determine, in preliminary fashion, the characteristics underlying peoples' implicit theories of exceptionally intelligent individuals at 30, 50, and 70 years of age.

Materials for the experiment consisted of a subset of the 250 behaviors compiled from experiment 1. Because of the large number of unintelligent behaviors gathered in experiment 1, and because our primary interest was in intelligent behaviors, a panel of three raters (ages 28, 55, and 70) judged how important each behavior was in defining unintelligent individuals in general. Behaviors that received a mean and median rating of 5 or over (on a scale of 1 to 9) were retained.

Twenty-two volunteers comprising each of three age groups (24 to 36, 39 to 58, and 60 to 84) served as paid participants. All individuals were selected from the membership list of a large church. These individuals were asked to complete six different questionnaires. All involved ratings on a rating scale of 1 (low) to 9 (high). Questionnaire 1 dealt with ratings of the importance of behaviors in defining an exceptionally intelligent 30-year-old individual. Questionnaire 2 required the same ratings for an exceptionally unintelligent 30-year-old individual. Questionnaires 3 and 4 required ratings for an exceptionally intelligent and unintelligent 50-year-old, respectively. Similarly, questionnaires 5 and 6 dealt with ratings for an exceptionally intelligent and unintelligent 70-year-old, respectively. Questionnaires 1, 3, and 5 contained the same list of intelligent behaviors, and questionnaires 2, 4, and 6 contained the same list of unintelligent behaviors. The order in which behaviors were presented in each questionnaire was randomized, and the order of questionnaires was counterbalanced across subjects.

We did a factor analysis on the data for a subset of 55 intelligent behaviors that received the highest mean importance ratings on at least one questionnaire. This method of compilation was chosen so that certain behaviors deemed important for one age-specific intelligent prototype would be included in the analysis, even though they may not have been deemed important at the other age levels.

The inputs to the various data analyses were three sets of correlation coefficients. One set involved the intercorrelations of the 55 variables for questionnaire 1. The second set involved the intercorrelations of the 55 variables for questionnaire 3. The last set involved the intercorrelations of the 55 variables for questionnaire 5. Principal-component factor analysis was done with varimax rotation of the axes.

Factor labels for the exceptionally intelligent 30-year-old prototype were *verbal facility, novelty in problem solving, practical problem solving, social competence,* and *problem-solving ability*. Factor labels for the exceptionally intelligent 50-year-old prototype were *social competence, novelty in problem solving, intellectual investment, verbal facility,* and *knowledge store*. Factors for the ratings of the exceptionally intelligent 70-year-old prototype were labeled *general intellectual activity, knowledge and novelty in problem solving, everyday confidence,* and *verbal ability*.

Comparisons between the factors were made by correlating factor scores on the varimax-rotated factors computed for each subject separately for the three questionnaires. Several points are worth noting about these factor-score intercorrelations.

First, those factors that had been given similar interpretations were significantly correlated. For example, factor 4 (social competence) from questionnaire 1, characterizing the 30-year-old prototype, was significantly related to factor 1 (social competence) from questionnaire 3, characterizing the 50-year-old prototype ($r = .54$).

Second, although factors similar in interpretation were significantly correlated, there were often interesting differences in the behaviors loading on the factors. If one were to characterize the general nature of this difference, it would be in terms of the greater importance of real-world adaptive behavior in the behaviors loading on the factors for the older as opposed to the younger individuals.

Third, the intercorrelations demonstrate the similarities in the types of abilities underlying people's conceptions of intelligent individuals of various ages. The importance or rank of the various abilities, though, seems to differ from one age to the next, given that importances are reflected in the order in which the factors are listed. The sixth study was useful in pinning down these differences in importance. Thus, somewhat different sets of abilities are more or less salient in determining people's conceptions of intelligent individuals, depending on the age represented by the exceptionally intelligent prototype.

Study 6

The specific goals of this study were (1) to determine what factors are most capable of distinguishing individuals of average and exceptional intelligence at 30, 50, and 70 years of age; (2) to compare the characteristics deemed most apt for discriminating between individuals of exceptional intelligence and individuals with average intelligence at 30, 50, and 70 years of age; (3) to compare these characteristics to those discovered in Study 5 via different rating procedures; and (4) to determine whether implicit theories of intelligence across the adult life span are influenced by other beliefs about properties of intelligence, such as its heritability.

Sixty-nine volunteers from three age groups served as paid participants. All individuals were selected from the membership lists of two large churches. The youngest group had a mean age of 34.8 with a range of 26 to 40. The middle-age group had a mean age of 48.6 with a range of 41 to 59. The oldest group had a mean age of 67.6 with a range of 61 to 85.

Materials for the study consisted of the intelligent behaviors from Study 5 that received the largest mean importance ratings on questionnaire 1, 3, or 5 and the unintelligent behaviors, also from Study 5, that received the largest mean importance ratings on questionnaire 2, 4, or 6. The result was 55 intelligent behaviors and 14 unintelligent behaviors. This method and rationale for selecting these behaviors were the same as for Study 5.

Individuals were asked to complete three different rating questionnaires and one open-ended questionnaire. All items on the rating questionnaires involved ratings on a scale from 1 (low) to 9 (high). Questionnaire 1 dealt with ratings of the likelihood of 30-year-old individuals of exceptional and of average intelligence being engaged in the behaviors. Questionnaire 2 was comparable for 50-year-old individuals, and questionnaire 3 was comparable for 70-year-old individuals. All questionnaires contained the same intelligent and unintelligent behaviors.

Materials for the open-ended questionnaire consisted of questions designed to address the following issues: the constancy or malleability of intelligence across the adult life span, hereditary versus environmental influences on intelligence, the appropriateness of typical measures of intelligence for assessing the intellectual capabilities of older adults, the modifiability of intelligence through education, the multidirectionality of intelligence, explicit definitions of intelligence, depictions of the most intelligent and unintelligent individuals that subjects knew, and familiarity with average and exceptionally intelligent individuals at each of the three ages.

The order in which the behaviors were presented in each questionnaire was randomized, and the order of questionnaires was counterbalanced across subjects. The open-ended questionnaire was always given after the subjects had finished the rating questionnaires.

The main variable of interest in the factor analysis was the difference between ratings of the likelihood that individuals of exceptional and average intelligence would be engaged in a given behavior (i.e., likelihood for exceptional intelligence minus likelihood for average intelligence). These difference variables were calculated separately by the age of the prototype rated. Each difference variable reflects the degree to which a particular behavior can discriminate between individuals with average intelligence and individuals of exceptional intelligence at any particular age level.

The inputs to the various data analyses were the sets of correlation coefficients for the difference scores generated from questionnaires 1, 2, and 3. Principal-component factor analysis was done with a varimax rotation of factorial axes.

Three interpretable factors emerged, *novelty in problem solving, crystallized intelligence,* and *everyday competence,* from the differences between ratings of the prototypes of exceptional intelligence and of average intelligence at 30 years of age, accounting for 26, 17, and 16 percent of the variance in the data, respectively. Examples of high-loading behaviors for each of these three factors were *has an active mind, displays curiosity, challenges what is presented to him or her in the media,* and *is able to learn and reason with new kinds of concepts* for novelty in problem solving; sample behaviors were *are experienced in their field, is well educated in career choice,* and *displays the knowledge to speak intelligently* for crystallized intelligence. Sample behaviors were *displays good common sense, adjusts to life situations,* and *acts responsibly* for everyday competence. These three factors are quite similar to the five factors obtained from the analysis in study 5 of the ratings of the importance of behaviors in defining an exceptionally intelligent 30-year-old prototype. In both analyses, the first two factors to emerge were factors dealing with crystallized intelligence and novelty in problem solving.

Three interpretable factors also emerged from the differences between ratings of the prototype of exceptional intelligence and of average intelligence at 50 years of age, *novelty in problem solving, everyday competence,* and *social competence,* accounting for 26, 21, and 14 percent of the variance in the data, respectively. The behaviors characterizing the social competence factor differed from those characterizing everyday competence factor in being more interpersonally oriented. These three factors are quite similar to the factors obtained in study 5 for the 50-year-old prototype.

Finally, three interpretable factors emerged from the differences between the ratings of the prototype of exceptional intelligence and of average intelligence at 70 years of age, *composite fluid and crystallized intelligence, everyday competence,* and *cognitive investment,* accounting for 28, 18, and 11 percent of the variance in the data, respectively. *Cognitive investment,* a factor different from most of those described before, includes behaviors such as *displays curiosity, appreciates young and old individuals,* and *is interested in one's family and home life*. These factors are very similar to the four factors that emerged in study 5.

Comparisons between the factors obtained in this study were made by computing factor scores on the varimax rotated factors obtained for each of the 67 subjects, separately for each of the three questionnaires. Several findings were worthy of note. First, those factors that had been given similar interpretations were substantially correlated. Second, although factors similar in interpretation were substantially correlated, there were often slight differences in the behaviors loading on the factors, with higher age levels stressing more the everyday aspects of adaptation. Third, the intercorrelations demonstrated that there are similarities in the types of characteristics that are capable of distinguishing individuals of average and exceptional intelligence at different ages.

We also examined the relationships between the age of the subjects and the factor structures underlying the age-specific prototypes. The results of these factor analyses were quite similar to those described above. In general, older individuals view everyday competence as more important in characterizing the difference between individuals of average and exceptional intelligence than do younger individuals. Moreover, middle-aged and older individuals tend to combine crystallized intelligence with problem-solving abilities for most age-specific prototypes. Thus, the distinction between fluid and crystallized abilities seems less important to the older individuals than to the younger ones.

The open-ended questionnaire revealed some interesting results. Individuals who believe that the level of one's intelligence remains constant over the life span of an adult believed crystallized intelligence to be a more important discriminator between prototypes of average and exceptional intelligence at 30 years of age than do individuals who believe that the level of one's intelligence changes over the adult life span. Also, subjects who think that one's intelligence cannot decrease over the life span view everyday competence and cognitive investment to be more important in characterizing the difference between prototypes of average and exceptional intelligence than do the subjects who think that one's intelligence can decrease over the adult life span. In short, the more importance one places on everyday intellectual abilities in one's conception of intelligence, the more likely one is to hold a view of stability in intellectual development during adulthood. Yet another interesting finding was that subjects who believed that intelligence and unintelligence remain constant over the adult life span were more likely to hold a heredity-based view of intelligence. Finally, subjects who felt individuals can become more intelligent over time were more likely to hold an environmentally determined view of intelligence and to believe that intellectual abilities can be improved through practice and training.

To conclude, implicit theories of intelligence change over the life span, with greater emphasis on everyday abilities both for older subjects and for prototypes of older individuals.

Intelligence, Wisdom, and Creativity

Can the implicit-theory approach be extended to study wisdom and creativity as well as intelligence? The final set of studies addresses this question.

Study 7

In Study 7, a brief questionnaire was filled out by 25, 26, 20, and 26 professors in the fields of art, business, philosophy, and physics, respectively, at a variety of U.S. universities (representing a return rate of 17 percent on questionnaires sent out). The questionnaire was also given to 17 nonstudent adults who answered a newspaper advertisement. The questionnaire asked respondents to spend a few minutes listing whatever behaviors they could think of that were characteristic of an ideally intelligent, wise, or creative person in their respective fields of endeavor (or, in the care of laypersons, in general). Those behaviors listed at least twice served as a basis for the subsequent investigations. The total numbers of behaviors obtained were 119 for art, 131 for business, 107 for philosophy, 138 for physics, and 156 for laypersons.

Study 8

Method

Two hundred professors in art, business, philosophy, and physics were asked to rate the characteristicness of each of the behaviors obtained in Study 7 from the corresponding population with respect to their conception of an ideally intelligent, wise, and creative individual in their occupation. Laypersons (nonstudent adults) also provided these ratings, but for a hypothetical ideal individual without regard to occupation. Ratings were on a scale of 1 (low) to 9 (high), with a rating of 1 meaning *behavior extremely uncharacteristic* and a rating of 9 meaning *behavior extremely characteristic*. Of course, not all 200 solicitees in each field responded. There were 65 respondents for the art questionnaire, 70 for the business questionnaire, 65 for the philosophy questionnaire, 85 for the physics questionnaire, and 30 for the laypersons' questionnaire. Each participant provided all three ratings (of intelligence, wisdom, and creativity), but with the order of the three ratings counterbalanced across subjects.

Means

Mean ratings for all three psychological constructs from all three occupations ranged from 5.8 to 7.1, with a median of 6.4. Ratings were quite similar in value across constructs and fields. Reliabilities of the ratings were high, ranging from .88 to .97 with a median of .92.

Correlations

Correlations between pairs of ratings of attributes for the various groups of subjects revealed some interesting patterns. First, correlations between intelligence and wisdom (across groups of subjects) ranged from .42 to .78 with a median of .68. Correlations between intelligence and creativity ranged from .29 to .64 with a median of .55. Correlations between wisdom and creativity ranged from −.24 to .48 with a median of .27. Clearly, the rank ordering of the three possible relations between constructs is that intelligence and wisdom are most closely related, intelligence and creativity next most closely related, and wisdom and creativity least related. The only departure from this pattern was for philosophers, for whom intelligence and creativity were more highly related (a correlation of .56 versus one of .42) than were intelligence and wisdom.

Second, all correlations were positive and statistically significant except for the correlation between wisdom and creativity for the business professors, which was significantly negative. In other words, business professors saw greater amounts of wisdom as associated with lesser amounts of creativity.

Third, there were some interesting differences among magnitudes of correlations across groups. Members of all groups saw intelligence and wisdom as fairly highly related. But for professors in art and physics, as well as for laypersons, the relations were very substantial ($r = .6$ to $.8$). For business professors, the relation was a bit weaker ($r = .5$), and for professors of philosophy, the relation was still weaker ($r = .4$). Also, the art, philosophy, and physics professors all saw intelligence and creativity as highly related ($r > .5$), but the business professors and laypersons saw them as only weakly to moderately related ($r = .3$). The relation between creativity and wisdom reached moderate levels for the art professors ($r = .5$) and philosophy professors ($r = .4$), but was low for the other groups and, as mentioned earlier, actually negative for the business group.

Summary

Although the various groups do not differ substantially in the absolute magnitudes of their ratings, they do differ in the perceived relations between constructs rated. In general, intelligence and wisdom are seen as closest and wisdom and creativity as furthest from each other, but there are differences in magnitudes of relations across fields.

These correlations tell us something about the interrelations of constructs, but not about the constructs themselves. The next study was designed to provide information about the internal structure of each construct.

Study 9

Method

Forty undergraduates were asked to sort three sets of 40 behaviors into as many or as few piles as they wished on the basis of which behaviors are "likely to be found together" in a person. These behaviors were from the listings for intelligence, wisdom, and creativity, respectively, from Study 8. Only the top 40 behaviors (in terms of laypersons' characteristicness ratings from Study 8) were used in each sorting task. Order of sortings for behaviors from the intelligence, wisdom, and creativity lists was counterbalanced. Subjects were not told in advance what the behaviors had in common (i.e., intelligence, wisdom, or creativity).

Nonmetric multidimensional scaling (ALSCAL) was used to analyze the ratings. Stress, or badness of fit, was calculated via stress formula 1, and the primary method was used for resolving ties. All scalings were principal-axis solutions. Hence, each dimension accounted for the maximum possible variance, controlling for earlier dimensions, with dimensions extracted in order of strength.

Intelligence

The solution for intelligence accounted for 82 percent of the data in three dimensions, with a stress of .15. Because the scaling was a principal-axis solution, it tended to yield bipolar dimensions in which positive and negative polarities lent themselves to separate but related interpretations.

The first dimension yielded two interpretations: practical problem-solving ability for the positive polarity (e.g., tends to see attainable goals and accomplish them; has the ability to change directions and use another procedure; able to apply knowledge to particular problems) and verbal ability for the negative polarity (e.g., can converse on almost any topic; has demonstrated a good vocabulary; has a good command of language).

The second dimension also lent itself to two interpretations. The positive polarity of this dimension was labeled *intellectual balance and integration* (e.g., has the ability to recognize similarities and differences; listens to all sides of an issue; is able to grasp abstract ideas and focus his or her attention on those ideas), and the negative polarity was labeled *goal orientation and attainment* (e.g., tends to obtain and use information for specific purposes; possesses ability for high achievement; is motivated by goals).

The third dimension yielded two interpretations. The positive polarity was *contextual intelligence* (e.g., learns and remembers and gains information from past mistakes or successes; has the ability to understand and interpret her or his environment; knows what is going on in the world), and *fluid thought* was the negative polarity (e.g., has a thorough grasp of mathematics and/or good spatial ability; has a high IQ level; thinks quickly).

Wisdom

The scaling for wisdom accounted for 87 percent of the variance in three dimensions, with a stress of .14. The first dimension yielded two interpretations, *reasoning ability* for the positive polarity (e.g., has the unique ability to look at a problem or situation and solve it; has good problem-solving ability; has a logical mind) and *sagacity* for the negative polarity (e.g., considers advice; understands people through dealing with a variety of people; feels he or she can always learn from other people; is fair).

The second dimension also yielded two interpretations, *learning from ideas and environment* for the positive polarity (e.g., attaches importance to ideas; is perceptive; learns from other people's mistakes) and *judgment* for the negative polarity (e.g., acts within own physical and intellectual limitations; is sensible; has good judgment at all times; and thinks before acting or making decisions).

The third dimension yielded two interpretations, *expeditious use of information* for the positive polarity (e.g., is experienced; seeks out information, especially details; learns and remembers and gains information from past mistakes or successes) and *perspicacity* for the negative polarity (e.g., can offer solutions that are on the side of right and truth; is able to see through things—read between the lines; has the ability to understand and interpret her or his environment).

Creativity

The scaling for creativity accounted for 93 percent of the variance in the data in four dimensions, with a stress of .08. The first dimension yielded two interpretations, *nonentrenchment* for the positive polarity (e.g., makes up rules as she or he goes along; has a free spirit; is unorthodox), and *integration and intellectuality* for the negative polarity (e.g., makes connections and distinctions between ideas and things; has the ability to recognize similarities and differences; is able to put old information, theories, etc., together in a new way).

The second dimension was also interpreted in terms of two polarities: *aesthetic taste and imagination* for the positive polarity (e.g., has an appreciation of art, music, etc.; can write, draw, compose music; has good taste) and *decisional skill and flexibility* for the negative polarity (e.g., follows his or her gut feelings in making decisions after weighing the pros and cons; has the ability to change directions and use another procedure).

The third dimension was interpreted in terms of *perspicacity* for its positive polarity (e.g., questions societal norms, truisms, assumptions; is willing to take a stand) and *drive for accomplishment and recognition* for its negative polarity (e.g., is motivated by goals; likes to be complimented on her or his work; is energetic).

The fourth and weakest dimension was interpreted in terms of *inquisi-*

tiveness (positive polarity) and *intuition* (negative polarity). The dimension was weak and did not have many salient weights on either polarity.

Summary

Excellent fits to the nonmetric multidimensional scaling model were obtained for intelligence, wisdom, and creativity. Thus, one can have a reasonably high degree of confidence in the interpretation of the data, especially because the dimensions do, in fact, seem to capture people's intuitions about the respective natures of the three psychological constructs. Moreover, the substantive dimensions are consistent with the earlier correlational data (from Study 8), indicating that of the implicit theories for the three possible pairs of attributes, the greatest similarity is between the implicit theories for intelligence and wisdom, whereas the least similarity is between the implicit theories for wisdom and creativity. Finally, the results for intelligence largely replicate those of Sternberg et al. (1981), who used a different methodology (factor analysis), a different set of subjects, and a different (but related) set of behaviors to study people's conceptions of intelligence. Thus, at least for the one psychological construct that has been subject to implicit theoretical analysis before, the present results appear to be robust.

Study 10

Method

In an attempt to relate implicit to explicit theories, 30 adults were administered four psychometric tests: the Cattell and Cattell Test of *g*, the Group Embedded-Figures Test, the George Washington Social Intelligence Test, and the Chapin Social Insight Test. These tests have been widely used in psychometric investigations of cognitive and social intelligence and have been shown to have reasonable construct validity. Paper-and-pencil creativity tests were not employed because of the common view (e.g., Amabile, 1983; Cronbach, 1984; Feldman, 1980; Simonton, 1984) that such tests capture, at best, only the most trivial aspects of creativity. In addition, subjects were asked to fill out all three of the questionnaires from Study 8—those for intelligence, wisdom, and creativity—as they pertained to themselves (rather than as they pertained to an ideal individual, as in Study 8). The same subjects filled out all three questionnaires in counterbalanced order. Only those questionnaire items were retained that had received principal-component loadings of .50 or greater in Study 8. Subjects used a scale of 1 to 9, where 1 indicated a behavior that was extremely uncharacteristic of the individual and 9 indicated a behavior that was extremely characteristic. Subjects were given as long as they needed to complete the questionnaires.

Convergent-Discriminant Validation

Questionnaires were scored by correlating each subject's response pattern on each questionnaire he or she completed (intelligence, wisdom, or creativity) with the "prototype" questionnaire obtained from the laypersons in Study 8. The prototype contained the set of ratings for the hypothetical ideal individual, with respect to intelligence, wisdom, or creativity. Thus, the correlation measured the degree of resemblance between the actual individual in this experiment and the hypothetical ideal individual emerging from Study 8. A higher correlation thus indicated greater correspondence to the hypothetical ideal, whereas a lower correlation indicated lesser correspondence to the ideal. A negative correlation would indicate an inverse relationship.

The strongest correlations were obtained for intelligence. A correlation of .48 was obtained with the Cattell and Cattell Test of *g*, which is a nonverbal intelligence test. This result replicates the correlation with the verbal Henmon-Nelson Mental Ability Test obtained by Sternberg et al. (1981), which was just as high (.52). The intelligence prototype correlation thus measures characteristics that overlap with those measured by intelligence tests, although the prototype measures social competence aspects of intelligence that are not measured by traditional psychometric intelligence tests (Sternberg, 1985a). Significant correlations were also obtained with the embedded-figures test (.54), which is a measure of field independence that tends to correlate with spatial ability and with the Chapin Social Insight Test (.43), a measure of social intelligence and competence. Meaningful correlations were obtained for the wisdom prototype scores and the George Washington Social Intelligence Test (.38) and the Chapin Social Insight Test (.46), both of which measure those aspects of intelligence that would seem most akin to wisdom. Finally, no significant correlations were obtained for creativity; but, then, there were no creativity tests included in the battery.

Summary

The multidimensional scaling results of the previous experiment showed the high "internal validity" of the implicit theories described in the experimental results. To be of psychological interest, however, implicit theories should also have external validity (i.e., relations to other theories), and measures based on implicit theories should have external validity as well (i.e., relations to measures based on other theories). The results of the present experiment show that the proposed implicit theories and the measures based on them do indeed have external as well as internal validity. Prototype scores derived from the implicit theories were shown to have sensible correlations with measures based on external theories, with the correlations falling into a pattern suggesting both convergent and discriminant validity for the proposed measures. Thus, implicit theories of intelligence, wisdom, and creativity do not occur in a vacuum and are not isolated from explicit theories. Rather, implicit theories appear to be quite compatible with explicit theories, at least in the present results.

Study 11

Method

In an attempt to determine whether people use their implicit theories in evaluating others, 40 nonstudent adults were presented with 54 simulated letters of recommendation. Two typical letters would be:

Gerald:
He possesses ability for high achievement.
He has the ability to grasp complex situations.
He has good problem-solving ability.
He attaches importance to well-presented ideas.

Doris:
She is motivated by goals.
She questions societal norms, truisms, and assumptions.
She thinks quickly.
She is not materialistic.
She is totally absorbed in study.

Descriptions were generated so as to vary predicted levels of intelligence, wisdom, and creativity. Each description was four, five, or six sentences long and was paired equally often with names of males and with names of females. A given subject saw a given description only once—either with a male name or with a female name. The subject's task was to rate the intelligence, wisdom, and creativity of each of the described individuals. Each rating occurred approximately equally often in each ordinal position across subjects. Ratings were made on a 9-point scale, where 1 indicated that the individual to be rated was not at all intelligent, wise, or creative and 9 indicated that the individual was extremely intelligent, wise, or creative.

It was possible to obtain predicted ratings of intelligence, wisdom, and creativity by summing the ratings of laypersons from Study 8 on each attribute for each subject and then dividing by the number of attributes given for the hypothetical individual. Averages rather than sums of ratings were used because the number of behaviors was not the same for each of the descriptions.

Suppose, for example, that five behaviors were given for Susan. The predicted intelligence rating would be the mean of the characteristicness ratings for intelligence in Study 8 (plus a constant). The predicted wisdom rating would be the mean of the Study 8 ratings for wisdom (plus a constant). The predicted creativity rating would be the mean of the Study 8 ratings for creativity (plus a constant). Thus, the more closely the description of the hypothetical individual resembles the ideal (of Study 8) on each of the three attributes of intelligence, wisdom, and creativity, the higher should be the rating that hypothetical individual receives in the present experiment.

Means

Mean ratings of hypothetical individuals were 5.8 for intelligence, 5.3 for wisdom, and 5.0 for creativity. The ratings were highly reliable, with split-half reliabilities of .84 for intelligence, .85 for wisdom, and .93 for creativity.

Intercorrelations of Ratings

Intercorrelations of ratings were .94 between intelligence and wisdom, .69 between intelligence and creativity, and .62 between wisdom and creativity. Thus, the rank order of correlations was the same as that in past experiments, although in this experiment intelligence and wisdom were almost indistinguishable. Use of male versus female names had no effect.

Simple Correlations between Predicted and Observed Ratings

The correlations between predicted and observed ratings generally showed the expected fit of the model to the data. In each case, the correlation between the predicted and observed values of a given attribute was substantial: .89 for intelligence, .96 for wisdom, and .89 for creativity. Moreover, the correlation between predicted and observed values for a given attribute was always higher than the correlation of predicted with observed values across attributes (e.g., predicted values for creativity with observed values for wisdom). Thus, people seem not only to have implicit theories of intelligence, wisdom, and creativity, but also to use these implicit theories in predictable and discriminating ways to judge others.

Multiple Regressions of Observed on Predicted Ratings

How well could the observed ratings for each attribute be predicted if all three predicted ratings (intelligence, wisdom, and creativity) were allowed to enter into each regression equation? Multiple regressions were used to answer this question. The squared multiple correlations between observed ratings for intelligence, wisdom, and creativity, on one hand, and the predicted values, on the other, were .85, .92, and .87, respectively. In other words, the observed ratings could be predicted very well from the combined predictions. In each regression, the highest standardized regression coefficient was for the attribute being predicted. Thus, for example, in predicting the wisdom rating, the highest weight was for the predicted wisdom rating, rather than for the predicted intelligence rating or the predicted creativity rating.

Summary

People not only have implicit theories, but also use their implicit theories in predictable ways. It is possible to predict their evaluations of others on the basis of knowledge about their implicit theories. Despite the seeming omnipresence of standardized tests in our society, most evaluations of people's abilities are still done informally—through informal conversations, interviews, letters of recommendation, second-hand comments, and the like. Psychometric tests tell us nothing about how these informal evaluations are made. But the results of implicit theoretical evaluations do. It is possible to predict a person's evaluation of the intelligence, wisdom, or creativity of another by knowing the evaluator's implicit theory and the information available about the person to be evaluated.

Overview

Previous research has given us some sense of the nature of intelligence, wisdom, and creativity, but different methods, instruments, subjects, and experimenters have made comparisons across these three constructs difficult. The research described here has made it possible more directly to compare the natures of the three constructs, at least as they are perceived by four groups of people. Consider each of the three constructs in turn and what we have learned about it.

Intelligence: Laypersons

People's conceptions of intelligence overlap with, but go beyond, the skills measured by conventional intelligence tests. Thus, the problem solving (fluid ability) and verbal comprehension (crystallized ability) skills measured by intelligence tests appear most prominently in the dimensions of the derived implicit theory of intelligence. The intelligent individual is perceived to solve problems well, reason clearly, think logically, use a good vocabulary, and draw upon a large store of information—just the kinds of things conventional intelligence tests measure. But also embedded within people's conceptions of intelligence are one's ability to balance information, to be goal-oriented and to aim for achievement of one's goals, and to show one's intelligence in worldly, as opposed to strictly academic, contexts. People, in general, thus seem to be more concerned with the practical and worldly side of intelligence than are the creators of intelligence tests.

Intelligence: Specialists

Whereas professors of art emphasize knowledge and the ability to use that knowledge in weighing alternative possibilities and in seeing analogies, business professors emphasize the ability to think logically, to focus on essential aspects of a problem, and both to follow others' arguments easily and to see where these arguments lead. The emphasis on assessment of argumentation in the business professors' implicit theories is far weaker in art professors' implicit theories. Philosophy professors emphasize critical and logical abilities very heavily, especially the ability to follow complex arguments, to find subtle mistakes in these arguments, and to generate counterexamples to invalid arguments. The philosophers' view very clearly emphasizes those aspects of logic and rationality that are essential in analyzing and creating philosophical arguments. Physicists, in contrast, place more emphasis on precise mathematical thinking, the ability to relate physical phenomena to the concepts of physics and to grasp quickly the laws of nature.

Wisdom: Laypersons

The wise individual is perceived to have much the same analytical reasoning ability that is found in the intelligent individual. But the wise person has a certain sagacity that is not necessarily found in the intelligent person: she or he listens to others, knows how to weigh advice, and can deal with different kinds of people. In seeking as much information as possible for decision making, the wise individual reads between the lines as well as uses the obvious information. The wise individual is especially able to make clear, sensible, and fair judgments and in doing so takes both a long- and a short-term view of the consequences of the judgments made. The wise individual is perceived to profit from the experience of others and to learn from others' mistakes, as well as from his or her own. This individual is not afraid to change his or her mind as experience dictates, and the solutions that are offered to complex problems tend to be the right ones.

Wisdom: Specialists

Implicit theories of wisdom show considerable overlap across fields of specialization. Nevertheless, there are some differences in implicit theories. Art professors emphasize insight, knowing how to balance logic and instinct, knowing how to transform creativity into concepts, and sensitivity. These aspects of wisdom would seem quite relevant in the mature appreciation and evaluation of art. Business professors emphasize maturity of judgment, understanding of the limitations of one's own actions and recommendations, knowing what one does and does not know, possession of a long-term perspective on things, knowing when not to act as well as when to act, acceptance of reality, good decision making, the ability to distinguish substance from style, and appreciation of the ideologies of others. These aspects of wisdom would seem particularly relevant in making and evaluating business decisions.

Philosophy professors emphasize balanced judgment, nonautomatic acceptance of the "accepted" wisdom, concentration on fundamental questions, resistance to fads, looking for fundamental principles or intuitions behind a viewpoint, concern with large purposes, openness to ideas, ability to use facts correctly, avoidance of jargon, possession of a sense of where future progress is possible, unwillingness to become obsessed with a single theory, attention to both scope and detail, and a sense of justice. All these talents would seem relevant to the construction and evaluation of philosophical arguments. Finally, physicists emphasize appreciation of the various factors that contribute to a situation, familiarity with previous work and techniques in the field, knowing if solving a problem is likely to produce important results, awareness of the important problems in the field, knowledge of the human and political elements of scientific work, contemplation, and recognition of aspects of physical phenomena that underlie the concepts of physics. These skills would seem to be helpful in attaining a deep understanding of the nature of physics and of its place both in science and in the world.

Creativity: Laypersons

Conceptions of creativity overlap with those of intelligence, but there is much less emphasis in implicit theories of creativity on analytical abilities, whether they be directed toward abstract problems or verbal materials. For example, the very first dimension shows a greater emphasis on nonentrenchment, the ability and willingness to go beyond ordinary limitations of self and environment and to think and act in unconventional and even dreamlike ways (Sternberg, 1981). The creative individual has a certain freedom of spirit and unwillingness to be bound by the unwritten canons of society, characteristics not necessarily found in the highly intelligent individual. Implicit theories of creativity encompass a dimension of aesthetic taste and imagination that is absent in implicit theories of intelligence and encompass aspects of inquisitiveness and intuitiveness that do not seem to enter into the implicit theories of intelligence. Implicit theories of creativity go far beyond conventional psychometric creativity tests. A person's ability to think of unusual uses of a brick, or to form a picture based on a geometric outline, scarcely does justice to the kind of freedom of spirit and intellect captured in people's implicit theories of creativity.

Creativity: Specialists

Implicit theories of creativity in the specialized fields were highly overlapping across fields and with the implicit theories of laypersons; nevertheless, there were some differences worthy of note. Professors of art placed heavy emphasis on imagination and originality as well as on an abundant willingness to try out new ideas. The creative artist is a risk taker and persists in following through on the consequences of risks. Such a person thinks metaphorically and prefers forms of communication other than strictly verbal ones. Business professors also emphasize the ability to come up with new ideas and to explore these ideas, especially as they relate to novel business services and products. The creative individual escapes traps of conventional thinking and can imagine a possible state that is quite different from what exists. Philosophy professors emphasize the ability to toy imaginatively with notions and combinations of ideas and to create classifications and systematizations of knowledge that differ from the conventional ones. Creative individuals never automatically accept the "accepted," and when they have novel hunches, these hunches often pay off. The creative person is particularly well able to generate insights regarding connections between seemingly unrelated issues and to form useful analogies and explanations. The physics professors share many of these same ideas about the creative individual, but show a particular concern with inventiveness, the ability to find order in chaos, and the ability to question basic principles. The physicists emphasize creative aspects of problem solving, such as the ability to approximate solutions, the ability to find shortcuts in problem solving, and the ability to go beyond standard methods of problem solving. Finally, the physicist looks in a creative person for the ability to make discoveries by looking for reasons why things happen as they do. Such discoveries may result from the perception of physical and other patterns that most others simply overlook.

In conclusion, people have implicit theories of intelligence, wisdom, and creativity, and they use these theories both in conceptualizing the constructs and in evaluating themselves and others. To understand these conceptions and their use and to attain some appreciation of the psychological constructs themselves, it is useful to study people's implicit theories of the nature of their minds.

Conclusions

The purpose of this chapter has been to argue that implicit theories provide a valuable means for studying cognition and its development. Development, of course, can be of many kinds. Our own studies have focused on differences in implicit theories that characterize nonexpert and expert groups. We have also examined development across the life span via implicit theories, in terms of both how people's implicit theories change as they grow older and how implicit theories about people change with increasing age of the subjects rated.

This last kind of research would seem particularly important in studying hypothetical constructs whose nature may change with age, where the nature of the change is not readily ascertained. In the literature on intelligence, for example, it has often been assumed that what changes over age is the factor structures or scores, or the process structure or scores, of a fixed set of tasks. Thus, the set of tasks is held constant over ages, and the structure of performance is allowed to vary. This procedure may be inappropriate, however. Certainly, no one would believe it should apply at the earlier end of the age distribution (e.g., for the tasks given 2- and 12-year-olds), and perhaps it should not apply at the later end of the age distribution either (e.g., for the tasks given 20- and 80-year-olds).

Our cross-sectional data on implicit theories of intelligence suggest that, at least from an implicit theoretical standpoint, intelligence is not quite the same thing at various age levels. People stress progressively more the everyday aspects of intelligence with increasing age both of raters and ratees. This change in stress is consonant, perhaps, with the changing life requirements of individuals of different ages. The academic aspects of intelligence are quite important during the early years, and the stress on school achievement both in its own right and as a criterion against which to evaluate intelligence tests shows just how important school achievement is to children and to society in judging these children. Intelligence test scores predict school achievement quite respectably. At the same time, school achievement is not important for older adults or for society's judgments of these adults. What matters later is life achievement, which is not predicted very well by scores on intelligence tests (Wagner & Sternberg, 1985).

Obviously, implicit theories do not provide the final word on what is intelligent (or wise or creative or whatever) at any given age. They provide just one source of information. Indeed, they should complement, not replace, explicit theories. But they do seem useful in suggesting where explicit theoretical conceptualizations of a phenomenon may simply be too narrow, or too broad, or simply off base.

Although the focus of this chapter has been on intelligence, the implicit theoretical approach applies to other constructs as well, such as wisdom and creativity. Presumably the approach can be applied to any cognitive construct at all, although it would seem to have its greatest use for constructs whose formulation is fuzzy and in need of converging operations for clarification.

To conclude, the study of implicit theories can provide a valuable supplement to the armamentarium of cognitive and cognitive-developmental psychologists who seek an understanding of cognition and its development. Implicit theoretical modeling is underexplored at present, but I would like to believe that data such as those reviewed in this chapter show that there is much to be gained from more intensive study of people's implicit theories of cognition and its development.

Acknowledgments

Preparation of this article was supported by Contract N0001483K0013 from the Office of Naval Research and Army Research Institute.

References

Amabile, T. M. (1983). *The social psychology of creativity*. New York: Springer.

Berg, C. A., & Sternberg, R. J. (1985a). Response to novelty: Continuity versus discontinuity in the developmental course of intelligence. In H. Reese (Ed.), *Advances in child development and behavior*. New York: Academic.

Berg, C. A., & Sternberg, R. J. (1985b). A triarchic theory of intellectual development during adulthood. *Developmental Review, 5,* 334–370.

Berry, J. W. (1984). Towards a universal psychology of cognitive competence. In P. S. Fry (Ed.), *Changing conceptions of intelligence and intellectual functioning*. Amsterdam: North-Holland.

Cattell, R. B. (1971). *Abilities: Their structure, growth and action*. Boston: Houghton Mifflin.

Cronbach, L. J. (1984). *Essentials of psychological testing* (4th ed.). New York: Harper & Row.

Eysenck, H. J. (Ed.) (1982). *A model for intelligence*. Berlin: Springer-Verlag.

Feldman, D. H. (1980). *Beyond universals in cognitive development*. Norwood, NJ: Ablex.

Fry, P. S. (1984). Changing conceptions of intelligence and intellectual functioning: Current theory and research. In P. S. Fry (Ed.), *Changing conceptions of intelligence and intellectual functioning: Current theory and research*. Amsterdam: North-Holland.

Gorsuch, R. L. (1983). *Factor analysis* (2d ed.). Hillsdale, NJ: Erlbaum.

Hartigan, J. A. (1975). *Clustering algorithms*. New York: Wiley.

Heath, S. B. (1983). *Ways with words*. New York: Cambridge University Press.

Horn, J. L. (1968). Organization of abilities and the development of intelligence. *Psychological Review, 75,* 242–259.

Jerison, H. (1982). The evolution of biological intelligence. In R. J. Sternberg (Ed.), *Handbook of human intelligence*. New York: Cambridge University Press.

Kruskal, J. B., & Wish, M. (1978). *Multidimensional scaling*. Beverly Hills, CA: Sage.

Laboratory of Comparative Human Cognition (1982). Culture and intelligence. In R. J. Sternberg (Ed.), *Handbook of human intelligence*. New York: Cambridge University Press.

Neisser, U. (1979). The concept of intelligence. *Intelligence, 3,* 217–227.

Simonton, D. K. (1984). *Genius, creativity and leadership*. Cambridge, MA: Harvard.

Sternberg, R. J. (1981). Intelligence and nonentrenchment. *Journal of Educational Psychology, 73,* 1–16.

Sternberg, R. J. (1985a). *Beyond IQ: A triarchic theory of human intelligence*. New York: Cambridge University Press.

Sternberg, R. J. (1985b). Implicit theories of intelligence, creativity, and wisdom. *Journal of Personality and Social Psychology, 49,* 607–627.

Sternberg, R. J., Conway, B. E., Ketron, J. L., & Bernstein, M. (1981). People's conceptions of intelligence. *Journal of Personality and Social Psychology, 41,* 37–55.

Wagner, R. K., & Sternberg, R. J. (1985). Practical intelligence in real world pursuits: The role of tacit knowledge. *Journal of Personality and Social Psychology, 49,* 436–458.

6. Modeling X-Linked Mediated Development: Development of Sex Differences in the Service of a Simple Model

Hoben Thomas

It might be appropriate to define a formal model's usefulness by the following criteria. First, it must be simple and plausible. Although plausibility is often in the mind of the beholder, certainly simplicity is another matter. Complicated models are often quickly forgotten or ignored. Second, it must be testable and falsifiable. Any useful model must be able to be tested and rejected with data; the more readily testable a model is, the better. Third, it must generate new and unique predictions which set it apart from rival models.

A model is presented which appears to satisfy these criteria. The development of the model was motivated by certain persistent, orderly, yet often unexpected and usually unexplained findings in the psychological literature concerned with sex differences in development.

There are striking sex differences at both ends of the ability continuum. Lehrke (1978) provided extensive documentation that at the bottom of the IQ scale the number of mentally retarded males far exceeds the number of females. At the other extreme are differences in mathematical giftedness. In the United States talent searches such as the Johns Hopkins studies of mathematically precocious youth (Benbow & Stanley, 1980, 1983) show large sex differences. The Scholastic Aptitude Test (SAT) mathematics scores for gifted boys are higher and more variable than for girls (Benbow & Stanley, 1980, 1983). This finding is not unique to the United States. Less well known are the large-scale Australian and New Zealand studies which show the same orderly sex differences (O'Halloran, Over, & Edwards, 1982).

Other sex differences may not seem as dramatic, but are often just as orderly and persistent. For example, except for standardized IQ and achievement testing, perhaps the most frequently used psychological tests are cognitive style measures, particularly the rod-and-frame task (RFT) and the embedded-figures test (EFT) pioneered by the late Herman Witkin and his associates (Witkin, Lewis, Hertzman, Machover, Meissner, & Wapner, 1954; Witkin & Goodenough, 1981). Literally hundreds of cognitive style studies have been completed worldwide. So extensive is the literature that the Educational Testing Service has published several bibliographies (e.g., Cox & Gall, 1981). What is intriguing about this literature is that sex differences, which in most of the literature almost always refer to average differences, are typically small. If the between-sex differences are statistically different, they tend to favor males—and if they are not statistically different, they still tend to favor males (e.g., van Leeuwen, 1978). The picture is clear for the RFT data where sex differences favor males usually from childhood on. The EFT data are less clear-cut; significant differences may not emerge until adulthood (Witkin & Goodenough, 1981). Adding more intrigue is the finding that significant sex differences are found typically only in agricultural cultures, not in hunting or food-gathering cultures (Witkin & Berry, 1975).

The sex differences literature of current research focus tends to be defined by those content domains where (1) large differences are noticed and cannot be avoided or "overlooked," such as the Benbow and Stanley data (1980, 1983), or (2) where the magnitudes of the differences, while small, tend to persist and thus get noticed in literature reviews. My suspicion, however, is that there are very few tasks where one hypothesis or another regarding sex differences (in some distributional parameter) is not likely to be tenable. In the older literature where summary statistics and data tended to be published, one does not have to look far before finding many variables, physical as well as psychological, that reveal persistent age-related sex differences in both sample standard deviations and sample mean (Thomas, 1980). The consistency of the empirical facts does not, however, imply consistency of causes. But a useful parsimonious theory would be one that linked between-sex differences reported in different areas.

What is proposed is basically a very simple model that accounts for a large body of sometimes seemingly disparate empirical facts. It also provides clearly falsifiable predictions, thus avoiding what Box (1976) calls "mathematistry"—theory for theory's sake with no empirical tentacles. Indeed, some of the predictions are so trivially simple that the theory can be falsified both rationally (thinking about it tells you it is wrong) and empirically.

The theory is unabashedly biological in its driving mechanism: A putative sex-linked, i.e., X-linked gene is viewed, in its recessive form, as facilitating certain task performances. This notion, when captured in a simple formal model, immediately implies certain data relationships.

The idea that sex differences can be explained by X-linked genetic factors is hardly a popular position, and in the last decade or so it has received a lot of bad press (e.g., Boles, 1980). Some of the reasons for its unpopularity are, to my mind, clearly emotionally or politically motivated. One of the more polite comments recently received came from a colleague who observed, "I like the model, but I do not like the idea."

The scientific reasons for the unpopularity of the X-linked hypothesis are easy to state. Very few recent studies have reported support for the hypothesis. Unfortunately, however, almost all this literature is irreparably flawed. With rare exception, the hypothesis thought to have been tested was not the hypothesis actually tested. Said differently, tests of the X-linked hypothesis have not been conceptualized properly.

Traditionally, the psychological approach for evaluating the X-linked hypothesis has been through the study of familial correlations, e.g., brother-sister correlations on some test. Under a simple genetic model (e.g., Thomas, 1983) there are indeed familial patterns of X-linked correlations that would be expected, and investigators looking for such patterns in Pearson test score correlations have not typically found them. But the distributional structure that underpins the genetic correlations is assumed to be a four-point distribution in the plane! Figure 6.1 illustrates the assumed structure. That is, *all* pairwise data (brother-sister test scores, for example) must be assumed to take on one of four pairs of values! Of course, real data are not of this form: Test score distributions are continuous, and individual test scores are measured imperfectly. Thus the genetic theory needs to be embedded in some theory of real test scores where observations are subject to error as well as other influences. When this is achieved and an appropriate model is constructed that reflects reality more satisfactorily, the Pearson correlations, computed on real data, do not estimate the genetic X-linked correlations at all (Thomas, 1983). Only if one assumes that measurement error is negligible (i.e., the

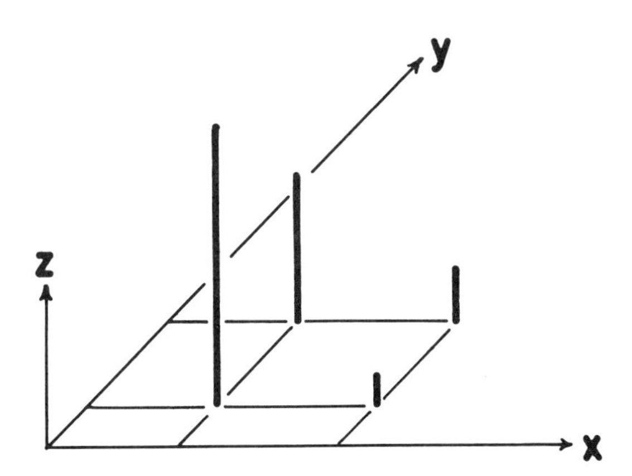

FIGURE 6.1. To expect r among test score pairs to estimate the genetic X-linked correlation requires a test score distribution of this form (for example, x = a sister's score may take on one of two values and similarly for y = her brother's score). All observations must therefore take on one of four coordinate pairs of test scores, as the figure shows. The assumption, of course, is absurd; z is the probability axis.

score distributions are "almost" four point masses) will the Pearson r estimate the genetic correlation. Thus, such reviews as Boles (1980) simply miss the point: It has been assumed for too long that Pearson test score r's estimate genetic correlation coefficients. In general they do not.

It is curious that within the last several decades of on-again, off-again interest in X-linked influences attention has focused on bivariate data structures, i.e., where correlation dominates. Yet even a very simple genetic model that considers measurement error leads to a very complicated structure where conventional bivariate normality collapses. Why not explore the implications of X-linked influences in a univariate setting first? It is almost always easier to deal with one random variable than with a pair. Furthermore, the first sign of sex differences usually shows up when the sample means are examined.

Before the simple theory is developed, there is some interesting history to recite that may make the model more intellectually attractive. Few persons seem to be aware just how many human characteristics, many physical, are mediated by X-linked genes, recessive and dominant. In Figure 6.2 are graphed data from McKusick (1983). The middle curve shows for the years tabulated the number of "proven" traits with an X-linked basis. The top curve graphs the combined "proven" and "suspected" traits. A conservative estimate is that roughly three traits per year have been discovered within the last 25 years or so, so that anywhere

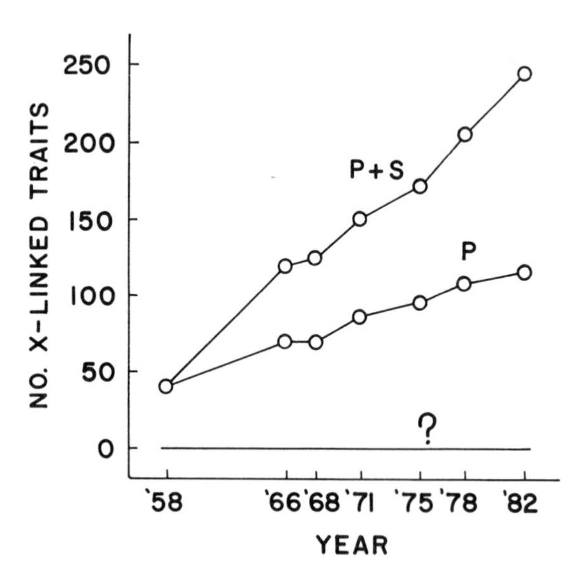

FIGURE 6.2. The number of "proved" (P) and "proved plus suspected" (P + S) X-linked traits recorded by McKusick (1983) for the years specified. The number of behavioral traits psychologists would agree are X-linked is denoted by ? and is likely to be constant at zero over the same period.

from 115 to 250 traits have been recognized as having an X-linked basis. Although I have no data, the bottom line graphs the number of behavioral traits I suspect psychologists might have agreed have an X-linked basis: The line is constant at zero. This figure proves nothing, but it does raise some interesting questions. Why should there be no evidence for X-linked mediated behavioral traits? Several answers are possible. My answer is that we have failed to conceptualize the problem properly and that our investigative strategy has been fundamentally wrong.

A brief overview of what follows may be useful. In the theory section, the simple model is developed. Its empirical consequences are stated in the following section in the form of five easily performed tests. Because these tests require rather weak model assumptions, failure of the model to survive the tests will surely falsify it. These two sections represent the heart of the chapter.

To approach the problem of parameter estimation, the model must be strengthened (and thus made more vulnerable to falsification). Strengthening of distributional assumptions is considered in the section on the distribution of *W*. Then parameter estimation and model fitting are illustrated with an analysis of the published Witkin et al. (1954) RFT data. A number of issues are considered in the general discussion, the last section, including a call for a more broadened perspective as to how data are to be viewed.

The Theory

Assume the simplest model: There exists an X-linked gene with two alleles, where *a* is recessive and *A* is dominant. Focus on the recessive gene which is assumed to facilitate (not jeopardize) performance on some task. All hemizygous *a* males and homozygous *aa* females would demonstrate facilitated performance on certain tasks. The remaining *A* males and *Aa* and *AA* females would show no X-linked facilitation. Let the population frequency of *a* be q, with $0 < q < 1$. Assuming random mating and independent assortment, the population proportion of individuals with X-linked facilitation would be q for males and q^2 for females. A very elementary but critical fact that forces all the model constraints is that $q^2 < q$ for all q.

Because there are obvious improvements in virtually all task performances over age, define a growth parameter π_i, $0 < \pi_i \leq 1$, where i indexes age. If age j is younger than age k, then $\pi_j < \pi_k$, so that at age j, $\pi_j q$ males and $\pi_j q^2$ females will display task facilitation. The π_i have a clear frequency interpretation and represent the proportion of persons with gene-facilitated potential (that is, *a* or *aa*) that display task-facilitated performance. Note that under this model individuals do not improve gradually; either they display facilitated performance, or they do not. Increases in the population mean, for example, reflect increasing numbers of individuals with task-facilitated performance.

To summarize, define a pair of discrete random variables, B_{mi} for males and B_{fi} for females, with functions g_{mi} and g_{fi}, respectively, where

$$g_{mi}(o) = \begin{cases} \pi_i q & \text{if } o = v \\ 1 - \pi_i q & \text{if } o = t \neq v \\ 0 & \text{otherwise,} \end{cases} \tag{1}$$

where $0 < \pi_i q < 1$. The function g_{fi} is identical to g_{mi} except that q^2 replaces q. The outcomes o are numerically defined dependent variable measurements. For instance, in tasks where small scores represent superior performance, as in the RFT, v would be "almost vertical" and t "tilted," when we refer to the subject's angular positioning of the rod inside the tilted frame (vertical is perfect performance). Note that B_{mi} and B_{fi} are not, in general, familiar Bernoulli variables because the outcomes are not typically defined on 0 and 1.

At this point all individuals display one of two values, v or t; this is hardly reality, but B does model the X-linked influence. Let other sources of influence including measurement error be summarized in a random variable N that might be regarded as a composite of several sources of influence. It is possible to index N so that the influence of N depends on development. Here it is assumed that N is fixed in its parameters at all ages. Let N be independent of B (actually, for much of what follows, B and N need only be assumed to be uncorrelated). Define W, the random variable on which observations are made. For males

$$W_{mi} = B_{mi} + N \tag{2}$$

and for females

$$W_{fi} = B_{fi} + N \tag{3}$$

for each individual at age i. No assumptions have been made about N except that it has moments $E(N) = \mu$ and var $(N) = \sigma^2 > 0$.

Model Properties with Empirical Implications

Even with very light machinery it may seem surprising how many varied constraints are imposed on the model that have implications for data. I regard these constraints as "stethoscopic tests" in the sense that one may easily check data sets to see whether the hypothesis of X-linked facilitated performance seems appropriate. If the tests are positive, then it may be worthwhile to look more deeply by using heavier machinery.

Means

Some of what follows is described in Thomas (1982). The expectations of Equations 2 and 3 are

$$E(W_{mi}) = vq\pi_i + (1 - q\pi_i)t + \mu$$

and (4)

$$E(W_{fi}) = v\pi_i q^2 + (1 - \pi_i q^2)t + \mu.$$

It follows that

$$E(W_{fi} - W_{mi}) = (t - v)(q - q^2)\pi_i > 0 \quad \text{if } v < t$$

and (5)

$$E(W_{fi} - W_{mi}) < 0 \quad \text{if } v > t.$$

Thus, at all ages the mean differences should be consistently ordered. If small scores are better scores ($v < t$), average female scores should always be larger than average male scores, independent of other model parameters. The obvious data implication is that the sample means should be consistently ordered for males and females at all ages. If this feature of data fails to hold, the model is falsified. Although the ordering of means is forced by Equation 4, the magnitude of the differences is another matter and depends on parameters q and π_i. The difference $q - q^2$ is largest at $q = \frac{1}{2}$. Since the growth parameter π_i increases with age, the mean differences between the sexes should increase with age. Of these two ordinal predictions, clearly the consistency of the sample mean differences, allowing for sampling error, is the critical one.

Test 1: Mean differences should always favor males.

Variances

Consider next the variances of Equations 2 and 3:

$$\begin{aligned} \text{var}(W_{mi}) &= q\pi_i(1 - q\pi_i)(v - t)^2 + \sigma^2 = \sigma_{mi}^2 \\ \text{var}(W_{fi}) &= q^2\pi_i(1 - q^2\pi_i)(v - t)^2 + \sigma^2 = \sigma_{fi}^2. \end{aligned} \tag{6}$$

In most discussions, sex differences mean mean differences. Nobody seems to know just what to do with variance differences except to ignore them. This model clearly implies order properties on the variances. From Equations 6 it follows easily that

$$\text{var}(W_{fi}) < \text{var}(W_{mi}) \quad \text{iff} \quad q(1 + q) < \frac{1}{\pi_i} \quad \text{iff}$$

$$q < \frac{-\pi_i + [\pi_i(\pi_i + 4)]^{1/2}}{2\pi_i}. \tag{7}$$

If $\pi_i = 1$ for the moment, then Equation 7 becomes

$$\text{var}(W_{fi}) < \text{var}(W_{mi}) \quad \text{iff} \quad q < \frac{5^{1/2} - 1}{2} = .618,$$

Thus $\sigma^2_{mi} > \sigma^2_{fi}$ if q is less than the famous number $(5^{1/2} - 1)/2$, and $\sigma^2_{mi} < \sigma^2_{fi}$ if q is greater than $(5^{1/2} - 1)/2$. The obvious data implication is to check the sample variances (for the behavior under scrutiny) at maturity. The variances should be ordered in a consistent way that depends on q.

Although q is never known precisely, one generally knows intuitively whether q must be large or small for the model to make sense. Consider the RFT task, for example, and specifically the data of Witkin et al. (1954, pp. 137–138) reproduced in Table 6.1. The variable is absolute angular error, in degrees, with a perfect vertical rod setting defined as zero. Thus small scores are better scores, and the sample means, as Table 6.1 reveals, for both within-sex and between-sex comparisons are nicely ordered, except for the 17-year-old females and the adult data. But how should one expect the variances to be ordered? There are large numbers of male field-independent subjects (i.e., those who do well on the task)—it is not a rare trait—and similarly there are large numbers of females who perform well on the task. Thus, for the model to be plausible, q, the proportion of males with X-linked facilitation, must be relatively large; clearly q cannot be small, such as .08, its approximate value for colorblindness in the United States (Post, 1962). Hence from Equation 7 the best guess is that the variance of females should exceed the variance of males. The data in Table 6.1 are consistent with this expectation, a finding consistent with most other RFT data and from the water-level task as well (Thomas & Jamison, 1975).

Now suppose $\pi_i < 1$ in Equation 7. Since $q(1 + q)$ is in the interval $(0, 2)$ while $1/\pi_i$ is in the interval $[1, \infty)$, the variance of females will exceed the variance of males for all $0 < q < 1$ when $\pi_i \leq \frac{1}{2}$ and, of course, for q small enough the variance of males will exceed the variance of females at all ages. It is interesting, in Table 6.1, that for the 8-year-old children the sample variances (from the grouped data) are exactly the same for both sexes. Perhaps among children younger than 8 years, the variance for boys exceeds the variance for girls.

As another example, consider the sex differences on the Scholastic Aptitude Test mathematics section (SAT-M) among precocious youth (e.g., Benbow & Stanley, 1980). The variance for the boys is, unlike the RFT data, much larger than the variance for the girls in every talent search. Under this model, this result is expected. After all, the talent search youth are already scoring in the top 5 percent or so of an achievement test before they are eligible to take the SAT-M, so they are a very bright group. And being able to score, without formal training, at levels often exceeding that of the typical college student must be a rare ability. Consequently for the theory to be sensible, q must be small, quite small.

TABLE 6.1. Tables 7.6 and 7.7 series 3 body upright rod-and-frame data, summary statistics, estimates, and model fits from Witkins et al. (1954).

		Ages of males						Ages of females					
Mean score	Interval	8	10	13	15	17	Adults	8	10	13	15	17	Adults
0–3.4	1	0	0	6	10	7	17	0	0	2	5	1	3
3.5–7.4	2	3	3	12	8	13	17	1	3	10	11	9	10
7.5–11.4	3	2	7	7	5	3	10	2	6	8	6	10	13
11.5–15.4	4	3	5	1	1		1	1	2	5	1	4	8
15.5–19.4	5	7	6	3	1		2	3	2	2	1	1	11
19.5–23.4	6	7	2	1			4	5	5	1	1		3
23.5–27.4	7	4	7				1	12	9	0			1
27.5–31.4	8							2	2	1			0
31.5–35.4	9								1				0
35.5–39.4	10												1
39.5–43.4	11												1
	N	26	30	30	25	23	52	26	30	29	25	25	51
	$\bar{x}$	17.35	15.90	7.68	5.60	4.88	7.22	21.65	18.83	9.88	7.15	8.66	12.76
	s^2	37.51	45.44	26.85	17.14	5.98	38.68	37.51	66.49	35.40	22.49	12.66	60.98
	$\widehat{\pi_i q}, \widehat{\pi_i q^2}$	.24	.59	.82	.94	—	—	.16	.38	.78	.90	—	—
	$\hat{\sigma}$	3.59	3.79	3.50	4.29	—	—	3.33	3.55	3.31	3.91	—	—
	$\hat{v}$	8.50	11.25	5.47	3.42	—	—	9.93	9.53	7.36	5.56	—	—
	$\hat{t}$	20.14	22.59	16.62	11.24	—	—	23.91	24.63	15.68	16.04	—	—
χ^2 (normality)		5.70	7.37	7.49	4.37	—	20.10	15.25	15.09	3.11[a]	10.09	.96	3.68[b]
df		4	4	3	2		4	5	6	3	3	2	4
p (upper-tail)		.22	.12	.06	.11		.001	.01	.02	.37	.02	.62	.45[b]
χ^2 (mixture)		1.51	4.09	1.50	—	—	—	3.08	2.44	.70[a]	1.90	—	—
df		2	2	1	0	—	—	2	4	1	1	—	—
p (upper-tail)		.47	.13	.22	—	—	—	.21	.66	.40	.17	—	—
Convergence satisfactory?		yes	yes	?	?	no	no	yes	yes	yes[a]	?	no	no

[a] Without observation in eighth interval.
[b] Without observations in intervals 10 and 11; with these observations, $\chi^2(8) = 79.28$, $p < .001$.

Other empirical facts suggest it may well be less than .07 (Thomas, 1985). The variances are similarly ordered in other mathematical talent searches (e.g., O'Halloran et al., 1982).

Test 2: The variances should be consistently ordered, at least in maturity. For rare traits the male variance should exceed the female variance; for common traits the reverse should hold.

Effect Size

A commonly used meta-analytical statistic is effect size, an estimate of which is simply the difference between two sample means scaled by a pooled estimate of the presumably common population standard deviation. Let $\bar{X}_f$, $\bar{X}_m$, and S_f^2 and S_m^2 be the sample means and unbiased sample variances for females and males, respectively. Then define the estimated effect size $\widehat{\mathrm{ES}}$ as

$$\widehat{\mathrm{ES}} = (\bar{X}_f - \bar{X}_m)/[S_f^2 + S_m^2)/2]^{1/2}, \tag{8}$$

which is essentially the estimate Hyde (1981) used to compare the sexes on a variety of cognitive tasks. Hyde emphasized that the effect sizes were small, perhaps thinking small differences were not significant in any sense, empirical or conceptual.

It is of interest to consider just how large the (approximate) expected effect size is, that is, $E(\widehat{\mathrm{ES}})$ under the model of Equations 2 and 3. By using an almost identical argument from Thomas (1982), effect size is largest when σ^2 is zero, $\pi_i = 1$, and $q = .366$, which implies that $E(\widehat{\mathrm{ES}}) \leq .57$. Thus, under the model the (absolute value of) $E(\widehat{\mathrm{ES}})$ is in the interval (0, .57]. Of course, this value is the maximum value to be expected. Gene frequencies departing from .366 will cause ES to become smaller, and the larger σ^2 is, the smaller must be ES. Consequently, ES would be expected to be small under the model; in fact, large effect sizes would falsify the model!

Similarly, if one considers the expected value of the two-sample t test, under the proposed model (cf. Thomas, 1982) where t is not t-distributed regardless of the distribution of N, the conventional table-valued t critical value will fail to achieve "significance" at the two-tailed .05 level unless there are about 26 females and 26 males. In general, much larger sample sizes are needed to achieve significance.

Test 3: Effect sizes should be quite small, and mean differences should be insignificant except in large samples; but mean differences should consistently favor males.

In an extensive review of the cross-cultural literature on EFT and RFT data, van Leeuwen (1978) found data precisely in accord with the expectation of small, often insignificant differences that nonetheless favored males.

Correlations

While the main thrust so far has been on unidimensional structures, consider individuals providing two measurements, j and k, that denote two tasks assessed at possibly different ages. Think of j as denoting a particular task and age combination, if desired, and similarly for k. Ignore for the moment which sex is of concern, and let $W_j = B_j + N_j$ denote the model for j; and similarly define W_k for task k. Consider the correlation between W_j and W_k, corr $(W_j, W_k) = \rho_{jk}$. Assume the correlation between B_j and N_k and the correlation between B_k and N_j are zero, consistent with the earlier development. Then

$$\rho_{jk} = \rho'_{jk} + \rho''_{jk} \tag{9}$$

where $\rho'_{jk} = \text{cov}(B_j, B_k)/(\text{var } W_j \text{ var } W_k)^{1/2}$ and $\rho''_{jk} = \text{cov }(N_j, N_k)/(\text{var } W_j \text{ var } W_k)^{1/2}$. Both ρ'_{jk} and ρ''_{jk} are assumed to be nonnegative, a weak assumption for most psychological variables. Let m and f denote, as before, males and females, respectively. If var $(W_{mi}) <$ var (W_{fi}) for both $i = j$ and $i = k$, then $\rho''_{mjk} > \rho''_{fjk}$.

Under the most general conditions there is no simple ordering of ρ_{mjk} and ρ_{fjk}. However, note that ρ'_{jk} approaches zero while ρ''_{jk} approaches corr(N_j, N_k) as var(N_j) and var(N_k) both become large. Furthermore, ρ'_{jk} is likely to be much smaller than ρ''_{jk} because cov(B_j, B_k) will be small. This is because by letting $\rho = \text{corr}(B_j, B_k)$ the covariance of B_{mj} and B_{mk} is

$$q\pi_j(1 - \pi_j q)(v_j - t_j)^2]^{1/2}[q\pi_k(1 - \pi_k q)(v_k - t_k)^2]^{1/2}.$$

This covariance has maximum value $.25\rho[(v_j - t_j)^2(v_k - t_k^2)]^{1/2}$ and will almost certainly, in reality, be much smaller than this maximum value depending, of course, on π and q. Thus, since a substantial proportion of test score variability surely will be represented in N_i and thus in cov(N_j, N_k), because B represents only X-linked influences, the contribution of ρ'_{jk} to ρ_{jk} in Equation 9 is likely to be negligible. If so,

$$\begin{aligned} &\text{If var } (W_{mi}) < \text{var } (W_{fi}) \text{ for } i = j,k, \text{ then } \rho_{mjk} > \rho_{fjk} \\ &\text{If var } (W_{mi}) > \text{var } (W_{fi}) \text{ for } i = j,k, \text{ then } \rho_{mjk} < \rho_{fjk}. \end{aligned} \tag{10}$$

The male RFT and EFT sample variances are typically smaller than the female RFT and EFT sample variances of (cf. Witkin et al., 1954, p. 93), and the male between-task correlations are larger than the female between-task correlations. Witkin et al. (1954, p. 85) reported correlations between EFT and RFT ranging from .43 to .76 for men and .03 to .26 for women. These ranges are strikingly disjoint. Thus, the empirical facts are in agreement with the theoretical prediction from Equation 10.

Recall from Equation 7 that the ordering of the variances of W is dependent on the gene frequency q and thus Equation 10 is also dependent on the gene frequency.

Also observe that the above development has implications for predicting sex differences in task reliability coefficients as well. Simply regard j and k as two measurements of the same task. For instance, it might be expected that the male RFT reliability should exceed the female RFT reliability for which there is evidence (Witkin et al., 1954, p. 73).

To summarize this development:

Test 4: Between-task sample correlation coefficients for males should exceed the correlation coefficients for females on tasks where superior performance is not rare.

Distributions

These ordinal tests are nonparametric in the sense that no assumption has been made about the distribution of W, and the tests must be viewed as exploratory, not confirmatory. The tests are all of the "if, . . . then" variety. For example, if the model holds, then the male average performance will exceed the female average performance. Obviously, the converse does not hold. But because the tests are largely independent of one another, a positive confirmation of all the tests would signal a very strong suggestion.

In general, to make further headway and to provide definitive estimates of the model parameters, additional assumptions need to be made regarding the distribution of N, so that the distribution of W may be specified. However, there is an additional test which, perhaps surprisingly, follows without any assumptions whatever regarding the distribution of N if N and B are independent.

Test 5: Because the distribution of W can never be normal, sample data should always reject normality.

Of course, in practice real data may appear normal, so the sample size might need to be large. There are, however, some quite powerful tests of normality (Filliben, 1975).

That W cannot be normal follows from a classical characterization theorem of the normal distribution. Let W be the additive composition of two independent random variables. Then W is normal if and only if each (nondegenerate) component is normal (Cramér, 1946, p. 212). Thus, the fact that W cannot be normal follows immediately, given that B is not normal. Given the pervasive application of the normal model in our thinking, this result may seem unsettling.

Distribution of W

Consider the distribution of the sum of two random variables

$$W = B + N. \tag{11}$$

It is instructive to derive this distribution intuitively; a formal argument can be essentially identical. Let B, independent of N, have the simple two-outcome distribution

$$\begin{aligned} B = 0 = v \quad &\text{with probability } p \\ B = 1 = t \quad &\text{with probability } 1 - p \,. \end{aligned}$$

And assume N is a familiar standard normal variable, $E(N) = 0$, $\text{var}(N) = 1$. If $B = 0$, then $W = 0 + N$ and the distribution of W is clear: It is a standard normal variable. Alternatively, let $B = 1$; then $W = 1 + N$ and W is again normal, but with mean 1. Now since B is a random variable, it will put part of the probability distribution around 0 and the other part around 1; and the proportions of the probability distribution around 0 and 1 will be given by p and $1 - p$, respectively. To provide an empirical example, sample four observations from a table of standard normal numbers (deviates). Add 1 to each of the four sampled values. Sample another 16 observations; to these add nothing. Consider the combined sample of 20 observations. They have been sampled from a two-component normal mixture distribution, the components are centered at 0 and 1, and the weights of these components are $\frac{1}{5}$ and $\frac{4}{5}$. The density is given by

$$g(w) = 0.8f_1(w) + 0.2f_2(w),$$

where f_1 is a standard normal density and f_2 is a normal density with mean and variance 1. Figure 6.3(a) illustrates this distribution; it may look normal, but it is, in fact, quite far from normal.

Thus, in general, the distribution of W in Equations 2, 3, and 11 if N is normal will be a two-component normal mixture distribution with component means centered at $v + E(N)$ and $t + E\,(N)$ with common component variance σ^2 and with weights p and $1 - p$, where $p = \pi_i q$ and $p = \pi_i q^2$, for males and females, respectively. (In a formal argument the conditional distribution of W given $B = 1$, for example, would be considered.) The means and variances of W have already been given in Equations 4 and 6, respectively. Note that (1) Equation 11 can generate a broad class of mixture distributions, and N does not need to be normal; (2) B could be defined to have several outcomes, so a multiple-allele model can be easily handled; (3) if B, as in Figure 6.1, is bidimensional and if N is bivariate normal, then the model easily generates a bivariate normal mixture distributions in the plane (Thomas, 1983). In general, however, W can be

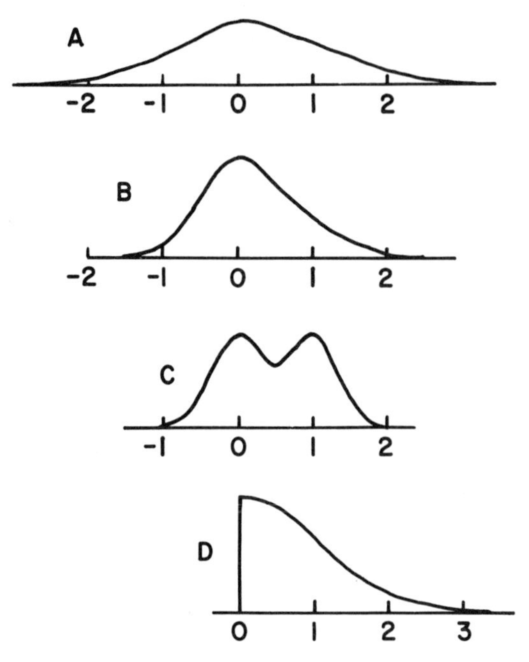

FIGURE 6.3. Two-component normal mixture distributions with component means at 0 and 1 and common component variance. (A) Left and right components weights are .8 and .2, respectively; component variance is 1. (B) Same as (A) but variance is $\frac{1}{4}$ (C) Weights are $\frac{1}{2}$, variance is $\frac{1}{9}$. (D) Folded density of (A). Normal mixtures will always be unimodal unless the component means are separated by more than two-component standard deviations, and then for some weights the distribution may be bimodal.

intractable unless N has certain desirable features, which is the case if N is assumed normal. A normal N makes a reasonable distribution in many settings.

Parameter Estimation and Model Fitting

The most interesting parameters of the model are π_i and q because of the clear frequency interpretation of each and because there are clear order constraints imposed on them, for example, $\pi_j < \pi_k$ if j is younger than k. Once estimates of these parameters are obtained, along with estimates of v, t, and σ [$E(N)$ is assumed to be zero], the data may be fitted to the hypothesized mixture model by using conventional χ^2 tests.

To illustrate the general approach to parameter estimation, the Witkin et al. (1954) RFT data in Table 6.1 are used. These data are not optimal for the purpose desired; there are far too few subjects at each age, and the data are grouped. However, the data are public, there are several age groups spanning a satisfactory age range, and the data analyses reveal certain important difficulties.

The goal in this effort is not to test and likely reject the strong model proposed. Rather, the purpose is to illustrate a general research strategy that I would like to encourage and that I believe might move us closer to understanding certain empirical facts regarding the development of sex differences which have never been explained or understood.

Recall in the RFT data that the subject's goal is to position the rod to a vertical setting defined as 0° error, when the frame is tilted to several different positions. The grouped data in Table 6.1 are based on the average of eight absolute error settings.

Under the model, each subject's RFT error score is sampled from a density $g_i(w)$ defined by

$$g_i(w) = p_i f_1(w) + (1 - p_i) f_2(w), \tag{12}$$

where f_1 and f_2 are normal densities with (component) means v and t, respectively, and (component) variance σ^2. For males $p_i = \pi_i q$, and for females $p_i = \pi_i q^2$. However, Equation 12 is not quite suitable. Recall that the scores for each subject were absolute values, not signed errors. This fact is important because if X is normal, then the absolute value of X is a *folded* normal (i.e., where the negative mass is "folded" into the positive mass). This fact makes life more difficult because $g_i(w)$ in Equation 12 for the RFT data is a *folded* two-component normal mixture and f_1 and f_2 are folded normal components (cf., Leone, Nelson, & Nottingham, 1961). An example of a folded two-component normal mixture is shown in Figure 6.3(D). Thus, all estimation assumed $g_i(w)$ was a folded two-component normal mixture distribution.

Estimation in mixture settings almost always requires an iterative approach because the derivatives of the likelihood equations cannot be solved in closed form. However, the EM algorithm (Aitkin & Wilson, 1980; Everitt & Hand, 1981) works well in these applications and is very easily programmed. In addition, several normal mixture algorithms are available (e.g., Macdonald, 1980; Wolfe, 1970) although these programs were not used here (for the folded mixture problem). Maximum likelihood estimation was achieved by using the EM algorithm with solution criterion minimizing minus the log likelihood, when several different starting values (guesses) were entered. The EM algorithm can be slow, but often only 6 to 10 iterations are necessary to converge, i.e., to approach the same solution values *if* there is convergence at all!

The approach used was the approach one might typically employ given the availability of normal mixture routines: Estimate parameters v, t, σ, and $\pi_i q$ or $\pi_i q^2$ separately for each data set. With this approach π_i and q, within each age group, are not identifiable (i.e., there are many combinations of π_i and q that produce the same $\pi_i q$). If, however, the estimates are properly constrained (for example, $\widehat{\pi_i q^2} < \widehat{\pi_i q}$), then estimates of q and π_i are possible from $\widehat{\pi_i q^2}/(\widehat{\pi_i q}) = \hat{q}$ and from $\widehat{\pi_i} = \widehat{\pi_i q}/\hat{q}$. Note that the parameters were estimated without constraint (except that $\sigma > 0$ and $0 < \widehat{\pi_i q}, \widehat{\pi_i q^2} < 1$), so it could well happen that $\widehat{\pi_j q^2} > \widehat{\pi_j q}$ while the theory requires $\pi_j q^2 < \pi_j q$. Thus in some ways the test of the theory is a demanding one: With no constraints and small data sets, Murphy's law certainly should be expected to hold!

This estimation strategy is not the favored one. A more efficient and powerful approach would be to simultaneously estimate all the parameters from the entire data set, in which case π_i and q are identifiable, with the solution constraints so that for example, $\widehat{\pi_j} < \widehat{\pi_k}$ for j younger than k. However, because there are no such general-purpose routines available, few other researchers are likely to approach the problem in this way. So this more desirable approach was not used here.

The results of the analysis are shown in the lower portion of Table 6.1. The top portion simply reproduces the grouped frequency data of Witkin et al. (1954). Since the analyses required individual scores, the midpoints of the grouped frequency intervals defined each individual's score. The sample sizes and ordinary sample means and standard deviations are given. Below these are the parameter estimates for ages 8 to 15 years.

The routine did not converge properly for the 17-year-old and adult groups, and thus no estimates are given for these groups. Convergence failure for these ages was not unexpected: There are, with these grouped data, very few frequency intervals, and many scores were identical. Among the 17-year-old males, for example, only three different scores are represented. For the younger age groups, particularly the 8- and 10-year-old groups, convergence was excellent and very fast. Thus, these are the results to be trusted. For the 13- and 15-year-old groups, convergence was slow and less stable; the solutions are more problematic. For the 13-year-old females, convergence was not possible with the one extreme observation, but a replicable solution was achieved when this observation was deleted. The solution given is based on 28 girls.

Collectively, the parameter estimates appear to be quite orderly. In all cases $\widehat{\pi_i q^2} < \widehat{\pi_i q}$, and within each sex these estimates monotonically increase with age, as required. If the ratios $\widehat{\pi_i q^2}/\widehat{\pi_i q}$ for ages 8 through 15 years are formed, they are, respectively, .66, .64, .95, and .96; these may be taken, under the model, as independent estimates of q. Stability here is about what one should expect, given these data. Hill (1963) has shown that for the two-component normal mixture case, depending on the size of $(t - v)/\sigma$, from 1600 to 6400 observations would be needed to reduce the variance of the mixing parameters to .1, and this result is for the case when all other parameters are known!

These estimates of q are interesting because an estimate of of .9 (Thomas, 1982) was obtained for Oltman's (1968) RFT data, a college sample. [For extensive water-level data, the estimate of q is about $\frac{2}{3}$, given entirely different estimation procedures (Thomas & Jamison, 1981).] If the mean or median of these four estimates is taken as the representative value $\hat{q} = .80$, then for 8-year-olds $\hat{\pi}$ is $= .28$, and for 10-year-olds $\hat{\pi} = .66$ (by averaging the values obtained for both sexes). For ages 13 and 15, however, estimates of π_i exceed 1, suggesting either a model failure or estimation difficulties.

For the remaining estimates, $\hat{\sigma}$ seems quite stable; the estimates of t and v are less so, particularly $\hat{t}$, and there appears the suggestion that t and v become smaller with age. Either model failure or estimator variability could be the cause.

A critical concern is to provide estimates of the variability of the parameter estimates; asymptotic estimates are achievable, with considerable programming effort (cf. Everitt & Hand, 1981), but typically are not provided in mixture decomposition programs. There may be a very simple alternative: the bootstrap (Efron, 1982). This procedure is designed to provide standard errors in difficult analytical settings. Computationally, the bootstrap is trivially simple: Define a vector of the test statistics for which a standard error is desired. Sample *with* replacement from the vector k times, where k is usually 50 to 200 or so. Compute the mean of each bootstrap sample, obtaining k means; compute the standard deviation among these k means, and call this number the bootstrap standard error. The bootstrap assumes that the observations are identically distributed, an assumption not obviously satisfied here. If the assumption is plausible, under the model the bootstrap estimated standard errors of $\hat{\sigma}$, $\hat{t}$, and $\hat{v}$ are, with $k = 50$ and bootstrap sample size 8, respectively, .12, .96, and 1.65. These numbers are to be viewed suspiciously. To recommend it, the bootstrap procedure would require systematic exploration with Monte Carlo methods. But the approach does appear attractive.

Table 6.1 also provides ordinary χ^2 goodness-of-fit tests under the normal model and under the assumed folded mixture model. Most of the data sets reject normality or have marginal fits; the fit under the folded mixture model appears satisfactory in most cases.

Overall, given the small sample sizes and convergence problems caused largely because the data were grouped, the results seem encouraging.

General Discussion

Combining the results of a more rigorous mixture decomposition analysis of Oltman's (1968) college student RFT data, where the model made a respectable showing (Thomas, 1982), with the results of the preceding analysis suggests that further research may be quite worthwhile. A number of content domains might be explored, including measures of cognitive style, certain specialized ability measures, and, as will be noted momentarily, conventional IQ test scores.

Although the methodology discussed here applies to continuously distributed random variables, fairly straightforward maximum likelihood estimation may be employed (Thomas & Jamison, 1981), for certain tasks, such as the water-level task, where at some ages the data are sufficiently discrete that the responses may be defined as counts. In these analyses data from seven water-level studies provided positive support for the hypothesis that performance on the water-level task may be under X-linked control. At least there is no other explanation to account for the data. Incidentally, the present model reduces to the count data Bernoulli case when N becomes a degenerate variable, that is, var $(N) = 0$, in which case the observations may be arbitrarily defined to be distributed on 0 and 1 and without loss of model generality.

One should harbor no illusions about the outcome to be expected when the model is subjected, through mixture decomposition analyses, to the power of a large data set. It will most likely be hammered down. That is the vulnerability of a strong model. If desired, the model could certainly be weakened in perhaps obvious ways, e.g., by allowing different parameters to vary between sex and over age.

It is interesting, however, what a simple model can achieve. It has provided an explanation (Thomas, 1985) for all the high mathematical aptitude sex differences facts reported in the Johns Hopkins talent search data (Benbow & Stanley, 1980, 1983). The empirical SAT-M facts are that (1) the boys' means and variances have always been larger than the girls' means and variances; (2) greater numbers of eligible boys have been selected on the achievement pretests; and (3) the ratio of the proportion of boys to girls with SAT-M scores above a fixed score c increases as c increases. When time $c = 700$, the ratio is about 13 : 1.

Alternate explanations have been offered for some of these facts. It may be true, e.g., that boys are more likely to enter talent search competition than girls and that girls are less likely to receive encouragement to study mathematics. Such theories are almost always very vague, however, and have no clear implications for data. Why, for example, should the variances be ordered as they have been in each search? The model proposed does provide a coherent, compact explanation.

There are several relevant empirical facts of theoretical interest when IQ scores are considered. Among the mentally retarded there are greater numbers of males represented than females (e.g., Lehrke, 1978). Also, as is generally well known, there are more retardates than would be expected by assuming a normal distribution (Jensen, 1980). Zigler, Balla, and Hodapp (1984) have proposed that two different clusters of factors can lead to low IQs, thereby accounting for the slight bulge in numbers of extremely retarded persons. In the language used here, Zigler et al. are proposing that IQ is a mixture distribution.

At the other end of the IQ scale there are similar facts: There are more exceptional individuals than a normal model would permit, and there is other evidence that the proportion of male high scorers exceeds the proportion of females (Terman, 1925). In addition, when the entire IQ spectrum is considered, males remain slightly more variable than females (Jensen, 1980), although even in large samples there are no mean differences between the sexes. These facts are quite consistent with the general ideas proposed and could be modeled easily. Of course, a simple one-gene two-allele X-linked model cannot account for discrepancies from the normal density at both ends of the distribution, but a three-allele model might easily do so. Consequently, IQ would be conceptualized as a three-component normal mixture with two very small components, one at each end of the continuum, and one large component, in the middle. In effect, an X-linked structure of rare recessive genes mediating inferior and superior performance would be superimposed on a model of polygene intelligence. In a large sample the components and their parameters should be easy to estimate.

An important feature of the theory is that it forces a change in perspective as to how we view and interpret data. To illustrate, consider 100 girls and 100 boys with measurements on a trait of interest. The sample statistics are as follows: boys, $\bar{x}$ = 1.66 and s = 1.11; girls, $\bar{x}$ = 1.44 and s = 1.12. The data do not appear very exciting. A conventional t test with .198 degrees of freedom (df) yields an unimpressive t = 1.24; the effect size of .198 is also unimpressive. Suppose, however, that an additional fact were mentioned, that 66 boys and 44 girls possessed the target trait and the remaining subjects did not. Because the ratio of boys to girls with the trait is 1.5, that might command attention.

Of course, one cannot, in general, retrieve frequency data from sample means. But our conventional mind set is to visualize two identical normal densities with the same shape (constant variance) shifted by .22, the mean difference. In the proposed model that mind set is wrong. Here the component means, t and v, are identically positioned for both sexes; thus the densities are not shifted. But the densities are different in shape; i.e., the sizes of the components are different. The spirit of the mean difference in this model is much more a difference of proportion or rate.

Our training and experience are so steeped within an additive-effects perspective that our view of the world may often be characterized by what G. E. P. Box (1976) calls "cookbookery": It is the tendency to force everything into the same familiar mold. By doing so we may fail to recognize what may be important about the data. A careful exploratory data analytical perspective may be the only cure.

Incidentally, the "sample values" reported above are simply from Equations 4 and 6 with $\pi_i = \sigma = v = 1$, $t = 0$, and $q = \frac{2}{3}$, while the frequencies are simply $100q$ and $100q^2$.

All models are wrong models. The issue therefore is not whether the present model is wrong, but where it is importantly and fundamentally wrong and in most urgent need of repair. Two features seem particularly suspect. First, the usefulness of a decomposition analysis is critically dependent on how carefully one selects the distribution N. Even when the exact mixture model is known to be true, estimation can be difficult unless the component means are well separated and the sample size is moderately large. Thus one might expect that although the issue of "robustness" in decomposition analysis has not been studied, probably certain small departures from the assumed model may make important differences in solutions. Under the proposed model, EFT data should yield a two-component mixture distribution. But to regard N as normal would not be sensible because the EFT data which are latency (time) scores are known to have a long tailed distribution. A mixture of log-normal components might be a plausible distribution for N.

A second possibly major problem concerns the genetic model. This model ignores dosage compensation mechanisms, i.e., the Lyon effect (Lyon, 1972) which is now fairly well accepted by geneticists. This hypothesis states that for females, in the case of X-linked genes, one of the two alleles in each cell in each genotype is deactivated, possibly in a random manner. The implication of this hypothesis for model construction is that the pairs Aa and AA would not have the same value as under the current model. If AA had value t and aa had value v, then Aa would have some intermediate value between t and v; if there is an equal probability of A or a being deactivated, the value for Aa would be in the middle, say, $|t - v|/2$. Under such a model there are interesting consequences for theory. For one, if Aa has a midpoint value, then the mean difference between males and females vanish. The variances are still ordered, but the picture is more complicated. However, it is unclear whether this effect holds for all X-linked genes, whether or not the deactivation probabilities are equal, and thus whether Aa should have a midpoint value. Of course, apart from dosage compensation considerations, other alleles or other genes may be involved. Such models can become quite complicated. There seems, at the moment, little reason to consider more complicated models.

Although the model is conceptually neutral regarding the content domain to which it could be applied, it was stimulated by persistent sex differences on certain tasks, such as the RFT, which seemed largely independent of cultural or learning experiences. Perhaps because the model is so readily evaluated in data, the concern has been expressed that one might be inclined to feverishly sift through data in the hopes of finding, by chance, support for the model. Although this was never the intent, there is little to fear: Remember the model is a strong model, which means that it can be falsified. Even in its weaker version, where the distribution of W is left unspecified, it makes a unique set of predictions, possibly matched by no other model. After all, what other model predicts, for example, that sex differences between the means should be persistent and small? Furthermore there are predictions concerning how data should be structured not only at some fixed age but also over age. For example, the mean differences must increase in magnitude, and the variance for males at some point in early development *must* be larger than the variance for females, another consequence of Equation 7 (cf. Thomas, 1982).

Of course, such predictions are model predictions, and the variability of real data must be considered. Thus the issue of testing statistical hypotheses under the model arises. Clearly conventional normal theory-based small-sample procedures would be inappropriate because not only does normality fail but also the model is not an additive model, as the above illustration made clear. However, virtually all conventional test procedures are essentially distribution-free in large samples. Although the issue of what sample size sample is large is a difficult one and would need to be studied, the guess would be that for most applications sample sizes of about 50 for each sex would allow for most conventional two-group comparisons to be made without leading to gross statistical decision errors.

Finally, if the theory appeals to your scientific sense, fine. Even if it does not appeal to you scientifically, it will certainly appeal to your aesthetic sense because at its core is a golden number. Recall that the ordinal tests hinged on the gene frequency q and that these inequalities turned on the critical number $(5^{1/2} - 1)/2$, the golden ratio. This number is historically very famous and ranks right up there with π or e. The number turns up in many aesthetically pleasing physical and biological settings, and it has lovely mathematical properties as well (Huntley, 1970). Is it possible there may be some deeper meaning to its appearance here?

References

Aitkin, M., & Wilson, G. T. (1980). Mixture models, outliers, and the EM algorithm. *Technometrics, 22,* 325–331.

Benbow, C. P., & Stanley, J. C. (1980). Sex differences in mathematical ability: Fact or artifact? *Science, 210,* 1262–1264.

Benbow, P. C., & Stanley, J. C. (1983). Sex differences in mathematical reasoning: More facts. *Science, 22,* 1029–1031.

Boles, D. B. (1980). X-linkage of spatial ability: A critical review. *Child Development, 51,* 625–635.

Box, G. E. P. (1976). Science and statistics. *Journal of the American Statistical Association, 71,* 791–799.

Cox, P. W., & Gall, B. E. (1981). *Field dependence-independence and psychological differentiation: Bibliography with index* (Supplement No. 5, Research Rep. 81–29). Princeton, NJ: Educational Testing Service.

Cramér, H. (1946). *Mathematical methods of statistics.* Princeton, NJ: Princeton.

Efron, B. (1982). *The jackknife, the bootstrap and other resampling plans.* Philadelphia: Society for Industrial and Applied Mathematics.

Everitt, B. S., & Hand, D. J. (1981). *Finite mixture distributions*. London: Chapman & Hall.
Filliben, J. J. (1975). The probability plot correlation coefficient test for normality. *Technometrics, 17,* 111–117.
Hill, B. M. (1963). Information for estimating the proportions in mixtures of exponential and normal distributions. *Journal of the American Statistical Association, 58,* 918–932.
Huntley, H. E. (1970). *The divine proportion: A study in mathematical beauty*. New York: Dover.
Hyde, J. S. (1981). How large are cognitive gender differences? A meta-analysis using ω^2 and *d*. *American Psychologist, 36,* 892–901.
Jensen, A. R. (1980). *Bias in mental testing*. New York: Free Press.
Lehrke, R. G. (1978). Sex linkage: A biological basis for greater male variability. In R. T. Osborne, C. E. Noble, & N. Weyl (Eds.), *Human variation: The biopsychology of age, race, and sex* (pp. 171–198). New York: Academic.
Leone, F. C., Nelson, L. S., & Nottingham, R. B. (1961). The folded normal distribution. *Technometrics, 3,* 543–550.
Lyon, M. F. (1972). X-chromosome inactivation and developmental patterns in mammals. *Biological Reviews, 47,* 1–35.
Macdonald, P. D. M. (1980). A Fortran program for analyzing distribution mixtures (Statistics Technical Rep.). McMaster University, Hamilton, Canada, Department of Mathematical Sciences.
McKusick, V. A. (1983). *Mendelian inheritance in man* (6th ed.). Baltimore, MD: Johns Hopkins.
O'Halloran, P., Over, R., & Edwards, J. (1982). *Achievement of New Zealand boys and girls in the Australian Mathematics Competition*. Canberra College of Advanced Education, Canberra, A.C.T. 2616, Australia, School of Information Sciences.
Oltman, P. K. (1968). A portable rod-and-frame apparatus. *Perceptual and Motor Skills, 26,* 503–506.
Post, R. H. (1962). Population differences in red and green color vision deficiency: A review and query on selection relaxation. *Eugenics Quarterly, 9,* 131–146.
Terman, L. M. (1925). *Studies of genius*. Stanford, CA: Stanford.
Thomas, H. (1980). A theory of growth. In R. Kluwe & H. Spada (Eds.), *Developmental models of thinking* (pp. 43–76). New York: Academic.
Thomas, H. (1982). A strong developmental theory of field-dependence-independence. *Journal of Mathematical Psychology, 26,* 169–178.
Thomas, H. (1983). Familial correlational analyses, sex differences, and the X-linked gene hypothesis. *Psychological Bulletin, 93,* 427–440.
Thomas, H. (1985). A theory of high mathematical aptitude. *Journal of Mathematical Psychology, 29,* 231–242.
Thomas, H., & Jamison, W. (1975). On the acquisition of understanding that still water is horizontal. *Merrill-Palmer Quarterly, 21,* 31–44.
Thomas, H., & Jamison, W. (1981). A test of the X-linked genetic hypothesis for sex differences on Piaget's water-level task. *Developmental Review, 1,* 274–283.
van Leeuwen, M. S. (1978). A cross-cultural examination of psychological differentiation in males and females. *International Journal of Psychology, 13,* 87–122.

Witkin, H. A., & Berry, J. W. (1975). Psychological differentiation in cross-cultural perspective. *Journal of Cross-Cultural Psychology, 6,* 4–87.
Witkin, H. A., & Goodenough, D. R. (1981). *Cognitive styles: Essence and origins.* New York: International Universities Press.
Witkin, H. A., Lewis, H. B., Hertzman, M., Machover, K., Meissner, P. B., & Wapner, S. (1954). *Personality through perception: An experimental and clinical study.* New York: Harper & Brothers.
Wolfe, J. H. (1970). Pattern clustering by multivariate mixture analysis. *Multivariate Behavioral Research, 5,* 329–350.
Zigler, E., Balla, D., & Hodapp, R. (1984). On the definition and classification of mental retardation. *American Journal of Mental Deficiency, 89,* 215–230.

7. Geometric Methods in Developmental Research

Kevin F. Miller

One need not look far to find spatial analogies applied to phenomena that are not inherently spatial. Terms with a spatial flavor, such as "close friends," "deep problems," "knowing one's way around," or "one need not look far" are used with neither literal referents nor ambiguity. This ready metaphorical use of spatial relations led Lakoff and Johnson (1980, p. 17) to assert that "most of our fundamental concepts are organized in terms of one or more spatialization metaphors." The pervasive nature of spatial analogies makes the geometric techniques described in this chapter both powerful and dangerous. Procedures for turning behavioral data into maps, clusters, and tree structures tap into our tacit knowledge about the meaning of distances and directions in space. Where the implicit assumptions we bring to interpreting geometric representations hold, these techniques provide powerful methods for reducing otherwise overwhelming sets of data into coherent structures. Where these assumptions are violated, the potential for misleading or trivial results is, if anything, greater than with more familiar statistical procedures.

In this chapter I describe several geometric approaches to capturing the structure of children's knowledge and behavior. Such procedures are fundamentally descriptive, having as their goal the reduction of data on the proximities between psychological objects to a more accessible format. The terms "proximities" and "psychological objects" are both used quite generally. Psychological objects can include stimuli, subjects, or tasks. Proximities can include all measures of similarity *or* distance that show the relations between these objects. Measures of proximity between objects can be as varied as judgments of similarity between pairs of stimuli, frequencies of confusions between stimuli, or measures of the similarity in performance of different children across situations. Geometric models use such proximity data to represent psychological objects as points in space (so that distances and directions between points correspond to relations among the objects) or members of clusters (so that all members of a cluster share common features distinguishing them from nonmembers). Techniques for providing geometric models of psychological data have proliferated in the last 20 years. I do not attempt to provide a detailed map of the entire field of geometric modeling, because thorough reviews are available elsewhere (Carroll & Arabie, 1980; Davison, 1983; Shepard, 1974, 1980). Instead I discuss two basic approaches to geometric modeling that are particularly applicable to developmental issues. The first approach, *nonmetric multidimensional scaling* (MDS), produces a continuous spatial representation of the relations among psychological objects. The second approach, *nonhierarchical clustering,* describes similarity as the result of (possibly) overlapping sets of features. Within each general approach, models have been developed to account for individual or developmental differences, and these individual differences approaches are particularly applicable to developmental research.

The chapter is divided into two main sections, one dealing with general issues in geometric representation and the other with applications of specific procedures to developmental research. Discussion of general issues in geometric modeling begins with consideration of Galton's (1881) "direct" spatial description of visual representations of numbers. Limitations of this approach are described and used to motivate consideration of the assumptions behind current geometric procedures and the consequences of failing to meet these assumptions. Strategies for collecting data suitable for geometric representation are also considered in this section.

Specific techniques and their developmental applications are considered in the second section. The general nonmetric MDS approach devised by Shepard (1962a, 1962b) and extended by Kruskal (1964a, 1964b) is described with reference to a specific example demonstrating the ability of this technique to recapture a known data structure from only the order of distances among points. Developmental applications of MDS in the areas of semantic development, spatial representation, and number development are then described.

The general nonmetric MDS method has no direct way of comparing different configurations, which limits its ability to describe developmental change. This limitation can be overcome to some extent by statistical procedures for comparing two configurations, but the weighted or individual-differences MDS procedures of the INDSCAL model (Carroll & Chang, 1970) provide a more general method for describing developmental changes. These procedures assume that individuals differ in terms of the weight or emphasis they place on the dimensions of a common representational space. INDSCAL is a powerful model for representing change. Illustrative applications are discussed in which INDSCAL was used to describe aspects of semantic development, face perception, and the cognitive consequences of expertise.

Spatial models of MDS are often usefully complemented with clustering techniques that describe similarity in terms of discrete sets of shared features. Clustering methods vary according to whether they require that clusters be nested (hierarchical clustering) or whether overlapping clusters are permitted (nonhierarchical or additive clustering). Although most developmental applications have involved the computationally simpler hierarchical clustering methods, more general nonhierarchical clustering methods are now available based on the ADCLUS model of Shepard and Arabie (1979) and its individual-differences generalization, the INDCLUS model of Arabie & Carroll (1980). Developmental applications of the INDCLUS model in number development are considered and contrasted with the results of hierarchical analyses. Given the prevalence of developmental models that rely on analyses of distinctive features (e.g., Gibson, 1969), nonhierarchical clustering methods are a particularly important tool for describing developmental changes.

By revealing structure not previously hypothesized by the researcher, geometric procedures can provide an important alternative to the "20 questions" hypothesis-testing model criticized by Newell (1973), in which studies either confirm or disconfirm a preexisting hypothesis.[1] Methods such as MDS and clustering can have a decentering effect on developmental research, by revealing unexpected structure and complexity in children's knowledge and behavior. In this chapter applications are described in spatial processing, face representation, and number development where geometric techniques have contributed to changing perceptions of the nature of development. These results are encouraging, but geometric procedures have yet to be widely applied to developmental problems.

General Issues in Geometric Techniques

Galton's Approach to Representation

The notion that spatial representations can capture important relations within domains of knowledge is an old and powerful idea. One intriguing early use of a spatial representation to describe psychological phenomena is Galton's (1881) description of visual representations for numbers. Galton collected a series of drawings from adults who reported experiencing striking visual images of numbers, some of which are reproduced in Figure 7.1. Galton's procedure differs in several critical ways from the modern procedures described below. He treated these spatial images quite literally, viewing them as direct reports of his subjects' experience. Furthermore, although his technique produced spatial representations, it is not readily quantified; there is no apparent way to aggregate or compare the drawings shown in Figure 7.1. These drawings do represent a number of reasonable features of numerical structure. Reference points such as 12 and 20 are usually marked, but Galton's figures are most striking for the diversity of images they display. Furthermore, these images contain a great deal of presumably superfluous information, such as the unexplained meanderings of W.S.'s report.

The difficulty of describing Galton's results brings into focus some of the requirements that geometric methods must meet to be of general use in analyzing psychological data. Galton assumed that there was a direct relation between location of numbers in his drawings and subjects' images. Current applications of geometric methods use distance and direction to model meaningful relations among objects, but do not assume that the correspondence between locations of objects in a reconstructed space and their psychological representations is more than metaphorical (see Shepard, 1975; Shepard & Chipman, 1970). Rather, if relations among stimuli correspond to relations among their representations, then a geometric model may be useful in describing the structure of a domain without presumption that the underlying psychological processes are in any sense "spatial."

Another limitation of Galton's method is the demands made on subjects. He reported that only about 1 in 30 of his male subjects and 1 in 15 of his female subjects experienced these visual images of numbers. To be generally useful, a geometric model must be applicable to the kinds of proximity data psychologists are likely to gather, such as similarity judgments, correlations, confusions, or the results of sorting.

A problem Galton avoided by assuming his subjects could directly describe their representations of numbers was the need to describe the axiomatic basis for his technique. If geometric models for knowledge are to take advantage of our tacit knowledge about space, it is important that the data being described at least roughly conform to these assumptions.

The procedures described below have largely overcome these limitations of Galton's study. They are applicable to a wide range of phenomena beyond those with obvious spatial organization. They can be applied to a wide variety of measures of similarity that need have no more than an ordinal relation to the true similarity between objects. Finally, much of the axiomatic basis for these procedures has been stated explicitly.

Spatial Models as Representations for Psychological Processes

In order for geometric models to usefully depict psychological processes, the data they describe must conform to our implicit assumptions concerning spatial relations. For example, since the time of the French Revolution it has been a common practice to describe politicians and political parties as falling along a continuum from Left to Right. Weisberg (1974) has shown that it is often possible to recapture such a structure (or a

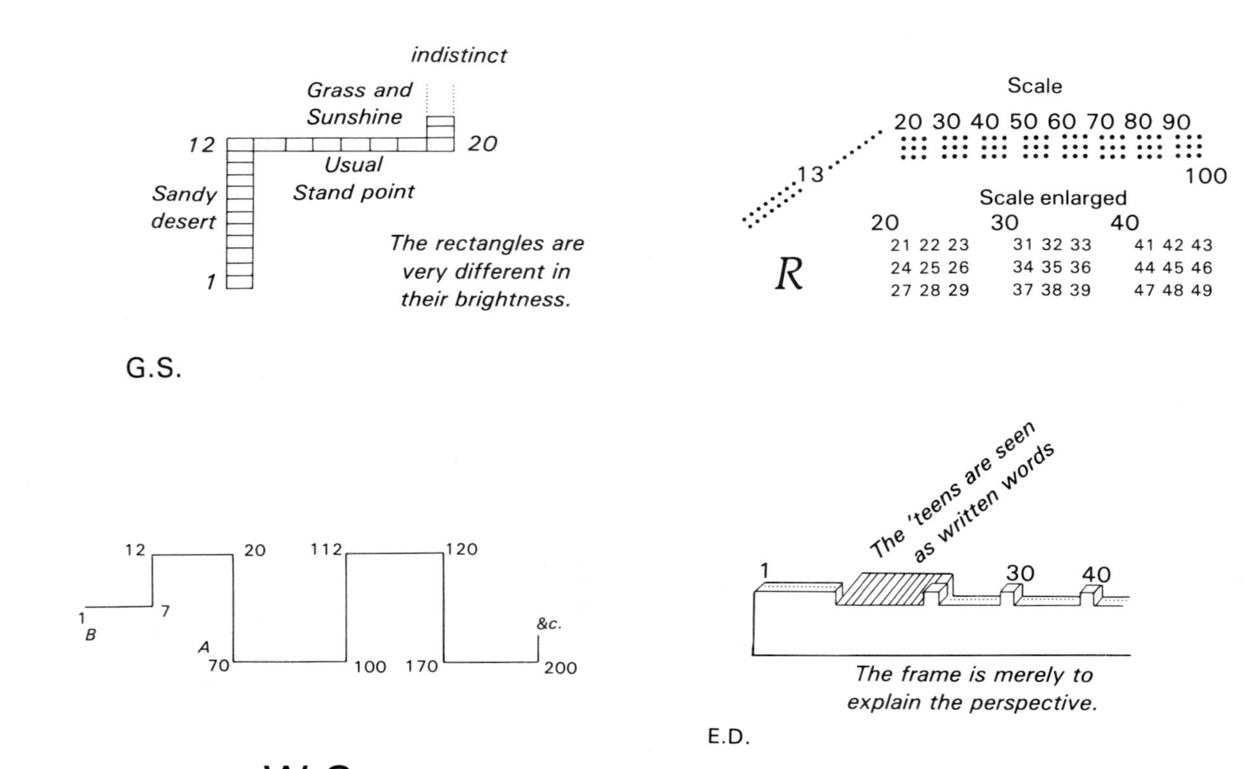

FIGURE 7.1. Drawings of "visualized numerals," adapted from Galton (1881).

circular one in which "radicals" on both ends of the spectrum are united in their opposition to centrist parties) from proximity measures of the frequency with which two politicians or parties cast the same votes. What does it mean to say that some politician or party can be placed at some particular point along this continuum? If such a representation is to be coherent, these political positions (and the data on which they are based) must conform to the three metric axioms of *positivity, symmetry,* and the *triangle inequality* (Beals, Krantz, & Tversky, 1968).

The first axiom, positivity, holds that objects must be maximally similar to themselves. Expressed in terms of distances d rather than similarities, the positivity axiom requires that for all objects i distinct from j

$$d_{ij} > d_{ii} = 0, \qquad (1)$$

where d_{ij} is the distance between i and d_{ii} is the distance between i and itself. Positivity is a trivial requirement in this case, because politicians have yet to determine a way to vote differently from themselves. As Tversky (1977) has pointed out, however, there is at least one interpretation of the positivity axiom that is not generally true. If confusion is taken as a measure of proximity, it is *not* the case that ease of identifying two identical stimuli as the same is constant across all stimuli, and circumstances exist in which an object is more likely to be identified as another object than as itself.

The second axiom requires that there must be only one distance between two objects. Proximities must be symmetric, or

$$d_{ij} = d_{ji}. \qquad (2)$$

In terms of similarities, symmetry holds that object i must resemble object j roughly as much as j resembles i. The distance between two politicians moving from left to right along a political spectrum must be identical to the distance between them moving in the other direction.

Although positivity is often a trivial requirement, in many instances similarity data violate the requirement of symmetry. Rosch (1975) reported that subjects show systematic asymmetries in completing sentences of the form ____ *is virtually* ____ such that prototypical stimuli are more likely to be in the second position than in the first. For example, subjects were more likely to assert that *11 is virtually 10* than the reverse. Because most of the procedures described in this chapter assume that proximity relations are symmetric, highly asymmetric data are not represented well by these geometric procedures.[2]

The third metric axiom, the triangle inequality, concerns the additivity of proximity relations. The triangle inequality requires that distances between two objects be no larger than the sum of the distances between each and a common third entity. This requires that

$$d_{ij} \leq d_{ih} + d_{hj} \qquad (3)$$

with $d_{ij} = d_{ih} + d_{hj}$ only for the case where the entity h falls between i and j on the shortest path between i and j. In terms of similarity, the triangle inequality implies that if two objects i and j are very similar, then some h similar to i cannot be very dissimilar to j. For the political example, the triangle inequality implies that a politician similar to one of two politicians whose voting patterns were highly similar to each other would have a voting pattern at least moderately similar to the other of the pair.

As with symmetry, real data may well not conform to the triangle inequality. Tversky and Gati (1982) showed violations of the triangle inequality for judgments of objects that vary along separable dimensions, such as schematic houseplants differing in the form of pot and shape of leaves. More generally, Shoben (1976, 1983) has argued that similarity relations between subordinate and superordinate members of a categorical hierarchy show systematic violations of this condition. Specifically, Shoben (1976) found that even atypical exemplars of a category were judged to be highly similar to the category name. Although *robin* and *goose* are judged to be quite different, both are judged to be highly similar to *bird*. It is not possible for them to be simultaneously close to *bird* and far from each other. Shoben's practical solution to this problem was to construct two MDS representations of the same data. In addition to a standard MDS solution in which all relations are equally weighted, he reanalyzed his results after weighting the relations between superordinate and subordinate members to ensure that these relations were accurately reconstructed. The second solution, but not the first, provided a good prediction of reaction time for determining whether two animals belong to the same category.

Shoben's approach is an ingenious method for adapting geometric procedures to describe data that do not conform to the underlying model. It should also suffice to warn potential users of geometric techniques that these spatial models are not the most appropriate models for all proximity matrices. Particularly in cases where proximity measures are highly asymmetric, users should be aware of the assumptions underlying these procedures and consider whether their data are appropriately represented by particular geometric models. Where, however, data are at least approximately consistent with the metric axioms, MDS and clustering procedures are often successful at revealing structure in an otherwise bewildering array of data.

Issues of Data Collection

Perhaps the thorniest issue facing developmental applications of geometric methods is the problem of finding appropriate tasks to use for collecting data. Although profile similarity measures can be derived from comparing subjects' performances across tasks (Carroll & Kruskal, 1978;

Shepard, 1972), most applications of geometric techniques involve data collected from some form of similarity judgment task. Choice of a task for collecting proximity data involves consideration of two factors: the difficulty that the judgment task may pose children and the number of judgments that must be made to gather a representative set of data. Three widely used procedures are mentioned briefly: pairwise comparison, ranking, and triadic comparison.

Pairwise Comparison

Perhaps the most straightforward and efficient method of collecting data on the proximities among a set of psychological objects is simply to solicit judgments of the proximity among the pairs of items. This is the most efficient of the three procedures, with the fewest judgments required to obtain a full proximity matrix for a given set of stimuli. If we assume that order of presentation does not affect judgment, there are $(N - 1)*N/2$ unique pairs for N objects. This procedure has been used with apparent success with children as young as 5 years in tasks involving judging distance (Newcombe & Liben, 1982) or similarity of colors (Cirrin & Hurtig, 1981).

Rank Ordering

Despite the apparent success of procedures involving the direct rating of similarity among pairs of objects, researchers have attempted to come up with simpler judgment tasks for young children. One procedure that remains relatively efficient (it doubles the number of judgments that must be made compared with pairwise comparison) while appearing to simplify the child's judgment task is ranking relations among stimuli. Subjects are presented with a target stimulus and then asked to rank all remaining stimuli for similarity to the target. This task might seem particularly appropriate for young children, but it runs the risk that subjects may shift targets. Having judged that the item most similar to *a* is *b*, they may then seek the item most similar to *b* rather than to *a*, resulting in a chain as subjects in effect work their way around the stimulus space. In a study comparing ranking with direct estimation of physical distances between pairs of objects, Newcombe and Liben (1982) found that children were more likely to chain their responses when ranking than when directly judging distances between pairs of points. Thus despite the apparent simplicity of the ranking task, questions exist concerning its appropriateness for use with young children.

Triadic Designs

A final attempt to simplify the child's judgment task uses triads rather than pairs of stimuli. This procedure asks subjects to pick the most similar and least similar pairs from triads of stimuli, rather than to directly rate similarity among pairs.

Triadic procedures can simplify the child's judgment task, but this simplification comes at the expense of greatly increasing the number of stimulus combinations, from $N^*(N - 1)/2$ to $N^*(N - 1)^*(N - 2)/6$, for N stimuli. More manageable sets of stimuli can be created by selecting balanced subsets from this cumbersome set, such that each pair of numbers appears equally often.[3] Triadic judgment tasks have been successfully used with children as young as 5 years in a study of visual memory for block figures (Arabie, Kosslyn, & Nelson, 1975) and in a study of number development (Miller & Gelman, 1983) that is discussed in more detail below.

Issues of data collection and the axiomatic basis for a model are subsidiary to the question of whether an approach yields new insights into the characteristics of children and the nature of developmental processes. Although geometric methods have not been widely applied to developmental issues, applications to date have yielded new results in several important areas. In the remainder of this chapter issues are described in the application of geometric models to developmental research. Two complementary approaches, MDS and clustering, are considered. Emphasis is placed on individual-differences generalizations of basic scaling and clustering models, for these individual-differences methods are particularly relevant to describing devlopmental change.

Applications of Geometric Techniques

Multidimensional Scaling Models

A Simple Application: Real Distances in a Fantastic Space

Because MDS procedures produce maplike representations of stimuli, an example is given in terms of the ability of MDS procedures to reproduce a known spatial configuration from ordinal information about the distances among points. The ability to recapture metric structure from ordinal information is an attractive feature of many geometric techniques, because it means that one need only assume an ordinal measurement scale for the data analyzed by most MDS procedures. This nonmetric feature is particularly attractive for developmental research, where it may be particularly problematic to assume the subjects at differing ages use the same subjective scale in making similarity judgments (e.g., Surber, Chapter 4, this volume).

The actual calculation of a solution is an iterative procedure. Nonmetric MDS algorithms attempt to construct spatial representations in which the order of distances corresponds to the order of proximity relations in the data. Starting from some initial configuration, MDS procedures repeatedly modify the configuration to improve the fit between the order of the proximity measures and the distances between the corresponding points in the representation. Kruskal (1964a, 1964b) developed a badness-of-fit measure, termed *stress,* to describe the extent to which the ordinal relations among proximity measures are violated in the solution. The specific measures of stress used vary across different MDS algorithms and the programs that fit them (see Kruskal & Carroll, 1969), but all work in an iterative fashion to alter the representation to decrease the stress between the proximity data and reconstructed distances. When further changes in the configuration of points will not result in appreciable decreases in stress, the final value of stress is a measure of how well the original data are described by the reconstructed configuration. High values of stress can be due to errors in the data as well as to systematic violations of the assumptions, such as the metric axioms, that underlie the geometric model.

One critical implication of the iterative strategy used in MDS programs is the possibility of running into "local minima," situations where further changes in the configuration of points will not lead to lower stress, although alternate configurations exist that would yield a better fit between model and data. Kruskal and Wish (1978) described this problem, using the analogy of a blindfolded parachutist trying to make her way down a hill. She might, like MDS procedures, follow a strategy of moving in the direction of steepest descent until she reached a position where all directions led upward. This would be a position of local minimum height (lower than all nearby points), but it might not be the global minimum (the bottom of the hill).

The likelihood of becoming entrapped in this problem of local minima is reduced for both program and parachutist if they repeat the procedure, starting from several different starting configurations (or landing positions for the parachutist). Most MDS programs contain procedures for obtaining a series of solutions starting from different initial configurations. Typically the same final configuration results from all starting configurations, but replicating the analysis from different initial configurations is the best safeguard against entrapment in a configuration with merely locally minimum stress (Arabie, 1977).

To illustrate the process by which MDS procedures reconstruct locations of points by using only the orders of proximities, I have taken a series of 16 points from Fonstad's (1981, pp. 52–53) atlas representing Tolkien's (1977) fictional Middle Earth. The lower section of Table 7.1 shows map distances between a series of points taken from this map. The upper section of Table 7.1 shows the ranks of the distances, which were

TABLE 7.1. Middle Earth distances.

	Location	Ordinal distance information used as input to KYST-2A														
A	Grey Havens															
B	Eryn Vorn	9														
C	Carn Dum	41	47													
D	Rivendell	46	38	7												
E	Isengard	51	23	47	21											
F	Galadon	61	37	31	5	6										
G	Rhosgobel	72	59	30	6	17	1									
H	Erebor	85	79	28	15	48	20	7								
I	Iron Hills	99	96	52	40	71	42	26	4							
J	Sea of Rhun	106	102	87	68	75	54	39	33	19						
K	Dead Marshes	88	67	66	34	16	11	13	35	49	35					
L	Dol Amroth	81	50	83	60	12	32	43	76	89	80	18				
M	Tolfalas	93	70	92	73	27	44	55	83	91	78	22	3			
N	Umbar	103	90	105	95	61	77	86	100	104	97	56	22	8		
O	Osgiliath	94	74	82	53	24	25	29	56	64	44	2	14	10	36	
P	Mordor	107	101	98	84	69	62	58	70	65	24	24	57	45	63	19
		A	B	C	D	E	F	G	H	I	J	K	L	M	N	O

		Actual distances														
A	Grey Havens															
B	Eryn Vorn	114														
C	Carn Dum	228	250													
D	Rivendell	246	223	103												
E	Isengard	262	170	250	162											
F	Galadon	290	222	194	95	97										
G	Rhosgobel	329	279	192	97	150	57									
H	Erebor	382	357	187	138	252	159	103								
I	Iron Hills	472	445	266	227	327	234	176	90							
J	Sea of Rhun	553	498	390	316	341	270	224	206	156						
K	Dead Marshes	396	314	312	212	144	122	129	214	254	214					
L	Dol Amroth	365	259	374	283	125	199	238	344	400	362	153				
M	Tolfalas	430	322	428	333	185	240	272	374	420	356	165	65			
N	Umbar	513	401	538	443	290	350	386	486	526	446	274	165	111		
O	Osgiliath	438	339	370	267	173	174	190	274	306	240	62	131	116	217	
P	Mordor	625	492	470	376	321	292	278	322	310	173	173	276	244	303	156
		A	B	C	D	E	F	G	H	I	J	K	L	M	N	O

Note: Distances measured from map published in Fonstad (1981, pp. 52–53) used as data by the KYST-2A nonmetric MDS procedure (Kruskal, Young, & Seery, 1977) for purposes of reconstructing this known spatial configuration.

The program began with an initial, randomly constructed configuration of points, with a relatively high value of stress (Kruskal's stress formula one 1 equals .426 in two dimensions).[4] The program rearranges the configuration of points along the steepest gradient to reduce stress. The four panels of Figure 7.2 show the progressive adjustments in the configuration of points. In each panel, a lowercase letter indicates the position of the first of two iterations, while an uppercase letter indicates the position of the same point at the second iteration. Where the location of the point was identical across the two iterations, only the uppercase letter is shown.

The top left panel shows the relatively small rearrangements between the initial configuration (lowercase letters) and the first iteration (uppercase letters), which yield a reduction in stress from .426 to .396. The top right panel compares the configuration after iteration 1 with iteration 10, at which point stress has been lowered to .061. To make sure that the program converged to an absolute minimum value of stress, a strict stopping criterion was specified. The program would continue attempting to improve the configuration until (1) 100 iterations were computed, (2) an extremely small value of stress was obtained (.0001), or (3) there was no improvement in stress between iterations (ratio of stress across iterations = .9999). An additional 39 iterations were required to reach this stress value. The lower left panel of Figure 7.2 shows the change between iteration 10 and the final configuration (iteration 49), which has a stress of .0001.

The lower right panel of Figure 7.2 compares the final reconstructed solution (lowercase letters) with actual locations (uppercase letters).[5] Figure 7.2 provides a graphic illustration of how well ordinal information about proximities constrains the reconstruction of a metric space.

Corresponding to changes in the configuration of points charted in Figure 7.2 are changes in the function relating the input data with their corresponding distances in the reconstructed configuration. Figure 7.3 shows the Shepard diagram plots, which illustrate the monotonic regression that lies at the heart of nonmetric MDS procedures. These diagrams relate input proximities data (ranked distances in Middle Earth) on the X axis to two values on the Y axis. Distances among the points in the reconstructed configuration are plotted as D's. Figure 7.3 shows the success with which reconstructed distances fit the monotonicity requirement (that no point be lower than any on its left) at various points in the analysis. Dashes show the best-fitting monotonic function relating input data to reconstructed distances. Stress is a function of the vertical distances between the reconstructed distances and this monotonic function (divided by a scale factor), and thus stress measures the extent to which the reconstructed distances violate a general monotonic relation with the

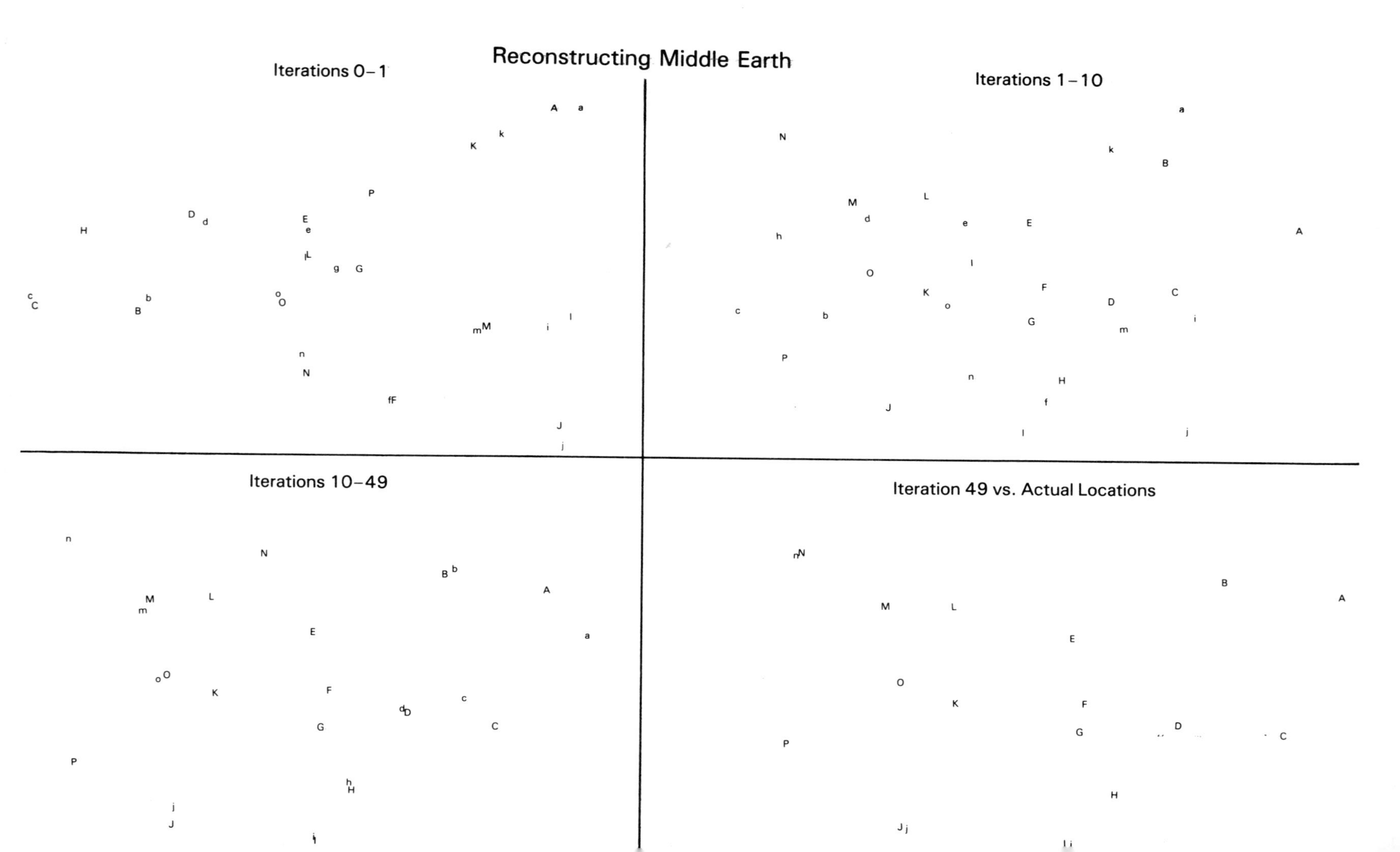
Reconstructing Middle Earth
Iterations 0–1
Iterations 1–10
Iterations 10–49
Iteration 49 vs. Actual Locations

input data. The four panels of Figure 7.3 clearly show the program's progress in decreasing stress. In the upper left panel (the random configuration of iteration 0 with stress = .426), there is the expected random relation between input data and output distances. The upper right panel shows the slight improvement after iteration 1 (stress = .396). The relation between input data and output distances is much clearer after 10 iterations (lower left panel, with stress = .0610), while the almost perfect monotonic fit between the data and reconstructed distances is shown by the presence of only one *D*, close to the curve, in the stress function for the final configuration (lower right panel of Figure 7.3).

Careful consideration of the Shepard diagram reveals a number of problems with the data. Jagged step functions with lengthy horizontal segments (as in the upper panels of Figure 7.3) result from equating a large number of distances in the reconstructed space that corresponded to distinct entries in the data. The shape of the Shepard diagram can also suggest the possibility of stronger forms of regression (such as linear regression) which can be specified as alternatives to monotonic regression in several MDS programs. Making stronger assumptions about the relations between data and distances can often permit one to describe a data structure that does not emerge from the weaker assumptions of monotonic regression. (See Arabie & Soli, 1982, for a thorough discussion of this issue.)

Issues of Dimensionality and Statistical Significance

In this example, it was known a priori that the data could be accounted for in two dimensions. This is often not the case, and the problem is complicated by the fact that unless data are perfectly fit in a given dimensionality, more dimensions will lead to lower values of stress. Tests to evaluate whether one MDS configuration (say, in a higher dimension) is an improvement over another have been developed (Hubert & Golledge, 1981; Schönemann & Carroll, 1970), along with tests for the significance of specific levels of stress (Klahr, 1969; Levine, 1978; Spence & Ogilvie, 1973). The number of stimuli also imposes an upper limit on the number of dimensions that are meaningful. In an excellent practical guide to MDS methods, Kruskal and Wish (1978) suggested that the number of objects

---

◁ Figure 7.2. MDS reconstruction of Middle Earth locations using the KYST2A program. Letters correspond to those locations designated in Table 7.1. The top left panel compares locations in an initial random configuration (lowercase letters) with locations of the corresponding points after iteration 1 (uppercase letters). The top right panel compares positions after iteration 1 (now in lowercase) with positions after iteration 10 (uppercase). The lower left panel compares positions after iteration 10 (lowercase) with positions after iteration 49 (uppercase). The program converged after 49 iterations. The lower right panel compares the final reconstructed configuration (lowercase) with the actual locations (uppercase).

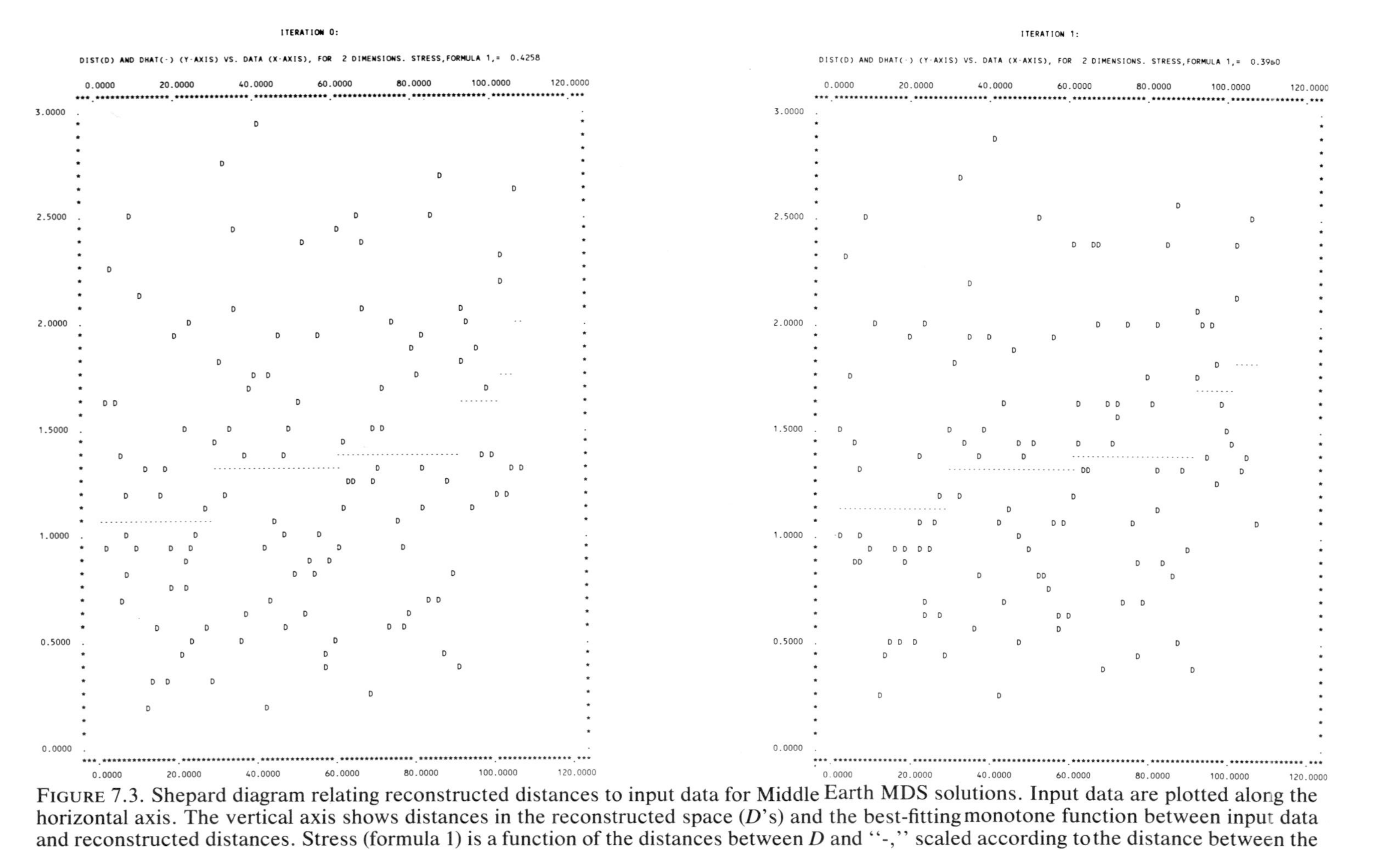

FIGURE 7.3. Shepard diagram relating reconstructed distances to input data for Middle Earth MDS solutions. Input data are plotted along the horizontal axis. The vertical axis shows distances in the reconstructed space (D's) and the best-fitting monotone function between input data and reconstructed distances. Stress (formula 1) is a function of the distances between D and "-," scaled according to the distance between the point and the X axis. The top left panel shows the randomly determined iteration 0 (stress = .4258). The top right panel shows iteration 1

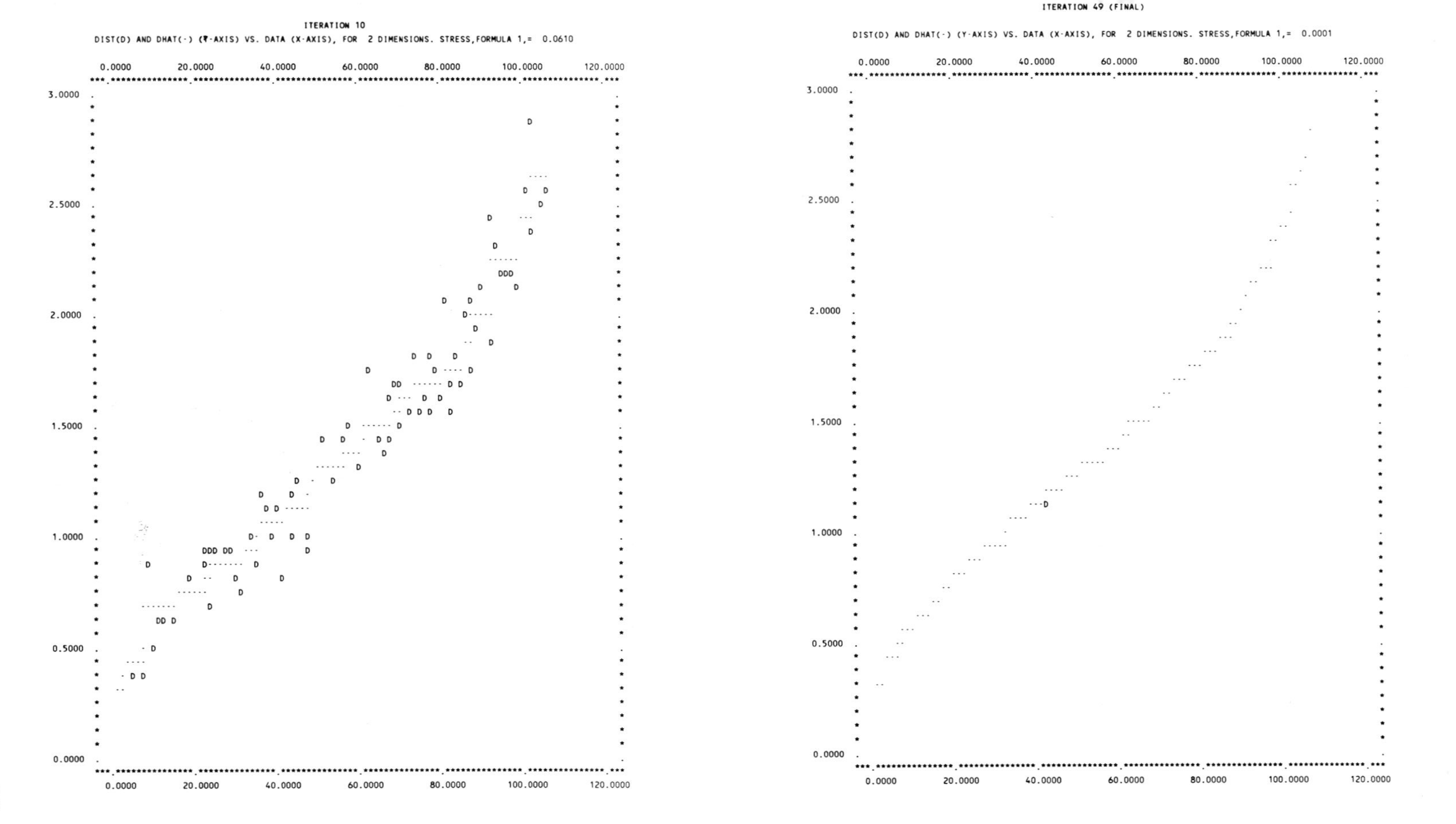

ITERATION 10
DIST(D) AND DHAT(-) (Y-AXIS) VS. DATA (X-AXIS), FOR 2 DIMENSIONS. STRESS,FORMULA 1,= 0.0610
0.0000 20.0000 40.0000 60.0000 80.0000 100.0000 120.0000
3.0000 2.5000 2.0000 1.5000 1.0000 0.5000 0.0000
ITERATION 49 (FINAL)
DIST(D) AND DHAT(-) (Y-AXIS) VS. DATA (X-AXIS), FOR 2 DIMENSIONS. STRESS,FORMULA 1,= 0.0001
0.0000 20.0000 40.0000 60.0000 80.0000 100.0000 120.0000
3.0000 2.5000 2.0000 1.5000 1.0000 0.5000 0.0000

being scaled should always exceed 4 times the number of dimensions used in representing those objects. Finally, attaining low-dimension solutions where feasible should be a goal in itself, because MDS procedures lose much of their accessibility when the number of dimensions employed exceeds what can be readily displayed or visualized.

Once a solution in a given dimensionality is obtained, interpretation can involve finding relations that correspond to coordinates of dimensions (which can be measured through regression techniques, e.g., Kruskal & Wish, 1978) or interpreting groups of neighboring points. As is described in several examples, distances in the resulting configuration can themselves be used to predict results from other psychological tasks.

Applications of Unweighted Multidimensional Scaling

Developmental research using the basic MDS model described above has typically involved finding separate representations to describe judgments of subjects at different ages. These solutions can then be used to generate hypotheses concerning the developmental changes that could transform one structure to another. Three applications are described, in semantic development, spatial representation, and number development.

Relations between Semantic and Physical Spaces

A novel application of MDS procedures that used real maps as a point of comparison is a study by Magaña, Magaña, and Ferreira-Pinto (1982). Arguing that spatial layouts of educational environments ought to conform to the cognitive representations of learners, Magaña et al. compared MDS analyses of children's judgments of similarity between animals to maps of the actual locations of these animals in various zoos. Figure 7.4 represents both children's judgments of similarity among animals (top part) and the locations of these same animals in the Los Angeles zoo (bottom part). Although some aspects of zoo placement are in agreement with children's representations, such as the proximity between *lion* and *tiger* in both structures, others differ greatly, such as the dispersal of the primates (*gorilla, monkey,* and *chimpanzee*) throughout the zoo.

Although the Magaña et al. study used actual spatial locations as referents, these were compared with a space generated from semantic rather than spatial judgments. It is thus an example of the applicability of MDS procedures to developmental issues beyond the representation of spatial information. Two other applications of MDS procedures show how these techniques can reveal the existence of complexity in children's representations of familiar domains.

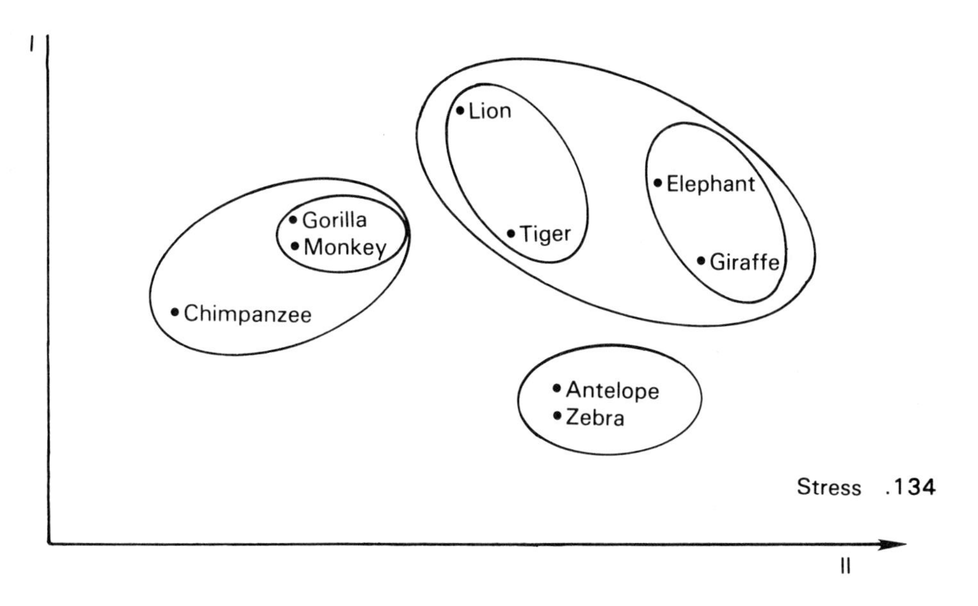

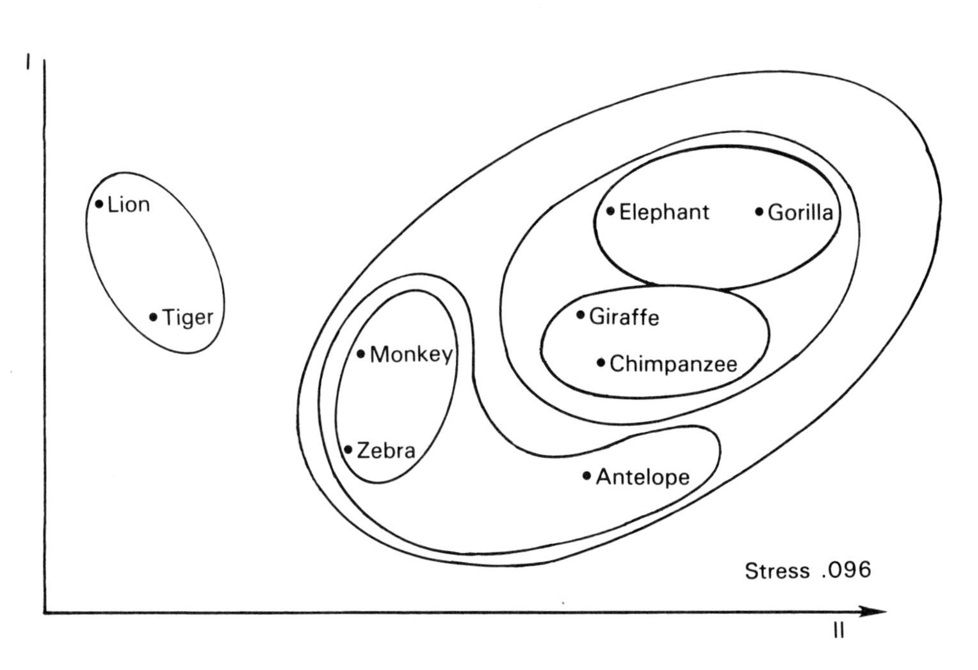

FIGURE 7.4. MDS (KYST) representation of children's judgments of relations among animals (upper panel) compared with MDS representation of the physical layout of the Los Angeles Zoo (lower panel) (adapted from Magaña, Magaña, & Ferreira-Pinto, 1982). Those items that clustered in a hierarchical clustering analysis are enclosed by closed curves.

Object Perception and Geometry

Piaget and Inhelder (1967) asserted that there is a development sequence in children's understanding of spatial relations corresponding to successive mastery of the geometric transformations of topological, projective, and Euclidean geometries. Supporting this theory, Laurendeau and Pinard (1970) reported that children's errors on a visual-haptic matching task were more likely than expected to involve changes of Euclidean than topological features. Rieser and Edwards (1979) used MDS procedures to reanalyze Laurendeau and Pinard's data, using frequency of confusion as an index of similarity. Figure 7.5 shows the solution obtained for the 4-year-old subjects, with closed curves demarcating topologically equivalent figures. Clearly features other than topological transformations contribute to young children's judgments. The curved C figures in the top right, for example, were more likely to be confused with the unbroken "doughnut" shape than with the other solid figures to which the C's are topologically equivalent. The globally circular figures were quite likely to be confused with each other, despite the fact that the presence of varying numbers of holes made them topologically distinct. Rieser and Edwards went on to collect direct similarity judgments from children and adults on a set of figures chosen to represent a variety of geometric transformations

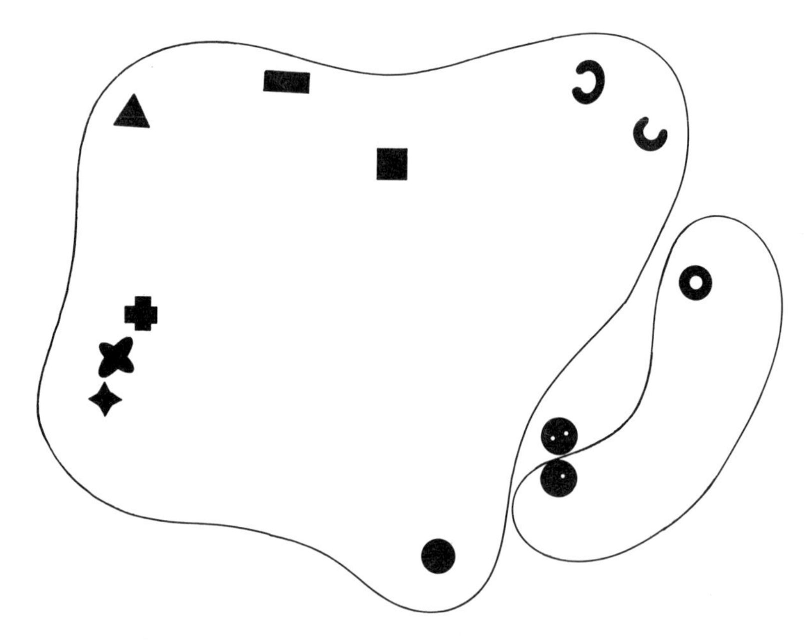

FIGURE 7.5. MDS representation from Rieser and Edward's analysis of Laurendeau and Pinard's (1970) data on confusion errors by 4-year-olds on a cross-modal matching task. Figures that are topologically equivalent are indicated by closed curves. (Taken from Rieser & Edwards, 1979.)

of an original parallelogram. With these new stimuli as well, they found that children's judgments were determined by Euclidean factors such as curvature or number of sides. To the extent that topological features emerged, they were present in the judgments of adults rather than children—just the opposite of the predicted developmental pattern. Children's representations of the shapes of objects are certainly more complex than a simple dichotomy between topological and nontopological transformations would imply, but this very complexity points up the utility of MDS procedures for representing the structure of semantically rich domains.

Number Development

Research on the development of number concepts has focused on children's understanding of a very small set of numerical relations. After Piaget's (1965) demonstration of young children's failure to realize that one-to-one correspondence between the members of sets always implies numerical equality, a vast body of research has accumulated on children's understanding of the features that define number (see Brainerd, 1979; Gelman & Gallistel, 1978). Perhaps because of this focus on the development of the basic number concept, there has been little research on how children's conceptions of number develop beyond the point at which they conserve numerosity. Further development might consist merely of learning new applications for this number concept, with these new *uses* for numbers distinguished from children's conceptions of what numbers *are*.

Alternatively, learning new uses for numbers might also affect the ways in which children represent numbers. Research with adults by Shepard, Kilpatric, and Cunningham (1975) implies that the latter alternative is more likely. Shepard et al. found that adults use a variety of multiplicative and other relations to make judgments of similarities between numbers. Once children know what numbers are, how do children develop and elaborate an understanding of what numerical features are salient characteristics of numbers?

To explore this question, Miller and Gelman (1983) collected developmental data on perceived similarity of numbers from adults and from children aged 5, 8, and 12 years. Because we were concerned about the ability of 5-year-olds to meaningfully use a rating scale with such an abstract concept, we abandoned the task of judging similarities among pairs of numbers used by Shepard et al. in favor of a triadic judgment approach. Sets of balanced incomplete triads were developed, so that children saw each pair of numbers equally often and were asked to pick from triads of numbers the most similar and least similar pairs. The resulting choices were then summed to produce a proximity matrix by incrementing an index of similarity for each pair picked as most similar and decrementing this index for each pair picked as least similar.

Separate MDS analyses were conducted for each age group, and they are presented in Figure 7.6. Both the 5- and 8-year-old subjects produced essentially one-dimensional configurations reflecting numerical magnitude. The kind of bending into a horseshoe configuration seen in these two solutions is frequently found when a basically one-dimensional configuration is mapped in two dimensions (Shepard, 1974). Some 5-year-olds were unsure whether 0 or 1 was the smallest number, and the small disruption in its spatial location is consistent with this consideration. In general, the solutions for both 5- and 8-year olds were quite similar in indicating judgments of similarity between numbers based on differences in magnitude.

Solutions for 12-year-old and adult subjects were quite different from those for younger children. For both groups, the dimension of basic magnitude (represented by a dashed axis) has been supplemented by a division into odd and even numbers as children begin to represent multiplicative relations as well as those based solely on magnitude.

These findings suggest that substantial development occurs in children's conceptions of numbers beyond the point at which they can conserve number in an adultlike manner. These changes were mapped in a series of static representations of children's performance at different ages. What is lacking in the techniques described thus far, however, is any systematic method for comparing performance across individuals or groups of subjects.

Weighted or Individual-Differences Scaling

Concordance Statistics

Calculating a rank-order correlation such as τ_b between sets of responses or matrices provides a convenient index of relation. Significance testing of the resulting statistic may be problematic, because often entries within the matrices were not independently sampled. Hubert (1978, 1979; Schultz & Hubert, 1976) has developed procedures for determining a conservative approximation of the probability of achieving a given concordance between two matrices. This is based on comparing the likelihood of a given level of concordance over random permutations of the rows and columns of the matrices being compared. These procedures can be used to determine significance levels for a variety of concordance statistics, including the Pearson product-moment correlation. One way to compare the similarity of matrices of judgments or scaling configurations is to use Hubert's procedure to determine the significance level of some concordance statistic. Table 7.2 shows the concordance between the number similarity judgments of different groups of subjects. As one would expect from the MDS analyses, significant correlations were found between judgments of 5-, 8-, and 12-year-olds and of 12-year-olds with adults. These results suggest that there is an adult pattern of number representation different from that

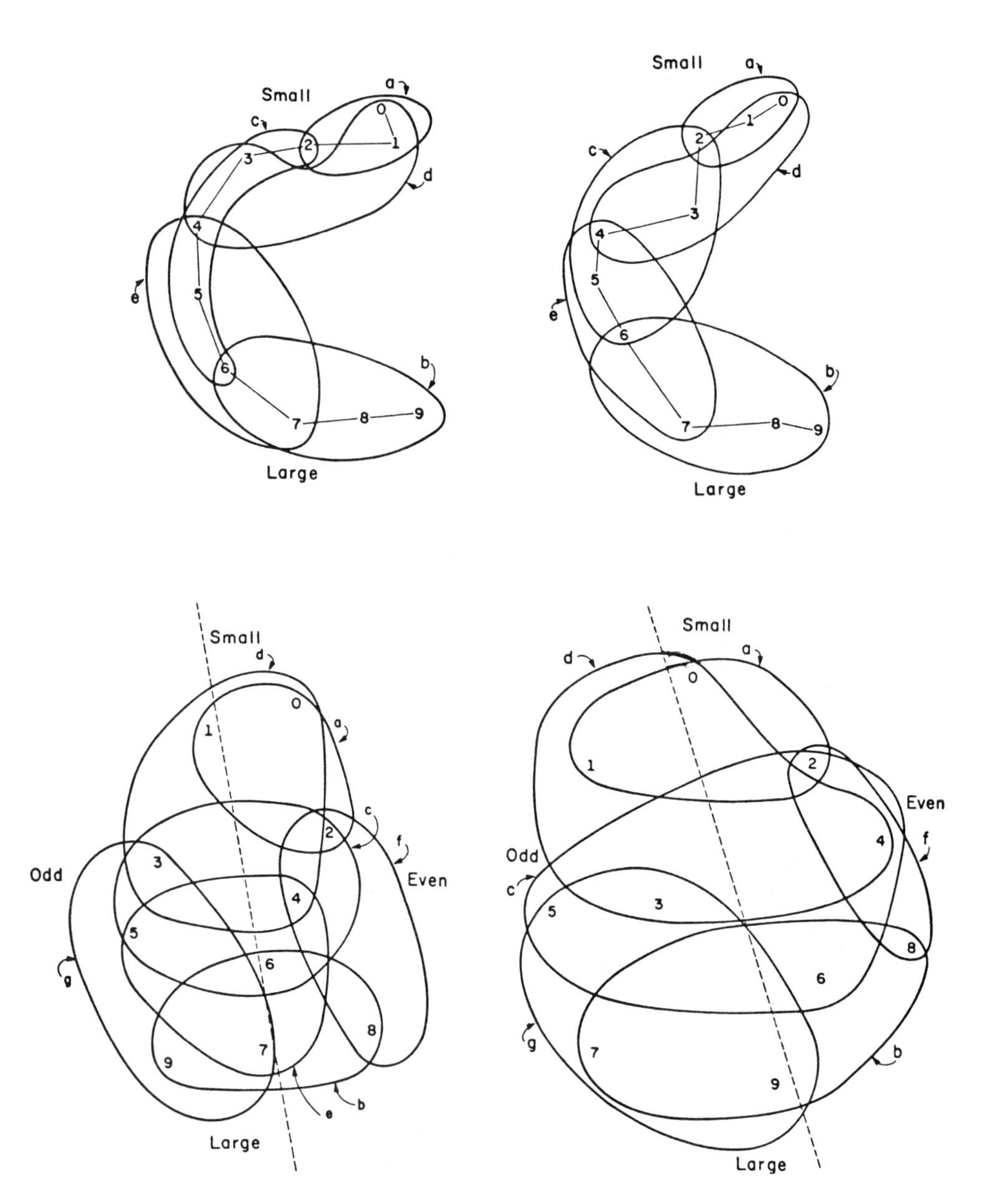

FIGURE 7.6. MDS representation of children's number-similarity judgments in the Miller and Gelman (1983) study. Top left panel shows 5-year-olds' results. Top right panel shows results from 8-year-olds. Bottom left panel shows 12-year-olds' solution. Adult solution is shown in bottom right panel. Those items that clustered in a nonhierarchical clustering analysis are enclosed in closed curves as follows: *a,* small numbers (0, 1, 2); *b,* large numbers (6, 7, 8, 9); *c,* middle numbers (2, 3, 4, 5, 6); *d,* small numbers excluding 2 (0, 1, 3, 4); *e,* moderately large numbers (4, 5, 6, 7); *f,* powers of 2 (2, 4, 8); *g,* odd numbers excluding 1 (3, 5, 7, 9).

TABLE 7.2. Concordance between number-similarity judgments.

	Kindergarten	Third grade	Sixth grade	Adults
Kindergarten				
Third grade	.987**			
Sixth grade	.776*	.814*		
Adults	.435	.465	.776*	

Note: The concordance statistic is identical to the Pearson product-moment correlation coefficient. Statistical significance was assessed by using Hubert's (1979) generalized concordance procedures.
* $p < .05$.
** $p < .025$.

of young children, with 12-year-olds demonstrating a combination of the two patterns.

INDSCAL AS A DEVELOPMENTAL MODEL

Concordance statistics for matrices of proximity judgments provide an important tool for evaluating developmental changes in representations, but it would be useful to be able to represent developmental changes directly in MDS procedures. The individual-differences model INDSCAL developed by Carroll and Chang (1970) provides a means of doing so. This mathematical model entails a psychological assumption about how individual differences affect representation of stimulus domains, namely that individuals differ by differentially emphasizing common stimulus dimensions.[6] The INDSCAL model is a *weighted* Euclidean model, because it stretches or contracts distances in an ordinary Euclidean space according to the comparative salience that a subject (or group of subjects) places upon that dimension. Mathematically, the familiar Euclidean distance model relates distance d to the absolute value of the differences in the K=dimensional coordinates of two points (i,j), such that

$$d_{ij} = \sqrt{\sum_{k=1}^{K} (x_{ik} - x_{jk})^2}. \tag{4}$$

INDSCAL weights these distances by multiplying distances along a dimension by each subject's (m) emphasis upon that particular dimension w_{mk}:

$$d_{ij}^{m} = \sqrt{\sum_{k=1}^{K} w_{mk}(x_{ik} - x_{jk})^2}\ . \tag{5}$$

An important distinction between the INDSCAL model and most other MDS models is that because subject (or other "individual") variation occurs by weighting dimensions, INDSCAL solutions are invariant up to a reflection or permutation of the axes but are specifically not preserved across an arbitrary rotation. Although dimensions are developed with respect to subject variation, Carroll and Wish (1974) and Shepard (1980) assert that INDSCAL dimensions generally correspond to important stimulus features. That is, dimensions along which subjects or groups of subjects vary typically correspond to meaningful stimulus dimensions.

Algorithms for fitting the INDSCAL model, most notably SINDSCAL (Pruzansky, 1975), or options in MDS procedures such as the ALSCAL (Takane, Young, & de Leeuw, 1977) or MULTISCALE (Ramsay, 1977, 1978) programs, provide the user with two spatial representations. One display represents the location of stimulus points in a common psychological space (with coordinates given for each object i and dimension k by the x_{ik}'s in Equation 5), while the subjects (or other sources of data) are represented as points in a separate space having the same dimensionality as the stimulus space (with coordinates given for each subject m and dimension k by the weights w_{mk} in Equation 5). Subjects whose data are well explained by an INDSCAL analysis will be located a relatively long distance from the origin, and the extent to which a subject emphasizes a particular dimension will be reflected by the subject's coordinate on that dimension.

Two methodological issues arise with INDSCAL that do not occur with other MDS techniques. In contrast with nonmetric MDS programs such as KYST-2A, most programs for fitting the INDSCAL model assume a *metric* rather than merely monotonic relation between data and recovered distances (an exception is ALSCAL, which optionally provides monotonic regression for the individual-differences model). Thus transformations of the data can sometimes affect the resulting configuration (see Arabie & Soli, 1982, for an example). The second issue concerns whether proximity judgments are assumed to be comparable across subjects. Typically (and presumably in most developmental applications), data are assumed to be conditional on each matrix; that is, judgments by one subject or a group of subjects are not assumed to be directly comparable to those of others. Under this assumption of matrix conditionality, each subject's data matrix is normalized so that each subject contributes an equal amount of variance to the resulting solution. Working with simulated data, MacCallum (1977) has argued that the assumption of matrix conditionality may interfere with the recovery of data structure, although how representative his data set is of those that would be obtained empirically is unclear. In any case, there are substantive grounds for arguing that matrix conditionality is the appropriate assumption for most developmental applications, because it avoids the danger that one extreme subject or age group will dominate the entire solution.

As a developmental model, INDSCAL posits that development is associated with changes in the salience of dimensions in representational spaces (including the case where zero weight indicates the irrelevance of a dimension). Cases where developmental change is orderly should produce subject spaces showing correspondingly orderly transformations from the weights of one set of subjects to another. Although significant assumptions are made concerning the representation of individual differences, INDSCAL can provide a powerful tool for describing developmental change, as the following examples demonstrate.

INDSCAL Analysis of Number Judgments

A reanalysis of the Miller and Gelman data on developmental changes in number representation provides a comparison between the information gained from weighted (INDSCAL) versus unweighted MDS (as presented in Figure 7.6). These data were reanalyzed with the SINDSCAL program, and a two-dimensional solution is presented in Figure 7.7. The resulting two dimensions are immediately interpretable as magnitude (on the X axis) and odd versus even numbers on the Y axis. These two dimensions of magnitude and odd/even were previously used to interpret the individual solutions from the KYST-2A analyses of the individual matrices, but they are unambiguously present in the INDSCAL analysis.

Turning to the subject space presented in the lower panel of Figure 7.7, one sees a pattern predictable from the individual KYST-2A solutions. Only the positive quadrant of the two-dimensional plane is plotted, because SINDSCAL weights are expected (but not required) to be nonnegative. Total distances from the origin are of approximately equal length, indicating that all age groups were comparably well fit by the model (the values of Pearson's r between normalized scores and the scalar product of dimensions by age group ranged from $r = .870$ for adults to $r = .899$ for 5-year-olds). The 5- and 8-year-old subjects showed a similar weighting of dimensions, which essentially involves a zero weight on the odd/even dimension, coupled with a substantial weight on the magnitude dimension. The INDSCAL model provides a convenient way of summarizing the relations between the individual data matrices, while showing the increase in salience of multiplicative relations that occurs with development. Over time, an initial reliance of young children upon magnitude information alone (shown by essentially zero coordinates on the odd/even dimension coupled with large projections on the magnitude dimension) is supplemented by consideration of additional numerical relations in judging similarity of numbers.

Other developmental research using the INDSCAL model has shown substantial developmental shifts in the dimensions children use to judge similarity of animal names (Howard & Howard, 1977) and to represent faces (Pedelty, Levine, and Shevell, 1985). The Pedelty et al. study is particularly interesting, because it leads to a modification of the account for age-related changes in face perception described by Carey (1982; Diamond and Carey, 1977). Carey and Diamond (1977) proposed that it is not until children are about 10 years old that they use configurational informa-

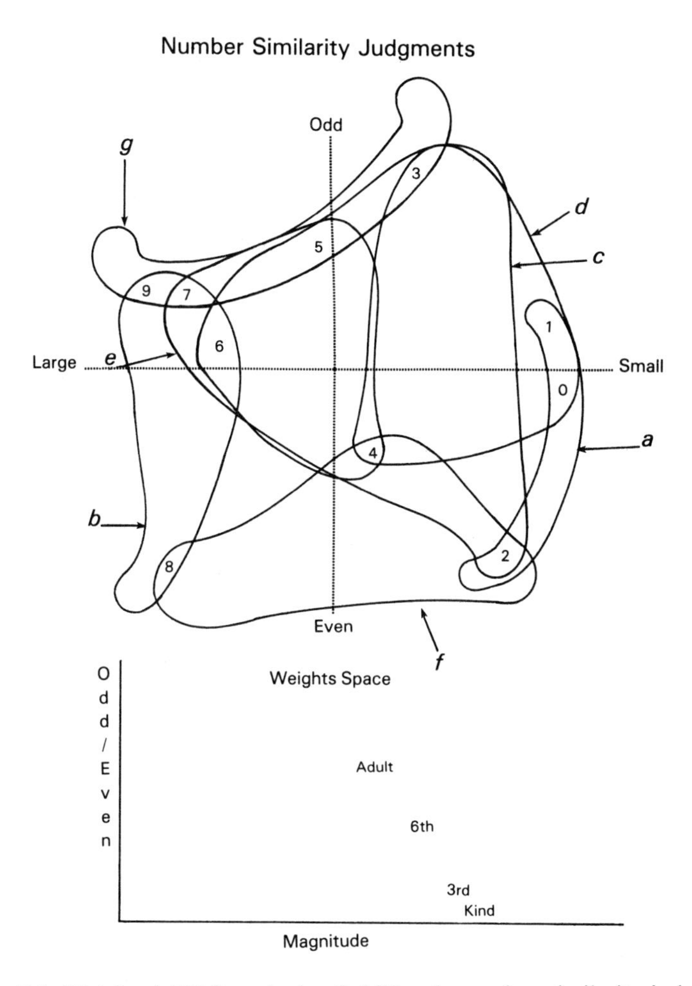

FIGURE 7.7. Weighted MDS analysis of children's number-similarity judgments. Top panel shows stimulus space, with closed contours enclosing items that clustered in nonhierarchical clustering. Lower panel shows subject or weights space, which indicates the salience of each dimension for a particular age group. (Data from Miller & Gelman, 1983.)

tion rather than isolated features to recognize unfamiliar faces. In a developmental study of similarity judgments of faces presented in either upright or inverted orientation, Pedelty et al. found that although face similarity judgments of subjects from 7 years through adulthood could be described in terms of a common set of dimensions (corresponding to hair color, facial width, and nose-lip distance), younger children tended to disregard some one of these dimensions in making judgments. Pedelty et al. argue that the development of face perception is described best in terms of a change in the quantity of information that can be perceived, rather than as a change in the kind of information (piecemeal versus configurational) to which children are responding. The conclusion that the development of face processing involves an increased ability to simultaneously consider a number of different features parallels results for the development of number judgments, although the apparent lack of precedence among the specific dimensions that young children emphasized is an interesting aspect of the Pedelty et al. study.

Representation and Skill: Number and the Abacus

The INDSCAL model has been used to describe developmental changes in number development, semantic representation, and face processing in terms of increases in the number of dimensions to which children simultaneously attend. The INDSCAL model can also be applied to the description of representational differences associated with varying levels of expertise.

It has frequently been asserted (Chase & Simon, 1973; Chi, Glaser, & Rees, 1982) that one consequence of expertise is a more functional representation of the domain in question. Studies of skilled memory in areas as diverse as circuit diagrams (Egan & Schwartz, 1979) and chess (Chase & Simon, 1973) show that experts organize their recall along functional lines, responding to those features that are most salient for the particular domain.

The assertion that experts' knowledge is more functional than that of novices becomes ambiguous when one considers the relation among different but related skills. Where those relations that are functional for some skill contrast with relations that are meaningful in a broader context, how does the expert's representation differ from the novice's? Two quite different predictions are possible, and neither is a new idea.

Extension of Expertise

The first view was most eloquently described by Bryan & Harter (1899). Discussing the process of acquiring skills such as telegraphy, Bryan and Harter (1899, p. 348) wrote, "In the measure that he has mastered the occupation, it has mastered him. Body and soul from head to foot, he has—or one may say he *is*—the array of habits which constitutes proficiency in that sort." According to this view, a mastered skill should color one's perception of all domains it touches upon. A skilled pianist, for example, should view music through the filter of those features relevant to piano playing.

Circumscription of Expertise

A second view holds that mastering a skill may make it possible to move beyond the constraints of those features uniquely relevant to the skill. If the knowledge of experts were truly functional, they might have integrated knowledge only relevant to their domain of specific skill with other knowledge, transcending the limitations of their skill. In his study of blindfold chess, Binet (1966/1893) asserted that developing expert knowledge of chess involves moving beyond the limitations of the spatial aspects of chess. Describing the chess expert's skill, Binet (1966/1893, p. 149) wrote:

> He remembers not that he moved his king to a certain square, but that, at a given moment, he had a particular plan of attack and defense which required the movement of his king. The move itself is only the conclusion of an act of thinking; that act must first be recaptured; the recall of its manifest result—the particular move—follows from it.

According to this view, the musical representation of the expert pianist might deemphasize those features unique to piano playing, emphasizing musical features of more general applicability.

Miller, Stigler, Houang, and Lee (1986) used the INDSCAL model to describe the effects on number representation of expertise at a culture-specific numerical skill, mental abacus calculation. Prior research has documented the impressive computational skills developed by adults and children who receive extended practice in abacus calculation (Hatano, Miyake, & Binks, 1977; Hatano & Osawa, 1983; Stigler, 1984). Perhaps the most intriguing aspect of this skill is the development of "mental abacus calculation," in which subjects calculate with reference to an image of the abacus. Prior to describing data supporting these claims, a brief review of how the abacus works may be in order.

Figure 7.8 shows how a variety of numbers are represented on the Japanese abacus used throughout Asia. Beads "count" as they are pushed toward the center (horizontal) bar by the thumb (lower beads) or forefinger (upper bead). The upper bead represents 5, while the lower beads represent 1 each. The value represented by a column is the sum of the top bead (0 to 5) and the lower bead (0 to 4). Within a column, the abacus is a modulo 5 number system, while remaining a base-10 system between columns.

The structure of the abacus is reflected in subjects' performance in a number of ways. Stigler (1984) reported that for abacus-trained children the number of steps involved in an abacus calculation was associated with reaction time for mental calculation among subjects who received abacus training, that these children could distinguish true intermediate states from foils, and that they made abacus-specific errors. Data on error patterns are particularly convincing in indicating that the abacus makes salient different features of numbers than does the ordinary system of numerals. Stigler found that abacus calculators (but not U.S. college students) were prone to make errors in which the answer was off by 5 in some column from the correct sum, as though they had mistaken the location of

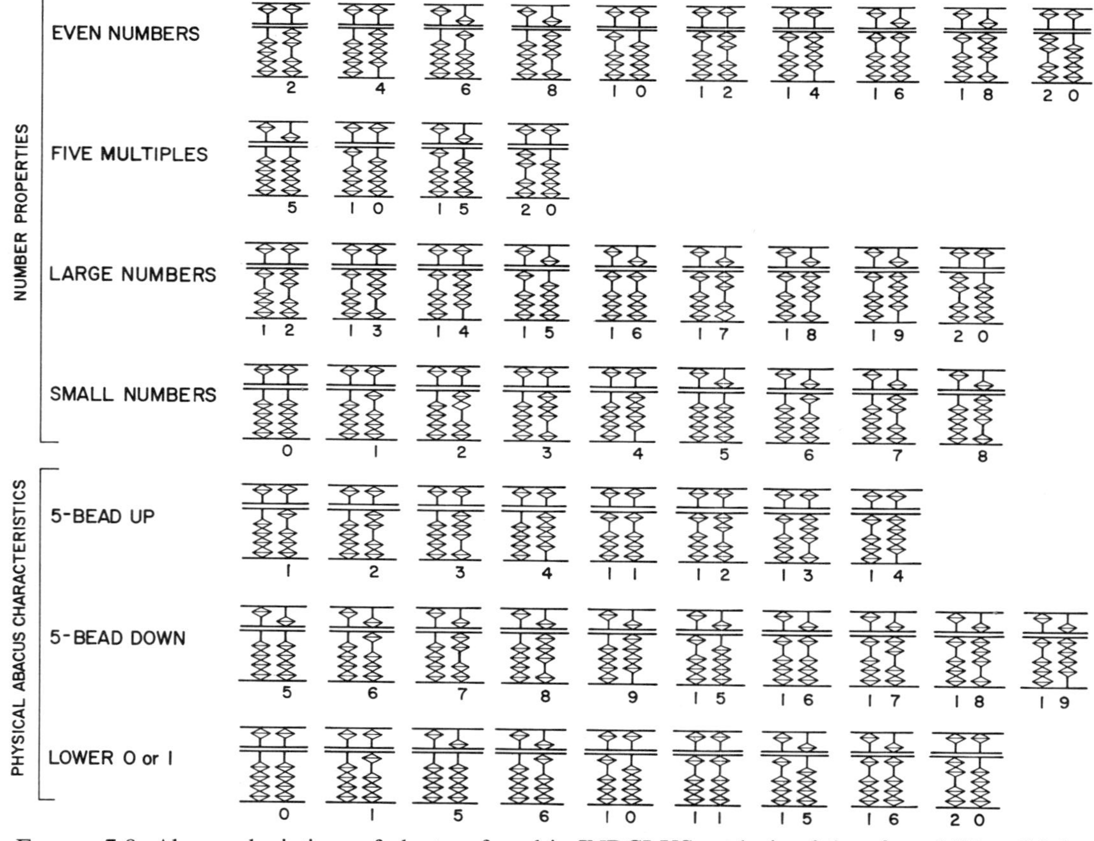

FIGURE 7.8. Abacus depictions of clusters found in INDCLUS analysis of data from Miller, Stigler, Houang, & Lee (1986). The Japanese abacus shown here is a modulo 5 system within a column. Beads "count" as they are moved toward the center (horizontal) bar. The top bead represents 5, while the lower beads represent 1.

the 5 bead. As the second row of Figure 7.8 demonstrates, the abacus represents numbers that differ by 5 in a similar way, increasing the likelihood that two numbers differing by ±5 might be confused in the course of calculation.

The different view on the relations between representation and expertise make opposite predictions on how experts will judge those features unique to the abacus. On the Bryan and Harter view, one would expect that abacus experts will in effect "see the abacus in every number." Thus the ±5 relation that emerges in their performance should also be evident in their judgments of similarity among numbers. According to the view suggested by Binet, one would expect just the opposite. The experts should deemphasize abacus-specific features, or "see the number in every abacus."

To evaluate the impact of abacus skill on children's representation of number, we collected similarity judgments for abacus and numeral pairs from three groups of subjects varying in degree of familiarity with the abacus. We collected data in Taiwan from expert abacus subjects (who regularly attended an after-school program in abacus calculation and had received high rankings in a national abacus test) and from novices (who had some exposure to abacus calculation as part of their school curriculum but had not taken part in after-school programs) and in the United States from children who had no experience with using the abacus as a tool for calculation. Parallel forms using abacus versus numeral representation were developed, presenting pairs of stimuli from the set 0 to 20. Each subject saw only one type of stimulus, making judgments of the similarity of 105 pairs of numbers presented either as numerals of abacus forms.

A SINDSCAL analysis of the aggregated similarity judgments indicated that three dimensions provided a reasonable balance of interpretability and variance accounted for. These dimensions correspond to magnitude (dimension 1), even versus odd (dimension 2), and a modulo 5 dimension (dimension 3). Figure 7.9 presents the planes produced by combining each pair of dimensions in this stimulus space.

Two of the dimensions, magnitude and even/odd, resemble those found in Miller and Gelman (1983). The third dimension, marked 0 mod 5 to 4 mod 5, deserves some elaboration. Looking at the top right panel of Figure 7.9, showing the magnitude dimension crossed with the mod 5 dimension, one can count from 0 to 4 by moving consistently downward before jumping back down to the bottom of the panel for 5. This process is repeated for 6 to 9, with a drop to 10, although it is not as well supported for the sequences 11 to 15 and 16 to 20. The third dimension provides support for the view that the modulo 5 feature of abacus representations of numbers finds it way into subjects' similarity judgments. Consideration of subject spaces is necessary to determine the role that these various dimensions play in judgments by subjects in the different groups. Figure

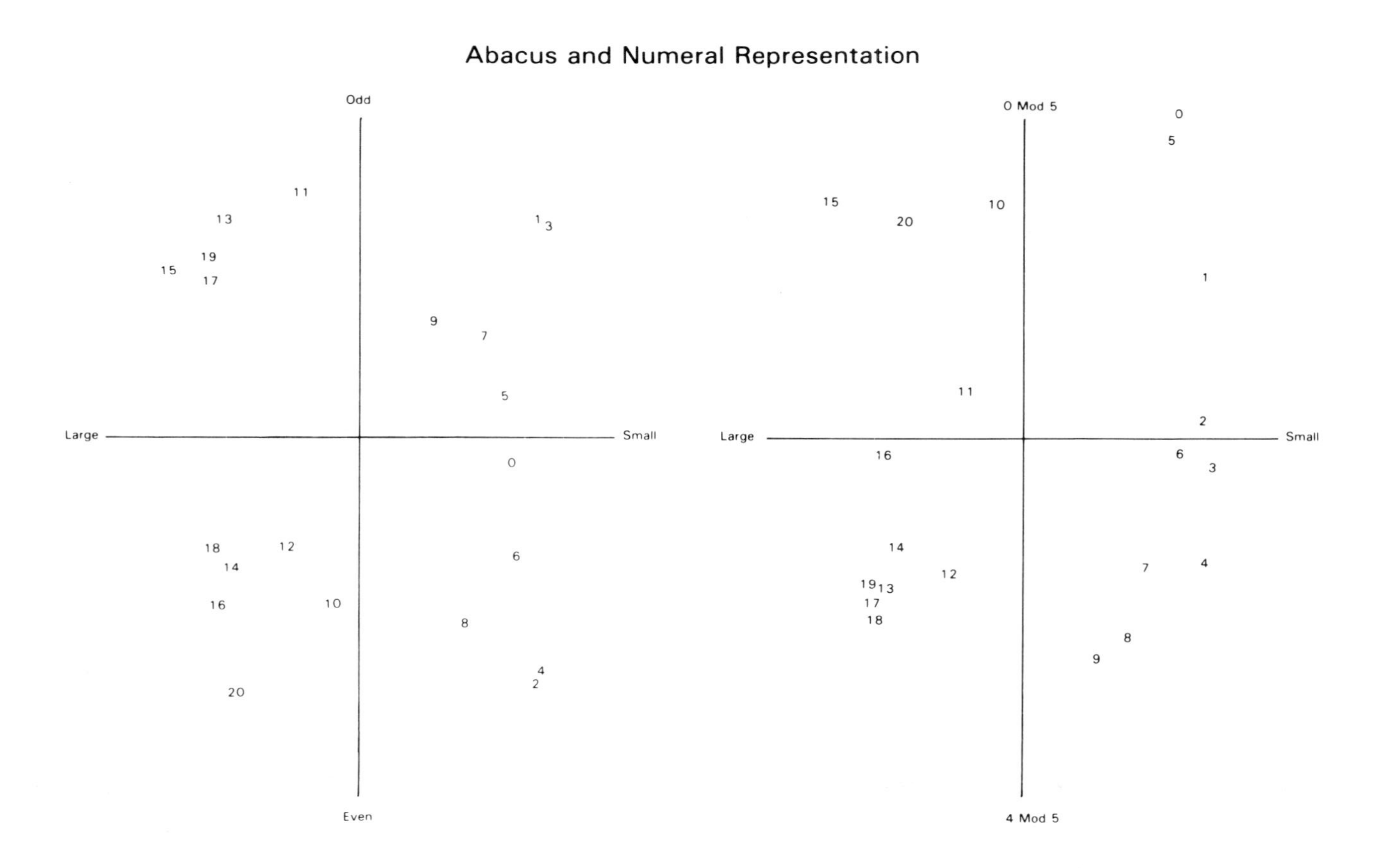
Odd
Even
Large
Small
0 Mod 5
4 Mod 5
Large
Small

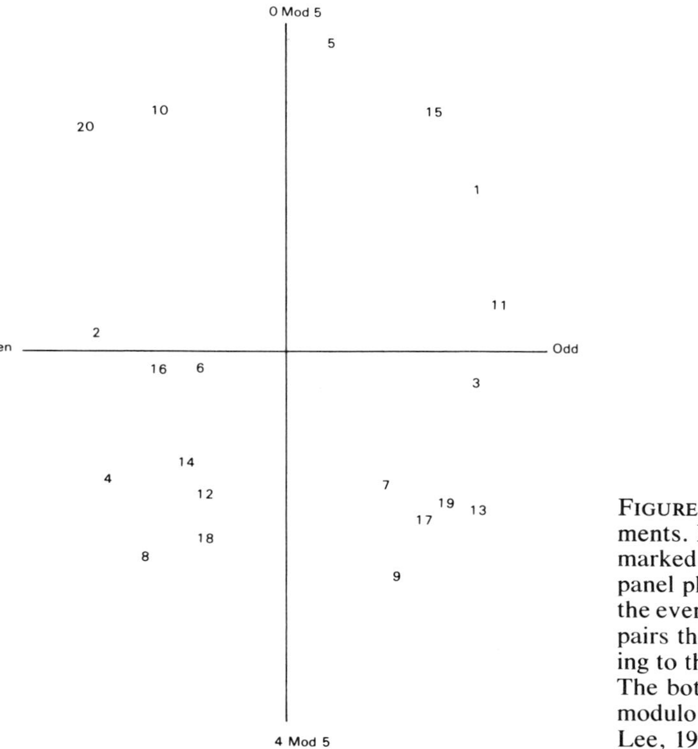

FIGURE 7.9. Weighted MDS analysis of abacus-numeral similarity judgments. Planes in this three-dimensional solution are shown, with axes marked according to the interpretation given in the text. The top left panel plots the magnitude dimension (dimension 1 on the *X* axis) with the even/odd dimension (dimension 2 on the *Y* axis). The top right panel pairs the magnitude dimension (*X* axis) with a dimension corresponding to the modulo 5 value of each number (dimension 3 on the *Y* axis). The bottom left panel pairs the odd/even dimension (*X* axis) with the modulo 5 dimension (*Y* axis). (Taken from Miller, Stigler, Houang, & Lee, 1986.)

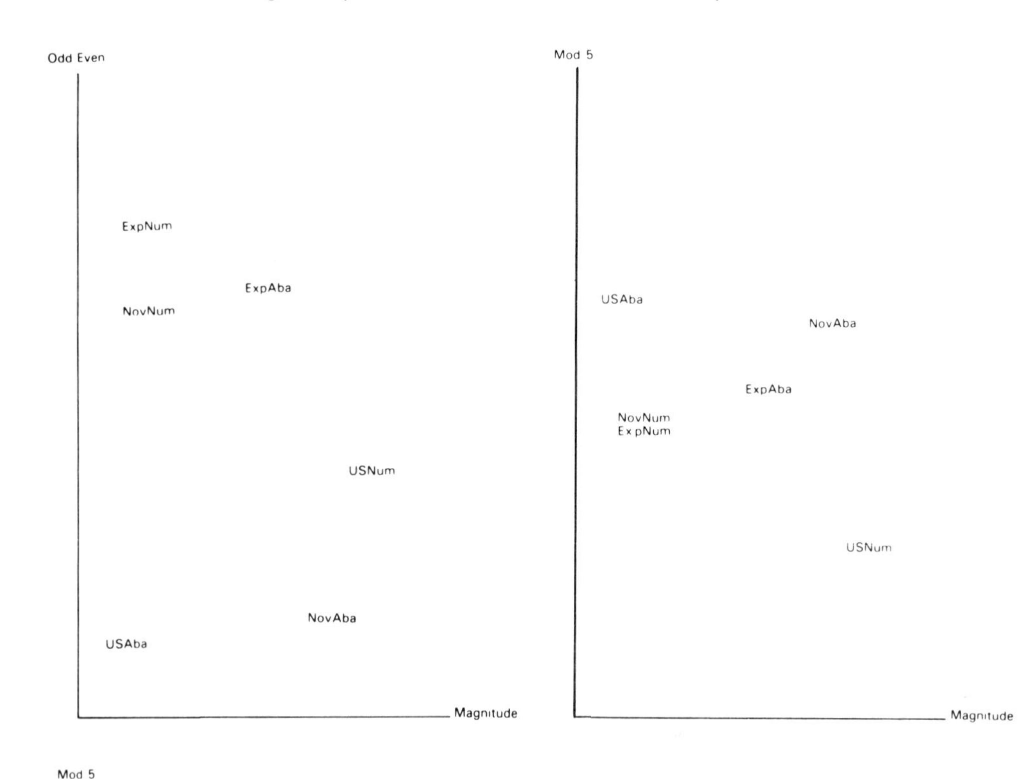

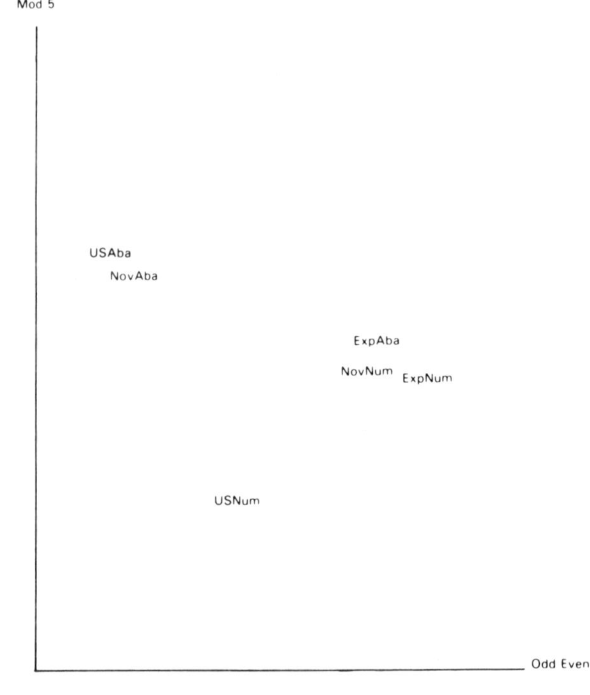

FIGURE 7.10. Subject or weight spaces from the abacus-numeral similarity judgments shown in Figure 7.9. Weights spaces show how much emphasis each group of subjects placed on the corresponding dimensions from the stimulus space shown in Figure 7.9. The top left panel plots subject weights on the Magnitude dimension (dimension 1 on the X-axis) with those on the Even/Odd dimension (dimension 2 on the Y-axis). The middle panel pairs the Magnitude dimension weights (X-axis) with those on the Modulo 5 dimension (dimension 3) on the Y-axis. The bottom left panel pairs weights on the Odd/Even dimension (X-axis) with those on the Modulo 5 dimension (Y-axis).

7.10 shows the subject spaces for the dimensions represented in Figure 7.9.

Considering, first, the top left panel of Figure 7.10, one sees that novices and people in the United States judging the abacus placed very little salience on the odd/even dimension. The novice and U.S. subjects differed in their weighting of the magnitude dimension. Given the modulo 5 nature of the abacus, it does not represent magnitude particularly clearly (as the U.S. results show). Novices "enriched" their judgments of the abacus with magnitude information, while experts in both conditions and novices judging numerals emphasized the odd/even dimension.

In the top right panel of subject weights, the mod 5 dimension is emphasized most heavily by the U.S. subjects and novices judging the abacus figures and least heavily weighted by the U.S. subjects judging numerals. This is consistent with its interpretation as an abacus feature. Finally, the third panel contrasts a clear abacus feature (mod 5) with a feature not represented on the abacus feature (odd/even). As one would expect, the U.S. subjects and novices judging the abacus showed similar patterns of dimension weights, with comparatively high weights on the mod 5 dimension and low weights on the odd/even dimension. Experts in both conditions and novices judging numerals showed a greater emphasis on the odd/even dimension than on the mod 5 dimension. United States subjects judging numerals placed greater weight on the odd/even dimension as well, but their position closer to the origin indicates that these two dimensions accounted for relatively little of the variance in their judgments.

The pattern of similarity shown in the weights space of the SINDSCAL analysis is supported by analysis of the original similarity judgments. Using Hubert's (1979) technique for assessing the significance of concordance between two matrices, one can see in Table 7.3 that only for the experts was there a significant correlation within expertise level between judgments of numbers presented in the two forms. The U.S. subject's

TABLE 7.3. Concordance between number-similarity judgments.

	American		Novice		Expert	
	Abacus	Number	Abacus	Number	Abacus	Number
American						
Abacus						
Number	.138					
Novice						
Abacus	.432*	.517*				
Number	.060	.299	.127			
Expert						
Abacus	.163	.601*	.429*	.419*		
Number	−.034	.360*	.124	.521*	.641*	

Note: The concordance statistic is identical to the Pearson product-moment correlation coefficient. Statistical significance was assessed by using Hubert's (1979) generalized concordance procedures.
* $p < .05$.

abacus judgments, based on abacus features alone, were significantly related only to the novice's abacus judgments. A somewhat surprising finding was that U.S. numeral judgments showed higher concordances with the abacus rather than the numeral judgments of the Taiwan groups. This may relate to the relative emphasis by U.S. subjects on the magnitude dimension in judging numerals, because magnitude was more heavily weighted by the novices and experts when judging the abacus than when judging numerals. This finding in turn may be best explained with reference to other research (particularly Stigler, Lee, Lucker, and Stevenson, 1982) indicating a generally greater mathematical sophistication on the part of children in Taiwan.

Results of this study suggest that expertise at abacus calculation is associated with greater consistency in judging numerical relations across changes in mode of presentation. What is of particular interest is how this occurs. Abacus experts are more likely to view nonabacus features such as odd/even as being salient to judging number similarity even when they are presented with abacus stimuli. In this case, mastering a skill is associated not with a universally greater emphasis on the features important to that skill, but rather with a declining emphasis on those dimensions unique to the skill.

As the above examples illustrate, the INDSCAL model provides a useful method of simultaneously representing the structure of a stimulus domain and changes in the ways in which subjects represent it. Although more general models of individual differences exist (reviewed in Carroll & Arabie, 1980) that permit subjects to differ by using different dimensions, rather than through subjective weighting of common dimensions, the INDSCAL model has been quite successful in representing developmental changes in the representation of complex domains.

Clustering Models of Development

General Issues: Clustering and Overlap

Several of the studies described thus far have supplemented MDS analyses with various cluster analyses of the data, a practice recommended by Shepard (1974). It may seem peculiar that a model describing similarity as a continuous function in space could coexist with a representation based on the idea that a set of discrete clusters or distinctive features account for similarity. Empirically, however, it has frequently proved useful to perform both analyses. One can see these alternate procedures as different "views" of the same set of data.

The vast majority of cluster analyses in developmental research have employed some variation of hierarchical clustering (Hartigan, 1967; Jardine, Jardine, & Sibson, 1967; Johnson, 1967). This adherence to hierarchical models is probably a matter of availability and familiarity rather than the result of substantive considerations. Hierarchical clustering algorithms generate a hierarchy of nested clusters, such that there can be no overlap within any level of the category. The methods used (e.g., Johnson, 1967) involve an iterative process of finding the highest similarity level among items in a proximity matrix and clumping them into one new entity. Having produced a new clustered entity, one needs a measure of distance between it and all remaining stimuli. Two different nonmetric techniques are generated according to whether one chooses to use the largest (complete-link or diameter method) or smallest (single-link or connectedness method) distance between any cluster member and each stimulus not in the cluster. In addition to satisfying the metric axioms described above, both measures also satisfy the ultrametric inequality that

$$d_{ik} \leq \max (d_{ij}, d_{jk}), \tag{6}$$

but the choice of metric typically has consequences for the kind of clusters one finds. Choosing the single-link method tends to result in *chaining* of clusters, long series in which one item is added to one of a small number of clusters at each level. Perhaps because of this, studies using hierarchical clustering have tended to use the complete-link method.

A serious concern about the use of hierarchical clustering relates to the applicability of the basic assumption of nonoverlap between clusters within levels of the hierarchy. It is not hard to generate stimuli that cluster in obviously nonhierarchical ways. Imagine trying to cluster data on similarity among four family members designated *mother, father, sister,* and *brother.* If one used a generational principle to cluster mother + father with sister + brother, the nonoverlapping principle of hierarchical clustering would preclude representing any increased similarity based on sex (father + brother, sister + mother). Even where there are substantive reasons to expect hierarchies to obtain [such as in Keil's (1979) model of constraints on predicability], the fact that hierarchical clustering forces such a result limits the utility of this procedure.

ADCLUS Model

An alternative model for describing nonhierarchical clusters was developed by Shepard and Arabie (1979) and termed the *ADCLUS model.* The ADCLUS model asserts that membership in a particular cluster adds a constant weight to the predicted similarities of all pairs of stimuli within that cluster. Given some stimuli i and j and a set of R clusters, the similarity between them s_{ij} should be predictable from

$$s_{ij} = \sum_{r=1}^{R} w_r p_{ir} p_{jr} , \tag{7}$$

where w_r is the weight of cluster r and p_{ir} and p_{jr} are 0 or 1, respectively, according to whether i and j are members of cluster r. Summing the weights associated with each cluster containing both objects should yield the total similarity between them.

Although the model is straightforward, fitting it requires identifying potential candidates for clusters from an enormous set. The ADCLUS model limits consideration to those sets of clusters whose members show a rise in similarity (measured by the lowest similarity measure among the pairs of items) when compared to any larger cluster containing this particular cluster.

A relatively efficient program for fitting the ADCLUS model, termed *MAPCLUS,* was developed by Arabie and Carroll (1980). The MAPCLUS procedure begins with continually varying values for the cluster membership variables p_{ir} and p_{jr} in Equation 7 (in effect, an object can be partially in a cluster). MAPCLUS then uses a mathematical programming approach to optimize two constraints, increasing variance accounted for by cluster weights and turning the cluster membership variables into 0 and 1.

Weighted or Individual-Differences Clustering

Carroll and Arabie (1983) extended the ADCLUS model to include individual differences, expressed as subjective variation in the weights of a set of constant clusters. This model treats clusters in a manner analogous to the treatment of dimensions in INDSCAL. Clusters are constrained to be common across subjects, but the weights placed on them are free to vary over subjects. The individual-differences clustering model and the algorithm developed to fit it are both termed *INDCLUS*.

In practice, MAPCLUS often produces cluster solutions that reflect more subtle aspects of data structure than those that result from hierarchical clustering. As an example, Figure 7.11 shows a hierarchical clustering of the Miller and Gelman (1983) number similarity data (based on an aggregate matrix summed across all ages), by the complete-link method. The clusters are drawn as contour plots on the SINDSCAL solution for these same data. Each closed curve represents one level of agglomeration, so those points joined inside many curves represent higher levels of judged similarity.

The hierarchical clustering groups small, medium, and large numbers. The first cluster formed is 0,2, but otherwise the clusters consist of series of numbers that grow gradually by adding their neighbors. In contrast, the closed curves on Figure 7.7 present an INDCLUS solution for these same data. Although the clusters of small, middle, and large numbers are found in both analyses, the hierarchical clustering algorithm is unable to "break into" these clusters to find the multiplicative and odd/even clusters (2,4,8, 3,5,7,9) found in the INDCLUS solution.

INDCLUS was also used in analyzing the effects of abacus expertise on number similarity judgments. The abacus figures in Figure 7.8 show mem-

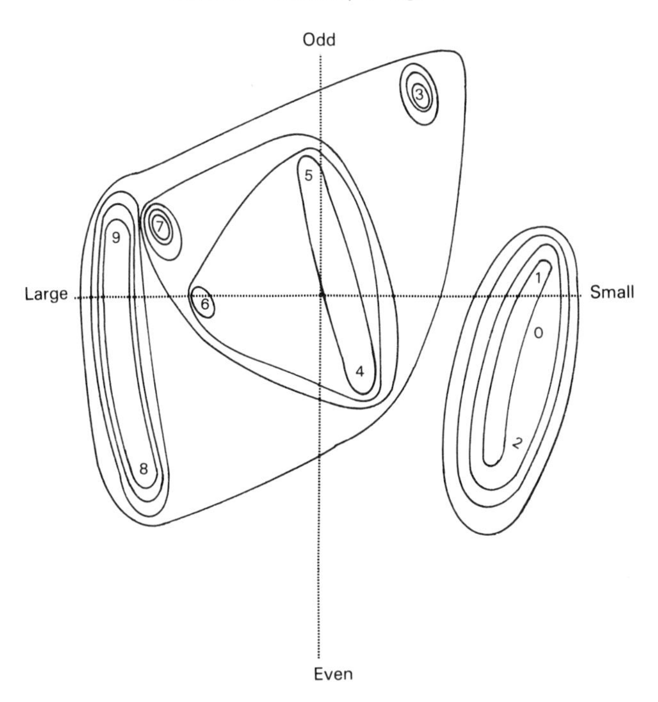

FIGURE 7.11. Hierarchical clustering solution for number-similarity judgments embedded in solution for data from Miller and Gelman (1983). Items enclosed inside many ovals are those that were most highly related. Comparison with Figure 7.7 shows advantages of nonhierarchical clustering in showing a variety of overlapping relations.

bers of the resulting clusters. In general, they can be clearly classified as numeral or physical abacus properties on the basis of inspection alone. The even numbers, for example, share no common feature in their representation on the abacus. The physical abacus properties such as "5 bead up," "5 bead down," and "0 or 1 lower bead up" are clearly evident in the abacus figures.

One cluster, the 5 multiples, that does share a common abacus representation is classified as a numeral property. This was done based on consideration of the weighting of different clusters by the various groups of subjects, which are shown in Figure 7.12. Abacus-related features are shown by dashed lines, and solid lines indicate the numeral clusters. Comparing weights on this cluster across the two modes of presentation shows there was an overall decrease in weight for the 5-multiples cluster for numerals compared with abacus stimuli (as though it were an abacus rather than a numeral feature). For the novices, however, this cluster received a substantially higher rating in the numeral than in the abacus

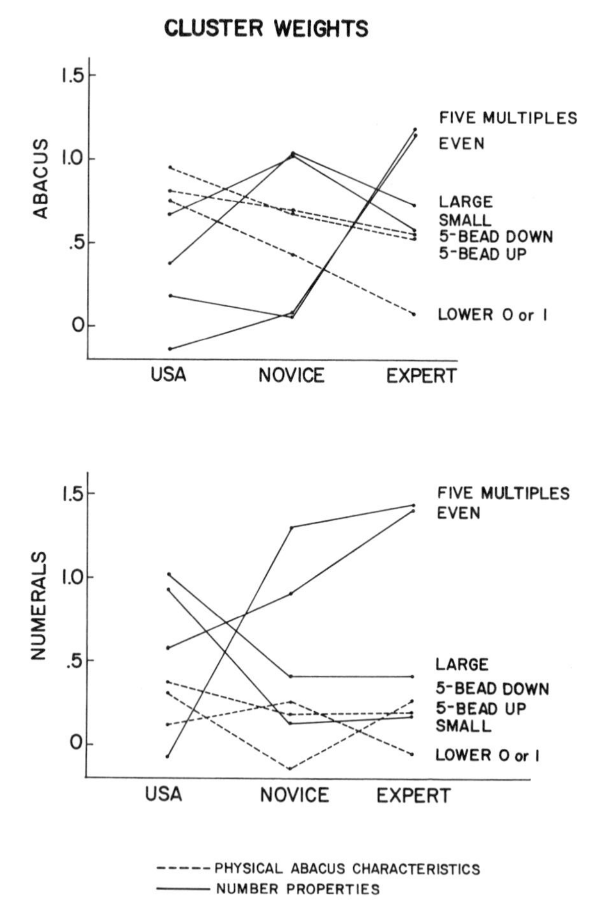

FIGURE 7.12. Results of an INDCLUS analysis of abacus and numeral similarity judgments. The INDCLUS algorithm determines separate weights for individual subjects (or groups) of a common set of overlapping clusters. Results for abacus judgments are shown in the top panel, and numeral judgments are shown in the bottom panel. Features of the physical abacus are shown by dashed lines; other number features are connected with solid lines.

condition (suggesting that it was primarily a numeral feature for these subjects). The experts' judgments are uninformative in this regard, because in both conditions this cluster received the highest weight.

There is an apparent contradiction between the interpretation of the 5-multiples cluster as a numeral feature and the prior assertion that the mod 5 dimension of the INDSCAL solution reflected the structure of the abacus. The apparent contradiction nicely illustrates the difference between a (continuous) dimension and a (discrete) cluster. All stimuli are represented along the mod 5 *dimension,* although the *cluster* of 5 multiples is a relation limited to a set of numbers that share a multiplicative relation in addition to their mod 5 relation. As this example shows, consideration of the weight of dimensions and clusters among different subject groups helps enormously in interpreting the significance of the stimulus relations that emerge from individual-differences scaling and clustering analyses.

The INDCLUS results correspond to those obtained with SINDSCAL in documenting an overall decline in the importance of physical abacus properties with the acquisition of expertise. This is particularly clear in the top panel of Figure 7.12, which shows the consistent decline in weight for abacus features across expertise groups, while there is an overall increase in the weights of numeral-related clusters. Ironically, those subjects who have spent the most time mastering the details of the abacus are those who seem least affected by its structure. Results of these analyses suggest that it is meaningful to maintain a distinction between the features that are meaningful in using a system such as the abacus and those that are meaningful in reflecting on it.

Given the importance of identifying distinctive features of stimuli and situations in developmental psychology, researchers should be familiar with nonhierarchical clustering techniques. These procedures are based on a geometric model different from the MDS procedures discussed previously, and their use can sometimes provide a different but complementary perspective on the structure in a set of data.

General Issues in Developmental Applications of Geometric Methods

The geometric techniques described in this chapter provide powerful descriptive tools that can permit the reduction of daunting matrices of data to reveal the organization of complex skills, domains of knowledge, or social structures. MDS procedures have been used to describe the structure of representation in a number of complex domains, documenting changes with development and skill in the processing of stimuli as diverse as faces, numbers, and geometric figures. Results of these studies could provide the basis for more complex models of developmental change. With few exceptions, however, results of studies using MDS and clustering procedures have not been incorporated into detailed developmental models. The ultimate utility of the kinds of geometric methods considered in this chapter may hinge upon (1) further development of procedures for evaluating competing representations (2) further development of individual-differences models and further applications of the general INDSCAL/INDCLUS approach to describing development, and (3) description of more specific connections between psychological processes and the results of MDS and clustering analyses.

Hybrid Models and Evaluation of Alternate Models

In addition to the basic models described above, new geometic methods continue to proliferate. A theoretically derived model that is neither a multidimensional scaling nor a clustering model is Sattah and Tversky's (1977) additive-trees model for the representation of similarity in semantic domains. Based on Tversky's (1977) model of similarity, the additive-trees procedure produces a family of different hierarchies, each of which roots to the tree at a different point. Additive trees have N external nodes representing the N stimuli, and the distance between two objects is measured by the length of the paths connecting them.

Pruzansky, Tversky, and Carroll (1982) have explored the utility of two different geometric models (two-dimensional Euclidean distance models such as those used in MDS and Tversky's additive-tree model) to develop a description of properties that might render one or the other model more suitable in a particular domain. In applying the models to real data, Pruzansky et al. note a tendency for tree structures to provide a better fit to similarity judgments in conceptual categories skewed toward typical instances. An example might be judgments of similarity among the stimuli judged to be the most frequent or familiar instances of categories such as *vehicles* or *tools*. Pruzansky et al. found that judgments of similarity among a variety of perceptual domains or factorial stimulus designs were better fit by the MDS model. Beyond the specific models tested in the Pruzansky et al. study, the study is noteworthy for its attempt to develop procedures for diagnosing the appropriateness of different geometric models for a given set of data.

Individual-Differences Procedures as Models for Development

The models of individual differences embodied in the INDSCAL and INDCLUS approaches contain interesting assumptions about the nature of development. In particular, both models assume that development can be described as changes in emphasis within a common developmental space. This assumption has proved useful in a number of specific applications, yet major issues in applying this technique to developmental data remain unexplored. In particular, the extent to which it will be meaningful to consider both developmental and individual differences simultaneously within a model such as INDCLUS or INDSCAL is not clear.

Relating Geometric Methods to Psychological Theories

Researchers have begun to move beyond considering the results of MDS analyses as static representations of knowledge to considering the cognitive processes that might have led to these relations. An important example connecting processing to a geometric representation of knowledge is the model of analogical reasoning developed by Rummelhart and Abrahamson (1973). In their model, solving a four-part analogy (*cat* is to *lion* as *dog* is to ____) can be represented as a process of searching along vectors in a semantic space to find that answer which completes a parallelogram mapping one relation (*cat* is to *dog*) onto the other (*cat* is to *lion*). Similar geometric representations of knowledge (and, more specifically, animal names) have been used to predict processing in a speeded categorization task (Rips, Shoben, & Smith, 1973) and series completion problems (Sternberg & Gardner, 1982). Within developmental research, the work by Bisanz and Voss (1982) stands as an example of using MDS procedures as the basis for measuring parameters of processing models. Bisanz and Voss were able to use changes in the perceived macrostructure of stories (Kintsch & van Dijk, 1978) coded from INDSCAL analyses of similarity judgments of the protagonists of stories to predict the probability of recalling particular story propositions.

The degree to which researchers are successful in getting more work out of geometric models, in the sense of using them as the basis for theories of psychological process, may be the test of the ultimate utility of geometric models to developmental psychologists. Geometric models provide an important technique for describing the organization of complex sets of data, reducing them to accessible geometric displays. As such, they provide a foundation for moving beyond these displays to more sophisticated models of psychological processes.

Acknowledgments

Preparation of this chapter was supported by grants from the University Research Institute of the University of Texas at Austin and the National Science Foundation (BNS-8510546). Phipps Arabie, Steven Gregorich, Kelly Madole, Sara Halpern, and Stephen Sobek provided helpful comments on an earlier draft. Address correspondence to: Kevin F. Miller, Department of Psychology, Mezes 330, The University of Texas at Austin, Austin, TX 78712.

References

Arabie, P. (1977). Some precautions concerning the solution. In J. B. Kruskal, F. W. Young, & J. B. Seery (1977). *How to use KYST-2, a very flexible program to do multidimensional scaling and unfolding*. Murray Hills, NJ: Bell Laboratories.

Arabie, P., & Carroll, J. D. (1980). MAPCLUS: A mathematical programming approach to fitting the ADCLUS model. *Psychometrika,45,* 211-235.

Arabie, P., Kosslyn, S. M., & Nelson, K. E. (1975). A multidimensional scaling study of visual memory in 5-year-olds and adults. *Journal of Experimental Child Psychology, 19,* 327–345.

Arabie, P., & Soli, S. D. (1982). The interface between the type of regression and methods of collecting proximities data. In R. G. Golledge & J. N. Rayner

(Eds.), *Proximity and preference: Multidimensional analysis of large data sets* (pp. 90–115). Minneapolis: University of Minnesota Press.

Ball, W. R. (1914). *Mathematical recreations and essays* (6th ed.). London: Macmillan.

Beals, R., Krantz, D. H., & Tversky, A. (1968). Foundations of multidimensional scaling. *Psychological Review, 75,* 127–142.

Bentler, P. M., & Weeks, D. G. (1978). Restricted multidimensional scaling methods. *Journal of Mathematical Psychology, 17,* 138–151.

Binet, A. (1966/1893). Mnemonic virtuosity: A study of chess players. *Genetic Psychology Monographs, 74,* 127–162 (first published in 1893).

Bisanz, G. L., & Voss, J. F. (1982, June). *Developmental changes in understanding story themes: Scaling and process analysis.* Paper presented at the annual meeting of the Canadian Psychological Association, Montreal.

Borg, I., & Lingoes, J. C. (1980). A model and algorithm for multidimensional scaling with external constraints on the distances. *Psychometrika, 45,* 25–38.

Brainerd, C. J. (1979). *The origins of the number concept.* New York: Praeger.

Bryan, W. L., & Harter, N. (1899). Studies on the telegraphic language. The acquisition of a hierarchy of habits. *Psychological Review, 6,* 345–375.

Burton, M. L., & Nerlove, S. B. (1976). Balanced designs for triads tests: Two examples from English. *Social Science Research, 5,* 247–267.

Carey, S. (1982). Face perception: Anomalies of development. In S. Strauss & R. Stavy (Eds.), *U-shaped behavioral growth* (pp. 169–190). New York: Academic.

Carey, S., & Diamond, R. (1977). From piecemeal to configurational representation of faces. *Science, 195,* 312–314.

Carroll, J. D., & Arabie, P. (1980). Multidimensional scaling. *Annual Review of Psychology, 31,* 607–649.

Carroll, J. D., & Arabie, P. (1983). INDCLUS: An individual differences generalization of the ADCLUS model and the MAPCLUS algorithm. *Psychometrika, 48,* 157–169.

Carroll, J. D., & Chang, J. J. (1970). Analysis of individual differences in multidimensional scaling via an *N*-way generalization of Eckart-Young decomposition. *Psychometrika, 35,* 283–319.

Carroll, J. D., & Kruskal, J. B. (1978). Multidimensional scaling. In W. H. Kruskal & J. M. Tanur (Eds.), *International encyclopedia of statistics* (Vol. 2, pp. 892–907). New York: Free Press.

Carroll, J. D., Pruzansky, S., & Kruskal, J. B. (1980). CANDELINC: A general approach to multidimensional analysis of many-way arrays with linear constrains on parameters. *Psychometrika, 45,* 3–24.

Carroll, J. D., & Wish, M. (1974). Models and methods for three-way multidimensional scaling. In D. H. Krantz, R. C. Atkinson, R. D. Luce, and P. Suppes (Eds.), *Contemporary developments in mathematical psychology* (Vol. 2, pp. 57–105). San Francisco: Freeman.

Chase, W. G., & Simon, H. A. (1973). Perception in chess. *Cognitive Psychology, 4,* 55–81.

Chi, M. T. H., Glaser, R., & Rees, E. (1982). Expertise in problem solving. In R. Sternberg (Ed.), *Advances in the psychology of human intelligence* (Vol. 1). Hillsdale, NJ: Erlbaum.

Cirrin, F. M., & Hurtig, R. R. (1981). Accessing mental representations of mentally retarded children. *American Journal of Mental Deficiency, 86,* 188–193.

Davison, M. L. (1983). *Multidimensional scaling*. New York: Wiley.
Diamond, R., & Carey, S. (1977). Developmental changes in the representation of faces. *Journal of Experimental Child Psychology, 23,* 1–22.
Egan, D., & Schwartz, B. (1979). Chunking in recall of symbolic drawings. *Memory and Cognition, 7,* 149–158.
Fonstad, K. W. (1981). *The atlas of Middle-earth*. Boston: Houghton Mifflin.
Galton, F. (1881). Visualized numerals. *The Journal of the Anthropological Institute of Great Britain and Ireland, 10,* 84–102.
Gelman, R., & Gallistel, C. R. (1978). *The child's understanding of number*. Cambridge, MA: Harvard.
Gibson, E. J. (1969). *Principles of perceptual learning and development*. New York: Appleton Century Crofts.
Hartigan, J. A. (1967). Representation of similarity matrices by tress. *Journal of the American Statistical Association, 62,* 1140–1158.
Hatano, G., Miyake, Y., & Binks, M. G. (1977). Performance of expert abacus operators. *Cognition, 5,* 47–55.
Hatano, G., & Osawa, K. (1983). Digit memory of grand experts in abacus-derived mental calculation. *Cognition, 5,* 95–110.
Hubert, L. J. (1978). Generalized proximity function comparisons. *British Journal of Mathematical and Statistical Psychology, 31,* 179–192.
Hubert, L. J. (1979). Generalized concordance. *Psychometrika, 44,* 135–142.
Hubert, L. J., & Baker, F. B. (1979). Evaluating the symmetry of a proximity matrix. *Quality and Quantity, 13,* 77–84.
Hubert, L. J., & Golledge, R. G. (1981). A heuristic method for the comparison of related structures. *Journal of Mathematical Psychology, 23,* 214–226.
Jardine, C. J., Jardine, N., & Sibson, R. (1967). The structure and construction of taxonomic hierarchies. *Mathematical Biosciences, 1,* 173–179.
Johnson, S. C. (1967). Hierarchical clustering schemes. *Psychometrika, 29,* 1–27.
Keil, F. C. (1979). *Semantic and conceptual development: An ontological perspective*. Cambridge, MA: Harvard.
Kintsch, W., & van Dijk, T. A. (1978). Toward a model of text comprehension and production. *Psychological Review, 85,* 363–394.
Klahr, D. (1969). A Monte Carlo study of the statistical significance of Kruskal's nonmetric scaling procedure. *Psychometrika, 34,* 1–27.
Kruskal, J. B. (1964a). Multidimensional scaling by optimizing goodness of fit to a nonmetric hypothesis. *Psychometrika, 29,* 1–27.
Kruskal, J. B. (1964b). Nonmetric multidimensional scaling: A numerical method. *Psychometrika, 29,* 115–129.
Kruskal, J. B., & Carroll, J. D. (1969). Geometrical models and badness-of-fit functions. In P. R. Krishnaiah (Ed.), *Multivariate analysis II*. New York: Academic.
Kruskal, J. B., & Wish, M. (1978). *Multidimensional scaling*. Beverly Hills, CA: Sage.
Kruskal, J. B., Young, F. W., & Seery, J. B. (1977). *How to use KYST-2, a very flexible program to do multidimensional scaling and unfolding*. Murray Hills, NJ: Bell Laboratories.
Lakoff, G., & Johnson, M. (1980). *Metaphors we live by*. Chicago: University of Chicago.
Laurendeau, M., & Pinard, A. (1970). *The development of the concept of space in the child*. New York: International Universities Press.

Levelt, W. J. M., van de Geer, J. P., & Plomp, R. (1966). Triadic comparisons of musical intervals. *British Journal of Mathematical and Statistical Psychology, 19,* 163–179.

Levine, D. M. (1978). A Monte Carlo study of Kruskal's variance based measure on stress. *Psychometrika, 43,* 307–315.

MacCallum, R. C. (1977). Effects of conditionality on INDSCAL and ALSCAL weights. *Psychometrika, 42,* 297–305.

Magaña, J. R., Magaña, H. A., & Ferreira-Pinto, J. B. (1982). A comparison of children's cognitive structuring of animal terms and the design of three zoo environments: Implications for planning educational environments. In A. D. Lutkus & J. C. Baird (Eds.), *Mind, child, architecture* (pp. 161–173). Hanover, NH: New England University Press.

Miller, K. F., & Gelman, R. (1983). The child's representation of number: A multidimensional scaling analysis. *Child Development, 54,* 1470–1479.

Miller, K. F., Stigler, J. W., Houang, R. T., & Lee, S-Y. (1986). *Representation and skill: Abacus effects on number representation.* Unpublished manuscript, The University of Texas at Austin.

Newcombe, N., & Liben, L. S. (1982). Barrier effects in the cognitive maps of children and adults. *Journal of Experimental Child Psychology, 34,* 46–58.

Newell, A. (1973). You can't play 20 questions with nature and win: Projective comments on the papers of this symposium. In W. G. Chase (Ed.), *Visual information processing.* New York: Academic.

Pedelty, L., Levine, S. C., & Shevell, S. K. (1985). Developmental changes in face processing: Results from multidimensional scaling. *Journal of Experimental Child Psychology, 39,* 421–436.

Piaget, J. (1965). *The child's conception of number.* New York: Norton.

Piaget, J., & Inhelder, B. (1967). *The child's conception of space.* New York: Norton.

Pruzansky, S. (1975). *How to use SINDSCAL: A computer program for individual differences in multidimensional scaling.* Murray Hill, NJ: Bell Laboratories.

Pruzansky, S., Tversky, A., & Carroll, J. D. (1982). Spatial versus tree representations of proximity data. *Psychometrika, 47,* 3–24.

Ramsay, J. O. (1977). Maximum likelihood estimation in multidimensional scaling. *Psychometrika, 43,* 241–266.

Ramsay, J. O. (1978). *Multiscale: Four programs for multidimensional scaling by the method of maximum likelihood.* Chicago: National Educational Resources.

Rieser, J., & Edwards, K. (1979). *Children's perception and the geometries: A multidimensional scaling analysis.* Paper presented at the annual meeting of the American Psychological Association, New York.

Rips, L., Shoben, E., & Smith, E. (1973). Semantic distance and the verification of semantic relations. *Journal of Verbal Learning and Verbal Behavior, 12,* 1–20.

Rosch, E. (1975). Cognitive reference points. *Cognitive Psychology, 7,* 532–547.

Rummelhart, D. E., & Abrahamson, A. A. (1973). A model for analogical reasoning. *Cognitive Psychology, 5,* 1–28.

Sattath, S., & Tversky, A. (1977). Additive similarity trees. *Psychometrika, 42,* 319–345.

Schönemann, P. M., and Carroll, R. M. (1970). Fitting one matrix to another under choice of a central dilation and a rigid motion. *Psychometrika, 35,* 245–256.

Schultz, J., & Hubert, L. J. (1976). A nonparametric test for correspondence between two proximity matrices. *Journal of Educational Statistics, 1,* 59–67.

Shepard, R. N. (1962a). The analysis of proximities: Multidimensional scaling with an unknown distance function. I. *Psychometrika, 27,* 125–140.

Shepard, R. N. (1962b). The analysis of proximities: Multidimensional scaling with an unknown distance function. II. *Psychometrika, 27,* 219–246.

Shepard, R. N. (1972). A taxonomy of some principle types of data and of multidimensional methods for their analysis. In R. N. Shepard, A. K. Ronmeny, & S. B. Nerlove (Eds.), *Multidimensional scaling: Theory and applications in the behavioral sciences: Vol. 1. Theory*. New York: Seminar.

Shepard, R. N. (1974). Representation of structure in similarity data: Problems and prospects. *Psychometrika, 39,* 373–421.

Shepard, R. N. (1975). Form, formation, and transformation of internal representations. In R. Solso (Ed.), *Information processing and cognition: The Loyola symposium (pp. 87–122). Hillsdale, NJ: Erlbaum.*

Shepard, R. N. (1980). Multidimensional scaling, tree-fitting, and clustering. *Science, 210,* 390–398.

Shepard, R. N., & Arabie, P. (1979). Additive clustering: Representation of similarities as combinations of discrete overlapping properties. *Psychological Review, 86,* 87–123.

Shepard, R. N., & Chipman, S. (1970). Second-order isomorphism of internal representations: Shapes of states. *Cognitive Psychology, 1,* 1–17.

Shepard, R. N., Kilpatric, D., & Cunningham, J. (1975). The internal representation of numbers. *Cognitive Psychology, 7,* 82–138.

Shoben, E. J. (1976). The verification of semantic relations in a same-different paradigm: An asymmetry in semantic memory. *Journal of Verbal Learning and Verbal Behavior, 15,* 365–379.

Shoben, E. J. (1983). Applications of multidimensional scaling in cognitive psychology. *Applied Psychological Measurement, 7,* 437–490.

Spence, I. (1982). Incomplete experimental designs for multidimensional scaling. In R. G. Golledge & J. N. Rayner (Eds.), *Proximity and preference: Multidimensional analysis of large data sets* (pp. 29–46). Minneapolis: University of Minnesota Press.

Spence, I., & Ogilvie, J. C. (1973). A table of expected stress values for random rankings in nonmetric multidimensional scaling. *Multivariate Behavioral Research, 8,* 511–517.

Sternberg, R. J., & Gardner, M. K. (1982). A componential interpretation of the general factor in human intelligence. In H. J. Eysenck (Ed.), *A model for intelligence*. Berlin: Springer-Verlag.

Stigler, J. W. (1984). "Mental abacus": The effect of abacus training on Chinese children's mental calculation. *Cognitive Psychology, 16,* 145–176.

Stigler, J. W., Lee, S-Y., Lucker, G. W., & Stevenson, H. W. (1982). Curriculum and achievement in mathematics: A study of elementary school children in Japan, Taiwan, and the United States. *Journal of Educational Psychology, 74,* 315–322.

Takane, Y., Young, F. W., & de Leeuw, J. (1977). Nonmetric individual differences multidimensional scaling: An alternating least squares method with optimal scaling features. *Psychometrika, 42,* 7–67.

Tolkien, J. R. R. (1977). *The Silmarillion.* Boston: Houghton Mifflin.

Tversky, A. (1977). Features of similarity. *Psychological Review, 84,* 327–352.

Tversky, A., & Gati, I. (1982). Similarity, separability, and the triangle inequality. *Psychological Review, 89,* 123–154.

Weisberg, H. F. (1974). Dimensionland: An excursion into spaces. *American Journal of Political Science, 18,* 743–776.

Notes

1. Recent developments in constrained MDS (Bentler & Weeks, 1978; Borg & Lingoes, 1980; Carroll, Pruzansky, & Kruskal, 1980) provide methods for using known or hypothesized relations to partially constraining the obtained solution.
2. The additive-tree procedure of Sattath and Tversky (1977) is an exception to this general statement, because it explicitly represents asymmetry in proximity relations. An inferential test for the symmetry of a matrix has been described by Hubert and Baker (1979).
3. The combinatorial problem of producing balanced incomplete subsets is known as *Kirkman's schoolgirls problem,* and techniques have been developed to produce such balanced subsets for some numbers of stimuli (Ball, 1914; Burton & Nerlove, 1976; Levelt, van de Geer, & Plomp, 1966). More general procedures for producing incomplete sets of stimuli are described by Spence (1982).
4. Kruskal's stress formula 1 measures the magnitude of violations of the ordinal constraint that recovered distances must increase monotonically with increases in the input data, relative to the sum of squares of all distances. On a Shepard diagram, such as those shown in Figure 7.3, stress formula 1 relates the length of vertical segments connecting each D and the dash directly above or below it to the distance between D and the X axis.
5. Because the goodness of fit of a nonmetric MDS solution is not affected by rotations or changes in scale, the real locations were constructed by submitting the actual distances in Table 7.1 to the KYST-2A program by using linear rather than monotonic regression. Through this procedure, the map of Middle Earth used in this example was rotated approximately 135° in a clockwise direction and rescaled to conform to the MDS reconstruction.
6. The "individual" of the INDSCAL technique is a generic individual, referring to separate sources of data. In particular these individuals may often meaningfully be *groups* of individuals who share particular characteristics (such as age, interests, or skill levels).

8. Computer Simulation, Cognition, and Development: An Introduction

F. Michael Rabinowitz, Malcolm J. Grant, and H. Louis Dingley

In 1950, British mathematician A. M. Turing wrote a paper in which he addressed the question, Can machines think? For Turing, the question was important but ambiguous. To minimize the ambiguity, he proposed an operational definition that came to be called *Turing's test.* Turing began by considering a situation in which an interrogator poses a series of questions to a man and a woman. Using only the verbal content of their replies, the interrogator tries to decide who is the man and who is the woman. Either the man or the woman may be designated as the target person whose task is to formulate replies that will cause the interrogator to make an incorrect decision. The nontarget or anchor person must try to answer in such a way as to facilitate the interrogator's task. What percentage of the time would an interrogator in this kind of game correctly distinguish the man's replies from the woman's? And, of more interest to Turing, would this percentage be different if the behavior of the target person were simulated by an intelligent computer?

The task of programming a computer to simulate the behavior of a man trying to imitate a stereotypic woman would be daunting, to say the least. To our knowledge there have been no serious attempts to implement a literal version of Turing's imitation game, although the principle of indistinguishability implied by the game has continued to play an important role in the development and evaluation of simulation models (Lehman, 1977). In addition, Abelson (1968) has offered some interesting suggestions about how an "extended Turing test" might be of considerable methodological value.

It is clear that Turing's own reasons for proposing the imitation game were more dialectical than methodological. His purpose lay in refuting various philosophical and religious objections to the notion of a thinking machine. These objections need not concern us; our interests in this chapter lie in the implications of the game for the implementation and validation of computer simulation models of cognition and development. The chapter comprises five sections. In the first section, we provide some background on two cognitive architectures, production systems and schema systems, that have been most influential in the cognitive and developmental literature. In the second section, we explore some of the diversity of opinion concerning the most appropriate unit of analysis and methods of evaluation. In the third section, four sets of issues implicated in the earlier sections are examined. In the fourth section, we discuss computer simulations of cognitive development. In the final section, an overview of the earlier sections is presented.

Cognitive Architectures

Langley (1983) has used the term *cognitive architecture* to refer to those aspects of the human information processing system that remain constant "across subjects, across task domains, and over time" (p. 289). Thus, an architecture represents a framework of assumptions within which specific theories and models can be developed. In this section we examine two cognitive architectures: production systems and schema systems.

Production System Architecture

Newell and Simon's (1972) introduction of production systems had a major impact on the subsequent development of psychological simulations. A *production* is a rule stated as a condition-action or if-then pair. A set of such productions in long-term memory comprises a *production system*. When the data pattern specified in the condition portion of a production matches a data pattern in working memory, the action portion of the production is triggered. The following is an English translation of a simple LISP production system function. The function operates on a set of letters in working memory. If the elements in working memory satisfy the conditions of any of the first three productions, the appropriate production fires. As a result, the contents of working memory are altered, and the entire production system begins again.

Define P-SYSTEM [working memory]

Production 1

If there are more than five elements in working memory, *then* apply P-SYSTEM to the first five elements.

Production 2

If the letter c occurs more than once in working memory, *then* delete all c's from working memory and apply P-SYSTEM to the result.

Production 3

If the letter d is present in working memory, *then* insert the letter a at the front of working memory and apply P-SYSTEM to the result.

Production 4

If none of the productions has been triggered, *then* return the current contents of working memory and stop.

In the first production, the length of working memory is examined to see whether it exceeds 5. If it does, the function P-SYSTEM is applied recursively to the first five items in working memory. This production effectively limits the size of working memory to five items. The second production determines whether the letter c occurs more than once in working memory. If it does, all instances of the letter c are deleted from working memory and the function P-SYSTEM is applied recursively to the result. The third production determines whether the letter d is present in working memory. If it is, the letter a is inserted at the beginning of working memory and P-SYSTEM is applied recursively to the result. Note that adding an item to the beginning of working memory may, in conjunction with the first production, cause an item to be lost from the end. Finally, if none of the first three productions is applicable, the last production simply returns the contents of working memory. When applied to working memory in which the letters a, b, c, c, d, and e are present, the function P-SYSTEM causes working memory to undergo the following transformations: (a b c c d e), (a b c c d), (a b d), (a a b d), (a a a b d), (a a a a b d), and (a a a a b).

This function illustrates several important features of production systems. Production systems affect, and are affected by, the contents of working memory. Each time a production system is applied, the first production with a true condition portion is triggered. The action portion of this production alters the contents of working memory and calls the production system again. Evaluation of the productions begins again with the first production and continues until no production in the system is triggered. Note that in P-SYSTEM the productions are listed in order of priority, thus, avoiding the situation where conflicting productions can be simultaneously triggered. Methods of conflict resolution that do not depend on a simple ordering are sometimes used and have been discussed in detail by Anderson (1983).

According to Newell (1973), production systems can be viewed as a type of control structure in that they contain all the organization necessary for effective information processing. There is no need for a separate executive function calling isolated subroutines or a distinction between control and computation processes. There is, however, a need to specify how production systems are acquired and modified. Although they reside in long-term memory, production systems can presumably be brought into working memory and operated on either by other systems or by productions within themselves. Some models involving self-modifying production systems are described later in this chapter.

Production system models have been created to operate in a variety of problem domains. For example, the work of Newell and Simon (1963, 1972) involved a series of computer programs they called the *general problem solver* (GPS). In part, this work fell within the domain of artificial intelligence since the goal was to program a computer to solve problems in an efficient manner. The work, however, was guided by, and contributed to, extensive psychological theorizing. Much of the effort involved writing production systems that simulated the problem solving of human subjects. The problems were frequently drawn from the areas of mathematics and logic and involved establishing the identity of two given symbolic expressions. GPS programs were goal-oriented in that they tried to solve problems by breaking them down into smaller and smaller problems, applying operators at each step to reduce the differences between the present state and what was needed. This approach is often referred to as *means-ends analysis*.

One of the most extensive applications of a production system architecture can be found in the ACT models developed by Anderson (1976). One aspect of ACT* (Anderson, 1983), the most recent version of the ACT models, involves pattern-matching productions, represented as nodes in hierarchically organized systems called *data flow networks*. Each production in the network is activated when the productions beneath it, which test for simpler subpatterns, are activated. In this way, patterns of increasing complexity are recognized. For example, recognition of the word *ACT* depends on recognition of the letter T, which in turn depends on recognition of a horizontal and vertical line intersecting in a particular way.

A notable feature of Anderson's model is the notion that each production has a level of activation that determines the relative frequency at which it carries out tests on its condition portion. The level of activation of a production increases each time it is triggered, and it depends on the activation of productions both above and below it in the data flow network.

Schema System Architecture

The term *schema* was used by Bartlett (1932) in connection with his classic research on subjects' memory for stories. Subjects, in recounting a story they had read, showed evidence of systematic distortions in the direction of greater consistency with their cultural stereotypes or schemata. More recent research has produced a considerable body of evidence consistent with predictions from schema theories (Anderson, 1980).

Anderson (1980) defined *schemata* as "large, complex units of knowledge that organize much of what we know about general categories of objects, classes of events, and types of people" (p. 128). This definition may be made clearer by a consideration of some of the functions and characteristics most often attributed to schemata. Our discussion in this section draws heavily on the work of Rumelhart and Ortony (1977).

Schemata Have Variables

Schemata are general in form, but when they are applied to specific situations, their variables become bound to particular values. For example, a birthday party schema may have, as variables, celebrant, host, guests, and food. When one encounters a room of noisy children, seated around a table eating cake while a haggard-looking adult looks on, the birthday party schema may well be invoked. Each variable in a schema has associated with it a distribution of values that it can assume. These distributions, derived from and updated with experience, act as constraints in the application of the schema. In the present example, the adult would likely be assumed to be the host; the child at the head of the table, the celebrant; and the other children, the guests. Cake is a typical value for the food variable in this schema; thus, the presence of cake makes the application of the schema more likely. If instead of cake, the observed food were spinach, an alternative schema such as family dinner might be invoked.

Schemata Can Incorporate Other Schemata

Schemata exist within a hierarchical framework. At the bottom of the framework are atomic schemata, or *primitives,* that involve sensory-motor processes. These primitives are the subschemata of more encompassing, "dominating" schemata. For example, the birthday party schema might have a host schema and a gift-giving schema beneath it in the hierarchy and a social function schema above it.

Schemata Guide Inferences

Once a schema has been applied to a particular event or situation, elements of the situation that have not actually been observed may be inferred. Having applied a birthday party schema, for example, we may infer that games will be played and party favors distributed. Had the family dinner schema been applied, a very different set of inferences would likely be drawn.

Schemata Affect Memory Processes

According to Rumelhart and Ortony (1977), fragments of instantiated schemata rather than raw input data are stored in memory. When these fragments are retrieved later, additional schemata may be involved in their interpretation. Thus, the original comprehension of an event and its later retrieval from memory may both involve comparable schematic processing. In each case, a schema is used to organize, interpret, and draw inferences concerning incomplete and possibly ambiguous information. Considerable research evidence supporting a schema interpretation of memory processes has accumulated over the past decade (Taylor & Crocker, 1981).

Schemata Can Be Modified by Experience

Schemata may become either more specific or more general as the result of experience. Specialization may occur if a schema variable is found repeatedly to take the same value. In this case, the variable may be replaced by a constant, making the schema apply more quickly but to a narrower range of situations. Conversely, generalization may occur when a schema is found to apply to a wide variety of situations in all but one respect. The discrepant aspect may become a variable in a new, more general schema.

Both production system and schema system architectures appear sufficiently comprehensive to be useful frameworks for cognitive and developmental models. Of the two architectures, production systems have usually been more clearly articulated and more easily translated into efficient computer programs. We agree with Anderson (1980), however, that the two systems are better viewed as complementary rather than competing formulations. In Anderson's view, "production systems are models for skills while schemas are patterns for recognizing recurring sets of features" (p. 254). We turn now to some general methodological considerations in the construction and evaluation of computer simulation models.

Methodology

In proposing the imitation game, Turing (1950) evidently intended that the computer should be programmed to simulate the behavior of the target person. It is unclear from his description, however, whether Turing meant some particular target person or someone who typified a general class of persons. The important question of unit of analysis arises in connection with simulation efforts and theory development in general. The answer to the question influences the nature of the processes incorporated in the theory or model as well as the type of evaluation strategy pursued.

Unit of Analysis

Group Models

Psychological theorists usually emphasize explaining the behavior of the average case rather than the behavior of any single individual. The situation today is not very different from what it was over 50 years ago when Lewin (1931) lamented the prevalence of "Aristotelian modes of thought." According to Aristotle, lawfulness was a property of classes of events but not of individual cases. Today, few psychologists would wish to deny the lawfulness of individual behavior. The variability of individual cases is attributed not to the inherent randomness of the underlying processes, but to the operation of variables that the theorist either cannot or is unwilling to incorporate in the theory. By ignoring the influence of extraneous variables, the goal of a parsimonious theory can be achieved more easily.

When psychologists focus on aggregate data, differences between subjects contribute to error variance. The researcher assumes that the process of interest is sufficiently powerful and general to account for an amount of variance several times the size of the error term. For example, Feigenbaum (1963), referring to a model of verbal learning processes, asserted that "there are certain elementary information processes which an individual must perform if he is to discriminate, memorize and associate verbal items, and that these information processes participate in all the cognitive activity of all individuals" (p. 299).

Single-Subject Models

A less common approach in psychology involves a focus on the behavior of one or a very few individuals, disregarding or postponing consideration of individual differences. The research programs of Newell and Simon (1963, 1972) and Baylor, Gascon, LeMoyne, & Pothier (1973) illustrate this approach. These researchers wrote programs to match the behavior protocols of specific individuals. On the subject of individual differences, Newell and Simon (1963) wrote:

> Given enough information about an individual, a program could be written that would describe the symbolic behavior of that individual. Each individual would be described by a different program, and those aspects of human problem solving that are not idiosyncratic would emerge as the common structure and content of the programs of many individuals (p. 284).

In their later description of the GPS research program, Newell and Simon (1972) expanded on this theme by pointing to a number of dimensions along which human problem solvers can vary (e.g., in the way they initially characterize a problem, in the priorities they assign to various problem-solving strategies). In general, the degree of similarity among human problem solvers was considerable, a fact that Newell and Simon attributed to the strong constraints of the task environment.

In the research by Baylor et al. (1973), individual differences were tied to differences in developmental stages. Once a program for an individual had been formulated and found to reproduce that subject's behavior, it was compared with the program formulated for another subject at a different developmental stage. Differences between the programs were assumed to reflect the nature of what had developed.

Single-Subject Models with Individual-Difference Parameters

Relatively rare in psychology are detailed process models of individual behavior that include adjustable individual-difference parameters. This approach is illustrated in a recent model of choice behavior in the game of Nim. Grant, Rabinowitz, and Dingley (1985) investigated the interaction between search and knowledge by studying and simulating the way people learn to play Nim. Nim is a two-person game in which players alternate in drawing one or more counters from any one of several groups of counters. In the version of Nim employed, the game began with five piles containing 5, 4, 3, 2, and 1 counter, respectively. The player who removed the last counter lost the game. In this game, a position is a winner if at least one of the positions that can be reached from it is a loser. Conversely, a position is a loser if all the positions that can be reached from it are winners. Thus, a player can categorize a position by searching the game tree below the position. Simple positions (e.g., only one pile of counters remaining), which occur late in the game, can be categorized readily, providing the basis for categorization of more complex positions farther up the tree.

In the computer model of Nim playing behavior, a recursive search process is used to simulate the subject's logical analysis of game positions. The number of positions assessed in a single search, including those assessed more than once by recursion, is limited by a parameter called *searchdepth*. When the capacity for logical analysis has been exhausted (i.e., when the number of positions assessed exceeds the value of searchdepth), the search terminates and the position currently under evaluation remains uncategorized.

When an individual plays several games of Nim, positions may be categorized as winners or losers, as the result of not only logical analysis but also experience. Positions that the person faces during a winning game are more likely to be categorized as winners, and those encountered in losing games are more likely to be categorized as losers. The categorization process is reversed for positions encountered by the opponent. In the model, it is assumed that the assessment of a position can be represented as a point on a continuous scale of confidence, with the negative extreme reflecting certainty that the position is a winner and the positive extreme reflecting certainty that it is a loser. A position moves down the confidence scale by a fixed amount each time it is faced by the player in a winning game and by the opponent in a game the player loses. A position moves up the scale by the same amount each time it is faced by the player in a losing game and by the opponent in a game the player wins. When a position reaches a critical distance from the middle point of the scale, the position is categorized as either a winner or loser. The critical distance at which categorization occurs is represented by a second parameter in the model called the *confidence criterion*. An important aspect of the model is that during logical search, positions categorized by experince are treated in the same way as positions categorized on the basis of logical search. Thus, the interaction of the parameters and their relative weights influence the course of the simulation.

In the evaluation of the Nim playing model, a parameter estimation procedure (see Rabinowitz, Grant, & Dingley, 1984, for a description of the computer program) was used to find the two parameter values for each subject that yielded the maximum similarity between the performance of the model and the behavior of the subject. Two aspects of each subject's protocol were used in the estimation procedure: the particular moves made throughout the entire set of games played and the number of games won. Despite the complexity of the behavior being simulated and the small number of parameters in the model, a high level of congruence was achieved between the output of the model and the behavior of approximately 90 percent of the subjects tested in three experiments.

Lewin (1931) believed, and we agree, that detailed process models of individual behavior are long overdue in psychology. We see the technique of computer simulation as a major aid in developing models that focus on the individual and, at the same time, specify important dimensions of variation from one individual to the next.

Evaluation

A notable feature of Turing's imitation game is the way in which the odds are weighted heavily against the computer. Both the interrogator and the anchor person are obligated by the rules of the game to do everything they can to make the simulation fail. The output of a successful simulation must be literally indistinguishable from the empirical data. This is certainly an ambitious goal, but one that Turing believed would be within the grasp of the scientific community by the end of the century.

The optimistic view held by many researchers during the 1960s was that computer simulation techniques would inject a new standard of rigor into hypothesis testing and theory development. This view needs to be understood in the context of the methodological thinking of the time. During the 1960s psychology was coming under increasing criticism for what many believed was an overreliance on statistical tests of significance (e.g., Bakan, 1962). Meehl (1967) echoed this same concern and went further to draw attention to the contrasting approaches to theory testing in psychology and physics. Meehl noted that theories in the physical sciences typically made point predictions that were increasingly likely to be falsified as experiemental sophistication and precision improve. In contrast, psychological theories are usually associated with imprecise predictions (e.g., population means will be unequal) that are more likely to be confirmed with improvements in experimental techniques (see Meehl, 1978, for a more recent discussion of similar issues).

One solution to the problem raised by Meehl is to encourage the development of psychological theories that make point predictions. (For a different solution, see Serlin and Lapsley, 1985.) Computer simulations can be and have been, useful in this type of theory construction. There is, however, in some applications of both computer simulations and mathematical models, a reversal of the usual role of significance testing. A goodness-of-fit test is used to evaluate the difference between predicted and observed results, and lack of statistical significance is taken as corroboration of the model from which the prediction was derived. The theoretical prediction becomes, in effect, the null hypothesis.

Not all researchers have been comfortable with this approach to model evaluation. For example, Gregg and Simon (1967) objected to the procedure because small samples and noisy data, as compared to large samples and clean data, are more likely to result in the acceptance of the theory. How is it that Gregg and Simon could object to those characteristics of the hypothesis-testing situation that Meehl admired most in the physical sciences? The answer lies in the emphasis psychologists have traditionally placed on positive, theory-supporting results. The overrepresentation of such results in our journals is well known and has been a concern to several authors (e.g., Rosenthal, 1979). When the theoretical hypothesis is the null hypothesis, the system, in effect, rewards sloppy, imprecise methods. The concern is real. Lehman (1977), in reviewing the validation techniques used in computer simulation research, concluded that "much of the treatment of results appears unsophisticated and almost cursory; often it seems that validation, although recognized as important, is treated in a highly subjective or informal fashion" (p. 233).

What Meehl (1967) advocated was not simply the development of theories that make point predictions, but also a fundamental change in the current ethos such that the goal of research becomes one of falsifying, rather than confirming, the theory or model under consideration (cf. Popper, 1959). It is unfortunate that Meehl's recommendation has had relatively little influence in psychology so far.

Group Models

When computer models of the behavior of the average person are formulated, the approach to evaluation may differ little from that taken by traditional theorists evaluating verbal theories. Predictions are derived from the theory or model about average behavior in various experimental conditions. If those predictions are confirmed by empirical data, confidence in the model increases. Simon and Feigenbaum (1964) took this approach in evaluating their model of verbal learning behavior. The performance of the model was examined under varying conditions of inter- and intralist similarity by using nonsense syllables that varied in familiarity and meaningfulness. The results of the simulation were used to predict group performance differences in actual experiments.

Single-Subject Models

In cases in which computer models of the behavior of specific individuals have been formulated (e.g., Hayes-Roth & Hayes-Roth, 1979; Newell & Simon, 1963), the approach to evaluation, as noted by Lehman (1977), has often been subjective. For example, Newell and Simon (1963) reported a comparison between the solution to a logic problem generated by the GPS program and the verbal protocol generated by a human subject who had been encouraged to think aloud while attempting to solve the same problem. The authors noted some encouraging similarities between the computer and human approaches to the problem. They also noted various discrepancies. For example, at one point while working on the problem, the human subject appeared to realize that an earlier step had been ill advised and proceeded to back up and alter that step. Nothing in the GPS output corresponded to this result. Although this kind of evaluation may be adequate and even necessary in the very preliminary stages of model development, it is clearly not a substitute for an objective assessment of a model under conditions where it can demonstrably fail.

There appears to be no reason why a rigorous approach to evaluation cannot be applied to models of individual behavior. We make two suggestions. First, once a model of an individual's behavior has been developed, predictions should be derived and tested concerning that person's behavior on later occasions when working at the same or related tasks (Kail & Bisanz, 1982). Second, the behavior of one or more other people should be studied in the same task to determine what, if any, modifications are necessary to generalize the model across individuals.

Single-Subject Models with Individual-Difference Parameters

As we have suggested, the most promising research direction, in our view, involves the development of process models of individual behavior that include individual-difference parameters. The existence of parameter-fitting programs now makes possible the estimation of optimal parameter sets for each subject tested. The resulting models have two major advantages: (1) Those aspects of a model believed to be general can be distinguished from those specific to a particular individual, and (2) point predictions can be generated at the individual level, while both point and distribution predictions can be generated at the group level.

There are constraints on the inclusion of individual-difference parameters in any model: the number of free parameters in relation to the size of the data base, the replicability of parameter values across relevant tasks, and the generality of parameter values across a broader theoretical domain that subsumes the parameter-based model. The first constraint is that the number of such parameters is small relative to the number of possible behavior outcomes. Consider a model that predicts the probability of each of n behavior oucomes. Because the probabilities must sum to 1, a model with $n - 1$ free parameters would fit the data perfectly. Such a model, however, would have little or no value. Wickens (1982) suggested that successive comparisons be drawn between pairs of models that differ in their restrictiveness. In these comparisons, if the more restricted model (i.e., the one with fewer free parameters) fits the data as well as the more general one, the more general model is rejected.

The second constraint involves parameter reliability. If the model and its parameter values are viewed as more than a descriptive summary of a single data set, then consistency must be demonstrated in the parameter values that characterize a person's behavior over time and across related task domains. For similar reasons, Sternberg (1963) recommended that invariance of parameter values across experiments be one of the criteria used to evaluate models. The third constraint involves parameter validity. If the model is part of a more general theory, then relationships between parameter values and behavior on tasks not directly related to the model may be specified. To the extent that the parameters fail to meet this constraint, the model must be modfied.

Issues

In the prior section we described several major conceptual contributions to computer simulation and the central role of validation in the history of computer simulation. Concurrent with conceptual and methodological development there arose a large number of related issues. Computer scientists, linguists, philosophers, and psychologists have disputed these issues. The variance in opinions seems to be almost as great within as between disciplines (e.g., Pylyshyn, 1978a and related commentary). The range of issues extends from philosophical (e.g., can machines think?) to technical (e.g., choice of a programming language). The following discussion is limited to issues (or pseudo-issues) that appear to be relevant to the psychologist interested in modeling cognitive development. Four broad categories of issues are addressed: why simulate?, technical issues, conceptual issues, and development.

Why Simulate?

To simulate or not to simulate is a question that has been discussed broadly in the literature: Feigenbaum (1963) anticipated many of the arguments that appeared later; Naylor, Balintfy, Burdick, and Chu (1966), in a book devoted largely to computer simulations of economic models, enumerated 15 reasons for simulating, many of which are as relevant to psychology as to economics; and in a thoughtful review of the question, Neches (1982) related issues to particular simulations. There are three self-evident reasons for *not* attempting a simulation of a psychological model: No new consequences will be discovered, the model can be expressed mathematically (which is succinct, formally elegant, and unambiguous as compared to a computer program), and the theoretical assumptions are sufficiently imprecise to make a simulation impossible. A fourth reason for choosing not to simulate involves temporal cost. It can take considerable time to formulate precise hypotheses and then implement them in a computer program. If this time were spent in other activities, such as preparing manuscripts, the researcher's productivity might be enhanced. Johnson-Laird (1981) argued, however, that "the single most important virtue of programming should come not from the finished program itself, or what it does, but rather from the business of developing it" (p. 186). Although we and other authors (e.g., Naylor et al., 1966) concur that the programmer may benefit by writing a computer simulation (e.g., by checking the internal consistency of the assumptions), this benefit lacks external validity.

It seems to us that computer simulations must be subjected to the same external criteria as other attempts to model psychological processes. These criteria involve assessing both the heuristic impact and the validity of the model. Because psychological simulations are often of interest to computer scientists, as well as psychologists, it is reasonable to evaluate the two criteria across both disciplines. Thus, there are two important reasons to write a computer simulation: The algorithms and/or concepts introduced are important enough to stimulate interest in the scientific community, and the model provides an adequate description of the empirical phenomenon of interest.

Technical Issues

Three technical issues and related problems are discussed here: choice of problem, program implementation, and program communication. Some technical problems associated with program validation were discussed earlier.

Choice of Problem

Considering the diversity in both scope and topic of actual computer simulations, most problems seem to be amenable to computer modeling. The programmer's interests and abilities are the major determinant of problem choice. As can be seen in the section on simulations of cognitive development, most programmers attempt to consider relevant data and theoretical ideas in constructing their models. In general, more attention is paid to empirical data in model construction than in model evaluation.

To highlight the flexibility of computer simulation as a formal method, the differences between nomothetic and idiographic approaches to studying behavior are considered. Windelband (1904) equated the nomothetic approach with seeking general laws and the idiographic approach with a search for structural patterns. Psychologists generally associate nomothetic with abstraction and generalization and idiographic with individual behavior. Kearsley (1976) argues that the two terms confuse a number of orthogonal issues: the number of individuals (one or many), explanatory level (structural or functional), and temporal focus (state or dynamic properties). He argues further, and we concur, that computer simulations can be developed for any of the eight possible orthogonal combinations. However, we believe that the most promising applications of computer simulations will be in the construction of single-subject models, particularly those that include individual-difference parameters.

Program Implementation

When one chooses to implement a model, a computer language must be selected, one needs to have skill with this language, and a "cognitive architecture" has to be either borrowed or developed. None of these is trivial. Judging by our experiences, becoming fluent in the LISP language is more difficult than in the BASIC language. Although programming in LISP eventually becomes easy and aesthetically pleasing, many will be unwilling to expend the initial effort. Furthermore, if one chooses to implement a program in a high-level symbolic language, one must have access to appropriate software and hardware. The hardware-software problem abated somewhat in 1984 with the availability of useful LISP and PROLOG interpreters that run on microprocessors.

A primary consideration in choosing a computer language for most psychological simulations is the range of symbol manipulation functions built into the language. Because LISP has a variety of symbol manipulation functions and can treat functions as objects, it is preferred by many researchers in both artificial intelligence and cognitive psychology (Simon, 1979; Winston & Horn, 1981). The functions-as-objects feature makes it possible for programs written in LISP to be self-modifying. According to Neches (1982), IPL, SNOBOL, and LISP are historically the computer languages of greatest importance in psychological simulations. The key concepts of list processing, pattern matching, and function notation were introduced in these languages. Neches (1982) suggests that contemporary preference for LISP occurred because the language is easy to use. The recent agreement to adopt Common LISP (Steele, 1984) as the standard LISP dialect will eventually ensure that programs written in Common LISP will run on a variety of different computers. Since the Japanese chose PROLOG, rather than LISP, as the symbolic language to be implemented on their fifth-generation computers, it is likely that an increasing number of investigators will use the PROLOG language in their psychological simulations. However, in the near future, we expect the majority of psychological simulations to be written in LISP. We recommend that investigators learn LISP as their first symbolic language.

In addition to using general symbolic languages for psychological simulations, several investigators have developed specialized languages for this purpose. Neches (1982) briefly describes three specialized languages designed to simulate cognitive processes (Newell, 1973, PSG production system; Norman & Rumelhart, 1975, MEMOD interpreter for the language SOL; and Anderson, 1976, ACT model). These specialized languages are large systems that occupy a substantial amount of computer memory and constitute complex cognitive architectures (assumptions about a variety of psychological processes are embodied in the programs). The investigator must decide whether to adapt one of these specialized languages (i.e., large systems) or to write the program in a general symbolic language such as LISP. Neches (1982, pp. 86–87) outlines four factors that lead researchers to abandon large systems:

(1) The systems become slow and expensive to run. . . . (2) The problems of developing and debugging grow as the system increases in complexity. . . . (3) Demand from others for chances to use the system are generally low. Many researchers, even if they have the facilities to bring up the program at their own site, are hesitant to do so due to the theoretical unwillingness to buy an entire set of assumptions, and to the pragmatic fear of poor maintenance. (4) At the same time, the demands of the few who are interested in adopting the system can become burdensome. One hesitates to commit the resources required for documenting and extending a system in order to make it useable outside the laboratory.

Neches acknowledges that the trend favors small simulations written in LISP. However, Neches points out that "there are some benefits to the whole-system approach in terms of generality and understanding of unexpected interrelations between components of the information processing system" (p. 87). Neches recommends a compromise approach in which a modifiable cognitive architecture written in LISP is available. The advantages of such an approach are that the programmer can specify the architecture consistent with her or his theoretical preference by setting parameter values, modify the program by adding or deleting LISP functions, enjoy the advantages of whole-systems architecture, and not have to invent or reinvent a "cognitive architecture" every time a new problem is investigated. The PRISM program (Langley, 1983; Neches, 1982) is written in LISP and features a fairly complete, modifiable architecture. Although we hesitate to recommend that programmers adopt PRISM, or some alternative, because of the computer overhead involved, there is a great need to improve communication about program theories. Without a semiuniversal adaptation of a modifiable cognitive architecture, communication about program theories will sometimes appear unfathomable to the uninitiated and will be difficult for individuals using different systems.

Since the publication of Kuhn's (1962) account of the development of science, there has been a great deal of discussion in the literature about the influence of paradigms on the work of scientists (see Gholson &

Barker, 1985, for a recent review). It is not difficult to construct parallel arguments about the influence of the computer language chosen on the psychological model produced. Programs that can be easily implemented in one language may be difficult or impossible to produce in another. Languages differ in the data types that can be used, algorithms that can be written, self-modifiability of algorithms, and the psychological assumptions that either can be or already are implemented. A programmer may choose a particular language for implementation because it is suitable, it is familiar, or it is the best language available. One can only estimate the relative influence of the language chosen on the product produced. Consider the programs written by Klahr and Siegler (1978) and Sage and Langley (1983) as an illustration of the difficulty of assessing the influence of the language chosen on the simulation. Both pairs of investigators have produced interesting models of the balance-scale problem by using production systems. Klahr and Siegler wrote their simulation in PSG, while Sage and Langley used PRISM. PSG, unlike PRISM, does not include self-modifying algorithms. In justifying their four stage models, Klahr and Siegler argued that adequate state descriptions were a prerequisite to understanding developmental transitions. However, Sage and Langley emphasized that the self-modifying discrimination algorithm used in their simulation passed through two of the four stages and terminated in a third stage described by Klahr and Siegler. It is left for the reader to assess the influence of the language of implementation on the particular aspect of the balance-scale problem that each pair of investigators chose to focus on.

Program Communication

Programmers who wish to communicate about their program theories need to do so at two levels. First, sufficient information must be presented that the program can be recreated at other sites. Second, the psychological principles incorporated in the program theory must be explained with sufficient clarity that they can be subjected to empirical scrutiny. Even a casual survey of the simulation literature reveals that a large percentage of authors fail on both criteria. Neches (1982) notes the related problem of "determining whether the program performs as it does for the reasons claimed by the author" (p. 78). There are at least three ways in which archival access to programs can be improved: creation of a document center from which programs can be obtained, inclusion of the programs in the published papers, and inclusion of the portions of the programs containing innovative programming techniques and central theoretical implementations in the published papers. In all cases, the author should include extensive annotations in the program. Only careful editing can ameliorate problems associated with vague program descriptions of verbal theories or distorted descriptions of mechanisms that account for program performance.

Conceptual Issues

In this section, four conceptual issues are discussed that are relevant to the production and evaluation of computer simulations of cognitive processes. Investigators, whether they are interested in producing or evaluating simulations of cognitive development or some other facet of cognition, must make choices that relate to these issues. Specific implications of these issues for cognitive development are considered in later sections.

Rationalism versus Empiricism

Pylyshyn (1978a) argued that the differences between artificial intelligence and cognitive simulation were stylistic rather than substantive. Many of his critics (e.g., Hayes, 1978) appropriately noted that the criteria for success are quite different in these enterprises, that it is easier to write artificial intelligence than cognitive simulation programs, and that a priori it is rather unlikely that an artificial intelligence program will successfully simulate cognitive performance. To better appreciate the position advocated by Pylyshyn and others (see Miller, 1978), consider Pylyshyn's (1978b, p. 124) definition of cognitive science:

> Essentially, cognitive science seeks to understand, not to *match* anything (not withstanding the ubiquity of the "variance accounted for" criterion, a methodological throwback from the positivist era). It does this by searching for general principles and showing how these, in combination with particular knowledge, particular goals and tasks, and particular mechanisms, are able to account separately for different aspects of a phenomenon. Errors and imperfections are not the primary phenomena to be accounted for; rather, it is the competence to deal with the task.

Thus, according to Pylyshyn, cognitive science becomes a rational rather than an empirical science; it does not attempt to predict (match) empirical phenomena, but attempts to generate general principles that can accomplish the tasks of interest. The outcome to be explained is competence rather than performance. The paradigm for understanding is nonpositivistic and is presumably based on evaluations of whether a computer model is *sufficient* to account for the phenomenon of interest. Evaluation depends more on rational judgment than on the match between empirically derived data and predictions of the model.

Miller (1978) analyzed the rationalist-empiricist controversy in cognitive science. He argued that the protagonists have different criteria of scientific progress. The rationalists believe it is difficult to create adequate cognitive theories but simple to demonstrate their "validity." Thus, rationalists think progress will occur through *theory development*. Their premises are (1) that we know a great deal about our minds without needing to gather cognitive facts and (2) that we need to describe the mechanisms that can accomplish these cognitive facts. However, empiricists believe it is easy to construct psychologically plausible theories, but it is difficult to demonstrate that the theories mirror reality. Thus, empiricists think progress will occur through *theory demonstration*. Their premises are (1) that some hypotheses are empirically viable while others are either false or vacuous and (2) that evaluation of hypotheses does not depend on individual judgment but is in the public domain of science.

Both rationalist and empiricist perspectives should be considered by those interested in simulating behavior. We share the empiricist's belief that empirical viability should be the criterion for cognitive science and the study of cognitive development. The rationalist's frustration with nonmechanistic, static models is also understandable. Even most models of cognitive development are state descriptions that fail to provide mechanisms to account for transitions from one state (or stage) to another. These types of nonmechanistic models cannot be translated to computer programs capable of simulating cognitive growth. The rationalist's desire to create models capable of performing cognitive tasks, particularly tasks which involve "cognitive change," should be, and perhaps is, shared by all. A reasonable goal is to create "sufficient" simulations that model behavior. Cognitive scientists of all persuasions will need to collaborate if we are going to achieve this goal (see Mandler, 1984).

Stochastic versus Deterministic Models

Cotton (1982) offered an interesting analysis of the issues related to preferences for stochastic or deterministic models. He suggested that empiricists are probabilists offering a variety of justifications for the stochastic assumptions in their models. Their arguments range from assertions that the best predictions of behavior that one can offer are probabilistic to assertions that the invocation of stochastic processes is both a convenience and an expression of ignorance. In contrast, Cotton argues that rationalists are determinists. Our own experience with computer modeling suggests that their philosophical determinism is tainted with methodological necessity. At present, it is difficult, perhaps impossible, to develop sufficient models that simulate successive changes in an individual's behavior if the "central psychological processes" in the model are assumed to be stochastic. The problem is that the relationship of the model's behavior to the actual subject's behavior would also be a stochastic process, the complexity of which would depend on the location of the stochastic mismatch between the model and actual subject in the logical chain developed in the model. For example, we considered adding a stochastic parameter to our Nim model, described earlier in the chapter. The parameter would have represented the probability of overlooking a position in a chain of logical search. Overlooking a position sometimes would lead the subject to arrive at an erroneous conclusion from his or her chain of logical search. However, even if the subject did make these sorts of errors stochastically, adding a stochastic parameter to the model would not help account for the data because the sequence of errors generated by the program would be independent of the sequence of errors generated by the subject.

We concur with Cotton's (1982) advocacy of methodological determinism. He wrote, "By this, I mean that our preference should be to state and test very specific deterministic models because of the possibility of describing individual persons' moment-by-moment behavior with such models" (p. 68). At this point, one might ask how deterministic models can handle both between- and within-subjects variability? Four solutions have been implemented: (1) Deterministic assumptions can sometimes generate stochastic models; (2) to the extent that the behavior of the subject or model is data driven, variability is associated with the stimulus sequence presented; (3) pseudorandom generators can be associated with responses or the output of the model without altering the deterministic structure of the program; and (4) parameters can be incorporated in the model to simulate individual differences. Cotton (1982) provided an example of deterministic assumptions generating a stochastic model. Our work on Nim illustrates the last three solutions. Because moves were stochastically generated by a computer opponent, each subject experienced a unique sequence of games. To the extent that subjects' responses were influenced by the positions presented by the computer opponent, between- and within-subjects variability occurred in the data. The subjects' moves predicted by the computer simulation (a different program from that used as the computer opponent) were influenced by the positions that the subjects experienced. Furthermore, the simulation generated a set of predicted moves that contained from 1 to 15 moves. If the subject made one of these moves, the prediction was considered to be correct. In this manner, a pseudorandom generator was associated with the subjects' responses. Finally, two parameters were included in the model. Best-fitting parameter values were obtained for each subject. The Nim model demonstrates that both between- and within-subjects variability can be accounted for by deterministic models. Because it appears that deterministic process models are needed to generate point predictions that simulate successive changes in an individual's behavior, investigators should be encouraged to find additional ways to account for between- and within-subjects variability from deterministic assumptions.

Is a Computer Simulation Conceptually Different from the Verbal Theory That Is Implemented?

Johnson-Laird (1981) recommended that we distinguish between the program and the theory that is modeled. There are a number of reasons for maintaining this distinction (Neches, 1982): Simplifying or psychologically implausible assumptions might be invoked to facilitate program implementation, the program might function with only a restricted set of problems, parameters might be surreptitiously introduced by manipulating either data or procedures, and data or procedures might be eliminated to ensure that the program functions. Note each of these reasons reflects the programmer's inability to adequately represent theoretical conceptions.

This problem is, in principle, not different from that experienced by a theorist using another medium of expression (e.g., mathematics). Two cases merit consideration. First, if the programmer's goal is to translate a vague verbal theory to a testable program and the program is not verified because it really was not a good translation, then a second translation can be attempted. Because the program, *not* the unspecified theory, is tested, for all practical purposes the program is the theory. In this case, rejecting the program theory is tantamount to rejecting the verbal theory. With the important exception of the theorist, the verbal theory is superfluous. Second, the programmer might explicate a testable verbal theory and wish to explore how the variables in the theory interact. In this case, it might be possible to empirically evaluate the basic assumptions in the verbal theory, but impossible to test the interactive assumptions without the aid of a computer model. Rejection of a poorly translated computer model would, in this instance, not result in the rejection of the verbal theory, but would result in the rejection of the program theory.

The Computer Metaphor

We argued earlier that computer simulation is one of the modeling techniques available to the theorist and that program theories should be evaluated in the same way as other attempts to model psychological processes. Other investigators have argued that computer simulation is more than a modeling technique, that it is also a metaphor for human cognition (see Kolers & Smythe, 1984). In our opinion, the introduction of the computational metaphor produced some unfortunate consequences. The distinction between many of the hypothetical constructs used in simulations and the program theories that evolved has become blurred to the extent that some critics assert that it is impossible to model, for example, creativity (Brown, 1982), human growth (Neisser, 1976), or symbolic capabilities (Kolers & Smythe, 1984). Thus, program theories become confused with and lost in a maze of arguments about hypothetical constructs.

At present we are *not* sufficiently knowledgeable about the functioning of the human brain to evaluate most of the aspects of the computer metaphor, so we should concentrate on evaluating the adequacy of the theories generated from computer simulation. Furthermore, program theories may continue to be useful even when we become capable of falsifying the hypothetical constructs contained in the theories. Mandler (1985) provided an example that illustrates the unproductivity of most current arguments about the computer metaphor. He used consciousness in the example, but creativity, human growth, or symbolic capabilities would have served as well. He considered two questions. Can computers be conscious? Can computers be pregnant? Because computers neither have the necessary equipment nor engage in the prerequisite activities, pregnancy is impossible. At present we do not know about the equipment or activities necessary to be conscious. Therefore, questions about computer consciousness are empty. To reiterate, investigators should concentrate on constructing and evaluating computer simulations as they would other types of models. Metaphors should be left to the poets.

Development

Two broad related questions have been addressed. Should cognitive scientists simulate development? How adequately have computer programs simulated development? Not surprisingly, opinions vary widely on both questions. Pylyshyn (1978b) argues that ontogenetic evidence gathered from children is of only incidental interest in cognitive science. Neisser (1976) suggests not only that cognitive scientists should be interested in development, but also that one of the main deficiencies of cognitive science is a failure to simulate development. Brown (1982) argues that computer simulations are interesting, but seriously limited, models of human growth. Chi and Rees (1983) are optimistic. They suggest that for the time being either production (e.g., Anderson, 1983) or schema (e.g., Rumelhart & Norman, 1978) models, currently the two preferred types of cognitive architectures, are "perfectly adequate to simulate development" (p. 94). Finally, Klahr (1982) claims that information processing models are the only theoretical formalisms that presently model the centrality of the child's own activity in development.

The diversity of opinions reflects disagreements about the goals of cognitive science and the meaning of development. However, these problems are overshadowed by psychologists' vague conception of what cognitive development *really* is about. If one defines development as age-correlated changes in physical growth and behavior, then one needs to consider development in a broad conceptual framework involving biological and psychological variables (for example, Hebb, 1966). None of the investigators discussed in this section treats development or cognitive development in this broad framework, although both Brown (1982) and Neisser (1976) claim computer programs do not adequately represent the child's environment. For example, Neisser (1976, p. 144) wrote, "The development of human intelligence occurs in a real environment with coherent properties of its own. . . . As long as programs do not represent this environment systematically, in at least some of its complexity, they cannot represent cognitive growth either." This criticism is almost certainly correct, but it is difficult to abstract the environment in a computer program if you cannot specify the class of relevant environmental variables. Thus, the criticism appears to be a valid assessment of current ignorance, rather than a particular shortcoming of computer simulation.

Accommodation and Conventionalism

Our collective conception about what development is really about has been influenced, or perhaps determined, by Piaget's concepts of assimilation and accommodation. Brown (1982, p. 101) offered representative definitions of these two concepts: "Assimilation is the function by which the events of the world are incorporated into preexisting knowledge structures while accommodation is the process by which the existing knowledge structures are modified in accordance with novel events."

The most common objection to computer simulations of developmental tasks is that the simulations do not accommodate (e.g., Brown, 1982; Neisser, 1976). How is this complaint to be interpreted? Since Samuel's (1963) pioneering work on the game of checkers, it is clear that computer programs can learn from experience by modifying parameters in mathematical functions. Furthermore, Brown (1982) was aware that programs can learn through acquisition by modifying and extending the data base. However, based on Brown's definitions, these types of modifications constitute assimilation, not accommodation. Evidently, computer simulations must be capable of modifying the procedures used in order to demonstrate accommodation. Programs including heuristics that modify procedures are referred to as *self-modifying*. Waterman (1975) developed such a program, and there have been a number of attempts to use self-modifying heuristics to model children's language acquisition (Anderson, 1983; Langley, 1982) and acquisition of arithmetic skills (Resnick & Neches, 1984). Whether critics such as Brown and Neisser will or should consider these self-modifying programs as "accommodating" is problematic.

The idea that a scientist's task is to discover the meaning of a concept, usually a commonly used word, is referred to as *conventionalism*. The accommodation question suggests that "conventional" thinking has infiltrated developmental psychology. A group of psychologists is attempting to discover, define, or find evidence relating to accommodation. In this light, it is easy to appreciate Klahr's position. He wrote (1982, p. 80):

> The capacity for adaptive self-modification is essential to developmental theory, but until recently, there have been no well-specified ideas about how this self-modification takes place. For 40 years now, we have had *assimilation* and *accommodation,* the mysterious and shadowy forces of *equilibration,* the "Batman and Robin" of developmental processes. What are they? How do they operate? Why is it that after all this time, we know no more about them than when they first sprang upon the scene? What we need is a way to get beyond vague verbal statements of the nature of the developmental process. Perhaps the most impor-

tant merit of production systems is that they provide a basis for modeling self-modification.

Klahr argues further that production systems currently are the only models that provide such a basis. Although it may be possible to write self-modifying schema models (discussed below), we agree with his evaluation that self-modifying production systems are a promising tool for developmental theorists.

Realism

Besides the conventionalism endemic to the controversy surrounding accommodation, the arguments reflect a philosophical realism that is disturbing. Both computer simulators (e.g., Wallace, 1982) and their critics (e.g., Brown, 1982) sometimes treat programs as objects of interest rather than as attempts to model cognition. The computational metaphor seems to be either the only or the most relevant issue. Although it is an impressive intellectual achievement to produce a self-modifying program, it is quite a different thing to demonstrate that the model predicts the behavior of one child, several children, or the average performance of several children. Writing computer algorithms and writing computer simulations of cognitive behavior are both useful enterprises that should be encouraged, not confused. In this light, consider Brown's (1982) complaint that machines can not capture "meaning" and "intentionality." It is difficult to believe that Brown would have voiced such a complaint when criticizing a verbal theory or a stochastic mathematical model. Computer simulations should be evaluated in terms of how accurately they model behavior. Attempts to simulate the acquisition of meaning and the ability to plan are challenging issues of current interest to cognitive scientists.

Mechanisms of Learning and Transition

Given contemporary developmental interest in accommodation and that much is to be learned about self-modifying programs, it is surprising that Chi and Rees (1983) consider that either the Anderson (1983) production model or the Rumelhart and Norman (1978) schema model currently is adequate to simulate development. Rumelhart and Norman (1978) offered only a vague set of mechanisms for self-modifying schemas, and the four learning-transition mechanisms implemented by Anderson (1983)—proceduralization, composition, generalization, and specialization—in his production system would not seem to be the stuff that constitutes accommodation. Although these four mechanisms do produce new procedures, the resulting procedures are closely tied to either declarative knowledge or other procedures and probably would not be considered adequate representations of altered knowledge structures by accommodation theorists. For example, the composition mechanism combines two or more procedures that usually occur serially into a single new procedure. If antecedent *a* led to the firing of procedure *A* that produced consequence *b* which, in turn, led to the firing of procedure *B* that produced consequence *c*, then the composition mechanism would create procedure *AB* such that antecedent *a* would cause procedure *AB* to fire, producing consequence *c*.

Chi and Rees are not particularly concerned about self-modifying models because they conceive of cognitive development as a learning process involving the gradual acquisition and structuring of knowledge. Chi's (1978) finding that children who played chess were better at recalling chess positions, but poorer at recalling digits, than non-chess-playing adults was an important catalyst in formulating a knowledge-based conception of development. Chi and Rees (1983, pp. 97–98) summarize:

> stages and decalage are really manifestations of a few underlying assumptions. . . : (1) only a small amount of new knowledge can be learned at any one time; (2) this new knowledge must be interpreted by and stored in existing knowledge structures; (3) new structures, when they are needed, are created from old ones; and (4) knowledge tends to be specific to the context in which it was learned.

It is possible to write computer programs, consistent with Chi and Rees' assumptions, that do not employ self-modifying heuristics. Consider the simulations written by Langley (1979, Kepler's third law of planetary motion) and Lenat (1977, number theory). Even though self-modifying heuristics were not used, these simulations defined new concepts and subsequently used them in making new discoveries, suggesting that self-modifying programs may not be needed to simulate development. Whether computer simulations can be produced that accurately model cognitive development, but do not include self-modifying heuristics, remains to be determined. However, this possibility complements the Chi and Rees knowledge-based conception of development and provides an alternative to self-modifying heuristics for those interested in simulating developmental transitions.

Over the past 15 years most researchers interested in cognitive development have ignored learning-transition mechanisms and have concentrated on describing the rules, strategies, and structures available to children at different ages (see Chapter 3 by Wilkinson and Haines, this volume). A similar trend seems to characterize research in adult cognition (Langley & Simon, 1981). Dissatisfaction with traditional learning theories, a developing interest in basic cognitive structures, and an increasing recognition of Piaget's work all fostered the disinterest in learning-transition mechanisms (also see Siegler, 1983). As can be seen in the above discussion, a revival of interest in learning-transition is apparent, particularly among those researchers familiar with the computer simulation literature. If the goal of cognitive science is to describe "mind" and the ability to learn is a central (or *the* central) feature of both cognition, in general, and development, in particular, then the study of cognitive development is central to cognitive science. Suppose we accept Pylyshyn's (1978b) conceptual framework and grant that expert performance is of primary interest to cognitive science. Even then, his assertion that developmental research is of only incidental interest is unacceptable if expertise is modifiable by experience (i.e., it does not reach a ceiling), and the learning transition mechanisms do *not* vary across development. If, as Chi and Rees (1983) argue, the cognitive structures of children are less elaborated than those of adults and the learning-transition mechanisms are invariant across development, then developmental research should be central to cognition. This follows because, in principle, it should be easier to both simulate cognitive structures and measure the products of transition in children than in adults. The awareness of issues in cognitive development shown by many cognitive scientists over the last 5 years probably reflects their recognition of the importance of developmental research in the construction and evaluation of computer models of learning-transition mechanisms. Likely their awareness will grow, and attempts to simulate developmental processes will become more frequent.

Simulation Models of Cognitive Development

Although relatively few computer simulations appear in the cognitive-development literature, interest in computer simulation as a formal method in developmental psychology appears to be growing. The number of published papers has doubled since 1980 (see Table 8.1). In this section, simulations of cognitive development are examined in relation to issues introduced earlier in the chapter. For reference purposes and to facilitate our discussion, models are classified in Table 8.1 according to the type of cognitive architecture, the task domain, the type of developmental model, and the type of methodology used to guide the creation and evaluation of the models.

Static and Dynamic Models of Development

Simon (1962) made two suggestions that influenced the type of information processing models constructed to simulate cognitive development. The first suggestion was to develop state theories that specified the knowledge structures and procedures needed to account for task performance at different stages of cognitive development. These state theories then could be implemented as process models (computer simulations) that would behave as children at the different stages. The second suggestion was that efforts be made to discover the learning-transition processes that would transform the model from one state to the next.

Klahr and Wallace (1970a, 1970b; state models) wrote the pioneering simulations of cognitive development. They used task-specific routines, which consisted of collections of hierarchically ordered, goal-directed

TABLE 8.1. Classification of developmental simulation models.

Authors	Domain	Type of model	Methodology
Production system architectures			
Anderson (1983)	Language acquisition	Transition	Idealized
Baylor and Gascon (1974)	Seriation	State	Individual
Baylor, Gascon, LeMoyne, and Pothier (1973)	Seriation	State	Individual
Baylor and LeMoyne (1975)	Seriation	State	Individual
Klahr (1973a)	Quantification	State	Idealized
Klahr (1973b)	Quantification	State	Idealized
Klahr and Siegler (1978)	Balance scale	State	Idealized
Klahr and Wallace (1972)	Quantification	State	Idealized
Klahr and Wallace (1973)	Quantification	State	Idealized
Klahr and Wallace (1976)	Quantification	State	Idealized
Langley (1982)	Language acquisition	Transition	Idealized
Resnick and Neches (1984)	Addition	Transition	Idealized
Sage and Langley (1983)	Balance scale	Transition	Idealized
Young and O'Shea (1981)	Subtraction	State	Group
Schema Architectures			
Greeno, Riley, and Gelman (1984)	Arithmetic word problems	State	Idealized
Hill (1983)	Language acquisition	Transition	Idealized
Kintsch and Greeno (1985)	Arithmetic word problems	State	Idealized
Riley, Greeno, and Heller (1983)[a]	Arithmetic word problems	State	Idealized
Task-specific Architectures			
Ashcraft (Chap. 9, this volume)	Addition	State	Group
Brown and Burton (1978)	Subtraction errors	State	Group
Brown and VanLehn (1980)	Subtraction errors	State	Group
Burton (1981)	Subtraction errors	State	Group
Klahr and Wallace (1970a)	Series completion	State	Idealized
Klahr and Wallace (1970b)	Classification	State	Idealized
VanLehn (1983)	Subtraction errors	State	Group

[a] This model is composed of both production system and schema components.

processes, to simulate series completion (1970a) and classification (1970b). Following the introduction of production systems, Klahr and Wallace (1972, 1973, 1976; state models) employed this architecture in their simulations of quantification skills. Klahr and Wallace placed constraints on the developmental sequencing of their state models. In modeling the older child, changes were made to the knowledge structures of models representing the younger child. These changes were consistent with hypothesized transition mechanisms, even though these mechanisms were not implemented in the model. Their sequencing strategy appears to have influenced the formulation of state models that followed (e.g., Baylor & Gascon, 1974; Baylor et at., 1973; Baylor & LeMoyne, 1975; Klahr & Siegler, 1978; Riley, Greeno, & Heller, 1983; Young & O'Shea, 1981).

In Table 8.1 there are only five developmental simulations in which transition mechanisms were employed. The earliest of these papers was published in 1982 (Langley, 1982). The introduction of self-modifying procedures (Waterman, 1975), in part, made it possible to include transition mechanisms in developmental models. However, transitions can also be modeled by changing knowledge structures. Although Simon (1962) may be correct in arguing for the priority of state models of development, it appears to us that theorists must use transition mechanisms to account for "assimilation" and "accommodation" (i.e., development). We encourage authors to include transition mechanisms in their developmental simulations.

Type of Problem

Cognitive developmental simulations have been written to model childrens' performance on logical, arithmetic, and language acquisition tasks. Most of these simulations are attempts to represent performance at a particular stage of development. However, models that simulate developmental transistions are beginning to appear. A brief description and discussion of simulations representing each of these tasks are provided below.

Logical Tasks

Inspection of Table 8.1 reveals that most of the simulations written before 1980 were designed to explain performance on logical tasks. The work of Klahr (1973a, 1973b) and Klahr and Wallace (1970a, 1970b, 1972, 1973, 1976) contributed substantially to the development of models in this area. In their 1976 book, Klahr and Wallace provided detailed descriptions of production systems and how they were changed to generate a variety of states. Their book should be a useful source for investigators interested in related undertakings. A review of the work of Klahr and Wallace and its contribution to our understanding of cognitive development can be found in Siegler (1983).

Diagnosis is essential to developmental theory construction (see Flavell, 1977). It is our opinion that in the short run, the major empirical contribution to cognitive development, associated with computer simulations, will be in the diagnosis of cognitive structures. The work of Baylor and his colleagues (Baylor & Gascon, 1974; Baylor et al., 1973; Baylor & LeMoyne, 1975) illustrates this point. They developed five state models to diagnose the cognitive structures children use in weight seriation. The models did not learn (i.e., transition mechanisms which would permit the model to generate successive states were not included). Each state was represented as a production system. Developmental changes were assumed to involve the successive acquisition of three or more seriation strategies. Stage 1 was associated with rules that allow a child to compare only two blocks at a time. Children at this stage seriate three or more blocks in a haphazard manner. Stage 2 was associated with rules that enable a child to seriate a subseries of three or four blocks. Stage 3 was associated with three different rule systems (states in the model), each of which permits a child to operate on a series of any length. The five states were developed to emulate the protocols obtained from five children. One of the state models was able to account for the behavior of a child on three different seriation problems: weight, hidden length (the child was allowed to see only two objects at a time), and length (all objects were visible).

Sage and Langley (1983) implemented a self-modifying production system to model childrens' rule acquisition on the balance-scale task. In doing so, they demonstrated that such programs can provide a mechanism for constructing nonstatic developmental theories. A computer simulation was used to determined whether a model that employed a discrimination learning mechanism would emulate children's development on this task. The model began by making random predictions about when a scale would balance or which side would go down. The discrimination process was invoked when the model made an incorrect prediction. By comparing the situation when a rule was applied incorrectly to the last correct application, a new, more specific production was created. The model progressively generated productions that were similar to the first three rules described by Siegler (1976) and the state production systems of these rules formulated by Klahr and Siegler (1978). However, the model was unable to generate the final rule, the torque rule, because the knowledge structures used did *not* include the necessary arithmetic.

Arithmetic Tasks

Young and O'Shea (1981) wrote production system models of subtraction. The correct subtraction production system was devised by using the decomposition technique for borrowing, one of two methods taught to children in Britain (Williams, 1971). The incorrect subtraction production systems were derived from inspection of errors produced by 10-year-olds on a corpus of 1500 subtraction problems (Bennett, 1976). To model the errors, Young and O'Shea added rules appropriate to other arithmetic tasks or omitted rules from the correct procedure. About two-thirds of the errors generated by each of 51 children were matched by the model. By isolating the missing or inaccurate knowledge that causes particular subtraction errors, Young and O'Shea provided an additional demonstration of the diagnostic capabilities of computer simulations. It should be possible to implement this model, as well as related models generated by Brown and his colleagues (Brown & Burton, 1978; Brown & VanLehn, 1980; Burton, 1981; and VanLehn, 1983), in teaching programs that first diagnose each child's missing or inaccurate subtraction rules and then train the child to use the correct rules. We encourage the authors to generalize their approaches to other arithmetic tasks.

Resnick and Neches (1984) developed two self-modifying production system models to simulate the developmental change from a SUM to a MIN addition strategy. The *SUM strategy* involves counting separate sets of objects to represent each addend, combining the sets, and then counting the total set. Children usually abandon this strategy spontaneously before their seventh birthday. They replace it with a counting-on procedure that involves counting the smaller addend onto the larger. This is called the *MIN procedure* because only the lesser of the two addends needs to be recounted (for example, 5 + 2 yields 5, 6, 7). Each of the Resnick and Neches models began by using the SUM procedure and, without any external input, changed to using the MIN procedure. The transformation of SUM to MIN was accomplished by three self-modifying heuristics used in conjunction with knowledge about numbers described by Gelman and Gallistel (1978). This work provides a second example of how self-modifying production systems can be used to model transitions in cognitive development.

The application of computer simulations to another class of arithmetic tasks deserves to be noted. Greeno and his colleagues (Greeno, Riley, & Gelman, 1984; Kintsch & Greeno, 1985; Riley et al., 1983) developed schema-architecture state models of children solving word arithmetic problems. Of particular interest is the Kintsch and Greeno (1985) simulation. The general principles from a theory of text processing (van Dijk & Kintsch, 1983) were incorporated in the Kintsch and Greeno (1985) model. This enabled the model to interpret word problems and generate plans for solving these problems. The formulation of computer simulations that incorporate a theory of text processing in conjunction with task-specific knowledge should enable researchers to explore the relationship between comprehension of task instructions and problem-solving ability in children's performance.

Language Acquisition

Langley used the PRISM architecture to create a self-modifying simulation (AMBER) that models the learning of speech generation strategies. AMBER begins with the ability to make one-word utterances and adds rules for ordering goals and producing longer strings of grammatical morphemes. Langley's main goal was to model the learning of content and function words and the order in which grammatical morphemes are mastered. AMBER learns to generate sentences by beginning with three performance rules: a rule for establishing subgoals, a rule for saying words, and a rule for noting when goals are satisfied. AMBER's initial self-modifications result from failures to produce content words. The failures can occur either before or after a particular word is correctly produced. A designation process is applied if one of these errors of omission occurs. The designation processes attempt to avoid errors of omission in the future by building new productions. Once AMBER begins to produce content words correctly, it can learn rules for producing morphemes. If the system incorrectly produces a morpheme that does not occur in adult speech, it makes an error of commission. Following these errors, the second self-modifying process, discrimination learning, creates more specific productions with additional conditions. AMBER learned six classes of morphemes in the following order: plural, present progressive, articles, past tense, third person plural, and uncontractible auxiliary.

Another process model of language acquisition was reported by Hill (1983) and Hill and Arbib (1984). These authors presented a schema model of the acquisition of language by a 2-year-old child. This model incorporated the following assumptions: The child has schemata for and talks about relations, the child has schemata for and employs word order, the child employs concatenating and deletion rules, the child forms classes of concepts and classes of words, and the classifying processes cause successive reorganization of the information stored. The model is a repetition-and-response model. It takes, as input, adult speech and a context and produces either a repetition of the adult sentence or a response to it. The model begins with a rudimentary notion of a sentence (i.e., two-word utterances containing a relation) and learns to generate utterances with a maximum of six words. The model has four dynamic data structures that grow as it acquires language: the lexicon; the grammar, to which the model adds templates for expressing the concepts salient to the child; conceptual knowledge of the world; and specific information about the present context that is necessary to choose between a set of alternative responses to questions asked. The model can learn information about new words, concepts, and templates for expressing relations. The model generates a flat template structure of syntax rather than the hierarchical structure generated by production system models (e.g., Anderson, 1983). Hill argues that this flat structure, although typical of the speech of 2-

year-old children, is inadequate to model the hierarchical structure of adult language. An interesting feature of Hill's model is that it is the only transition model appearing in Table 8.1 that does not employ self-modifying procedures to learn.

Cognitive Architectures, Program Implementation, and Communication

The developmental simulation literature is representative of the cognitive simulation literature in choice of architecture, programming language, and communication. As can be seen in Table 8.1, authors of developmental simulations have used a variety of cognitive architectures. Most of these simulations were implemented in high-level symbolic languages, but even the BASIC language has been used effectively (see Ashcraft, Chapter 9, this volume). These simulations demonstrate that the choice of cognitive architecture and language of implementation usually reflects the availability of hardware and software, the problem of interest, and the author's programming skill and theoretical preference. Unfortunately, the failure to communicate adequately is characteristic of the reports of developmental simulations. With few exceptions, the authors fail to provide a detailed description of their models and how they were implemented. Even the computer language used is often not mentioned. The communications gap creates a major obstacle to validating the models and assessing their generality.

Methodology, Rationalism, and Empiricism

In Table 8.1, simulations are categorized by methodology according to whether they were written to characterize the performance of an individual subject, as distinguished from a group of subjects, or an idealized subject. The type of methodology used is closely related to the method of evaluation. In the reports that presented simulations of idealized subjects, minimal attention was paid either to relating the models directly to the behavior of children or to conducting statistical tests. There is a danger in such an approach because in the absence of empirical tests, simulation models may reflect only theoretical fantasies. The quantification model of Klahr and Wallace (1976) seems to be a case in point. They assumed a developmental sequence in which class inclusion is followed by conservation which, in turn, is followed by transitivity. There is, however, considerable evidence that transitivity is the first, not the last, of these skills acquired (e.g., Brainerd, 1973; 1978; Bryant & Trabasso, 1971; Riley & Trabasso, 1974). For a different view of this model see Siegler (1983).

The authors who presented simulation models of individual subjects and groups of subjects formally evaluated their models by using empirical data. The method of evaluation varied as a function of the type of computer model. Baylor and his colleagues (Baylor & Gascon, 1974; Baylor et al., 1973; Baylor & LeMoyne, 1975) implemented the two validation strategies we suggested in the methodology section for computer models written for individual subjects. Without changing the basic productions, two of the models were modified to fit an additional child (generalization across individuals), and one model was able to account for the behavior of a child on three different seriation problems (generalization across tasks). The authors reported nearly perfect agreement between the traces of the appropriate simulation and the series of moves made by each of the five children studied.

The production system models of subtraction formulated by Young and O'Shea (1981) were fitted to error data generated by each of 51 children. Error-generating productions were treated as parameters in the model, and an individual subject's errors were fitted to the different versions of the model so as to optimize the match between the model and data. With this procedure, the model matched about two-thirds of the errors generated by the children. Brown and VanLehn (1980) constructed a different kind of simulation to account for children's subtraction errors. This model was devised after an inspection of protocols obtained from a large number of children. The model generated 32 types of subtraction errors as well as correct performance. The authors reported that 21 of the types of errors appeared in children's performance, 1 type of error was absurd, and the remaining 10 types of errors had not yet been identified in children's performance. Ashcraft's (Chapter 9, this volume) chronometric model of addition is another example of a formally evaluated simulation of a group of subjects. Response times generated by a model based on a spreading-activation search of long-term memory were compared to those generated by children.

Conclusions

The computer has become an important tool in cognitive science. However, a number of theoretical, methodological, and technical issues need to be addressed if computer simulation is to become an important formal method in psychology, in general, and developmental psychology, in particular.

Computer Simulation: Rationalist's Toy or Empiricist's Tool?

The hybrid nature of the computer simulation literature is apparent in this review. Most researchers attempt to empirically justify the processes used in their simulations, but rarely attempt to match the output of their model to behavior. Statistical tests, and other standard validation procedures, are rarely used. Even the word *empirical* sometimes refers *not* to the behavior of people but rather to the testing of a computer program:

Does the program run as intended? Does the program embody procedures sufficient to accomplish some goal? What effects result from changing designated procedures? Although the distinction between artificial intelligence research (in which the goal is to develop programs that are both efficient and sufficient) and computer simulation of psychological processes (in which the goal is to develop programs that account for behavior) seems clear in principle, it has often been blurred in practice. We believe that Pylyshyn's (1978a) assertion that the differences between artificial intelligence and cognitive simulation are stylistic rather than substantive is an accurate characterization of the two disciplines at present, but a poor prescription for their future development.

Over the past 25 years, investigators in both psychology and artificial intelligence have spent enormous amounts of energy writing programs that are sufficient to solve problems. Some of these programs constitute viable psychological theories, but most do not. The concepts generated in this work, however, have influenced the thinking of many cognitive psychologists. It is clear from our review that considerable progress has been made in developing heuristics that will *eventually* be useful to empirically minded psychologists. Furthermore, the steady development of complex cognitive architectures is a laudable feat. We remain optimistic that the mainly rational enterprise described in this chapter will bear empirical fruit.

Single-Subject Models

Theoretical accounts of individual behavior are not common in cognitive psychology. A major reason is that traditional experimental and statistical methods are not easily applied when the unit of analysis is one person. We believe that computer models, particularly those that include individual-difference parameters, can be used to make major contributions to our understanding of individual behavior. Unfortunately, only a few investigators have exploited this technology. For example, Baylor and his colleagues (Baylor & Gascon, 1974; Baylor et al., 1973; Baylor & LeMoyne, 1975) are the only investigators who wrote computer simulations to model the behavior of individual children (see Table 8.1). Even though the evaluation of single-subject simulations requires some departures from tradition, both in the statistics employed and in the value attached to disconfirming evidence, we encourage researchers to use computers to model individual behavior.

Communications Revisited

In putting together this review, we have been continually frustrated by the difficulty of determining what particular simulation models do and how they do it. Very often, models are described in vague generalities that provide little more than a general impression, prone to misinterpretation.

It is ironic that computer models, once heralded for their potential contribution to theoretical clarity and precision, should be described in terms likely to engender only confusion. There are many problems, although some, such as the lack of standardized languages and compatible hardware, are in the process of being solved. However, the intrinsic complexity of the models being developed will likely continue to challenge the communication talents of the most articulate among us, as well as the comprehension abilities of the most gifted. We reiterate that an archival system for programs and community adoption of a flexible cognitive architecture will reduce the communication gap.

Cognitive Development

Computer simulations have been used rarely to model cognitive development. Some reasons for this neglect also characterize other areas of psychology: the difficulty of acquiring programming skills, the lack of widely accepted techniques for empirically validating computer models, the difficulty of communicating the important features of the models, and the extensive time and effort demanded of those who wish to use simulation techniques. In addition, and perhaps most important, heuristics that could be applied to modeling developmental transitions have become available only recently. Despite these difficulties, progress has been made. As in the computer simulation field in general, most of the progress is associated with devising heuristics that can be applied to developmental modeling. However, several investigators (e.g., Baylor et al., 1973; Young & O'Shea, 1981) have used production systems to diagnose cognitive structures. Their success should encourage others to try. The advent of self-modifying heuristics is particularly important to developmental theorists. These heuristics provide a mechanism for creating nonstatic program theories of developmental changes (e.g., Sage & Langley, 1983). In time we will know if these powerful tools can be used to create viable theories of developmental transitions.

Acknowledgments

The preparation of the paper was supported by a grant from the Natural Sciences and Engineering Research Council of Canada. We would like to thank Rita Anderson for her helpful suggestions.

References

Abelson, R. P. (1968). Simulation of social behavior. In G. Lindzey & E. Aronson (Eds.), *The handbook of social psychology*, (2d ed., Vol. 2, pp. 274–356). Reading, MA: Addison-Wesley.

Anderson, J. R. (1976). *Language, memory, and thought.* Hillsdale, NJ: Erlbaum.

Anderson, J. R. (1980). *Cognitive psychology and its implications*. San Francisco: Freeman.

Anderson, J. R. (1983). *The architecture of cognition*. Cambridge, MA: Harvard.

Bakan, D. (1962). The test of significance in psychological research. *Psychological Bulletin, 66,* 423–437.

Bartlett, F. C. (1932). *Remembering*. New York: Cambridge.

Baylor, G. W., & Gascon, J. (1974). An information processing theory of aspects of the development of weight seriation in children. *Cognitive Psychology, 6,* 1–40.

Baylor, G. W., Gascon, J., LeMoyne, G., & Pothier, N. (1973). An information processing model of some seriation tasks. *Canadian Psychologist, 14,* 167–196.

Baylor, G. W., & LeMoyne, G. (1975). Experiments in seriation with children: Towards an information processing explanation of the horizontal decalage. *Canadian Journal of Behavioural Science, 7,* 4–29.

Bennett, M. (1976). *SUBSTITUTOR: A teaching program*. Unpublished project report. University of Edinborough, Department of Artificial Intelligence.

Brainerd, C. J. (1973). Order of acquisition of transitivity, conservation, and class inclusion of length and weight. *Developmental Psychology, 8,* 105–116.

Brainerd, C. J. (1978). *Piaget's theory of intelligence*. Englewood Cliffs, NJ: Prentice-Hall.

Brown, A. L. (1982). Learning and development: The problem of compatibility, access and induction. *Human Development, 25,* 89–115.

Brown, J. S., & Burton, R. B. (1978). Diagnostic models for procedural bugs in basic mathematical skills. *Cognitive Science, 2,* 155–192.

Brown, J. S., & VanLehn, K. (1980). Repair theory: A generative theory of bugs in procedural skill. *Cognitive Science, 4,* 379–426.

Bryant, P. E., & Trabasso, T. (1971). Transitive inference and memory in young children. *Nature, 232,* 456–458.

Burton, R. B. (1981). DEBUGGY: Diagnosis of errors in basic mathematical skills. In D. H. Sleeman & J. S. Brown (Eds.), *Intelligent tutoring systems*. London: Academic.

Chi, M. T. H. (1978). Knowledge structures and memory development. In R. S. Siegler (Ed.), *Children's thinking: What develops?* (pp. 73–96). Hillsdale, NJ: Erlbaum.

Chi, M. T. H., & Rees, E. T. (1983). A learning framework for development. *Contributions to Human Development, 9,* 71–107.

Cotton, J. W. (1982). Where is the randomness for the human computer? *Behavior Research Methods and Instrumentation, 14,* 59–70.

Feigenbaum, E. A. (1963). The simulation of verbal learning behavior. In E. A. Feigenbaum & J. Feldman (Eds.), *Computers and thought* (pp. 297–309). New York: McGraw-Hill.

Flavell, J. H. (1977). *Cognitive development*. Englewood Cliffs, NJ: Prentice-Hall.

Gelman, R., & Gallistel, C. R. (1978). *The child's understanding of number*. Cambridge, MA: Harvard.

Gholson, B., & Barker, P. (1985). Kuhn, Lakatos, and Laudan: Applications in the history of physics and psychology. *American Psychologist, 40,* 755–769.

Grant, M. J., Rabinowitz, F. M., & Dingley, H. L. (1985, June). *Knowledge and search in the game of Nim*. Paper presented to the meeting of the Canadian Psychological Association, Halifax.

Greeno, J. G., Riley, M. S., & Gelman, R. (1984). Conceptual competence and children's counting. *Cognitive Psychology, 16,* 94–143.

Gregg, L. W., & Simon, H. A. (1967). Process models and stochastic theories of simple concept formation. *Journal of Mathematical Psychology, 4,* 246–276.

Hayes, P. J. (1978). Doing AI but saying CS. *The Behavioral and Brain Sciences, 1,* 108.

Hayes-Roth, B., & Hayes-Roth, F. (1979). A cognitive model of planning. *Cognitive Science, 3,* 275–310.

Hebb, D. O. (1966). *A textbook of psychology* (2d ed.). Philadelphia: Saunders.

Hill, J. C. (1983). A computational model of language acquisition in the two-year-old. *Cognition and Brain Theory, 6,* 287–317.

Hill, J. C., & Arbib, M. A. (1984). Schemas, computation, and language acquisition. *Human Development, 27,* 282–296.

Johnson-Laird, P. N. (1981). Mental models in cognitive science. In D. A. Norman (Ed.), *Perspectives on cognitive science* (pp. 147–191). Norwood, NJ: Ablex.

Kail, R., & Bisanz, J. (1982). Cognitive development: An information-processing perspective. In R. Vasta (Ed.), *Strategies and techniques of child study* (pp. 209–243). New York: Academic.

Kearsley, G. P. (1976). Individuality, individual differences, and computer simulation. *Educational and Psychological Measurement, 36,* 811–823.

Kintsch, W., & Greeno, J. G. (1985). Understanding and solving word arithmetic problems. *Psychological Review, 92,* 109–129.

Klahr, D. (1973a). A production system for counting, subitizing, and adding. In W. G. Chase (Ed.), *Visual information processing* (pp. 3–34). New York: Academic.

Klahr, D. (1973b). Quantification process. In W. G. Chase (Ed.), *Visual information processing* (pp. 527–544). New York: Academic.

Klahr, D. (1982). Nonmonotone assessment of monotone development. In S. Strauss (Ed.), *U-shaped behavioral growth* (pp. 63–86). New York: Academic.

Klahr, D., & Siegler, R. S. (1978). The representation of children's knowledge. In H. W. Reese & L. P. Lipsitt (Eds.), *Advances in child development and behavior* (Vol. 12, pp. 62–116). New York: Academic.

Klahr, D., & Wallace, J. G. (1970a). The development of serial completion strategies: An information processing analysis. *British Journal of Psychology, 61,* 243–257.

Klahr, D., & Wallace, J. G. (1970b). An information processing analysis of some Piagetian experimental tasks. *Cognitive Psychology, 1,* 358–387.

Klahr, D., & Wallace, J. G. (1972). Class inclusion processes. In S. Farnham-Diggory (Ed.), *Information processing in children* (pp. 144–175). New York: Academic.

Klahr, D., & Wallace, J. G. (1973). The role of quantification operators in the development of conservation of quantity. *Cognitive Psychology, 4,* 301–327.

Klahr, D., & Wallace, J. G. (1976). *Cognitive development: An information processing view.* Hillsdale, NJ: Erlbaum.

Kolers, P. A., & Smythe, W. E. (1984). Symbol manipulation: Alternatives to the computational view of mind. *Journal of Verbal Learning and Verbal Behavior, 23,* 289–314.

Kuhn, T. S. (1962). *The structure of scientific revolutions.* Chicago: University of Chicago Press.

Langley, P. (1979). Rediscovering physics with BACON.3. *Proceedings of the Sixth International Joint Conference on Artificial Intelligence,* 505–507.
Langley, P. (1982). Language acquisition through error recovery. *Cognition and Brain Theory, 5,* 211–255.
Langley, P. (1983). Exploring the space of cognitive architectures. *Behavior Research Methods and Instrumentation, 15,* 289–299.
Langley, P., & Simon, H. A. (1981). The central role of learning in cognition. In J. R. Anderson (Ed.), *Cognitive skills and their acquisition* (pp. 361–380). Hillsdale, NJ: Erlbaum.
Lehman, R. S. (1977). *Computer simulation and modeling: An introduction.* Hillsdale, NJ: Erlbaum.
Lenat, D. B. (1977). Automated theory formation in mathematics. *Proceedings on the Fifth International Joint Conference on Artificial Intelligence,* 833–842.
Lewin, K. (1931). The conflict between Aristotelian and Galilean modes of thought in contemporary psychology. *Journal of General Psychology, 5,* 141–177.
Mandler, G. (1984). Cohabitation in cognitive sciences. In W. Kintsch, J. R. Miller, & P. G. Polson (Eds.), *Methods and tactics in cognitive science* (pp. 305–315). Hillsdale, NJ: Erlbaum.
Mandler, G. (1985). *Cognitive psychology: An essay in cognitive science.* Hillsdale, NJ: Erlbaum.
Meehl, P. E. (1967). Theory testing in psychology and physics: A methodological paradox. *Philosophy of Science, 34,* 103–115.
Meehl, P. E. (1978). Theoretical risks and tabular asterisks: Sir Karl, Sir Ronald, and the slow progress of soft psychology. *Journal of Consulting and Clinical Psychology, 46,* 806–834.
Miller, L. (1978). Has AI contributed to our understanding of the human mind? A critique of the arguments for and against. *Cognitive Science, 2,* 111–128.
Naylor, T. H., Balintfy, J. L., Burdick, D. S., & Chu, K. (1966). *Computer simulation techniques.* New York: Wiley.
Neches, R. (1982). Simulation systems for cognitive psychology. *Behavior Research Methods and Instrumentation, 14,* 77–91.
Neisser, U. (1976). General, academic, and artificial intelligence. In L. B. Resnick (Ed.), *The nature of intelligence* (pp. 135–144). Hillsdale, NJ: Erlbaum.
Newell, A. (1973). Production systems: Models of control structures. In W. G. Chase (Ed.), *Visual information processing* (pp. 463–526). New York: Academic.
Newell, A., & Simon, H. A. (1963). GPS, a program that simulates human thought. In E. A. Feigenbaum & J. Feldman (Eds.), *Computers and thought* (pp. 279–293). New York: McGraw-Hill.
Newell, A., & Simon, H. A. (1972). *Human problem solving.* Englewood Cliffs, NJ: Prentice-Hall.
Norman, D. A., Rumelhart, D. E., & the LRN Research Group (1975). *Explorations in cognition.* San Francisco: Freeman.
Popper, K. R. (1959). *The logic of scientific discovery.* New York: Basic Books.
Pylyshyn, Z. W. (1978a). Computational models and empirical constraints. *The Behavioral and Brain Sciences, 1,* 93–99.
Pylyshyn, Z. W. (1978b). The A. I. debate: Generality, goals, and methodological parochialism. *The Behavioral and Brain Sciences, 1,* 121–127.
Rabinowitz, F. M., Grant, M. J., & Dingley, H. L. (1984). Fit: An iterative

parameter-estimation function in LISP. *Behavior Research Methods, Instruments, and Computers, 16,* 307–314.
Resnick, L. B., & Neches, R. (1984). Factors affecting individual differences in learning ability. In R. J. Sternberg (Ed.), *Advances in the psychology of human intelligence* (Vol. 2, pp. 275–324). Hillsdale, NJ: Erlbaum.
Riley, C. A., & Trabasso, T. (1974). Comparatives, logical structures, and encoding in a transitive inference task. *Journal of Experimental Child Psychology, 17,* 187–203.
Riley, M. S., Greeno, J. G., & Heller, J. I. (1983). Development of children's problem-solving ability in arithmetic. In H. P. Ginsburg (Ed.), *The development of mathematical thinking* (pp. 153–200). New York: Academic.
Rosenthal, R. (1979). The "file drawer problem" and tolerance for null results. *Psychological Bulletin, 86,* 638–641.
Rumelhart, D. E., & Norman, D. A. (1978). Accretion, tuning, and restructuring: Three modes of learning. In J. W. Cotton & R. Klatzky (Eds.), *Semantic factors in cognition* (pp. 37–53). Hillsdale, NJ: Erlbaum.
Rumelhart, D. E., & Ortony, A. (1977). The representation of knowledge in memory. In R. C. Anderson, R. J. Spiro, & W. E. Montague (Eds.), *Schooling and the acquisition of knowledge.* Hillsdale, NJ: Erlbaum.
Sage, S., & Langley, P. (1983). Modeling cognitive development on the balance scale task. *International Joint Conference on Artificial Intelligence, 7,* 94–96.
Samuel, A. L. (1963). Some studies in machine learning using the game of checkers. In E. A. Feigenbaum & J. Feldman (Eds.), *Computers and thought* (pp. 71–105). New York: McGraw-Hill.
Serlin, R. C., & Lapsley, D. K. (1985). Rationality in psychological research: The good-enough principle. *American Psychologist, 40,* 73–83.
Siegler, R. S. (1976). Three aspects of cognitive development. *Cognitive Psychology, 8,* 481–520.
Siegler, R. S. (1983). Information processing approaches to development. In P. H. Mussen & W. Kessen (Eds.), *Handbook of child psychology: History, theory and methods* (Vol. 1, pp. 129–211). New York: Wiley.
Simon, H. A. (1962). An information processing theory of intellectual development. In W. Kessen & C. Kuhlman (Eds.), Thought in the young child. *Monographs of the Society for Research in Child Development, 27* (2, Serial No. 83), 150–162.
Simon, H. A. (1979). Information processing models of cognition. *Annual Review of Psychology, 30,* 363–396.
Simon, H. A., & Feigenbaum, E. A. (1964). An information processing theory of some effects of similarity, familiarization, and meaningfulness in verbal learning. *Journal of Verbal Learning and Verbal Behavior, 3,* 385–396.
Steele, G. L., Jr. (1984). *Common LISP: The language.* Billerica, MA: Digital Press.
Sternberg, S. (1963). Stochastic learning theory. In R. D. Luce, R. R. Bush, & E. Galanter (Eds.), *Handbook of mathematical psychology* (pp. 1–120). New York: Wiley.
Taylor, S. E., & Crocker, J. (1981). Schematic bases of social information processing. In E. T. Higgins, C. P. Herman, & M. P. Zanna (Eds.), *Social cognition: The Ontario symposium* (pp. 89–134). Hillsdale, NJ: Erlbaum.
Turing, A. M. (1950). Computing machinery and intelligence. *Mind, 59,* 433–460.

van Dijk, T. A., & Kintsch, W. (1983). *Strategies of discourse comprehension.* New York: Academic.

VanLehn, K. (1983). On the representation of procedures in repair theory. In H. P. Ginsburg (Ed.), *The development of mathematical thinking* (pp. 201–253). New York: Academic.

Wallace, J. G. (1982). An information processing viewpoint on nonmonotone assessment of monotone development. In S. Strauss (Ed.), *U-shaped behavioral growth* (pp. 87–99). New York: Academic.

Waterman, D. A. (1975). Adaptive production systems. *Proceedings of the Fourth International Joint Conference on Artificial Intelligence,* 296–303.

Wickens, T. D. (1982). *Models for behavior: Stochastic processes in psychology.* San Francisco: Freeman.

Williams, J. D. (1971). *Teaching techniques in primary maths.* Windsor: National Foundation for Educational Research in England and Wales.

Windelband, W. (1904). *Geschitchte und Naturwissenschaft* (3d ed.).

Winston, P. H., & Horn, B. K. P. (1981). *LISP.* Reading, MA: Addison-Wesley.

Young, R. M., & O'Shea, T. (1981). Errors in children's subtraction. *Cognitive Science, 5,* 153–177.

9. Children's Knowledge of Simple Arithmetic: A Developmental Model and Simulation

Mark H. Ashcraft

This chapter is about children's mental arithmetic, the knowledge that is acquired across the school years, the early representation of that knowledge in memory, and the evolution of the mental representation and processes across childhood. The largest portion of the chapter is devoted to a model of children's knowledge and performance in a simple addition task. I propose that knowledge in the domain of arithmetic is, in principle, similar to other long-term memory knowledge, both in its representational format and in the processes used to access the knowledge. The computer simulation based on the model successfully predicts the major empirical effects found in the literature and generates new predictions about the nature of memory retrieval across the developmental span.

For the sake of clarity, I do not segregate the brief review of the literature from my description of the model. Instead, I describe the empirical work in a nearly chronological order, weaving into this review the essential elements that form the model and the simulation. By "recapitulating ontogeny" in this fashion, I hope to portray the structure and functioning of the model in such a way that its evolution from an early set of speculations to the current, articulated simulation is clear, reasonable, and compelling. The literature review is highly selective and limited, for the most part, to my own work; more inclusive reviews (see Ashcraft, 1982; Resnick & Ford, 1981) are available elsewhere. I divide this review into five sections: early studies on the problem size effect, the network representation and spreading activation hypotheses, developmental effects in declarative and procedural knowledge, a formal presentation of the simulation model of mental arithmetic development, and a brief discussion of more general issues related to the computer simulation approach.

Prior to the review, it seems appropriate to describe the purpose of generating this model and simulation. The model is not a comprehensive theory of human information processing or its development; I have considered only numerical and arithmetic knowledge. Nor is it a model of *problem solving* in the classical sense of that term. The model is pertinent to the arithmetic knowledge used in arithmetic word problems, but not to the language or problem-solving domains involved (see Kintsch & Greeno, 1985, for instance). Instead, the model is a theory of the development of simple arithmetic performance. My goal has been to characterize the knowledge that children possess at various stages of their formal education in arithmetic and to explore the processes they use to access that knowledge. The simulation is a particular instantiation of the model. It implements the important hypotheses of the model in the formalism of a computer program, and it provides a means of assessing those hypotheses and, by extension, the adequacy of the model.

The tradition into which this work falls is the information processing tradition of cognitive psychology as applied to child development. My own research has relied very heavily on the chronometric approach to mental processing (e.g., Posner, 1978). Not surprisingly, then, the predictions of greatest interest in the simulation model involve latency differences among conditions and across ages. Furthermore, the model concerns the underlying mental representation of numerical knowledge, in the tradition of semantic long-term memory models (e.g., Anderson & Bower, 1973; Collins & Quillian, 1972; Schank & Abelson, 1977). Finally, both the model and the simulation are developmental. Knowledge structures and processes available at different ages are described, and of course predictions for different ages are generated. The central developmental process in the model and simulation is a reasonable and familiar psychological construct, learning.

To close this introduction, my goal is to develop a model of children's arithmetic knowledge, tracking from first grade through the college level the several mental processes used to access and apply this knowledge. The simulation model is designed to solve addition problems in a developmentally correct fashion, predicting various reaction time, strategy, and error effects. An equally important goal in developing the simulation is to generate quantitative predictions that can be tested empirically. At a general level, the model is a verbal statement of process and structure, a framework for understanding children's mental arithmetic development. The computer simulation is a functioning instantiation of the model that predicts not only results reported in the literature but also patterns of performance not yet tested.

Early Studies on the Effect of Problem Size

I begin with an anecdote, not merely because it illustrates the occasionally positive role of happenstance in research, but also because it reveals several important pretheoretical assumptions that characterized my thinking at the beginning of this project. I stumbled upon the area of mental arithmetic research by accident, while grading final examinations. As I computed the grades, I noticed how easily I could subtract the number missed from a total of 50 on one examination, compared to the difficulty of subtracting the number missed from 75 possible on the other examination. Quite suddenly, I realized the importance of this casual observation—I was performing a purely mental task with the mundane facts of subtraction and "discovered" the obvious fact that some problems were more difficult and required more time than others. I had stumbled on a phenomenon at the heart of cognitive psychology—mental processing of symbols, coordinated sequencing of retrieval and rule application, and a rich system of facts and procedures represented in memory. Within a matter of weeks, this insight was translated into a reaction time (RT) experiment on simple addition (Ashcraft & Battaglia, 1977, 1978).

At the time of this incident (December, 1976), I was working on issues of semantic distance, typicality, and their effects on the structure of semantic representation and the processes of retrieval (e.g., Ashcraft, 1976, 1978). As I began to think through the same issues for mental arithmetic, I hypothesized initially that simple arithmetic facts must serve an analogous function to the conceptual entries or nodes in semantic memory, the basic information stored in the system from which more complex relationships are derived. Because it was quite natural to think of semantic knowledge as represented in a network structure (e.g., Collins & Loftus, 1975), I hypothesized the same kind of representation in mental arithmetic. Evidence at the time pointed to the importance of semantic distance or relatedness as the basic metric of semantic memory (e.g., Glass, Holyoak, & O'Dell, 1974; Kintsch, 1974), so I assumed there must be some analogous metric in the mental representation of arithmetic as well. Finally, the fundamental mechanism by which semantic knowledge was accessed was claimed to be a process of spreading activation, where activation from separate sources may intersect during a search, allowing retrieval of the information stored at that intersection (e.g., Anderson & Bower, 1973; Collins & Quillian, 1972; Norman & Rumelhart, 1975). So, at the outset, three related theoretical assumptions dominated my speculations about mental arithmetic: first, the simple arithmetic facts are stored in a memory network; second, this network is dimensioned in some fashion analogous to the semantic distance or relatedness effect; third, the process of spreading activation is the basic mechanism of memory retrieval from the network.

In the first studies on mental addition (Ashcraft & Battaglia, 1978), we speculated about long-term memory storage of the simple addition facts. This speculation was based largely on one empirical effect observed in that first research, the increase in RT as a problem increases in size (see Figure 9.1). The fundamental result is termed the *problem-size effect,* a robust effect in every study of arithmetic processing. In most important respects, I speculated, this effect is entirely analogous to the semantic distance effect: Mental distance between concepts is represented in the

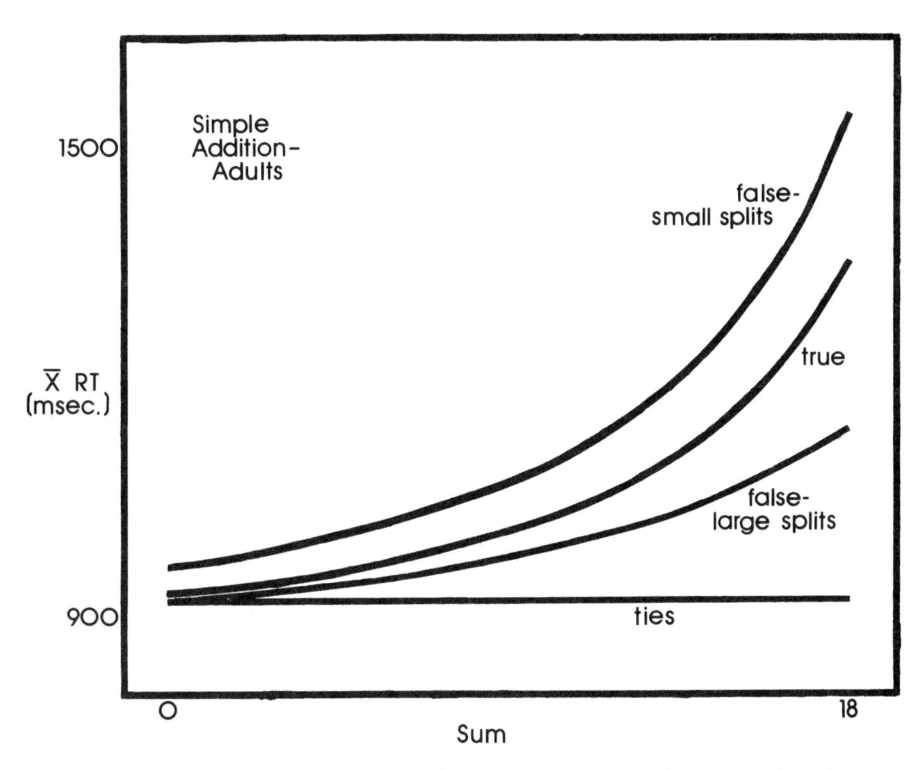

FIGURE 9.1. Idealized problem-size effect for the basic addition facts for adults.

memory structure, and this distance determines retrieval speed through the structure. The effect can be likened to the word frequency or typicality effects, in which more frequent or typical items can be judged more rapidly in a variety of situations (e.g., Ashcraft, 1978; Rosch, 1975; Whaley, 1978). Yet in a way, the effect is counterintuitive. Why should adults require longer for the problem 7 + 6 than they do for the problem 4 + 3? Would not years of experience with simple addition facts have yielded a leveling effect, such that they are all of equal difficulty?

As a point of minor historical interest, the empirical result we reported for the problem-size effect involved a specific regression analysis predictor variable termed *correct sum squared.* Because a scatter plot of the data yielded a nonlinear relationship between problem sum and RT, an exponential version of the sum was computed and found to be a superior predictor. The dominant model of addition performance at that time, the Groen and Parkman (1972) counting model, predicted a strictly linear problem-size effect. Thus, our exponential factor disconfirmed a major prediction of this counting model. We argued that the exponential effect implicated retrieval as the primary mental process used by adults. Thus, "correct sum squared may be interpreted as an index of search time here. . . . Such an interpretation suggests that RT performance on these problems reflects retrieval of stored information, with retrieval time increasing as a function of the magnitude of the problem. Aside from the retrieval time interpretation of the correct sum squared, no special significance of the squared term, as oposed to some other power greater than 1.0, is intended" (Ashcraft & Battaglia, 1978, p. 532). Critics have routinely ignored the notion that the sum squared was an *index* of something, search time as a function of problem difficulty, and instead have tried to relate the squaring directly to some mental mechanism. One reviewer, for example, demanded to know how a subject could possibly be thought to find the answer to a problem by first having to compute the square of that answer.

Such concerns miss the point. In the left panel of Figure 9.2, adults' RTs are plotted for the simple addition problems 0 + 0 up through 9 + 9, the "basic addition facts." Points that are circled are tie problems, such as 2 + 2; points with flanking dashes are "0 addend" problems, such as 5 + 0. Above the graph is the empirical regression equation for these data (Ashcraft & Stazyk, 1981, experiment 1): RT is composed of both an intercept, attributed to encoding, decision, and response execution times (see Ashcraft, 1982, for a discussion of the additive-factors logic in the model), and a weighted contribution of the correct sum squared. The curved function in the left portion of the figure is the plotted regression equation.

In the right panel of Figure 9.2 is a scatter plot of corresponding data, generated by the computer simulation. At the heart of the model, and the simulation, is the notion of problem difficulty. As we became more convinced that problem difficulty was the basic metric embedded in the memory structure, we abandoned the sum-squared predictor in favor of a normative set of difficulty ratings. Adults rated each problem's difficulty on a scale from 1 to 9, and these ratings were transformed to what I will call *strength values*. Depicted in the right panel of Figure 9.2 is the set of predicted data points when these strength values are used as the index of retrieval time in the simulation. Plotted through the simulated points is the same empirical function that appears on the left. By inspection alone, predicting performance based on strength values of the individual problems appears reasonable, providing a close fit to the bulk of the data. The most systematic lack of fit obtains with the 0 addend problems, flanked by dashes. I return to this deviation from the predicted values later, because it is an important indicator of rule-based performance.

The prediction of the problem-size effect by means of strength values is the first important feature of the model and the computer simulation. Each basic addition problem is assumed to be stored in a memory representation that, for purposes of illustration, may be thought of as a printed addition table. Digits 0 through 9 are both the column headings and the row headings in this table and are the memory nodes where the spreading-

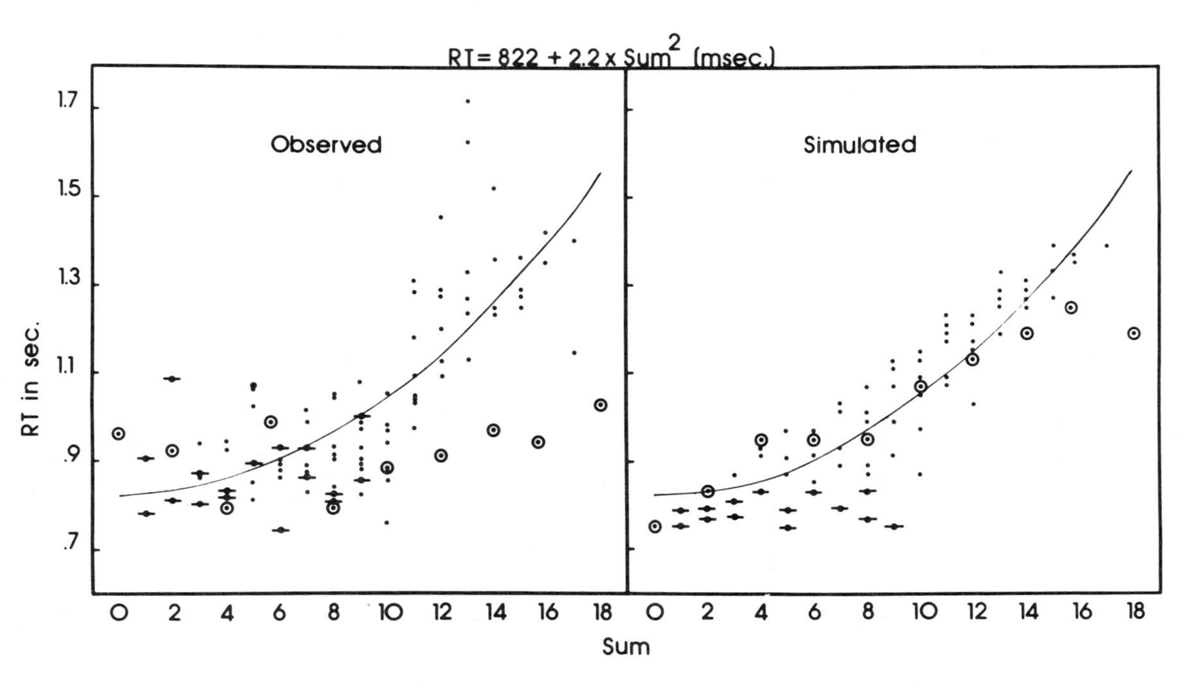

FIGURE 9.2. Observed and simulated problem-size effect for addition for adults.

activation search originates. These nodes are referred to as *parent nodes*. Each of the 100 intersection nodes in this 10×10 table represents the answer to a problem. These are termed *family members,* where each parent node has connecting pathways down the column or across the row to 10 such family members. Each of these 100 nodes has a particular strength value associated with it; at present, assume these strength values to be the adult ratings just described. During processing, a stimulus such as $4 + 3$ is presented to the simulation. After encoding, the search phase of processing begins. Parent nodes 4 and 3 are activated by the encoded representation of the problem, and they begin to spread activation to their respective family members. The amount of activation accumulating at any family member is a direct function of its strength value and the frequency with which the node is a target of the activation spread. Thus, the intersection node of 7, a family member of both parent nodes 4 and 3, is activated twice, once from each parent.

A second feature of the spreading-activation process bears mention as well. Because we often test arithmetic performance with the true/false verification task, in which an answer is supplied along with the problem, it is convenient to refer to those nodes within the network that match the answer stated in a stimulus. Thus, when we test $4 + 3 = 7$ as a stimulus, the set of intersection nodes representing 7 is of interest. These nodes are referred to as *C nodes,* because in general the simulation processes problems of the form $A + B = C$ (or $A \times B = C$). Presenting an answer to a subject supplies an extra source of information that is functional during search (see Campbell, 1985; Campbell & Graham, 1985). Thus, the simulation also activates *C* nodes when an answer is presented in the stimulus. This amount of activation is less than that passed by a problem's addends, however. That is, in the true/false task, addends 4 and 3 are more important, or informative, than the possibly incorrect answer (for example, $4 + 3 = 8$; see Campbell & Graham, 1985, for evidence that retrieval is more addend-driven than answer-driven). In the simulation, this activation amount is arbitrarily set at one-half of that passed by the parent nodes.

Despite the advantage given to the answer nodes, the simulation still predicts the true/false verification task to be slower than the somewhat simpler production task in which subjects merely generate the answer to a stimulus problem. The reason is fairly straightforward. Neither subjects nor the computer simulation needs to pass through a yes/no decision stage in the production task, so the absence of decision time renders production trials faster overall (Ashcraft, 1982). Our data (Ashcraft, Fierman, & Bartolotta, 1984) indicate just this sort of main effect for production versus verification tasks, with the only exception being first graders' latencies (but cf. Campbell, 1985).

To recap, the problem-size effect—an increase in RT as problems grow larger—is the fundamental effect in this area of research, and it is the target of different theoretical mechanisms across models of arithmetic performance. It is well predicted by rated difficulty measures and in the present model is taken as evidence for an underlying difference in strength or accessibility among the stored arithmetic facts. The usual strength-speed assumption is incorporated in the model, that nodes of greater strength are more rapidly accessed during search (e.g., Anderson, 1983).

Network Representation and Spreading-Activation Hypotheses

At this point, we were convinced that adults' performance was not explainable in terms of simple counting models (Groen & Parkman, 1972). The nonlinear RT effect had been replicated in two more studies (Ashcraft & Battaglia, 1978, experiment 2; Ashcraft & Stazyk, 1981, experiment 1). Furthermore, we had tested adults with somewhat larger addition problems, such as $15 + 12 = 27$ versus 28. We found that the size of the problem in the 1s column (the $5 + 2$) was an important contributor to overall RT. This suggests, of course, that even complex arithmetic performance still requires reference to a memory representation of the basic addition facts (Ashcraft & Stazyk, 1981, experiment 2).

We advanced the specific hypothesis that adults store simple addition problems in a network representation and retrieve them by means of a spreading-activation search. At this point, evidence of a very similar nature came to our attention. Winkelman and Schmidt (1974) presented simple addition or multiplication problems with answers correct under the other operation, and they observed a significant slowing of RT. In other words, adults were slowed when they received problems such as $5 + 3 = 15$ or $7 \times 4 = 11$. Winkelman and Schmidt speculated that associations among problems in memory were responsible for this confusion effect. The presence of associations among problems or, stated more generally, interconnections among memory nodes is a hallmark assumption of network models.

Our own study of the confusion effect (Stazyk, 1980; also Stazyk, Ashcraft, & Hamann, 1982) was limited to multiplication problems, to avoid a possible weakness in the Winkelman and Schmidt report (simply that subjects might easily misperceive the operator sign, + or ×, on confusion problems, yielding spurious RT effects). We first replicated the problem-size effect for multiplication problems, and we demonstrated the incompleteness of previous regression analyses of such data (e.g., Parkman, 1972). We extended the generality of a hypothesized decision-stage mechanism by finding a similar effect to that obtained in addition: The more incorrect an answer, the more quickly subjects can reject it (see the "split" curves in Figure 9.1). For now, however, the most important effect was the confusion effect. We presented simple multiplication problems with two kinds of false answers, multiples and nonmultiples. Thus, a problem such as 7 × 4 appeared not only with its correct answer 28 but also with an incorrect answer that was a multiple of one of the problem's digits, say 24, and with an answer that was merely incorrect, say 25. The effect of such confusion answers was quite pronounced; small problems showed a significant slowing of about 75 ms, large problems showed up to a 300-ms slowing (see figure 1 in Stazyk et al., 1982). The effect was still sizable when subjects had 600 ms of advance exposure to the problem before the answer to be verified was presented.

Until this point, our evidence for the hypothesis of interrelatedness in the memory network had been extremely indirect; we had shown the inadequacy of counting approaches, had shown how the components of larger problems played a role in verification, and had obtained the basic problem-size effect in multiplication as well as addition. Yet, any one of several theoretical mechanisms could predict those patterns. As Stazyk et al. noted, however, only a memory representation with explicit connections or pathways between related problems seemed adequate to account for the obtained confusion effects. Thus, the explicit notion was proposed that simple arithmetic facts are stored in an interconnected network representation in memory (Ashcraft, 1982). Each fact was assumed to be a distinct node in the network, with access to individual nodes provided by the process of spreading activation. This scheme was advanced as the basis for Stazyk et al.'s confusion effect with the multiplication operation as well as the cross-operation effect obtained by Winkelman and Schmidt. When a stimulus is presented, related concepts in memory are activated by the encoded representation of the stimulus. Such activation, if strong enough, may affect processing in exactly the same fashion as is found in the semantic literature, i.e., facilitating responses to positives but slowing responses to negatives (e.g., Kintsch, 1974). Thus, a stimulus such as 4 × 8 = 24, when presented to the simulation, generates a confusion effect. The *C* node 24 receives considerable activation, because it is a family member of both 4 and 8 and because *C* nodes themselves are activated. The accumulated activation at that node is nearly as high as the activation at the correct *C* node 32. During the decision stage, the discrimination between these two nodes is slow, because their activation levels are so close.

Note that no extraordinary processes or assumptions need to be made for a network model to explain the confusion effect. The effect is a normal by-product of the usual spreading-activation search: Related nodes become primed and then match a stated but false answer, generating interference. An early critical test of the simulation model, then, was the following: With only the basic spreading-activation mechanism as outlined above, would the simulation predict the empirically observed confusion effect on multiples? The answer to this question was a straightfor-

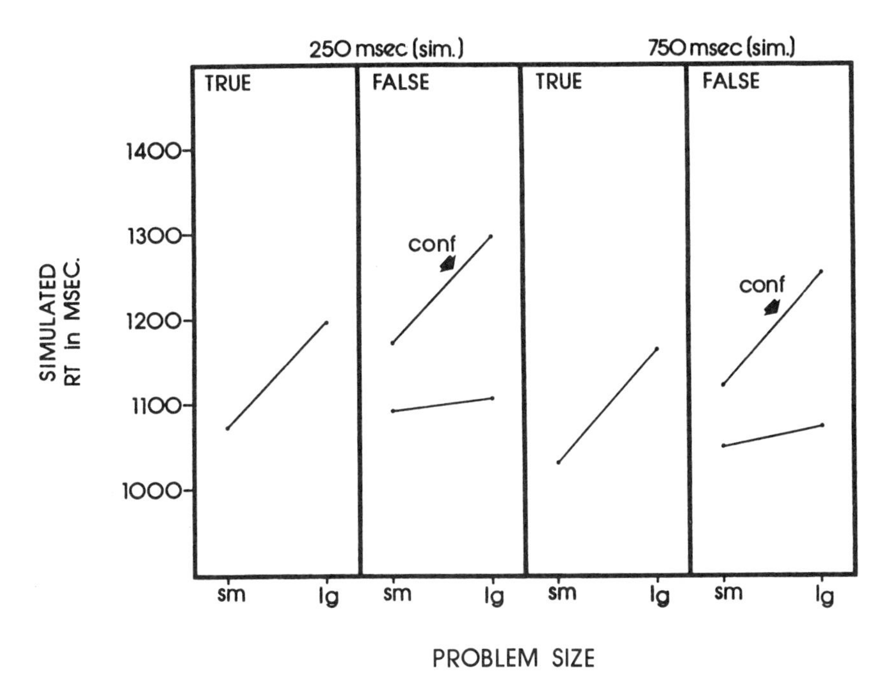

FIGURE 9.3. Predictions for confusion versus nonconfusion RTs based on the simulation.

ward yes, as illustrated in Figure 9.3. Recall from the description above that each parent node spreads activation down the connecting pathways to its family members. In the proposed structure, an answer node such as 24 is therefore a family member of several parents, specifically 3, 4, 6, and 8. A problem such as 8 × 4, consequently, not only primes the correct intersection node 32 but also primes the *C* nodes 24 along both the parent node vectors (literally, in a printed table, the 8s row and the 4s column). When the distractor answer is then presented, its corresponding nodes in the structure have received some nontrivial amount of activation. This degree of priming yields a competitionlike effect during the decision stage, slowing the process because of a related but incorrect node.

Let me reiterate an important point here: No special process was added to the simulation to generate this effect. It is generated by the normal spreading-activation search that operates on all trials. The situation is largely analogous to semantic priming. Priming of related semantic nodes is generally beneficial, supporting retrieval and context effects, but is occasionally responsible for interference. Similarly, priming of related nodes in arithmetic occasionally exerts a deleterious effect, when distractor answers in the verification task have been activated during search.

[Incidentally, largely the same kind of effect is observed in a purely production task; i.e., subjects' occasional errors in producing answers to problems such as 8 × 4 and 3 × 5 are usually multiples, or sometimes answers under another arithmetic operation, say, 24 or 8, respectively. See Campbell and Graham (1985) and Miller, Perlmutter, and Keating (1984).]

In sum, by 1982 not only had we advanced the basic notion of a network representation of arithmetic fact knowledge, but also in the Stazyk et al. confusion effect paper we had confirmed a critical prediction of that approach. The simple facts of addition and multiplication seemed to be stored in a network representation, accessible by means of a spreading-activation search. Adults' performance was well predicted by a measure of problem difficulty, interpreted as a search distance effect in the network. These effects and hypotheses were described in two papers that year (Ashcraft, 1982; Stazyk et al., 1982) and were successfully demonstrated in a simulation model the following year (Ashcraft, 1983). Since the early 1970s, the research area had shifted from a theoretical commitment to counting models to a consideration of fact retrieval as the basic process in adults' mental arithmetic.

Developmental Effects in Declarative and Procedural Knowledge

We viewed developmental investigations of mental arithmetic as particularly important from the very outset of the project, if for no other reason than the obvious educational and practical importance of arithmetic. By 1982, four separate developmental studies either had been conducted (Ashcraft & Fierman, 1982; Fierman, 1980, reported in Ashcraft et al., 1984; Hamann, 1981, reported in Hamann & Ashcraft, 1985) or were in progress (see Ashcraft et al., 1984, experiment 2).

A fundamental aim was to correct what we viewed as an imbalance in the empirical literature. That is, there had been extensive investigations into early number knowledge, such as the Gelman and Gallistel (1978) work on counting (also Ginsburg, 1977), and several studies of simple addition performance from first through third grades (e.g., Svenson, 1975; see Ashcraft, 1982, for a review). In contrast, there were no studies, to our knowledge, that involved children older than about the third grade. There was a theoretical lapse as well: In essence, theory in the area had not progressed beyond the simple counting model approaches. Our research with adults showed the inadequacy of counting as an explanation of adult performance and implied, of course, that children must shift at some point from the early counting processes to more mature retrieval processes.

Our first developmental study indicated that this shift is noticeable as early as the third grade and is largely accomplished by the end of fourth grade (Ashcraft & Fierman, 1982). Children in later grades were subsequently found to be faster overall, of course, (e.g., Fierman, 1980; Hamann & Ashcraft, 1985), but their data still demonstrated the same basic processes that we had identified for adults. We obtained evidence of counting-based performance at the first-grade level, relatively slow retrieval at the third- and fourth-grade levels, and a continued speeding of retrieval processes beyond that (Hamann, 1981).

Two important developmental issues emerged from these studies: first, the issue of the growth of strength values in the proposed network representations and, second, the issue of nonretrieval processing. These issues correspond directly to two categories of knowledge in the model I proposed—declarative knowledge in the network representation and procedural knowledge of "how to do arithmetic" (Ashcraft, 1982). Both categories are present in the simulation model. The first is quite explicit in the network strength values and the predictions of performance as discussed above. The second, procedural knowledge, is represented in only an abbreviated fashion in the simulation. Predictions from the simulation for certain classes of experimental conditions, for instance, young children working on large problems, show an interplay of the two knowledge sources and suggest a particular temporal relationship between the two. I describe the simulation and its incorporation of these two knowledge sources in some detail, because this involves the developmental heart of the model. I then discuss briefly the other procedural knowledge assumed by the model but not present in the simulation.

Declarative Knowledge and Associative Strength

When we deal with the development of the declarative knowledge store, the network representation of arithmetic facts, we confront a basic question of learning and acquisition. At what point can a child be said to have stored an arithmetic fact in memory at some useful level of strength? The earlier arithmetic literature suggested that first graders follow a "counting on" strategy when they add, incrementing the larger number in a problem by 1s in a 4–5, 6, 7 fashion for the problem 4 + 3 (Groen & Parkman, 1972; Svenson, 1975). This mental counting approach is an entirely reconstructive process; that is, children need only have the counting string stored in memory, along with procedures for keeping track of the incrementing process. The major exception to this strategy, even as early as first grade, involves performance with tie problems such as 2 + 2 or 6 + 6. Even first graders show no problem-size effect on tie problems, demonstrating an essentially flat RT profile. The strong suggestion here was that ties have been "memorized" and therefore need only some constant amount of time for their retrieval (Groen & Parkman, 1972). No compelling reason was offered to suggest why first graders were able to memorize tie problems but needed an entirely different and reconstructive method for nontie problems.

If ties were already memorized by the end of first grade, then it seemed quite natural to suppose that other simple addition problems might also be memorized that early. One attempt we made to evaluate this possibility (Ashcraft et al., 1984) involved a specific examination of mental counting speed. We reasoned that children's mental counting speed should correspond to their speed of adding simple numbers, if they were performing addition by a reconstructive counting process. Alternately, if children's addition involves a significant component of retrieval, then their rates of counting and adding should differ. Our results revealed no difference for first graders: Their mental counting rate was about 1000 ms per increment, not appreciably different from their rate of addition under the hypotheses of Groen & Parkman's (1972) min model (for minimum addend, the smaller number being added). In contrast, the second graders' counting rate was considerably slower than their rate of addition. Furthermore, not only had their counting processes become faster, but also their performance to the "count by 5s" condition revealed a strong influence of memorized information: They could count by 5s on the normal 5s sequence much more rapidly than off the usual sequence.[1] The mismatch between rates of counting and addition and the involvement of memorization in the second graders' counting suggested strongly that retrieval from memory was an important component of early addition performance (see Ashcraft et al., 1984; Siegler & Shrager, 1984).

A second attempt to assess the role of memory retrieval among first graders was even more definitive. Hamann and Ashcraft (1985; also Hamann, 1981) showed first graders a set of simple addition problems in the standard RT task and then showed the problems again in a postexperimental interview. First graders, as well as fourth graders, revealed a particularly interesting pattern of spoken responses to the interview problems. To a problem such as 4 + 3, they often responded that they had counted out the answer; but to a problem such as 14 + 13, they responded, "Well, 4 + 3 = 7, and then . . . " In other words, even at the first-grade level there was evidence of memory retrieval when the problem was more than minimally taxing.

I wish to discuss one more body of evidence concerning early memory retrieval. Siegler and Shrager (1984) described the incidence of different problem-solving strategies among a sample of kindergarten children. Based on the results of a "speeded guess" procedure, they estimated the degree to which very simple addition problems were already represented in memory for these children. For problems no larger than 5 + 5, associative strengths between pairs of addends and their correct sums were appreciable, especially for $N + 1$ and tie problems. Siegler and Shrager proceeded to integrate these strength values into an elegant simulation of children's early strategy choice under simple addition. Based on the strengths, the Siegler and Shrager model makes successful predictions concerning children's performance on addition problems; higher levels of strength generally predict retrieval performance and lower error percentages, whereas lower levels of strength generally predict unsuccessful retrieval, which is then followed by some overt strategy such as counting aloud or counting on fingers. A central notion in the model is the assumption that retrieval is the most basic strategy of all, that it predates other strategies such as counting developmentally, and that it precedes them during arithmetic processing.

For our purposes, the source of the Siegler and Shrager strength values is critical. These authors presented compelling evidence about the growth of these strength values. In brief, three sources of association strengths were identified: the influence of the child's own experience with counting and sums, the positive and negative effects of counting string associations, and the frequency with which parents present problems to their children.

In my simulation, I have taken the Siegler and Shrager strength values for correct associations as the memory strength values for a hypothetical child of kindergarten age.[2] These values are then modified across development according to a simple rule, which for ease of presentation is described in two parts. The first part of this rule is that during each simulated year, nodes are strengthened in an incremental fashion. That is, each strength value in the network is increased according to the formula $\Delta s = g(100 - s)$. Each simulated year sees an increment in memory strength Δs equal to a fixed proportion g of the difference between asymptote and current strength. The fixed proportion g is the growth rate, estimated from Fierman's (1980) first-grade and college data to be .20. This equation is, of course, no more than a restatement of the incremental learning theory (e.g., Estes, 1964).

The second part of the rule seems less intuitively obvious but is supported by data (Hamann, 1983; see also Hamann & Ashcraft, in press). Each increment in strength value is weighted according to the problem's frequency of presentation, with more frequent problems receiving a higher weight. In other words, the full equation for strength values is $\Delta s_{ij} = gf_{ij}(100 - s_{ij})$, where f_{ij} is a frequency weight that varies for each problem, expressed as a proportion of the maximum observed frequency. This weighting involves a larger increment in strength for small problems but then a diminishing increment in strength as the problems get larger. Hamann's data in support of this part of the rule are remarkably straightforward. She tabulated the frequency of presentation of the 100 addition facts in a sample of 12 texts, 3 each for kindergarten through third grade. She found an overwhelming tendency to present smaller problems more frequently, such that the larger problems never achieve the frequency of smaller problems. The frequency distribution across addend sizes, with all 4 years combined (see Figure 9.4), shows a low point (150 presenta-

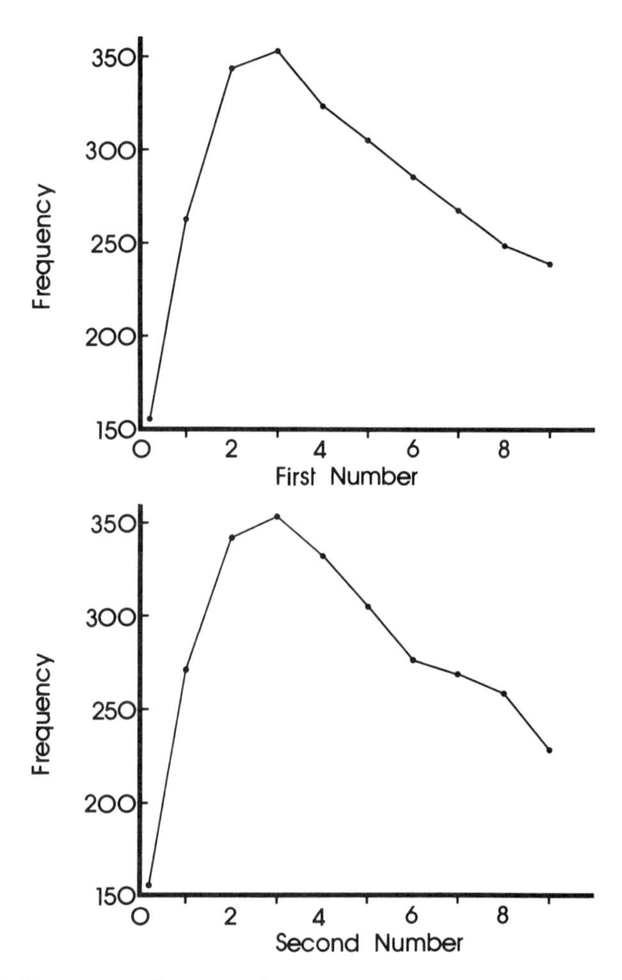

FIGURE 9.4. Frequency of presentation of basic addition facts by first and second number, accumulated across grades K to 3 (after Hamann, 1983).

tions) for problems with 0s as addends, a peak (350 presentations) for an addend of 3, and a dwindling (225 presentations) for an addend of 9.

The consequence of this developmental rule in the simulation is a memory representation with great diversity in the individual nodes' strength values. In general, strength values are a weighted function of age and problem size, that is, of the growth rate g and frequencies of presentation f_{ij}. One indication of the adequacy of this developmental growth function is presented in Figure 9.5, a scatter plot of rated difficulty values, based on adult norms, versus the values generated in the simulation. To simulate growth from kindergarten to college (grade 13), the strength value equation was applied repeatedly to the initial kindergarten strength value matrix, one repetition per simulated year. The correlation between the

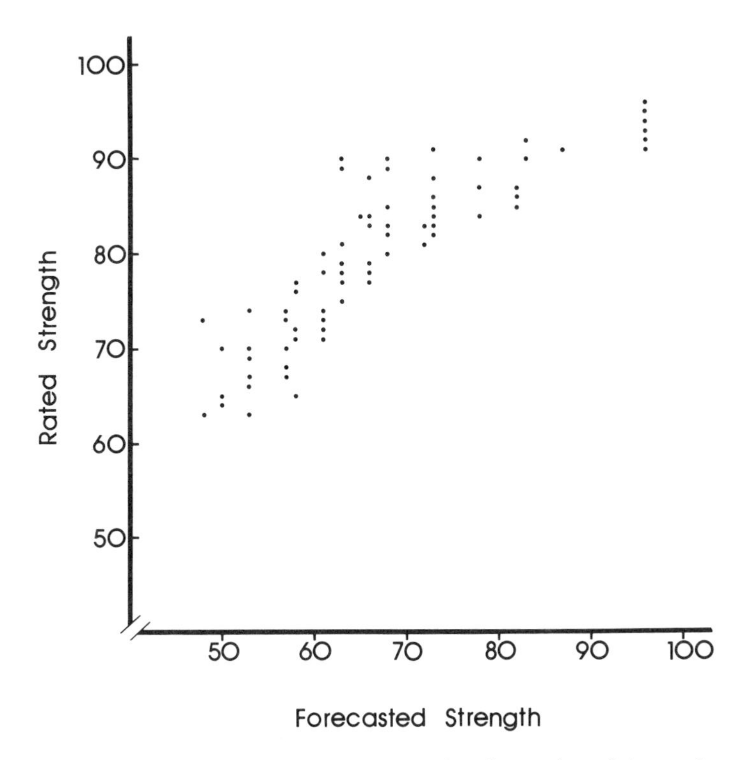

FIGURE 9.5. Scatter plot of forecasted strength values x by adult rated strength values y.

normative and forecasted measures is .901. Figure 9.6 shows the processing consequences of this developmental growth function, observed RTs to small and large problems (one- and two-digit sums, respectively) on the left (from Hamann & Ashcraft, 1985) and simulated RTs to the same problems on the right. Although the growth function here is only an approximation, it does model a great deal of the developmental change that occurs across these ages.[3] Table 9.1 presents the relevant correlations among empirical RTs, forecasted strength values, and empirical predictors.

Procedural Knowledge and Nonretrieval Processing

Although both our research and the important paper by Siegler and Shrager indicate a greater reliance on memory retrieval than had previously been proposed, it is nonetheless certain that much of a young child's performance is due to processes other than fact retrieval. Indeed, clear instances of processing have been documented in which retrieval is not involved. In general, I refer to this class of solution methods as *procedures* and their representation in memory as *procedural knowledge*. I have suggested that, in addition to the stored facts, children acquire a

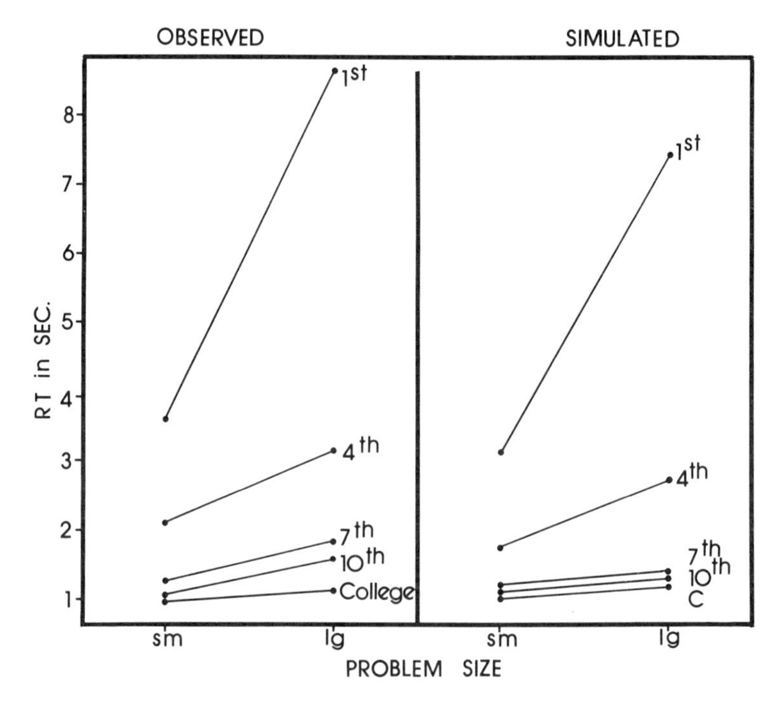

FIGURE 9.6. Observed and simulated problem-size effects across grades (observed points from Hamann & Ashcraft, 1985).

variety of rules, algorithms, heuristics, and other strategies for doing arithmetic (Ashcraft, 1982). These procedures often provide a completely separate method of obtaining the answer to a simple arithmetic problem (e.g., counting on). I have argued further that, on any trial, overall RT will be a function of the faster of the two kinds of performance. That is, if a problem is represented with sufficiently high strength, it will be retrieved

TABLE 9.1. Correlations between RT and various predictors.

Grade	Min	Wheeler	Forecasted strength
1	.774	.804	−.747
4	.379	.610	−.557
7	.413	.674	−.528
10	.468	.688	−.540
College	.326	.523	−.616

Note: College data are from Ashcraft et al. (1984), and other data are from Hamann and Ashcraft (1985). The Min predictor is the smaller of two numbers being added (Groen & Parkman, 1972). The Wheeler predictor is a measure of difficulty based on mastery during acquisition (Wheeler, 1939; see Hamann & Ashcraft, 1985, in press). The forecasted strength variable is the measure of accessibility or strength as generated by the simulation.

successfully from the network representation. If a problem's strength is too low or if it is not represented at all, then a procedural solution will prevail. I have hypothesized that procedural solutions will be slower than retrieval for any arbitrarily selected addition fact (Ashcraft, 1982; but cf. Baroody, 1983, 1984). Siegler and Shrager's (1984) results seem to confirm this assumption rather directly. Mean retrieval time in their data was 4s, whereas mean latency under the counting strategies ranged from 7 to 13s.

The procedural knowledge component I proposed (Ashcraft, 1982) contains a variety of methods for reconstructing an answer. Nonetheless, I have included only one major reconstructive procedure in the simulation, the counting-on procedure. This procedure is by far the most documented of all strategies for doing addition, and it is the one for which definite temporal parameters are known. In the simulation, there is a call to the search process for all trials (and for all ages). If the initial spread of activation through the network does not activate any node above threshold, then the search procedure is terminated and procedural knowledge governs the processing. Then the simulation attempts to solve the problem by using its knowledge of counting principles, and it predicts considerably longer latencies owing to the slowness of young children's mental counting processes. In the simulation, counting solutions are the norm for problems larger than 1 + 1 at the first-grade level; 0 addend problems and ties up to 3 + 3 are performed by retrieval. The proportion of trials completed via counting decreases steadily, until only one problem is solved by counting at the simulated fourth-grade level (8 + 9 = 17). This developmental progression from counting to retrieval, hypothesized and documented in earlier studies (e.g., Ashcraft & Fierman, 1982), is produced by the simulation according to a simple principle—strength of the problem node in memory. When a problem has insufficient strength to achieve threshold, its solution requires procedural knowledge. As the problem node grows in strength, it exceeds threshold during search and is consequently accessible to the search and retrieval process.

A detail or two about the involvement of procedural knowledge are in order. As currently implemented, the simulation does not add aborted search time to the latency estimate for counting. Instead, the simulation predicts parallel operation of the declarative and procedural components, simultaneous retrieval attempt and counting-on. This is a minor but definite difference between my approach and that of Siegler and Shrager. They interpret their data as suggesting a sequential operation of aborted search and then counting. It is not clear that existing data are precise enough to discriminate between the sequential and parallel processing alternatives.

The simulation is incomplete in its declarative and procedural knowledge components in at least one other sense. The adult model predicts performance to either addition or multiplication problems; these are merely two interrelated bodies of knowledge in the networks. We have only recently collected developmental data on multiplication (Koshmider, 1986; but cf. Campbell & Graham, 1985), and so we have little basis for specifying initial strength values for multiplication facts. Furthermore, we have no clear idea at all as to the kinds of procedural strategies children might use for multiplication. An inference from our counting studies (Ashcraft et al., 1984) is that multiplication is not performed via a counting strategy among adults, because the counting rates were much too slow in comparison to adult multiplication rates. It remains to be seen whether counting is a viable explanation for multiplication at elementary school levels. At present in the simulation, the procedural route simply fails when a multiplication problem is presented.

Let me consider one loose thread here concerning procedural knowledge. I have argued that both addition and multiplication problems that contain a zero are "special cases" (Ashcraft, 1983). The most compelling evidence for this conclusion was presented by Stazyk et al. (1982), where zero problems were among the slowest and most error-prone of all the basic multiplication facts (but this slowess may be limited to the verification task; see Miller et al., 1984). One of our adult subjects even persisted through the session in believing that problems such as $7 \times 0 = 0$ were incorrect. We suggested that these problems are generally learned by a taught rule, such as "anything times zero is zero," rather than by the extensive practice devoted to other problems. As a consequence, these entries in the network are rather weak (Stazyk et al., 1982). In the simulation, I have included zero problems in the networks and have used the generally high association values for these problems as if they were comparable to values for other problems. Through this scheme, predicted performance to these problems is too fast (Figure 9.2). Hamann's (1983) analysis of textbooks confirms our suspicion: Zero problems are the lowest in frequency of presentation. They are rated high in accessibility (low in difficulty), undoubtedly because of the accessibility of the taught rule, but they are performed via procedural knowledge rather than network retrieval. Treating the zero problems the same as all other problems in the simulation yields a substantial inaccuracy in prediction for these problems. In combination with Hamann's frequency data, this confirms the need for procedural knowledge in performance and indirectly supports the learning strength hypothesis in the model.

In summary, the model contains two distinct sources of arithmetic knowledge—a declarative structure that represents known facts in a network of interrelated nodes and a procedural knowledge component that contains various rules and other reconstructive procedures. A relatively straightforward developmental increase in the strength of declarative knowledge is implemented in the simulation, along the lines suggested by incremental learning models, with the important qualification that a child's lesser experience with larger problems yields an overall advantage for small versus large problems. A failed attempt at retrieval results in reliance on procedural knowledge for a reconstructive solution to the problem, with consequent increases in latency. In practice, such reconstructive solutions based on simple counting drop out completely after the fourth grade in runs of the simulation. At younger ages, however, counting is a prominent feature of predicted performance. This involvement of counting exaggerates the slope of the problem-size effect, both in the simulation and in the obtained data, because counting is a slower process than retrieval.

Simulation Model of Mental Arithmetic Development

Having presented various aspects of the model and simulation in piecemeal fashion, I now describe the model and simulation more formally, highlighting the critical assumptions and the consequences of those assumptions. In general, I include specific details about the simulation program only where ambiguity might otherwise result. Appendix 9A contains a pseudocode summary of the search and decision stage processes and the developmental rule for forecasting strength values. A flowchart summary of the processing activity is presented at the close of this section.

The model and the computer simulation rest on three critical and interrelated assumptions. First, the basic facts of addition and multiplication (0 + 0 and 0 × 0 through 9 + 9 and 9 × 9) are stored in long-term memory as a network of interconnected nodes. Access to the network is gained by means of parent nodes, digits 0 through 9, linked by directed pathways to nodes that represent answers; for convenience, the set of nodes linked to a parent is referred to as that parent's *family members,* e.g., the 4 + family or the + 3 family. Each directed pathway from a parent to a family member has a particular strength value s_{ij} associated with it, where i is the index for the first addend or parent and j for the second. Access or retrieval time for any node is a function of the strength value for the corresponding pathways (*strength of pathways* is the same concept as *strength of nodes*). For purposes of illustration, this network structure is isomorphic with a printed table of addition or multiplication facts, where each intersection of row i and column j contains two values, the correct answer and the strength value for the pathway leading to that answer. The important qualification here is that a square printed table implies an equidistant node structure, whereas the present structure is "distorted" from true square by the strength or distance values s_{ij}.

Second, it is assumed that the basic facts of addition and multiplication are acquired and consequently stored in this memory representation as a function of frequency and practice. In the model, strength values reflect this acquisition process. Strength for any problem node is a function of experience or practice with that problem, broadly defined. In other words, any relevant experience with a basic fact is assumed to influence the strength of that fact in memory. This assumption includes not only those factors identified by Siegler and Shrager (1984), but also specifically such categories of experience as classroom practice, individual problem solution, whether formal or informal, and a "bootstrapping" effect on memory strength from reconstructed answers for unknown (or low-accessibility) problems. The overall effect of this practice—the learning curve for arithmetic—is simulated by the joint influence of two parameters: g, the constant yearly growth rate, and f_{ij}, the relative frequencies of presentation for the addition problems $0 + 0$ through $9 + 9$ (as noted, the multiplication network is implemented for adults, but not developmentally). Each year sees an increment in strength values for each problem, modeled by an incremental learning theory equation[4] and governed by the parameter g. This increment in strength is never as great for larger problems as it is for smaller problems, however, based on the textbook survey data mentioned above. This differential frequency is represented as a matrix of relative frequency values f_{ij}.

Part of the importance of the strength value construct is that it provides a more adequate explanation of the ties effect. That is, tie problems have often been classified as special cases, largely because their problem-size effect does not match the results for other problems. The relatively flat RT pattern to these problems, however, is generated by the same simulation mechanism that generates RTs for all problems, spreading-activation search through nodes of varying strength. In other words, ties are not "exceptions" to the problem-size effect when that effect is indexed by strength values.

The third critical assumption is that the normal process of retrieval is one of spreading-activation search. That is, a problem's answer is assumed to be retrieved from the network by first activating the problem's addends (parents A and B). This activation spreads to related nodes, i.e., family members, in the network and eventually culminates in retrieval of a stored answer. In the simulation, activation is propagated from the parent nodes to their respective family members: In situations where a stimulus problem is presented with an answer for true/false verification, the stated answer C also triggers a spread of activation. The critical point here is that the spread of activation from A and B parent nodes, and the C nodes, sums during this process, yielding a set of activated nodes at the several intersections that will compete for selection as the correct answer to the problem. The most highly activated node in this set continues to propagate activation,[5] according to the principle that the amount of activation passed through the network is a negative function of distance; that is, less activation is spread to more distant nodes (Collins & Loftus, 1975; see *proximity* in Appendix 9A). At the end of the search, the simulation identifies the most highly activated node in the entire network as the correct answer, in a Pandemoniumlike fashion (Selfridge, 1959; see also

Rumelhart & McClelland, 1982), and computes the simulated RT based on this node's level of activation (see Appendix 9A, search step 7). This retrieved answer is then passed along for further processing (e.g., decision in a verification task).

Embodied in this third assumption about spreading activation is the notion of threshold of activation. As mentioned above, a node must exceed threshold during search for it to be accessed, that is, to be identified as a candidate answer to the presented stimulus problem. Threshold is defined in the same percentage metric as strength values. To be concrete, the maximum possible strength value is 100, so the accessibility threshold is also 100. In practice, this means that a node may achieve threshold if it was the target of activation from any two sources, parent nodes or C nodes. For example, the adult strength value for $2 + 3 = 5$ is 82. This C node 5 will be activated to its strength value by each parent node and so will achieve an activation level of 164 (then further modified by the activation spread from C nodes on a verification trial). Conversely, any trial that does not yield a node at or above threshold results in nonretrieval processing; quite literally, the information stored at the node is not accessible during search, so some other method must be applied to arrive at the answer. As it is currently programmed, nonretrieval processing is an application of the counting-on process for addition; no analogous process for multiplication is yet implemented. Counting, if this method is called, proceeds at an age-appropriate rate (see Ashcraft et al., 1984), but is invariably slower than successful retrieval would have been. More complex forms of procedural knowledge, both informal and formal (e.g., estimation strategies, rules for carrying in complex addition or multiplication), represent an important avenue for further development of the simulation model.

Let me describe one final bit of machinery, the decision stage, because it is important to understand its operation for certain tests of the simulation. To begin, the decision stage is called only when a true/false decision is required. During simulation runs of the production task (for example, $4 + 3 = ?$), the decision stage does not operate. When a decision is required, however, the search stage is completed as described above. At the conclusion of search, two values are passed to the decision stage for evaluation. One is the activation level ACT_x of the most activated node, the node identified by the simulation to be the correct answer. The second value is the activation level of the answer stated in the problem, or more precisely the activation level ACT_c of the most highly activated C node, where the set of C nodes is the set that matches the answer C stated in the stimulus. Of course, when the problem presented to the simulation is true, these two activation values are identical, and it is exactly this match that causes the simulation to decide the problem is true. When a false problem is presented, such as $4 + 3 = 8$ (or $4 \times 8 = 24$), then two distinct values are transmitted to the decision stage, the activation value for the stated answer 8, ACT_c, and the activation value ACT_x. Under these conditions of mismatching activation values, the simulation attempts to discriminate between the two values. As is generally the case for symbolic comparisons (e.g., Banks, 1977), time for discrimination here is a negative function of the distance or difference between the two values. Thus, the attempt to distinguish same and different during the decision stage adds merely a constant decision time to true trials but a differential amount of time to false trials, depending on the degree of mismatch between stated and retrieved answers' levels of activation.[6]

This discrimination process is the basis for the prediction of a confusion effect in the simulation. The slowing of RT to problems such as $4 \times 8 = 24$ is due to the interrelatedness of nodes within multiplication, and slowing of performance to problems such as $3 \times 5 = 8$ is due to the interrelatedness between addition and multiplication operations. In both cases, sufficient activation at the distractor *C* nodes has accumulated during search to slow the discrimination process. For several reasons, however, it is not clear whether the label *confusion effect* should be applied to the slowing of RT to addition problems such as $4 + 3 = 8$. In the past, this slowness has been attributed to the operation of a decision-stage mechanism (e.g., Ashcraft & Stazyk, 1981), which functions on the basis of the difference, or *split,* between the retrieved answer and the stated answer (see Figure 9.1 and Appendix 9A). Interestingly, the same general predictions are made by the simulation with this split-driven discrimination process turned off. That is, this split effect is also predicted based on activation and then competition among neighboring nodes (see Ashcraft, 1983, for instance).

The situation is somewhat more indeterminate under the multiplication operation, however; a purely network-based confusion for these predictions is insufficient. If only the network confusion effect is operative, then the simulation incorrectly predicts rapid rejection of false problems such as $4 \times 5 = 23$. The reason for this incorrect prediction is quite straightforward: 23 is not in the basic (i.e., single-digit) multiplication table, so no *C* node 23 exists to accumulate activation. Empirically, however, such answers do slow the verification process, though possibly not to the same degree as legal entries in the table (e.g., Duffy & Fisher, 1980; Stazyk et al., 1982). A computational change in the simulation would resolve this difficulty immediately: Computing RT as the longer of the two decision processes would in effect merge the network-competition and the distance-based discrimination processes, modeling the fragmentary data that exist on this topic. I have resisted such a change since it lacks theoretical motivation and solid empirical backing (but see Campbell & Graham, 1985, for a careful analysis of errors made in a production task).

Figure 9.7 presents an overview of the simulation model, in the form of a flowchart summarizing the two solution methods, network retrieval and procedural solution. Consider network retrieval first. For any problem

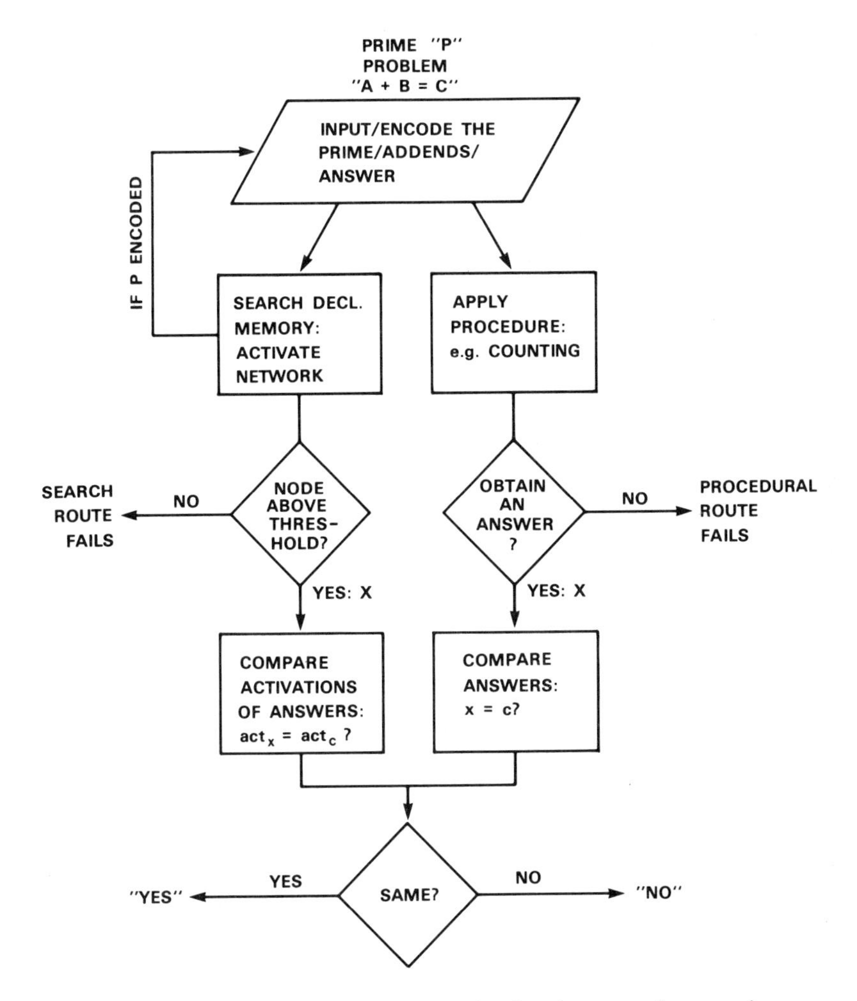

FIGURE 9.7. Flowchart summary of simulated stages of processing.

$A + B = C$, both addends and the answer are encoded and then passed to the search stage. Search consists of the spreading-activation mechanism described above. In situations where a prime P precedes the stimulus problem, the parent node and C node spread of activation is triggered by the prime and is then followed by encoding of the problem. At the conclusion of the search stage, the set of nodes activated above threshold is examined, and the most highly activated of these is selected as the correct answer to the problem. If no node has achieved threshold, then the search route fails. Assuming the most highly activated node is indeed above threshold, processing shifts to the decision stage. Decision consists of the comparison of two values, the activation level of the retrieved node ACT_x and the activation level of the node corresponding to the stated answer C

in the problem, ACT_c. If these two activation values are the same, the simulation concludes that the problem $A + B = C$ is correct. The RT in this situation is a constant, composed of encoding, decision, and response time, plus a variable search time that varies as a function of the activation level (see Appendix 9A). If the two activation values differ, then the overall RT contains an additional component, the decision-stage time necessary to discriminate between ACT_x and ACT_c. As stated, this discrimination time is a negative function of the difference between the two magnitudes (e.g., Banks, 1977).

Now let us consider the alternate processing route, procedural solution. Although this route is called on every trial, it is considerably slower than the retrieval route, because counting is a slower process (Ashcraft et al., 1984). Thus the overall RT is governed by procedural solution only when the search route fails, that is, when no node achieves threshold. When this circumstance holds, as is often the case for simulations of young children's performance, then the procedure that is applied is a simple counting-on process (e.g., Groen & Parkman, 1972), in which the larger of A and B is incremented by 1s. At the end of counting, the simulation advances X as the correct answer to the problem $A + B$ and shifts to a decision mechanism. During decision, the obtained answer X is compared to the stated answer C. The predictions for decision time here are similar to those for the activation-based decision mechanism, that is, a constant time when the two values match and a variable time when they mismatch, where time is a negative function of the difference between the two magnitudes. The predicted RT under a procedural solution is a constant for encoding, decision, and response times, plus an amount of time due to the counting mechanism, counting rate r times the number of increments counted on (counting rates from Ashcraft et al., 1984). Again, when X and C differ, then the time for the discrimination is also a component of RT.

The major new predictions generated by the simulation have to do with automatic versus conscious retrieval processes within simple arithmetic, using the priming paradigm developed by Posner (1978; see also Posner & Snyder, 1975). In particular, the simulation permits primes P to be presented for variable durations and demonstrates the effects on latency when primes of differing relationships to the target problems are presented. For instance, activation of the network by a relevant prime (for example, 5 as a prime for $5 + 3 = 8$) facilitates subsequent processing, because a set of nodes relevant to the upcoming search (the 5 + family) has been activated. Conversely, activation from an irrelevant or "misleading" prime (for example, 8 as a prime for $3 \times 4 = 8$) can inhibit processing (for example, Figure 9.3). The predicted amounts of facilitation depend critically on two variables, time duration between prime and target and network strength values. The latencies that are predicted show effects of problem size and simulated age (see Ashcraft, 1985a, for details). There are little data on the development of automaticity, regardless of area (but see Simpson & Lorsbach, 1983), so there are literally no such data on the development of automatic retrieval in arithmetic. Because we are just now beginning to collect such data, at present there is no basis for evaluating the accuracy of the simulation's predictions.

Issues in Simulation Modeling

Because simulation models are not the norm in developmental work, it seems appropriate in a book like this to discuss some advantages and disadvantages of this approach. I do not present a formal consideration of these topics, because excellent sources of such discussions are available elsewhere (e.g., Kieras, 1984). Instead, I summarize several benefits and drawbacks of a computer simulation approach, discuss some difficulties related to model evaluation, and propose a more modest role for simulations than is often claimed, the simulation as a demonstration of a theory.

A major advantage of computer simulation involves the issue of concreteness. As Kieras (1984) put it, "Constructing a rigorously specified computer program is an excellent way to convert a set of vague ideas into a more specific and precise theory" (p. 2). However clear the notions of network storage and spreading activation were to me, these hypotheses were not sufficiently specified in the verbal statement of the model (Ashcraft, 1982). Computer simulation, however, provides a formalism in which theoretical constructs must be completely specified. The endeavor forces the theorist to be quite explicit about every process and mechanism. This precision is often quite lacking in verbal theories (see Ashcraft, 1985b; Baroody, 1985).

A simulation is very heuristic to the theorist, in the sometimes embarrassing sense that it illuminates gaps in current knowledge or the theorist's own conceptualization. For instance, I claim in my theory that multiplication is acquired and performed in an entirely analogous fashion to addition. I am not compelled, in this verbal statement, to specify when multiplication facts begin to acquire strength in memory, what those strengths might be, or how they might grow across the developmental span. In a verbal theory, these questions might go unnoticed. They confront me directly in a simulation, however; unless they are addressed adequately, the simulation simply will not run. The simulation theorist is therefore painfully aware of the lapses in available data and the elements in the simulation which reflect those lapses. A salutary effect, however, is that further empirical work can be targeted more usefully once the lapses are revealed.

A third advantage involves the complexity of the behavior being modeled. Computer simulation permits the modeling of highly complex systems and processes and is often considerably more ambitious than traditional mathematical modeling techniques (see, for instance, Schank &

Riesbeck, 1981). With the present model, I attempted to predict latencies on simple arithmetic problems in production and verification tasks for subjects in grades 1 through college. These predictions are a function of particular theoretical assumptions about storage format, retrieval processes, and acquisition history. As the empirical results flowed in, it became clear that a formal model of the various hypothesized components would be substantially more complex than is customarily handled with traditional mathematical modeling techniques. Short of reducing the scope of the modeling effort, simulation seemed the only formalism in which such complexity could be embedded conveniently.

Notice further that the dependent measure studied in this empirical literature is most often reaction time, and theoretical predictions about the nature of processing generally translate to empirical predictions of the duration of different mental events. Only computer simulation seemed to have the potential for modeling the hypothesized behavior of a process model, for specifying the underlying knowledge representation, and for predicting RT patterns dependent on those hypothesized processes and structures. This level of complexity matches a second argument that Kieras (1984) made in favor of constructing a simulation: "To account for empirical data. . . . The fact that such accounting can be done at a very fine level of detail is important because the level of detail possible with modern on-line data collection methods is simply not exploited by conventional verbal or mathematical models, whereas simulation models are intrinsically committed to a very high level of detail" (p. 3).

A final strength, in my opinion, is the clarity with which a simulation can make predictions and the flexibility it permits in testing components of an overall process. In a simulation, the causes of the predicted effects can be stated exactly; there are no "emergent" properties in a simulation, by definition (in the sense proposed by Hempel & Oppenheim, 1953), although unexpected outcomes may abound, as in the present case with split effects. This is not to say that the causes will necessarily be simple, merely that the causes are known, in principle, by virtue of having been programmed and that their actions can be interpreted precisely. Furthermore, the exactly specified relationships may then be used to generate new predictions, testable both empirically and within the simulation itself. Thus, in the current simulation, the root cause for the interaction between age and problem size is precisely the effect of experience on strength values in the network. We might test the strength value to the problem-size hypothesis on a set of arithmetic problems known to be of minimal strength, first exploring the behavior of the simulation and then evaluating the hypothesis empirically. Contrast such statements and predictions with those of a verbal theory, which often makes only qualitative predictions based on vaguely defined processes. Finally, the simulation permits a novel way of evaluating components in the model. We can simply turn the component off and observe the resulting behavior of the simulation. This approach was used, for example, to contrast retrieval and counting mechanisms, and it revealed substantially incorrect predictions for the problem-size effect beyond the third grade when the retrieval component was omitted.

Whereas computer simulation is an appropriate and useful formalism for many situations, the approach is not without its limitations. First, the approach can be expensive, in terms of both equipment costs and the theorist's time (although the present simulation is implemented on an ordinary microcomputer, cutting both kinds of costs at once). Second, the flexibility of the method is such that a simulation is never "finished," in the sense that additional components and modifications are always possible. This has implications, of course, for evaluating the adequacy of a simulation model. To aggravate the situation, few sources of practical or theoretical advice exist to guide the theorist; because simulations vary so widely in topic, scope, and intent, however, it is doubtful that any one set of guidelines for writing a simulation model could be proposed. The most serious drawback involves the issue of evaluating the simulation as a psychological model. Indeed, the greatest strengths of the simulation approach—versatility and power—are often the primary sources of this concern. Given the ambitious scope of many simulation models, a distinct worry is that computational power may be seductive, leading a theorist to ever-more complex solutions rather than ever-more parsimonious models and theories (see especially Loftus, 1985). I illustrate how difficult it can be to evaluate simulations and then comment on the status of simulation models as psychological theories.

A major concern in mathematical models, of course, is the number of parameters that must be assigned values and how those assignments or estimates are made. This problem is, if anything, a thornier issue in simulation work. A simulation invariably contains decisions about many parameters or weights, probably more than typical mathematical models given the generally larger scope of simulations. It can be surprisingly difficult both to gauge the gradations of psychological importance of all these parameters and weights and to anticipate their joint effects under different circumstances. It can be equally difficult to maintain the distinction between true parameters and mere computational values, particularly as the simulation grows larger. This creates a serious problem if we wish to test the simulation against standard criteria of goodness of fit and parsimony. I would not consider my simulation to be "disconfirmed" if the growth rate g were eventually found to be .30 instead of .20. Yet the estimate of .20 is critically involved in the latency predictions, which *are* taken seriously as evidence in evaluating the simulation.

I have adopted two guidelines in an attempt to deal with this issue (although I do not claim they are necessarily unique to my own work, general to other simulation efforts, or completely adequate to solve the problem). To minimize the number of "free" parameters in the simulation, I have (1) relied extensively on parameter values from empirical studies and (2) adopted an internal metric within the simulation, a single parameter in a sense, that in turn is responsible for many other computational values. To illustrate (1), strength values in my simulation are from empirical rating studies or published association strength data, and counting rates are also obtained from published studies. Because a goal of the simulation is realistic prediction of RT effects, it makes no sense to omit such empirical values out of a sense of theoretical purity. This approach is in contrast to a view that such values in a model should derive from more basic principles or processes. As applied to the current simulation, this view would dictate, for example, that counting rates themselves be derived from a more basic "primitive," say a central "rate of information processing." My choice here is related to a particular role for simulations, described below. To illustrate (2), the internal metric I have adopted throughout the simulation is based on the quantification of strength or accessibility. Stated simply, strength is quantified as a percentage, and the various processes that operate on or use the strength values are expressed as a function of this percentage metric (e.g., threshold, the proportional frequencies f_{ij}, the amount of activation, the decreasing gradient of activation as a function of proximity, etc.). At a minimum, deriving such parameters from a common "ancestor" makes it simpler to identify values that do *not* derive from that scheme (e.g., the decision-stage weights for discrimination time).

I turn now to the role of simulation theories, because this issue has implications for the kinds of evaluations that are appropriate. It is often claimed that the simulation itself is the testable, concrete statement of a theory, that the theory and the simulation are equivalent. This claim seems mistaken to me, or at least overstated, for several reasons. A theory is generally a statement of a set of principles, sometimes formulated mathematically, that is open for inspection and testing by impartial investigators. Few, if any, computer simulations meet the criteria of openness and testability, except to their own creators. Tests of the simulation by others, as in all hypothesis testing, involve deductions from the theory's principles to a set of testable hypotheses. Furthermore, equating the theory with the simulation is taken seriously at the level of theoretical constructs and basic assumptions, but is never taken seriously at the level of programming statements. Any simulation (and simulation language) includes programming "overhead" and devices that are necessary computationally but irrelevant psychologically. As before, we rely on the verbal statement of the theory to tell the difference between psychologically important and computationally necessary propositions. It is the task of the theorist here both to discern the difference and to maintain a level of scientific integrity sufficient to guard against computationally convenient but psychologically implausible mechanisms.

Another manifestation of the same issue is somewhat more subtle. Few simulations embody all the mechanisms, principles, or processes hypothesized by a theory. Instead, certain important or central parts of the theory are implemented, and the simulation is an instantiation of only this subset of the theory. An unfortunate consequence is that, whereas successful predictions from the simulation can be taken as support for the theory, unsuccessful predictions can reflect an inaccurate theory, an inadequate translation to program code, or an irrelevant test because a component is not yet fully implemented. There is often no firm basis to distinguish between the first two alternatives, given the subset relationship of the simulation to the theory. And the third alternative can render the simulation nearly impervious to disconfirmation.

In the face of this uncertainty, I argue for a more limited role for simulation models than the traditional claim that "the simulation is the theory." In my view, simulations have a vital role as illustrations or demonstrations. That is, a simulation can illustrate the plausibility of theoretical constructs or principles and can demonstrate how a set of assumptions will (or will not) successfully model some aspect of behavior. An anonymous reviewer once commented that a counting model could predict the basic set of arithmetic effects more parsimoniously than a network model and could also predict an effect I had advanced as a definitive test of network approaches. My simulations of various counting models told me that, although they are certainly more parsimonious, they are in fact not able to predict the basic results reported in the literature (especially the problem-size effect across different ages; see Ashcraft & Stazyk, 1981; Ashcraft et al., 1984). Simulation of a network representation not only predicted these basic effects but also generated more differentiated predictions of the definitive network test, predictions that were supported by the data (especially the confusion effect; see Stazyk et al., 1982, for a thorough discussion of the alternative models' predictions). My simulation, I believe, has demonstrated the plausibility of a theory based on the assumptions of network storage and spreading activation. For reasons discussed above, this demonstration is more powerful than claims that could be made about a verbal theory which has not been implemented in a simulation.

Conclusion

Returning to the substantive issues, I wish to conclude on a theoretical note that unifies this model of arithmetic performance with the larger literature on cognitive processing. The theoretical point concerns automaticity of mental processes and the necessary condition for automatic processing to occur. A study reported by Shiffrin and Schneider (1977) serves nicely for this point. A group of subjects given consistent mapping between stimuli and responses developed automatic detection processes across 2400 trials; when the mapping was reversed, a subsequent set of 2400 trials had still not overcome the initial, massive dose of practice. In short, automaticity develops with consistent, massive, repetitive practice. In my simulation, automatic retrieval characterizes all network retrieval processing, based on strength values that indicate accessibility. Thus the same underlying force, practice or learning, is implicated both in the strength values of nodes in the simulation and in theoretical accounts of automaticity. Whereas in most discussions of automaticity, performance is categorized into a dichotomy of automatic versus conscious, from the empirical work clearly automaticity develops continuously, even incrementally, as a function of practice. Significantly, memory strength in the simulation develops continuously, also as a function of practice. Thus, routine retrieval from long-term memory networks is automatic to the extent that practice has strengthened the memory nodes. Automatic retrieval in the model is inseparable from the impact of practice or learning on strength values. In the present framework, then, development is learning.

Acknowledgments

The research and simulation model described in this chapter were partially supported by a grant from the National Science Foundation, SED-8021521. Initial work on the simulation was completed at the Learning Research and Development Center (LRDC), University of Pittsburgh, supported in part by the National Institute of Education (NIE), Department of Education. I am indebted to James Greeno for the opportunity to study at the LRDC during my sabbatical. I am also indebted to Charles Brainerd for the invitation to describe an earlier version of the current model in a special issue of *Developmental Review* devoted to quantitative models of development (1982). I also wish to acknowledge the important contributions of my several student colleagues, John Battaglia, Ed Stazyk, Ben Fierman, Mary Sue Hamann, Robin Bartolotta, John Koshmider, and Joan Roemer, and to thank Marjorie Reed for several discussions of priming and developmental mechanisms.

References

Anderson, J. R. (1983). *The architecture of cognition*. Cambridge, MA: Harvard.
Anderson, J. R., & Bower, G. H. (1973). *Human associative memory*. Washington: Winston-Wiley.
Ashcraft, M. H. (1976). Priming and property dominance effects in semantic memory. *Memory & Cognition, 4,* 490–500.
Ashcraft, M. H. (1978). Property dominance and typicality effects in property statement verification. *Journal of Verbal Learning and Verbal Behavior, 17,* 155–164.
Ashcraft, M. H. (1982). The development of mental arithmetic: A chronometric approach. *Developmental Review, 2,* 213–236.
Ashcraft, M. H. (1983). *Simulating network retrieval of arithmetic facts*. Learning Research and Development Center Publication Series, University of Pittsburgh, 1983/10.

Ashcraft, M. H. (1985a, April). *Children's mental arithmetic: Toward a model of retrieval and problem solving*. Paper presented at the meetings of the Society for Research in Child Development, Toronto.

Ashcraft, M. H. (1985b). Is it farfetched that some of us remember our arithmetic facts? *Journal for Research in Mathematics Education, 16,* 99–105.

Ashcraft, M. H., & Battaglia, J. (1977, November). *Cognitive arithmetic: Evidence for two-stage decision and search*. Paper presented at the meeting of the Psychonomic Society, Washington.

Ashcraft, M. H., & Battaglia, J. (1978). Cognitive arithmetic: Evidence for retrieval and decision processes in mental addition. *Journal of Experimental Psychology: Human Learning and Memory, 4,* 527–538.

Ashcraft, M. H., & Fierman, B. A. (1982). Mental addition in third, fourth, and sixth graders. *Journal of Experimental Child Psychology, 33,* 216–234.

Ashcraft, M. H., Fierman, B. A., & Bartolotta, R. (1984). The production and verification tasks in mental addition: An empirical comparison. *Developmental Review, 4,* 157–170.

Ashcraft, M. H., & Stazyk, E. H. (1981). Mental addition: A test of three verification models. *Memory & Cognition, 9,* 185–196.

Banks, W. P. (1977). Encoding and processing of symbolic information in comparative judgments. In G. H. Bower (Ed.), *The psychology of learning and motivation* (Vol. 11, pp. 101–159). New York: Academic.

Baroody, A. J. (1983). The development of procedural knowledge: An alternative explanation for chronometric trends of mental arithmetic. *Developmental Review, 3,* 225–230.

Baroody, A. J. (1984). A reexamination of mental arithmetic models and data: A reply to Ashcraft. *Developmental Review, 4,* 148–156.

Baroody, A. J. (1985). Mastery of basic number combinations: Internalization of relationships or facts? *Journal for Research in Mathematics Education, 16,* 83–98.

Campbell, J. I. D. (1985). *Associative interference in mental multiplication*. Unpublished doctoral dissertation, University of Waterloo, Ontario, Canada.

Campbell, J. I. D., & Graham, D. J. (1985). Mental multiplication skill: Structure, process, and acquisition. *Canadian Journal of Psychology, 39, 338–366.*

Collins, A. M., & Loftus, E. F. (1975). A spreading-activation theory of semantic procesing. *Psychological Review, 82,* 407–428.

Collins, A. M., & Quillian, M. R. (1972). How to make a language user. In E. Tulving & W. Donaldson (Eds.), *Organization of memory*. New York: Academic.

Duffy, S. A., & Fisher, D. L. (1980, May). *The organization and processing of multiplication facts*. Paper presented at the meetings of the Midwestern Psychological Association, St. Louis.

Estes, W. K. (1964). All-or-none processes in learning and retention. *American Psychologist, 19,* 16–25.

Fierman, B. A. (1980). *Developmental mental addition: A test of two models and two methods*. Unpublished master's thesis, Cleveland State University, Cleveland, OH.

Gelman, R., & Gallistel, C. R. (1978). *The child's understanding of number*. Cambridge, MA: Harvard.

Ginsburg, H. (1977). *Children's arithmetic: The learning process*. New York: Van Nostrand.
Glass, A. L., Holyoak, K. J., & O'Dell, C. (1974). Production frequency and the verification of quantified statements. *Journal of Verbal Learning and Verbal Behavior, 13,* 237–254.
Groen, G. J., & Parkman, J. M. (1972). A chronometric analysis of simple addition. *Psychological Review, 79,* 329–343.
Hamann, M. S. (1981). *Cognitive processes in simple and complex addition.* Unpublished master's thesis, Cleveland State University, Cleveland, OH.
Hamann, M. S. (1983, May). *Acquisition and practice of addition and quasi-addition facts*. Paper presented at the Pittsburgh-Carnegie-Mellon Conference on Cognition, Pittsburgh.
Hamann, M. S., & Ashcraft, M. H. (1985). Simple and complex mental addition across development. *Journal of Experimental Child Psychology, 40,* 49–72.
Hamann, M. S., & Ashcraft, M. H. (in press). Textbook presentations of the basic addition facts. *Cognition and Instruction.*
Hempel, C. G., & Oppenheim, P. (1953). The logic of explanation, In H. Feigl & M. Brodbeck (Eds.), *Readings in the philosophy of science*. New York: Appleton Century Crofts.
Kieras, D. (1984, November). *The why, when, and how of cognitive simulation: A tutorial.* Paper presented at the meetings of the Society for Computers in Psychology, San Antonio, TX.
Kintsch, W. (1974). *The representation of meaning in memory*. Hillsdale, NJ: Erlbaum.
Kintsch, W., & Greeno, J. G. (1985). Understanding and solving word arithmetic problems. *Psychological Review, 92,* 109–129.
Koshmider, J. W. III (1986). *Development of children's multiplication skills.* Unpublished master's thesis. Cleveland State University, Cleveland, OH.
Loftus, G. (1985). Johannes Kepler's computer simulation of the universe: Some remarks about theory in psychology. *Behavior Research Methods, Instruments, & Computers, 17,* 149–156.
Miller, K. F., Perlmutter, M., & Keating, D. (1984). Cognitive arithmetic: Comparison of operations. *Journal of Experimental Psychology: Learning, Memory, and Cognition, 10,* 46–60.
Norman, D. A., & Rumelhart, D. E. (1975). *Explorations in cognition. San Francisco: Freeman.*
Parkman, J. M. (1972). Temporal aspects of simple multiplication and comparison. *Journal of Experimental Psychology, 95,* 437–444.
Posner, M. I. (1978). *Chronometric explorations of mind.* Hillsdale, NJ: Erlbaum.
Posner, M. I., & Snyder, C. R. R. (1975). Facilitation and inhibition in the processing of signals. In P. M. A. Rabbitt & S. Dornic (Eds.), *Attention and performance V* (pp. 669–682). New York: Academic.
Resnick, L. B., & Ford, W. W. (1981). *The psychology of mathematics for instruction*. Hillsdale, NJ: Erlbaum.
Rosch, E. (1975). Cognitive representations of semantic categories. *Journal of Experimental Psychology: General, 104,* 192–233.
Rumelhart, D. E., & McClelland, J. L. (1982). An interactive activation model of context effects in letter perception: Part 2. The contextual enhancement effect and some tests and extensions of the model. *Psychological Review, 89,* 60–94.

Schank, R., & Abelson, R. (1977). *Scripts, plans, goals and understanding—An inquiry into human knowledge structures*. Hillsdale, NJ: Erlbaum.
Schank, R. C., & Riesbeck, C. K. (Eds.) (1981). *Inside computer understanding*. Hillsdale, NJ: Erlbaum.
Selfridge, O. G. (1959). Pandemonium: A paradigm for learning. In *The mechanisation of thought processes*. London: H. M. Stationery Office.
Shiffrin, R. M., & Schneider, W. (1977). Controlled and automatic human information processing: II. Perceptual learning, automatic attending, and a general theory. *Psychological Review, 84,* 127–190.
Siegler, R. S., & Shrager, J. (1984). Strategy choices in addition and subtraction: How do children know what to do? In C. Sophian (Ed.), *Origins of cognitive skills*. Hillsdale, NJ: Erlbaum.
Simpson, G. B., & Lorsbach, T. C. (1983). The development of automatic and conscious components of contextual facilitation. *Child Development, 54,* 760–772.
Stazyk, E. H. (1980). *A network approach to mental multiplication*. Unpublished master's thesis, Cleveland State University, Cleveland, OH.
Stazyk, E. H., Ashcraft, M. H., & Hamann, M. S. (1982). A network approach to mental multiplication. *Journal of Experimental Psychology: Learning, Memory, and Cognition, 8,* 320–335.
Svenson, O. (1975). Analysis of time required by children for simple additions. *Acta Psychologica, 39,* 289–302.
Whaley, C. P. (1978). Word-nonword classification time. *Journal of Verbal Learning and Verbal Behavior, 17,* 143–154.
Wheeler, L. R. (1939). A comparative study of the difficulty of the 100 addition combinations. *Journal of Genetic Psychology, 54,* 295–312.
Winkelman, H. J., & Schmidt, J. (1974). Associative confusions in mental arithmetic. *Journal of Experimental Psychology, 102,* 734–736.

Appendix 9A: Pseudocode Description of Development, Search, and Decision

Development

1. Input the Siegler and Shrager (1984) "association values" multiplied by .33 to standardize strength to the age range kindergarten through college.
2. Input number of years Y to be forecasted (Y will correspond to grade).
3. Iterate Y times through rule 4.
4. Add Δs_{ij} to current strength, where

$$\Delta s_{ij} = g f_{ij}(100 - s_{ij}) \quad \text{and} \quad f_{ij} = \frac{100 - (i + j)}{100}.$$

Search

For a network with elements n_{ij} and a stimulus problem $A_i + B_j = C_k$:

1. Activate nodes $n_{i\cdot}$ (parent A) to strength s_{ij}.
2. Activate nodes $n_{\cdot j}$ (parent B) to strength $s_{ij,}$ and sum with previous activation, if any.
3. Activate nodes $C_{k,}$, and sum with previous activation, if any.
4. Select highest valued ACT_{ij} to be X, with address (i, j) (see footnote 5).
5. Spread activation from X_{ij} to all $n_{i\cdot}$ and $n_{\cdot j}$ such that activation at any node n_{ij} = proximity ($\mathrm{ACT}_{x_{ij}}$) + previous activation, where $\mathrm{ACT}_{x_{ij}}$ is the activation level of X_{ij} and proximity is a weight score of .9, .8, .7, etc., for nodes 1, 2, 3, etc., horizontal or vertical steps away from the intersection (steps computed on vaues of i and j).
6. Select node with highest activation as X, the correct answer, with activation ACT_x.
7. Simulated RT = 1000 − ACT_x. Note: The activation score ACT_c for the answer stated in the problem (C) is also saved for further processing.

Decision

For the problem $A + B = C$, with X as the retrieved answer:

1. Compute the difference $D = \mathrm{ACT}_x - \mathrm{ACT}_c$.
2. Transform to proportional difference $\mathrm{PD} = (\mathrm{ACT}_x - D)/\mathrm{ACT}_x$.
3. Simulated RT for the discrimination is a decision weight w, times PD, with w estimated at 300 (from Ashcraft & Stazyk, 1981; Stazyk et al., 1982).

Note: Under counting solutions, substitute the stated and counted answers for ACT_c and $\mathrm{ACT}_{x,}$, respectively. This is also the *split* decision mechanism, described in the text.

Notes

1. Our first graders could do some rudimentary counting by 5s on the usual 5-10-15 string, but they were unable to count off the string by 5s at all. Their counting by smaller unit sizes was extremely slow, and their counting by 1s yielded a rate of 1000 ms per increment.
2. The Siegler and Shrager values must be rescaled before being used as percentage-based accessibility or strength values. That is, their values are probabilities derived from tests of kindergarten children, e.g., a probability of .86 for responding 2 to the problem 1 + 1. To use these in a model that spans first-grade through college levels, I have multiplied all the correct response probabilities by the constant .33, this constant based on the 3 : 1 ratio of first graders' to adults' fastest RTs (Fierman,

1980). If this adjustment were not made, the .86 would indicate a strength value of 86 out of a possible 100, a clearly unreasonable strength for a kindergartener when adult strengths are measured on the same scale. Problems that were not tested by Siegler and Shrager, i.e., those with addends larger than 5, were arbitrarily assigned a strength of 1 (out of 100) in the kindergarten matrix of strength values.

3. An alternate developmental scheme would not merely increment the strength values for each simulated year, but would vary the rate of information processing across ages. That is, the overall speeding of RT across developmental levels is due to increased strength values at present, but could be simulated by assuming that older children also have a faster rate of search and retrieval from memory (and faster encoding, decision, and response times as well). I have elected the incremental strengthening approach because it requires fewer assumptions and because no clear-cut source of data is available to estimate the slower rates of information processing for younger ages.
4. In most learning theory accounts (e.g., Estes, 1964), the incremental model was held to be true only in the aggregate, i.e., that individual subjects' performance supports an all-or-none conditioning conclusion, but that averaged together this performance resembles the negatively accelerated function predicted by incremental models. Although the present simulation indeed makes predictions for an aggregate or typical case, I do not subscribe to an underlying all-or-none interpretation for strength values for individual subjects. I assume that node strength is a continuous variable, receiving genuine increments as a function of experience and learning.
5. Why should not *all* nodes that have received activation, all family members and C nodes alike, propagate a spread of activation to their neighbors, instead of the current scheme of all C nodes but only the highest node of intersection from the family members? The two reasons entail economy of program execution and net effect on processing. Because the first parent activates an entry in each "column" of the table and the second parent an entry in each "row," each of the 100 nodes in the network is a "grandchild" of each parent (i.e., parent activates 10 "children," each child activates 10 "grandchildren," and similarly for the other parent). An initial version of the simulation did propagate activation from each family member (i.e., to each grandchild). This scheme required excessive amounts of execution time for the program, because each of the 200 nodes (100 in addition, 100 in multiplication) was being updated once as a grandchild of parent A and once as a grandchild of parent B (and then often as a neighbor of the C nodes as well). This massive activation spread, furthermore, had no functional effect on later processing; the entire network was boosted with this exhaustive spread, but the *relative* levels of activation for any pair of nodes were not appreciably different from those found with the

simpler scheme now used. The present scheme should therefore be viewed as a functionally equivalent shortcut for the full spread of activation.

6. I have not included any error-generating processes in the simulation, preferring instead to focus on latency predictions. Nonetheless, the simulation does address an important source of errors, at least indirectly. Campbell and Graham (1985) have shown that the majority of errors in multiplication problems can be accounted for by associative or network relatedness, for example, 24 as a highly probable error to $4 \times 8 = ?$. Whereas the simulation does not generally make such errors, an examination of the network after search does reveal substantial activation of the nodes that occur most frequently as errors. Under unusual circumstances, however, the simulation does occasionally retrieve an incorrect answer and proceeds to make an incorrect decision. For the most part, these circumstances involve target nodes only marginally above threshold, at ages lower than third grade, where a neighboring node, for instance a tie, overpowers the target because of the neighbor's appreciably greater strength value. See Siegler and Shrager (1984) for a careful analysis of situations where an incorrect value can temporarily exceed the strength of correct values and the self-correcting influence of further experience.

10. Mechanisms of Visual Development: An Example of Computational Models

Martin S. Banks

For centuries, philosophers and scientists have been fascinated by the development of visual perception. Doubtless, this continued interest stems in large part from the fact that we are highly visual creatures. We use our eyes to acquire information about innumerable aspects of our surroundings. For example, vision informs us of the presence, location, and identity of objects and of the rules governing the interactions of one object and another. Vision steers interactions with our surroundings by guiding reaching, locomotion, and posture. It also provides important information about the social environment. Thus, any description of early human development must include a description about how infants and children use their eyes to gather information about their surroundings. I argue in this chapter that the study of visual development is important for an additional reason: The growth of visual perception provides a unique opportunity to examine mechanisms that underlie developmental transitions from one level of performance to another.

A chapter on visual development could be out of place in a book, like this one, that emphasizes cognitive development. Hoping to avoid this, I have chosen material that does not require expertise in visual science and should be of general interest to developmentalists. The chapter consists of four parts. The first is a highly abridged and selective summary of the current understanding of visual development. We have learned a great deal about the status of various visual capabilities at different ages. Unfortunately, we have not learned nearly so much about the mechanisms that underlie transitions from one age to the next. In the second part I describe an approach that might be useful for examining developmental mechanisms. This computational approach is similar to the one advocated by David Marr (1982). In the third part I provide background material necessary for the reader to understand the computational models presented later. Finally, in the fourth part I describe an intriguing developmental problem and present computational models of how the problem might be solved. The problem is how the visual system deduces the characteristics of its early optical and neural processing in order to compensate for distortions caused by these factors. Solutions to the problem involve interaction with the environment, recalibration to compensate for physical growth, and other factors of interest to any developmentalist.

A Brief Review of Our Understanding of Visual Development

Truly remarkable progress has been made in the last 15 years in describing the development of a large number of visual capabilities (Banks & Salapatek, 1983; Gibson & Spelke, 1983). There is now an excellent data base on the development of pattern vision (Banks & Dannemiller, 1986), color vision (Teller & Bornstein, 1986), depth perception (Yonas & Owsley, 1986), and eye movement control (Aslin, 1986). Clearly the field is maturing rapidly in many ways. I think, however, that not much progress has been made in another domain: We do not have very adequate theories of the means by which visual capabilities change from one age to another. In other words, our understanding of the mechanisms of development is patchy at best.

To make clear why I think this is the case, I discuss three popular theories of perceptual development. I have chosen these theories not because they are poor exemplars of perceptual developmental theories, but rather because they are good exemplars and as such illustrate my claim that the field has not formulated adequate theories of developmental mechanisms. Two of the theories, the differentiation theory of Gibson (1969) and the integration theory of Cohen (Cohen, DeLoache, & Strauss, 1979), are stated in terms of psychological mechanisms. Another, the two visual systems theory of Bronson (1974), is stated in terms of psychological and neurophysiological mechanisms. All three theories have served useful functions. They are consistent with large amounts of data. They have also guided empirical research and aided its interpretation. I emphasize, however, what these theories have not done: They have failed to delineate in clear terms the mechanisms by which visual capabilities change from one age to another.

According to Gibson's differentiation theory, the developing child learns to make finer distinctions among visual stimuli by learning to extract the *distinctive features* of those stimuli. Distinctive features are properties that distinguish an object from other objects despite changes in irrelevant variables such as distance, orientation, slant, and context. Gibson's theory has allowed the synthesis of a number of empirical findings, but it is unsatisfying in many ways. For instance, the set of distinctive features for a given class of stimuli is not specified. If they are simply those properties that allow one to categorize stimuli correctly, the theory is tautological. Gibson also did not specify how the distinctive features are extracted from everyday visual inputs, and because some of the features (symmetry, for example) are fairly high-order, extraction might be quite difficult indeed. Most important for this chapter, however, are the developmental aspects of the theory, and they, too, are vague. Gibson stated that the child learns the distinctive features for various objects through multiple exposures to the objects. But how? In particular, what is the source of candidate features? How are candidate distinctive features extracted by the naive child who has little idea of what to look for? By what mechanism are useful features reinforced and useless ones discarded? Gibson stated that the selection of distinctive features depends on reduction of uncertainty rather than on external reinforcement, but this tack simply sidesteps the key issue. How does the child know when she or he has hit upon a feature that allows useful generalizations and distinctions among stimuli? These are important developmental questions that are not addressed in any clear fashion.

Gibson argued that the visual environment is rich and provides ample information to uncover useful distinctive features. This statement is undoubtedly true. Unfortunately, this argument has been used to suggest that the problem of explaining how the child learns to extract such features is trivial. In fact, it is not trivial at all. Perhaps the clearest evidence to that effect (other than the absence of clear hypotheses in the presentation of differentiation theory) comes from research on artificial intelligence showing, for example, that simple learning machines based on associative networks could not, and presumably cannot, learn to categorize anything but the simplest stimuli (Minsky, 1961). More successful machines have quite sophisticated structures built in. Thus, the explanation of how differentiation occurs through repeated exposure to visual stimuli will assuredly be quite difficult.

Another influential theory of early perceptual development is Cohen's integration theory (Cohen et al., 1979). According to this view, infants become more and more able, as they grow older, to perceive parts of an object as a unified whole. There is quite a bit of empirical evidence consistent with this viewpoint, but the theory is vague in some important respects. The definition of what constitutes a part and what constitutes a whole is not made explicit, but rather is left to intuition. More importantly, the theory is vague about the developmental mechanisms that move infants from perceiving parts to perceiving wholes. For instance, Cohen does not state how the infant comes to appreciate that certain parts belong together (such as the cheek and mouth of a face) whereas other parts do not (such as the cheek of a face and some background feature). Is experience with everyday stimuli required, or does appreciation unfold according to a genetic maturational program? If experience is required, what structures have to be built in for the infant to learn to make this distinction? What kinds of experience are needed?

Another influential theory is Bronson's (1974) two visual systems theory. Bronson noted an interesting and important correlation between changes in visual behavior from birth to 3 months and changes in the relative maturity of cortical and subcortical mechanisms. Once again, this theory has served a very useful function. It has directed attention to the neurophysiological literature and led to a synthesis of several empirical findings involving eye movement control and pattern vision capabilities. It also provides a fairly clear developmental mechanism: maturation of the visual cortex. In an important sense, though, the theory does not explain how these visual capabilities develop. It is fine to note that the visual cortex is important to pattern vision and that it appears to develop rapidly at a time when pattern vision capabilities are improving. But this hypothesis alone does not explain how pattern vision develops because the link between the neural structures involved and the ability to discriminate, recognize, and identify patterns has not been specified. How does the visual cortex provide the capability to discriminate and categorize patterns properly despite changes in size, orientation, and other mostly irrelevant variables? How does experience with particular classes of objects enhance this capability? In other words, noting a correlation between a perceptual capability and a neurophysiological structure does not explain how the capability works. It only tells us what particular pieces of neural machinery are involved. Thus, Bronson's theory does not tell us how pattern vision and eye movement control develop. It only points to changes in the nervous system that are probably involved in the development of those skills.

Again, I should emphasize that these three theories were singled out not because they are poor theories but rather because they are among the best and most influential in the field of perceptual development. As such, they illustrate the status of the field's understanding of mechanisms of development. Put simply, our models of developmental mechanisms are disappointingly vague. This observation is rather embarrassing because the aspect of perceptual developmental psychology that should set it apart from the rest of perceptual psychology is the explanation of how development occurs, and such an explanation is precisely what is lacking.

A Computational Approach to Studying Mechanisms of Perceptual Development

How, then, should we go about developing more explicit theories of developmental mechanisms? There is not a single right answer to such a question, but I argue for an approach that might be extremely useful. Indeed, the approach has already been applied successfully in another field. The approach is computational and is based on the one David Marr and others have described for the study of mature vision (Barrow & Tenenbaum, 1979; Marr, 1982).

There are two important facets to Marr's approach. First, one has to recognize that vision (and its development) is complicated and subtle, and consequently the scientific investigation of vision requires work in at least three levels of analysis. To illustrate what one should try to accomplish at each level, I borrow an analogy from Marr (1982). The question raised in the analogy is, How does an electronic hand calculator work? One could not understand the calculator by studying its light-emitting diodes and integrated circuits alone. One would also have to understand addition, subtraction, multiplication, and division; that is, one would have to understand what the calculator is designed to do. Only then would the structure and behavior of the calculator's components make sense. The study of arithmetic would, in Marr's terminology, involve the computational theory of hand calculators. This is the highest level of investigation at which one attempts to answer fairly abstract questions concerning the mechanisms under study. What task must be performed by the mechanism under investigation? What physical laws or constraints are involved? What computations need to be performed? Marr argues that work at this level is sorely needed in the study of mature vision, and I think the same applies to the study of perceptual development. Consequently, the models described in the fourth section of this chapter are computational theories.

The next level is that of algorithm and representation. In studying the hand calculator, we would find that it represents numbers internally in binary and that computations are performed in binary arithmetic. Thus, the following sorts of questions are considered at the level of algorithm and representation: How is the computational theory implemented? In what form is the information represented? How is the information transformed during processing?

The final and lowest level in Marr's scheme is that of hardware. In studying the hand calculator at this level, we would find that electric current rather than mechanical force is used, that transitors rather than vacuum tubes are basic components, and so on. Thus, questions like the following are asked at this level: How is the task performed by the device implemented physically, or physiologically? That is, what does the circuit diagram look like? What kinds of chips are used?

Separating the task of understanding vision into these distinct levels allows us to see more clearly the implications of particular findings. For example, finding that simple cells in the visual cortex respond to edges and bars (Hubel & Wiesel, 1962, 1968) may help us understand the hardware and perhaps even the algorithms and representations of visual processing, but it does not help us understand vision at the level of computational theory.

The second facet of Marr's scheme is perhaps more controversial. He argues that the proper approach to studying vision is to quantify one's models with the goal of implementing the models in some explicit form. Marr argues, in fact, that if researchers really understand the mechanisms under study, then they should be able to write a computer program or design a machine that actually performs the task done by the visual mechanism.

I should emphasize here some critical differences between this view and the view of more traditional quantitative modeling. Let me characterize the traditional modeling approach in developmental psychology first. Several researchers have modeled age-related changes in particular cognitive skills (see Chapter 9 by Ashcraft and Chapter 8 by Rabinowitz, Grant, & Dingley, this volume). They have developed computer programs that attempt to fit a set of data acquired in specific experimental situations. In a prototypical case, the data might be the percentage of correct performance in a number of cognitive tasks. Those data would, of course, be collected at more than one age. The simulation program would contain equations with several variables representing particular psychological mechanisms. A successful outcome would be a satisfactory fit between the simulation's behavior and the observed data. These sorts of quantitative models can be criticized on several grounds. For one thing, they often contain several parameters that are allowed to vary in order to maximize the correspondence between predicted and observed behavior. In such cases, a successful outcome is almost guaranteed, at least for a particular set of data. For another thing, the programs are frequently designed to simulate behavior in only certain experimental situations. Thus, they may not inform us about how the simulated perceptual or cognitive processes operate in general.

The computer implementation approach advocated by Marr is dissimilar from the traditional modeling approach in several ways. Most important, the implementations do not attempt simply to generate data (percentage of correct responses, for example) to fit observed data. Rather, they are designed to accept input information, much as humans do, and then to make perceptual decisions or categorizations, much as humans do. For example, the input to Grimson's (1981) implementation of Marr and Poggio's (1979) theory of stereopsis is two-dimensional intensity distributions, viewed from two vantage points. The output is a description of the three-dimensional layout of the scene that produced the intensity distributions.

The computational approach advocated by Marr and more traditional modeling approaches also differ in their generalizability. To use Grimson as an example again, his implementation is intended to work for a wide variety of visual scenes, viewed from two vantage points. In contrast, many quantitative models of developmental processes are intended only to generate behavior for particular experimental situations.

Keeping in mind these differences between the computational approach and more traditional approaches, I argue that the computational approach is attractive for the study of visual development for three reasons. (The intended contrast here is between the computational approach and the less quantitative approaches commonplace in developmental psychology. In other words, this section does not contrast the computational approach and the traditional quantitative modeling approaches discussed above.)

(1) If you intend to program a computer to actually do what the mechanism of interest is supposed to do, the following things happen. This task forces you to be explicit about the relevant aspects of the environment. It forces you to be explicit about what computations have to be performed on those environmental aspects to encode the information the mechanism requires. It also forces you to be explicit about how the information is to be represented and transformed during processing and how it is to be compared to other information to make a decision or categorization. Failures to be explicit are far too common among perceptual developmental theories. One wonders if Gibson (1969) would have underestimated the difficulty of extracting invariant information in everyday settings if she had tried to implement her differentiation theory. Attempts to implement developmental theories should minimize the likelihood of such oversights.

(2) When the implementation does not perform properly, you know immediately that something is wrong with the model. This, too, could serve us well because most of our theories, as they are currently stated, are too vague to disprove. It is essential, of course, that the implementation be sufficiently constrained by environmental restrictions and by empirical observations. Otherwise, it would be too difficult to isolate erroneous assumptions. When an implementation is reasonably constrained and does not perform properly, you should be able to pinpoint the sources of difficulties. Perhaps you have been too vague about the aspects of the environment that are involved. Or perhaps you have not incorporated enough sources of environmental information to allow the program to arrive at unambiguous solutions. Or perhaps the representations of environmental information used are not rich enough or do not capitalize sufficiently on invariant properties.

(3) If the program works properly, you may be able to make nonobvious predictions and then collect more data to see whether the predictions are accurate. This sort of evidence can be used to argue persuasively that the model is on the right track.[1]

The computational approach to the study of vision has been quite successful in recent years. It has yielded important insights into stereopsis (Longuet-Higgins, 1982; Mayhew, 1982), the perception of motion (Ullman, 1979), the perception of depth from optic flow (Clocksin, 1980; Prazdny, 1980), the perception of biomechanical motion (Hoffman & Flinchbaugh, 1982; Webb & Aggarwal, 1982), the extraction of shape from shading (Horn, 1979), and so on.

This, then, is the main thesis of this chapter: A computational approach may be very fruitful to the investigation of perceptual development, just as it has been fruitful to the investigation of mature vision. In particular, such an approach might allow us to make headway on the difficult problem that has eluded us: the description of mechanisms of perceptual development.

By this point the reader might question my sanity. After all, most of the capabilities developmental psychologists study simply do not lend themselves to the kind of quantitative rigor this computational approach demands. Consequently, the approach may be attractive in principle but unfeasible in practice. A lack of enthusiasm for quantitative approaches may be appropriate for many areas of developmental research, but I do not think it is necessarily appropriate for the study of visual development.

First, the properties of the environment that are important to vision and visual development may be easier to describe and quantify than those important to other domains of development. We know, for example, that sharp, vertically oriented contours are important for stereopsis and that horizontal retinal disparities between such contours are the primary cue to depth. These properties can be measured quantitatively. The important environmental properties for the development of particular cognitive and social skills are not nearly so clear.

Second, many characteristics of visual mechanisms that might be important to one's model can be measured quantitatively. For example, we can obtain quantitative, replicable estimates of how visual acuity, optical quality, receptor distributions, and other properties of the eye and central visual system change with age. Knowledge of such properties is crucial to successful modeling; as mentioned above, any model, quantitative or otherwise, requires empirical observations to constrain its parameters and allow strong hypothesis testing. Because so many important aspects of visual processing can be measured reliably, vision is probably better suited for quantitative modeling than is cognition, language, or social behavior.

Third, we have fairly clear ideas of what various visual capabilities are for; without such clarity, it is very difficult to model performance for everyday settings. We know, for example, that stereopsis is for perceiving three-dimensionality. We know that eye movements are used to keep the fovea on a moving target or to move the fovea to a different target when desired. This knowledge of functions aids modeling because it specifies the proper domain for the implementation. For example, an implementation of stereopsis should be able to describe three-dimensional layout for a variety of scenes. It should not be able to recognize and identify objects in those scenes. For these three reasons, visual development may be an excellent research area in which to use the computational approach.

Background Material for a Specific Developmental Problem

I now illustrate how this approach can be used by giving concrete examples of computational models I have developed for one aspect for visual development. At this time, the models are not completely refined, but they are mature enough to serve as illustrations. Before I present the models, however, it is useful to define some basic issues in perceptual development and to provide background material for the particular developmental problem addressed by the models.

There are, of course, many challenging problems in perceptual development. One classic problem is the explanation of how infants acquire the ability to recognize and identify objects in everyday settings. Well before they enter school, children can recognize and identify objects reliably despite dreadfully complicating factors such as changes in an object's position, orientation, slant, distance, and context. (Indeed, even 4- to 6-month-old infants can recognize some familiar objects, such as their mothers, in a variety of situations; Fagan, 1976; Fagan & Shepherd, 1979.) Because changes in position, orientation, slant, distance, and context are mostly irrelevant to an object's identity, the visual system must use recognition and identification schemes that are not misled by such changes. The question for perceptual developmentalists is, How do infants acquire this ability? This is, of course, a very difficult question because we do not even have a good idea of how object recognition and identification occur in adults. But let us consider the developmental question anyway.

One might argue that the requisite skills are simply built in so that infants can recognize and identify objects properly right from the start. This view is almost certainly wrong. As Gibson (1969) and others have documented, considerable experience with a class of stimuli is often needed in order to recognize and identify them properly.

Alternatively, one might adopt a less extreme position. Gibson (1969), for example, argued that the ability to categorize particular objects was not built in. Rather, the infant comes into the world with structures that allow him or her to detect the invariant properties that uniquely identify particular objects. Once the child is exposed to an object enough times, the invariant properties are detected and the object is identified properly. This hypothesis may be correct but, as it is currently stated, is not very interesting. The fundamental elements of the hypothesis are unspecified. What are the built-in structures? What are the invariant properties? How are they detected?

Despite these problems, perceptual developmentalists agree that visual experience is important to the acquisition of object recognition and identification. Indeed, I bolster this position later in the chapter by presenting evidence that some basic visual mechanisms are controlled by visual experience. So at least some aspects of the ability to recognize and identify objects are acquired through experience.

We are quite far from understanding in detail how the ability to recognize and identify objects is acquired, and so it is probably useful to split the problem up for the time being. One can do this by considering the processes underlying object recognition and identification in terms of specific invariances. *Slant invariance,* for example, refers to the ability to recognize an object when it is viewed at different slants. *Distance invariance* refers to the ability to recognize an object when it is viewed at different distances, and I focus on this skill for the remainder of the chapter.

The computational models presented here concern one aspect of how the distance invariance property of object recognition is acquired. However, before distance invariance and the models are discussed, it is necessary to provide some more background material. Specifically, I must describe linear systems analysis and contrast sensitivity functions. Readers familiar with these topics may skip ahead to page 353.

My discussion of linear systems analysis and contrast sensitivity functions is brief and conceptual. Cornsweet (1970), Gaskill (1978), and Georgeson (1979) provide more comprehensive and rigorous treatments. Linear systems analysis is based on Fourier's theorem, which implies that any two-dimensional, time-invariant visual stimulus can be exactly described by combining a set of more basic stimuli. These basic stimuli are sine wave gratings, examples of which are shown in Figure 10.1. A sine wave grating is a pattern of light and dark stripes whose intensity varies sinusoidally with position. These gratings are specified by four parameters: (1) spatial frequency, the number of pattern repetitions (or cycles) per degree of visual angle; (2) orientation, the grating's tilt to the left or right of vertical; (3) contrast, which is related to the difference between maximum and minimum intensities of the grating [contrast is equal to $(I_{max} - I_{min})/(I_{max} + I_{min})$] and (4) phase, the grating's position with respect to some reference position. Startling as it sounds, even a complex, two-dimensional visual stimulus, such as a face, can be described exactly by the combination of a set of sine wave gratings of various frequencies, orientations, contrasts, and phases.

Linear systems analysis uses Fourier's theorem to predict a system's response to arbitrary two-dimensional stimuli. Because any stimulus can be represented by the addition of various gratings, the response or output of a linear system can be determined by the addition of the responses to the constituent gratings of the input stimulus. Consider a simple optical system: a camera. The camera's response or output for various spatial frequencies is its *modulation transfer function* (MTF), the proportion of input contrast that is transmitted onto the film as a function of spatial

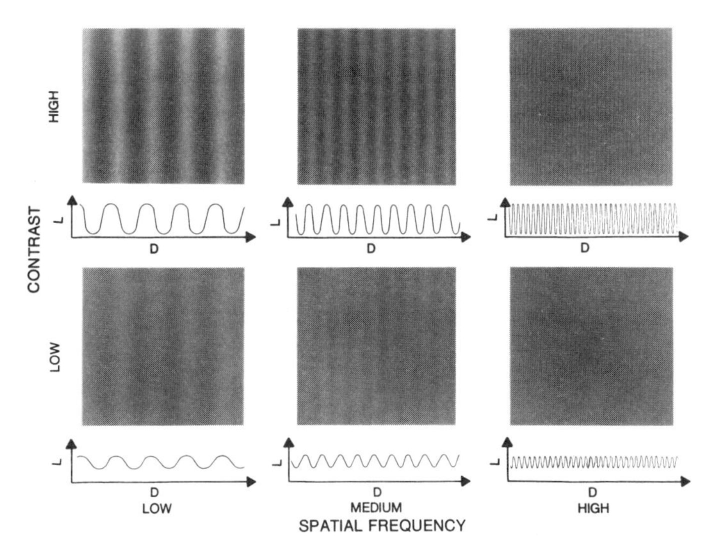

FIGURE 10.1. Six sine wave gratings differing in spatial frequency and contrast. From left to right, the gratings increase in spatial frequency. From bottom to top, they increase in contrast. If the figure is held at arm's length, the gratings have spatial frequencies of 2.5, 5, and 16 c/deg.

frequency. The relationship between input and output for the camera is described by the equations

$$A_o(u, v) = A_i(u, v) \cdot A_h(u, v) \quad (1)$$

$$P_o(u, v) = P_i(u, v) + P_h(u, v). \quad (2)$$

These equations are derived by Fourier transformation. Thus, the argument of each variable is spatial frequency. Equation 1 relates the amplitudes or contrasts of the input and output sine wave grating components; $A_h(u, v)$ is the lens' modulation transfer function in two dimensions (u and v). And $A_i(u,v)$ is the amplitude spectrum of the input stimulus; an amplitude spectrum is the contrasts of the constituent sine wave gratings at different spatial frequencies. Thus, multiplication of the input's sine wave components $A_i(u,v)$ by the appropriate weighting factor $A_h(u,v)$ yields the amplitude spectrum of the output. Inverse Fourier transformation (the operation involved in Fourier synthesis) can then be used to convert the output spectrum $A_o(u,v)$ into spatial coordinates to predict the appearance of the image on the film. Equation 2 relates the phases of the input and output spatial frequency components. Most optical systems and visual systems do not change the phase of a stimulus or its components during processing. Therefore, the phase transfer function of a system $P_h(u,v)$ is generally zero, which implies that the output and input phases are identical. For this reason, I disregard phase transfer functions and their effects henceforth.

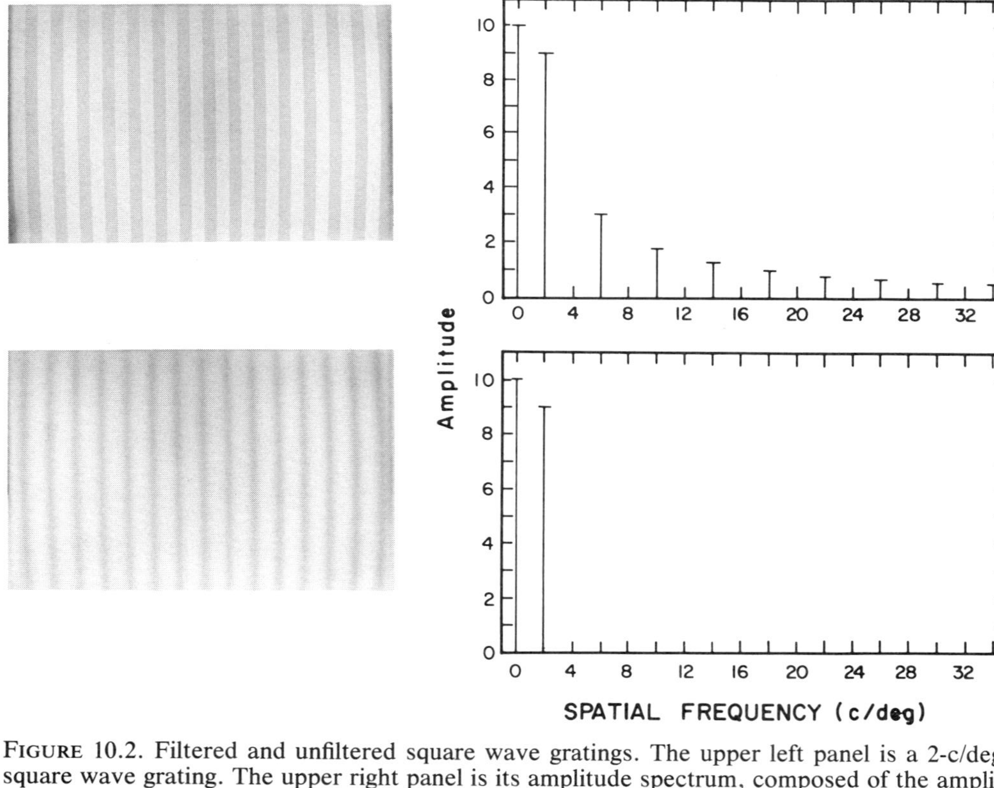

FIGURE 10.2. Filtered and unfiltered square wave gratings. The upper left panel is a 2-c/deg square wave grating. The upper right panel is its amplitude spectrum, composed of the amplitudes of the grating's sine wave components. The lower right panel is the amplitude spectrum that results once the components above 3 c/deg are filtered out. The lower left panel illustrates the resultant pattern.

Figure 10.2 illustrates how linear systems analysis is used to predict the output of an optical system to a particular input: a square wave grating. Suppose that the MTF of the system is a simple low-pass filter. In other words, the lens transmits spatial frequencies lower than 3 cycles/degree (c/deg) perfectly and does not transmit higher spatial frequencies at all. In that case, Equation 1 implies that the amplitude spectrum of the output contains all the spatial frequencies of the original square wave except those above 3 c/deg (see upper right graph in Figure 10.2). One can then use the inverse Fourier transformation to calculate the predicted output (lower right graph in Figure 10.2). A lens that transmits only low spatial frequencies would thus produce a noticeably degraded version of the original square wave.

Now let us turn to vision. Linear systems analysis has been used to good effect in the investigation of visual performance (e.g., Cornsweet, 1970; Ratliff, 1965). The contrast sensitivity function (CSF) is used instead of the MTF to represent the visual system's ability to detect and transmit information as a function of spatial frequency. The CSF is determined by measuring an observer's contrast sensitivity to sine wave gratings of various spatial frequencies. This measurement is made by presenting gratings of a number of different spatial frequencies, one at a time, and determining the least contrast necessary to detect the grating at each of those frequencies. The CSF of an adult with good vision is shown in the lower portion of Figure 10.3. Contrast sensitivity, the reciprocal of the minimum contrast required for detection, is plotted as a function of spatial frequency. Note that sensitivity is greatest for intermediate spatial frequencies (2 to 6 c/deg) and lower for low and high frequencies. A grating, varying in spatial frequency and contrast, is displayed in the upper portion of the figure, to illustrate what the CSF represents. The grating increases in spatial frequency from left to right and increases in contrast from top to bottom. The physical contrast of the grating is constant along any horizontal line in the photograph, but its perceived contrast is not. Clearly, perceived contrast is greater at intermediate frequencies than at low and high frequencies. Note the correspondence between the visibility of the grating at different frequencies in the upper part of Figure 10.3 and the CSF in the lower part.

The CSF's of young infants have been measured by three research groups. Atkinson, Braddick, and colleagues have used behavioral and evoked-potential techniques to measure CSFs in infants from a few days to 6 months of age (Atkinson, Braddick, & Moar, 1977; Harris, Atkinson, & Braddick, 1976). Banks and Salapatek (1978) used a behavioral technique to measure CSFs in 1- to 3-month-olds. Pirchio and colleagues measured these functions in 2- to 10-month-olds by using evoked potentials (Pirchio, Spinelli, Fiorentini, & Maffei, 1978). These data agree remarkably well in light of the differences in technique and stimuli. The agreement suggests that age-related shifts in these functions are fairly robust.

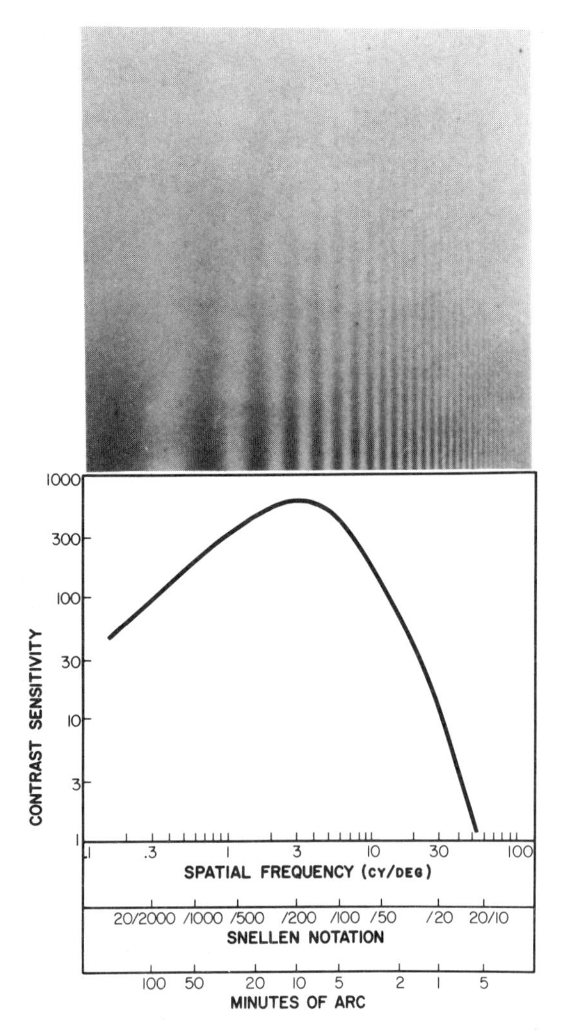

FIGURE 10.3. A sine wave grating and a typical adult CSF. The upper part of the figure displays a sine wave grating in which spatial frequency increases from left to right and contrast increases from top to bottom. The lower part of the figure shows a typical adult CSF. Contrast sensitivity, the reciprocal of contrast at threshold, is plotted as a function of spatial frequency. Scales relating spatial frequency to Snellen equivalents and stripe width in minutes of arc are shown for comparison. If the figure is viewed from a distance of 70 cm, the scales at the bottom indicate the actual frequency values of the grating in the upper part of the figure.

Figure 10.4 shows the group average data of Banks and Salapatek (1978). Comparing these functions to the adults' in Figure 10.3 reveals striking differences. Infants' CSFs are clearly shifted to lower spatial frequencies. Indeed, the highest detectable frequency, the acuity cutoff, is a factor of 10 to 20 below that for adults. Likewise, infants' CSFs exhibit a large sensitivity deficit relative to adults. These deficits may reflect motivational differences between infants and adults, but the similarity of behavioral and evoked-potential results suggests that motivation is not the primary cause.[2] This research suggests a distinct lack of clarity in the infant's visual world: The young infant's visual system is able to detect only fairly large, high-contrast patterns in the environment. This ability improves gradually until at least 6 months of age, when infants are about a factor of 2 less sensitive than adults (Pirchio et al., 1978; Harris et al., 1976).

The height and shape of the CSF at any age reflect the operation of several basic visual mechanisms. Consider, for example, the steady loss in adults' contrast sensitivity that accompanies increases in spatial frequency. Measurements of the optical quality of the mature eye reveal that less than 100 percent of the contrast of a stimulus is transmitted to the retina. This percentage depends heavily on the spatial frequency of the stimulus. For example, the retinal image contrast of a 5-c/deg grating is about 70 percent of the stimulus contrast under normal viewing conditions, whereas the retinal contrast of a 20-c/deg grating is merely 15 per-

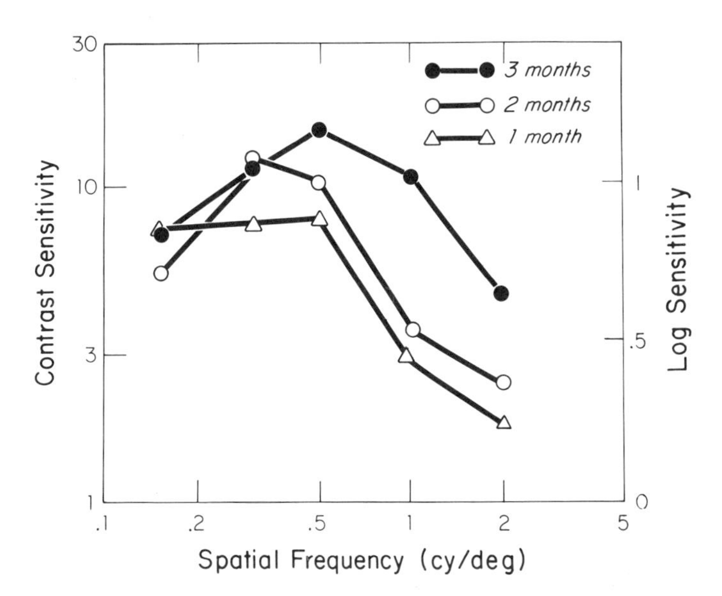

FIGURE 10.4. The average CSFs for 1-, 2-, and 3-month-olds as reported by Banks and Salapatek. The average contrast sensitivity for each age group is plotted as a function of spatial frequency. (From Banks & Salapatek, 1978.)

cent of the stimulus contrast (Campbell & Green, 1965; Campbell & Gubisch, 1966). In other words, the contrast of very fine pattern information is reduced much more by the eye's optics than is the contrast of coarser pattern information. This optical effect accounts for most of the high-frequency loss in adults' contrast sensitivity illustrated in Figure 10.3. Additional losses occur because of the spatial summating properties of early neural processing (Campbell & Green, 1965).

The visual system's differential sensitivity to spatial frequency poses a problem: How is constant perception of an object at various distances achieved? That a problem of this sort exists can be illustrated by considering a simple object viewed at two distances. Consider an object, a bright filled square on a dark background, viewed at 1 m. Its amplitude spectrum at this distance is shown in Figure 10.5(*a*); notice that several spatial frequencies are present at various amplitudes. Figure 10.5(*b*) displays the amplitudes of those frequency components once they are processed by the optics of a hypothetical eye; notice that the contrast of the object, higher spatial frequencies in particular, has been attenuated by the optics. Now we move the object to a distance of 4m. The amplitude spectrum of Figure 10.5(*c*) results. The same spatial frequencies are present but are simply shifted to values 4 times higher than when they are viewed at 1m.

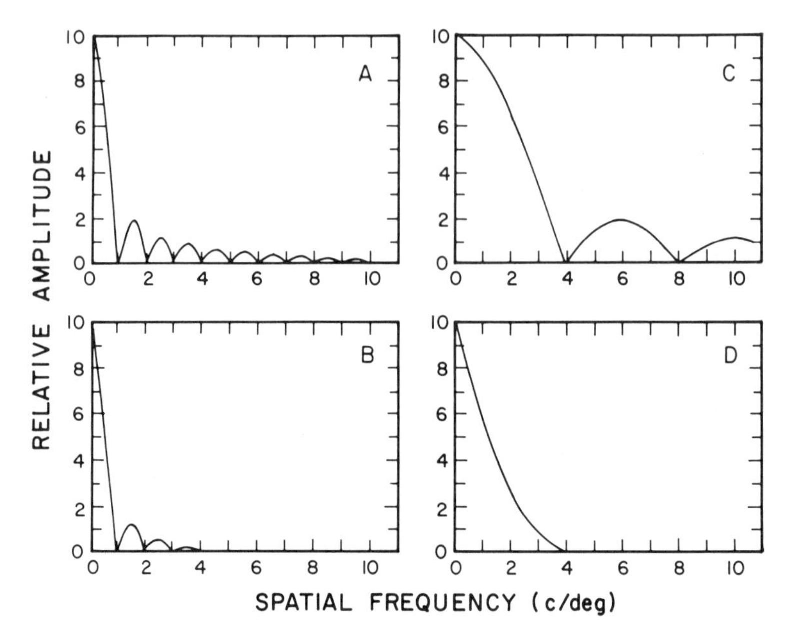

FIGURE 10.5. The amplitude spectra of a bright filled square on a dark background. (*a*) The spectrum of the square viewed at 1 m; (*b*) the spectrum of the square viewed at 1 m once it is filtered by the optics of a hypothetical eye; (*c*) the spectrum of the square viewed at 4 m; (*d*) the spectrum of the square viewed at 4 m once it is filtered by the optics of the eye.

Figure 10.5(*d*) shows the amplitudes of those frequency components once they are processed by the eye's optics. The relative amplitudes in the retinal image are quite different from those at a 1-m viewing distance. If the visual system could not compensate for the differences in relative retinal image contrasts at the two distances, it should be quite difficult to determine whether an object is the same when it is viewed at different distances. Fortunately, the mature visual system does compensate in a useful way.

Before describing how the visual system performs this compensation, I should point out that the problem of recognizing objects at various distances is a general one. It arises, for example, in satellite photography. Pictures of objects on the earth are significantly degraded by the defocusing effects of the camera's optics and the earth's atmosphere. These effects can be minimized, however, by "deblurring" the photograph through computer-enhanced imaging techniques. The deblurring is accomplished in the following way. First, the defocusing effects of the camera's optics and the earth's atmosphere are represented as a blur function. This function simply describes how much the contrasts of various spatial frequencies are attenuated by the defocusing agents. Then the Fourier transform of the original photograph is computed, and the amplitudes of the resulting spatial frequency components are multiplied by the inverse of the blur function.[3] The result is a much improved image that represents the objective structure of objects on the earth more veridically than the original did. An example is shown in Figure 10.6. The left half of the figure shows the original blurred photograph. The amplitude spectrum of this photograph is computed and multiplied by the inverse of the blur function. Fourier synthesis is then used to reconstruct the photograph in such a way that the attentuated high spatial frequencies are amplified relative to the unattenuated low spatial frequencies. The result is illus-

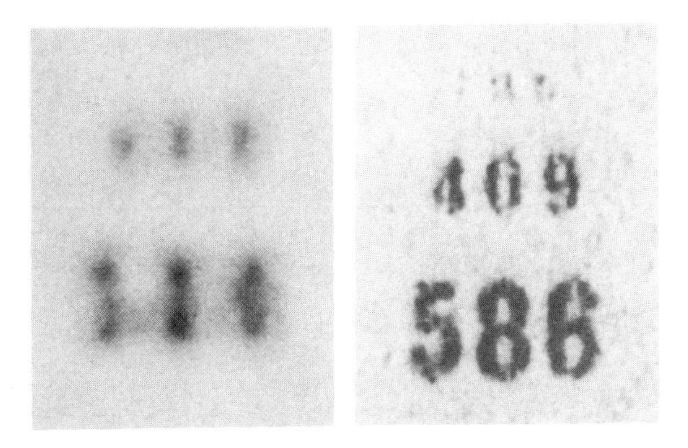

FIGURE 10.6. Demonstration of deblurring by using Fourier technique. On the left is the blurred original. On the right is the deblurred version produced by compensating for the attenuation of the original blurring. (Adapted from Gennery, 1973.)

trated in the right half of the figure. The enhanced photograph is a much more veridical representation of the original object.

The mature visual system appears to perform a similar form of contrast compensation in order to "deblur" stimuli. This compensation has been demonstrated in several experiments on adults' processing of pattern information under suprathreshold conditions (e.g., Blakemore, Muncey, & Ridley, 1973; Georgeson & Sullivan, 1975; Kulikowski, 1976; Watanabe, Mori, Nagata, & Hiwatashi, 1968). Georgeson and Sullivan (1975) asked adults to adjust the contrast of a sine wave grating of one spatial frequency (the "comparison" grating) until it appeared to match the contrast of a sine wave grating of a different frequency (the "standard" grating). In their main experiment, the standard was a grating of 5 c/deg, a value near the peak of the adult CSF. The results are illustrated in the right panel of Figure 10.7. When the contrast of the standard was low (that is, when the grating was near threshold), adults set the contrast of the comparison gratings to higher values. Those values were predictable from the CSF. For example, when asked to match apparent contrasts, adults set the contrast of a 20-c/deg comparison grating to a value 8 times higher than the contrast of the 5-c/deg standard. This ratio was equal to the ratio of

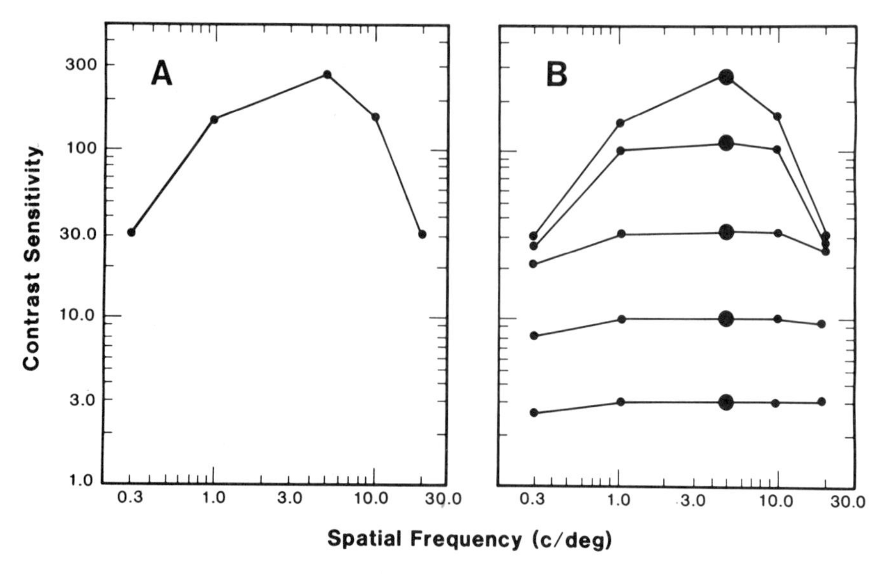

FIGURE 10.7. Adult CSF and contrast-matching data from Georgeson and Sullivan (1975). (*a*) CSF. (*b*) Contrast-matching data. The procedure by which these data were obtained is described in the text. The reciprocal of the contrasts of the standard and comparison gratings is plotted as a function of spatial frequency. The large symbols represent the reciprocals of the contrasts of the 5-c/deg standard. The small symbols represent the reciprocals of the contrasts of the comparison gratings when they matched the standard in apparent contrast. (From Stephens & Banks, 1985.)

contrast thresholds for 5 and 20 c/deg. The most interesting result in this experiment occurred when the contrast of the standard was set to a value well above threshold. Adults in this situation adjusted the contrast of the comparison to the same physical value as the contrast of the standard. This result is surprising because, as mentioned above, two gratings of equal contrast but different spatial frequencies will produce different retinal image contrasts. In other words, when the adults set 5- and 20-c/deg gratings to equal physical contrasts, they were accepting as equal in apparent contrast two gratings whose retinal image contrasts differed substantially. This implies that the mature visual system compensates at suprathreshold contrasts for the defocusing effects of the eye's optics.

Georgeson and Sullivan called this phenomenon *contrast constancy* and noted an important perceptual consequence. As an object moves away from an observer, its spatial frequency content shifts to progressively higher values. For medium- and high-contrast (suprathreshold) objects, apparent contrast would not change. Thus, contrast constancy confers a useful property on the perception of real objects: As long as the contrast that defines an object and its features is above threshold, apparent contrast remains invariant across a wide range of distances.

How is contrast constancy achieved? Georgeson and Sullivan pointed out that the central visual system must in some way undo the optical attenuation that occurs in the formation of the retinal image and the neural attenuation caused by peripheral neural summation. They proposed a simple model based on multiple spatial-frequency channels with narrow tuning. These channels are mechanisms that respond to a narrow range of spatial frequencies only. There is considerable psychophysical and physiological evidence for their existence (e.g., Braddick, Campbell, & Atkinson, 1978). According to Georgeson and Sullivan's model, high-frequency channels have steeper contrast-response functions than medium-frequency channels. In other words, as the contrast of a target is raised, the activity of high-frequency channels increases more rapidly than the activity of medium-frequency channels. Consider how this model could be used to explain apparent contrast matches between a medium- and a high-frequency grating at low and high contrasts. At near-threshold contrasts, apparent contrast matches would reflect differences in the contrast thresholds of the two gratings; observers would require more contrast in the high-frequency grating before they could appear equal in contrast because high-frequency channels have higher contrast thresholds than medium-frequency channels. As one raised the contrast of the targets, however, apparent contrast matches would become veridical because the activity of high-frequency channels increases more rapidly than that of medium-frequency channels. Experimental evidence suggests that this differential response to contrast is mediated by the visual cortex (Georgeson & Sullivan, 1975; Hess, Bradley, & Piotrowski, 1983).

Banks, Stephens, & Hartmann (1985) demonstrated that 12-week-olds, but not 6-week-olds, possess multiple spatial-frequency channels with narrow tuning. In the first of their two experiments they used a masking paradigm. The detectability of sine wave gratings of different spatial frequencies was measured in the presence and the absence of a narrowband visual noise masker. The 12-week-olds exhibited adultlike, spatial-frequency-dependent masking. In other words, the presence of the noise masker decreased the detectability of sine wave gratings whose spatial-frequency content was similar to that of the masker, whereas the presence of the masker did not affect the detectability of gratings whose frequency content was dissimilar from that of the masker. The masking effects observed in the 6-week-olds were not spatial-frequency-dependent. In other words, the younger infants did not provide evidence for multiple spatial-frequency channels. In the second experiment, Banks et al. used a composite grating paradigm. The results were entirely consistent with those of experiment 1. The performance of the 12-week-olds, but not of the 6-week-olds, was consistent with the presence of narrowband spatial-frequency channels.

Stephens and Banks (1985) noted that if Georgeson and Sullivan's hypothesis is correct, contrast constancy should not be observed at 6 weeks of age but might be observed at 12 weeks of age. To test this possibility, Stephens and Banks used a visual preference procedure to measure an analog to apparent contrast matches in 6- and 12-week-olds. Two sine wave gratings, differing in spatial frequency by a factor of 3, were presented side by side. They referred to the lower-frequency grating as F and to the higher-frequency grating as $3F$. From previous experiments they knew that the contrast threshold for $3F$ was about 4 times greater than that for F. For a given experimental session, the contrast of $3F$ was fixed at either a near-threshold level or one of two suprathreshold levels. Then the contrast of F was varied in order to estimate the contrast at which preference for the two gratings was equal. Stephens and Banks assumed that the equal-preference point corresponded to an apparent contrast match. The equal-preference points for 6-week-olds were always predictable from their contrast thresholds. That is, the younger infants required 4 times more contrast in $3F$ than in F, at all three contrast levels of $3F$, in order to distribute their looking time equally to the two stimuli. Some of the 12-week-olds' equal-preference points were also predictable from their contrast thresholds. For near-threshold stimuli, they required 4 times more contrast in $3F$ than in F for equal preference. However, the equal-preference points were not predictable from contrast thresholds at suprathreshold contrasts. Indeed, equal preference occurred when the two stimuli had the same physical contrast. If one accepts the assumption that the equal-preference point in infants is analogous to an apparent contrast match in adults (Stephens & Banks, 1985, evaluate the validity of this assumption in some detail), these data imply that contrast constancy is present at 12, but not 6, weeks of age. The presence of contrast constancy at this age suggests that the perceived contrast of objects and their features should remain reasonably constant across a range of viewing distances.

Computational Models of How Contrast Constancy Develops

Before presenting the computational models that I have developed recently, let me review the major points concerning the phenomenon of contrast constancy and its development.

(1) Under suprathreshold conditions, the apparent contrasts of gratings of different spatial frequencies are the same when the physical contrasts of the gratings are the same. This behavior implies that the perceived contrasts of suprathreshold features in an object should be invariant when the object is viewed at different distances. Assuredly, such invariance aids the recognition and identification of objects in various spatial locations.

(2) The optics of the eye attenuate high spatial frequencies more than low ones. Consequently, contrast constancy can be achieved only if the contrast of high-frequency targets is amplified later in the visual system relative to the contrast of low-frequency targets.

(3) Stephens and Banks (1985) demonstrated behavior in 12-week-olds, but not 6-week-olds, that is analogous to veridical contrast matching. Thus, contrast constancy may develop quite early in life.

Now consider the question of how the visual system must amplify high frequencies relative to low ones in order to achieve contrast constancy. To aid the discussion, I refer to attenuation of high frequencies caused by the eye's optics and by peripheral neural summation as the *blur function*. This function simply represents the loss of contrast as a function of spatial frequency. I refer to the postretinal amplification of high frequencies relative to low ones as the *gain function*. This function represents the relative enhancement of perceived contrast as a function of spatial frequency. (Recall that the mechanism of postretinal amplification is the increased slope of the contrast-response functions. Therefore, amplification occurs at suprathreshold contrasts only. The gain function describes this amplification at contrasts reasonably well above threshold.) Note that veridical contrast matching implies that the gain function is the inverse of the blur function; any other form would lead to under- or overcompensation for attenuation owing to the blur function.

The developmental question of interest is, How does the gain function come to be the appropriate one? Four models of how this might be achieved are listed in Table 10.1. There are two general classes of models that, for want of better terms, I have called *genetic* and *experiential* models. These terms are, of course, too simple because all four models

TABLE 10.1. Models of the Development of Contrast Constancy

Genetic Models
- Model 1: Prespecified gain function is inverse of blur function.

Experiential Models
- Model 2: Distribution of environmental information is known. Blur function is deduced by comparing distribution of output information to distribution of environmental information.
- Model 2A: One type of environmental feature is known. Blur function is deduced by comparing output distribution for that feature to known input distribution.
- Model 3: Distribution of environmental information is not known nor is a particular environmental feature. Blur function is deduced by comparing output distribution for an object undergoing a smooth change in distance.

require both genetic and environmental influences. I use the terms simply to convey the nature and relative importance of environmental factors for each.

In the genetic model the gain function is assumed to be prespecified genetically. Visual experience is required to sustain visual function, but is not crucial to setting how much high frequencies are amplified relative to low ones. According to this viewpoint, contrast constancy develops once multiple spatial-frequency channels emerge.

There are two arguments against this sort of model. First, the genetic model has difficulty explaining how contrast constancy emerges at 12 weeks of age. The infant's blur function is presumably quite different from the adult's. This age difference is illustrated by the differences between infant and adult CSFs. Twelve-week-olds are most sensitive to 0.5 c/deg and quite insensitive to spatial frequencies from 3 to 4 c/deg (Atkinson et al., 1977; Banks & Salapatek, 1978). The peak of the adult CSF, however, is at 3 to 4 c/deg, with sensitivity falling to the acuity cutoff at 40 to 50 c/deg. Changes in the optics of the eye probably cause differences in high-frequency sensitivity between infants and adults, but there are no definitive data yet. Additional neural differences are implied by the striking immaturity of the infant's retina (Abramov et al., 1982; Hendrickson & Youdelis, 1984). Whatever the cause, the blur functions of the mature and immature eyes are assuredly dissimilar. Consequently, the gain functions in 12-week infants and in adults would have to be rather different to achieve veridical contrast matching at both ages. The genetic code could conceivably carry information to reset the gain function at various ages. To accomplish this resetting, however, the code and the resulting maturational plan would have to be rather complex. This requirement for complexity makes the genetic model somewhat unattractive.

Additional, and perhaps more persuasive, evidence against a simple genetic model comes from studies of contrast matching in adults with amblyopia. Amblyopia is a condition of reduced visual acuity in one eye that is generally caused by anisometropia (different refractive errors in the two eyes) or by strabismus (crossed eyes). Hess and Bradley (1980)

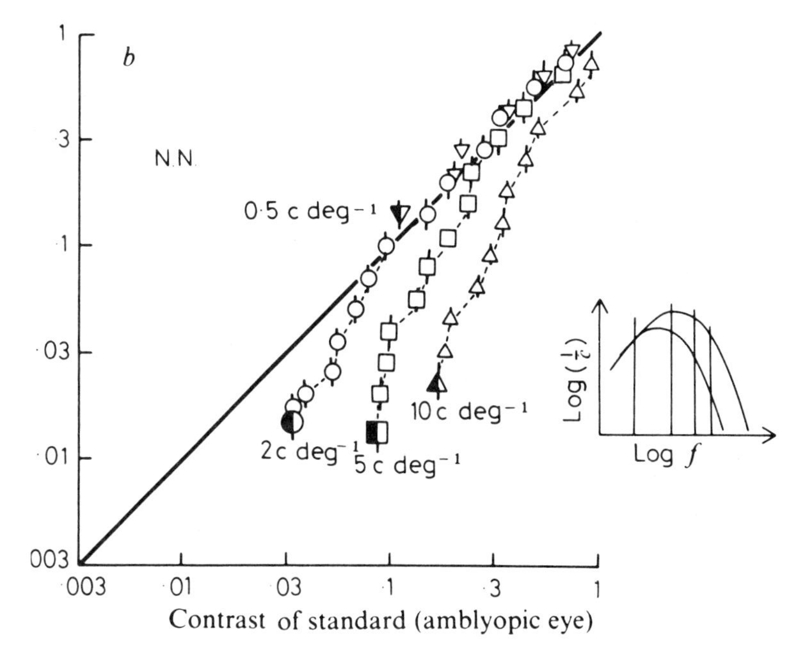

FIGURE 10.8. Contrast-matching data from one amblyopic observer in the Hess and Bradley (1980) report. The CSFs for the amblyopic and nonamblyopic eyes are shown in the inset to the right. The large graph plots the contrast of the grating presented to the nonamblyopic eye, when it appeared to match the contrast of the grating presented to the amblyopic eye, on the vertical axis. The contrast of the grating presented to the amblyopic eye is plotted on the horizontal axis. The solid line indicates where the data would lie if matches occurred at equal physical contrasts. The half-filled symbols represent the matches at threshold. The open symbols represent the matches at suprathreshold contrasts. (From Hess & Bradley, 1980.)

measured the CSFs and contrast matching of amblyopic adults. Their results are illustrated in Figure 10.8. The CSFs of the observers' amblyopic and normal eyes were rather dissimilar. The amblyopic eye exhibited reduced contrast sensitivity to high spatial frequencies. Bradley and Hess asked their observers to match a high-frequency grating presented to the normal eye with a grating of the same spatial frequency presented to the amblyopic eye. When the grating presented to the normal eye was near threshold, the observers required more contrast in the target presented to the amblyopic eye. When the grating presented to the normal eye was suprathreshold, however, observers reported identical apparent contrasts when the two gratings were, in fact, equal in contrast. Clearly these amblyopic observers were using different gain functions for the two eyes to compensate for the poorer contrast sensitivity of the amblyopic eye. Genetic models would have difficulty explaining these data because the genetic code would have to carry information about not only how the blur function changes with age in normal children, but also how it changes between eyes in amblyopic children and adults. This seems quite implausible and leads one to suspect that visual experience is involved fundamentally in the acquisition of the proper gain function.

Before describing the three experiential models in Table 10.1, let me characterize clearly what they have to explain. Allow me, for the moment, to use a homunculus (see Figure 10.9) to represent the information gathering and decision making that must be performed in the central visual system. The homunculus is used only to clarify the discussion. In using him, I am not making a theoretical claim that the information gathering and decision making are performed by a high-level mechanism.

The homunculus' job is to adjust the parameters of the gain function to render it the inverse of the blur function. In the experiential models, the blur function is assumed to be unknown initially, so the homunculus needs information that will allow him to measure it. How should he proceed? The difficulty in answering this question is illustrated by the equation

$$O(u,v) = I(u,v) \cdot B(u,v), \tag{3}$$

where $O(u,v)$ represents the output of the peripheral visual system as a function of spatial frequency in two dimensions, $I(u,v)$ represents the input to the visual system as a function of frequency, and $B(u,v)$ represents the blur function, that is, how much the contrast of various spatial frequencies is reduced during peripheral processing. The experiential

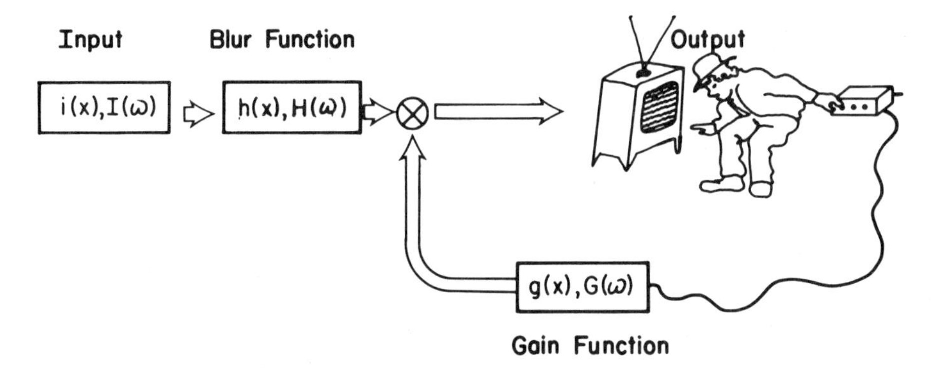

FIGURE 10.9. A schematic of the feedback mechanism that is presumably involved in adjusting the contrast compensation (or gain) function. The input to the visual system is represented by the box on the left. The blurring caused by optical imperfections and peripheral neural summation is represented by the next box. The output of the blur process is depicted by the image on the TV screen. The evaluation of that output is represented by the homunculus who adjusts the parameters of the gain function to compensate for attenuation due to the blur function.

models assume that the homunculus has direct access to $O(u,v)$ only, so he has to solve one equation with two unknowns. This is, of course, impossible unless some additional constraints can be brought to bear. The three experiential models postulate different constraints.

Model 2 assumes that the input $I(u,v)$ is known in a statistical sense, so the equation reduces to

$$B(u,v) = \frac{O(u,v)}{I(u,v)}, \tag{4}$$

where $O(u,v)$ and $I(u,v)$ are known. Model 2 does not assume that every input presented to the visual system is known; such an assumption would be absurd because the purpose of visual perception itself is to determine what specific inputs are. Instead, it is assumed that the average distribution of spatial frequency information in the environment is known. For instance, the homunculus might assume that the average contrast of 20 c/deg information in the environment is 50 percent of the average contrast at 5 c/deg. We can rewrite Equation 4 to express this model more clearly:

$$B(u,v) = O_a(u,v)/I_a(u,v) \tag{5}$$

where $I_a(u,v)$ represents the expected average input amplitudes as a function of spatial frequency and $O_a(u,v)$ represents the output amplitudes the homunculus observes on the TV screen. The blur function is deduced by comparing the expected average input distribution to the observed average output distribution. The homunculus can deduce the correct blur function in this manner, but only if the actual input information corresponds on average with his expectations. Is this plausible? If the distribution of spatial-frequency information in the environment were simple (that is, could be described by a few parameters), the model could be implemented readily. Unfortunately, the distribution is not simple. Switkes, Mayer, and Sloan (1978) have shown that the distribution of amplitudes as a function of spatial frequency varies from one sort of environment to another. Urban environments, for example, appear to have relatively greater amplitudes at high spatial frequencies and at vertical and horizontal orientations than rural environments do. Thus, model 2 requires in practice a detailed expectation of the average distribution of amplitudes across spatial frequencies in the environment, and this expected distribution would have to vary depending on the kind of environment. The combined requirements for detail and flexibility seem unfeasible and decrease the attractiveness of this model.

Another version of model 2 is more plausible, however. This model, which I call model 2A, assumes that the homunculus knows the spatial-frequency distribution of a particular feature in the environment and can identify that feature unambiguously for the range of blur functions he has to deal with. Equation 5 applies for this model, but now the expected input is a particular feature rather than some time average for all inputs.

The known feature would have to contain a broad range of spatial frequencies in order to provide information at all the spatial frequencies the homunculus needs to do his job. An example illustrates how this model works. Suppose that the known feature is a sharp light-dark transition (an edge). In the interest of simplicity, I just consider the edge in one dimension. The one-dimensional Fourier transform of an edge of amplitude k is

$$I(v) = \frac{k}{\pi j v}, \tag{6}$$

where j is the square root of -1 and v is spatial frequency. From Equation 3, we have

$$O(v) = B(v) \cdot I(v) \tag{7}$$

$$O(v) = B(v) \cdot \frac{k}{\pi j v} \tag{8}$$

which implies that

$$B(v) = O(v) \cdot \pi \cdot \frac{jv}{k}. \tag{9}$$

Because π and j are constants and $O(v)$ can be measured, the homunculus could determine $B(v)$ to within a scale factor $1/k$. In other words, he could deduce in principle the blur function by simply monitoring the output due to a known feature. This model seems feasible. Perhaps the greatest uncertainty is whether the homunculus could reliably identify a particular feature in the environment from the ouput information provided. For example, without knowing the blur function, the homunculus might be unable to discriminate a diffuse edge, such as a shadow, from a sharp edge. If he mistakenly chose the diffuse edge as the known feature, he would err in his computation of the blur function and adjust the gain function inappropriately.[4] Whether reliable identification of a particular feature is possible could be asked by using a computer implementation of model 2A. The fact that a computer implementation is possible enhances the utility of these computational models; the performance of the implementation would be an extremely useful index of the model's feasibility. If the implementation could not successfully identify a particular feature embedded in everyday settings, the model should not be pursued further. If it could identify the feature reliably for a reasonably broad range of blur functions, we would know that the model can work in principle.

Model 3 represents a different tack altogether. It assumes that the homunculus deduces the blur function by noting how the output changes as an object undergoes a smooth transition in distance. Figure 10.10 illustrates how the model works. Consider a particular input stimulus $i(x,y)$ and its amplitude spectrum $I(u,v)$. When the stimulus is viewed at 1 m, its amplitude spectrum is the solid line in Figure 10.10. When the stimulus is viewed at 2 m, all the spatial-frequency components are shifted upward in frequency by a factor of 2. This shifted amplitude spectrum is illustrated by the dashed line in the figure. The homunculus could deduce the blur function if he could determine that the stimuli at 1 and 2 m were actually produced by the same object and that the change in distance was a factor of 2. The equations on page 366 show how. In deriving the equations, I assumed that the visual system processes images by using separate spatial-frequency-selective mechanisms (an assumption for which there is overwhelming psychophysical and physiological evidence). The mechanisms are roughly one octave wide (that is, they respond to a twofold range of spatial frequencies). The outputs of the various mechanisms are represented by $W(u,v)$, $X(u,v)$, $Y(u,v)$, and so forth. The W mechanism responds to a one-octave band centered at a spatial frequency of v_1. The X mechanism also responds to a one-octave band, but the center of the band is v_2, a spatial frequency 2 times higher than v_1. The center of the Y mechanism's band is v_4, which is 4 times higher than v_1, and so on. The outputs of the three mechanisms are shown in Table 10.2 for the object presented at two distances d_1 and d_2. The second distance in this example is twice the first, but the algorithm will work for other distances, too.

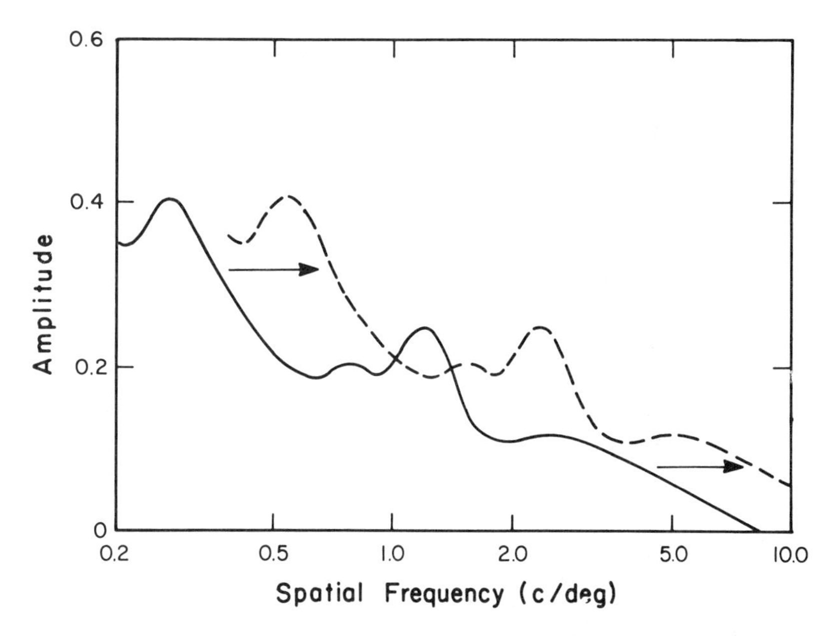

FIGURE 10.10. The amplitude spectra of an object when it is viewed at two different distances. The solid line represents the amplitude spectrum when the viewing distance is 1 m, and the broken line represents the spectrum when the viewing distance is 2 m. Notice that all the sine wave components simply shift upward in spatial frequency by a factor of 2.

TABLE 10.2. Model 3

Distance 1		Distance 2	
$W(v_1, d_1)$	$= H(v_1) \cdot I(v_1, d_1)$ ←	$W(v_1, d_2)$	$= H(v_1) \cdot I(v_1, d_2)$
$X(v_2, d_1)$	$= H(v_2) \cdot I(v_2, d_1)$ ←	→ $X(v_2, d_2)$	$= H(v_2) \cdot I(v_2, d_2)$
$Y(v_4, d_1)$	$= H(v_4) \cdot I(v_4, d_1)$	→ $Y(v_4, d_2)$	$= H(v_4) \cdot I(v_4, d_2)$

Once the homunculus determines the distance ratio, he can deduce the blur function by comparing one mechanism's output at one distance to another's output at the second distance. In the example, he should compare W's output at d_1 to X's at d_2 and X's ouput at d_1 to Y's at d_2. The following equations illustrate how he estimates the blur function by making these comparisons:

$$\frac{W(v_1, d_1)}{X(v_2, d_2)} = \frac{H(v_1) \cdot I(v_1, d_1)}{H(v_2) \cdot I(v_2, d_2)} \tag{10}$$

$$\frac{X(v_2, d_1)}{Y(v_4, d_2)} = \frac{H(v_2) \cdot I(v_2, d_1)}{H(v_4) \cdot I(v_4, d_2)} . \tag{11}$$

But we know that

$$\frac{I(v_1, d_1)}{I(v_2, d_2)} = \frac{I(v_2, d_1)}{I(v_4, d_2)} = 1 . \tag{12}$$

Therefore,

$$\frac{H(v_1)}{H(v_2)} = \frac{W(v_1, d_1)}{X(v_2, d_2)} \quad \text{and} \quad \frac{H(v_2)}{H(v_4)} = \frac{X(v_2, d_1)}{Y(v_4, d_2)} . \tag{13}$$

These ratios are the relative loss of contrast from one band of spatial frequencies to the next. This information is all the homunculus needs to adjust the gain function appropriately.

This model is more attractive than models 2 and 2A because it does not require too much knowledge about the input stimulus. However, the homunculus does need to know when and where to apply the algorithm, and this decision may not be easy. I propose the following strategy. The homunculus monitors the output of the TV screen for a particular type of event: a smooth, symmetric change in the angular subtense of a closed figure (note that he does not actually have to compute the change in distance, only the change in angular subtense). He applies the algorithm of Equations 10 and 11 to only those events because they are generally caused by an object moving smoothly in distance and not tilting or slanting toward or away from the eye as it does so. If he could reliably identify such cases, the algorithm could be used to compute the blur function and thereby adjust the gain function. When he identifies a proper event, the change in distance could be determined by the ratio of angular subtenses at the two distances.

The next step in the development of these computational theories will be computer implementation using visual scenes as input. The successes or failures of the implementations should indicate which models are worth pursuing. Finally, the computational theories should be tested empirically in restricted rearing experiments. For example, model 3 would predict that a kitten raised in a situation that did not allow the viewing of objects undergoing smooth transitions in distance would not exhibit contrast constancy.

Summary

I have argued here that the field of perceptual development has been primarily concerned with describing perceptual capabilities at various ages. Missing are clear explications of developmental mechanisms. In other words, we do not have adequate theories of the means by which perceptual capabilities improve over time. I have argued that a rigorous computational approach might yield important insights. In particular, computational theories would help us characterize rigorously (1) what the young child learning to perceive has to do, (2) the sorts of information available to accomplish this task, (3) how the information is used, and (4) the problems imposed by physical growth. To illustrate the computational approach, I described how the mature visual system compensates for distortions caused by optical blur and peripheral neural summation, and I asked how the visual system might attain the information it needs to adjust the compensation mechanisms appropriately. I proposed three computational models of the developmental mechanisms, but only two seemed feasible. These models are quite different from those proposed by Gibson, Cohen, and Bronson. Of course, the scope of the computational models proposed here is more restricted. In addition, the computational models are designed to address the problem at issue at the level of computational theory and, therefore, do not specify the precise mechanisms or neural structures involved. Specification at those levels of analysis should await refinement of an appropriate computational theory. Another difference is the degree of explicitness. Gibson's and Cohen's theories, for example, are frustratingly vague and, consequently, are exceedingly difficult to test scientifically. It is not clear how one could implement either of the theories physically, and it is also not clear how to test them empirically. In contrast, the computational theories presented here are reasonably explicit and testable. Both models could be implemented as computer programs, and the performance of such implementations would tell us how feasible they are. Furthermore, it should be possible to test the computational models experimentally.

How useful might this quantitative, computational approach be to other areas of developmental psychology? For reasons stated earlier, it is fruitful, in any scientific domain, to quantify one's models as much as possible. Unfortunately, quantification entails two clear risks. First, in quantifying variables, one might oversimplify or distort the phenomena of interest. Second, in developing a quantitative model, one might have to make several untested assumptions. As more and more assumptions enter the model, its successes and failures become less and less informative. Thus, the utility of the computational approach depends critically both on whether the perceptual, cognitive, or social constructs under study can be quantified without losing their essence and on whether enough constraints can be brought to bear to restrict the number of untested assumptions. Cognitive and social constructs are generally more complex, or difficult to define, than perceptual constructs, and clear-cut environmental and empirical constraints are more difficult to come by. I am, consequently, less optimistic about the promise of the computational approach for the study of cognitive and social development. As I said above, the study of visual development may be unusually well suited for the approach and consequently may provide a unique opportunity for the study of development in action.

Acknowledgments

This research was supported by NIH Research Grant HD-19927 and by NIMH Research Scientist Development Award MH-00318. Ben Stephens collaborated on much of the empirical and theoretical work described here. I thank Pat Bennett for helpful comments on an earlier draft.

References

Abramov, I., Gordon, J., Hendrickson, A., Hainline, L., Dobson, V., & LaBossiere, E. (1982). The retina of the newborn human infant. *Science 217,* 265–267.

Aslin, R. N. (1986). Motor aspects of visual development in infancy. In P. Salapatek & L. B. Cohen (Eds.), *Handbook of infant perception.* New York: Academic.

Atkinson, J., Braddick, O., & Moar, K. (1977). Development of contrast sensitivity over the first 3 months of life. *Vision Research 17,* 1037–1044.

Banks, M. S., & Dannemiller, J. L. (1986). Infant visual psychophysics. In P. Salapatek & L. B. Cohen (Eds.), *Handobok of infant perception.* New York: Academic.

Banks, M. S., & Salapatek, P. (1978). Acuity and contrast sensitivity in 1-, 2-, and 3-month-old human infants. *Investigative Ophthalmology and Visual Science 17,* 361–365.

Banks, M. S., & Salapatek, P. (1983). Infant visual perception. In P. H. Mussen (Ed.), *Handbook of child psychology* (Vol. 2). New York: Wiley.

Banks, M. S., Stephens, B. R., & Hartmann, E. E. (1985). The development of basic mechanisms of pattern vision: Spatial frequency channels. *Journal of Experimental Child Psychology 40,* 501–527.

Barrow, H. G., & Tenenbaum, J. M. (1979). Recovering intrinsic scene characteristics from images. In E. Riseman & A. Hanson (Eds.), *Computer vision systems*. New York: Academic.

Blakemore, C., Muncey, J. P. J., & Ridley, R. M. (1973). Stimulus specificity in the human visual system. *Vision Research 13,* 1915–1931.

Braddick, O., Campbell, F. W., & Atkinson, J. (1978). Channels in vision: Basic aspects. In R. Held, H. W. Leibowitz, & H.-L. Teuber (Eds.), *Handbook of sensory physiology. Perception* (Vol. 8). New York: Springer-Verlag.

Bronson, G. W. (1974). The postnatal growth of visual capacity. *Child Development 45,* 873–890.

Campbell, F. W., & Green, D. G. (1965). Optical and retinal factors affecting visual resolution. *Journal of Physiology 181,* 576–593.

Campbell, F. W., & Gubisch, R. W. (1966). Optical quality of the human eye. *Journal of Physiology 186,* 558–578.

Clocksin, W. F. (1980). Perception of surface slant and edge labels from optical flow: A computational approach. *Perception 9,* 253–269.

Cohen, L. B., DeLoache, J. S., & Strauss, M. S. (1979). Infant visual perception. In J. D. Osofsky (Ed), *Handbook of infant development*. New York: Wiley.

Cornsweet, T. N. (1970). *Visual perception*. New York: Academic.

Fagan, J. F. (1976). Infants' recognition of invariant features of faces. *Child Development 47,* 627–638.

Fagan, J. F., and Shepherd, P. A. (1979). Infants' perception of face orientation. *Infant Behavior and Development 2,* 227–234.

Gaskill, J. D. (1978). *Linear systems, Fourier transforms, and optics*. New York: Wiley.

Gennery, D. B. (1973). Determination of optical transfer function by inspection of frequency-domain plot. *Journal of the Optical Society of America 63,* 1571–1577.

Georgeson, M. (1979). Spatial Fourier analysis and human vision. *Tutorial Essays in Psychology 2,* 39–88.

Georgeson, M. A., & Sullivan, G. D. (1975). Contrast constancy: Deblurring in human vision by spatial frequency channels. *Journal of Physiology 252,* 627–656.

Gibson, E. J. (1969). *Principles of perceptual learning and development*. New York: Appleton Century Crofts.

Gibson, E. J., & Spelke, E. S. (1983). The development of perception. In P. H. Mussen (Ed.), *Handbook of child psychology* (Vol. 3). New York: Wiley.

Grimson, W. E. L. (1981). *From images to surfaces*. Cambridge: MIT Press.

Harris, L., Atkinson, J., & Braddick, O. (1976). Visual contrast sensitivity of a 6-month-old infant measured by the evoked potential. *Nature 274,* 570–571.

Hendrickson, A., & Youdelis, C. (1984). The morphological development of the human fovea. *Ophthalmology 91,* 603–612.

Hess, R. F., & Bradley, A. (1980). Contrast perception above threshold is only minimally impaired in human amblyopia. *Nature 287,* 463–464.

Hess, R. F., Bradley, A., & Piotrowski, L. (1983). Contrast-coding in amblyopia I. Differences in the neural basis of human amblyopia. *Proceedings of the Royal Society of London 217,* 309–330.

Hoffman, D. E., and Flinchbaugh, B. E. (1982). The interpretation of biological motion. *Biological Cybernetics 42,* 195–204.

Horn, B. K. P. (1979). Hill shading and the reflectance map. *Proceedings IEEE 69,* 14–47.
Hubel, D. H., & Wiesel, T. N. (1962). Receptive fields, binocular interaction and functional architecture in the cat's visual cortex. *Journal of Physiology 160,* 106–154.
Hubel, D. H., & Wiesel, T. N. (1968). Receptive fields and functional architecture of monkey striate cortex. *Journal of Physiology 195,* 215–243.
Johnston, I. R., White, G. R., & Cumming, R. W. (1973). The role of optical expansion patterns in locomotor control. *American Journal of Psychology 86,* 311–324.
Kulikowski, J. J. (1976). Effective contrast constancy and linearity of contrast sensation. *Vision Research 16,* 1419–1431.
Longuet-Higgins, H. C. (1982). The role of the vertical dimension in stereoscopic vision. *Perception 11,* 377–386.
Longuet-Higgins, H. C., & Prazdny, K. (1980). The interpretation of a moving retinal image. *Proceedings of the Royal Society of London, Series B 208,* 385–397.
Marr, D. (1982). *Vision: A computational investigation into the human representation and processing of visual information.* San Francisco: Freeman.
Marr, D., & Poggio, T. (1979). A computational theory of human stereo vision. *Proceedings of the Royal Society of London B 204,* 301–328.
Mayhew, J. (1982). The interpretation of stereo-disparity information: The computation of surface orientation and depth. *Perception 11,* 387–403.
Minsky, M. (1961). Steps toward artificial intelligence. *Proceedings of the Institute of Radio Engineers 49,* 8–30.
Pirchio, M., Spinelli, D., Fiorentini, A., & Maffei, L. (1978). Infant contrast sensitivity evaluated by evoked potentials. *Brain Research 141,* 179–184.
Prazdny, K. (1980). Egomotion and relative depth map from optical flow. *Biological Cybernetics 36,* 87–102.
Ratliff, F. (1965). *Mach bands: Quantitative studies on neural networks in the retina.* San Francisco: Holden-Day.
Regan, D. (1972). *Evoked potentials in psychology, sensory physiology, and clinical medicine.* London: Chapman & Hall.
Regan, D., & Beverley, K. I. (1982). How do we avoid confounding the direction we are looking and the direction we are moving? *Science 215,* 194–196.
Stephens, B. R., & Banks, M. S. (1985). The development of contrast constancy. *Journal of Experimental Child Psychology 40,* 528–547.
Switkes, E., Mayer, M. L., & Sloan, J. A. (1978). Spatial frequency analysis of the visual environment: Anisotropy and the carpentered environment hypothesis. *Vision Research 10,* 1393–1399.
Teller, D. Y., & Bornstein, M. H. (1986). Infant color vision. In P. Salapatek & L. B. Cohen (Eds.), *Handbook of infant perception.* New York: Academic.
Ullman, S. (1979). *The interpretation of visual motion.* Boston: M.I.T. Press.
Warren, R. (1976). The perception of egomotion. *Journal of Experimental Psychology: Human Perception and Performance 2,* 448–456.
Watanabe, A., Mori, T., Nagata, S., & Hiwatashi, K. (1968). Spatial sine wave responses of the human visual system. *Vision Research 8,* 1245–1263.
Webb, J. A., & Aggarwal, J. K. (1982). Structure from motion of rigid and jointed objects. *Artificial Intelligence 19,* 107–130.

Yonas, A., & Owsley, C. (1986). Development of spatial vision in infants. In P. Salapatek & L. B. Cohen (Eds.), *Handbook of infant perception. New York: Academic.*

Notes

1. Recently, I stumbled on an excellent example. I have written a computer implementation of equations developed by Longuet-Higgins and Prazdny (1980). These equations concern the use of optic flow in the retinal image to judge the three-dimensional layout of the environment and to judge one's motion through the environment. I discovered that the computer program generally could not determine the direction of self-motion unless the scene provided multiple-depth planes. This seemed odd at the time. I learned later, however, that human observers also have difficulty judging the direction of self-motion toward a single flat surface in the frontoparallel plane (Johnston, White, & Cumming, 1973; Regan & Beverley, 1982). Humans can judge the direction of motion accurately only when different depth planes are present (Warren, 1976).
2. The reasoning behind this argument is the following. The steady state, visually evoked potential seems to be unaffected by motivation to view a target (Regan, 1972). Thus, when behavioral and evoked-potential measurements agree, both measurements probably index visual mechanisms per se.
3. When the amplitude of the blur function is zero or nearly zero, multiplying by the inverse is impossible. Furthermore, the amplitude of the input is sometimes zero or nearly zero in a particular spatial-frequency band. In those cases, multiplying by the inverse of the gain function is inappropriate because it leads to amplification of noisy data. In either case, the best strategy is simply to set the output amplitudes at the affected spatial frequencies to zero.
4. Although this sort of detail is beyond the scope of this chapter, I should at least point out that different adjustment strategies could be used. For example, proportional adjustment, in which each adjustment is some proportion less than 1, minimizes undesirable oscillations.

11. Monte Carlo Simulation as a Method of Identifying Properties of Behavioral Organization

C. Donald Heth and Edward H. Cornell

Models provide a framework for understanding a psychological process, often by identifying components of that process. Models permit cogent and precise communication of theoretical concepts and often serve as analytical descriptions of behavioral observations.

Here we describe one class of psychological models that we have found especially useful for the analysis of children's behavior. We develop a modeling technique that facilitates three functions of a model: understanding, communication, and description. We apply this technique to a phenomenon of cognitive development, the growth of the ability to organize efficient search for resources. Our intention is to provide a set of modeling modules or tools that can be extended to other situations by other investigators. Although the models are framed in a particular computer language, we develop these modules in a very general manner, so that they are comprehensible independent of a computer language.

Orienting Attitudes

Psychological models have been built in many media and with many techniques, ranging from mathematical formalisms such as Hull's system of behavior (Hull, 1952) to physical constructions of mechanical, chemical, or electrical parts, such as the conditioning machine of Baernstein and Hull (1931). In essence, however, a model is meant to exhibit an explicit action or computation that represents some psychological phenomenon. According to this broad characterization, then, psychological models are devices that simulate the action of the psychological system. It is this sense of models as simulations that has guided the work we report here.

Simulation is a multidisciplinary topic that has evolved primarily in response to practical concerns about the behavior of complex systems (see, e.g., Bratley, Fox, & Schrage, 1983). A paradigmatic simulation situation, for example, is the queue at a bank wicket. The manager of the bank, faced with the problem of reducing customer complaints of long lines, might be interested in the effect of reassigning responsibilities among the tellers of the bank. Rather than implementing a costly experiment in staffing, the manager may simulate the behavior of customers and tellers by a computer program that produces changes in the values of the program's variables analogous to the changes that occur on the floor of the bank. Policy decisions can then be made on the basis of the outcome of the program.

Clearly, the manager must address some important issues if the simulation is to be useful. The components of the physical system being simulated must be clearly identified and their interrelationships adequately specified. The computer program (which specifies a series of *state changes* in the machine) must mimic these components and relationships in all important respects. And the outcome of the simulation program must be properly interpreted. Although many subtle issues arise in such cases, computer simulation has proved to be a highly effective tool in the practical and theoretical understanding of large systems.

However, in psychological inquiry, simulation techniques are generally used at a different stage of research than commonly seen in systems theory research. Psychologists are rarely in the position of the bank manager, who understands the general configuration of the system. Instead, psychological theorists are more often in a position analogous to an outside examiner trying to understand how the bank works and what the responsibilities of the tellers are.

It seems reasonable that simulation could help such a naive observer understand the workings of the system in the following way. Repeated simulations of the bank situation could be performed with different assumptions of teller and customer relations. The observer would conclude that he or she had a good description of the bank's structure when a given simulation matched the bank's operation well. In a similar way, simulation of psychological systems has been used to develop approximate descriptions of many cognitive phenomena (see Chapter 8, this volume).

In this chapter, we outline such a procedure. We describe a data-driven methodology in which models of children's behavior can be tested against empirical outcomes. This method will put a strong premium on the construction and testing of simulation models. Consequently, we develop a set of simulation tools that can be easily adapted to different theoretical statements. Although we develop these tools in the context of a specific application, we believe that this approach can be used in a variety of contexts.

Before describing this approach in detail, it is worthwhile to examine several methodological orientations that have shaped it. Consider the outside observer using simulation to understand the operation of the bank. One issue is the possible stochasticity of the system. Clearly customers and tellers behave in ways that are not completely predictable;

this variability must be represented in some way by the simulation. A second issue is the selection of criteria to use for a "match" between simulation and system—a problem often referred to as *validation of the model*. Finally, the observer must consider whether the goal is to describe banks in general or one in particular. That is, the simulation will be characterized by certain parameters in the computer program that produces it. At issue is whether these parameters are meant to describe aggregate or specific cases. Our approach is likewise characterized by these issues.

A Monte Carlo Technique

Our specific application involves a choice task. We start with the assumption that organized or strategic behavior would not produce a random series of choices. Sequences of activities are structured for the purpose of adapting to environmental contingencies that are themselves structured by physical and biological laws. The challenge for any theorist, then, is to identify the regularities produced by such systematic processes.

Many theories and models, including those that rely on simulation, represent the regularities of a system in terms of deterministic statements about the underlying processes (see Cotton, 1982). Rabinowitz, Grant, and Dingley (Chapter 8, this volume), for example, advocate such an approach. However, in some situations a probabilistic expression in a simulation model may be more appropriate. For example, a particular component of a simulation may be of little intrinsic interest and hence might be modeled by a general statement of probability. Alternatively, the theorist may wish to avoid a commitment to any particular assumption about some part of the process or system. Finally, probabilistic expressions can serve a useful methodological function. When simulation of psychological processes is used, as a form of hypothesis testing, then a probabilistic or *Monte Carlo* technique can serve as a useful null hypothesis. A Monte Carlo simulation represents a provisional statement about the psychological process under study. In a way, it is an expression of uncertainty about the process or system.

To the extent that the empirical indices of the system differ from the Monte Carlo simulation, we can recognize that our theoretical explanation requires more elaboration.

Elaboration can take the form of introducing successive refinements to the Monte Carlo model. For example, consider behavior in a two-choice probability learning procedure. A preliminary model of behavior in such a procedure might assume that choices are made randomly. If the results produced by simulations of this model are compared to the behavior of a child in an actual study, there may very well be a large difference between the simulation and the child's protocol. The model of choice could be elaborated by the addition of a short-term memory to the simulation model. Choices in the elaborated model would now be a joint function of the random process and the memorial process. A developmental theorist would then test to determine whether the elaborated model provided a more valid model relative to the purely random model.

Model Validation

The type of hypothesis testing that we suggest above relies heavily on measures of goodness of fit between the results of a simulation and empirical data. Simulation models must be testable, in the sense that their respective abilities to match the data are distinguishable.

In a highly deterministic model containing no stochastic components, goodness-of-fit measures may limit the type of analysis that can be accomplished. A χ^2 statistic, for example, could be computed by using the outcome of the simulation as the *expected* term and a given empirical datum as the *observed*. However, this index would require multiple observations. For reasons discussed in the next section, we find this restriction too severe.

The Monte Carlo simulation techniques, however, have the advantage of producing outcomes that are themselves random variables. Consequently, a model can be simulated many times to produce a distribution of outcomes. A given empirical outcome, even that from a single observation of a subject, can be compared to this distribution. The comparison provides a measure of the likelihood of the datum under the assumptions of the model.

Later in this chapter we discuss a formal treatment of this likelihood. For now, we only indicate how it can serve as a rough index of the validity of a model. Briefly, given a model of a behavioral process, we can estimate the probability that the record of choices exhibited by a child would fall into a distribution produced by the outcomes of many runs of our Monte Carlo, or random, method of producing choices. If the likelihood of the child's performance was low, we could reject that particular expression of the model. Depending on this decision, we could introduce successive refinements, the addition of memories or strategic algorithms, for example, to the Monte Carlo system. As the system output begins to approximate closely the behavioral record, we can consider whether such mnemonic or strategic algorithms might characterize the system of directing choice.

In many respects, this approach to simulation is characteristic of many attempts to model psychological phenomena. For example, using the vocabulary of information theory, we could say that before a simulation is attempted, we have maximum uncertainty concerning the outcome. "Good" models help us to remove the uncertainty, in the same way that "good" simulations transform the random output of a Monte Carlo process to structured sequences. We have used Monte Carlo simulation in this way to provide a method for assessing how much organization characterizes behavior, for example, identifying the spatial patterns of search by children of different ages (Cornell & Heth, 1983, in press).

Case Description Modeling

The approach that we illustrate here is case-descriptive (Starbuck, 1971), in that we apply these techniques to the modeling of individual response histories. We can therefore identify, for each child, whether a cognitive process or strategy is required to model that child's behavior. The purpose of this approach is to build a normative description of a general class (e.g., characteristic strategies of an age group) from idiographic decisions about the members of the class. We feel that this approach provides some additional information to the usual technique of modeling the class as an aggregation.

For example, individual descriptions can sometimes produce different functional relationships from those of aggregate descriptions. Bakan (1967) has distinguished those descriptions that characterize the general class from those that describe the aggregation. As he noted, individual case descriptions can refine the boundaries of a particular class. Hence, case descriptions can be collated to provide information about the relative presence of strategies in different age groups or ecologies. This is done by enumerating the subjects who manifest identifiable strategies. The coappearance of strategies that can be identified separately by the simulation can also be determined, illustrating the confluence of abilities that may characterize the development of problem-solving skills both within and between children (Cornell & Heth, 1983).

Case-descriptive procedures also allow for the isolation of unique strategies used by particular individuals. For example, when searching for objects she has seen hidden, a girl may discover that it is useful to recapitulate the serial order of hidings rather than check sites that are close to one another. Once isolated, the strategy can lead to training procedures to boost the performance of other children who have not yet discovered it. Siegler's (1976) identification of encoding strategies for the balance-scale problem exemplifies this approach.

Finally, at the level of case description, a variety of analytical procedures can be used to validate a strategy that has been isolated by the model. A simple technique is to interrogate the particular child as to the solution she or he has created. The interpretation of the answers to such an interrogation, however, is a complicated matter (Nisbett & Wilson, 1977). Another method is to design a new problem or place the child in a different ecology where use of the strategy would have unambiguous results. Training procedures that affect the use of the strategy also serve as converging operations to identify a strategy isolated by the model.

An Illustrative Application

Our general orientation to modeling has evolved in response to the complexity of data produced when toddlers search for hidden objects, as in an Easter egg hunt (Cornell & Heth, 1983; Heth & Cornell, 1985). Searching and gathering techniques are revealing indices of early cognitive development. In particular, efficient search indicates inferential, planning, and mnemonic abilities of preschool and early primary school children (for reviews, see Wellman, 1985). Young children typically enjoy looking for hidden treats, and tasks can easily be arranged to match the natural contingencies experienced by many species that must find resources. One treasure hunt we devised required that the child select 20 of 100 possible hiding sites (envelopes) that were spread in various configurations along the perimeter of a large playroom (Heth & Cornell, 1985). The choice of sites was particularly challenging because the child had to anticipate recall of 20 caches and had to distribute the treasure to avoid plundering by another youthful pirate. Of particular interest to us as students of comparative development is whether and how the series of choices made by both children was organized to address contingencies of hoarding and predation.

In our initial studies of how children search, we were struck by the variety of analyses that a series of choices afforded. Our first tendency was to examine gross performance measures related to efficiency. We calculated summaries of the number of items found per search, repetitious visits to previously checked sites, and visits to sites that had never contained a target object (intrusive searches). Not surprisingly, older children were generally superior to younger children when these variables served as dependent measures in analyses of aggregate data.

Next we attempted to relate these results to specific rules or strategies used by the children within different age groups. For example, older children might avoid repetitious searches because they employ mnemonic strategies that allow them to identify sites grouped around landmarks. Younger children might be using movement algorithms that only reduce backtracking when sites are distributed in regular arrays. These possibilities required that we be able to identify organization within each child's search path.

Our solution was to employ a simulation technique that would generate stochastic information about various null hypotheses. The presence of nonrandom responses was tested for separate dependent measures, representing processes of discriminating hiding sites, memories of searches, and minimalization of distance traveled (Cornell & Heth, 1983, in press). Here, we use a search problem that approximates one faced by many foraging organisms and extend this approach to isolate rules or strategies.

Consider an individual who must allocate search effort over a large and heterogeneous spatial arena. The individual could be a child hunting Easter eggs, an aboriginal Australian looking for wood, or a bumblebee gathering nectar. If search effort is costly in terms of energy or time expended, then the individual should concentrate activities in regions of high payoff and minimize return visits to places already exploited. The structure of the spatial array will determine to a large extent how these requirements can be satisfied. There have been formal descriptions of different types of spatial configurations, ranging from highly regular tesselations (Pyke, 1978) to heterogeneous, "patchy" environments (Charnov, 1976). For example, a field of clover may have a very even distribution of blossoms used by bumblebees, while a leopard might find its prey clustered around water holes. Formal treatments of these situations have used the mathematical tools of systems theory and microeconomics to examine the optimal solutions for a forager (Kamil & Sargent, 1981).

Unfortunately, these treatments often concentrate on the molar efficiency of the organism and only indirectly address the processes (either psychological or physiological) that may generate efficient exploitation (but see Orians, 1981). Ollason (1983) has suggested an alternate approach, in which the behavior of the forager is determined by molecular mechanisms such as memories for previous movements and the reinforcement effects of found resources.

Our approach is similar to Ollason's; accordingly, for the present application we devised a search problem similar to the ecology he has described. In this problem, many similar target objects are distributed randomly throughout a region and are gathered when the searcher visits an obvious target site. Once its contents are gathered, a target location is empty; however, there are no obvious cues that the site has been exhausted, and the site remains a possible candidate for later visits. As in most environments, the search region is demarcated by boundaries, some prohibiting travel. Delimiting the search region allows us to work with well-defined sets of locations.

In our procedure, the set consisted of 50 sites, each consisting of an inverted opaque cup. They were placed in a large (13.7 × 8.5 m) empty room according to the following procedure. A grid was imposed on a scale drawing of the room. A grid square represented 0.36 m^2 of the room. The grid provided Cartesian coordinates that were used to generate a random configuration of the hiding sites. The cups were then placed in corresponding positions in the room, and a penny was placed under each cup. The task was presented to a 7-year-old girl who was asked to gather the pennies under each cup. The cardinal number of each choice was announced after she had replaced a chosen cup to its original position. The gathering session was videotaped, and the sequence of choices transcribed in accord with the spatial coordinates of each cup.

A General Technique for Simulation of Performance

Our first objective was to develop a set of computer algorithms that would produce a sequence of choices like that exhibited by the child in this search situation. That is, we begin simulation in a rather unconstrained manner, in that our initial goal is to model the performance of the child rather than a putative cognitive architecture. Our hope is that the types of decisions necessary to model behavior adequately will elucidate the psychological processes involved and provide hypotheses for empirical validation.

Simulation methods include a number of tools for the analysis of deterministic phenomena (Bratley et al., 1983), including specialized simulation languages, computer hardware, and analytical techniques. For our purposes we wanted to develop a set of simulation modules that could be added or subtracted to a simulation model to reflect different assumptions concerning the complexity of the behavior being modeled. That is, a particular series of choices may exhibit a complicated pattern, reflecting sequential dependencies between choices. We would like to factor this complexity into several simulation constructs to isolate possible psychological sources.

Our solution is a kit of modules that implement a stream-based program. *Streams* are programming constructs that can be used to produce a computable item (e.g., an integer) whenever the stream is activated (Charniak, Riesbeck, & McDermott, 1981). In a sense, a stream can be viewed as an indefinite list of items; whenever the rest of the stream-processing program needs a new item, the object is computed from the contents of the stream. The principal component of a stream is a *generator* that constructs the items of the stream according to specified steps (usually written in the language in which the stream is implemented). The fate of the items produced by the generator is determined by the other constructs of the program, which can be viewed as *stream transformers*. That is, these constructs alter the products of a stream in various ways, by applying functions to them, by screening them according to certain rules, or by combining them with other streams.

We start with a generator module that is essentially an algorithm for computing random numbers. The result is a stream of choice activity, which is subsequently transformed by additional transformer modules.

These additional modules alter the sequence of random numbers in various ways. Some modules may exclude certain numbers from the sequence. For example, we might stipulate that hiding locations on the periphery of the search region not be chosen. A module that excludes certain numbers on the basis of some test is generically referred to as a *filter*. Another type of module applies some function to the numbers of the generator. For example, certain functions map a uniform distribution from the random number generator into a normal or other type of distribution (Pritsker & Pegden, 1979). This type of module is known as a *map* and is used to mimic the outcome of processes that may be involved in systematic response algorithms, such as when a forager exhausts a circular array of sites by moving to the right after completing each additional search. Odette (1984) describes how filters and maps can be used in a wide variety of computational situations.

For our purpose, we also include three additional stream transformers that increase the power of the simulation kit. In contrast to filters and maps, which take only a single stream as an input, these transformers combine or merge two streams. One, which we designate as an *accumulator,* alters a stream on the basis of the last item produced by the accumulator. For example, in our situation, an accumulator could be used to produce a choice that is based on the previous choice. With this transformer, the last choice is an additional stream. Another transformer, which we designate as a *sieve,* works by filtering a stream on the basis of another stream. This additional stream could be considered a parameter to the test used by the filter part. Actually, the parameter could be a simple integer, a list, or another stream. We allow the possibility that the parameter to this filter can be modified by the sieve and "fed back" for the next occasion. For example, the immediately preceding three choices made in our foraging task could be kept as a list and used by the sieve to filter out choices that repeat one of these three. As a new choice is made, the list is updated and fed back to the sieve for the next item in the stream. The size of the list used by the sieve therefore reflects the size of a short-term memory. The last construct, which we term a *combiner,* merges a parameter with the stream. The parameter can be a list or another stream. For example, during searching for previously cached resources, only a subset of possible hiding places may have been used, such as a group of hiding places next to a window of the room. Choices generated by the random stream could be mapped onto the list of remembered locations to determine the child's overall performance. If the random stream generated the number 6, for example, the combiner would produce the "6" member of the list of remembered places.

Our simulation model, then, is a specific composition of a generator and a set of filters, maps, accumulators, sieves, and combiners. The combination produces a stream of numbers corresponding to simulated choices. The numbers correspond to the constraints and transformations imposed by modules of the model. We can then evaluate the correspondence between the stream from the simulation model and the stream of choices made by a child in our foraging study.

Several caveats are noted here. First, we emphasize again that we begin by simulating the child's performance rather than the processes underlying it. We do not necessarily assert that a child uses a generate-and-test decision process in which choices are randomly produced and then filtered or mapped. Rather, the modular decomposition is a convenient way to isolate components that may be sufficient to produce data like those produced by the child. Second, we use the different modules to explore the extent of the putative organization in the data. The number of items in short-term memory, for example, is limited in human cognition. We would be especially interested, then, to see whether the performance of the simulation model overpredicts performance when we use a large "memory" component in the stream. Finally, our approach places strong emphasis on an aspect of modeling methodology known as validation, the correspondence of the model to its real-world analog. In our present case, we require an assessment of when the inclusion of a module increases the match between simulation and observation. However, once a model produces patterns of output that have good validity, additional questions can be explored. In operations analysis, simulation models are used to explore questions of optimization. For example, when a refinery operation has been simulated and the simulation is properly validated, the refinery management can examine whether a change in operation will increase efficiency (see Pritsker & Pegden, 1979). In a similar manner, if our model indicates a module as having especially strong leverage in the determination of performance, it may lead to the development of procedures to improve particular cognitive skills.

Data and Analysis

Figure 11.1 shows the search path of the 7-year-old girl in our treasure hunt. With 50 choices she gathered 45 pennies and made 5 repetitious searches. She traveled an average distance of 1.88 m between choices.

Appendix 11A contains our simulation of the sequence of choices. The simulation is written in Logo; however, the general techniques can be implemented in a variety of programming languages (e.g., LISP, FORTH). Here, we demonstrate their use by applying modules to the simulation of the performance of our child in the search task.

Step 1

We construct a stream of choices with no sequential dependencies. This step illustrates the application of the stream modules and introduces some simple notational devices to summarize these modules.

We begin with a composition of modules that generates random numbers uniformly distributed over some interval and builds a stream of search choices from this random generator. A variety of computational techniques are suitable for the generation of random integers (Bratley et al., 1983; Heth, 1984); for simplicity, we employ here the function used by our particular implementation of Logo, which computes a pseudorandom number between 0 and 1 less than the number supplied as a parameter to the function. This function is then used in a generator; we denote the

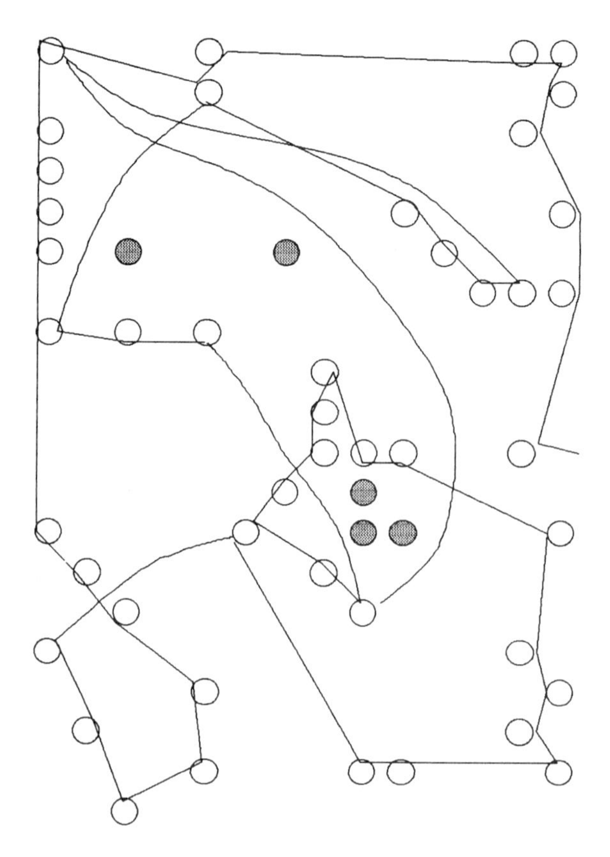

FIGURE 11.1. The search path produced by Shannon, a 7-year-old girl, on her first attempt at the gathering problem. Open circles represent cups that were checked; filled circles were not visited.

generator by a symbol that suggests its recurrent properties, and we label it G_1. Under it, we give the Logo function that defines it.

The generator G_1 produces a stream of random integers uniformly distributed over a range determined by a constant. In this example the constant is 50, which restricts the set of integers to the range 0 to 49. We then use this generator to select choices from a set of 50 possible hiding places. We accomplish the selection by transforming the stream of integers into the set of actual hiding places, represented as ordered pairs of X and Y coordinates in our treasure hunt. Two additional modules, illustrated in Figure 11.2, are required. One is another generator, G_2, which simply produces the same list of 50 hiding places each time it is called. The other is combiner C_1, which combines the stream of random integers with the pool of hiding places produced by G_2. Combiners are given their own symbols to emphasize how they merge two streams. In the case of C_1, this merger selects one hiding place from the list, determined by the random number. For example, if the number is 5, then the sixth element of the list is selected. The result is a new stream, consisting of hiding places that are selected with replacement from the list. Although the selection of hiding places could be done in another way (for example, by having the initial generator randomly compute hiding places), we adopt this composition of modules both to demonstrate the action of a generator and a combiner and to allow for possible modifications in the set selected from.

To recapituate, we now have a stream of ordered pairs [for example, (14 6) (5 1) (11 10) . . .] that are selected randomly from any place in the hiding place list. The stream corresponds to a Monte Carlo selection of choices and could be used as a first approximation to the child's behavior. For example, if we simulate 50 searches with this construction, we might find several repetitions. In fact, in over 100 such simulations of a 50-search session, we obtained a mean of 18.2 repetitions, with a 5th percentile of 15. The mean distance traveled between successive choices was 5.74 m, with a 5th percentile of 4.84 m. A representative search path produced by the model is given in Figure 11.3. Recall that the girl of our

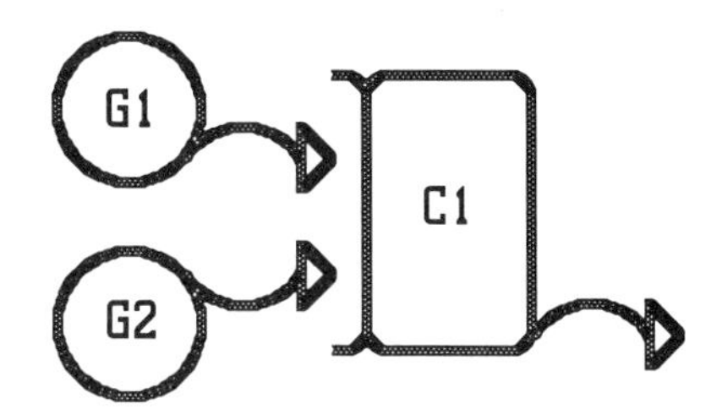


```
to C1 :stream1 :stream2
repeat (sar :stream2) [make stream1 (sdr :stream1)]
(sar :stream1)
end

to G1 :k
(list random :k (generator 'G1 (list :k)))
end

to G2 :hidinglist
  (list first :hidinglist (generator 'G2
    (list (if emptyp bf :hidinglist
        [:sitelist]          {Note global parameter.}
      [bf :hidinglist] )) ))
end
```

FIGURE 11.2. The model instance of step 1. Modules G_1 and G_2 are generators; C_1 is a combiner. The Logo code for each is presented below the diagram. *Sitelist* is a global parameter that contains the coordinates of all sites located in the room.

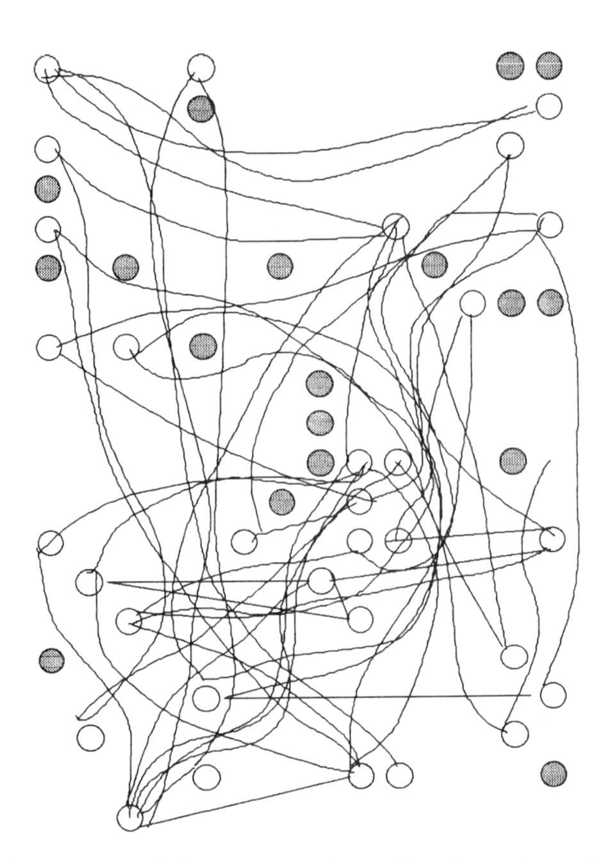

FIGURE 11.3. A representative search path resulting from the model of step 1, including modules to produce random choices of sites. Open circles represent cups that were checked; filled circles were not visited.

treasure hunt made 5 repetitions and traveled only 1.88 m between searches. Relative to the distribution produced by the 100 simulations of the step 1 model, this level of performance would be very unlikely. Therefore, we conclude that the step 1 model is inadequate and must be modified to produce better performance.

STEP 2A

One way to improve performance would be to use memories of searches to guide choices. We introduced a short-term memory by passing the stream of choices from the step 1 model through a sieve. As a first approximation, the module that is incorporated as a sieve does not allow immediate choice of the preceding five locations. A short-term memory capacity of 5 items seemed to be a minimal assumption, given the serial recall

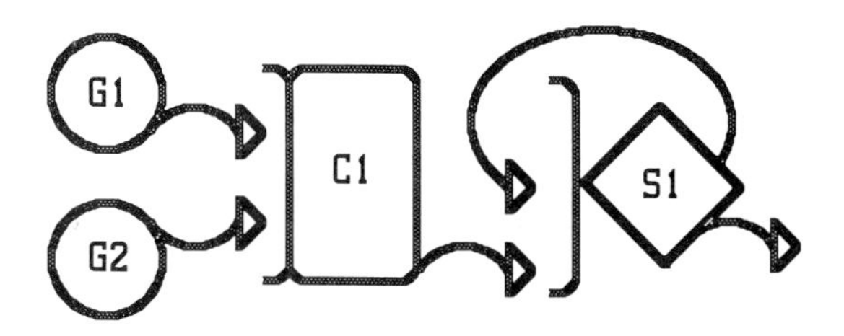


```
to S1 :stream1 :stream2
  if (member (sar :stream2) :stream1)
     [nil]
     [fput (sar :stream2) (bl :stream1)]
end

to C1 :stream1 :stream2
  repeat (sar :stream2) [make stream1 (sdr :stream1)]
  (sar :stream1)
end

to G1 :k
  (list random :k (generator 'G1 (list :k)))
end

to G2 :hidinglist
  (list first :hidinglist (generator 'G2
    (list (if emptyp bf :hidinglist
       [:sitelist]       {Note  global   parameter.}
      [bf :hidinglist] )) ))
end
```

FIGURE 11.4. The model instance of step 2A. Modules G_1 and G_2 are generators, C_1 is a combiner, and S_1 is a sieve. The Logo code is presented below the diagram.

abilities of 7-year-old children (Dempster, 1981). Figure 11.4 depicts the action of the sieve, labeled S_1. Figure 11.5 depicts a representative search path that resulted when the sieve was added to the initial model. Repetitious searches dropped to a mean of 16.5 redundant choices with a 5th percentile of 12. The distance traveled between successive choices averaged 5.82 m, with a 5th percentile of 5.08 m. The addition of a short-term memory module facilitated the reduction of redundant searches, but it produced little effect on distance traveled and did not yield the low number of repetitions shown by the child. Extension of the capacity of this short-term memory module to the last 10 choices made little difference. This outcome is somewhat surprising because efficient avoidance of depleted sites is often attributed to mnemonic capacity (e.g., Kamil, 1978; Shettleworth & Krebs, 1982). Later, we explore the effect of increasing memory capacity in more detail.

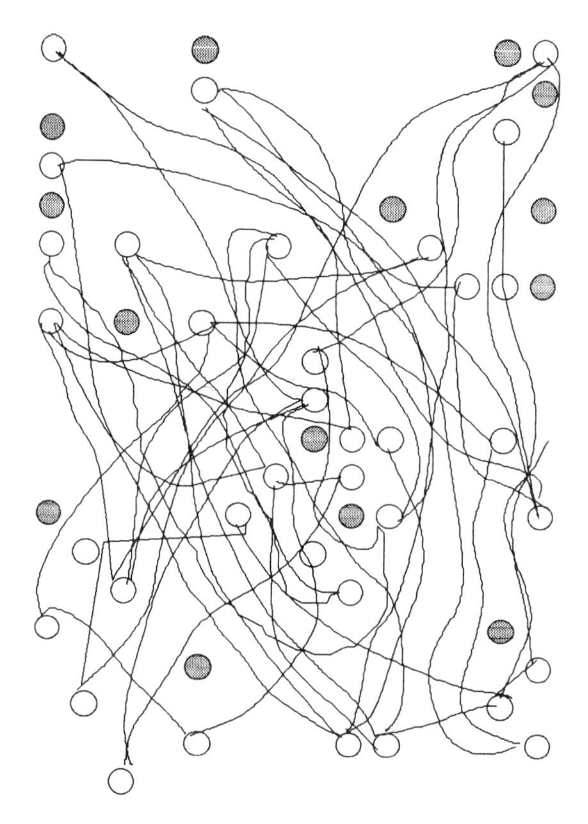

FIGURE 11.5. A representative search path resulting from the model of step 2A, including a module of a working memory of five choices. Open circles represent cups that were checked; filled circles were not visited.

STEP 2B

One possible modification is the inclusion of a simple algorithm that corresponds to many seen in foraging situations (e.g., Pyke, 1978). A forager looking for food will sometimes confine search to a delimited region or "patch." Accordingly, choices are generally made to adjacent sites, or sites that are close to a previous choice. We can examine the impact of such an algorithm by defining a composition of modules including an accumulation that generates choices according to some criterion distance from the last choice. That is, the accumulation selects the next choice from those that are close to the last choice made.

In step 2B we explored the effects of this least-distance module independent of the 5-item memory module. We also included the constraint that the last two choices (the immediate site and the preceding one) not be repeated by using a sieve like that of step 2A, to prevent alternation between two locations. We also allowed for some switches from one patch to another by making the neighborhood accumulation probabilistic, such that a choice beyond the criterion distance has a small ($p=.10$) chance of being produced by the accumulation. A composition to accomplish this function is illustrated in Figure 11.6 with the label A_1 denoting the neighborhood or least-distance accumulation. This accumulation works in the following way: One input is a stream of random numbers between 0 and 9. The other input is the last choice made. Also, A_1 has a table of sites that lists the sites closest to a given site, next closest, and so on, to the fifth closest sites. Based on the value of the random stream, A_1 selects one of these sets, or the complement of all of them, and chooses the next site to visit. That choice is then screened by the sieve to ensure that one of the immediately two preceding responses is not repeated. An interesting feature of this model is that the neighborhood computed by A_1 is from the last choice of A_1, not of S_1. This corresponds to a search algorithm in which the child considers a neighboring cup, decides if she had already checked it, and then chooses a neighbor of that cup.

The results of step 2B are illustrated in Figure 11.7. There were 23.1 revisits to sites, with a 5th percentile of 18 revisits. The large number of repetitions indicated that the simple constraint of avoiding the present and last choice was inadequate to minimize redundant searches. However, the mean distance between successive choices was 1.92 m, with a 5th percentile of 1.34 m. The mean was considerably lower than that of the previous models and very close to the distance traversed by the young girl.

We conclude that the independent models of step 2 are inadequate by themselves to account for both distance traveled and number of repetitious searches. In step 3, we explore more elaborate models.

Step 3

Here we simply combined the modules of steps 2A and 2B with the neighborhood accumulation introduced after the stream of random numbers. The resultant stream of sites is then passed through the short-term memory sieve. The series of modules is illustrated in Figure 11.6 and a representative search path appears in Figure 11.8. Over 100 simulations there was a mean of 20.0 revisits to sites, with the 5th percentile of 13 repetitions. There was a mean of 2.10 m traveled between searches, with the 5th percentile of 1.56 m. Although the results of these simulations appear closer to the young girl's performance than the results of steps 1, 2A, and 2B, one dependent measure (actual repetitions) is outside the 5th percentile indicated by the model.

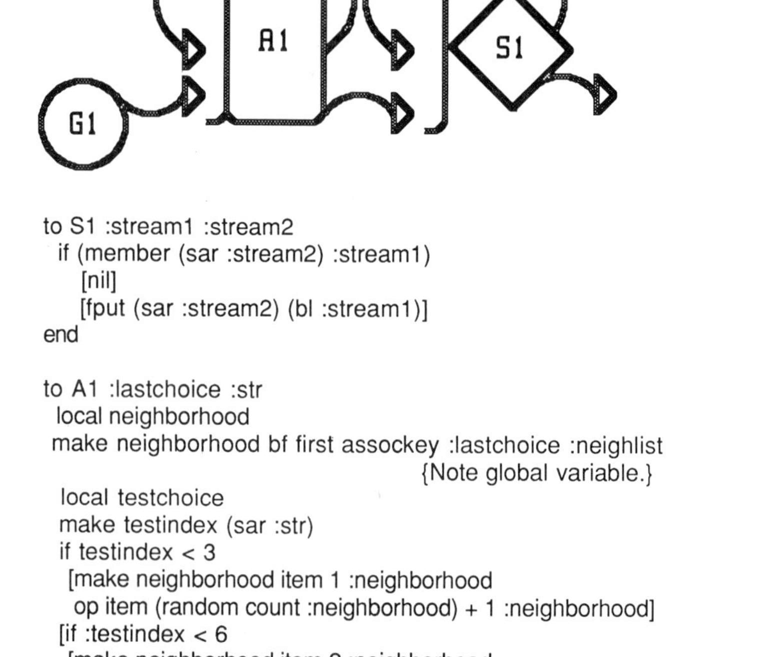


```
to S1 :stream1 :stream2
  if (member (sar :stream2) :stream1)
     [nil]
     [fput (sar :stream2) (bl :stream1)]
end

to A1 :lastchoice :str
  local neighborhood
  make neighborhood bf first assockey :lastchoice :neighlist
                                                  {Note global variable.}
   local testchoice
   make testindex (sar :str)
   if testindex < 3
    [make neighborhood item 1 :neighborhood
     op item (random count :neighborhood) + 1 :neighborhood]
   [if :testindex < 6
    [make neighborhood item 2 :neighborhood
     op item (random count :neighborhood) + 1 :neighborhood]
   [if :testindex < 7
    [make neighborhood item 3 :neighborhood
     op item (random count :neighborhood) + 1 :neighborhood]
   [if :testindex < 8
    [make neighborhood item 4 :neighborhood
     op item (random count :neighborhood) + 1 :neighborhood]
   [if :testindex < 9
    [make neighborhood item 5 :neighborhood
     op item (random count :neighborhood) + 1 :neighborhood]
    [op disregard :neighborhood :sitelist] ]]]]  {Note global parameter.}

to G1 :k
  (list random :k (generator 'G1 (list :k)))
end
```

FIGURE 11.6. The model instance of step 2B and step 3. Module G_1 is a generator, A_1 is an accumulator, and S_1 is a sieve. The models of steps 2B and 3 differ with respect to the size of the list bound to the first parameter of S_1. The Logo code is presented below the diagram. the variable *neighlist* is a list that gives the five nearest neighbors of a given site. *Disregard* is a user-defined function that excludes items listed in the first argument from the list of the second argument.

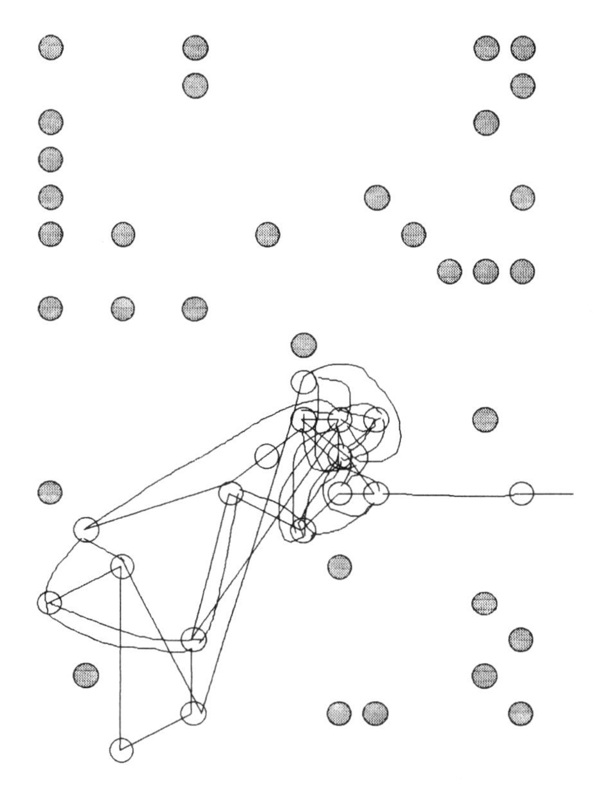

FIGURE 11.7. A representative search path resulting from the model of step 2B, including a module producing least-distance choices. Open circles represent cups that were checked; filled circles were not visited.

Validation of a Model

Up to this point, we have judged each model by the general congruence of the simulated output and the actual dependent measures of distance traveled and number of repetitious searches. Our intention has been to provide a rough assessment of the adequacy of each step, with a view to realizing a plausible model. From our inspection of the two dependent variables of our search situation, model 3 seems worthy of more exacting tests of the match between simulations and the child's performance. We now attempt such tests.

Although there are several approaches to the validation of simulation models, we regard a technique proposed by Hanna (1971) as especially appropriate to the stochastic models we have developed. Briefly, Hanna regards a model as a theoretical tool that reduces the uncertainty of empirical data. Models are viewed as containing information about the experimental situation; the task of model validation is to measure and com-

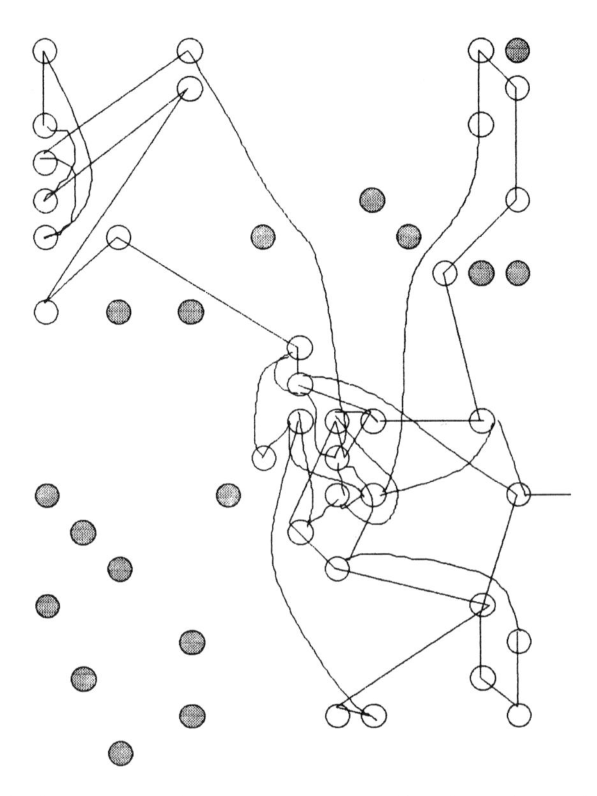

FIGURE 11.8. A representative search path resulting from the model of step 3, including modules producing least-distance choices and a working memory of five choices. Open circles represent cups that were checked; filled circles were not visited.

pare the informational content of alternate models. For this purpose, Hanna derives entropy measures of three characteristics of a model:

1. A coefficient of predictive power ρ that measures the information in the child's protocol that can distinguish in favor of a model over a "random model"
2. A coefficient of descriptive power δ that is the coefficient of predictive power associated with the maximum likelihood estimates of the model's parameters
3. A coefficient of parameter effect ε that is the difference between ρ and δ and that measures the amount by which the model can improve if the parameters are chosen post hoc

Hanna (1971) defines certain dominance relationships between models depending on the relation of the respective parameters. As applied to our simulations, Hanna's method could serve to evaluate the relative contribution of additional modules of a model. That is, the impact of an additional module could be used to determine whether that module increases predictive power, descriptive power, or both.

Two decisions were necessary in order to implement Hanna's (1971) measurements of the information provided by a model. His techniques required that we specify the parameter space, or possible values, of the constants within a model. Points representing specific model instances are necessary to estimate the coefficients of predictive and descriptive power. Thus, we first decided to constrain the parameter space of our models to make estimation procedures more tractable. The second decision was to constrain the outcome space for our models. The outcome space here is a two-dimensional representation of two dependent variables: the number of repetitious searches and distance traveled between searches. Hanna's techniques require nonzero probabilities for outcomes. To meet this requirement, for both variables we collapsed the outcomes into two categories. This ensured that the categories were broad enough to provide some outcomes in each.

The procedure is first illustrated by assessing the information provided when memory components are added to the model of random choice. We examined 10 model instances in which there were memories of 0, 5, 10, . . . , 45 past choices excluded from the set of current choices. These instances represent different capacities of a short-term memory module that is used to avoid repetitious searches. The performance of each model instance was estimated by running 100 simulations. The outcome of each simulation was categorized in terms of the number of repetitions and the average distance between choices. A particular simulation was classified as matching the empirical outcome of our gathering task when the number of repetitions and the distance traveled produced by the simulation were both less than the median of the random model.

The proportion of the 100 simulations matching the empirical outcome was used to calculate a value for ρ according to Hanna's (1966) equation 3:

$$\rho = 1 - \log_r \frac{1}{P(\omega^*)}$$

Here r is the number of possible empirical outcomes, and $P(\omega^*)$ is the probability of the particular empirical outcome. In our case, r is 4, due to the 2×2 classification according to the median of the random model, and $P(\omega^*)$ is the proportion of the simulations matching the empirical outcome. The mean value of ρ over the 10 possible instances defines ρ for the memory module. This value for ρ is given in the first row and column of Table 11.1.

The ability of the memory module to account for our data can be appreciated by considering what the value of ρ would be under different outcomes of the simulation. If the memory module were a particularly successful model of our 7-year-old's performance, then 100 percent of the

TABLE 11.1. Coefficients of information content of models.

	ρ	δ	ε
Memory model	.268	.582	.314
Neighborhood model	−.116	.391	.507
Combined model	.745	1.000	.255

simulations would produce repetitions and distances below the median of the random model; in this case, ρ would equal 1. If the memory module were no better (and no worse) than the random model, then only 25 percent of the simulations would produce repetition and distance data below the median number of repetitions and the median distance "traveled" by the random model. In this case, ρ would equal 0. Finally, if the memory module were a particularly poor model of search behavior, it would produce few simulations below the median repetitions and distance of the random model. A module for which only 5 percent of the simulations matched our child's data would result in a value of -1.16 for ρ. As can be seen in Table 11.1, changes in the capacity of the memory module in general do not provide a very powerful model of our child's search behavior.

The next coefficient to be computed in Hanna's (1971) analysis is δ, which measures the descriptive power of the model. Delta is the maximum value of ρ across all possible instances of the model. In our case, the model incorporating a short-term memory capacity of 45 items generated the highest value of ρ. The resultant value of δ is given in the first line and second column of Table 11.1.

Together, ρ and δ define the coefficient of parameter effect, which describes how a model is affected by changes in the values of its constituent parameters. This coefficient, ε, is given in the first line and third column of Table 11.1.

We interpret these values in relation to those of our neighborhood module, which models a very different kind of choice process. This module stipulates that the child decides to search on the basis of distance relationships among possible search sites. We examined three model instances that differed in the probability of choosing distance relationships. For example, the model instance tested in step 2B assumed that the searcher chooses sites closest to the last one searched with probability of .3. Next closest sites are chosen with probability of .3; third, fourth, and fifth closest sites are chosen with probability of .1, and sites farther away are grouped into a single category and chosen with probability of .1. This set of values corresponds to a type of strategy often seen in gathering tasks, in which the searcher tends to check adjacent sites.

We wanted to distinguish broad classes of neighborhood models; hence we examined two other instances with different parameter values. In one we reversed the values of the parameters of the above model by using values of .1, .1, .1, .1, .3, and .3 for choosing sites that range from the nearest to the farthest set, respectively. This stimulates a tendency to check one site in a neighborhood and then move to a more distant neighborhood rather than to continue checking adjacent sites. The third instance of neighborhood models assumed that the searcher chooses sites closest to the last one searched with a probability of .3, chooses sites beyond the five closest sites with probability of .3, and chooses the four intermediate sites with equal probability of .1. This model approximates a strategy that organizes search in reference to groups of sites. There is a total probability of .7 of searching within a group of five adjacent sites, with the most adjacent site given priority. The remaining .3 probability of moving to a more distant site mimics such occurrences as leaving when a neighborhood is perceived to be exhausted.

The values for the coefficients of the predictive, descriptive, and parameter effects of the neighborhood module are given in the second row of Table 11.1. When they are compared to the corresponding values for the memory simulations, the values suggest that our child's protocol was not characterized solely by proximity organization. Indeed, the average value of ρ is negative, indicating that the simulations produce outcomes like the child's less often than a equiprobable assignment to the cells of the 2×2 table. Interestingly, the simulations are quite sensitive to the parameters of the module. As reflected by the value of ε, the informativeness of the module can be improved with the right choice of parameter values; indeed, the module is more sensitive than the memory module.

In the third step of the analysis, we examined the effect of combining the memory module with the neighborhood module. The combination can be tested with Hanna's procedure. The results of this analysis are presented in Table 11.1. An interesting form of interaction appears, in that the combined effect is much larger than would be expected from the two modules considered separately. The average value of ρ is very high, and the best set of parameters results in a simulation with perfect prediction (in the sense that all outcomes of this composition of modules are in the appropriate cell of the 2×2 table). Furthermore, this composition is not affected very much by different values of the parameters of the modules. In other words, the combination of memory and neighborhood modules produces a simulation model that is highly predictive and robust with respect to different parametric assumptions.

Summary and Conclusions

We have presented an approach to modeling in which a single-case protocol is evaluated against a Monte Carlo outcome of a computer simulation. In our illustration, the protocol is a record of visits to sites by a child who searched for hidden treats. The simulation begins with a program that generates a stream of random numbers. The numbers represent choices or responses available in the environment. This permits a first analysis to determine whether the behavioral record could have been produced by chance. Examination of two dependent measures, the distance traveled between searches and the number of repeated visits to sites, indicated that the child's performance was extremely rare within the distribution of chance outcomes.

In the subsequent analyses we introduced various programming modules in addition to the stream generator. These modules provide constraints or algorithms that modify the output of the simulation. The design of a module is derived from psychological theory. For example, one module alters the stream by rejecting choices that have occurred recently. We consider this to model a short-term memory of previously visited sites. A second module constrains the choice of sites on the basis of proximity relationships. The algorithm reduces travel and is compatible with practices of optimal foraging when resources are distributed in patches.

Two advantages of the modular approach were illustrated. The parameters of a theoretical process, such as the capacity of short-term memory, can be studied independently of the operations of other processes. Or, different theoretical processes may be combined, as were the memory and neighborhood modules. The evaluation of the models indicated that this combination had properties that are not obvious from analysis of the output of the separate modules.

Although psychological theory aids in the design of processing modules, in practice we view our form of simulation as very data-driven. The outcome of the various modules is tested to determine their application to the child's protocol. Hence, our model building proceeds in a number of distinct steps, in which we introduce a module to determine its effects on a simulated protocol, and we evaluate the effectiveness of this module relative to other models.

We illustrated a quantitative evaluation originally formulated by Hanna (1971). Hanna's approach is to view the modeling process as involving the extraction of information from the situation being modeled. In the context of simulation, this approach involves the use of an entropy statistic to measure the match of a model to the empirical outcome. Hanna's technique yields three coefficients that index the precision of our modules.

The results of this evaluation suggest a characterization of the relative attributes of the processing modules. Specifically, Table 11.1 indicates that the memory model provides more predictive and more descriptive power than the neighborhood model, as we have defined them. However, not only is the combined model better than either alone on both counts, but also it exhibits less effect due to variation in the parameters of the model, despite the fact that it has the additional module.

We conclude that our 7-year-old gatherer organized her search with two cognitive components: memories of previous visits to sites and estimates of the spatial proximity of sites. We arrived at this conclusion by means of a method that placed minimal restrictions on the experimental regimen but that still permitted the quantitative assessment of different theoretical interpretations. In this sense, our technique provides one very important function often ascribed to scientific models—their ability to bridge the gap between field observation and laboratory analysis.

We view the general techniques we have described here as appropriate in a variety of situations. Monte Carlo simulation is useful when the stochastic complexity of a theory makes purely analytic treatments difficult. The stream-based simulation "toolbox" that we have developed would be most applicable in situations where the data consist of a series of observations similar to the series of choices we used in our Easter egg hunt. Streams are also useful when the investigator wishes to evaluate the effect of incorporating additional complexity into a model; a working state description of cognitive development may be simulated by a system of processing modules. The effects of adding to the model may be as revealing as the match of simulated and empirical performance.

Acknowledgments

This research was supported by grants to the authors from the Natural Sciences and Engineering Research Council of Canada.

References

Baernstein, H. D., & Hull, C. L. (1931). A mechanical model of the conditional reflex. *Journal of General Psychology, 5,* 99–106.

Bakan, D. (1967). *On method: Towards a reconstruction of psychological investigation.* San Francisco: Jossey-Bass.

Bratley, D., Fox, B. L., & Schrage, L. E. (1983). *A guide to simulation.* New York: Springer-Verlag.

Charniak, E., Riesbeck, C. K., & McDermott, D. V. (1981). *Artificial intelligence programming.* Hillsdale, NJ: Erlbaum.

Charnov, E. L. (1976). Optimal foraging: The marginal value theorem. *Theoretical Population Biology, 9,* 129–136.

Cornell, E. H., & Heth, C. D. (1983). Spatial cognition: Gathering strategies used by preschool children. *Journal of Experimental Child Psychology, 35,* 93–110.

Cornell, E. H., & Heth, C. D. (in press). The spatial organization of hiding and recovery of objects by children. *Child Development.*

Cotton, J. W. (1982). Where is the randomness for the human computer? *Behavior Research Methods and Instrumentation, 14,* 59–70.

Dempster, F. N. (1981). Memory span: Sources of individual and developmental differences. *Psychological Bulletin, 89,* 63–100.

Hanna, J. F. (1966). A new approach to the formulation and testing of learning models. *Synthèse, 16,* 344–380.

Hanna, J. F. (1971). Information-theoretic techniques for evaluating simulation models. In J. M. Dutton & W. H. Starbuck (Eds.), *Computer simulation of human behavior* (pp. 682–692). New York: Wiley.

Heth, C. D. (1984). A Pascal version of a pseudorandom number generator. *Behavior Research Methods, Instruments, & Computers, 16,* 548–550.

Heth, C. D., & Cornell, E. H. (1985). A comparative description of representation and processing during search. In H. M. Wellman (Ed.), *Children's searching: The development of search skill and spatial representation* (pp. 215–249). Hillsdale, NJ: Erlbaum.

Hull, C. L. (1952). *A behavior system.* New Haven, CN: Yale.

Kamil, A. C. (1978). Systematic foraging by a nectar-feeding bird, the Amakihi (*Loxops Virens*). *Journal of Comparative and Physiological Psychology, 92,* 388–396.

Kamil, A. C., & Sargent, T. D. (Eds.) (1981). *Foraging behavior: Ecological, ethological, and psychological approaches.* London: Garland Press.

Nisbett, R. E., and Wilson, T. D. (1977). Telling more than we can know: Verbal reports on mental processes. *Psychological Review, 84,* 231–259.

Odette, L. L. (1984). Computing with streams. *Dr. Dobb's Journal, 9(9), 50–56.*

Ollason, J. G. (1983). Behavioral consequences of hunting by expectation: A simulation study of foraging tactics. *Theoretical Population Biology, 23,* 323–346.

Orians, G. H. (1981). Foraging behavior and the evolution of discriminatory abilities. In A. C. Kamil & T. D. Sargent (Eds.), *Foraging behavior: Ecological, ethological, and psychological approaches* (pp. 389–405). London: Garland Press.

Pritsker, A. A. B., & Pegden, C. D. (1979). *Introduction to simulation and SLAM.* New York: Wiley.

Pyke, G. H. (1978). Optimal foraging: Movement patterns of bumblebees between influorescences. *Theoretical Population Biology, 13,* 72–98.

Shettleworth, S. J., & Krebs, J. R. (1982). How marsh tits find their hoards: The roles of site preference and spatial memory. *Journal of Experimental Psychology: Animal Behavior Processes, 8,* 354–375.

Siegler, R. S. (1976). Three aspects of cognitive development. *Cognitive Psychology, 4,* 481–520.

Starbuck, W. H. (1971). Testing case-descriptive models. In J. M. Dutton and W. H. Starbuck (Eds.), *Computer simulation of human behavior* (pp. 674–681). New York: Wiley.

Wellman, H. M. (Ed.). (1985). *Children's searching: The development of search skill and spatial representation.* Hillsdale, NJ: Erlbaum.

Appendix 11A

The following defines a set of Logo functions that implement the stream-based simulation package described above. These functions and the specific simulation modules described in the text are written in ExperLogo—a commercial Logo package available from ExperTelligence of Santa Barbara, California. Readers familiar with Logo programming will notice two special functions used in ExperLogo: *apply* and *funcall.* Both apply the first argument (a function) to the remaining argument or arguments. For example, (funcall :sum 2 2) evaluates to 4. In ExperLogo, all functions return values, so that the function "output" or "op" is rarely used.

The specific definitions given here were developed along the lines of a stream manipulation program discussed by Charniak et al. (1981). The function *sar,* when it is applied to a stream, returns the first element or head of the stream; the function *sdr* returns the tail. The function *normalize* ensures that the stream does not start with a generator.

Program comments are contained within braces (e.g., {comment}). The specification of stream transformers is described in the text.

```
to generator :fun :args                 {Used to construct a stream gener-
  (fput 'gen(fput :fun :args))             ator.}
end

to isgenerator :exp                     {Tests a list to determine if it is a
  (equalp(first :exp) 'gen)                generator.}
end

to fungenerator :l                      {Returns the function of a genera-
  (first(bf :l))                           tor.}
end

to argsgenerator :l                     {Returns the arguments of a gener-
  (bf(bf :l))                              ator.}
end

to sar :s                               {Returns the head of a stream.}
  (first(normalize :s))
end

to sdr :s                               {Returns the tail of a stream.}
  (normalize(bf(normalize :s)))
end

to append :lis1 :lis2                   {Utility function.}
  if(emptyp :lis1)[op :lis2]
  (fput(first :lis1)(append(bf :lis1) :lis2))
end

to normalize :s                         {Expands any generators at the
                                           head of s.}

  if(or(emptyp :s)(wordp(first :s))(not(isgenerator(first :s))))[op :s]
  make rest nil                         {Rest is a utility variable, not used
                                           in this application; see Charniak
                                           et al. for details.}
```

```
  label loop
  test(and :s(listp(first :s))(isgenerator(first :s)))
  iffalse[op :s]
  make rest(bf :s)
  make s(append(apply(thing(fungenerator(first :s)))
    (argsgenerator(first :s))) :rest)
  go loop
end

to map :func :str                    {Definition of the map trans-
                                       former.}
  (list(funcall(thing :func)(sar :str))
    (generator 'map(list :func(sdr :str))))
end

to filter :pred :str                 {Definition of the filter trans-
                                       former.}
  label loop
  test(funcall(thing :pred)(sar :str))
  iffalse[op(list(sar :str)(generator 'filter
    (list :pred(sdr :str))))]
  make str(sdr :str)
  go loop
end

to accumulate :func :str1 :str2      {Definition of an accumulator.}
  make str1(funcall(thing :func) :str1 :str2)
  (list :str1
    (generator 'accumulate(list :func :str1(sdr :str2))))
end

to combine :func :str1 :str2         {Definition of a combiner.}
  (list(funcall(thing :func) :str1 :str2)
    (generator 'combine(list :func(sdr :str1)(sdr :str2))))
end

to sieve :func :param :str           {Definition of a sieve.}
  local paramlist
  make paramlist(funcall(thing :func) :param :str)
  label loop
  if :paramlist[op(list(sar :str)
    (generator 'sieve
    (list :func :paramlist(sdr :str))))]
  make str(sdr :str)
  make paramlist(funcall(thing :func) :param :str)
  go loop
end
```

Author Index

Page numbers set in italic type refer to pages on which complete reference information appears.

Subject Index

Springer Series in Cognitive Development

Series Editor: Charles J. Brainerd
(recent titles)

Adult Cognition: An Experimental Psychology of Human Aging
Timothy A. Salthouse

Recent Advances in Cognitive-Developmental Theory: Progress in Cognitive Development Research
Charles J. Brainerd (Ed.)

Learning in Children: Progress in Cognitive Development Research
Jeffrey Bisanz/Gay L. Bisanz/Robert Kail (Eds.)

Cognitive Strategy Research: Psychological Foundations
Michael Pressley/Joel R. Levin (Eds.)

Cognitive Strategy Research: Educational Applications
Michael Pressley/Joel R. Levin (Eds.)

Equilibrium in the Balance: A Study of Psychological Explanation
Sophie Haroutunian

Crib Speech and Language Play
Stan A. Kuczaj, II

Discourse Development: Progress in Cognitive Development Research
Stan A. Kuczaj, II (Ed.)

Cognitive Development in Atypical Children: Progress in Cognitive Development Research
Linda S. Siegel/Frederick J. Morrison (Eds.)

Basic Processes in Memory Development: Progress in Cognitive Development Research
Charles J. Brainerd/Michael Pressley (Eds.)

Cognitive Learning and Memory in Children: Progress in Cognitive Development Research
Michael Pressley/Charles J. Brainerd (Eds.)

The Development of Word Meaning
Stan A. Kuczaj, II/Martyn D. Barrett (Eds.)

Formal Methods in Developmental Psychology: Progress in Cognitive Development Research
Jeffrey Bisanz/Charles J. Brainerd/Robert Kail (Eds.)